Communication Law
in America

Communication Law in America

Third Edition

PAUL SIEGEL

ROWMAN & LITTLEFIELD PUBLISHERS, INC.
Lanham • Boulder • New York • Toronto • Plymouth, UK

Published by Rowman & Littlefield Publishers, Inc.
A wholly owned subsidary of The Rowman & Littlefield Publishing Group, Inc.
4501 Forbes Boulevard, Suite 200, Lanham, Maryland 20706
http://www.rowmanlittlefield.com

Estover Road, Plymouth PL6 7PY, United Kingdom

British Library Cataloguing in Publication Information Available

Library of Congress Cataloging-in-Publication Data

Siegel, Paul, 1954–
    Communication law in America / Paul Siegel.—3rd ed.
        p.   cm.
    Includes bibliographical references and index.
    ISBN 978-1-4422-0938-1 (pbk. : alk. paper)—ISBN 978-1-4422-0939-8 (electronic)
    1. Mass media—Law and legislation United States.   2. Press law—United States.
3. Freedom of speech—United States.   I. Title.
KF2750.S53   2011
343.7309′9—dc22

                                                                            2010053894

♾ ™ The paper used in this publication meets the minimum requirements of
American National Standard for Information Sciences—Permanence of Paper for
Printed Library Materials, ANSI/NISO Z39.48-1992.

Printed in the United States of America

Brief Contents

Detailed Contents

To the several tech gurus who helped me along the way, and to whom I will very likely turn for guidance in the future, as I am nudged or dragged into the digital age:

Ryan Hollister
Mike Mullins
Maeve Ryan
Joshua Singer
Lisa Tassinari
Lorelle Wilson
Michael Wilson

Preface to the Third Edition

The book you have in front of you (or on your digital device) represents a thorough updating of the previous edition of *Communication Law in America*. Discussions of literally hundreds of new court cases, statutes, regulations, and secondary sources appear in these pages, including more than 150 citations for 2010 and 2011. The current edition may very well represent a crossroads, in that the media themselves are at a crossroads. "Media convergence" has been a buzz phrase for several decades. The phrase refers to the notion that where we receive our media content is becoming less and less important, in that the same device (such as a very "smart" phone) can behave not only like a telephone but also like a TV, radio, newspaper, and computer.

But the law has not yet caught up with the reality. There are still several important regulations that apply to broadcast media, but not to print or to the Internet. To be fair, courts are beginning to understand this disjointedness. In 2010 the D.C. Circuit Court of Appeals cited as one reason for invalidating the Federal Communication Commission's sanctions against TV stations for broadcasting the "fleeting expletives" uttered by such celebrities as Cher and Nicole Richie the fact that other media (print, cable, and the Internet) can drop the occasional "f-bomb" with impunity, and that consumers often access all such media content from a single device, just by clicking once or twice.[1] If that court's reasoning catches on, this may be the last edition of the textbook to merit a separate chapter for Internet law, or even for broadcast and cable law.

The textbook is at a crossroads for another reason as well. Its full value cannot be appreciated without frequent visits to my website, www.paulsiegelcommlaw.com, where you will find not only updates to the text but also hundreds of images, and over fifty scenes from TV shows and movies that were the reason for a lawsuit discussed in the book. Throughout the text you will see the icon as shown in the margin whenever we wish to invite you to visit the site to see the relevant video clips.

Perhaps more to the point of media convergence, this is the first edition of the text

---

1. *Fox TV, Inc. v. FCC*, 613 F. 3d 317, 326 (2010).

offered digitally through any of various "e-book" hardware devices. Some readers of the text will thus have the benefit of live hyperlinks to the website. Such a seamless experience is sure to become the norm in the future.

But more about the website, which gets over a thousand visitors each month. Not exactly the traffic experienced by a Justin Bieber fan site, but give us time. Among the dozens of video clips now available on the site are scenes from *Borat* (there were multiple lawsuits); Michael Moore's *Fahrenheit 911*, *Bowling for Columbine*, and *Sicko*; *Law and Order*; *Family Guy*; *American Gangster*; *Disturbia*; and *Hillary: The Movie* (which resulted in a Supreme Court decision that has already dramatically changed the political landscape). There is even a campaign commercial that resulted in a libel suit, in which one senate candidate accused another of being an atheist. The E-Trade babies commercial that prompted a short-lived lawsuit from Lindsay Lohan is here, as well as a Cocoa Pebbles commercial that angered Hulk Hogan enough to litigate.

I had much help in collecting the visuals found in the text and on the website. Among those who helped are Jeffrey Fister and Eileen Dugan of *West End Word*, attorney "RMJ" from Missouri, *Reader's Digest*'s and *Conservative Digest*'s Larry Abraham and Scott Stanley, Tracey McIntire from People for the Ethical Treatment of Animals, Roger Vann of the ACLU of Connecticut, Helen Harris of RP International, Daniel Shelton of Shelton Brothers Importers, Diana Palmentiero of what was then Court TV, Michelle Sievers of ESPN, Glenn Gilbert of the *Lake County News Herald*, James Mc-Mullan, Hugo Zacchini (the "Human Cannonball"), James Earl Reid, Jeff Koons, Matthew Hunsberger, Tom Forsythe, Johnnie Luevanos of Universal Studios, David Pahl, Jim Hemphill, Mike Sandusky, Frank Goodenough, Dan Frazier of http://carryabig sticker.com, Jane Stevens, Stephen Hornyak, Andrew van den Houten, Cindy McMahan and Daniel Ferrell of Elmo's Diner, Anne Rajotte, Benjamin Reed, and Jay Herzog.

Many of the cartoons from the second edition appear here as well. The soon-to-be-famous Katie Osowiecki, then a student of the Hartford Art School, is the creator.

Additional individuals helped tremendously with research for this book, sometimes pointing me in the right direction, sometimes, I admit, doing my homework for me. Among these were Camille Broadway, Bill Buell, Jim Hemphill, Thomas E. Hemstock Jr., Ella Holst, Bruce Lockard, Roger Mellen, Pat Petit, Lawrence Rosenfeld, Edward Samuels, Mike Sandusky, Stuart Sigman, Art Spitzer, Alex Tang, Lee Templeman, John Vivian, Kaitlin Walsh, and Lorelle Wilson. Special thanks are due to Kris and Paul Oehlke, who spent the better part of a day at the Library of Congress for me, when they really should have been seeing the sights.

University of Hartford graduate student Alexandra Frisbie was invaluable in the finishing stages of the current edition, especially in creation of the case index and proofreading the glossary.

A special note of thanks is due a young lady I have never met. Emily Egan, while a high school student, created a wonderful mini-documentary about the New York State "I Love New York" public relations campaign, at least some familiarity with which is essential to understanding the copyright infringement suit against *Saturday Night Live* for its "I Love Sodom" parody described in chapter 6. She graciously gave me permission to upload her work to my website, so as to give students a more complete understanding of the court case. I hope all is going well for you at NYU, Ms. Egan.

Chapter 1

INTRODUCING THE AMERICAN LEGAL SYSTEM

Those who watched President Obama's 2010 State of the Union address got a mini-lesson about the American legal system when he departed a bit from protocol by criticizing a recent Supreme Court decision while standing within spitting distance of the justices. "With all due deference to separation of powers," he said, "last week the Supreme Court reversed a century of law [in a decision] that I believe will open the floodgates to special interests." He was making reference to the Court's decision in *Citizens United v. Federal Elections Commission*,[1] about which more will be said in chapter 10. That the Supreme Court can "reverse" prior decisions—their own or those of lower courts—hints at the structure of the judiciary, which will be an important subject in this opening chapter. Obama's reference to "separation of powers" reminds us that in our legal system we have three separate branches of government that all can have an impact on the law, including communication law.

Why Are You Here?

That you are reading this book likely means you are enrolled in a college course such as Mass Media Law, Journalism Law, or Freedom of the Press. One reason you should have a strong background in communication law is that legal questions arise every day in the workplace, and relatively few media organizations have in-house legal counsel to answer questions on a moment's notice. The course you are taking now will offer you the facts you need and the tools to research new facts so that you can

---

1. 130 S. Ct. 876 (2010).

avoid or minimize legal liability. Perhaps the most important reason for becoming familiar with the major concepts of communication law is that the U.S. political system works best if citizens participate actively in decision making. Our representative democracy works to the extent that we all take responsibility for using our freedom of speech (and the corollary freedoms to listen and to learn) forcefully and frequently. In doing so, it surely helps to know the full gamut of our legal rights, as well as the limitations on those rights.

Sources of Communication Law

President Obama's State of the Union reference to separation of powers was designed to demonstrate awareness that the executive branch (the president) should not step on the toes of the judicial branch (the courts, and especially the Supreme Court). Our system of government also includes Congress, the legislative branch. Each of these three branches of government is mimicked in state government and to an extent in local government as well. As we will see, they each have a role to play in the creation and interpretation of communication law. The main sources of law are **constitutions**, **statutes**, **executive orders**, decisions by **administrative agencies**, and the **common law**. Let us take a look at each source.

Constitutions

One source of communication law is constitutions. Notice the use of the plural here. Every state has its own constitution. So although we start our discussion here with a summary of important features of the *federal* Constitution, we say more about state constitutions later.

The First Amendment To be sure, the section of the U.S. Constitution of most relevance to the act of communication is the First Amendment, which is part of the Bill of Rights. Here is the wording of that provision, which was adopted on December 15, 1791:

> Congress shall make no law respecting an establishment of religion, or prohibiting the free exercise thereof; or abridging the freedom of speech, or of the press; or the right of the people peaceably to assemble, and to petition the Government for a redress of grievances.

The first thing apparent from the text is that the amendment is not talking to *us*, but rather to our elected representatives. It does not tell us what we have or do not have a right to do. It is in the form of a list of admonitions to Congress, warning that *its* right to pass certain kinds of laws is restricted.

Although the First Amendment's reference to Congress has always been taken to refer to the entire federal government, individual states and localities were free to regulate the speech of their own citizens without running afoul of the First Amendment, at least until a U.S. Supreme Court ruling handed down more than 130 years after ratification of the Bill of Rights.[2] That decision is discussed in chapter 2.

The First Amendment's prohibitions apply even today only to *governmental* entities. When private individuals or companies prohibit us from engaging in some kinds of speech—perhaps our parents demand that we not talk about religious differences with them, or our employer (unless our employer *is* the government) asks that we not talk about politics with our coworkers—they are not in violation of the First Amendment. Perhaps surprisingly, it is not always easy to decide whether a specific entity is part of the government for constitutional purposes. For example, even though Amtrak was set up as a private corporation, it is considered a "state agent" for some purposes and must thus abide by the First Amendment.[3]

Look again at the wording of the First Amendment. It contains five specific admonitions: five clauses. The first two—the **Establishment Clause** and the **Free Exercise Clause**—are often referred to together as the "religion clauses." The Establishment Clause is sometimes described as providing freedom *from* religious indoctrination and is frequently invoked in educational settings. This clause led federal courts to forbid public school administrators from leading students in prayer,[4] and from including units in "scientific creationism"[5] or "intelligent design"[6] in public school science classrooms. The Free Exercise Clause gives us the freedom *to* practice our religions to the extent that such practice does not interfere with a compelling governmental interest. The two religion clauses often seem to conflict. Deferring to litigants' freedom of religion might seem appropriate under the Free Exercise Clause, but that very deference may raise Establishment Clause issues by showing favoritism to one religion over another, or to religion over nonreligion.

Although journalism law cases rarely invoke the religion clauses, one of the most important Supreme Court cases of the 1990s, which concerned the rights of newspaper editors, involved both of the clauses.[7] By a 5–4 vote, the Court ruled that the University of Virginia could not refuse to help fund a Christian students' group's cost of publishing its newspaper, called *Wide Awake*.

Let us skip ahead for a moment to the First Amendment's last clause, the one that gives us the right to "peacefully assemble" and to "petition the government for redress of grievances." Despite the comma between them, these two rights are usually thought of as part of the same whole. Traditionally the people's right to assemble has

---

2. *Gitlow v. New York*, 268 U.S. 652 (1925).

3. *Lebron v. National Railroad Passenger Corporation*, 513 U.S. 374 (1995).

4. *School District v. Schempp*, 374 U.S. 203 (1963); *Engel v. Vitale*, 370 U.S. 421 (1962).

5. *Edwards v. Aguillard*, 482 U.S. 578 (1987).

6. *Kitzmiller v. Dover Area School District*, 400 F. Supp. 2d 707 (M.D. Pa. 2005).

7. *Rosenberger v. University of Virginia*, 515 U.S. 819 (1995).

been seen as limited to gatherings with a political purpose—that is, to express grievances, not to have a volleyball game. First Amendment decisions also often include reference to the "**freedom of association**," a related right not explicitly listed in the Constitution but which the Supreme Court has borrowed from labor law (a right to form unions) and interpreted over time as a First Amendment right applicable to both political and nonpolitical associations. Association is related to speech, the courts have told us, in that we often need to work together with others, perhaps protected from the watchful eyes of opponents, to most effectively make arguments in the public forum.[8] Freedom of association seems logically related to freedom of assembly as well. After all, an association can be thought of as "an assembly dispersed over time and space."[9]

On at least one occasion the **Petition Clause** featured prominently in a libel decision from the Supreme Court. The plaintiff was an attorney whose name had surfaced as a possible high-level governmental appointee, with the defendant an acquaintance (hardly a friend) who engaged in a negative campaign of writing letters about the plaintiff to many government officials, from the president on down.[10] Petition Clause claims may become more frequent in future years because of a phenomenon called the **SLAPP suit**. The acronym stands for "strategic lawsuit against public participation." SLAPP suits are similar to libel suits, but they are aimed at preventing citizen activists from speaking out against businesses and even government officials. Many social critics argue that these suits are inconsistent with the spirit of the Petition Clause, in that they often result from citizens' comments at public hearings, the kind of forums that are specifically designed to have elected officials listen to grievances. Many states have created "anti-SLAPP laws," with California's among the strongest.[11] While SLAPP statutes are most frequently used in libel suits (including in pretrial motions to reveal anonymous sources), in 2010 the Washington statute was used by a federal judge to throw out a copyright infringement suit against Michael Moore over a snippet in his film *Sicko*.[12]

We will not spend much time here on the **Free Speech Clause** and the **Free Press Clause**, because they are the focus of almost this entire book. When courts are asked to determine whether a specific governmental action violates the First Amendment rights of media professionals, it is virtually always these two clauses that are at issue.

8. See, for example, *Perry v. Schwarzenegger*, 38 Media L. Rep. 1107 (9th Cir. 2009).

9. C. Edwin Baker, "Scope of the First Amendment Freedom of Speech," 25 *UCLA Law Review* 964, 1032 (1978).

10. *McDonald v. Smith*, 472 U.S. 479 (1985).

11. *Club Members for an Honest Election v. Sierra Club*, 196 P.3d 1094 (Cal. 2008) (social critics need not have completely pure motives in order to be protected by the anti-SLAPP law); see also *John Doe #1 v. Cahill*, 884 A. 2d 451 (Del. 2005) (refusing to unmask an individual who had posted strongly worded criticisms of a city councilman on a weblog).

12. *Arsonson v. Dog Eat Dog Films*, 2010 U.S. Dist. LEXIS 91417 (W.D. Wash. 2010). The case was on appeal as we were going to press.

One point does deserve special attention—we are talking about two clauses rather than one. Does freedom of speech not include both oral and written communication? How can we explain this apparent redundancy in the Bill of Rights? Whatever may have been on the minds of our Founding Fathers, one school of thought today suggests that freedom of the *press* refers to the professional journalist.

Certainly members of the working press, with credentials, are able to go places and do

Washington's anti-SLAPP statute was used to throw out a copyright infringement suit against Michael Moore for his having used in *Sicko* the homemade film submitted to him from which this still photo was taken.

Remember to visit www.paulsiegel commlaw.com and click on "Video Clips" to see this and other visual material.

things that other people cannot. Police will often permit only emergency personnel and reporters near the scenes of accidents. There is a separate section of desirable seats for members of the working press to watch the Supreme Court conduct **oral arguments**. In most states, members of the working press are given some form of statutory immunity from having to testify about their news sources. The name we give to such statutes—**reporter shield laws**—is a clear indication that here too we have an example of freedom of the press meaning something different from and more than freedom of speech.

Former Supreme Court justice Potter Stewart thought it very appropriate that media professionals be given more First Amendment rights than the rest of us. He argued this position forcefully in an address at Yale Law School, later reprinted as a law review article. The title of the lecture and article consists of four words taken from the text of the First Amendment itself—*or of the press.* Stewart says that "the publishing business is, in short, the only organized private business that is given explicit constitutional protection."[13] Whether the working press should enjoy First Amendment protections above and beyond those of ordinary citizens—and who should be considered a member of that "working press"—is a continuing focus of debate among legal scholars.[14] It is clear, however, that from time to time the Supreme Court has singled out the media for a special measure of freedom, as seen throughout this book.

Other Sources of Communication Law in the Federal Constitution

The First Amendment is not the only part of the Bill of Rights of relevance to communication law. Consider the Fourth Amendment's protection against "unrea-

---

13. Potter Stewart, "Or of the Press," 26 *Hastings Law Journal* 631, 633 (1975).

14. *Too Much Media v. Hale*, 37 *Media Law Reporter* 1994 (N.J. Super. Court 2009) (struggling with whether a blogger can be protected by a state reporter shield law); see generally, Dean C. Smith, "*Price v. Time* Revisited: The Need for Medium-Neutral Shield Laws in an Age of Strict Construction," 14 *Communication Law & Policy* 235 (2009); Anthony L. Fargo, "Analyzing Federal Shield Law Proposals: What Congress Can Learn From the States," 11 *Communication Law and Policy* 35 (2006).

THINGS TO REMEMBER

The Five Clauses of the First Amendment

- ESTABLISHMENT CLAUSE (Freedom *from* religious indoctrination)
- FREE EXERCISE CLAUSE (Freedom *to* practice religion)
- FREE SPEECH CLAUSE (Freedom of expression)
- FREE PRESS CLAUSE (Freedom for the press as an institution)
- PETITION CLAUSE (Freedom to complain to government officials)

sonable searches and seizures." This means that law enforcement officials generally may not detain us, frisk us, or rummage through our personal effects without first obtaining a **search warrant**. To get a search warrant, an officer must persuade a judge that there is probable cause to believe that important and clearly definable evidence will be uncovered by the search. Frequently, law enforcement officials, persuaded that the offices of a newspaper or television station are harboring evidence crucial to a criminal investigation, will search the premises of these media outlets. As we will see in chapter 9, the Supreme Court has said that the media have no special immunity from such searches,[15] and media outrage over that decision led Congress to pass a major piece of legislation called the Privacy Protection Act. The Fourth Amendment is of relevance to communications professionals for yet another reason. As will be made clear in chapter 5, there have been times when media have cooperated so closely with law enforcement officials—accompanying them on raids, for example—that the reporters themselves may later be sued for violating the target's Fourth Amendment privacy rights. It is also clear that police may be in violation of the Fourth Amendment if they bring reporters along as they arrest a suspect or search his home.[16]

The Fifth and Fourteenth Amendments are also very relevant. The Fifth Amendment is probably best known for its protection against self-incrimination—thus the countless times we hear courtroom witnesses, real and fictional, "plead the Fifth." This amendment also tells the federal government—the Fourteenth Amendment has parallel wording applicable to the states—that it may not deprive persons of "life, liberty, or property without due process of law." It is this last provision that is most often of relevance for us, because one aspect of **due process** is that laws and regulations must be worded precisely enough so that we know *how* to obey them, or they will be found "void for vagueness." If your hometown had a law saying that businesses could be regulated as "adult" if a "substantial or significant" portion of their

---

15. *Zurcher v. Stanford Daily*, 436 U.S. 547 (1978).
16. *Wilson v. Layne*, 526 U.S. 693 (1999).

wares were sexually oriented, how would you know if your business was covered by the law?[17]

So important is a working knowledge of the Sixth Amendment for the professional communicator that this book devotes chapter 8 to the subject. The Sixth Amendment ensures criminal suspects the right to a speedy and public trial by an impartial jury. There has likely always been a good deal of tension between First and Sixth Amendment guarantees—for example, what kinds of pretrial reportage might make it difficult to impanel an impartial jury? Once a trial has begun, may the trial judge impose restrictions on the press so that jurors do not learn in their living rooms things that would be inadmissible as evidence in the courtroom? The Supreme Court and lower courts have struggled with these kinds of questions for decades.[18]

The Fourteenth Amendment, passed shortly after the end of the Civil War, is important to professional communicators for at least two reasons. First, that same due process language has been treated by the Supreme Court as a kind of funnel through which many provisions of the Bill of Rights—including freedom of speech and freedom of the press—have been applied to the states. This process is known as the **doctrine of incorporation**.[19] The Fourteenth Amendment also tells the states that they may not deny any person "the equal protection of its laws." This **Equal Protection Clause** has been the main grounds on which the media have successfully argued against statutes that single out media industries for special taxation or other obligations or that seem to discriminate among mass media.[20]

The Bill of Rights and later amendments are not the only federal constitutional provisions of relevance to the act of communication. Article I, Section 8 of the Constitution enumerates specific powers granted to Congress by the nation's founders. Here Congress is told that it may pass laws "to promote the progress of . . . useful arts, by securing for limited times to authors . . . the exclusive right to their respective writing and discoveries." This section is the basis for U.S. **copyright** law, the main subject of chapter 6.

State Constitutions and Communication Law

We must look not only to the federal Constitution but also to the various state constitutions as sources of communication law. Most state constitutional provisions concerning communica-

---

17. *VIP of Berlin, LLC, v. Town of Berlin*, 644 F. Supp. 2d 151 (D. Conn. 2009), overturned, 593 F. 3d 179 (2nd Cir. 2010); see generally Wade Kolb III, "*Caperton v. Massey*: The Due Process Implications of Contributions to Judicial Campaigns," 4 *Duke Journal of Constitutional Law and Public Policy Sidebar* 315 (2009).

18. *Presley v. Georgia*, 130 S. Ct. 721 (2010).

19. To cite one recent example, in 2010 the Supreme Court held that the Second Amendment right to bear arms is "incorporated," thus striking down a local Chicago handgun ordinance. *McDonald v. City of Chicago*, 130 S. Ct. 3020 (2010).

20. *Educational Media Company at Virginia Tech, Inc. v. The Cavalier Daily*, 2008 U.S. Dist. LEXIS 45590 (E.D. Va. 2008); *Arkansas Writers Project, Inc. v. Ragland*, 481 U.S. 221 (1987).

tion are coextensive with the First Amendment, granting no greater and no fewer rights than are given in the federal Constitution. Some states, however, have decided that their citizens will enjoy a larger measure of freedom of expression than will other Americans. Typically, the relevant sections of these state constitutions affirmatively give citizens the right to "freely speak, write, and publish." Notice that such wording is far more sweeping than the First Amendment, which tells Congress only that *it* may not abridge free speech. If citizens are told explicitly that they have a right to free speech, such a right would seem to prohibit even private individuals and corporations from abridging such a right. There need be no proof of "state action" to have an alleged infringement of freedom of speech taken seriously in a court of law.

The wording of state constitutional provisions often differs from that of the First Amendment in an opposite direction as well. Whereas the federal provision is worded quite absolutely—"Congress shall make *no* law" (emphasis added)—many state provisions put citizens on notice that they will be "responsible for any abuse" of their freedom of speech. Then, too, whereas the federal Constitution is silent with respect to the kinds of such abuses that might lead one individual to sue another, some state constitutions explicitly give citizens a right to sue for libel or invasion of privacy.

By far the most frequently recurring question related to state constitutional free speech provisions has been whether one has a right to engage in political dialogue with and hand out leaflets to shoppers in privately owned malls. The U.S. Supreme Court has made clear that there is no federal constitutional right to speak out on issues of one's choosing when at a mall. Yet in that very same decision, the Court made equally clear that the states may conclude that their own constitutions grant such a right.[21] In the years since that decision, several states have addressed the same issue, with mixed results. Some states have found in their constitutions at least a limited right to engage in expressive activity on the grounds of privately owned shopping centers,[22] while others have instead concluded that their own constitutional provisions go no further than the protections granted in the First Amendment.[23] Individual homeowners' state constitutional rights to freedom of expression regulated by their homeowners' associations is a newer area of litigation.[24]

---

21. *Pruneyard Shopping Center v. Robins*, 447 U.S. 74 (1980).

22. *Fashion Valley Mall v. NLRB*, 172 P.3d 742 (Cal. 2007), *Bock v. Westminster Mall*, 819 P.2d 55 (Colo. 1991); *Batchelder v. Allied Stores International*, 445 N.E.2d 590 (Mass. 1983); *State v. Schmid*, 423 A.2d 615 (N.J. 1980); *Alderwood Association v. Washington Environmental Council*, 635 P.2d 108 (Wash. 1981).

23. *Stanahan v. Fred Meyer, Inc.*, 11 P.3d 228 (Or. 2000); *Cologne v. Westfarms Association*, 469 A.2d 1201 (Conn. 1984); *State v. Lacey*, 465 N.W.2d 537 (Iowa 1991); *Woodland v. Michigan Citizens Lobby*, 378 N.W.2d 337 (Mich. 1985); *City of Billings v. Laedeke*, 805 P.2d 1348 (Mont. 1991); *SHAD Alliance v. Smith Haven Mall*, 488 N.E.2d 1211 (N.Y. 1985); *State v. Felmet*, 273 S.E.2d 708 (N.C. 1981); *Eastwood Mall v. Slanco*, 626 N.E.2d 59 (Ohio 1994); *Charleston Joint Venture v. McPherson*, 417 S.E.2d 544 (S.C. 1992); *Jacobs v. Major*, 407 N.W.2d 832 (Wis. 1987).

24. *Committee for a Better Twin Rivers v. Twin Rivers Homeowners' Association*, 929 A.2d 1060 (N.J. 2007). See generally the special issue of the *Rutgers Journal of Law and Public Policy* on homeowners' associations (volume 5, Spring, 2008).

THINGS TO REMEMBER

The U.S. Constitution and Communications Law:
Beyond the First Amendment

- FOURTH AMENDMENT
  - Search of newsrooms
  - Press has no constitutional right to avoid a legitimate search

- FIFTH AMENDMENT
  - Due process of law applied to federal government
  - Void for vagueness doctrine

- SIXTH AMENDMENT
  - Right to a speedy, public, and fair trial
  - Can conflict with press freedom

- FOURTEENTH AMENDMENT
  - Due process applied to the states
  - Equal protection of laws

- ARTICLE I, SECTION 8
  - Authorizes copyright laws

Statutes

The U.S. Constitution takes up only a few dozen pages of text. By bulk, and probably also in terms of impact on our daily lives, we are far more affected by the laws passed every year by Congress, state legislatures, city councils, and numerous other local legislative bodies nationwide. States pass obscenity laws, Congress creates the **Freedom of Information Act**, and perhaps your municipality has a local ordinance governing the size and aesthetics of billboard advertising or other outdoor displays.[25] In each of these instances, the enactment of the law might not be the last word on any particular issue, because laws are often challenged in court by affected parties, who will claim that the laws violate state or federal constitutional provisions. This process of **judicial review** resulted, to cite just one example, in the striking down by the Supreme Court in 2010 of some key components of the McCain-Feingold Act, which had required corporations to set up separate "political action committees" rather than spending directly from their own coffers if they wished to pay for advertising supporting or opposing a candidate for public office.[26]

---

25. In 2008, for example, real estate tycoon Donald Trump was fined $10,000 because his flagpole was found to be too large by the California Coastal Commission. Trump had similar difficulties the year before when Palm Beach, Florida, concluded his American flag was too large. Victoria Kim, "Stern Agency Meets Unflappable Mogul," *Los Angeles Times*, February 7, 2008, B1.

26. *Citizens United v. Federal Election Commission*, 130 S. Ct. 876 (2010).

This flag, displayed outside Donald Trump's Mar-a-Lago resort, was disapproved as too large by the Palm Beach, Florida, zoning commission.

Even if litigants do not seek to have a law declared unconstitutional, they will sometimes feel the need to ask a court to clarify a law's meaning. We call this process **statutory construction**. One notable example is comedienne Carol Burnett's libel suit against the *National Enquirer*, which had published an article alleging that Burnett behaved very strangely, as if intoxicated, in a fancy restaurant. In that California libel law for newspapers is slightly different than that for magazines, the court first needed to determine exactly what a newspaper *is* and how it differs from a magazine. Having done so, the court could then conclude that the *National Enquirer* is more of a magazine than a newspaper and could apply the appropriate state law.[27]

---

27. *Burnett v. National Enquirer*, 144 Cal. App. 3d 991 (1983). Whether a court would rule similarly today is anyone's guess. In recent years the *National Enquirer* has scooped the more mainstream press on some major stories, such as former vice presidential candidate John Edwards's affair.

Executive Orders

As a general principle, the separation of powers that defines our form of government provides that Congress makes the laws, the president carries out the laws, and the judiciary interprets and determines the constitutionality of the laws. In reality, however, the president—and at other levels of government, governors and mayors—can also make law. The president does so by appointing officials to the various regulatory agencies, negotiating treaties and trade agreements, and issuing executive orders. In addition, the president has an enormous long-term effect on the law through the process of nominating persons for lifetime appointments as federal judges.

In the aftermath of the terrorist attacks of 2001, very dramatic changes in American law, governing such matters as electronic surveillance and interrogation techniques, were accomplished through Bush administration executive orders. Soon after taking office, President Obama signed an executive order seeking the closing of the detention facility at Guantanamo Bay.[28] An older example, but one that still has an impact, is President Reagan's executive order imposing a "gag order" of sorts on persons, including physicians, who accept federal funds to aid in reproductive counseling overseas. Recipients of such grants would be forbidden not only from providing abortions, but also from advising patients about the procedure. That executive order was upheld by the Supreme Court against a First Amendment challenge.[29] The ruling said only that presidents *may* impose such a rule when doling out family planning funds, not that they *must* do so. And so it is that President Clinton rescinded the order, President George W. Bush reimposed it, and President Obama rescinded it yet again.

Administrative Agency Decisions

It was already mentioned that Article I of the U.S. Constitution enumerates the powers granted to Congress. These powers range broadly, from building roads to establishing procedures for immigration and naturalization, from printing money to maintaining the armed forces. Congress's power to regulate commerce among the states is also quite broad. The few hundred members of Congress could not possibly perform all of the many functions required of them without creating a sizable federal bureaucracy. So it is that Washington, D.C., is a veritable alphabet soup of hundreds of regulatory agencies and departments. Several of these agencies have responsibilities of direct relevance for the professional communicator.

Clearly the most important agency, especially if you plan a career in TV, radio, satellite communications, or cyberspace, is the **Federal Communications Commission (FCC)**. Chapter 12, where we examine those laws and regulations that apply exclusively to electronic media such as broadcasting and cable, also includes a detailed

---

28. This has not been accomplished, of course, and the Republican takeover of the House of Representatives will make it far more difficult. James Oliphant, "New House Has Its Own Agenda," *Washington Post*, January 2, 2011, A1.

29. *Rust v. Sullivan*, 500 U.S. 173 (1991).

description of this agency's history and powers. Another agency whose rulings are relevant to communication law is the **Federal Trade Commission (FTC)**, one of whose powers is to set forth rules and mediate disputes to protect consumers from deceptive advertising. The **Food and Drug Administration (FDA)** also has a voice in the regulation of advertising for and labeling of—you guessed it—food and drugs. In 2010, for example, the FDA indicated it might take action against tobacco companies, which had been put on notice that they would no longer be allowed to market cigarettes as "light" (because such a label falsely implied these cigarettes were less dangerous than others), yet were planning to maintain familiar visual cues (such as the color of packaging) to continue to steer consumers to those same "light" varieties.[30] (Some of the labeling that caught the FDA's eye can be found on page 342.) The rulings of numerous other federal agencies, from the Federal Elections Commission to the Securities and Exchange Commission, can also have an impact on communication.

Common Law and the Law of Equity

Anyone who has watched police and lawyer programs on prime-time TV knows the scene well. An attorney is making a motion to the court, asking the judge to take a particular action. The opposing attorney objects. The judge appears thoughtful, glances in the direction of the first lawyer, and asks, "Can you cite any relevant **precedents?**"

THINGS TO REMEMBER

Communication Law: Beyond the U.S. Constitution

- State constitutions are a source of communication law:
    - Some states simply mimic the wording of the First Amendment.
    - Other states affirmatively enumerate citizens' communication rights.
    - Often, states give more rights than the First Amendment does.

- Statutes are a source of communication law:
    - Legislative bodies at all levels of government may pass laws or regulations.
    - Courts sometimes must decide if they are constitutional (judicial review).
    - Courts also may tell us what a law really means (statutory construction).

- Executive orders are sources of communication law:
    - The president often has "wiggle room" in the enforcement of laws.
    - Presidents also affect law through appointments, and through international negotiations.

- Some of the many federal agencies that have an effect on communication law are the FCC, FTC, FDA, and FEC.

---

30. Duff Wilson, "Color Coding," *New York Times*, February 19, 2010, B1.

The judge in this scenario is seeking guidance from common law, sometimes called judge-made law. Common law really means to argue based on tradition and custom, ideally backed up with one or more prior court decisions on the same or a similar point. The U.S. legal system depends for its consistency upon a large body of common law, so that litigants can make some reasonable predictions about how courts will rule on specific issues today based on how they have ruled in the past.

Common law is not a uniquely American invention. Indeed, we imported the idea of lawmaking by precedent from English common law dating back many centuries before any British colonists set foot in the New World. Another less visible tradition that the United States borrowed from England is the right of litigants to seek a judicial remedy in **courts of equity** in situations where the common-law traditions cannot help. A detailed history of the relationship between the development of common law and the law of equity is beyond the scope of this book, in part because only a handful of states continue to maintain separate courts of equity. Still, it is important to realize that one impetus for the development of equity was a perceived dichotomy in English legal tradition between rights and remedies. Plaintiffs may have been able to establish to a court's satisfaction that they had been wronged, but no remedy existed in the law to make the plaintiff whole again.[31] The development of such remedies as **subpoenas** (compelling someone to appear before a court at a later date and to produce papers or otherwise give testimony in reply to specific judicial inquiries) and **injunctions** (ordering that a planned action not be taken, lest a litigant be irreparably wronged) was an outgrowth of the courts of equity. Whenever the phrase "common law" is used throughout the remainder of this text, reference will be made implicitly as well to the law of equity.

The common law should not be thought of as a judicial straitjacket, with no opportunity for evolution. The law does in fact change over time, in part because customs and traditions change. When faced with an arguably relevant precedent, a court always has several options available to it. The first option and the most likely one is to accept and follow the precedent. The Latin phrase *stare decisis,* or "let the decision stand," is often used as a catchphrase to refer to the practice of following precedent.

At the other extreme, a court may decide that the time has come to **overturn** a precedent, to admit forthrightly (at least sometimes it is done forthrightly) that the original decision was wrong. Occasionally a Supreme Court precedent in the field of communication law has been overturned. For example, the Supreme Court had held for many years that motion pictures were not deserving of constitutional protection. "The exhibition of moving pictures is a business, pure and simple, originated and conducted for profit like other spectacles," the Court said back in 1915, and "not to be regarded . . . as part of the press of the country, or as organs of public opinion" within the meaning of freedom of speech.[32] Not until the 1950s did the Supreme

---

31. See, generally, Eric A. White, "Examining Presidential Power through the Rubric of Equity," 108 *Michigan Law Review* 113 (2009).

32. *Mutual Film Corp. v. Industrial Commission of Ohio,* 236 U.S. 230, 244 (1915).

Court explicitly overrule its earlier decision, finding that motion pictures had become "a significant medium for the communication of ideas."[33] On rare occasions the Court has changed its mind without waiting for so many years to pass. The 2010 *Citizens United* case mentioned earlier (the one about corporations' expenditures on behalf of political candidates) effectively overruled portions of a precedent from only seven years earlier.[34]

Most of the time, courts follow precedents. Sometimes they overturn a precedent. In between these two opposite actions are two other options for dealing with a precedent. Often, one or the other is employed en route to an eventual overturning. The first of the two options is to **distinguish** the precedent, and the word means much the same in this context as it does in everyday conversation. When judges distinguish an earlier decision, they are really saying that the case is not a precedent worthy of following at all, *given the facts of the controversy now before them*. This last phrase is the key. The facts of the two cases are different. In communication law, the opportunities for building arguments in favor of distinguishing a precedent are many and varied. The earlier case might deal with a movie that has been found to meet the current definition of obscenity, whereas the case we are looking at today might involve a film that has some sexy scenes in it yet could not be considered so hard-core as to be obscene. The earlier decision might have been a libel case in which the plaintiff was a famous person, what the courts have come to call a **public figure**. If the case we are looking at today involves a libel plaintiff who is not at all famous, many features of libel law that were applied in the earlier case will be inapplicable.

The fourth and last option is to **modify** the earlier precedent. Knowing the dictionary definition of *modify* is not going to be much help here. In the law, to modify a precedent is to follow, in a very general way, the rule that seems to explain the earlier case but to at the same time show a recognition that something "out there, in the *real* world" has changed. Perhaps an example or two will clarify. In libel law, one of the things that plaintiffs must prove is that an utterance or publication was truly defamatory, that it damaged their reputations. Historically, falsely accusing someone of being homosexual would almost certainly be deemed libelous. Indeed, up until 2004,[35] when the Supreme Court struck down Texas's sodomy law, the charge amounted to one of criminality in several states. But societal values change over time, and most courts today will say that to be thought gay is not necessarily to have one's reputation damaged.[36] The general rule—libel demands a finding of **defamation**—still holds, and we are still following it in principle, but the world has changed to the point where what used to be thought of as defamatory might no longer be considered so.

33. *Joseph Burstyn, Inc. v. Wilson*, 343 U.S. 495, 501 (1952).

34. *McConnell v. Federal Election Commission*, 540 U.S. 93 (2003).

35. *Lawrence v. Texas*, 539 U.S. 558 (2003).

36. *Albright v. Morton*, 321 F. Supp. 2d 130, 136–139 (D. Mass. 2004), *aff'd sub nom. Amrak Productions v. Morton*, 410 F. 3d 69 (1st Cir. 2005).

The Supreme Court's changing thinking about TV in courtrooms provides another example of modifying a precedent. In the 1960s, the Court overturned the swindling conviction of one of President Johnson's Texas friends because the TV cameras permitted at his trial created a zoolike atmosphere.[37] Less than twenty years later, the Court upheld the **conspiracy** convictions of some Florida police officers who had argued unsuccessfully that TV at their trial was a violation of their constitutional rights.[38] How can we explain the two differing results, when the Court did not actually overturn the earlier case? Something "out there," in the real world, had changed. Television technology had grown more sophisticated and far less intrusive, to the point where the technology now could be introduced into the courtroom without disrupting the proceedings.

Having now reviewed the four options open to a court that is presented with a precedent for consideration, it should be emphasized that it is not always perfectly clear which option the court has exercised. Recall that we treated the question of whether films are protected by the First Amendment as an example of the Supreme Court's having overruled itself after a few decades had passed. That same constitutional history, however, could be seen as an example of modifying the earlier precedent. It could be argued that in the early days of motion pictures, films had no message to impart, no story to tell; they were merely toys. We flocked to the movie theaters because we were fascinated with the optical illusion itself. Perhaps, then, it would make no more sense to say that films are protected "expression" than to say that a kaleidoscope is protected expression. For the Court many years after that decision to recognize that motion pictures *now* were being used to tell stories, to delight but also to inspire and educate, would be more an example of modifying than of overruling. That which would have changed would not be the minds of the justices but the place of motion pictures in society.

Another reason it is not always clear which strategy a court has used is that there

---

THINGS TO REMEMBER

Common Law Precedents

- The common law, or "judge-made law," is the body of precedents that can inform a current controversy.
- When presented with a precedent, a court may do one of four things:
  - Follow it (the principle of *stare decisis*)
  - Distinguish it
  - Modify it
  - Overturn it

---

37. *Estes v. Texas*, 381 U.S. 532 (1965).
38. *Chandler v. Florida*, 449 U.S. 560 (1981).

is a strong tendency in the law toward a kind of inertia against the outright overturning of precedents. As one commentator put it, "Most of what seems essentially false in judges' opinions" is "the repeated insistence that they are not changing the law at all when they obviously are."[39]

An Overview of the American Judiciary

Now that we know what courts may do with common-law precedents, we need to develop an understanding of how the judiciary is structured in this country. In other words, what does it mean to "go to court"?

We should first realize that there is not one judicial system in the United States, but rather a federal system, a system for each of the states, and one for the District of Columbia. There are thus fifty-two systems in all, without even counting the courts governing such places as Puerto Rico or the Virgin Islands. It is important to keep that in mind throughout this book, because we will often be able to offer only generalizations rather than definitive answers about the status of a particular legal doctrine. The law varies from state to state and from one region of the federal judiciary to another.

While federal judges are appointed to life terms by the president, with the advice and consent of the Senate, the vast majority of state judges are elected. In states that elect their judges, a natural tension has long been recognized. On the one hand, if voters are to be called upon to elect their judiciaries, those voters should be fully informed about the candidates' backgrounds. But to many people the practice of electioneering and the seeking of campaign contributions seem inconsistent with the cherished tradition of an impartial and independent judiciary. States deal with the tension in a variety of ways. Some use "retention elections," in which voters are asked only whether a judge should get to retain her seat (there are no alternative candidates offered on the ballot). Other states permit competing candidates but conduct nonpartisan elections in which candidates' party affiliations do not appear on ballots. Most state judges also enjoy far longer terms—as long as fifteen years in some jurisdictions—than their counterparts in the other branches of government. Then too, judicial candidates are often held to eligibility requirements—a law degree, or having been approved by an appointed judicial commission—equally unparalleled in the other branches.

Sometimes courts have had to adjudicate the constitutionality of rules governing the election and performance of state judges. In 2008 the U.S. Supreme Court upheld New York State's mechanism for electing its state judges.[40] In that state, political par-

---

39. M. Shapiro, "Incremental Decision Making," in *Courts, Law, and Judicial Processes*, ed. S. Sidney Ulmer (New York: Free Press, 1981), 316

40. *New York State Board of Elections v. Torres*, 552 U.S. 196 (2008).

ties elect delegates who will in turn select the parties' candidate for judicial posts. There is nothing unsavory about allowing leaders of political parties to have nearly complete control over who their parties' judicial nominees would be, the majority held. Indeed, this is the essence of freedom of association.

A few years earlier the justices had struck down a Minnesota law that prohibited judicial candidates there from making utterances that might even *appear* to commit them to a point of view on matters likely to come before their court. As Justice Scalia indicated in his majority opinion, "there is almost no legal or political issue that is unlikely to come before a judge."[41] This is not to suggest that state judges' impartiality can always be assumed. Thus, in 2009 the Court held that there was enough of an appearance of judicial impropriety to overturn a West Virginia Supreme Court decision when the state's chief justice had benefited from some $3 million in "independent expenditures" by one of the litigants before him.[42]

A Three-Tiered Hierarchy

The structure of the judiciary itself need not be a source of complete bewilderment. Indeed, the hierarchy of courts in the states is almost without exception modeled after the federal system. There are three layers. At the bottom are the **trial courts**. In the federal system these are called **federal district courts**. The names of the trial courts vary greatly from state to state but are most frequently called **superior courts**.

Litigants who are unhappy with the trial court result have the option of bringing an appeal to the next layer of the judiciary. In the federal system, and in most states, these courts are called, intuitively enough, **appellate courts**. In the federal system these appellate courts govern a specific region of the country, called a **federal circuit**. There are thirteen such circuits. Eleven of them are given numbers. There is also an appellate court for the District of Columbia. That particular court has jurisdiction over most appeals from decisions of the FCC and other federal agencies. If you work in the electronic media or cable television industries, this court may thus be the most important one governing your professional life. The thirteenth federal appellate court is the one for the Federal Circuit, a special court created by Congress in 1982 to handle specialized appeals such as in patent and trademark cases.[43]

Litigants who are not satisfied with an appellate ruling can sometimes take their grievance one step higher. The pinnacle of the judiciary in both the federal and state systems is also an appellate court, but it goes by a special name. We have already made reference many times in this chapter to the U.S. Supreme Court. The highest court in most states is also referred to as a supreme court, although there are some exceptions; New York's highest court, for example, is its Court of Appeals.

---

41. *Republican Party of Minnesota v. White*, 536 U.S. 765, 772 (2002).

42. *Caperton v. A.T. Massey Coal Company*, 129 S. Ct. 2252 (2009).

43. For a full-color map of the federal appellate courts' **jurisdiction**, go to www.uscourts.gov/courtlinks/.

Although we often hear aggrieved parties vow that they will take their cases "all the way to the Supreme Court, if necessary," in fact this is romantic fancy because the justices of the Supreme Court have tremendous latitude about which of the thousands of appeals filed there will ever be heard. In recent years, the justices have issued opinions in far fewer cases than in the past, only seventy-three in their 2009–2010 term. Many state supreme courts have similar discretion to determine which cases they will hear. As a result, litigants are often limited to having their grievances heard in two, rather than three, rungs of the judicial system.

The Scope of a Precedent

Thus far we have used the word *precedent* to refer to an earlier court decision that might lead a court today to rule similarly. Not all precedents are equal, however. A precedent in a state court in Wisconsin, for example, even if decided by that state's highest court, has no *binding* precedential value on a state judge in California. The California court might be persuaded by the logic of the Wisconsin court's arguments, but it is not required to follow the precedent. If a judge hears a case that raises issues that have never been raised before in his or her jurisdiction, the controversy is often referred to as one of **first impression**. If you have ever seen the film *Whose Life Is It Anyway?*, you may recall the scene in which a trial judge comes to the hospital to decide whether Richard Dreyfuss's paraplegic character has a right to die. In this judge's jurisdiction, the issue was depicted as a case of first impression, although the judge was aware of precedents from other states.

Judges are bound by precedents only by higher courts in the same area, or jurisdiction, as their own. If you are a state trial court judge, you are bound by relevant decisions of the U.S. Supreme Court and by your state's supreme court, as well as by any appellate rulings from courts in the same appellate division (geographic region of the state) as your own. If you are a federal trial judge, you are bound by U.S. Supreme Court decisions, as well as by federal appellate decisions that come from the same circuit in which you find yourself. Until the U.S. Supreme Court gives guidance with a definitive ruling, there tend to be conflicting decisions among the circuits. We see frequent examples of this phenomenon throughout this book.

The U.S. Supreme Court is the ultimate arbiter of what the U.S. Constitution means. It must be emphasized, however, that the Court has no authority to interpret state constitutions; that is the province of the individual state supreme courts.

The Current U.S. Supreme Court

The most recent addition to the Supreme Court is Elena Kagan, who assumed her duties in 2010. An Obama appointee, she is one of four members of the Court—the others are Sonia Sotomajor, Ruth Bader Ginsburg, and Stephen Breyer—appointed by Democratic presidents. Chief Justice Roberts, as well as justices Samuel Alito, Anthony Kennedy, Antonin Scalia, and Clarence Thomas, were appointed by Republican presidents. U.S. Supreme Court justices are appointed, with the "advice and consent" of the Senate, to lifetime terms, as are all federal judges. The Senate confirmation process can be rather stormy, as evidenced in recent decades by the media spectacles surrounding Senate Judiciary Committee hearings on the candidacies of judges Robert Bork (rejected) and Clarence Thomas (ultimately confirmed by a slim 52–48 vote in the full Senate).

Going to Court: Civil or Criminal

Conflicts resulting in a trip to the courtroom are generally of two types, **civil** or **criminal**. The name of the proceeding is usually an indication of which category we have before us. Civil cases are given names of the form *A v. B* (e.g., *Smith v. Jones*), where person A is the **plaintiff** who is suing person B, the **defendant**. In criminal proceedings, the "plaintiff" becomes the government, which is said to **prosecute** the

From left to right: Standing: Sonia Sotomayor, Stephen Breyer, Samuel Alito, Elena Kagan. Seated: Clarence Thomas, Antonin Scalia, Chief Justice John Roberts, Anthony Kennedy, Ruth Bader Ginsburg. Photo by Steve Petteway, Collection of the Supreme Court of the United States.

case against the defendant. Thus we may have names such as *United States v. Dennis*, *Georgia v. Stanley*, or *State v. Dalton*.

In civil disputes, the case begins with the plaintiff filing a **complaint** with the court, which enumerates the specific allegations of misconduct against the defendant. The defendant then has an opportunity to file a response to the complaint, referred to as the **answer**.

The process of **discovery** then takes place, and it can be both lengthy and costly. The label makes sense because this step is when each side of the dispute discovers the nature of the other's case. Lawyers for one side will question the other's witnesses, and transcripts of such pretrial **depositions** are made and can be used later at trial to ensure that witnesses' stories remain consistent.

Typically a flurry of legal paper filings will then ensue. Some filings might seek to avoid a trial by having the court grant **summary judgment** to one side or the other (more frequently to the defense). Summary judgment for the defendant is appropriate when, taking into account all facts agreed to by defendant and plaintiff and presuming the truth of plaintiff's version of any disputed facts, the law requires that the defendant prevail. Keep in mind that mass media defendants are often very unpopular with juries. As a result, motions for summary judgment are very important to professional communicators.

Often, too, motions are made that are aimed at setting the ground rules, should a trial be necessary. Sometimes such motions concern the threshold issue of whether a specific court has a right to hear the case at all. One of the many disgruntled participants in the hit motion picture, *Borat*, for example, was told she could not sue in her home state of Alabama, in that the release form she had signed dictated that any legal disputes arising from the film would have to be brought in New York courts.[44] As we will see in chapter 4, one of the most important pretrial issues to have settled in libel disputes is whether the plaintiff is a public figure or an ordinary private citizen. The answer to that one question often determines the ultimate winner and loser of the case.

If you have ever been called for jury duty, you may have noted that legal disputes are often settled at the last minute, even on the day a trial is scheduled to begin. Indeed, a very tiny percentage of court cases, civil or criminal, ever actually come to trial. Sometimes these pretrial settlements (in criminal law, they usually involve **plea bargaining** to a lesser charge) occur at the very last minute, after the careful questioning of potential jurors (called **voir dire**) has been completed and both sides see the jury that will actually hear the case.

Criminal cases involve some unique features with which communication professionals should have at least some familiarity. Typically the prosecution of the case begins with the arrest of the suspect. The **arraignment**, at which a judge formally reads to the suspect the charges against him or her and at which the suspect may make an initial **plea**, follows soon after. Should the defendant plead guilty, sentencing may take place immediately or soon after additional facts about any mitigating or

---

44. *ex parte Cohen*, 998 So. 2d 508 (Ala. 2008).

aggravating circumstances surrounding the offense are brought to the judge's attention in the form of a presentencing report.

If the defendant pleads not guilty, there is usually at least one more major step in the process prior to a trial itself. In some settings this step is the **preliminary hearing**. In other jurisdictions, and in federal prosecutions, it is the seeking of an **indictment** by a **grand jury**. In either case, the purpose of this pretrial step is to ensure that the state does in fact have enough evidence against the defendant to justify "holding the defendant over" and that the taxpayers' money will not be wasted by going to trial. Al-

Etiquette teacher Katie Martin's suit against the producers of *Borat* was dismissed by the Alabama Supreme Court, because she had agreed in writing to bring any legal disputes to New York State courts.

though grand juries and "real" juries (usually called **petit juries**) are typically drawn from the same jury pools (e.g., from voter registration lists), there are two important differences between the two. First, whereas petit jurors hear full-blown criminal trials, traditionally open to the press and public, the evidence presented to a grand jury by a district attorney is traditionally kept secret. Second, the burden of proof demanded by petit jurors is that the state establish its case "beyond a reasonable doubt," whereas grand jurors, to indict a suspect, need only find that there is "**probable cause**" to believe that the defendant is guilty.

Not all trials are jury trials, of course. The rules governing when litigants in a civil case have a right to a jury trial vary among jurisdictions. Sometimes it may be wise for one or the other party in a lawsuit to forgo that right. It is commonly believed, for example, that libel plaintiffs prefer jury trials, whereas media defendants in such trials prefer judge, or bench, trials. Juries are more likely to be swayed by the emotionalism and immediacy of seeing a wronged plaintiff, or so the reasoning goes, whereas they might not be swayed by the more abstract philosophies in support of freedom of the press—especially if the press got its facts wrong and hurt someone in their community.[45]

The Appeals Process

Whichever side wins at the trial level in a civil dispute, or if a criminal prosecution results in a conviction, an appeal may be the next step. There are many differences between trials and appellate hearings. Trials typically take much longer than appellate hearings. Only trials can have jurors and witnesses. Appellate hearings are much less

---

45. Rodney A. Smolla, *Suing the Press: Libel, the Media, and Power* (New York: Oxford University Press, 1986), 194–95.

THINGS TO REMEMBER

The Basic Structure of the Legal System

- The federal judiciary has three levels—district courts, circuit courts of appeal, and the Supreme Court; most states mirror this system.
- The U.S. Supreme Court, as well as many other state supreme courts, is not required to accept any invitation to hear an appeal from lower courts.
- Lower court judges are legally *bound* to follow precedents only from higher courts in their own jurisdictions.
- Courts hear both civil cases (in which an individual plaintiff sues a defendant) and criminal prosecutions by the state.
- Prior to the convening of an actual trial, much discovery takes place, and there may also be motions to avoid a trial by seeking summary judgment.

populous affairs; typically one attorney for each side makes oral arguments in front of the court—which can be interrupted at any time by questions from the bench—for a half hour or so. The oral argument usually takes place weeks or months after lengthy position papers called **briefs** have been filed in court by each side. Sometimes parties beyond those immediately involved in the dispute file a brief. In a media law case, for example, organizations such as the American Society of Newspaper Editors or the National Association of Broadcasters may ask to have their thoughts on the controversy entertained by the court. The papers filed by such associations are called **amicus briefs**, *amicus* being Latin for *friend*. Sometimes you may encounter the phrase **amicus curiae** (friend of the court) to describe a group filing an amicus brief.

Although only trial courts have witnesses and jurors, in one sense it is the appellate courtroom that is more crowded. Trial courts generally are presided over by one judge, whereas at the appellate level a panel of judges is involved. In federal procedure, the appellate panels consist of three randomly assigned judges from that circuit. An **en banc** ruling by all the judges of a circuit (usually a dozen or more) may be sought as an intermediate level of appeal after an unsuccessful hearing in front of a three-judge panel and before a petition to the U.S. Supreme Court.

Another key difference between trial and appellate proceedings is the kind of issues addressed by the courts. Trial courts entertain questions of both fact and law, whereas appellate courts generally deal only with questions of law. One major exception to this general principle is the "**clearly erroneous rule**" of federal civil procedure. This rule permits a federal appellate court to look at the facts of the case independently if the court first determines that the trial judge made a clearly erroneous finding of fact. The rule is not often invoked. It is viewed as strong medicine, in part because leveling such an accusation against a lower court judge is rather insulting, and also because invoking the rule is itself ultimately reviewable by a yet higher court.

Questions of fact ask, "What happened?" In a homicide case, for example, we would ask if this criminal suspect emptied a revolver into the deceased, and if the victim died from the wounds thus inflicted or from some other cause. However, whether the answers to those and other facts demand a finding of first-degree or second-degree homicide, or involuntary manslaughter, is a **question of law**. In an obscenity prosecution, issues such as what kind of sexual acts are engaged in and with what frequency by the on-screen talent are questions of fact. Whether the film as a whole satisfies a statute's definition of obscenity and whether that definition in turn satisfies the requirements set forth by relevant Supreme Court rulings are questions of law.

Decisions and Opinions

Because appellate courts have several judges hearing a dispute, the permutations of votes for one side or the other and the reasoning behind each such vote become more complicated than in a single-judge trial. A whole nomenclature has developed to describe such matters. Let us use the nine justices of the U.S. Supreme Court as

It seems the speaker has been recently promoted to an appellate court, where, unlike at the trial level, there are no juries or witnesses for judges to scold (only lawyers).

the model in this discussion. We begin by emphasizing the rather intuitive distinction between a decision and an opinion. A **decision** tells us who wins the case, whereas an **opinion** tells us why. In the extreme, we might have a unanimous decision with nine separate opinions. Such a situation would tell us who prevailed, but would probably give lower courts little if any guidance as to what the decision really means or how to apply it to slightly different facts in the future.

First let us consider the **majority opinion**. (When you read actual Supreme Court cases, you will not find majority opinions referred to as such. Rather, you will typically find phrasing such as "Justice Green delivered the opinion for the Court, in which Justices Brown, White, Blue, and Orange joined.") U.S. Supreme Court majority opinions must command at least five votes, presuming that all nine members have participated in a case. For any number of reasons, however, fewer than nine may vote in any given case. Sometimes justices feel the need to **recuse** themselves—that is, to purposely decide not to participate in a case—for ethical reasons. Maybe one justice's daughter is a student at a university that is party to a case, or perhaps another owns stock in a corporation that is one of the litigants. If only seven justices participate in a case, four votes are all that are needed to produce a majority decision.

Majority opinions tend to have a certain structure. They will often begin by reciting the facts of the case, such as who did what to whom, who brought suit and why, and what the lower courts ruled. Typically at or near the very end of the opinion we will learn the Court's **holding**—what the case stands for, and what specific guidance the justices intend lower courts to take from their decision. The holdings of some landmark decisions are well known to most Americans, such as the *Gideon* holding that indigent criminal suspects must be provided with free legal counsel,[46] or the *Miranda* holding that information learned from suspects in police interrogations is inadmissible if the accused is not advised of certain of his or her constitutional rights prior to questioning.[47] Much of what appears in majority opinions between the recitation of the facts and the setting forth of the holding is called **dicta**. Some of the dicta may consist of reasoning in support of the Court's ultimate conclusion. Dicta often include predictable, almost formulaic repetitions of boilerplate paragraphs from previous cases. Virtually any case involving student newspapers, for example, no matter which side actually prevails, will include a famous dictum from the Vietnam War–era *Tinker* case to the effect that students do not "shed their constitutional rights to freedom of speech or expression at the schoolhouse gate."[48]

Dicta carry much less precedential value than the actual holding of a case, for at least two reasons. First, in our constitutional system of separation of powers, courts are empowered to decide immediate controversies set before them, not to create law in the abstract. Because dicta by their very nature often reach far beyond the immedi-

---

46. *Gideon v. Wainwright*, 372 U.S. 335 (1963).
47. *Miranda v. Arizona*, 383 U.S. 436 (1966).
48. *Tinker v. Des Moines Independent Community School District*, 393 U.S. 503, 506 (1969).

ate conflict being adjudicated, giving them too much weight would have the long-term effect of making the judiciary into a mini-legislature. Second, only the holding of a case tells the parties involved exactly why the one side has won, and only the holding is supposed to tell lower courts exactly what lesson to learn from the case at hand. Accordingly, judges do not have any immediate incentive to consider their dicta as carefully as they do their holdings, and the imprecision likely to result from this lack of incentive will ultimately be destructive. The two reasons for discounting dicta, then, concern issues of legitimacy and accuracy.[49]

A very special situation arises when the Supreme Court has only eight members sitting and produces a 4–4 tie vote. The lower court decision is affirmed, but that affirmance does not carry any binding precedential weight beyond the jurisdiction of the lower court; the Supreme Court's tie vote does not produce the "law of the land." Thus, if a case is appealed from the Wisconsin Supreme Court and results in such a 4–4 tie, the legal doctrine established by the lower court will be binding only in Wisconsin. In essence, the result is as if the case had never been heard by the U.S. Supreme Court. Typically, no opinion is written when a case produces a 4–4 tie.

From the vantage point of lower court judges looking to the U.S. Supreme Court for guidance, an especially troublesome result occurs when a clear majority decision is announced, but not enough justices can agree on the rationale behind the decision to produce a majority opinion. The opinion that commands the most votes—it might be three, it might be four—is referred to as a **plurality opinion**. The reasoning offered in such an opinion will not carry any precedential value, although it can offer some insights as to how the Court might react to slightly different situations in the future.

Assuming that a case does produce a clear majority opinion, some justices who voted with the winning side, and who even signed on to the majority opinion, may still feel the need to write a separate **concurring opinion** to indicate how their own views of the case may differ a bit from the view espoused by the majority. Then, too, a justice might "concur in the decision only," which means that the justice will vote with the majority but wants to emphasize that he or she wholly rejects the majority's reasoning. Concurring opinions are often written by the justice who provided the "swing vote" in a 5–4 decision. Justice Lewis Powell was famous for writing such opinions, and Justice Kennedy seems to be his successor in this regard.[50] As you may well imagine, the tone of such opinions frequently suggests that "I will go this far, *but no further.*"

The chance to write opinions is not restricted to those who vote on the winning side, of course. Those justices whose votes place them in the minority will produce at least one **dissenting opinion**. Sometimes the reasoning espoused by a dissenting justice today becomes the basis for a majority opinion tomorrow.

---

49. Michael C. Dorf, "Dicta and Article III," 142 *University of Pennsylvania Law Review* 1997 (1994); see also Pierre N. Leval, "Judging Under the Constitution: Dicta about Dicta," 81 *New York University Law Review* 1249 (2006).

50. Eric J. Segall, "Reconceptualizing Judicial Activism as Judicial Responsibility: A Tale of Two Justice Kennedys," 41 *Arizona State Law Journal* 709 (2009).

Two final categories of opinions you may encounter are the **per curiam opinion** and the **memorandum order**. *Per curiam* means "by the court," and a per curiam opinion is a majority opinion that is not signed by any particular justice. A memorandum order is a court decision that is not accompanied by an opinion; we learn who won, but little, if anything, else.

Legal Citations: How to Find the Cases

You have already been exposed in this chapter to examples of legal citations, which are designed to tell readers what court decided a case and how to find the full text of the decision. Legal citation formats traditionally follow this pattern, after the name of the case is given: volume number; abbreviation of the name of the publication; page number where the case begins; then, in parentheses, the name of the court (if not already clear from the name of the publication) and the date the case was decided. Look back at footnote 40, for example. It tells us that the citation for *New York State Board of Elections v. Torres* is 552 U.S. 196 (2008).

- We can find the case in Volume 321.
- The publication is *United States Reports* (one of the places you can find U.S. Supreme Court decisions).
- If you were looking for the case the old-fashioned way, in actual books on library shelves, you would find this court case beginning on page 196.
- The case was decided in 2008.

THINGS TO REMEMBER

Appellate Procedures, Decisions, and Opinions

- The losing party in a trial may bring an appeal to a higher court.
- Both parties will then file written briefs, followed by oral arguments before a panel of judges.
- Other parties may express their views through the use of amicus briefs.
- Losing parties in a federal appellate court can petition the entire court to hear the case again en banc, prior to contemplating a Supreme Court appeal.
- Generally appellate courts may only address questions of law, whereas trial courts look also at questions of fact.
- Decisions tell who wins a case; opinions tell why.
- The actual holding of a decision is its true precedential value; often the bulk of the text in an opinion consists of dicta, which have very limited precedential value.
- Depending on how many judges join an opinion, and which way they vote, the opinion may be referred to as majority, plurality, concurring, or dissenting.

A bit of truth in advertising is in order: The moment we talk about finding court cases in "volumes" of "publications," we are engaged in a bit of fiction for most readers of this book. Most college students are more likely to have online access to court cases (as through LEXIS/NEXIS) than they are to have ready access to a brick-and-mortar law library. For present purposes, then, it will suffice that you can recognize what "publications" the most frequently encountered citations refer to, even if you are not likely to ever read the court cases cited there in an actual printed volume.

The Torres example used earlier refers to *United States Reports*, which is one place we can find Supreme Court decisions. Others include *Supreme Court Reporter* (abbreviated S. Ct.) and *United States Supreme Court Reports, Lawyers' Edition* (L. Ed.). Federal appellate decisions are in the *Federal Reporter* (F.), with more recent cases in the second or third series of the publication (F. 2d and F. 3d, respectively). Fairly recent appellate decisions not directed to be officially published by judges may nonetheless be printed in the *Federal Appendix* (F. Appx.). Federal district opinions can be found in the *Federal Supplement* (F. Supp., and F. Supp. 2d for more recent cases).

Each state's judiciary publishes its own case reports. Thus we may see references, for example, to the *Wisconsin Reporter* or the *New York Supplement*. The West Publishing Company's "regional reporter" system conveniently breaks the fifty states' decisions down into seven areas—the Atlantic (A.), the Pacific (P.), the Northeastern (N.E.), the Northwestern (N.W.), the Southern (So.), the Southeastern (S.E.), and the Southwestern (S.W.). Keep in mind, however, that a case appearing in one West regional reporter and not another is not at all relevant to the precedential value of a

---

THINGS TO REMEMBER

Finding the Cases

- U.S. Supreme Court decisions can be found in many places:
  - *United States Reports* (abbreviated U.S.)
  - *Supreme Court Reporter* (S. Ct.)
  - *United States Law Week* (U.S.L.W.)
- Federal appellate decisions are most easily found in the *Federal Reporter* (F., F.2d, or F.3d).
- Federal district court decisions are found in the *Federal Supplement* (F. Supp. or F. Supp. 2d) or *Federal Appendix* (Fed. Appx. or F. App'x.).
- State decisions can be found in official state reporters or more frequently in academic libraries, in West Publishing's "regional reporters" (Atlantic, Pacific, Northeastern, Northwestern, Southern, Southeastern, and Southwestern).
- Legal citations are traditionally in the form of volume number, name of reporter, page number, court, and date decided, as in 878 S.W.2d 577 (Tex. 1994).
- The legal profession is in flux on the issue of citations, in that most research is done online nowadays, not from actual books with volume numbers.

case. In other words, do not confuse a federal appellate decision's *circuit* (very important to know when determining the case's precedential scope) and a state decision's West Publishing region.[51]

There is much more that could be said about legal citations, but whole treatises are devoted to the subject, and we just don't have enough space here to get bogged down. Moreover, the whole system is in flux, largely owing to that fiction mentioned earlier: If most folks find court cases and other legal documents on the Internet instead of in an actual "volume," do the numbers really mean anything anymore? Don't be surprised therefore when you encounter (even in this book) citations that refer only to LEXIS "page numbers" for court cases that are either not yet published or may never be published.[52]

Chapter Summary

What we call communication law actually comes from many sources, including the federal and state constitutions, statutes, actions by regulatory agencies, executive orders, and the common law.

With respect to the U.S. Constitution, the First Amendment—especially its Free Speech Clause and Free Press Clause—is of most importance to media professionals. Several other provisions of the Constitution have implications for the practice of journalism. Some state constitutions give individuals greater rights to free speech than does the First Amendment.

The common-law tradition of establishing and adjusting precedents is an important part of our jurisprudence. Courts may follow, modify, distinguish, or overturn an earlier case. Judges' decisions tell who wins a case; their opinions tell why they reached this result. Opinions may be majority, plurality, concurring, or dissenting. The federal judiciary, as well as most state systems, has three layers, a trial level and two appellate levels. Trial courts deal with questions of law and fact, whereas appellate courts are generally restricted to matters of law.

---

51. You can see a full-color map of the West regional reporter system at http://lib.law.washington.edu/ref/103590BKpage6.jpg.

52. Readers wishing to learn more about citations, and about the ongoing debates in legal circles about how to respond to the world of online legal research, are directed to Peter Martin's online treatise *Introduction to Basic Legal Citation*. Find it at www.law.cornell.edu/citation.

Chapter 2

THE DEVELOPMENT OF FREEDOM OF SPEECH

Reacting to an Italian court decision convicting Google executives of violating the privacy rights of an autistic youngster for failing to remove from YouTube (which is owned by Google) in a timely manner a video of the child being bullied, Indiana University law professor Fred Cates reminded us that in such Internet disputes, the First Amendment may as well be a "local ordinance."[1] Although the American press almost uniformly expressed outrage at the Italian decision, an equally valid lesson to draw from the case is that in our own country, compared to most other Western democracies, freedom of speech is revered almost to the point of fetishism. It is much harder for libel plaintiffs to win a judgment in the United States than in much of Europe. For better or worse, the United States is almost unique among Western democracies in the degree to which it tolerates hate speech. To the extent that freedom of the press conflicts at times with a criminal suspect's right to a fair trial, our country's weighing of the competing interests is far more tilted toward the press than it is in Canada, where it is assumed that the press will be prohibited from reporting anything about a high-profile trial until the jury's verdict is in.

Speech as *the* American Freedom?

An often-repeated story tells of nineteenth-century statesman Daniel Webster who, when asked which of the many freedoms enjoyed by Americans is most important, unhesitatingly replied that it must be freedom of speech. If stripped of all other freedoms, his reasoning went, this freedom is the one he could use to win each of the

---

1. Adam Liptak, "When Free Worlds Collide," *New York Times*, February 28, 2010, WK1.

others back. Along these lines, it is worth remembering also that when FDR delivered his famous "four freedoms" speech to Congress in 1941, the first of the "essential human freedoms" that he felt that all world citizens should be granted was freedom of speech.

Perhaps we should not carry this romance with free speech too far. The Founding Fathers have often had attributed to them the belief that freedom of speech was surely the most important of all the principles articulated in the Bill of Rights; after all, they did put it in the *First* Amendment. The facts get in the way of this assertion, however. What we now call the First Amendment was actually submitted as amendment number three in the Bill of Rights. The first two amendments failed to win approval.

Even if the "first-ness" of the First Amendment is a historic accident rather than a symbol of the founders' priorities, the wording of that constitutional provision seems to suggest that issues of freedom of speech and press were indeed very special to the document's drafters. The First Amendment is written as an absolute promise that Congress shall make *no* law abridging the freedoms enumerated within. Unlike the wording of many other nations' analogous guarantees and those in many state constitutions, there is no requirement that citizens behave "responsibly" to enjoy these rights. Think too of some of the other guarantees provided in the Bill of Rights. In the Fourth Amendment, for example, we learn that we are free only from "unreasonable" searches and seizures. The Fifth Amendment warns that our property, our liberty, and even our life can be taken away from us as long as the government follows an unarticulated set of rules that together constitute "due process." The Eighth Amendment does not, of course, protect us from any and all kinds of punishment, but only from the "cruel and unusual" ones; that same amendment also tells us that if we are suspected of a crime, we may be required to pay any amount of bail short of "excessive," should we wish to avoid staying in jail until our trial date.

If Americans revere freedom of expression so much, it behooves us to know something about the origins of that freedom. The discussion of that history is broken down into two time periods. The first covers the period from Europeans' arrival in the Americas up through World War I. Then the story is carried forward from that era—when the Supreme Court first began to give some guidance as to the meaning of the First Amendment—to the present.

Freedom of Speech from the Colonial Period through World War I

The Puritans who settled the Massachusetts Bay Colony were not especially noted for tolerance of diverse views. Banishments, excommunication, public whippings, and mutilations were common punishments for speaking out against the faith or against the colony's government. Similarly harsh sanctions were often imposed in Connecticut and throughout New England. Governor Dale's code governing Virginia as of 1610, for example, established the death penalty for anyone who spoke out against the tenets of Christian faith. Even the most tolerant of the colonies seem rather intolerant by today's standards in that freedom of religious expression was generally granted only to professed Christians.

Concerning the early colonists' respect for the working press, consider that the very first newspaper in the New World, Benjamin Harris's *Publick Occurrences Both Foreign and Domestic*, was shut down in Massachusetts after its very first issue was printed. When James Franklin's *New England Courant* published an article critical of the colony's government, he was promptly jailed (during which time his younger brother Benjamin took over the paper).

To be fair, there is some evidence of increasing tolerance for dissenting views during the colonial period. Even as early as the 1600s, there was a trend toward treating those judged guilty of seditious libel (i.e., criticizing the government) more and more leniently. Punishments such as physical violence (ear cropping, breaking arms and legs, tongue boring, and whipping) and public humiliation (use of the pillory or the stocks, or simply forcing the accused to recant publicly and beg for forgiveness) gave way over time to sanctions such as fines or the required posting of a bond that would be forfeitable only in the event of further transgressions.

Probably the most dramatic example of how strongly at least some of the colonists felt toward freedom of the press was the seditious libel prosecution in the 1730s of *New York Weekly Journal* publisher John Peter Zenger, who had been imprisoned for several months prior to his trial for publishing statements highly critical of the colony's governor, William Crosby. During this era, truth was not an accepted defense to the charge of sedition. Indeed, the logic of the day suggested that because the purpose of such laws was to avoid inflaming the passions of the people against the king and his governors, truthful criticisms would be all the more dangerous.

Andrew Hamilton, who made the closing arguments on behalf of Zenger, openly invited the jury to ignore the letter of the law and to find on behalf of Zenger precisely because he had not printed any substantial untruths. The jury did indeed acquit Zenger, to the delight of those assembled in the courtroom.

The founders would not have been able to muster the necessary votes to ensure the Constitution's adoption had they not assured their constituents that a Bill of Rights would be added. With respect to the First Amendment, there was considerable difference of opinion concerning whether the individual states should be enjoined from abridging citizens' freedom of expression or whether the proscription should apply only to the newly formed federal government. The latter view prevailed, and thus the amendment was phrased in terms of what *Congress* shall not do. Historians of the period point out also that it is not entirely clear what "freedom of speech" and "freedom of the press" meant to the drafters. Were citizens being promised freedom from any and all postpublication sanctions for communicative acts, or were they merely being assured that they would not be subject to **prior restraint**, to prepublication censorship? A later section of this chapter explores the issue of prior restraint in more detail.

Despite the First Amendment's strong wording, it took a rather short amount of time for the new Congress to enact laws that abridged freedom of speech. France and England were at war, and fears ran high that the United States would be drawn into the war. Congress passed and President Adams signed the **Alien and Sedition Acts**. Collectively, these acts gave the government increased powers to detain and deport noncitizens and criminalized the dissemination of some kinds of criticisms of the government.

Persons convicted under the Sedition Act could be fined heavily and imprisoned for up to five years. There were over a dozen prosecutions under the law, several directed against editors of the leading opposition newspapers of the day. Two lessons can be culled from the Sedition Act. First, the act compels us to remember that the same founders who had voted for the Bill of Rights also convinced themselves of the need to stifle political speech. Second, the act was a strategic failure in that those jailed for violating it became folk heroes; moreover, the demise of the Federalists resulted in large part from popular animosity toward that party's support of the act.

The period between 1801 (when the Sedition Act expired) and 1917 (when Congress passed the **Espionage Act**, discussed below) is characterized by a lack of major developments in First Amendment jurisprudence (even though the Supreme Court handed down dozens of decisions affecting the act of communication). Certainly there was much censorship in the Civil War era, especially directed against those speaking out against slavery.[2] And the latter portion of the nineteenth century required the courts to deal repeatedly with the issue of obscenity in response to congressional actions that, among other things, prohibited the use of the mails to send sexually oriented matter. By and large, at least with respect to definitive Supreme

---

THINGS TO REMEMBER

The Colonial Experience Forward

■ The early colonial experience included much political and religious intolerance.
■ The Zenger jury concluded that true speech should not be punished.
■ The founders chose not to apply the First Amendment to the individual states.
■ For at least some of the founders, freedom of speech and freedom of the press probably only meant freedom from prior restraint.
■ The fact that the First Amendment is *first* in the Bill of Rights is merely a coincidence.
■ Despite the First Amendment, Congress quickly enacted the Sedition Act.

---

2. Gautham Rao, "The Federal Posse Comitatus Doctrine: Slavery, Compulsion, and Statecraft in Mid-Nineteenth-Century America," 26 *Law and History Review* 1, 27 (2008).

Court interpretations of the First Amendment, these "forgotten years"[3] were not a time of much doctrinal advance and also not the focus of much scholarship. Therefore, a discussion of the Court's First Amendment doctrine as it developed in the World War I era and beyond is appropriate.

Freedom of Speech Doctrine Emerges

Call it *A Tale of Two Websites*. Actually, two tales, seven years apart. First we look at the Nuremberg Files website, which disseminated names and addresses of doctors who perform abortion in the form of online "wanted" posters and which expressed approval of those who carried out violent acts against such individuals. These features of the site were "true threats," a closely divided Ninth Circuit Court of Appeals ruled in 2002.[4]

Compare this to a 2009 decision from federal judge Lynn Edelman of Illinois. Matthew Hale, the leader of a white supremacist organization, was on trial for soliciting the murder of a federal judge. Soon after that trial's end, William White, one of Hale's followers, posted a notice on Overthrow.com, a website apparently popular with other white supremacists. This particular posting gave readers the name, address, telephone number, and many other identifying characteristics of the jury foreman from the Hale case—"the gay, anti-racist juror" who "convicted Matt Hale." But because the references to this particular juror did nothing more than give these factual details—even though earlier web postings from the defendant had suggested of other political opponents that they "should be lynched" or "should be drug out into the street and shot"—an indictment against White was dismissed.[5]

Taken together, these two decisions point to the difficulty of determining when political speech should be protected and when it crosses over the line into the kinds of incitement of illegal action the government has a right to prohibit. An appreciation of how courts attempt to resolve such difficult questions requires that we have some familiarity with the history of the Supreme Court's thinking about the First Amendment's protection for political speech. The Court's doctrine began to emerge in the World War I era and continued to emerge through the McCarthy period and beyond. It is not an exaggeration to say that the Court used the cases we discuss here to explain what the First Amendment means.

In the pages that follow you will learn much about antiwar activists, anarchists, and political dissidents of many persuasions. These early cases did not typically involve the mass media. Much of the doctrine that emerged from these cases, however, has laid

---

3. David M. Rabban, "The First Amendment in Its Forgotten Years," 90 *Yale Law Journal* 514 (1981).

4. *Planned Parenthood of the Columbia/Willamette, Inc. v. American Coalition of Life Activists*, 290 F. 3d 1058 (9th Cir. 2002).

5. *U.S. v. White*, 638 F. Supp. 2d 935 (N. D. Ill. 2009).

the foundation for contemporary applications of the First Amendment in a wide variety of circumstances, from regulation of advertising to broadcast station licensing.

The Clear and Present Danger Test: *Schenck v. United States*

The United States had entered into the "war to end all wars," which would later be known as World War I. Almost without exception, even the freest of nations curtail the amount of liberty enjoyed by their citizens the moment war is declared. The United States in 1917 certainly manifested this tendency when Congress passed the Espionage Act (amended in 1918). Not surprisingly, the act forbade any attempt to cause insubordination among the military or to in any way obstruct the draft. It also criminalized any speech or writing deemed "disloyal, profane, scurrilous, or abusive" of "the form of government of the United States . . . or the flag." The penalty for violating the law could be as severe as twenty years' imprisonment.

Charles Schenck, the general secretary of the Socialist Party, was convicted under the Espionage Act for sending leaflets to young men who had been called and accepted for military service, imploring them to resist the draft and to recognize that draftees are little more than slaves. Writing for a unanimous Supreme Court, Justice Holmes upheld Schenck's conviction. The only acceptable justification for suppressing political speech, Holmes concluded, is if the speaker's words "are used in such circumstances and are of such a nature as to create a clear and present danger that they will bring about the substantive evils that Congress has a right to prevent."[6] Holmes's opinion in *Schenck*—also remembered for having added to the lexicon the admonition that freedom of speech, although important, does not protect us from "falsely shouting fire in a theater"—was the birth of the "clear and present danger" test for measuring the scope of First Amendment freedoms. It is interesting that although the test's first appearance is in the context of an opinion *upholding* a criminal conviction for engaging in dissident speech, in later years the test evolved to emphasize that the state's power to punish such speech is very limited. The Supreme Court has cited *Schenck*'s famous phrase dozens of times in adjudicating First Amendment issues ranging from leased-access channels on cable TV systems and FCC broadcast indecency standards to regulation of advertising and campaign-finance reform.

The Marketplace of Ideas: *Abrams v. United States*

A few months after *Schenck*, the Supreme Court upheld another Espionage Act conviction. In this instance, however, Justice Holmes (joined by Justice Brandeis) dissented and in so doing gave birth to a metaphor more influential than any other in the history of First Amendment jurisprudence. At issue again were antiwar leaflets, this time printed by Jacob Abrams and four other Russian nationals living in the

---

6. *Schenck v. United States*, 249 U.S. 47, 52 (1919).

United States and distributed by such means as dropping them out of an office building window. Writing for a seven-person majority, Justice Clarke found that the intent of the offending literature was "to persuade the persons to whom it was addressed to turn a deaf ear to patriotic appeals in behalf of the government of the United States, and to cease to render it assistance in the prosecution of the war."[7]

Justices Holmes and Brandeis expressed dismay for the defendants' being sentenced to twenty years in jail "for the publishing of two leaflets that [they] had as much right to publish as the government has to publish the Constitution of the United States now vainly invoked by them." For them, the defendants' intent was to express support for the Russian Revolution, not hinder the U.S. war effort. The government's prosecution, the dissenters argued, did not seem aimed at the ends sought by the defendants, but rather at their political ideology itself. Holmes and Brandeis argued that such government actions, designed to "sweep away all opposition," ignore the "theory of our Constitution" that "the best test of truth is the power of [a] thought to get itself accepted in the competition of the market."

The "marketplace of ideas" metaphor has served as a rationale for dozens of Supreme Court and hundreds of lower court decisions. As expressed by Justice Holmes, it seems to be an instrumental value, one whose good comes from its likelihood to help the truth emerge. It can also be viewed as a good in and of itself. The FCC, for example, has claimed over the years to embrace the principle that a multitude of voices speaking over broadcast and cable channels is a desirable thing.

Not Only Congress, but the States, Too: *Gitlow v. New York*

The First Amendment, it will be recalled, tells only the *federal* government (indeed, only Congress) that it may not abridge freedom of speech and freedom of the press. This decision was a conscious one on the part of the drafters, who considered and rejected an alternate phrasing that would have restricted the power of each individual state government as well. In 1925, 134 years after the formal adoption of the Bill of Rights, the Supreme Court somewhat unceremoniously held that the First Amendment bars the states, too, from abridging Americans' freedom of expression. Justice Sanford accomplished this change in one sentence: "For present purposes we may and do assume," he said, "that freedom of speech and of the press—which are protected by the First Amendment from abridgment by Congress—are among the fundamental personal rights and 'liberties' protected by the due process clause of the Fourteenth Amendment from impairment by the States."[8]

---

7. *Abrams v. United States*, 250 U.S. 616, 620–621 (1919). For an intriguing variation on the marketplace of ideas metaphor, see Robert Jensen, "First Amendment Potluck," 3 *Communication Law and Policy* 563 (1998).

8. *Gitlow v. New York*, 268 U.S. 0652, 666 (1925). Which other Bill of Rights provisions would be "incorporated" so as to impose limitations not only on Congress but on the states too has been determined by the Supreme Court on a case-by-case basis. In 2010 the Court struck down a local

The context was the Supreme Court's decision to uphold Benjamin Gitlow's conviction, under New York's criminal anarchy statute, for having written a "Left Wing Manifesto" seeming to advocate the government's overthrow, by violent means if necessary. The majority opinion also posits a distinction between "abstract doctrine" or "academic discussion," which would presumably be protected by the First Amendment, and "language advocating, advising, or teaching the overthrow of organized government by unlawful means," which the New York law appropriately prohibited. The distinction was one that justices Holmes and Brandeis found unacceptable, and they once again dissented. Gitlow was not trying to "induce an uprising against government at once"; at most he sought such action "at some indefinite time in the future." The dissenters thus emphasized that a "clear and present danger" must in fact be *present*.

The "More Speech" Prescription: *Whitney v. California*

Two years after the *Gitlow* decision made clear that the First Amendment applied not only to federal but also state infringements on free speech, another criminal syndicalism prosecution, this time from the other coast, was before the Supreme Court.[9] Anita Whitney, who coincidentally was the niece of former Supreme Court justice Stephen Field, had been an active member of the Communist Labor Party in California. The immediate impetus for her prosecution seems to have been her attendance at the party's organizing convention, where, although she herself argued for a more moderate stance, the gathered delegates voted their full allegiance to the goal of an international workers' revolution.

The Supreme Court unanimously upheld Whitney's conviction under the state law, largely because her attorneys did not timely raise the federal constitutional issue that might have led to her vindication: whether her participation at the party convention constituted a "clear and present danger" to the state. Thus, even Justice Brandeis's stirring words from the case were part of a concurring rather than dissenting opinion:

> No danger flowing from speech can be deemed clear and present, unless the incidence of the evil apprehended is so imminent that it may befall before there is opportunity for full discussion. If there be time to expose through discussion the falsehood and fallacies, to avert the evil by the processes of education, *the remedy to be applied is more speech, not enforced silence.*[10]

The emphasized phrase carries enormous implications for First Amendment jurisprudence. Rather than prohibit political, religious, or similar charitable groups from

---

Chicago handgun ordinance, holding for the first time that the Second Amendment is applicable to the states. *McDonald v. City of Chicago*, 130 S. Ct. 3020 (2010).

9. *Whitney v. California*, 274 U.S. 357 (1927).

10. 274 U.S. at 377 (Brandeis, J., and Holmes, J., concurring) (emphasis added).

soliciting donations in airports, the "more speech, not enforced silence" prescription argues for the use of prominently placed signs and frequently made announcements to the effect that the solicitors are acting on their own behalf only, not with the approval of the airport's governing authority. Such additional speech might even caution the public to donate only to reputable organizations, to say "no" if in doubt. The *Whitney* rationale also seems to argue for permitting advertisers to use clever graphics and production techniques to make their print ads look almost like news articles and their infomercials resemble television interview programs, just as long as some additional speech explicitly alerting consumers that these are in fact advertisements is required. That same rationale suggests that attorneys who advertise that they will take cases on a contingency-fee basis—that clients "pay us nothing unless we win"—make clear somewhere in their ads the details of the promise. Does it apply only to the lawyers' own fees or also to reimbursement of out-of-pocket expenses such as court filing fees? In fact, courts and regulating agencies have used the *Whitney* rationale in all these kinds of situations and more.

The Smith Act Cases

The Cold War intensified in the late 1940s and throughout the 1950s. The atrocities that accompanied Joseph Stalin's reign began to come to light. Winston Churchill's famous "iron curtain" speech warned the free world that communism could be every bit as threatening as fascism. So it was that a statute passed by Congress in 1940 out of fear that radical right-wing politics could destroy the American way of life was now applied to the political left. The Alien Registration Act, popularly known as the **Smith Act**, criminalized advocacy of the government's overthrow as well as knowingly becoming part of a group whose members embraced such a goal. Eugene Dennis, the secretary-general of the American Communist Party, along with several other party officials, was prosecuted under the Smith Act. In upholding their convictions, Chief Justice Vinson wrote that the Smith Act was constitutional because it "is directed at advocacy, not discussion," that the clear and present danger test "cannot mean that before the Government may act, it must wait until the *putsch* is about to be executed, the plans have been laid and the signal is awaited." Rather, Vinson adopted the interpretation suggested by a lower court: "In each case [courts must decide] whether the gravity of the evil, discounted by its improbability, justifies such invasion of free speech as is necessary to avoid the danger."[11] There is always some competing interest to be balanced against free speech claims, Vinson was telling us, and one can hardly imagine a more serious counterweight than the fear that the government might be violently overthrown.

Whereas *Dennis* turned on the distinction between "advocacy" of revolution and mere "discussion" of revolution, six years later the Court shifted the line a bit, hold-

---

11. *Dennis v. United States*, 341 U.S. 494, 502, 509–510 (1951).

ing that advocacy of abstract doctrine would be permissible, but not advocacy of action. The occasion was the justices' reviewing the Smith Act convictions of fourteen leftists from California. The government's case against the accused consisted primarily of their having assumed leadership positions within the Communist Party and their having written some articles in the *Daily Worker*, the party's newspaper. This time, however, the Court overturned the convictions. Justice John Marshall Harlan's opinion criticized the lower court for having assumed that "advocacy, irrespective of its tendency to generate action, is punishable." Such an interpretation of the act is far too broad, Harlan concluded. Instead, the crucial distinction should be that "those to whom the advocacy is addressed must be urged to do something, now or in the future, rather than merely to believe in something."[12]

This doctrine was quite an advance over previous doctrine in terms of the amount of political speech it protected. The Court, however, had not yet completed its rewriting of the "clear and present danger" test. That task would have to wait another dozen years.

The *Brandenburg* Test: Imminent Lawless Action

At a Ku Klux Klan rally on a farm in Hamilton County, Ohio, Klan leader Clarence Brandenburg told his handful of supporters that "we're not a revengent organization, but if our President, our Congress, our Supreme Court, continues to suppress the white, Caucasian race, it's possible that there might have to be some revengeance taken." Participants were also overheard to offer such prescriptions for society's ills as "bury the niggers" and "send the Jews back to Israel."

Brandenburg was convicted of violating Ohio's criminal syndicalism statute. The Supreme Court's unanimous decision overturning that conviction established the test that to this day still determines when political speech is protected by the First Amendment. The test, appearing in a short per curiam opinion, says that "the constitutional guarantees of free speech and free press do not permit a State to forbid or proscribe advocacy of the use of force or of law violation except where such advocacy is directed to inciting or producing imminent lawless action and is likely to incite or produce such action."[13]

Notice that the test has elements of both content and context. As to content, the Court emphasizes that only very specific kinds of advocacy may be prohibited. The "imminence" requirement is a forceful restatement of the earlier "clear and *present* danger" test. We know from later decisions that the Court takes the imminence requirement very seriously. In 1973, for example, a unanimous Court overturned a Vietnam War protester's incitement conviction in large part because he told his cohorts, in response to the police having set up barricades, that they would all "take the

---

12. *Yates v. United States*, 354 U.S. 298, 320, 325 (1957).
13. *Brandenburg v. Ohio*, 395 U.S. 444, 447 (1969).

fucking street *later*." The Court's interpretation of this sentence was that "at best the statement could be taken as counsel for present moderation," and that "at worst it amounted to nothing more than advocacy of illegal action *at some indefinite future time*."[14] On the other hand, in 1997 the Fourth Circuit Court of Appeals managed to skirt the imminence requirement in the context of a book called *Hit Man*, which had apparently provided the blueprint for a grisly triple murder in Maryland. The book was published long before the hired killer purchased it and acted on its contents, but the court held that "imminence" was not an essential element in this civil suit by surviving family members, because the book offered detailed *instruction* rather than mere incitement.[15]

The *Brandenburg* test's contextual elements are apparent from the demand that words must be *likely* to result in the speaker's desired lawbreaking. Speakers must be addressing an audience sufficiently sympathetic to their cause and sufficiently aroused to action that imminent illegality is, in fact, a likely outcome of their advocacy. This requirement further demonstrates that the *Hit Man* case just described is an anomaly, the first time a mass-distributed book has ever been held to constitute "incitement" under the *Brandenburg* test. More typically, courts find that mass media artifacts are incapable of creating imminent lawless action. *Natural Born Killers*, for example, the 1994 Oliver Stone film depicting a couple's spree of violence and the media glorification surrounding it, was held to be incapable of inciting an Oklahoma couple's violent criminal actions conducted shortly after they saw the film "several times" in 1996.[16] The perhaps less familiar TV movie *Born Innocent*, which included a graphic rape scene that also apparently led to a copycat crime, was also deemed protected by the First Amendment.[17]

Go to www.paul siegelcommlaw .com and click on "Additional Images" to see the *Hit Man* cover.

Or consider the an article from the August 1981 issue of *Hustler* magazine, titled "Orgasm of Death," which explained to readers the joys and dangers of autoerotic asphyxiation (masturbating while hanging oneself so as to diminish the flow of blood to the brain and prolong an orgasm). The mother of a fourteen-year-old who died in his attempt to create the sexual rush described in the article sued the magazine, but U.S. District Judge Alvin Rubin determined there could be no liability; that there was no genuine incitement.[18] Popular music[19] and video games[20] have similarly been

14. *Hess v. Indiana*, 414 U.S. 105, 108 (1973) (emphasis added).

15. *Rice v. Paladin Enterprises*, 128 F. 3d 233 (4th Cir. 1997).

16. *Byers v. Edmondson*, 826 So.2d 551 (La. App. 2002). "Imminence" aside, the court held that the film was a fantasy, not to be taken as incitement at all.

17. *Olivia N. v. National Broadcasting Co.*, 178 Cal. Rptr. 888 (Ct. App. 1981). The case involved a TV movie.

18. *Herceg v. Hustler Magazine, Inc.*, 814 F. 2d 1017 (5th Cir. 1987).

19. *Davidson v. Time Warner, Inc.*, 1997 U.S. Dist. LEXIS 21559, 25 Media L. Rep. (BNA) 1705 (S.D. Tex. 1997); *McCollum v. CBS, Inc.*, 249 Cal. Rptr. 187 (Ct. App. 1988).

20. *James v. Meow Media*, 300 F.3d 683 (6th Cir. 2002); *Wilson v. Midway Games*, 198 F. Supp. 2d 167 (D. Conn. 2002); *Sanders v. Acclaim Entertainment*, 188 F. Supp. 2d 1264 (D. Colo. 2002); *Watters v. TSR, Inc.*, 715 F. Supp. 819 (W.D. Ky. 1989).

Even though the film *Natural Born Killers* apparently did inspire at least one couple to engage in violent crimes, courts that adjudicated the issue found that the film's producers could not be held liable for having incited such crimes.

deemed protected by the First Amendment against claims that their messages have led youngsters to act out what they took to be the messages found within, with tragic results.

Linda Blair's character (with back to us) in the TV movie *Born Innocent* is raped with a broom handle at a juvenile detainee facility. The California Supreme Court refused to find NBC liable for damages when a youngster engaged in a similar rape with a soda bottle.

Before moving on, it should be emphasized that the Brandenburg test demands that true illegality be sought by the speaker. This may explain why prosecutors refused to bring charges against Khalid Abdul Mohammad for a highly inflammatory speech he gave at the Million Youth March in New York City in 1998. (C-SPAN's coverage of the event did not provide sufficient lighting to give us a usable still photo for use in these pages, but the video of the speech is available on the author's website.) As the video makes clear, every time the speaker suggested that his followers might appropriately take some violent action against the police gathered to keep peace at the event, he predicated any such action upon the police's own violent instigation. Since violence waged only in self-defense might not be illegal, the "imminent *lawless* action" test likely would not be met.

The USA Patriot Act

The best-known legislative response to the terrorist attacks in 2001 was the almost immediate passage of the USA Patriot Act. Several features of the law have clear implications for the act of communication. First, the law strengthens the government's hand when it denies a Freedom of Information Act (FOIA) request, whether from journalists or others, about matters arguably raising issues of national security. While a more complete explanation of the FOIA is postponed until chapter 7, suffice it to say for now that the government has successfully withheld details about who is being held in the prison at the U.S. naval base in Guantánamo Bay, Cuba, and the identity of their attorneys,[21] whether the government has intercepted communications between those attorneys and their detainee-clients,[22] and key details concerning how often the Department of Justice has used some of the new powers granted to it under the Patriot Act.[23]

One of those new powers granted to the FBI is the ability to issue "national security letters" (NSLs) without getting a judge's approval and without even presenting evidence that a targeted individual is suspected of a crime. The recipient of an NSL, generally a business or library listing the target as a patron, is subject to a **gag order** and may not discuss the FBI's demand with anyone. A Connecticut-based library association received an NSL about one of its patrons and tried to have the associated gag order lifted so that it could speak out publicly, including in front of a congressional committee,

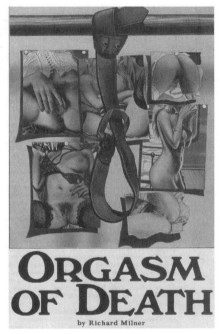

ORGASM OF DEATH
by Richard Milner

Although a young teenager followed the procedures described in "Orgasm of Death," the First Amendment precluded any finding of liability against the magazine.

about the Patriot Act. The library case, and related litigation involving Internet service providers' clients, has moved up and down the federal judiciary for a few years. Most recently, the Second Circuit Court of Appeals held that the FBI could not enforce an NSL-related gag order without automatically triggering **judicial review** of that order. Moreover, in the resulting judicial proceeding, the government must *demonstrate*, not merely assert, that enforcement of the gag order is necessary to further its investigation of a terrorist organization.[24]

In 2010 the Supreme Court upheld another Patriot Act provision, as applied to a particular litigant described by the *Washington Post* as "an unlikely scofflaw." Ralph Fertig, himself a former administrative law judge, sought a judicial ruling to the effect

---

21. *Center for National Security Studies v. U.S. Department of Justice*, 331 F.3d 918 (D.C. Cir. 2003). But see *Associated Press v. U.S. Department of Defense*, 410 F. Supp. 2d 147 (S.D.N.Y. 2006).

22. *Wilner v. National Security Agency*, 592 F. 3d 60 (2nd Cir. 2009).

23. *American Civil Liberties Union v. U.S. Department of Justice*, 321 F. Supp. 2d 24 (D.D.C. 2004); *American Civil Liberties Union v. U.S. Department of Justice*, 265 F. Supp. 2d 20 (D.D.C. 2003); *Gerstein v. U.S. Department of Justice*, 2005 U. S. Dist. LEXIS 41276 (N.D. Cal. 2005).

24. *Doe v. Mukasey*, 549 F. 3d 861 (2nd Cir. 2008).

THINGS TO REMEMBER

Evolution of First Amendment Doctrine

- The Court's First Amendment doctrine emerged from cases involving incitement to illegal action.
- The following cases have involved the Espionage Act, the later Smith Act, or various state criminal syndicalism laws:
  - *Schenck v. United States*
    - Birth of the clear and present danger test
    - Falsely shouting fire in a crowded theater metaphor
  - *Abrams v. United States*
    - Marketplace of ideas
  - *Gitlow v. New York*
    - First Amendment now applies to the states, too
    - Holmes's dissent says that "every idea is an incitement"
  - *Whitney v. California*
    - Proper remedy to bad speech is more speech, not enforced silence
  - *Dennis v. United States*
    - "The gravity of the evil discounted by its improbability"
    - Actual advocacy versus "mere discussion"
  - *Yates v. United States*
    - Advocacy of action versus advocacy of abstract doctrine
  - *Brandenburg v. Ohio*
    - Advocacy of "imminent lawless action"
    - Must also be "likely to produce such action"
- There is also much litigation involving the Patriot Act, Congress's response to the 9/11 attacks.

---

that a provision of the Patriot Act criminalizing the giving of "expert advice" to a group deemed by the Department of State to be a terrorist organization would be unconstitutional as applied to his planned offer of assistance to a Kurdish group called the PKK. Fertig wanted to offer the PKK help in drafting messages to the United Nations and other bodies, and perhaps even to challenge in court its having been listed as a terrorist organization. The Supreme Court held that Congress was within its rights to prohibit such activities.[25]

Theories of First Amendment Adjudication

As we have seen, the Supreme Court's First Amendment jurisprudence began in earnest in the World War I era. The cases that produced this body of case law, culminating in the *Brandenburg* test, generally have involved criminal defendants whose words

---

25. *Holder v. Humanitarian Law Project*, 130 S. Ct. 2705 (2010).

Attorney Ann Beeson together with Connecticut Library Connection plaintiff George Christian, who for many months was not permitted to tell anyone that he had received a national security letter from the FBI.

were uttered to incite presumably sympathetic listeners to engage in conduct that itself would likely be illegal. Such a scenario describes only one of many categories of conflict raising First Amendment issues. Most of the kinds of speech that define the scope of the chapters in this book—such as libel, invasion of privacy, and copyright and trademark infringements—do not involve speakers trying to incite others to take specific actions. It is no surprise, then, that there have been many different approaches to First Amendment litigation over the years. In this section several of the competing theories of First Amendment adjudication are presented.

Free Speech as the Absence of Prior Restraint?

Dating back at least to the sixteenth century, the preferred method of controlling the press in England had been to prevent offensive tracts from ever being published (rather than punishing the authors or the publishers after the fact). Either the Crown, the Church, or both controlled the printed word by licensing only a tiny group of publishing companies and requiring printers to post sizable monetary bonds that would be forfeited if their houses were ever to publish offensive materials.

The prevailing wisdom around the time of the American Revolution was that freedom of the press referred only to the absence of such prior restraints on the act of communication. The British jurist William Blackstone was a contemporary of the Founding Fathers, and James Madison, Thomas Jefferson, John Adams, and the others were quite familiar with Blackstone's *Commentaries on the Law of England*, published in 1769, which argued that the "liberty of speech . . . consists in laying no previous restraints upon publications, and not in freedom from censure for criminal matter when published."

There is much conflicting scholarship as to whether the men who ratified the First Amendment embraced this view of freedom of speech. In any event, the more modern view, embraced by the U.S. Supreme Court at least since the 1930s, is that the First Amendment protects against more than prior restraints but that prior restraints are so especially odious that they carry with them "a heavy presumption against [their own] constitutional validity."[26] The Supreme Court's modern prior-restraint doctrine is usually traced to a 1931 decision, *Near v. Minnesota*.[27] Jay Near, publisher of the controversial *Saturday Press*, was prosecuted as a "public nuisance" for publishing "malicious, scandalous, and defamatory articles" about the mayor of Minneapolis and other **public officials**, as well as the "Jewish race" in general. The case was one of prior restraint because the punishment meted out was an injunction that had the effect of closing down the newspaper. In holding the injunction unconstitutional, the Court allowed that freedom from prior restraints is not "absolutely unlimited," but it also made clear that such governmental censorship would be upheld "only in exceptional cases."

The 2010 documentary film *The Most Dangerous Man in America* tells the tale of former government contractor Daniel Ellsberg, who leaked classified documents collectively referred to as the Pentagon Papers to the *Washington Post* and the *New York Times*. The leaked documents showed some of the ways the government misled us about its participation in the Vietnam War. After two conflicting federal appellate decisions were handed down, one enjoining the *New York Times* from publishing the papers, the other refusing to enjoin the *Post*, the Supreme Court granted expedited review and produced a somewhat confusing 6–3 decision rejecting the government's claim that publication of the papers posed a serious threat to the national security.[28]

The majority's official pronouncement in the case was a surprisingly brief per curiam opinion, the thrust of which was that the government had not met the "heavy burden" of proof necessary to sustain a prior restraint on speech. The opinion does not, however, indicate exactly what the burden of proof should be or why in this case the government had failed to meet it.

Readers would have to muddle through nine separate opinions by the justices to make sense of the *Pentagon Papers* case. Two of the justices in the majority (Black and Douglas) espoused a rather absolutist view of the matter, suggesting that the government might never be able to justify a prior restraint on speech. Each of the other justices in the majority allowed that there might be circumstances in which prior re-

26. *Bantam Books v. Sullivan*, 373 U.S. 58, 79 (1963).
27. 283 U.S. 697 (1931).
28. *New York Times Company v. United States*, 403 U.S. 713 (1971).

straints are permissible. Justice Stewart offered a description of the government's burden of proof that has since been cited dozens of times by lower courts. Prior restraints, Stewart suggested, should be permitted only when the state can demonstrate that publication will cause "direct, immediate, and irreparable damage."

In the late 1970s, the government had occasion to argue that such serious harm would result if the *Progressive* magazine were permitted to publish an article about the hydrogen bomb. The thesis of the article was that Americans were being lulled into a false sense of security about the unlikelihood of nuclear disaster. The article's author, whose training in the hard sciences was limited to a bachelor's degree, was able to piece together from readily available public documents a blueprint for constructing a working nuclear device. Federal district judge Robert Warren issued a restraining order against the magazine.[29] Although he admitted that "cherished First Amendment rights" were at stake here, he feared that ruling for the magazine "could pave the way for thermonuclear annihilation for us all." The magazine appealed Judge Warren's ruling to the Seventh Circuit Court of Appeals in Chicago, which held oral arguments on the case in September 1979. The judges never had occasion to render their decision, however; while the case was pending, a handful of newspapers in other venues published essays highly similar to the one at issue in the case, and the government promptly dropped its case against the *Progressive*, which went to press with its hydrogen bomb piece in November, seven months later than it had planned.

The Supreme Court's aversion to prior restraints on speech was reaffirmed in 2010 in *Citizens United v. FEC*.[30] There the justices struck down key provisions of a federal campaign finance law, and even overturned a couple of its own precedents, refusing to allow the government to prevent corporations from engaging in political advocacy timed to affect a presidential primary campaign.

First Amendment Absolutism

Recall the first five words of the First Amendment: "Congress shall make no law," it tells us, before enumerating the kinds of rights (including freedom of speech and freedom of the press) that the government may not abridge. The wording is absolute. It is not surprising, then, that some jurists and scholars have been known as First Amendment absolutists. Supreme Court justice Hugo Black is probably most often associated with **absolutist theory**. When the founders drafted the First Amendment, Black said, "they knew what they were talking about." They consciously intended to prevent the government from telling its citizens "what they should believe or say or

---

29. *United States v. Progressive*, 467 F. Supp. 990 (W.D. Wis. 1979).

30. 130 S. Ct. 876 (2010). Individual states, under their own constitutions, are free to provide even more protection against prior restraints. The State of Washington notably claims that prior restraints are absolutely forbidden by article I, section 5 of its constitution. *Bradburn v. North Central Regional Library*, 231 P.3d 166, 172 (Wash. 2010).

In *Citizens United v. FEC,* the Supreme Court held that federal laws preventing a corporation from broadcasting during the 2008 primary election season a full-length film highly critical of Hillary Clinton constituted an unconstitutional prior restraint on speech.

publish." That the First Amendment says "no law" is appropriate, he added, and "that is what I believe it means."[31]

First Amendment absolutism has obvious problems. There are numerous things one can do via speech that almost any reasonable person would agree should be illegal. Committing perjury is one example. So too is bribery, as is threatening to kill another human being. One way around this problem is to decide, somewhat artificially, that certain kinds of utterances simply will not count as *speech.* This strategy has been embraced by the Supreme Court, for example, with sexual speech. Obscene messages have been declared outside the bounds of First Amendment protection. Period.

Another way to reconcile absolutism with practicality is to decide that the drafters of the Bill of Rights themselves had a relatively limited class of speech in mind when they used the phrase "freedom of speech." First Amendment theorist Alexander Meiklejohn is probably the best-known advocate of this approach. For Meiklejohn, "freedom of speech" refers only to political speech, speech on the kinds of matters upon which the electorate may be called to vote.[32] (In later writings, Meiklejohn softened his stance somewhat to include within his definition of "the political" such matters as the arts, education, and the sciences.[33]) Meiklejohnian theory posits that political speech is absolutely protected by the First Amendment, whereas other lesser kinds of speech (advertising, for example) will find some protection in the Fifth Amendment. Engaging in such speech is seen as one of the liberties that the government may not take away without due process of law.

In recent years, Supreme Court justice Anthony Kennedy has espoused a new kind of absolutism, what might be called "absolutism with exceptions." He argued that the First Amendment means what it says except for those categories of speech that the Court has long held fall outside the amendment's protection. Kennedy most clearly articulated his theory in a case that found the Court invalidating New York State's "Son of Sam" law, which prohibited criminals from making money by writing about their wrongdoing. Laws such as this one, Kennedy argued, amount to "raw censorship." For Kennedy, First Amendment adjudication should consist initially of asking whether the speech taken aim at by a particular law falls into the categorical excep-

---

31. Edmund Cahn, "Justice Black and First Amendment 'Absolutes': A Public Interview," 37 *New York University Law Review* 549, 554 (1962).

32. Alexander Meiklejohn, *Free Speech and Its Relation to Self-Government* (New York: Harper & Row, 1948).

33. Alexander Meiklejohn, "The First Amendment Is an Absolute," 1961 *Supreme Court Review* 245, 255–257 (1961).

True First Amendment absolutism would seem to demand that the court accept the accused's ludicrous defense.

tions to constitutional protection, such as knowing libel, obscenity, child pornography, and incitement to illegal action. If the speech does not fit into any of these categories, it enjoys absolute First Amendment protection.[34]

It is clear, then, that the "no" in "Congress shall make no law" is not to be taken literally. The legislative branch of government at all levels imposes a wide array of laws and regulations that may affect the act of communication. When deciding the constitutionality of such regulations, courts will first ask whether they are defective in some fairly generic way, such as vagueness. The notion here is that if a law is unclear, even law-abiding citizens will not know how to obey it. For example, a Massachusetts-

---

34. *Simon & Schuster, Inc. v. Members of the New York State Crime Victims Board*, 502 U.S. 105, 128 (Kennedy, J., concurring) (1991); see generally Helen J. Knowles, *The Tie Goes to Freedom: Justice Anthony M. Kennedy on Liberty* (Rowman & Littlefield, 2009), especially chapter 2. In 2010 the Supreme Court explicitly rejected Congress's invitation to add depictions of animal cruelty to the list of speech categories that are completely without First Amendment protection. *U. S. v. Stevens*, 130 S. Ct. 1577 (2010).

based beer importing firm sued Maine's Bureau of Liquor Enforcement for rejecting three beer-bottle labels as violative of the bureau's rule against "undignified or improper" illustrations. The plaintiff, Shelton Brothers of Belchertown, contended that the regulation was unconstitutionally vague. Other states that had rejected the same or similar labels from the same company had backed down after Shelton Brothers filed suit; Maine eventually backed down as well.[35] The State of Maine reversed its earlier decision soon after the ACLU-backed lawsuit was filed.

Another way in which statutes might be unconstitutional is if they are found **overbroad**. In the First Amendment context, **overbreadth** refers to laws that may be well intentioned, but that prohibit much more speech than is needed to further even a legitimate state interest. For example, in 2009 the Utah Supreme Court struck down the state's "sexually explicit business and escort service" tax because its definition of "escort service"—"any person who furnishes or arranges for an escort to accompany another individual for . . . companionship"—seemed to cover far too much ground. As Justice Durrant pointed out, the law would prohibit travel tour guides, among other quite legitimate enterprises.[36]

Yet a third way laws regulating communication might be found unconstitutional

The State of Maine initially rejected this beer label's Santa illustration as "undignified" and "improper," a standard challenged by the importer as unconstitutionally vague.

---

35. "Suds for Santa: Historically, Saint Nick has been Linked to Drink," *Philadelphia Daily News*, Dec. 21, 2009, 33.

36. *Bushco, DBA Babydolls Escorts v. Utah State Tax Commission*, 2009 UT 73 (Sup. Ct. Utah 2009).

is if they are what the courts have come to call **underinclusive**. The concept refers to times when Congress or some other legislature articulates what seems at first blush to be a good reason for passing a specific law, but where further reflection leads a court to ask, "if that was their concern, why did they only go after *this* kind of activity?" In 2007, for example, the Washington Supreme Court struck down a state law prohibiting candidates for public office from knowingly telling falsehoods about their opponents. To be sure, there were several reasons such a law, however well-intentioned, was almost certain to be struck down, not the least of which was the difficulty of having courts figure out what is true and false in the heat of a political campaign. The court also pointed to the law's underinclusiveness. If the state's reason for passing the law was to ensure the integrity of the electoral process, why prohibit only speech about an opponent, yet let candidates get away with blatant lies about their own backgrounds?[37]

If a statute survives review thus far in the model—if it is not vague, or overly broad, or underinclusive—courts next consider whether the conduct a law or regulation seeks to abridge is primarily expressive, whether it really triggers the First Amendment. That tax fraud or armed robbery may both involve speech does not make laws criminalizing such acts relevant to the First Amendment. Assuming that a law or regulation does implicate the First Amendment, courts will next consider whether the speech involved falls into categorical exceptions such as obscenity or deceptive advertising. If the answer is no, the final step is to apply whatever test or doctrine has been established by the courts to govern the kind of speech at issue. Commercial speech, for example, is generally governed by the *Central Hudson* test, presented in detail in chapter 10.

Access Theory

If the core purpose of the First Amendment is to foster communication, we need to fear not only government censors but also the huge corporations that each own so very much of the mass media and which might refuse to run a story or an announcement for purely business reasons rather than as a result of editorial judgment. So argue proponents of media access theory. Perhaps best known among such theorists is Professor Jerome Barron of the George Washington University Law School. In 1967, Barron published a seminal article in the *Harvard Law Review* that he later expanded into a book.[38] Barron bemoaned the concentration of media ownership, which he described as an "economic revolution" placing "with fewer and fewer persons the power to decide whatever a larger and larger number shall see, hear, and read."

---

37. *Rickert v. Public Disclosure Commission*, 168 P.3d 826 (Wash. 2007).

38. Jerome Barron, "Access to the Press: A New First Amendment Right," 80 *Harvard Law Review* 1641 (1967); Barron, *Freedom of the Press for Whom: The Right of Access to Mass Media* (Bloomington: Indiana University Press, 1973).

Access theorists have enjoyed only mixed success in the United States, depending on the specific medium involved. The print media are generally free from intrusions into their editorial discretion. Television and radio fare much differently. Section 315 of the Federal Communications Act, for example, provides a complicated array of rules and exceptions telling station managers that candidates for political office must be granted equal access to their airwaves. The cable television industry is also subject to some kinds of compelled access. In many locales, the city's contract with the cable franchise requires that a small number of stations be set aside for "community access," generally made available on a first-come, first-served basis to any community groups wishing to produce programming.

Although Barron was concerned primarily with the rights of the public to use the airwaves and the print media, another access issue is the relationship among reporters, editors, and publishers. Social critic A. J. Liebling reminds us that "freedom of the press is guaranteed only to those who own one," a lesson that media employees often learn the hard way. Not infrequently reporters and editors are disciplined for publishing stories that prove embarrassing to their employers or to a major advertiser. In the absence of a clear employment contract to the contrary, reporters and editors, like most employees in the United States, serve at the pleasure of their bosses and can be fired at any time for any reason not otherwise in violation of the law. That their transgression may have been to communicate with the public is generally deemed irrelevant.

Balancing Theories

The moment we reject absolutist positions, we are necessarily in the business of balancing of some kind. Courts engage in **ad hoc balancing** when they ask, "In this particular case, which is more important, freedom of speech or the competing interest?" One party's free speech claims will then be weighed against whatever interests form the opposing side's case. The competing interest might be to protect a plaintiff's reputation, as in libel cases. It could be to preserve the peace, as in incitement prosecutions. A state may have an antiobscenity law through which it seeks to preserve a certain moral climate. As Justice Harlan put it in a McCarthy-era case, First Amendment jurisprudence "always involves a balancing by the courts of the competing private and public interests at stake in the particular circumstances shown."[39]

One thing about real-world First Amendment adjudication is missing from the ad hoc balancing model: courts cheat a bit in favor of the litigants raising First Amendment claims. So important is freedom of speech in the calculus of rights Americans enjoy that courts purposely tip the scales. Judges do not simply ask, "Which interest is more important in this particular case?" Rather, they ask, "Does the anti–free

---

39. *Barenblatt v. United States*, 360 U.S. 109, 126 (1959).

speech litigant have a strong enough case to overcome the presumption in favor of free speech?"

This kind of inquiry is often referred to as **preferred-position balancing**. The Supreme Court has used the admittedly vague phrase "preferred position" to describe freedom of speech in over a dozen decisions since the 1940s. In a concurring opinion from a 1949 decision, Justice Frankfurter dismissed it as a "mischievous phrase" that "radiates a constitutional doctrine without avowing it . . . that any law touching communication is infected with presumptive invalidity."[40] Mischievous or not, the phrase does seem to mean something very much like what Frankfurter feared it had come to mean. When asked to determine the constitutionality of laws or regulations seeming to abridge a fundamental right such as freedom of speech (freedom of the press and freedom of religion are treated similarly), courts employ the highest level of scrutiny. Using this "strict scrutiny," courts demand that the state have a "compelling interest" to infringe on the right to communicate.

Preferred-position balancing is the theory of First Amendment adjudication most often employed by the modern Supreme Court (even though it does not use the phrase as often these days as in decades past). Indeed, in a 2010 decision the Court

---

THINGS TO REMEMBER

Some Approaches to First Amendment Adjudication

- PRIOR-RESTRAINT DOCTRINE
  - In colonial times, freedom of the press likely meant only freedom from prepublication censorship.
  - Although the First Amendment also applies to after-the-fact punishments, prior restraints are still viewed by the Supreme Court as especially odious.

- ABSOLUTIST THEORY
  - The "no" in "Congress shall pass *no* law" is emphasized.
  - Alexander Meiklejohn said that only political speech is absolutely protected.
  - Justice Kennedy embraces "absolutism with exceptions."

- ACCESS THEORY
  - Freedom of the press should not be just for those who own one.
  - Courts have generally rejected it for print but accepted it somewhat for broadcast media.

- AD HOC BALANCING
  - Which is more important in this case, free speech or the competing interest?

- PREFERRED-POSITION BALANCING
  - This frequently used approach consists of balancing with a dishonest scale, assuming that free speech will win.

---

40. *Kovacs v. Cooper*, 336 U.S. 77, 89–90 (1949) (Frankfurter, J., concurring).

explicitly rejects ad hoc balancing in favor of preferred-position balancing. As Chief Justice Roberts put it, "The First Amendment's guarantee of free speech does not extend only to categories of speech that survive an ad hoc balancing of relative social costs and benefits. The First Amendment itself reflects a judgment by the American people that the benefits of its restrictions on the Government outweigh the costs. Our Constitution forecloses any attempt to revise that judgment simply on the basis that some speech is not worth it."[41] But *why* is free speech so important that it occupies a preferred position? In the next section, an attempt to answer that question is offered.

The Value of Freedom of Expression

In the same concurring opinion from *Whitney v. California* that gave us the famous "more speech, not enforced silence" prescription, Justice Brandeis also provides us with an elegantly worded list of functions served by freedom of speech. "Those who won our independence," he wrote, believed that "freedom to think as you will and to speak as you think are means indispensable to the discovery and spread of political truth." He further contended that engaging in public discussion on the issues of the day is a "political duty" that should be recognized as a "fundamental principle of the American government." The opinion suggests too that law and order "cannot be secured merely through fear of punishment," that "it is hazardous to discourage thought, hope and imagination" because "fear breeds repression" and "repression breeds hate," the kind of hate that "menaces stable government."[42]

Freedom of speech, then, is important because it helps us find the truth; it is essential to our role as self-governors in a democracy, and it provides a kind of safety valve against possibly violent turmoil. Yale University law professor Thomas Emerson incorporated these three functions into his own theory of free speech and suggested also that free speech serves a more individual "self-fulfillment" function.[43]

Truth-Seeking

Nineteenth-century philosopher John Stuart Mill, in his essay *On Liberty*, asks us to consider whether societies are open to new ideas or whether they feel a need to censor potential heresies.

We cannot ignore the possibility that a new idea is more correct than our handed-down wisdom. For would-be censors "to refuse a hearing to an opinion because they are sure that it is false is to assume that their certainty is the same thing as absolute certainty."

41. *United States v. Stevens*, 130 S. Ct. 1577, 1585 (2010).
42. 274 U.S. 357, 375 (1927) (Brandeis, J., concurring).
43. Thomas I. Emerson, *The System of Freedom of Expression* (New York: Random House, 1970).

Suppose, however, that somehow we had a "God's eye view" and could report with confidence that our received truths are inarguably, unquestionably true. What benefit could possibly result from opening the door to heretics' falsehoods? Mill answers that we will gain a "clearer perception and livelier impression" of our own truths by their "collision with error"; failure to engage opposing views, Mill warns, will ensure that our own beliefs "will be held as a dead dogma, not a living truth, apt to give way before the slightest semblance of an argument. Truth thus held is but superstition."

In the real world, of course, we do not have the omniscience to know whose ideas are correct in advance of a full debate. Indeed, in most important clashes of ideas, the "truth" tends to be somewhere between the extremes.[44] Robert Jensen argues that ideas should not even be thought of as in competition with each other. He rejects a marketplace (of ideas) model in favor of a potluck dinner. Each idea is a contributor's dish: "My contribution doesn't fight with others'; the dishes aren't in a battle to determine which one is best, which one will win acceptance in the market. Each dish tells its own story, inviting the diners to taste."[45]

Self-Governing

First Amendment scholar Alexander Meiklejohn's theory of freedom of expression emphasizes Americans' role as "self-governors." We vote on important matters of the day, or at least choose among candidates in large part on what they promise to do about those same issues. For Meiklejohn, just as the **Speech or Debate Clause** in Article I of the Constitution gives our elected federal representatives an absolute right to free speech in carrying out their duties, so too should the First Amendment be interpreted to give all Americans an absolute right to speak out about political issues.

In Meiklejohnian theory, political speech is the core of the system of free expression, protected absolutely by the First Amendment, whereas more private speech enjoys the far lesser degree of protection offered by the Fifth Amendment's Due Process Clause. Although the Supreme Court rejects Meiklejohn's notion that the First Amendment applies only to political speech, it has on many occasions made clear that political speech is the most important kind. In 2010, for example, the Court overturned regulations governing corporations' expenditures for or against political candidates. Justice Thomas's concurring opinion in the case emphasized that the artifact in front of the Court, a full-length film criticizing Hillary Rodham Clinton, assumed through much of the 2008 primary season to be the front-runner for the Democratic Party's presidential nomination, was "core political speech."[46]

---

44. Benjamin DuVal, "Free Communication of Ideas and the Quest for Truth: Toward a Teleological Approach to First Amendment Adjudication," 41 *George Washington Law Review* 161 (1972). For DuVal, the devil gives us permission to make decisions and take actions, even based on inadequate and possibly conflicting data, as long as we promise not to censor any new ideas.

45. Robert Jensen, "First Amendment Potluck," 3 *Communication Law and Policy* 563, 582 (1998).

46. *Citizens United v. FEC*, 130 S. Ct. 876, 929 (2010) (Thomas, J., concurring).

Checking on Government Abuse

In the United States the press is often referred to as the fourth estate, a way of emphasizing that we depend on a free press to keep us informed about the performance of the three branches of government—legislative, executive, and judicial. Much of what we think of as hard news involves the press looking over the shoulders of government bureaucrats and reporting about their successes and failures. The CNN regular feature "Keeping Them Honest," which compares public officials' statements with what the network's research finds reality to be, is a clear example of this watchdog function.

A classic law review article by Vincent Blasi argued that empowering the press to keep a watchful eye on the government is the main reason for valuing freedom of speech. He calls it the "checking function." Abuses by the government are "an especially serious evil," Blasi argued, more serious than abuses by large corporations or other powerful agents. Government, after all, is unique in its "capacity to employ legitimized violence"—we give the police, not corporate CEOs, the right to use guns against us.[47] Lines blur, of course, when government gets entwined with the private sector, as when the federal government bailed out General Motors in 2009 by becoming its largest stockholder.

Letting off Steam

If we suppress a viewpoint that we despise, does it go away? Or do its proponents go underground and does their discontent fester until it is all the more likely to be manifested in violence? The safety-valve function of free speech stems from the latter hypothesis. As Emerson explains, freedom of speech "promotes greater cohesion in a society because people are more ready to accept decisions that go against them if they have a part in the decision-making process." Unsuccessful advocates of change are less likely to foment violent revolution if they are at least allowed to advocate.[48]

Self-Fulfillment

Comedian Jerry Seinfeld does a riff on the often reported finding that survey respondents report that they fear public speaking more than just about anything else,

---

47. Vincent Blasi, "The Checking Value in First Amendment Theory," 2 *American Bar Foundation Research Journal* 521, 538 (1977). For an intriguing argument that the fear of "legitimized violence" means that ordinary citizens should have a special measure of freedom to criticize police officers, see *Rodriguez v. Kyriacos*, 314 F. 3d 979, 989 (9th Cir. 2002) (Reinhardt, dissenting): "Police officers serve in unique positions of public trust. They are charged with protecting individual security and safe-guarding individual rights, and are therefore legally authorized to use a level of coercive force not afforded to the lay population."

48. Emerson, *The System of Freedom of Expression*, 7. See also Lee Bollinger, *The Tolerant Society* (New York: Oxford University Press, 1986).

even death. If we are invited to a funeral, we would rather be in the coffin than delivering the eulogy.[49] Seinfeld's observation obscures another reality about self-expression that may seem a contradiction yet is no less true: it feels good to express yourself.

Perhaps no event in recent times drives this point home more powerfully than the May 2006 sentencing of 9/11 conspirator Zacarias Moussaoui to life imprisonment without parole. When Moussaoui loudly suggested to those in court that he had "won," Judge Brinkema cut him off, pointing out that he was being taken to a maximum-security facility where he will essentially be prevented from speaking publicly ever again. Instead of achieving the martyrdom he had sought, he would "die with a whimper," the judge intoned, quoting from poet T. S. Eliot.

C. Edwin Baker, who was a student of Emerson's at Yale, later went on to create his own freedom of speech theory, which emphasizes the self-fulfillment function of expression above all others. His theory leads to some intriguing propositions, such as defining advertising and other commercial speech as generally outside the protection

---

THINGS TO REMEMBER

Functions of Free Speech

- **THE TRUTH-SEEKING FUNCTION**
  - John Stuart Mill emphasized the need to hear even false ideas to remind us why the true ideas are true.
  - Benjamin DuVal's "pact with the devil" allows us to make decisions only if we promise to remain open to new ideas.

- **THE SELF-GOVERNING FUNCTION**
  - Alexander Meiklejohn is most closely associated with the self-governing stance.
  - Political speech is an absolute First Amendment freedom.
  - Nonpolitical speech is a Fifth Amendment liberty.

- **THE CHECKING FUNCTION**
  - The free press is essential in a democracy as a fourth estate, the check on the other three branches of government.

- **THE SAFETY VALVE FUNCTION**
  - Political dissidents must be permitted to blow off steam.
  - Peaceful evolution helps avoid violent revolution.

- **THE SELF-FULFILLMENT FUNCTION**
  - Expressing ourselves feels good.
  - C. Edwin Baker's theory is based on this self-fulfillment function.

---

49. Ernie Harwell, "Keep It Short and Sweet, or Just Pick Up the Check," *Detroit Free News*, February 21, 2010, C12.

One of the traditionally accepted values of freedom of speech is self-fulfillment, that expressing ourselves feels good.

of the First Amendment, in that speakers sending such messages are motivated by potential profits rather than by a desire for individual self-fulfillment.[50]

Is Freedom of Expression Overrated?

All the First Amendment theories examined so far have in common an underlying assumption that free speech is a good thing. The theories differ only in terms of the answer they offer to the question of why it is a good thing. Many theorists, however, argue that freedom of expression is placed on too high a pedestal in the United States, that it is allowed to ride roughshod over more important rights and interests. In this section we examine the thoughts of some Marxist, feminist, and critical race theorists who agree that freedom of speech as we typically understand it in this country is indeed overrated.

Karl Marx said that religion is "the opiate of the people." An emphasis on the

---

50. C. Edwin Baker, *Human Liberty and Freedom of Speech* (New York: Oxford University Press, 1989). See also Tamara R. Piety, "Against Freedom of Commercial Expression," 29 *Cardozo Law Review* 2583 (2008).

afterlife, he suggested, is conveniently consistent with the need on the part of those in power to keep the masses contented with their small share of material resources in *this* life. Writing several generations later, a group of Marxists argued similarly that freedom of speech is an opiate, or at least a distraction. Chief among these writers was Herbert Marcuse, who pointed out that having the right to speak out against injustice is quite different from having any real power to change what he perceived as a fundamentally unjust system of allocating wealth.[51] For Marcuse and his followers, "free speech operates freely only because society realizes that free speech is devoid of any real power of change."[52]

One need not be a Marxist, of course, to level that same criticism against American journalism, especially TV news. That the main purpose of the news is not to inform but rather to entertain just enough so that viewers pay attention to the commercials is the thesis of Neil Postman's well-received book *Amusing Ourselves to Death*. Postman, who was a communications professor at New York University, described the "Now, this . . ." grammar of TV news. The phrase alerts us that the TV news item we have just seen "has no relevance to what one is about to see." It is the newscaster's way of saying "that you have thought long enough on the previous matter (approximately forty-five seconds), that you must not be morbidly preoccupied with it . . . and that you must now give your attention to another fragment of news or a commercial."[53]

Whereas Postman warns that the media discourage us from paying too close attention to the issues of the day, pioneering mass media theorists Paul Lazarsfeld and Robert Merton have argued that we may be guilty of paying such close attention to the information with which the media bombard us that we get lulled into political inactivity. We come to confuse *knowing* about social problems with *doing* something about them. They call this confusion the narcotizing dysfunction of media.[54]

To the extent that American media exist primarily to sell viewers' and readers' attentive eyeballs to advertisers, we expect to find a tendency to avoid airing any political views that would disturb consumers too much, that make us tune out. Such a criticism is reminiscent of Dorothy Parker's famously stinging remark about an actress of her day whose performance "ran the gamut of emotions from 'A' to 'B.'" If the marketplace of ideas offers only a very limited spectrum of viewpoints, one possi-

---

51. Herbert Marcuse, "Repressive Tolerance," in *A Critique of Pure Tolerance*, ed. Robert Paul Wolff, Barrington Moore, Jr., and Herbert Marcuse (Boston: Beacon Press, 1965), 81–123.

52. Joyce Flory, "Implications of Marcuse's Theory of Freedom for Freedom of Speech," in *Perspectives on Freedom of Speech*, ed. Thomas L. Tedford, John J. Makay, and David L. Jamison (Carbondale: Southern Illinois University Press, 1987), 77, 79.

53. Neil Postman, *Amusing Ourselves to Death: Public Discourse in the Age of Show Business* (New York: Penguin Books, 1985), 99–100.

54. Paul F. Lazarsfeld and Robert K. Merton, "Mass Communication, Popular Taste, and Organized Social Action," in *The Communication of Ideas*, ed. Lymon Bryson (New York: Harper, 1948), 95–118.

ble result could be what sociologist Elisabeth Noelle-Neumann has described as the "spiral of silence." Consumers of news who themselves favor political views more on the fringes than one typically sees described in the media will become hesitant over time, afraid to share their views with others for fear of being branded a radical. The media will thus be less and less likely over time to be able to identify and feature responsible spokespersons for any but the most mainstream of perspectives.[55] A countervailing trend should be noted, however, with respect to newer, more interactive media. The anonymity of the Internet chat room, it is argued, leads not to a diminution of political diversity, but rather a disinhibition, a rallying each other on, that is associated with political radicalism and cyberbullying.[56]

In recent years much scholarship has been written by feminists who, in the course of questioning the most basic assumptions of U.S. society, understandably have much to say about whether deference to First Amendment rights is always in women's best interests. Perhaps most relevant for the study of communication law are those feminists who have argued that we need to rethink our attitudes toward the use of pornographic images of women. Among the best-known writers in this area have been Andrea Dworkin,[57] Catherine MacKinnon,[58] and Gail Dines.[59] We examine their antipornography arguments in chapter 11, which deals with obscenity and other sexually oriented speech.

Feminists are not the only representatives of historically oppressed groups to question what they perceive as the U.S. legal system's tendency to value free speech interests above concerns about inequality. Critical race theorists such as Jeannine Bell,[60] Richard Delgado,[61] and Mari Matsuda[62] argue that the courts should not automatically assume that the First Amendment prohibits minority group members from bringing civil actions against persons who use racial epithets against them. These writ-

---

55. Elisabeth Noelle-Neumann, *The Spiral of Silence* (Chicago: University of Chicago Press, 1984).

56. See, for example, Karly Zande, "When the School Bully Attacks in the Living Room: Using *Tinker* to Regulate Off-Campus Student Cyberbullying," 13 *Barry Law Review* 103 (2009).

57. Andrea Dworkin, *Pornography: Men Possessing Women* (New York: Plume, 1989); Andrea Dworkin, "Against the Male Flood: Censorship, Pornography, and Equality," 8 *Harvard Women's Law Journal* 1 (1985).

58. Catherine MacKinnon, *Only Words* (Cambridge, Mass.: Harvard University Press, 1993); Catherine MacKinnon, *Toward a Feminist Theory of the State* (Cambridge, Mass.: Harvard University Press, 1989); Catherine MacKinnon, *Feminism Unmodified* (Cambridge, Mass.: Harvard University Press, 1987); Catharine MacKinnon, "Pornography, Civil Rights, and Speech," 20 *Harvard Civil Rights–Civil Liberties Law Review* 1 (1985).

59. Gail Dines, *Pornland: How Porn has Hijacked our Sexuality* (Boston: Beacon Press, 2010).

60. Jeannine Bell, "Restraining the Heartless: Racist Speech and Minority Rights," 84 *Indiana Law Journal* 963 (2009).

61. Richard Delgado, "Words That Wound: A Tort Action for Racial Insults, Epithets, and Name-Calling," 17 *Harvard Civil Rights–Civil Liberties Law Review* 133 (1982).

62. Mari Matsuda, "Public Response to Racist Speech: Considering the Victim's Story," 87 *Michigan Law Review* 2320 (1989).

THINGS TO REMEMBER

Some Criticisms of the American Style of Free Speech

- Some view free speech as an "opiate."
  - The right to complain is not as important as the power to change things.
  - We confuse knowing about problems with doing something about them.
  - Political dialogue in the United States is merely a commodity to attract eyeballs to ads.
  - The media cannot afford to offend us, so the marketplace of ideas is very narrow.

- Feminists and critical race theorists express concern:
  - We need to pay attention to the aggrieved person's narratives.
  - Free speech is not necessarily more important than equality.

ers emphasize that whites and people of color live in two very different perceptual worlds. When confronted by the same stories of hate speech incidents, people of color react with alarm, hurt feelings, and a desire for redress, whereas most whites seek to dismiss such occurrences as "isolated pranks." The whole process of telling and listening to stories is crucial for critical race theorists, who argue in favor of a new "outsider jurisprudence" that will be more sympathetic to historically powerless groups.

Some Transcendent First Amendment Doctrines

The remainder of this book's chapters are organized around either message-content issues (libel, invasion of privacy, advertising) or issues unique to specific communications media (broadcast and cable, the Internet). Other important communication law issues transcend these categories. We deal here with four of them: the right to hear, the right not to speak, the issue of symbolic conduct, and the kinds of content-neutral governmental policies often referred to as time, place, and manner regulations. This last issue will also necessarily involve a discussion of the Court's "public forum" doctrine.

A Right to Hear (and Read)

The First Amendment tells us that Congress shall not abridge the freedom to speak. Over the years, the judiciary has come to recognize that freedom of speech would be incomplete were it not to entail also a right to hear (or read). The Supreme Court has emphasized in more than a dozen of its free speech cases that the First Amendment protects the act of communication and that this act involves not only senders of messages but receivers as well.

The Court first made reference to a "right to hear" in the course of overturning a contempt of court judgment against the United Auto Workers president R. J. Thomas, who had delivered a speech, in defiance of a court order, to a group of Houston workers. Writing for a 5–4 majority, Justice Wiley Blount Rutledge found that both Thomas's right to speak and "the rights of the workers to hear what he had to say" were at issue.[63] Since the Thomas decision, the Court has applied this right to hear in a number of landmark cases. For example, the Court has said that although selling or distributing obscene works can be criminalized, one may own and read in the privacy of one's own home virtually any sexually oriented materials that do not include lewd depictions of children.[64] And in the Court's 1976 decision first holding that purely commercial advertising is protected by the First Amendment, that protection was based primarily on the consumers' interest in obtaining comparative pricing information.[65] More recently, the Court invalidated a federal statute that prohibited virtually all government workers above a certain salary scale from making any money "moonlighting" as writers or lecturers, even on matters wholly unrelated to their official job duties. The regulation, Justice Stevens found, imposed "a significant burden on the public's right to read and hear what the employees would otherwise have written and said."[66]

A Right *Not to Speak*

In recent years the issue of gay marriage has been very much in the news. In some states citizens have participated in a petition drive to get the issue on the ballot. Such petition sign-up sheets have generally been considered public documents. But what if some of the signatories fear reprisals if their neighbors learn that they have signed such a petition? Is there a right to "speak" anonymously in such circumstances? The Supreme Court ruled in 2010 that disclosure of signatories on a state of Washington anti–gay marriage petition serves several interests, including the ferreting out of any "bait and switch" signature gathering (wherein individuals are told they are signing one kind of petition but are actually signing something quite different). Although the Court therefore refused to strike down the state law providing for disclosure, the majority permitted plaintiffs a chance to prove that the revealing of their names would indeed lead to harassment.[67]

A "right not to speak" has been part of the Supreme Court's First Amendment doctrine—note we are not talking here about criminal suspects' more specific right

---

63. *Thomas v. Collins*, 323 U.S. 516, 534 (1945).
64. *Stanley v. Georgia*, 394 U.S. 557 (1969).
65. *Virginia State Board of Pharmacy v. Virginia Citizens Consumer Council*, 425 U.S. 748 (1976).
66. *United States v. National Treasury Employees Union*, 513 U.S. 454, 470 (1995).
67. *Doe v. Reed*, 130 S. Ct. 2811 (2010).

to "take the Fifth" (Amendment) to avoid incriminating themselves—for at least a half century. In the beginnings of the modern civil rights movement, some southern states felt threatened by the emergence of groups such as the NAACP and employed a number of tactics to stifle their growth. One such tactic was compelling the groups to disclose their membership lists. In a 1957 decision, the Supreme Court blocked such forced disclosure, ruling in essence that such organizations have a right not to speak, at least when speaking would likely bring violent reprisals upon their supporters.[68]

The Court recognizes not only a right to speak anonymously, but a right not to speak at all. A decision from the 1940s held that public school students could not be forced to utter the Pledge of Allegiance.[69] Most interesting about the case for communication law is that the plaintiffs, a group of Jehovah's Witnesses, argued that the compelled speech was a violation of their right to practice their religion, a Free Exercise Clause issue. Justice Jackson's opinion for the Court, however, was based on the far broader "right not to speak" implicit in the Free Speech Clause. If the First Amendment allows us to speak our mind, surely it must also mean that the government may not compel us to "utter what is not in [our mind]," he wrote at the time.

The right not to speak was emphasized even more forcefully in a later case involving another Jehovah's Witness, New Hampshire resident George Maynard, who strongly disagreed with the state motto ("Live Free or Die") and therefore covered up the words on his automobile license plate. In ruling for Maynard, the Supreme Court held explicitly that the First Amendment provides for "both the right to speak freely and the right to refrain from speaking at all."[70]

In 2001 the Supreme Court had to determine under what circumstances political candidates might be forced to "speak" about controversial issues. Voters in Missouri amended their state constitution to require that future ballots include a reference indicating which candidates had "DECLINED TO PLEDGE TO SUPPORT TERM LIMITS." The Supreme Court overturned the provision as a violation of the First Amendment (among other federal constitutional provisions). Not only was Missouri guilty of compelling candidates to speak out on an issue they might otherwise choose to avoid, but the state was planning to punish candidates who did not take the preferred stance on that issue.[71]

Also in 2001, the Court struck down 1996 amendments to the Legal Services Corporation Act forbidding LSC-funded lawyers to bring suits with the purpose of altering welfare laws (though attorneys could bring actions on behalf of specific clients who had been denied benefits).[72] The prohibited categories of lawsuits were them-

---

68. *NAACP v. Alabama*, 357 U.S. 449 (1958).

69. *West Virginia State Board of Education v. Barnette*, 319 U.S. 624 (1943).

70. *Wooley v. Maynard*, 430 U.S. 705, 714 (1977).

71. *Cook v. Gralike*, 531 U.S. 510 (2001).

72. *Legal Services Corporation v. Velazquez*, 531 U.S. 533 (2001).

The Supreme Court held in 2001 that the state of Missouri may not insert the words "DECLINED TO PLEDGE TO SUPPORT TERM LIMITS" on ballots, lest candidates be *forced* to speak about the issue.

selves instances of attorneys' speech, the Court majority concluded. The Court distinguished the case from its earlier decision in *Rust v. Sullivan*,[73] which forbade physicians who received federal family-planning funding to counsel patients about abortion. In *Rust* the government itself was "speaking" through its program. But when an LSC attorney sues the government, the administration in office already has the chance to speak (by contesting the lawsuit, both inside and outside the courtroom).

The next year, the Supreme Court invalidated an ordinance of an Ohio town that required individuals who planned to do door-to-door canvassing within the community to first fill out a form with identifying information in order to obtain a permit. The rule violated the First Amendment right not to speak, Justice Stevens held for the

---

73. 500 U.S. 173 (1991).

majority, in that it would even prevent a resident from making "a spontaneous decision to go across the street and urge a neighbor to vote against the mayor . . . without first obtaining the mayor's permission."[74]

Litigants have sometimes argued, with mixed results, that their First Amendment rights are violated when they are forced to support financially the speech of others whose views they find offensive. Teachers might be forced to join a union,[75] or lawyers a bar association;[76] their fees must be used for purposes directly germane to that membership, however, not for advocacy of political causes or candidates. Public universities, though, may use mandatory student activity fees to fund extracurricular student organizations—no matter how "offensive"—as long as funding is not a function of the groups' political viewpoints.[77] Later cases have suggested that student governments must be able to demonstrate that their fund allocation system is designed to address the risk of dollars flowing to some ideologies at the expense of others.[78]

There have also been a handful of Supreme Court cases involving government-mandated generic advertising campaigns touting the joys of eating fruit[79] or mushrooms[80] or beef. Whether farmers and ranchers can be forced to donate funds in support of such advertising campaigns seems to be a function of whether the Court frames the issue as one of a "right not to speak" or of "the government as

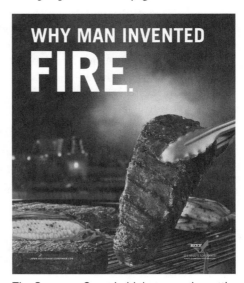

The Supreme Court held that even the cattle ranchers who did not support government sponsorship of this message, and whose government assessments were used to pay for this and other ads, had no valid "right not to speak" claim.

speaker." The Court's most recent decision in this area, from 2005, involved the "Beef: It's What's for Dinner" campaign, for which much of the funding came from a fee ($1 per head of cattle) assessed against ranchers by the U.S. Department of Agri-

---

74. *Watchtower Bible and Tract Society of New York v. Village of Stratton*, 536 U.S. 150, 167 (2002).

75. *Abood v. Detroit Board of Education*, 431 U.S. 209 (1977).

76. *Keller v. State Bar of California*, 496 U.S. 1 (1990).

77. *Board of Regents of the University of Wisconsin v. Southworth*, 529 U.S. 217 (2000).

78. See, for example, *Amidon v. Student Association of the State University of New York at Albany*, 508 F. 3d 94 (2nd Cir. 2007).

79. *Glickman v. Wileman Brothers and Elliott, Inc.*, 521 U.S. 457 (1997).

80. *United States v. United Foods*, 533 U.S. 405 (2001).

culture. The unsuccessful plaintiffs argued that the government advertising "pro-mote[d] beef as a generic product," thus "imped[ing] their efforts to promote the superiority of . . . American beef, grain-fed beef, or certified Angus or Hereford beef."[81] The Court's 6–3 decision treated the program as government speech, rather than as government-compelled private speech. As such, there was no First Amendment violation.[82]

Mass media litigants have benefited from a First Amendment right not to speak (or print). When the State of Florida tried to force the *Miami Herald* to publish a reply written by a candidate for office who had been criticized in the paper's editorial pages, the Supreme Court invalidated the statute that served as the state's basis for the request. The First Amendment prevents the government from compelling editors "to publish that which reason tells them should not be published," Chief Justice Burger wrote for the Court.[83]

Symbolic Conduct

Frequently theatergoers encounter a notice near the entrance advising that the actors in a particular production will be smoking. Have you ever wondered whether the government would have the right to ban stage smoking, in the same way that smoking has been banned by so many states in such public places as restaurants and even bars? The issue is just beginning to percolate through the courts. In 2009 the Colorado Supreme Court held that the state's Clean Indoor Air Act could be used to forbid onstage smoking.[84] Actors could always simply pretend to smoke—isn't pre-tending what acting is all about?

The Colorado antismoking case notwithstanding, the "speech" protected by the First Amendment need not involve spoken (or written) words. Human beings engage in many kinds of behaviors designed to send messages: marching, dancing, and sit-ting, as well as flag waving and flag burning. Over the years the courts have deter-mined that, depending on the context, all these behaviors and more are within the First Amendment's protection. Justice Jackson, in the case invalidating West Virgin-ia's requirement that public school students recite the Pledge of Allegiance, wrote that "symbolism is a primitive but effective way of communicating ideas, . . . a short cut from mind to mind."[85]

None of this is to suggest that all forms of symbolic conduct in all contexts will be granted First Amendment protection. This lesson was learned all too clearly by Viet-

---

81. *Johanns v. Livestock Marketing Association*, 544 U.S. 550, 555–556 (2005).

82. A similar decision was reached in a 2009 case involving generic advertising for table grapes. See *Delano Farms Company v. California Table Grapes Association*, 586 F. 3d 1219 (9th Cir. 2009).

83. *Miami Herald Publishing Co. v. Tornillo*, 418 U.S. 241, 256 (1974).

84. *Curious Theatre Company v. Colorado Department of Public Health and Environment*, 230 P. 3d 544 (Colo. 2009).

85. *West Virginia State Board of Education v. Barnette*, 319 U.S. 624, 632 (1943).

Theater audiences have always assumed that actors indulging in a joint onstage were really using some kind of legal prop, but if the logic of a Colorado Supreme Court decision becomes good law in many more states, actors would not be allowed to smoke tobacco, or "light up" in any way. Photo is from a Towson University production of *Landscape of the Body*. Reprinted with permission.

nam War protestor David Paul O'Brien, who was found in violation of a federal law that forbade the knowing destruction of one's draft card. Upholding his conviction, the Supreme Court set forth a list of criteria still often used to determine when laws or regulations affecting symbolic conduct are compatible with the First Amendment. The *O'Brien* test demands that any such regulations "further an important and substantial government interest," that the state's interest be "unrelated to the suppression of free expression," and that "the incidental restriction on alleged First Amendment freedoms [be] no greater than is essential to the furtherance of that interest."[86] The federal statute under which O'Brien was prosecuted was deemed an expression of several legitimate state interests that were themselves unrelated to the defendant's message, such as ensuring the effective functioning of the Selective Service System.

Even though Mr. O'Brien himself did not prevail, the *O'Brien* test has been used to protect litigants' rights to engage in symbolic conduct, as when a college student hung an upside-down flag with a peace symbol affixed to it in his protest of the U.S. military bombing of Cambodia and the killings at Kent State University.[87] Several times in recent years—most recently in 2008—the House of Representatives ap-

---

86. *United States v. O'Brien*, 391 U.S. 367, 376 (1968).

87. *Spence v. Washington*, 418 U.S. 405, 410–411 (1974). The Court also refused to permit punishing of flag desecrators in *United States v. Eichman*, 496 U.S. 310 (1990), and *Texas v. Johnson*, 491 U.S. 397 (1989).

proved wording of a constitutional amendment that would outlaw flag desecration, thus undoing the effects of these rulings. Each time, the amendment was killed in close Senate votes.

The *O'Brien* test has been employed by the Court to adjudicate zoning regulations affecting "adult" movie theaters,[88] and even an outright ban of nightclubs featuring nude dancing.[89] States have more freedom to regulate otherwise protected First Amendment activity, the Court reasoned, if the regulations are unrelated to the expression itself, but rather are aimed at the "secondary effects" of the expression (such as increases in prostitution and other crime). It should be noted, however, that much scholarly research has shown that neighborhoods boasting adult bookstores and similar businesses actually tend to have *lower* crime rates than similar areas without such businesses.[90]

A fascinating kind of symbolic conduct that has been the source of controversy and litigation in recent years is the "self-help remedy" of destroying every copy of a newspaper one can find, if offended by an article within. Only a tiny handful of states have passed legislation to criminalize such action when the perpetrator buys the copies legitimately or when the paper is designed to be distributed free of charge. How can one "steal" something that is free, after all?[91] There has been at least one successful civil suit against such "mass trashers," but this involved a sheriff and his deputies, so there was "state action" involved, and the officials violated the First Amendment rights of the local newspaper.[92]

Time, Place, and Manner Restrictions

The *O'Brien* test, we have seen, asks us to consider whether a governmental regulation is aimed at the expressive components of conduct. Many laws or regulations that may have the effect of stifling speech are not *designed* to keep any particular message from being heard. Suppose, for example, that you answer your door to a police officer advising you that your neighbors would appreciate it if you and your party guests make a bit less noise. The content of the message or messages being exchanged among your friends is not at issue in such a situation. The legal intervention stems instead from the *time* (late at night, perhaps, when neighbors are trying to sleep), *place* (a

---

88. *Young v. American Mini Theatres*, 427 U.S. 50 (1976).

89. *City of Erie v. Pap's A. M.*, 529 U.S. 277 (2000).

90. See, for example, Daniel Linz et al., "Peep Show Establishments, Police Activity, Public Place and Time: A Study of Secondary Effects in San Diego, California," 43 *Journal of Sex Research* 182 (2006).

91. Clay Calvert, "All the News That's Fit to Steal: The First Amendment, a 'Free' Press & a Lagging Legislative Response," 25 *Loyola of Los Angeles Entertainment Law Review* 117 (2004–2005).

92. *Rossignol v. Voorhaar*, 316 F.3d 516 (4th Cir. 2003). Upon remand, the plaintiff newspaper won a summary judgment ruling against the sheriff and the deputies. 321 F. Supp. 2d 642 (D. Md. 2004).

residential, as opposed to purely commercial, area of town), or *manner* (the decibel level itself) of the communication.

Although the Supreme Court has never ruled on a "noisy party complaint" case, it has upheld the notion that content-neutral limitations on a message's loudness or inappropriate choice of venue are permissible. In 1972, in his majority opinion upholding the conviction of a group of civil rights demonstrators for staging a potentially disruptive protest too close to a public school, Justice Marshall indicated why time, place, and manner restrictions were not only permissible but necessary. After all, "two parades cannot march on the same street simultaneously." Moreover, although "a silent vigil may not unduly interfere with a public library, making a speech in the reading room almost certainly would. . . . The crucial question is whether the manner of expression is basically incompatible with the normal activity of a particular place at a particular time."[93]

Over the years the Supreme Court has created a three-part test to determine the constitutionality of time, place, and manner restrictions on speech. First, the regulation must be content neutral. It must not be motivated by governmental displeasure at the specific message being sent. An ordinance forbidding the use of overly loud sound trucks, for example, passes this test in that it does not matter what is said, as long as it is not said at a deafening volume.[94] Similarly, a New York City regulation governing the loudness of amplified concerts in Central Park was upheld. After all, it did not prescribe one decibel level for rap music and another for the 1812 Overture.[95]

Second, the regulation must be narrowly tailored to further an important government interest. In 1939, the Supreme Court struck down as unconstitutional laws in a handful of cities that, in the interests of preventing littering, prohibited all distribution of printed literature on street corners. If these cities wanted to decrease littering, they should have more directly punished "those who actually throw papers on the streets," not persons engaged in otherwise protected First Amendment activity.[96] More recently, Richmond, Virginia's, practice of artificially privatizing streets immediately surrounding an inner-city public-housing complex and prohibiting entry to persons not having legitimate business to conduct within was upheld. The plan was narrowly tailored to further the government's interest in maintaining safety in an otherwise high-crime area.[97]

Finally, a restriction on the time, place, and manner of communication must permit ample alternative means for speakers to transmit their messages. Thus, much to the dismay of a homeless persons' advocacy group organizing a political demonstra-

93. *Grayned v. City of Rockford, Illinois*, 408 U.S. 104, 115–116 (1972).

94. *Kovacs v. Cooper*, 336 U.S. 77 (1948).

95. *Ward v. Rock Against Racism*, 491 U.S. 781 (1989); see also *International Action Center v. City of New York*, 587 F. 3d 521 (2nd Cir. 2009) (upholding the city's moratorium on "new" parades down Fifth Avenue beyond the fifteen traditionally permitted ones).

96. *Schneider v. New Jersey*, 308 U.S. 147, 162 (1939).

97. *Virginia v. Hicks*, 539 U.S. 113 (2003).

tion over several days in Lafayette Park (a small grassy area across the street from the White House), the Supreme Court upheld the constitutionality of a National Park Service regulation prohibiting sleeping overnight in the park. The regulation did not prevent the demonstrators from communicating the plight of the homeless, Justice White concluded. Indeed, as long as the participants were willing to take turns, they could collectively maintain a twenty-four-hour presence in the park.[98] Or consider Justice Marshall's reasoning in a decision invalidating a New Jersey municipality's law against posting For Sale signs on residential lawns. The law, which was aimed at curbing the practice of panic selling stemming from racial fears, was admittedly not content neutral in that it proscribed one specific message. Marshall went out of his way to point out that the law also could not pass the "ample alternative means of communication" requirement in that the signs reach a specific audience—the casual buyer, not necessarily looking to buy a home and thus not in the habit of reading the classified pages or consulting real estate agents—not easily reached via any other medium.[99]

Public Forum Analysis

As we have seen, the government may restrict or prohibit communication when the time, place, or manner is deemed inappropriate. There are also places where the government recognizes that communication is an especially appropriate activity. These are called **public forums**. The Court has recognized three kinds.

Quintessential Public Forums   Public parks and street corners (so long as speakers do not impede the flow of vehicular or pedestrian traffic) have "by long tradition . . . been devoted to assembly and debate,"[100] and the government is thus compelled to protect the rights of speakers in these forums. Thus, for example, those portions of Houston's ordinance prohibiting parades from taking place downtown any hours other than 10 to 11 a.m. and 2 to 3 p.m. were struck down, the court having found them far too restrictive on the First Amendment interests of demonstrators who want to reach a larger (read "rush hour") audience.[101]

Limited Public Forums   These include auditoriums and meeting rooms, which the government is not required to open up to outside use, but which once opened must be administered in an evenhanded way, similar to the rules required for the quintessential public forums. Certainly this means that viewpoint-based discrimination is not permitted and all potential users must be treated equally. Thus, Hastings College of Law could require that all student groups seeking official campus recognition must themselves not discriminate among students for purposes of member-

---

98. *Clark v. Community for Creative Non-Violence*, 468 U.S. 288 (1984).
99. *Linmark Associates v. Township of Willingboro*, 431 U.S. 85, 93 (1977).
100. *Perry Education Association v. Perry Local Educators' Association*, 460 U.S. 37, 45 (1983).
101. *SEIU, Local 5 v. City of Houston*, 595 F. 3d 588 (5th Cir. 2010).

ship,[102] and a school district in New York could not discriminate against a group of local Christians who wanted to use an elementary school's auditorium.[103] Also, the District of Columbia was sued successfully by People for the Ethical Treatment of Animals (PETA) when PETA's application to participate in the city's "Party Animals" public sculpture forum with a "sad elephant" was rejected, although a "happy elephant" (one lacking the sad elephant's political stance against animal abuse) would have been accepted.[104]

Public forums can legitimately be "limited" in the sense of being open only to certain categories of speakers or even categories of discourse. For example, state university student fees might be used to pay for offices, mailboxes, photocopying, and the like only for student groups, not for outside community groups. A school board or city council meeting might be willing to hear from only those citizens who have something to say that is germane to the evening's agenda.

Nonpublic Forums
This category refers to public property that is not by tradition or practice open as a speaking venue for all comers. The only constraint placed on the government in regulating the use of such property is that access to it should

not be based on a potential speaker's viewpoint. Automobile license plates are a good example. Their purpose is to alert law enforcement that a vehicle is properly registered (and with a little checking, in whose name it is registered), not to serve as a speech venue. But most states do use "vanity plates" as a way of raising revenue, and when they do so, the only restriction on them is that their rules not discriminate against registrants on the basis of the viewpoint expressed by their requested license plate wording.[105]

It is not always clear when a public forum has been created, and when in-

Once the D.C. government opened up a public forum for "party animal" sculpture designs, it could not discriminate against the viewpoint espoused here by PETA. The blanket reads: "The CIRCUS is coming. See SHACKLES! BULL HOOKS! LONELINESS! All under the 'Big Top.'"

---

102. *Christian Legal Society v. Martinez*, 130 S. Ct. 2971 (2010). The CLS refused to permit gay students to join. Hastings is a public law school, part of the University of California.

103. *Good News Club v. Milford Central School*, 533 U.S. 98 (2001). The group was very candid about its desire to hold an evening of prayer, singing, and reciting of Bible lessons, and the Court made clear that the public forum doctrine's requirement of nondiscrimination trumped any possible Establishment Clause considerations.

104. *PETA v. Gittens*, 360 F. Supp. 2d 28 (D.D.C. 2003).

105. *Children First Foundation v. Legreide*, 373 Fed. Appx. 156 (3rd Cir. 2010) (New Jersey may not prohibit "Choose Life" license plates if they permit other plates with explicit political messages.)

stead the government has chosen to create a forum for its own speech. Earlier in this chapter passing reference was made to *Rust v. Sullivan*,[106] where the Court ruled that the federal government was the speaker when it spent money in support of family planning clinics and forbade fund recipients from even talking about abortion. The logic is clear enough—if the government spends money on antismoking messages, it has not thus created a "forum" that must also welcome and fund those with opposing views.

What about states that give tax incentives to lure filmmakers to shoot their films in the sponsoring state? Who is the speaker—the film director or the state? Clearly there would be First Amendment implications if a state gave tax breaks to a documentary espousing the virtues of one political party, then refused to give similar incentives to a documentarian with an opposing agenda. More typical conflicts fall into a grayer domain. We have no case law on the issue yet, but consider the example of film director Andrew van den Houten. The letter rejecting his application for a grant from Michigan to help defray the expenses of producing *The Woman* made clear the decision was based at least in part on the film commission's determination that the movie was "unlikely to promote tourism in Michigan or reflect Michigan in a positive light."[107] Does state funding of filmmaking create a public forum, or is it akin to the state advertising itself as a vacation destination?

THINGS TO REMEMBER

Some Transcendent First Amendment Doctrines

- The First Amendment includes a right to hear.
- It also includes a right not to speak.
- Free speech includes some kinds of symbolic conduct.
- The *O'Brien* test determines constitutionality of regulations aimed at symbolic conduct:
  - The regulation must further an important interest.
  - That interest must not be simply to stifle a specific message.
  - The regulation must be narrowly drawn.
- Time, place, and manner restrictions are not subject to strict scrutiny:
  - The regulations must be content neutral.
  - They must be narrowly tailored.
  - They must permit sufficient alternative means of communication.
- Government property has sometimes been held to be a public forum open to expressive activity.
- Courts often have difficulty deciding when to apply public forum analysis and when to allow the government itself to speak.

---

106. 500 U.S. 173 (1991).

107. Michael Cieply, "State Backing Films Says Cannibal is Deal Breaker," *New York Times*, June 14, 2010, A1.

Regulating the Business of Communication

Not all legal interventions affecting communication industries should necessarily be considered communication law. If a local police chief, upset at the coverage given him by the town's "alternative" free weekly, effectively shuts down the paper by barging into the newsroom and confiscating the publisher's computer, we would have a clear (and clearly unconstitutional) example of "media law" at work. If that same publisher, however, is a divorced father who is tens of thousands of dollars behind in his child-support payments, the confiscation of that same computer through a judgment obtained by the Division of Family Services would not be at all relevant to the study of communication law. Media industries are governed by much the same legal environment affecting other businesses. They must pay their workers at least the minimum wage. They must provide safe and nonharassing working conditions. They must contribute their legally mandated share of employees' Social Security payments.

Andrew van den Houten, director of *Offspring*, a vampire-themed film which did receive funding from the state of Michigan. A sequel was denied funding in Michigan but received backing from the Massachusetts Film Office. Used by permission.

In this final section of the chapter, three areas of the law that are applied to media industries just as to other industries are examined. When applied to the media, however, they have a special impact on the act of communication by determining either who may speak or what may be said. The three topics to be addressed here are antitrust, taxation, and workplace laws.

Antitrust Laws

The Sherman Act of 1890 and the Clayton Act of 1914 give the Department of Justice license to bring both civil and criminal proceedings against businesses that function "in restraint of trade." Media outlets have often behaved in an anticompetitive manner, and sometimes this behavior has prompted the government to pursue them for antitrust violations. In 1951, the Supreme Court held that the Lorain Journal Company, a newspaper publisher in Ohio, was in violation of antitrust laws when it refused to accept advertising from businesses that had also advertised in competing local media.[108]

---

108. *Lorain Journal Co. v. United States*, 342 U.S. 143 (1951). See also, *United States v. Kansas City Star*, 240 F. 3d 643 (8th Cir. 1957) (newspapers had threatened companies who advertised with

Newspapers have not been the only media industries to become antitrust defendants over the years. The structure of the motion picture industry was shaped in large part by a 1948 Supreme Court decision holding that **block-booking** (whereby theater owners were forced by movie studios to exhibit their less desirable "B" movies along with the more popular films likely to produce a profit) was a violation of the Sherman Act.[109] Major Hollywood studios at the time also owned huge chains of theaters, an arrangement that produced its own host of anticompetitive practices. Independent theater owners naturally found it hard to get access to the best pictures, which the studios preferred to keep for their own screens. The government successfully pressured the studios to sell off their movie theaters in the late 1940s.

Perhaps the most dramatic litigation in recent years alleging anticompetitive practices on the part of a communications industry has been the Department of Justice's suit against Microsoft. The government alleged that Microsoft used its virtual monopoly in personal computer operating systems (Windows) to create an unfair advantage in marketing its own Internet browser (Internet Explorer). Microsoft argued that its browser is an integral part of its operating system and that to force it to remove Internet Explorer would be akin to forcing a cookie manufacturer to take the chocolate chips out of its cookies to protect the market share of companies that wished to sell consumers chocolate chips separately. A settlement was approved by the D.C. Circuit Court of Appeals in 2004, which effectively ended the federal suit and companion suits by a handful of states and computer trade groups.[110] The settlement requires Microsoft to allow computer manufacturers more flexibility to include rival software companies' products on their desktop displays. Microsoft has continued to encounter similar legal problems in European courts.[111]

Antitrust laws can be triggered not only when a company engages in specific anticompetitive practices but also when one or a small group of companies simply grows so big that a monopoly or quasimonopoly results. Such monopolies can happen with media outlets just as they can among car manufacturers or soft drink producers. The federal government has often brought actions against media companies that have achieved too large a market share. For example, in the 1960s the Times Mirror Company, the owner of the *Los Angeles Times* and other newspapers, was forced to divest itself of newspapers it had recently purchased in neighboring San Bernardino

---

competing publications that their ads would no longer be welcome, and threatened uncooperative individuals with negative press coverage).

109. *United States v. Paramount Pictures, Inc.*, 334 U.S. 131 (1948); see also *United States v. Loew's, Inc.*, 371 U.S. 38 (1962) (holding that movie studios' "block-booking" of films to TV stations violated antitrust laws).

110. *Massachusetts v. Microsoft Corp.*, 373 F.3d 1199 (D.C. Cir. 2004).

111. Charles Arthur and Jack Schofield, "Microsoft Forced to Offer Users a Choice of Web Browsers," *The Guardian* (London), March 2, 2010, 12.

County.[112] The government has also had to approve the many mergers that resulted from the Telecommunications Act of 1996, discussed in more detail in chapter 12.

In 1970 Congress adopted the **Newspaper Preservation Act**, which permitted competing newspapers in the same town to function under a **joint operating agreement (JOA)** whereby the advertising, circulation, and printing portions of the two papers would be joined, but each paper would maintain separate editorial functions. These exceptions to the usual behaviors one would expect under existing antitrust law were to be permitted only if at least one of the two newspapers was otherwise in danger of failing. The act was thus the federal government's way of expressing the value of having more than one major newspaper in a community. In the late 1970s there were functioning JOAs in twenty-eight cities nationwide, but as of 2009 the number had dwindled to nine.[113]

Taxation

Although the press may be taxed in the same way as any industry,[114] taxes that discriminatorily target media outlets may be found unconstitutional. This principle was established clearly in a 1936 case from Louisiana, whose legislature had enacted a tax on the advertising revenues from newspapers with circulations of more than twenty thousand subscribers. The tax seemed designed cleverly to burden, even silence, critics of Senator Huey Long, who was most vociferously challenged by editors of the state's largest newspapers. In his majority opinion striking down the law, Justice George Sutherland described the tax as "a deliberate and calculated device . . . to limit the circulation of information to which the public is entitled."[115]

Even in the absence of as colorful a figure as Huey Long, the Supreme Court reached a similar result in 1983, when it struck down a Minnesota tax on paper and ink that, by exempting the first $100,000 of use, effectively targeted the tax so narrowly that one newspaper paid almost two-thirds of it. Even if the legislature had no personal animus against the Minneapolis Star and Tribune Company, Justice O'Connor ruled, singling out only a few media companies for taxation presents too strong "a potential for abuse."[116]

The State of Arkansas was also held in violation of the First Amendment when it enacted a tax that at first blush would seem to be constitutional because it was aimed

---

112. *United States v. Times Mirror Co.*, 274 F. Supp. 606 (C.D. Cal. 1967), *aff'd*, 390 U.S. 712 (1968).

113. Laurie Kellman, "New Antitrust Relief for Newspapers Opposed," *Associated Press Financial Wire*, April 21, 2009.

114. *Arizona Publishing Co. v. O'Neil*, 304 U.S. 543 (1938); *City of Corona v. Corona Daily Independent*, 252 P.2d 56 (Cal. Ct. App. 1953).

115. *Grosjean v. American Press Co.*, 297 U.S. 233, 250 (1936).

116. *Minneapolis Star & Tribune Co. v. Minnesota Commissioner of Revenue*, 460 U.S. 575, 592 (1983).

at "tangible personal property" generally. The constitutional infirmity was in the tax's application to some magazines but its exemption for locally published "religious," "professional," and "trade and sports journals." Taxes may not discriminate on the basis of a publication's content, the Court ruled.[117] Similarly, Texas was not permitted to exempt only *religious* periodicals from a general sales tax. The Court's decision here rested upon the First Amendment's Establishment Clause.[118]

Taxes that apply to only some media industries do not necessarily violate the Constitution, however. In 1991, for example, the Supreme Court upheld an Arkansas sales tax levied against cable television companies but not magazines, newspapers, or even home satellite systems. Justice O'Connor's majority opinion indicated that "differential taxation of speakers, even members of the press, does not implicate the First Amendment unless the tax is directed at, or presents the danger of, suppressing particular ideas."[119] Whether a sales tax may constitutionally be applied to magazines while exempting newspapers is still an open question, however. Courts have come down on both sides of this issue.[120] It is likely that a sales tax reaching only "advertisers" and exempting "true newspapers" would be found constitutional.[121]

Workplace Law

Just as taxes that are applied to industry generally may be applied to media outlets, so must media industries obey relevant federal, state, and local labor laws in their relations with employees. Interesting questions often arise, however, when courts try to determine how to apply this body of law to professional communicators. In this section we look at two areas of labor law that have attracted much judicial attention: the Fair Labor Standards Act of 1938 (FLSA) and the National Labor Relations Act.

One of the key provisions of the FLSA is that employees not exempted from its scope must be paid overtime wages for work in excess of forty hours per week. Certain categories of professional employees are exempt from the act—thus the references to "exempt" and "nonexempt" employees in human resources offices nationwide—and courts have often been called on to determine when media employees should be considered exempt professionals. This body of case law often forces media litigants to make arguments contrary to their customary economic bargaining positions. Management must claim that the work of such employees is distinct and creative (and

---

117. *Arkansas Writers' Project, Inc. v. Ragland*, 481 U.S. 221 (1987).

118. *Texas Monthly, Inc. v. Bullock*, 489 U.S. 1 (1989); see also *Haller v. Commonwealth*, 728 A.2d 351 (Pa. Super. Ct. 1999).

119. *Leathers v. Medlock*, 499 U.S. 439, 453 (1991).

120. *Southern Living v. Celauro*, 789 S.W.2d 251 (Tenn. 1990) (striking down the differential taxation of magazines and newspapers); *Hearst Corp. v. Iowa Department of Revenue & Finance*, 461 N.W.2d 295 (Iowa 1990) (upholding such differential treatment).

121. *Arizona Department of Revenue v. Great Western Publishing*, 3 P.3d 992 (Ariz. Ct. of Appeals 1999); *H. J. Wilson Company v. State Tax Commission of the State of Mississippi*, 737 So. 2d 981 (Miss. 1998).

thus not qualifying for overtime pay), whereas workers counter that their output is routine and uninspired.[122]

Ever since the 1940s, the secretary of labor, who has initial responsibility for enforcement of the FLSA, has maintained that only a very small number of working journalists are "professionals" exempt from the act's overtime-pay provisions. Only "editorial writers, columnists, critics, and 'top-flight' writers of analytical and interpretative articles" should be considered exempt, the Department of Labor argues. Although it is fair to say that the vast majority of reporters are valued for their "intelligence, diligence, and accuracy," only these categories of employees are called on as their "primary duty" to produce work requiring "invention, imagination, or talent," work that is "original and creative in character." The Department also emphasizes that reporters, unlike other professionals such as doctors and lawyers, do not have to master a prescribed body of knowledge to function in their careers; they need not have journalism degrees and often do not have college degrees at all. Courts have generally accepted the Department of Labor's interpretation of the FLSA's applicability to the newsroom.[123] The one exceptional case involved *Washington Post* writers who were considered professionals exempt from the FLSA's overtime-wages provisions. In that case, the court emphasized that *Washington Post* reporters are very highly paid national leaders in the field of journalism, often called on to teach at universities, to write books, and to serve as guests on talk shows and public affairs programs. Moreover, these reporters functioned in a professionally collegial atmosphere that would be envied by their counterparts at other papers. They were encouraged to generate their own story ideas and to decide not only how to pursue stories but also when it might be wisest to "kill" a story.[124]

The National Labor Relations Act also has an impact on how media outlets are regulated as businesses. The act provides most employees with the right to organize, to form unions, to collectively bargain, and to engage in all these activities without fear of retribution from their employers. But what happens if the employer is a newspaper and the alleged retribution takes the form of reassigning a reporter to new duties? Such was the case when Mitchell Stoddard, a columnist for the *Passaic Daily News* in New Jersey, had been active in a union organizing drive and later learned that his employer no longer planned to run his weekly column. The National Labor Relations Board (NLRB) ordered the newspaper to restore the status quo, to continue to run Stoddard's column. The newspaper appealed, arguing that the NLRB's chosen

122. *Reich v. Newspapers of New England*, 44 F.3d 1060, 1075 n.12 (1st Cir. 1995); see also *Freeman v. National Broadcasting Co.*, 846 F. Supp. 1109, 1123 (S.D.N.Y. 1993).

123. *Reich v. Newspapers of New England*, 44 F.3d 1060 (1st Cir. 1995); *Reich v. Gateway Press*, 13 F.3d 685 (3d Cir. 1994); *Freeman v. National Broadcasting Co.*, 846 F. Supp. 1109 (S.D.N.Y. 1993); *Dalheim v. KDFW-TV*, 706 F. Supp. 493 (N.D. Tex. 1988), *aff'd*, 918 F.2d 1220 (5th Cir. 1990).

124. *Sherwood v. Washington Post*, 677 F. Supp. 9 (D.D.C. 1988), *rev'd and remanded on other grounds*, 871 F.2d 1144 (D.C. Cir. 1989).

remedy was a violation of its right to determine what will and will not run in its pages, the "right not to speak" corollary First Amendment right discussed earlier in this chapter. The D.C. Circuit Court of Appeals recognized that the NLRB's goals—to ensure both that the company not be allowed to retaliate against Stoddard and that "meaningful remedies for [future] victims of unlawful discrimination" be in place— were legitimate. Here, however, the NLRB went too far in that it injected itself "into the editorial decision-making process." The court remanded the case back to the NLRB, suggesting that an order "direct[ing] the Company to not discriminate against Stoddard on the basis of his union activity" might be a more appropriate remedy. On remand, the NLRB ordered the paper to restore Stoddard's "column-writing duties" but did not compel the paper to actually publish whatever columns he writes, just as long as that decision flows from considerations other than his union activities.[125]

The strained judicial compromise reached in this case underscores the more general proposition that deference to publishers' free press rights necessarily means that media company employees may have fewer free speech rights than workers in other industries.[126] Thus, for example, Washington's Fair Campaign Practices Act, which protects employees from retaliation for their off-the-job political activities, was held inapplicable to a newspaper reporter who had been dismissed by the Tacoma *Morning News Tribune* for having participated in a pro-choice abortion rally and for ignoring management's request that she refrain from any high-profile political activities. The newspaper's need to protect its reputation for objectivity in reporting the news must prevail over the reporter's interests, the court held.[127]

What of laws against race and gender discrimination in employment? With respect to the hiring and treatment of onstage or on-air media personalities, whether movie stars or news anchorpersons, the courts will generally permit employers to engage in discriminatory practices. All the employer need do is demonstrate that a particular "look" is a "bona fide occupational qualification" (in federal law, a BFOQ) of the job, for example, "Our ratings go down when an old, unattractive female is anchoring." More generally employers such as movie studios and theater companies (and perhaps broadcast news media) can argue that their own "artistic freedom" (protected by the First Amendment) would be abridged if the courts were to tell them whom to hire or to cast.[128]

---

125. *Passaic Daily News v. NLRB*, 736 F.2d 1543 (D.C. Cir. 1984).

126. Louis Day, "The Journalist as Citizen Activist: The Ethical Limits of Free Speech," 4 *Communication Law and Policy* 1 (1999).

127. *Nelson v. McClatchy Newspapers, Inc.*, 936 P.2d 1123 (Wash. 1997). See also John Paul Dilts, "The First Amendment and Credibility: Revisiting *Nelson v. McClatchy Newspapers*," 10 *Communication Law and Policy* 1 (2005).

128. Russell K. Robinson, "Casting and Caste-ing: Reconciling Artistic Freedom and Antidiscrimination Norms," 95 *California Law Review* 1 (2007).

THINGS TO REMEMBER

Regulating Media as a Business

- Federal antitrust laws have been used against
  - newspapers that refuse to accept advertising from businesses already advertising in competing media;
  - movie studios that demand theater owners to accept less-known "B" movies if they want to show the true blockbusters;
  - movie studios that own too many movie theaters; and
  - media companies that have grown so huge and command such a large market share that they threaten to stifle competition.
- The Newspaper Preservation Act sometimes permits otherwise competing newspapers to form joint operating agreements to share non-editorial costs.
- The media may be subject to the same kinds of taxes as any other business, but taxes that single out the media, or that discriminate among media outlets, might be found unconstitutional.
- Taxes that exempt only *religious* media are especially likely to be found unconstitutional.
- Most media employees are considered "nonexempt" and thus eligible for certain benefits such as overtime pay.
- Journalists can generally be prevented by their employers from engaging in overt political activity.

Chapter Summary

The Supreme Court had very little to say about the First Amendment's meaning until the World War I era, when, in a long series of cases continuing through the 1960s, the Court dealt with the issue of incitement to overthrowing the government or to other violent action. The current test for such speech is found in *Brandenburg v. Ohio*, a 1969 decision.

Over the years many competing First Amendment theories have been proposed, including absolutist theory, access theory, and various balancing approaches. Generally, the modern judiciary engages in preferred-position balancing.

Theorists have also identified many functions served by freedom of speech, including aiding in the search for the truth, enabling us to be better self-governors, acting as a check on government abuse, providing for individual fulfillment, and serving as a societal safety valve. Other theorists, including Marxists, feminists, and critical race theorists, have questioned the place of freedom of speech in the hierarchy of values.

The First Amendment has been interpreted to include a right to hear, a right not to speak, and a right to engage in symbolic conduct.

Government restrictions on speech that are not aimed at the actual content of the message do not require as exacting scrutiny as purer forms of censorship.

Chapter 3

DEFAMATION: COMMON-LAW ELEMENTS

L ibel law is designed to protect a person's reputation from blemish. In Shakespeare's *Othello*, the treacherous Iago famously reminds us that an ordinary thief, one who "steals my purse," "steals trash," but that a defamer, someone who "filches from me my good name," "makes me poor indeed." More routine though less poetic definitions of libel are readily available in standard legal publications. *Black's Law Dictionary* defines libel as "an intentional false communication . . . that injures another's reputation or good name." The *Restatement of Torts* reports that messages are libelous if they "tend so to harm the reputation of another as to lower him in the estimation of the community or to deter third persons from associating or dealing with him."

Sometimes it seems as if Hollywood celebrities who are offended by their media coverage are as likely to sue for libel as they are to simply have their publicists try to set the record straight with a press release. In recent years Britney Spears has sued *US Weekly* magazine for publishing an article alleging that she and her husband had produced a sex tape,[1] Tom Cruise has sued on more than one occasion when the media have suggested he is gay,[2] Ashley Olsen's lawsuit against the *National Enquirer* for claiming she had been involved in a drug scandal resulted in the publication retracting the story,[3] and in England (where libel law is more friendly to plaintiffs than here in the United States), Elton John won an undisclosed settlement from the *London*

---

1. Jessica Garrison, "Star's Sex Tape Suit is Dismissed," *Los Angeles Times*, November 7, 2006, B1.
2. "Gay Libel," *The Independent* (London), March 3, 2009, 28.
3. Matthew Belloni, "Media Trend of Celebrity Hit and Run Being Replaced by Attack Then Retract," *Hollywood Reporter*, November 26, 2008.

Times for alleging that he acted a bit snooty at an AIDS fund-raiser, asking attendees to speak to him only if spoken to.[4]

Libel suits stem not only from Hollywood gossip, of course. Often hard news stories prompt libel suits. In 2008, for example, the Supreme Court upheld a lower court's dismissal of the libel suit brought by Dr. Steven Hatfill, once thought by the FBI to have been responsible for the anthrax mailings that came on the heels of the

Britney Spears filed a $20 million lawsuit against *US Weekly* for this article, which alleges that she and then-husband Kevin Federline had produced a home sex tape. The case was dismissed.

---

4. Richard Eldredge, "Sir Elton Wins Award for Libel, Helps Charity," *Atlanta Journal-Constitution*, February 17, 2006, 2G.

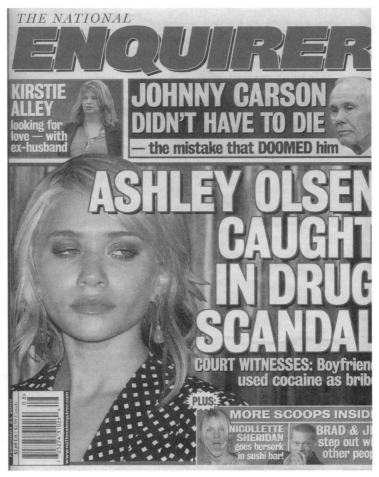

The cover story about Ashley Olsen prompted the former child star to sue for a reported $40 million. The paper settled out of court by publishing a retraction of the story.

9/11 attacks and which killed individuals in Florida and in Washington, D.C.[5] Also in 2008, incumbent senator Elizabeth Dole of North Carolina was sued by challenger Kay Hagan after Dole's campaign ran a TV spot that strongly implied Hagan was an atheist.[6] (Hagan is now *Senator* Hagan).

Ordinary people also sue for libel, and as you will see in chapter 4, the law is more

---

5. *Hatfill v. New York Times*, 532 F. 3d 312 (4th Cir. 2008), *cert. denied*, 2008 U.S. LEXIS 9136.

6. Hagan withdrew the suit immediately after the election. "Now That I've Won, It's No Big Deal," *The Hotline*, November 14, 2008.

WHAT DID HAGAN PROMISE IN RETURN?

PAID FOR BY THE ELIZABETH DOLE COMMITTEE, INC. APPROVED BY ELIZABETH DOLE.

A key element of Kay Hagan's suit against the Dole campaign was that this TV campaign ad falsely leads viewers to believe it is Hagan's own voice at the end saying, "There is no God."

in their favor than it is for celebrities and public figures. But the cost of mounting a libel case can be steep, which may explain why so many plaintiffs are well-heeled people whose names we already knew.

Media professionals are more likely to get into legal trouble over alleged libel than over any other issue this book addresses. The defendants' costs can be staggering. Jury awards in the millions of dollars are no longer especially newsworthy events. Even if the media defendant ultimately prevails, as typically happens at least on the appellate level, the legal fees involved and the enormous amount of time taken from writing new stories to defend old ones would alone constitute ample reason to avoid publishing defamatory materials.

For most of the country's history, that the press could be sued and even criminally prosecuted for libel—seventeen states still have **criminal libel** laws on the books, though they are rarely used—never seemed to raise any constitutional objections.[7] The First Amendment, it will be recalled, tells *Congress* that it cannot abridge freedom of speech and of the press. Defamation had always been handled at the state level. Moreover, that the founders clearly knew of the existence of libel laws and mentioned not one word about them in the text of the Constitution seems to suggest that they saw no philosophic conflict between the system of freedom of expression they intended to create and the continuing use of laws against defamation. In this chapter, we examine the traditional common-law definition of libel as it has evolved in the states. In 1964, the U.S. Supreme Court intervened, ruling that the First Amendment does impose significant restrictions on libel law.[8] So dramatic have been the changes

---

7. At least one author has suggested that criminal libel cases might be far more common than one would imagine. See David Pritchard, "Rethinking Criminal Libel: an Empirical Study," 14 *Communication Law and Policy* 303 (2009). The Reporters Committee for Freedom of the Press reported on half a dozen prosecutions for criminal libel nationwide in 2008.

8. *New York Times Co. v. Sullivan*, 376 U.S. 254 (1964).

in libel since that seminal ruling that we devote chapter 4 to an examination of the Supreme Court's libel doctrine as it has developed in the past few decades.

Elements of a Libel Suit

Defamation can be defined as false statements of fact disseminated about a person that result in damage to that person's reputation. Traditionally, the law recognized separate actions for libel (written defamation) and **slander** (spoken defamation). In the several centuries after the invention of the printing press but before the discovery of radio, this separation was logical for at least two reasons. First, the unamplified spoken word could damage a person's reputation in the minds of only those who were physically present to hear the speech. Unless the speaker had access to a physical setting with extraordinary acoustics, the audience would probably be a few hundred people at most. In addition, the spoken word has a more ephemeral quality than the written word. The expression "here today, gone tomorrow" actually exaggerates the life of the spoken word, which is more accurately described as gone in the *moment* after it is uttered. The written word, by contrast, has a life that transcends space and time. Recipients of the message can show it to others, and they can discuss it and amplify its effects. Libel could reach a larger audience and do much more lasting harm than slander.

The advent of the electronic mass media muddied the waters to the point where today the distinction between libel and slander has all but disappeared in law. Even the least viewed programs on national network television, after all, reach an audience many times the size of the circulation figures for the country's most popular magazines and newspapers. Moreover, the widespread use of recording equipment ensures that the spoken word now can have a shelf life as long as any written message. Although some states still make some parts of a libel suit easier to prove against a "libeler" than a "slanderer," such differences are few. Therefore, this book follows the lead of most courts and commentators by using the word *libel* to refer to both written and spoken defamatory utterances.

Generally speaking, libel plaintiffs must prove four elements in order to prevail.[9] They must establish defamation, of course, but also **publication**, **identification**, and **fault**. The discussion of the first three of these elements takes up the rest of this chapter. Because the Supreme Court's libel doctrine, which has been evolving since the

---

9. Some writers include *falsity* as a fifth element. This book does not do so, reflecting the fact that the common law traditionally placed the burden of proof instead on the defendant to establish the truth of the defamatory statements. Moreover, in some states, even today, truth is not an absolute defense to a libel action. Although the Supreme Court has had some things to say about this issue, it has not gone so far as to wholly reverse the common-law tradition. This point will be expanded upon when we discuss the Court's ruling in *Philadelphia Newspapers, Inc. v. Hepps* in chapter 4.

1960s, has focused almost entirely on the issue of fault, the discussion of that fourth element is necessarily rather lengthy and complex. Chapter 4 examines the Supreme Court's 1964 intervention into libel law as well as later cases that have fine-tuned and generally expanded the First Amendment protections provided in that case.

Defamation

Defamatory utterances are those that if believed will make a listener think less highly of the persons described, avoid their company in social situations, or avoid seeking out their services in business relationships. The following discussion of this first element examines several key questions courts address as libel plaintiffs try to build their cases. First, we consider whether the defamatory meaning is explicit and obvious, or whether readers would need additional information to understand the insult. Then we focus on the audience, as we try to ascertain *in whose minds* the complainant has been damaged. Next, with respect to the message itself, we will see that courts have sometimes excused arguably libelous statements as "rhetorical hyperbole." The focus then shifts to the relationship between the defamation element and the kinds and amounts of damages successful plaintiffs may be awarded. Finally, we will examine how corporations, and even products, can be libeled.

Libel Per Se, Libel Per Quod, and Implied   Traditionally, the common law of libel has recognized two categories of defamatory statements. Although Supreme Court intervention into libel law has made the distinctions less important to litigants than was once the case, the categories still help in understanding the overall concept of defamation. The first category of defamation is **libel per se**, allegations that would obviously, with no further embellishment by the speaker or special knowledge on the part of the listener, damage the reputation of the persons described. Examples of defamation that have generally been recognized as libel per se include allegations of criminal wrongdoing, of gross incompetence in one's chosen career, of such serious moral failings as being a chronic liar, and of having a loathsome and contagious disease. Though it may seem somewhere between quaint and offensive by contemporary standards, to accuse a woman of sexual misconduct has also been viewed as libelous per se.[10] The second broad category of defamation is **libel per quod**. At one level, this category includes all libelous statements that do not fit into the traditional libel per se category. Another way of defining libel per quod is as a statement that seems innocent enough on its face but that when added to specific facts presumably already known by readers would be injurious to reputation. Suppose that a campus paper were to write that "Professor Jones was seen gardening in her backyard yesterday and

---

10. For more on libel cases stemming from allegations of sexual impropriety, see Lisa R. Pruitt, "Her Own Good Name: Two Centuries of Talk about Chastity," 63 *Maryland Law Review* 401 (2004); and Diane L. Borden, "Patterns of Harm: An Analysis of Gender and Defamation," 1 *Communication Law and Policy* 105, 133–134 (1997).

appeared to be vigorous, energetic, and healthy." These would hardly seem to be defamatory statements, but what if Jones had recently filed for disability benefits? Knowledgeable readers might correctly surmise that the reporter had intended to suggest that Jones was engaged in fraud.

A concept often confused with libel per quod is **implied libel** (sometimes called **defamation by implication**). Libel per quod involves situations in which the plaintiff alleges that factual allegations were untrue. In the Professor Jones hypothetical in the above paragraph, the plaintiff would allege that it was actually someone else seen in her garden or that she was not "energetic" but rather was manifesting some very obvious difficulty bending down. By contrast, implied libel cases find plaintiffs admitting from the outset that the defendant's words are true. It is the *implication* of those admittedly true statements that burns, such plaintiffs allege. In a case from Iowa, for example, a sportswriter was accused in print of "rarely attending events on which he wrote columns." To the extent that words like "rarely" can be assigned a truth value, the claim was literally true, in that the plaintiff admitted that he attended fewer than one-fifth of the events about which he wrote. The implication of the admittedly true charge, the plaintiff alleged, was that it is customary for sportswriters to attend all or most events about which they write, or even that he was somehow unethical for writing about things of which he did not have direct knowledge.[11] Not all states or federal circuits are willing to adjudicate claims of implied libel. Some have held that only *explicit* falsehoods may be the subject of libel claims.

Who Has to Believe?   A report can be found defamatory even when plaintiffs fail to show that the vast majority of readers held them in lower esteem after seeing the charges. A subject matter might be sufficiently esoteric that only a small percentage of readers will understand a statement's libelous meaning. No matter. Courts will gauge the negative effects of the libel on any right-minded individuals who together constitute a community of relevance to the plaintiff.[12]

Adjudication becomes quite complicated if a plaintiff's "community" is an identifiable group with values far different from those of the society at large. Would it be defamatory for the press to report that world-famous safecracker "Frankie the Fingers" has "lost his touch"? Certainly such an allegation, if believed, would make pro-

---

11. *Stevens v. Iowa Newspapers, Inc.*, 711 N.W.2d 732 (Iowa Ct. App. 2006), *aff'd*, 728 N.W. 2d 823 (Iowa 2007); see also *Nichols v. Moore*, 477 F.3d 396 (6th Cir. 2007) (accepting that Michigan recognizes actions for "defamation by implication," but finding that the brother of convicted Oklahoma City bomber Terry Nichols failed to establish such a claim against filmmaker Michael Moore's *Bowling for Columbine*); *Tomblin v. WCHS-TV8*, 2010 U.S. Dist. LEXIS 4769 (S.D. W. Va. 2010) (libel-by-implication plaintiffs must show not only that the defendant's words would mislead viewers, but also that the defendant intended this to happen).

12. A very early case remains the classic example of this point. In *Ben-Oliel v. Press Publishing Co.*, 167 N.E. 432 (N.Y. 1929), only readers who were very knowledgeable about diverse Middle Eastern cultures would have understood why the article in question had defamatory elements.

THINGS TO REMEMBER

Libel Per Se, Libel Per Quod, and Implied Libel

■ Traditional libel per se categories include allegations of
  - CRIMINAL ACTIVITY ("Jones is an embezzler"; "Smith is an organized crime lynchpin")
  - PROFESSIONAL INCOMPETENCE ("Siegel has left more sponges inside his patients than most households go through in a year.")
  - SERIOUS CHARACTER FLAWS ("We would have loved to interview Chambers for this article, but he is such a chronic liar that it hardly seemed worth the effort.")
  - HAVING A "LOATHSOME, CONTAGIOUS" DISEASE ("Apparently the reason the star has not shown up on the set for the last two days is that he is dealing with his recent AIDS diagnosis.")
  - LACK OF CHASTITY ATTRIBUTED TO AN UNMARRIED WOMAN ("Accounts of their wedding in the society pages that described the bride as 'blushing' and 'virginal' were, at best, half truths.")

■ Libel per quod involves
  - defamatory allegations that do not fit these categories;
    or
  - defamation that can only be understood in conjunction with outside knowledge.

■ Implied libel refers to statements that
  - are literally true
    and
  - might be actionable because of their unspoken implications.

fessional criminals less likely to seek out Frankie's services. The charge would also seem to fit into the traditional libel per se category of attributing "professional incompetence" to the person described. More generally, Professor Lyrissa Lidsky of the University of Florida points out that in some neighborhoods and in some social circles, being accused of having "cooperated with the police" might diminish one's reputation greatly.[13] The courts' general reply to these insights is that libel law is not concerned with how esteemed one is in the eyes of criminals, but rather with an utterance's effect on one's reputation among a community of listeners that is both substantial and respectable.

Not all subaudiences are criminal, of course. A wounded soldier who felt he had been defamed by his depiction in the Michael Moore film *Fahrenheit 9/11* claimed that his brief appearance in the movie would give soldiers and their families (though not necessarily the average viewer, thus the cases' relevance to this discussion) the false impression that he had become an embittered critic of the war effort. A federal appellate court found, however, that even if the military could be considered a special sub-

---

13. Lyrissa Barnett Lidsky, "Defamation, Reputation and the Myth of Community," 71 *Washington Law Review* 1, 8 (1996).

community for purposes of evaluating the defamation element, here *no* reasonable audience could find that the film depicted the soldier in the way he claimed.[14]

Sometimes a potential libel plaintiff's reputation in the mainstream community, long before publication of allegedly defamatory remarks, is so irredeemable that a few more insults could not hurt. Such **libel-proof plaintiffs**, as they are known in the law, are generally not able to prevail in defamation cases. This reasoning may have been what prompted the jury in the libel suit pressed by known drug dealer Harry Perzigian to find for the defendant, actor Carroll O'Connor, who had accused Perzigian of being a "partner in murder" after his son committed suicide while stoned. That libel plaintiffs have a criminal record will likely not be sufficient to establish that they are "libel-proof"; typically it must also be shown that a plaintiff is generally *known* to be an established criminal.[15]

Another complication in adjudicating the defamation element of libel is that community standards are not static. To falsely assert that a person is black would surely not be considered defamatory today, but just as surely *was* considered defamatory in the first half of the twentieth century.[16] Similarly, for a long time it was assumed that to falsely call someone homosexual was libelous, in part because the charge amounted to allegation of criminal wrongdoing. But the U.S. Supreme Court has told us that it is not a crime to have gay sex,[17] and courts adjudicating libel claims stemming from allegations of homosexuality have to deal with the more progressive social climate

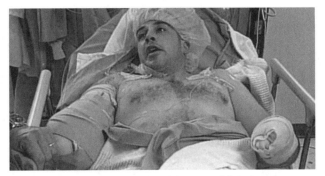

Sergeant Peter Damon was unable to establish that the average military member would erroneously interpret his appearance in *Fahrenheit 9/11* so as to suggest he had become an embittered opponent of the Iraq War.

---

14. *Damon v. Moore*, 520 F. 3d 98 (1st Cir. 2008).

15. *Thomas v. Telegraph Publishing*, 929 A. 2d 991 (N.H. 2007).

16. Samuel Brenner, "'Negro Blood in His Veins:' The Development and Disappearance of the Defamation Per Se by Racial Misrepresentation in the American South," 50 *Santa Clara Law Review* 333 (2010)

17. *Lawrence v. Texas*, 539 U.S. 558 (2003).

Defendant Carroll O'Connor on the witness stand in *Perzigian v. O'Connor*, a libel case brought by the drug dealer indirectly involved with the suicide of O'Connor's son. ©1997 Court TV (now truTV). Reprinted with permission.

implied by that decision.[18] In *Albright v. Morton*, for example, Madonna's former bodyguard and lover James Albright sued because his name was used in error in a caption to a photo in a Madonna biography that actually depicted another member of Madonna's entourage, an "outspoken homosexual" named José Guitierez.[19] The association of the incorrect caption with that photo, Albright claimed, falsely labeled him gay (even though the caption also explained that the person pictured was Madonna's "secret lover," with whom she had a "stormy three-year relationship" during which time "they [had] planned to marry, and had even chosen names for their children"). Judge Nancy Gertner ruled for the defendants, holding that community standards had progressed to the point where a false attribution of homosexuality could no longer be considered libelous.

What Does It All Mean?   Clarendon Hills, Illinois, resident John Green volunteered to coach his son's Little League team. His application was rejected. Green later heard indirectly that Little League president Steven Rogers may have been spreading rumors about him to the effect that he "exhibited a long pattern of misconduct with children" and "abused players, coaches and umpires." The state supreme court unanimously dismissed Green's libel suit against Rogers, in part because words like "misconduct" and "abuse" are open to many relatively innocent interpretations. Citing Webster's dictionary, the court pointed out that "abuse" can mean simply to "reproach" someone "coarsely."[20]

---

18. It may still be possible for libel plaintiffs who can prove that they were in fact damaged by a false attribution of homosexuality to prevail. See Anne Bloom, "To Be Real: Sexual Identity Politics in Tort Litigation," 88 *North Carolina Law Review* 357, 426 (2010).

19. 321 F. Supp. 2d 130 (D. Mass. 2004). A federal appellate court upheld the decision, but on the alternative grounds that the only readers who possibly would have inferred a defamatory meaning in the mislabeled photo were those who knew enough about Madonna's inner circle to know that the fellow pictured was gay (despite the very heterosexually focused attributions in the caption) but not enough to know that the person pictured was Guitierez rather than Albright. 410 F.3d 69 (1st Cir. 2005).

20. *Green v. Rogers*, 234 Ill. 2d 478 (Sup Ct. 2009). See also *Greenbelt Cooperative Publishing Association v. Bresler*, 398 U.S. 6 (1970), in which the Supreme Court ruled that accusing a real estate developer of "blackmailing" the city council really meant, in context, nothing more than that he drove a hard bargain. He was not an extortionist.

Madonna attends ex-lover Prince's concert with her secret lover and one-time bodyguard Jimmy Albright (left). Albright who bears an uncanny relationship to Carlos Leon, the father of Madonna's daughter, enjoyed a stormy three-year relationship with the star. They planned to marry, and had even chosen names for their children.

Plaintiff James Albright's libel suit failed because almost no one would infer that the person described in the photo's caption was gay, unless they already knew that the photo was actually of the gay Madonna entourage member José Guitierez. Such readers would also surely know that this was not a photo of Albright.

THINGS TO REMEMBER

Defamation and the Audience

- To be actionable, a libelous statement must be believed by a significant number of reasonable persons.
- That people who are themselves unsavory characters think less of you will not constitute your being libeled.
- Some libel plaintiffs are already held in such low esteem that they are deemed "libel-proof."
- Society's concept of what kinds of charges are libelous changes over time.

The original caption read: "Evel Knievel proves that you're never too old to be a pimp." The Ninth Circuit Court of Appeals held that the use of the word *pimp* in the context of over a dozen photos on an ESPN website with similarly irreverent captions could not be considered defamatory.

Do they make handcuffs this small? Be afraid of this little girl.

The over-the-top nature of this photo and caption, as well as numerous other textual cues, led the Texas Supreme Court to conclude that a *Texas Observer* article was not defamatory.

Colorful stuntman Evel Knievel sued ESPN because of a photo on one of its websites that showed him surrounded by his wife and an attractive young lady, with the caption "Evil Knievel proves that you're never too old to be a pimp." In dismissing his suit, the Ninth Circuit Court of Appeals concluded that no reasonable person could possibly believe that the word pimp was meant to accuse Knievel of criminal activity. The court cited a number of websites devoted to slang usage when it suggested that the word might actually have been intended as a compliment, suggesting that Knievel had achieved "mastery of a subject matter"—sex?—or was just plain "cool."[21]

Or consider a Texas case involving a satire on school "zero-tolerance policies" for student essays dealing with violent themes. The court held that no sensible reader would take seriously a *Texas Observer* article "reporting" that a six-year-old had been arrested for her book report on Maurice Sendak's classic, *Where the Wild Things Are.*[22]

21. *Knievel v. ESPN*, 393 F.3d 1068, 1077 (9th Cir. 2005).
22. *New Times, Inc. v. Isaacs*, 146 S. W. 3d 144 (Tex. 2004).

Headlines and Captions   Often TV news programs run crawls or insert captions on the bottom of the screen to give viewers, especially those tuning in late, a sense of what the talking heads are talking about. Can such network inserts be defamatory in and of themselves? Likely so, even though a 2009 decision in California held that the caption "MANHUNT ON THE BORDER" was not enough to result in liability for Fox News. On the network's *Hannity and Colmes* program there had been an interview with John Monti, an "anti–illegal immigration activist" who claimed that a number of illegal aliens whom he had photographed beat him up. When later investigations suggested to the police that it was Monti, if anyone, who had been guilty of battery, some of the individuals he had accused included Fox as a defendant in a libel suit (Monti's trial ended in acquittal). A 2–1 majority of the state appellate court rejected plaintiffs' claim that the Fox caption necessarily suggested the police, accepting Monti's version of the narrative, were indeed hunting them down.[23]

What about newspaper headlines? Can they be defamatory, even if the accompanying article as a whole would not be? Consider Brian "Kato" Kaelin's lawsuit against the publisher of the *National Examiner* tabloid. The week after O. J. Simpson was acquitted in the homicides of Nicole Brown Simpson and Ron Goldman, the paper ran a large headline proclaiming that the "COPS THINK KATO DID IT!" In overturning a lower court decision granting summary judgment to the defendant publishers, the Court of Appeals for the Ninth Circuit emphasized that readers would not learn until turning to the article itself, on page 17, that at worst Kaelin might be suspected of not telling all that he knows and thus of having derailed the prosecution's case. He was not a suspect in the homicides themselves. The amount of effort readers would need to expend to learn the true meaning of the headline was extraordinary, the court said, because the tabloid's layout is different and the headline "is unlike a conventional headline that immediately precedes a newspaper story."[24]

Sometimes a provocative headline combined with an otherwise unexceptional photograph may be defamatory, especially if added disclaimers are ineffective. This is what happened when the cover of *Boston* magazine's May 2003 issue boasted that readers would find inside an article headlined "The Mating Habits of the Suburban High School Teenager," with a "superhead" above, in an only slightly smaller font, adding: "They hook up online. They hook up in real life. With prom season looming, meet your kids—they might know more about sex than you do." The thrust of the article, according to the First Circuit Court of Appeals, was that "teenagers in the

---

23. *Balzaga v. Fox News Network*, 173 Cal. App. 4th 1325 (2009). The caption merely emphasized that the police were *investigating* the incident, the court found; it might even refer to Monti's own purported hunting down of the men he was describing as his assailants. A strongly worded dissenting opinion chides the majority for straining the definition of *manhunt* beyond all reason.

24. *Kaelin v. Globe Communications Corp.*, 162 F.3d 1036 (9th Cir. 1998). See also *McNair v. The Hearst Corp.*, 494 F.2d 1309, 1311 (9th Cir. 1974) (Headlines can themselves be libelous, because "what a newspaper regards as newsworthy usually makes its appearance in the headline and lead paragraphs. This is what is intended to compel the reader's attention.").

A California appellate court held that this particular on-screen caption was not itself defamatory, while allowing that there might be circumstances where a caption could lead to liability.

The *National Examiner* could be held liable for this headline alone, even though the article itself did not suggest that the "it" Kato Kaelin may have done was commit homicide.

greater Boston area have become more sexually promiscuous over the span of the last decade, . . . that high school has replaced college as the time for sexual experimentation, . . . [and] that, among teenagers, oral sex is the new second base and sex is the new kissing, that no strings 'hooking up' and Internet porn and online cybersex have often replaced dating," and that "today's eastern Massachusetts teens are both sexually advanced and sexually daring." Most of the first two pages of the article consisted of a photograph of five teens taken at a local prom, in which Ms. Stacy Stanton's face was most prominent. The photo's caption, which alerted readers that "the individuals pictured are unrelated to the people or events described in this story," was in such a small font that Ms. Stanton's libel suit would have to go to trial, the appellate court held.[25]

Defaming People, Corporations, and Products

Individuals are not the only potential libel plaintiffs. Corporations often sue for libel, as do nonprofit associations and labor unions. To falsely claim that an organization has engaged in fraudulent or deceptive practices can be, as one would expect, just as libelous as to make the same charges against an individual. The Church of Scientology, for example, has often sued for libel and under related causes of action.[26]

A federal appellate court held that together, this headline and photo suggested that the teens depicted (including the plaintiff) were themselves highly promiscuous. A disclaimer, which appears between the article text and the writer's byline, was deemed far too small and too oddly placed to dissuade readers from such an erroneous conclusion.

25. *Stanton v. Metro Corp.*, 438 F.3d 119 (1st Cir. 2006).

26. *Church of Scientology v. Behar*, 238 F.3d 168 (2d Cir. 2001); *Church of Scientology v. Daniels*, 992 F.2d 1329 (4th Cir. 1993); *Church of Scientology v. Flynn*, 744 F.2d 694 (9th Cir. 1984); *Church*

THINGS TO REMEMBER

Defamation and Meaning

- Highly inflammatory remarks that fall into the category of rhetorical hyperbole are generally not actionable as libel.
- A misleading newspaper headline can be libelous even if nothing in the article itself is libelous.
- A clarifying or disclaiming statement that does not appear until very late in an article might not save a publisher from liability for earlier sections of the article.
- Liability for a libelous photo might not be eliminated by a disclaiming caption that is not prominent enough to be seen along with the photo.

Corporations may also sue for libel if a story falsely alleges that the company is on the brink of financial disaster. Such a story prompted a legal dispute that reached the Supreme Court in 1985. A credit-reporting agency, in a newsletter with limited circulation, mistakenly reported that a construction company in Vermont had filed for bankruptcy. It seems that a teenager hired as a "stringer" for Dun & Bradstreet misinterpreted a document showing that a former employee of Greenmoss Builders had filed for *personal* bankruptcy.[27]

Sometimes corporations will sue because of negative comments made about their products or services themselves. In such situations, where there is not even a hint in the allegedly libelous report that the company itself has engaged in dishonesty, only that the product is an inferior one, the cause of action is called **trade libel**, or **product disparagement**. It is important to understand the difference between defaming the company and disparaging one of its products. If, through overreliance on misinformed sources or through other shoddy reporting, you publish an article alleging that a certain model of automobile is unsafe, you might open yourself up to a trade libel suit. If the same article alleges that the car's manufacturers likely knew that the car was a road hazard, but rushed to bring it to market anyway, the company would also be able to sue for ordinary libel.

How Much Does It Hurt?   When people bring civil suits against each other, the end result they seek is usually the awarding of money damages. How much money plaintiffs are awarded is, at least in part, a function of the ways in which and how badly they were hurt. As a result, in libel law the matter of damages is almost inextricable from the element of defamation.

Generally speaking, the law recognizes two broad categories of damages—

of Scientology v. Foley, 640 F.2d 1335 (D.C. Cir. 1981); *Church of Scientology v. Adams*, 584 F.2d 893 (9th Cir. 1978).

27. *Dun & Bradstreet v. Greenmoss Builders*, 472 U.S. 749 (1985).

compensatory and punitive. **Punitive damages** are designed to punish the defendants for outrageous behavior, as well as to make an example of them that may deter others. Juries may not reach the issue of punitive damages unless some form of **compensatory damages** are also granted. The logic here is straightforward enough: no matter how egregious the press's behavior, they should not be punished unless they did some harm by that behavior. As we see in the next chapter, the U.S. Supreme Court's intervention into the law of libel in recent decades has put additional limits on the kinds of situations that permit the awarding of punitive damages.[28]

Compensatory damages fall into three subcategories. **Presumed damages** are much what the name implies. Common-law practice is for juries to grant presumed damages without demanding that plaintiffs demonstrate how, specifically, they were harmed. In libel law, presumed damages tended to be sought in cases involving the libel per se category of defamation discussed earlier. Libel per se plaintiffs did not have to prove how or why the words written about them damaged their reputation, in that some categories of accusations, if believed, could be presumed to lower one's standing in a community.

The other two subcategories of compensatory damages have names that may seem counterintuitive. **Actual damages** can be distinguished from presumed damages in that the plaintiff must at least make some showing of harm. But the harm can be a rather intangible one. Defamation actions are quite different in this way from, say, medical malpractice suits. In the latter kind of case, we expect to see the crutches, the neck braces, the prognoses of expert witnesses. By contrast, libel plaintiffs need only show that they have suffered "impairment of reputation and standing in the community, personal humiliation, [or] mental anguish and suffering."[29]

Actual damages, then, do not require that plaintiffs demonstrate anything in the way of measurable, tangible harm. If a plaintiff *is* able to pinpoint actual dollar amounts of loss resulting from libel, such as from being terminated because an employer believed the lies or being thrown out by a landlord, we move into the realm of what are called **special damages**. References to special damages are most frequently seen in trade libel cases where a company tries to establish the specific amount of market share forfeited as a result of remarks disparaging of its products.[30]

Publication

The word *publication* is an unfortunate one as applied to libel law. It is misleading in two ways. First, it seems to suggest, erroneously, that only the mass media can possibly libel anyone, because we tend to think of "publishing" as something only

---

28. *Gertz v. Welch, Inc.*, 418 U.S. 323, 349 (1974).

29. 418 U.S. at 350.

30. See, for example, *Vascular Solutions, Inc. v. Marine Polymer Technologies, Inc.*, 590 F. 3d 56 (1st Cir. 2009).

THINGS TO REMEMBER

More on the Defamation Element

- Libel actions generally cannot be brought on behalf of deceased individuals.
- Corporations can sue for libelous remarks suggesting that their officers or employees have engaged in fraudulent or other reprehensible activities.
- Corporations can sue for trade libel or product disparagement when the offensive criticisms concern the product line itself, rather than its manufacturers.
- Libel plaintiffs may seek several categories of damages
  - **PUNITIVE**
    - Designed to punish the defamer and to deter others
  - **COMPENSATORY**
    - *Presumed*: no proof of harm needed
    - *Actual*: some proof of harm needed, but it does not need to be very tangible
    - *Special*: highly specific and measurable proof of harm required

media industries do (maybe only print media). Second, it suggests that defamatory comments must reach a huge audience before they can be actionable.

In libel law, however, *publication* has a very narrow and special meaning. It means that the speaker or writer has shared the allegedly defamatory comments about another person with at least one third party. (Of course, because the defamation element requires that many people actually believe the untruths, we assume here that the one person you tell in turn spreads the word to others.) If you complain directly to your teacher that you think he is having an affair with a classmate, that would be one-to-one communication, with no publication; if you share this same conjecture with your teacher's spouse, or the dean, the element of publication will have been established.

Legal doctrines that have evolved over centuries usually pick up a few exceptions along the way, and so it is with the concept of publication. There are times when person A saying something nasty to person B *about* person B can be sufficient to establish publication. Such is the case if the defamation is offered in a context where it is all but unavoidable that the recipient will himself have to share it with at least one third party. Such instances are collectively referred to in libel law as **self-publication**. For example, writing an insulting letter to a blind person could constitute publication, because the person will likely have to seek out a sighted individual to read the letter aloud. The same would be true of a letter written to and about a preliterate child. A more recent phenomenon is for courts to hold that an employer's letter of termination to an employee can be sufficient to find publication, because the fired employee will feel compelled to share the reasons for termination during interviews with potential future employers.[31]

---

31. Markita D. Cooper, "Between a Rock and a Hard Case: Time for a New Doctrine of Compelled Self-Publication," 72 *Notre Dame Law Review* 373 (1997).

It is important that we not confuse the elements of defamation and publication. Whereas publication requires that only one third party hear or read the libelous remarks, defamation requires that the remarks were capable of lowering the defamed person's status with an undefined but fairly sizable number of potential recipients of the message.

The element of publication becomes more complicated and also becomes of special relevance to media professionals when we recognize that the **republication** of a libel can be just as actionable as the original act of libel. Your printing or broadcasting that "Smith said Jones is a child molester" can create as much liability for you as had been created for Smith. You would similarly be in trouble if you reported, however matter-of-factly, that "there is a rumor floating about that Jones is a child molester."

There are exceptions to this general rule against republication. In some jurisdictions newspapers that publish stories from reputable wire services will escape liability. This wire services defense, dating from the 1930s, is actually a special instance of a more general rule that if the media outlet had legitimate cause to believe in the reliability of the original source, the dissemination of that source's words should not be actionable.[32]

Similarly, we do not expect bookstore and magazine rack managers to be personally responsible for every word and every picture in their entire inventory. Neither would the phone company be legally responsible for libelous remarks made over its wires.[33] Internet service providers (ISPs) are given similar protection from liability for nasty things their subscribers might say to and about each other (see chapter 13 for a more complete explanation).

Another way for the media to avoid liability after having republished a libelous statement is to invoke the **neutral reportage** defense. This defense, which is accepted in only a few jurisdictions, permits the press to report in a fair and unbiased manner newsworthy allegations made by any prominent and responsible speaker about public officials or well-known public personalities.[34] Another privilege, sometimes called **fair report**, can protect the media from a libel judgment when the defamatory statements republished were first made in an official government proceeding or document. The privilege seems logically consistent with the Speech or Debate Clause (Article I, Section 6 of the U.S. Constitution), as well as similar provisions in many state constitu-

---

32. Matt C. Sanchez, "Note: The Web Difference—A Legal and Normative Rationale Against Liability for Online Reproduction of Third-Party Defamatory Content," 22 *Harvard Journal of Law and Technology* 301, 306–7 (2008).

33. Richard J. Peltz, "Fifteen Minutes of Infamy: Privileged Reporting and the Problem of Perpetual Reputational Harm," 34 *Ohio Northern University Law Review* 717, 733 (2008).

34. *Edwards v. National Audubon Society*, 556 F.2d 113, 129 (2d Cir. 1977). The privilege has been embraced in California, the District of Columbia, South Carolina, and Utah. It has been explicitly rejected in Kentucky, Michigan, and Pennsylvania. See *Norton v. Glenn*, 860 A. 2d 48, 52 (Pa. 2004); *Schwarz v. Salt Lake Tribune*, 2005 UT App. 206 (2005). The Supreme Court has repeatedly rejected invitations to clarify the constitutional scope, if any, of the privilege.

tions, which gives legislators **absolute privilege** to say whatever they please *when conducting their official duties.*[35]

The fair report privilege applies to the proceedings of any legislative body, from Congress to the local school board, that is empowered to make public policy. The privilege protects accurate reports of statements made by those who convene such meetings and any member of the public who is authorized to speak to them. It also covers statements that originate in citizen petitions or similar documents that are recognized and "received" by governmental bodies.

The privilege is a qualified one. It can be overcome by a finding that the media's report of a proceeding was not "fair and accurate," such as going beyond the facts of a proceeding to offer possibly biased commentary about the credibility of the participants.[36]

Be careful also about quoting spontaneous statements, such as from the proverbial cop on the beat. It is one thing to report on some kind of official police document, quite another to base a story on informal statements. As a general rule, reporters hoping for the fair report privilege's protection should be more cautious the lower the rank of the source for the reprinted libel and the less formal the communication in which the libel originated.

That the fair report privilege is also applicable to judicial proceedings is especially important to the press since virtually every comment made about a defendant in open court beyond name, address, and age is likely to be defamatory in some way. Fortunately for the media, the privilege applies to any statements or official documents issued by any of the participants, including witnesses, jurors, the judge, and the litigating parties themselves. Moreover, the privilege has often been held to apply to documents that may or not themselves ever be read in open court.[37] In Nevada, the privilege applies even to *potential* litigants' communications about pending (or even merely *threatened*) litigation.[38]

Whether the fair report privilege extends to republication of documents from foreign countries is an issue that has produced contradictory results in different jurisdictions. The Fourth Circuit Court of Appeals was the first to rule on the question, in

---

35. The italicized phrase is important, in that the privilege does not necessarily apply to libelous statements uttered by members of Congress in settings other than actual Senate or House debates. See *Hutchinson v. Proxmire*, 443 U.S. 111, 116 (1979).

36. *Moreno v. Crookston Times Printing Co.*, 610 N.W.2d 321 (Minn. 2000).

37. *Salzano v. North Jersey Media Group*, 993 A.2d 778 (N.J. 2010) (privilege applies to documents filed with a court prior to any actual trial); *Abromats v. Wood*, 213 P.3d 966 (Wyo. 2009) (privilege adheres to statements made to a victims rights' organization, in preparation for future courtroom testimony); *Wilson v. Slatalla*, 970 F. Supp. 405 (E.D. Pa. 2007) (privilege applied to a book about college-age computer hackers, in that the allegedly libelous remarks, while written in colorful prose, were based on official judicial documents).

38. *Clark County School District v. Virtual Education Software*, 213 P.3d 406 (2009).

Lee v. Dong-A Ilbo.[39] That case involved several Korean American newspapers and a television station that had published or broadcast stories, based on documents from the South Korean government, alleging that a South Korean citizen living in the United States was viewed by South Korea as an enemy North Korean agent. The court held that the fair report privilege did not apply to documents from foreign governments.

But a federal district court in Pennsylvania (part of the Third Circuit) protected the *Boston Globe* and other media from a defamation suit stemming from reports that Howard Friedman, a U.S. citizen, would be denied future entry into Israel. The report was based on a press release issued by three ministers of the Israeli government, which claimed that Friedman had been "associated with planning illegal activities in Israel."[40]

Two additional caveats about the privilege are worth noting, which demand that the press "tell us where they got it" and that they "get it right." As to the first caveat, while there may be many times when the media can use anonymous sources, their use would seem to logically preclude a media defendant's invoking the fair report privilege. You can't base your defense on the claim that "I got this information from a government source" and then refuse to tell us specifics.

It is also crucial when using this defense to "get it right." The privilege is forfeited if your story is not an accurate report of an otherwise protected government proceeding or document. The Supreme Court of Ohio allowed a libel suit to go forward against a newspaper for having reported that "Amherst attorney James Young is facing a contempt of court citation." As it turns out, there was an Amherst attorney named James Young, and an attorney named James Young had in fact been held in contempt of court a few days prior to the story's run. But the attorney who had been found in contempt was a James H. Young, and *his* usual place of business was Cleveland.[41]

Making the right criticisms of the wrong person can not only defeat the chance to fall back on the fair report privilege but can also serve to establish for the plaintiff the third element of a libel case—identification.

Identification

The third element of libel in the common law is identification. While one might think intuitively that this element would be rather straightforward, in fact it carries its own complications. Three such complications are explored here: the relationship between naming and identifying, the special problems posed by fictional writing, and

---

39. 849 F.2d 876 (4th Cir. 1988); see also *Oao Alfa Bank v. Center for Public Integrity*, 387 F. Supp. 2d 20 (D.D.C. 2005) (document from Russian investigative service not protected by fair report privilege).

40. *Friedman v. Israel Labour Party*, 957 F. Supp. 701 (E.D. Pa. 1997).

41. *Young v. The Morning Journal*, 669 N.E.2d 1136 (Ohio 1996).

THINGS TO REMEMBER

The Publication Element

- To establish "publication," only one additional person needs to hear the libel.
- Republication of a libel can be just as actionable as the original publication.
- Wire services, common carriers, bookstores, and Internet service providers are generally excluded from republication liability.
- Some jurisdictions also offer the neutral reportage defense, protecting the press broadly against liability as long as they report in a fair and unbiased way the fact of person A's having criticized person B.
- A fair report privilege is also recognized concerning republication of libel initially made in an official meeting or publication.

problems that emerge when libel is attributed to only some members of identifiable groups of various sizes.

Naming and Identifying   The case of the Cleveland (not Amherst!) attorney just mentioned serves as a powerful reminder that libel suits are often prompted by an omitted middle initial, a misspelling, or some other misidentification. Misidentify one person and you may succeed in defaming another. Generally, reporters are wise to identify with a vengeance whenever anything potentially defamatory is being associated with a named individual. Such identification means using a person's full name (with middle initial where appropriate), age, and full address, and perhaps even occupation.

As you begin to read full texts of court opinions, either on the job or as a requirement of this course, the phrase you will most frequently encounter when judges make reference to the element of identification is that the allegedly libelous statements must be "of or concerning" the plaintiff. It is important to recognize that the element of identification can be proved even if you never once use the plaintiff's name in your story. In one case, for example, a Philadelphia police captain serving on the city's sex crimes squad implied that a young woman, described only as a "Bryn Mawr student," may have filed a false report alleging she had been carjacked, robbed, and raped. The woman sued not only the police captain but also the local media that had broadcast his allegations. In denying the defendants' motion for summary judgment, which was based in large part on the plaintiff's never having been named, the court reminded us that naming and identifying are two different things. There were simply too many details about the young woman in the story—that reported being raped on a particular day after attending a party at the University of Pennsylvania, that she was a student at a well-known and relatively small college, that she drove a Nissan, and so on—to deny the likelihood that she would be identifiable.[42]

---

42. *Weinstein v. Bullick*, 827 F. Supp. 1193 (E.D. Pa. 1993), *aff'd*, 77 F.3d 465 (3d Cir. 1996).

You might not need to include this much detail to avoid a misidentification, but at least provide some characteristics beyond the suspect's name.

Identification in Fiction   The whole notion of applying libel law to works of fiction is troubling. After all, for a journalist to admit that she has knowingly published falsehoods would be an odd thing indeed, an admission likely to help a libel plaintiff prevail. But novelists purposely write falsehoods. As a result, when libel suits are brought against fiction writers, the cases tend to focus intently on the element of identification.[43]

"Floater," the title of an episode of the TV series *Law and Order*, refers to how a murder victim's body found in the Hudson River leads to the exposure of a huge corruption scandal in New York City family and divorce courts. Take the "floater" herself out of the narrative, and the *Law and Order* story line follows faithfully several elements of a real-life judicial scandal involving a Brooklyn judge who, faced with arrest, agreed to wear a "wire" in an (unsuccessful) attempt to record testimony from a local attorney of Indian descent named Ravi Batra. Batra's name surfaced in several

---

43. Matthew Savare, "Falsity, Fault, and Fiction: A New Standard for Defamation in Fiction," 12 *UCLA Entertainment Law Review* 129, 138 (2004); Mark Arnot, "When Is Fiction Just Fiction? Applying Heightened Threshold Tests to Defamation in Fiction," 76 *Fordham Law Review* 1853, 1862 (2007).

Actor Erick Avari's lawyer character, "Ravi Patel," had a few too many similarities (including name) to real attorney Ravi Batra, thus leading to a plausible defamation-in-fiction claim.

media accounts suggesting that he was involved in some way with the scandal (even though no charges along those lines were ever brought against him). And in "Floater," a fictional attorney also of Indian descent ("Ravi Patel") is depicted as very much a part of the judicial corruption scandal. Batra sued, and the court found too many similarities between Batra and Patel to dismiss the case. There were only six attorneys in New York City at the time whose first names were Ravi, and only Batra at all resembled the actor who portrayed Patel in the *Law and Order* episode. Anyone who knew Batra could not help but associate him with "Patel," and thus wonder whether Mr. Batra had been involved in a grisly homicide.[44]

Sometimes a fictional character and a real-world plaintiff have identical names. Such was the case in *Bryson v. News America, Inc.*, in which a purportedly fictional short story about high school classmates appearing in *Seventeen* magazine accused a character—by the name of Bryson!—of being a "slut."[45] Ah, but every lesson seems to have an exception. Some courts have refused to assume that a libel plaintiff has been "identified" by a character name in a fictional work even when the surnames are identical, at least if the names are very common ones.[46]

The Numbers Game   Sometimes, libel plaintiffs cannot prove that they have been identified in a defamatory utterance *as an individual* and assert instead that they have been libeled by dint of their membership in a particular group. Predicting whether such plaintiffs will prevail sometimes may seem more art than science,[47] but some general principles can be culled from the case law.

First, membership in a very large group will not give one standing to sue for libel as a result of the group's having been defamed. No individual attorney or group of attorneys would be able to win damages by suing any of the authors or publishers of

---

44. *Batra v. Wolf*, 36 *Media Law Reports* 1592 (Sup. Ct. NY 2008). Notice an irony—the title and plot of "Floater" is a substantial departure from the real-world scandal, which did *not* involve a murder. The defendants could certainly point to this and other discrepancies to suggest that the story was not "of and about" the plaintiff. But if there are enough similarities between the fictional character and the plaintiff, such departures from reality might be, as here, the most defamatory "allegations" of the narrative. Such is the nature of defamation in fiction.

45. 672 N.E.2d 1207 (Ill. 1996).

46. *Allen v. Gordon*, 86 A.D.2d 514 (N.Y. App. Div. 1982).

47. Nat Stern, "The Certainty Principle as Justification for the Group Defamation Rule," 40 *Arizona State University Law Journal* 951 (2008); Jeffrey S. Bromme, "Group Defamation: Five Guiding Factors," 64 *Texas Law Review* 591 (1985).

the various "dead lawyer joke" compilations we find in most larger bookstores. Senator Jones could not win a suit against a radio talk show host for making on air the bald assertion that "all politicians are crooks." Do these examples sound outlandish and fantastic? In fact courts have frequently had occasion to rule that it is impossible in one broad stroke to defame all members of specified ethnic or religious groups.[48]

As a general rule, then, the larger the group, the more difficult it is for an individual plaintiff to prove identification. Similarly, the smaller the number of people in the group alleged to have a defamatory trait, the more difficult it will be for individuals within the group to prevail. Defamatory statements alleging that "one" or "a few" members of a group manifest a particularly loathsome quality will be less likely to lead to liability than statements claiming that "all" or "the vast majority of" a group's members can be so characterized. In some states, including New York, courts have fashioned what is called an **intensity of suspicion** test, which embraces a combination of those two principles.[49]

A libel case involving the film *American Gangster* emphasizes the first of the two "intensity of suspicion" principles (the large size of the plaintiff's membership group), but also includes a twist. In the end credits of the film, we learn that the main character's having "flipped" and cooperated with law enforcement led to "the convictions of three quarters of New York City's Drug Enforcement Agency." Part of the plaintiff's problem was the sheer size of the law enforcement entity allegedly being defamed. It has over four hundred special agents, and New York law has never permitted libel plaintiffs to win when allegations had been leveled at groups larger than even sixty. But there was another problem. The correct name of the (federal!) law enforcement agency at issue is the Drug Enforcement *Administration*. There is no Drug Enforcement *Agency*. And there is no New York City law enforcement unit with a name at all similar to the federal DEA.[50]

Our discussion of "the numbers game" in libel law would not be complete without at least brief mention of the issue of hate speech codes. Such regulations, adopted by many colleges, seem at first blush to have much in common with libel law, in that they typically prohibit speech that expresses very negative things about a person associated with or attributable to that person's race, religion, gender, or sexual orientation. These are really not libel provisions, however, for a number of reasons. First,

---

48. *Viola v. A&E Television Network*, 433 F. Supp. 2d 613 (W.D. Pa. 2006) (Catholics); *Dontigney v. Paramount Pictures*, 411 F. Supp. 2d 89 (D. Conn. 2006); *L & D of Oregon v. American States Insurance Company*, 14 P. 3d 617 (Ore. App. 2000) (African Americans).

49. *Brady v. Ottaway Newspaper*, 445 N.Y.S. 2d 786, 793–795 (App. Div. 1981). See also *Arcand v. Evening Call Publishing Co.*, 567 F.2d 1163 (1st Cir. 1977) (allegation that one out of twenty-one members of a local police force had to call for help after accidentally locking himself in the back of a police car failed to establish identification); *Chapman v. Byrd*, 475 S.E.2d 734 (N.C. Ct. App. 1996) (same result when one of nine deli employees was alleged to have AIDS).

50. *Diaz v. NBC Universal, Inc.*, 536 F. Supp. 2d 337 (S.D.N.Y. 2008), *aff'd*, 337 F. Appx. 94 (2nd Cir. 2009).

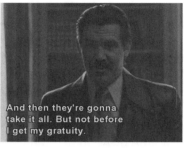

And then they're gonna take it all. But not before I get my gratuity.

A libel suit against the producers of *American Gangster* failed, in large part because the inaccurately referenced law enforcement organization to which Josh Brolin's character belonged in the film was so large.

such regulations are not designed to protect victims' reputations, but rather their feelings. Indeed, an insulting epithet generally will not trigger the rules unless the comment is made directly to a specific individual. Comments made *about* that individual, in front of others, would not be covered. Second, for such codes to have any chance of being found constitutional, they must be restricted to situations in which a violent breach of the peace is likely to occur. Although libel law may be thought of in a grand, historical way as an evolution away from violence such as dueling, contemporary libel plaintiffs need not establish the likelihood of violence as an element of their suits. Finally, whereas libel has been a respected area of tort law for centuries, with every state in the union boasting a libel statute, a complex mosaic of case law, or both, those few court decisions involving campus hate speech codes have uniformly struck down the rules as violations of the First Amendment.[51]

Fault

Suppose that you are the owner of a duplex, occupying one unit and leasing the other, in a relatively temperate climate such as in North Carolina. You go away on a vacation in October, and during your absence, your hometown experiences a freak ice storm. Your tenant's child slips and falls on the ice in front of your property. Does it seem fair that you can be sued in such a circumstance? You were not home and were thus unable to clear the sidewalk, and you had no reason to make arrangements for anyone else to do it for you. Yet in some jurisdictions in the United States, you could indeed be held liable for the child's injuries under the doctrine of **strict liability**, the notion that a person who causes injury to another should make retribution, even if no negligence is involved. A few generations ago, this doctrine was embraced throughout the country, and it has by no means disappeared from U.S. law. In some instances, such as product liability, the tendency over time has been to embrace strict liability rather than demand that the plaintiffs prove an article was manufactured negligently.[52] Other contemporary examples include workers' compensation laws as well as doctrines holding employers responsible for their employees' actions, even without a showing of corporate negligence. For example, in 2005 the Supreme Court let stand

---

51. *UWM Post, Inc. v. Board of Regents of the University of Wisconsin*, 774 F. Supp. 1163 (E.D. Wis. 1991); *Doe v. University of Michigan*, 721 F. Supp. 852 (E.D. Mich. 1989).

52. Larry S. Stewart, "Strict Liability for Defective Product Design: The Quest for a Well-Ordered Regime," 74 *Brooklyn Law Review* 1039 (2009).

THINGS TO REMEMBER

The Identification Element

- It is possible to be identified for the purposes of a libel case without having been explicitly named.
- Even purportedly fictional accounts, such as movies and novels, can lead to libel suits if an unsympathetically drawn character can be shown to be identifiable as a living real person.
- No single individual member will succeed as a libel plaintiff if a huge category of persons (such as lawyers, politicians, or Jews) is defamed.
- When dealing with smaller groups, the rules are a bit murkier, with some courts having depended on an "intensity of suspicion" test suggesting that plaintiffs become more likely to prevail when the number in the whole group is small and the number alleged to have a particularly unsavory characteristic is a high proportion of that larger group.

---

a $1 million judgment against Royal Caribbean stemming from the off-ship misconduct of one of its employees, without any finding of fault on the company's part.[53]

Now imagine for a moment a world in which the doctrine of strict liability were applied to defamation. Hurt someone's reputation by something you print or broadcast and you must pay, even if your error is an innocent one. Misidentify a criminal suspect by using the wrong middle initial, and no amount of apologizing will get you off the hook. In fact libel law operated this way in many jurisdictions prior to the Supreme Court's landmark decision in 1964, *New York Times Co. v. Sullivan*.[54] Although there are many ways of describing the significance of the case, one way is to say the Court constitutionalized the fault element of libel. An examination of *Sullivan* and its progeny is the subject of chapter 4. Before that, however, we examine some of the arguments available to libel defendants even before the Supreme Court made this whole area of the law more "speaker-friendly."

Some Common-Law and Statutory Defenses to Libel

You have already been exposed to at least some defenses available to communicators who are sued for libel. To argue that the plaintiff has failed to establish one or more of the elements of libel is, after all, a defense. Defendants, as seen in the discussion of the identification element, might argue that the seemingly libelous remarks were not

---

53. *Doe v. Celebrity Cruises*, 394 F.3d 891 (11th Cir. 2004), *cert. denied*, 2005 U.S. LEXIS 8179 (2005).

54. 376 U.S. 254 (1964).

"of or concerning" the plaintiff. Then, too, the fair report and neutral reportage privi-leges are often used to suggest that although *re*publication may have taken place, the libel suit should not be permitted to go forward. Several other libel defenses are avail-able to litigants, some unique to this particular tort, others more globally available to defendants in any kind of civil case.

One of the surest ways to defeat a libel suit is to point out that the plaintiff failed to honor the applicable **statute of limitations**. To avoid clogging the courts with "stale" claims—witnesses die, memories fade, evidence is lost—virtually all civil and criminal actions must be brought within a statutorily prescribed time limit. Statutes of limita-tions for libel vary from state to state, typically extending for one or two years after publication. A few states recognize a three-year limitation. In most jurisdictions, the clock starts running the moment the defamation is published, not when the potential plaintiff learns about the publication. In this context, "published" refers to when the material was made generally available. In the case of broadcast stations, this time is easy to figure out. The first broadcast is the date of publication. Things are a bit more complex with printed materials. We cannot always go by the copyright date or the cover date. Books that reach the bookstores late in the year often list the following year on the copyright page. Similarly, magazines are often postdated by several weeks so that they appear "fresher" on newsstands and in subscribers' homes.

The truth defense, demonstrating that allegedly defamatory statements are true, is a very powerful defense in defamation cases.[55] It may seem puzzling to describe truth as merely a *defense* in libel law, as if suggesting that the communicator is presumed guilty, that the article is presumed false. Should not the burden be on the plaintiff to *prove* that the story is false?

The courts have not yet provided a uniform answer to this question. Traditionally, in common law, a libel *was* presumed false. If that tradition seems quirky and unfair by today's standards, try thinking about it another way. In common law, Americans' reputations were presumed unsullied and pure until proven otherwise. In any event, because the Supreme Court has held in recent years that the First Amendment places some limitations on the common-law tradition of requiring the defendant to prove truth, we will have much more to say about this issue in the next chapter. For now, suffice it to say that in those situations where the plaintiff must prove falsity to prevail, it will not do to point out one or a handful of inconsequential errors extraneous to the libel alleged. If my story alleges that you have been prosecuted for embezzling $30,000 from one employer and $400,000 from another, you will not have proved falsity by showing that my figures are ever so slightly off, or that I spelled one of the

---

55. *Noonan v. Staples*, 556 F. 3d 20 (1st Cir. 2009) may be an aberration in this regard. The court here ruled that a disgruntled former employee can at least have his day in court on a libel claim, even though he was unable to demonstrate at a pretrial stage that any of the allegations made by his ex-boss were false. The court seems to have felt that the ex-boss had singled out the plaintiff for public humiliation.

employers' names wrong. You must prove that the gist or the "sting" of the article is false.

For example, James Nichols, brother of Oklahoma City bombing coconspirator Terry Nichols, sued Michael Moore for libel over several inaccurate or at least ambiguous statements in Moore's documentary film *Bowling for Columbine*. The suit was dismissed, however, in that even the questionable statements were *substantially* true. Was Nichols arrested "in connection to" the bombing, as the film asserts? Not if the intended meaning is that the police thought he was himself a part of the conspiracy. Indeed he was never so charged. But his arrest and detainment as a material witness did happen just a few days after the bombing, and it was a direct result of the FBI's investigation into the bombing.[56]

Consent is a rarely encountered but still respected libel defense. Should you interview a subject who, knowing full well the nature of the allegations you intend to print, expressly gives you permission to go ahead, the subject will not be able to prevail in a libel suit against you stemming from those allegations. Courts sometimes infer consent from the plaintiff's conduct. For example, if it can be shown that a plaintiff herself has told others of the yet-unpublished defamatory statements against her, some courts might hold that a defamation suit cannot stand. If the supposed libel had the power to damage her reputation, the reasoning goes, she would have kept them to herself. In one case involving the relationship between an employer and an employee rather than a reporter and source, a state appellate court held that there can be no

In this admittedly surreal scenario, the *Tribune*'s error would not open it up to damages for libel, because the gist or "sting" of what was said about the attorney's client was true.

---

56. *Nichols v. Moore*, 477 F. 3d 396, 401 (6th Cir. 2007).

James Nichols's suit against Michael Moore's interview excerpts and commentary from *Bowling for Columbine* was dismissed in that even the most "troubling" inaccuracies were "substantially true."

defamation in an employee's personnel file if the only additional pairs of eyes to have seen the alleged libel belonged to persons shown the file by the employee himself.[57]

In our earlier discussion of the element of defamation, we encountered cases where the defendant successfully argued that the alleged libel could not possibly have hurt the plaintiff's reputation because the statements were "mere hyperbole" and not to be taken literally. Hyperbole is really a special instance of the more general common-law defense called **fair comment**, which posits that to be defamatory, an utterance must make a specific factual claim. Opinions, if offered without any personal animus toward the person being judged (thus the "fair" in fair comment), cannot be the cause of a libel action. The fair comment privilege can be abused and thus disallowed if your opinion is presented in such a way as to suggest that you have certain facts at your disposal that you are choosing not to share with your readers and that these important but undisclosed facts form the basis for your negative assessment of a potential plaintiff. This approach might be called the "if you only knew what I know" posture. If, however, you either forthrightly reveal the facts that led you to your opinions or have cause to believe that those facts are already known to your readers (for example, if this one article concerns an incident so much in the news that only a hermit could have missed earlier accounts), the privilege will generally be respected.

Here too the Supreme Court (and some lower courts trying to make sense of relevant Supreme Court decisions) has made some moves toward constitutionalizing this common-law defense. Thus we discuss the fact-versus-opinion distinction again in chapter 4, this time from a First Amendment perspective.

Chapter Summary

Libel law has been around for many centuries and exists to enable persons who feel their reputations have been sullied to recover damages from anyone who has spread untruths about them.

---

57. *Pressley v. Continental Can Co.*, 250 S.E.2d 676 (N.C. Ct. App. 1979).

A plaintiff must generally establish four elements to prevail: that a specific allegation is in fact likely to damage his or her reputation, that the defamation was published (seen by at least one third party), that the plaintiff was identified in some way, and that the publisher manifested some degree of fault. Traditionally, falsity did not have to be proved; it was assumed, with truth being a common-law defense.

Phrases amounting to mere rhetorical hyperbole are not actionable. Republication of libels from other sources can be as actionable as the publication of the original statements. Exceptions are often made for the fair reporting of libelous statements made in official proceedings.

Not only individuals, but also corporations, can sue for libel. If a company's product rather than its officers has been maligned, the proper cause of action is product disparagement, rather than libel itself.

Identification can exist even if the plaintiff has not been explicitly named in the offensive publication and can result from the publication of a fictional work. A plaintiff's chances of prevailing in the case of a defamation aimed at a group of which he or she is part diminish as the group grows larger and the proportion of its members alleged to possess the defamatory quality grows smaller.

Plaintiffs can receive compensatory damages to make them whole. Sometimes such damages are presumed; or they might be actual damages, requiring at least some proof of harm. Special damages demand the most specific and tangible proof of harm. In some jurisdictions punitive damages are also permitted.

Even before the Supreme Court constitutionalized libel—the subject of the next chapter—several defenses were available to defamation suits. Defendants might be able to show that their publication was substantially true. It might be alleged that a plaintiff consented, explicitly or implicitly, to the publication. The defense called fair comment, which argues that the publication consisted of nothing more than opinion, rather than assertions of fact, might be invoked. In addition, defendants can always show that plaintiffs failed to establish one or more of the tort's elements, or that the suit was not filed timely (i.e., that the statute of limitations expired).

Chapter 4

DEFAMATION: FIRST AMENDMENT LIMITATIONS

A candidate for reelection to the Commack, New York, Board of Education sued because a campaign flier accused him of "breaking the law" by "awarding a lucrative food service contract to one of his business associates." The state's highest court reversed a $100,000 libel judgment in the case. Even though the flier was in several ways inaccurate—it lacked "verbal precision," in the court's words—the plaintiff could not prove that its drafters knew that its accusations were false. Public officials would be wiser to "develop a thicker skin" than to seek redress in the courts, Justice Smith wrote.[1]

A libel suit by a district attorney against best-selling author John Grisham, whose *The Innocent Man* tells of the wrongful prosecution and imprisonment of an Oklahoma man for a rape and murder, was dismissed without a trial. Although the book (and those of a handful of other authors of books on the same subject, also named as defendants) contained numerous errors, a federal appellate court emphasized that Grisham and the others "wrote about a miscarriage of justice and attempted to encourage political and social change." Even if some of their perceptions of the miscarriage of justice were inaccurate, Judge Lucero continued, "we depend on the marketplace of ideas—not the whim of the bench—to correct insidious opinions."[2]

What these two cases have in common is the presumption made by each court that the libel plaintiffs, because they are public officials, should have a very heavy burden of proof. This presumption is the legacy of *New York Times Co. v. Sullivan*, the U.S. Supreme Court's landmark libel ruling from 1964.[3]

To fully grasp the significance of the case, we have to remind ourselves a bit about the times in which it was decided. The 1960s will seem like ancient history to some

---

1. *Shulman v. Hunderfund*, 905 N.E. 2d 1159 (N.Y. 2009).
2. *Peterson v. Grisham*, 594 F. 3d 723 (10th Cir. 2010).
3. 376 U.S. 254 (1964).

readers. Blackberries were for eating, not web ("web"?) surfing. There were no cell phones and no CNN. Most Americans received three or four TV stations total. It is perhaps no surprise, then, that we were so dependent on newspapers of record, such as the *New York Times*, to stay abreast of the civil rights struggle being waged in the South.

The struggle was in full swing. The sixties were the decade in which Congress began the arduous task of dismantling our nation's long legacy of *institutional* racial discrimination. The Civil Rights Act, the Voting Rights Act, and the Fair Housing Act, all aimed at making "whites only" signs relics of the past, were crucial pieces of legislation that emerged from this era.

Introducing *New York Times Co. v. Sullivan*

It was against this backdrop that the Supreme Court found a vehicle by which to impose constitutional limitations on the tort of defamation: a jury award for libel in the amount of $500,000 to L. B. Sullivan, a city commissioner in Montgomery, Alabama, whose duties included oversight of the local police department. Sullivan's suit was prompted by the *New York Times* publication in March 1960 of a full-page paid political advertisement placed by a group of civil rights leaders calling themselves the "Committee to Defend Martin Luther King and the Struggle for Freedom in the South," which criticized police handling of protest rallies at the state capitol and the Alabama State College campus.

There were several inaccuracies in the advertisement, among them the following:

- The students sang "The Star-Spangled Banner," not "My Country, 'Tis of Thee."
- Police did not "ring" the campus (although they were deployed there in large numbers).
- Students were expelled not for leading this particular state capitol demonstration but for demanding service at a lunch counter in the county courthouse.
- The follow-up student protest against the expulsions involved most (but not all) of the student body and consisted of a one-day "strike," not a mass refusal to register.
- The student dining hall was never padlocked.
- The local police disputed the allegation that King had been "assaulted."
- Martin Luther King, Jr., had been arrested only four times, not seven.
- Sullivan had not been police commissioner at the time of three of these arrests, nor did he have anything to do with the perjury indictment against King.

Perhaps you found some of these errors substantive ones and others so innocuous as to be a waste of the Court's time. Would Sullivan's reputation have been damaged by the factual errors in the advertisement? The Court's review of the trial record suggests that Sullivan did not do a very good job of showing how he was harmed. He produced only one relevant witness on the point, a former employer who indicated that the allegations made in the advertisement were serious ones and that he would

Heed Their Rising Voices

from the *New York Times*, March 29, 1960

As the whole world knows by now thousands of Southern Negro students are engaged in widespread non-violent demonstrations in positive affirmation of the right to live in human dignity as guaranteed by the U.S. Constitution and the Bill of Rights. In their efforts to uphold these guarantees, they are being met by an unprecedented wave of terror by those who would deny and negate the document which the whole world looks upon as setting the pattern for modern freedom.

In Montgomery, Alabama, after students sang "My Country, 'Tis of Thee" on the State Capitol steps, their leaders were expelled from school, and truckloads of police armed with shotguns and tear-gas ringed the Alabama State College campus. When the entire student body protested to state authorities by refusing to register, their dining hall was padlocked in an attempt to starve them into submission.

Small wonder that the Southern violators of the Constitution fear this new, non-violent brand of freedom fighter. Small wonder that they are determined to destroy the one man who, more than any other, symbolizes the new spirit now sweeping the South—the Reverend Dr. Martin Luther King, Jr.

Again and again the Southern violators have answered Dr. King's peaceful protests with intimidation and violence. They have bombed his home, almost killing his wife and child. They have assaulted his person. They have arrested him seven times—for "speeding," "loitering," and similar "offenses." And now they have charged him with "perjury"—a felony under which they could imprison him for ten years.

We urge you to join hands with our fellow Americans in the South by supporting, with your dollars, this combined appeal for all three needs—the defense of Martin Luther King, the support of the embattled students, and the struggle for the right to vote.

be hesitant to hire anyone who was guilty of those allegations. This same witness, however, testified that he did not believe in the truth of the allegations, an admission that certainly helped the defendant more than the plaintiff. Add to the equation that Sullivan's name is not mentioned once in the advertisement, and you would correctly surmise that the Court could have overturned the Alabama jury's damages award of $500,000 without producing a memorable landmark decision. But if the Court found only that the Alabama courts did a bad job of applying that state's own law of defamation, there would have been no *federal* constitutional issue involved.[4] The Supreme Court, if it wanted to reverse the damages award, would probably have to say something about the relationship of the First Amendment to the law of defamation.

The Birth of the Actual Malice Rule

The U.S. Supreme Court unanimously overturned the libel judgment against the New York Times Company on the grounds the plaintiff had not established that the newspaper's level of fault was sufficient to justify liability. Writing for the Court, Justice Brennan set forth the central holding of the case: when a public official sues for damages because of an allegedly defamatory falsehood concerning his or her **official conduct**, the First Amendment demands that the plaintiff prove, with **convincing clarity**, that the statement was made with **actual malice**—that is, with knowledge that it was false or with reckless disregard as to whether it was true or false.[5] Several of these phrases require explication. Because later court cases have attempted to clarify the definitions of "public official," "official conduct," and even "actual malice" itself, those terms are discussed further when we begin to look at *Sullivan*'s progeny.

The term *convincing clarity* is a general legal term of art that tells us what the plaintiff's level of proof must be. You are likely already familiar with one or both of the other two levels of proof that together govern the vast majority of court proceedings in the United States—proof "beyond a reasonable doubt" and proof "by a preponderance of the evidence."

The government, when it prosecutes a criminal defendant, must establish its case beyond a reasonable doubt. How much doubt is "reasonable" doubt? There really is no one right answer to this question. Beyond *any* doubt would mean that you are 100 percent sure of the defendant's guilt. Does "beyond a reasonable doubt" mean 99 percent sure? Or 95 percent sure? Judges' instructions to jurors tend not to provide such mathematical equivalents. It is fair to say, however, that if your own internal mental rule translates into a probability of guilt much lower than 90 percent, a good criminal defense lawyer will do anything possible to keep you off the jury.

Plaintiffs in most civil suits—the kinds dealt with on TV by Judge Judy—must establish proof by a "preponderance of the evidence" to prevail. This level of proof has an intuitive, mathematical feel to it. Preponderance means "more than not," or any probability greater than 50 percent.

---

4. Richard A. Epstein, "Was *New York Times v. Sullivan* Wrong?" 53 *University of Chicago Law Review* 782, 790 (1986).

5. *New York Times Co. v. Sullivan*, 376 U.S. 254 (1964). Justices Black, Douglas, and Goldberg wrote or joined concurring opinions in which they argued for a more absolute rule than that espoused by Brennan. The concurrences interpreted the First Amendment as providing absolute immunity for any and all statements made about public officials' official conduct or even (in Justice Black's words) "about public affairs" generally.

What, then, is "convincing clarity"? You have probably already guessed correctly that it is defined as a standard somewhere in between "preponderance of the evidence" and "beyond a reasonable doubt." Sometimes it is defined as a level of evidentiary proof so clear as to leave no *substantial* doubt in your mind to the contrary. Although "substantial" doubt is clearly more than "reasonable" doubt, how much more is anyone's guess.

Applying the Rule

In finding that the *New York Times* did not manifest the high level of fault demanded by the actual malice standard, the Court emphasized two factors. First, the newspaper staff genuinely believed at the time of publication that the charges made in the advertisement were "substantially true." Second, the Court found that the most stinging charges did not refer to Sullivan, even obliquely.

Sullivan's attorneys successfully established at trial that had the *Times* staff responsible for accepting the advertisement taken the time to fact-check—simply by using the paper's own previous editions—they would have identified many of the falsities in the ad. The failure to check facts, however, was not sufficient evidence of actual malice, the Court held, in part because many of the signatories to the advertisement were very well-respected civil rights leaders.

New York Times Co. v. Sullivan is remembered as a landmark decision not only because of the establishment of the actual malice rule but also because much of Justice Brennan's language in other parts of the opinion has proved so very influential over the years. The next few sections describe the further significance of the *Sullivan* ruling beyond the holding itself.

THINGS TO REMEMBER

The *New York Times* Holding

- *New York Times Co. v. Sullivan* established the "actual malice" rule, which can be expressed as

$$PO \ (OC) \rightarrow AM \ (CC)$$

Translation: When *p*ublic *o*fficials sue because of *c*riticism about their *o*fficial *c*onduct, they must prove *a*ctual *m*alice with *c*onvincing *c*larity.
- "Actual malice" is defined as publishing a knowing falsehood, or publishing with "reckless disregard of truth or falsity."
- "Convincing clarity" is a level of proof somewhere between that required for a criminal prosecution ("beyond a reasonable doubt") and that required for an ordinary civil suit ("by a preponderance of the evidence").

Libel and Sedition

The Alien and Sedition Acts, discussed in chapter 2, prescribed jail terms of up to five years for "false, scandalous and malicious" statements made against the president, members of Congress, or the government itself. Libel suits brought by public officials angered by criticisms of their official conduct, Justice Brennan said in *Sullivan*, are uncomfortably reminiscent of such sedition prosecutions. The imposition of sanctions against those who criticize the government is "inconsistent with the First Amendment," he said. The spirit of the First Amendment is "a profound national commitment to the principle that debate on public issues should be uninhibited, robust, and wide-open, and that [such debate] may well include vehement, caustic, and sometimes unpleasantly sharp attacks on government and public officials."

That *Sullivan* was a civil libel case rather than a criminal prosecution was immaterial from the Court's perspective. "What a State may not constitutionally bring about by means of a criminal statute," Brennan admonished Alabama's public officials, "is likewise beyond the reach of its civil law of libel." To hold otherwise would open up "the possibility that a good-faith critic of government will be penalized for his criticism, [a] proposition [that] strikes at the very center of the constitutionally protected area of free expression."

Two Famous Metaphors

The actual malice test does not permit recovery of damages anytime defamatory falsehoods appear. Indeed, the test provides a high degree of protection for errors, as long as the publishers are neither liars nor wholly irresponsible. In *Sullivan*, Justice Brennan developed two metaphors to help explain why it is so important to permit citizen-critics such a high degree of latitude.

The first metaphor—"breathing space"—describes the latitude that must be provided to journalists commenting on public affairs. As Justice Brennan put it in *Sulli-*

THINGS TO REMEMBER

Memorable Dicta

- *New York Times v. Sullivan* is famous too for these observations:
  - The First Amendment is "a profound national commitment to the principle that debate on public issues should be uninhibited, robust, and wide-open."
  - Allowing public officials to sue for libel too easily is inconsistent with this commitment and uncomfortably reminiscent of sedition prosecutions.
  - The press must be granted a certain amount of wiggle room, called "breathing space," to make innocent errors.
  - Without such breathing space the press will experience the "chilling effect" of self-censorship, and we will all be deprived of valuable *true* speech.

van, "Erroneous statement is inevitable in free debate," and "it must be protected if the freedoms of expression are to have the breathing space that they need to survive."

The second metaphor—a "chilling effect"—is the opposite side of the coin. It represents journalistic timidity and the effect of making the avoidance of publishing any falsity one's most important governing principle. "There can be little doubt," Brennan warned, that reporters not given a bit of leeway will feel this chilling effect, and that "public debate and advocacy will be constrained."

Some Unanswered Questions from *Sullivan*

New York Times Co. v. Sullivan is certainly the most important U.S. libel decision to date. Indeed, much of contemporary libel doctrine can be seen as a fine-tuning or an elaboration of issues raised in the 1964 landmark opinion. For that reason, the majority of this chapter is devoted to examining a number of questions left unanswered in *Sullivan* but that have since received some additional explication from the Court.

Who Is a "Public Official"?

The actual malice rule applies only when libel plaintiffs are public officials. But who among those on the government payroll are public officials? Must they be elected, or can they be appointed? Is anyone who draws a public paycheck, from a state university president down to each of the school's department secretaries and janitors, to be included? The *Sullivan* Court decided not to decide. The 1964 decision was not the occasion "to determine how far down into the lower ranks of government employees the 'public official' designation would extend for purposes of this rule, or otherwise to specify categories of persons who would or would not be included," Justice Brennan said.

The truth is that there is no national consensus about who is and who is not considered a public official for purposes of the actual malice rule. Still, the Supreme Court gave some guidance in a 1966 case that came about because a columnist (Rosenblatt) for the *Laconia Evening Citizen* in New Hampshire, in the course of praising the new supervisor of the Belknap County Recreation Area, seemed to imply—the relevant section began, "What happened to all the money *last* year? And every other year?"—that the former supervisor (Baer) was a poor financial manager at best, an embezzler at worst. Reversing the jury's damage award imposed against the columnist, the Supreme Court sent the case back to the lower court to determine if the former recreation supervisor should be considered a public official and therefore if he should have had to prove actual malice.[6]

---

6. *Rosenblatt v. Baer,* 383 U.S. 75, 78 (1966). That Baer was a *former* supervisor was not deemed relevant, because the allegedly libelous remarks were made about his tenure as supervisor. Later cases make clear that *candidates* for public office can also be considered public officials for the purposes of applying the actual malice test.

The key to the *Rosenblatt* case for our purposes is the definition of "public official" the Supreme Court instructed the lower court to use. The phrase must apply "at the very least to those among the hierarchy of government employees who have, or appear to the public to have, substantial responsibility for or control over the conduct of governmental affairs. . . . The employee's position must be one which would invite public scrutiny and discussion of the person holding it, entirely apart from the scrutiny and discussion occasioned by the particular charges in controversy." This definition posits two related but distinguishable criteria. The first criterion is that the government employee must occupy a responsible enough position to have an effect on policies, to have "responsibility" or "control." Thus, while the case law is mixed as to whether public school teachers or even principals are public officials, there is little doubt that a school superintendent would have to prove actual malice.

The second criterion is perhaps best understood by conjuring up an image of two neighbors gossiping (about weighty public affairs, of course!) at the backyard fence. Public officials are those who occupy positions with responsibilities of sufficient concern that we are likely to gossip about them long before anyone publishes an allegedly libelous article about them, and certainly long before they ever bring suit for libel.

These criteria seem clear enough, but that does not mean that courts around the country have always been in agreement about how to apply them.[7] Some states apply the "public official" label only to elected public officials, even though this was not part of the Supreme Court's instructions in the *Rosenblatt* case.[8] Also, courts often disagree—sometimes within one state[9]—as to whether certain such categories of public employees as teachers or *deputy* public defenders should be considered public officials in libel law. A small handful of states goes further, making it impossible for teachers to sue when their pedagogic expertise is questioned.[10]

THINGS TO REMEMBER

Who Is a Public Official?

For purposes of the *Sullivan* rule, "public officials" are persons who have substantial responsibility over the conduct of governmental affairs and occupy positions that invite public scrutiny.

---

7. Danny R. Veilleux, "Who Is a Public Official for Purposes of Defamation Action?" 444 A.L.R. 5th 193 (2006).

8. *Mandel v. Boston Phoenix*, 322 F. Supp. 2d 39 (D. Mass. 2004); *McIntyre v. Piscottano*, 2005 Conn. Super. LEXIS 1526 (2005).

9. *Ghafur v. Bernstein*, 32 Cal. Rptr. 3d 626, 631 (Ct. App. 2005).

10. Joshua B. Orenstein, "Absolute Privilege from Defamation Claims and the Devaluing of Teachers' Professional Reputations," 2005 *Wisconsin Law Review* 261

What Is "Official Conduct"?

The paid advertisement that formed the basis of L. B. Sullivan's libel suit against the *New York Times* made specific allegations about police conduct in Montgomery, Alabama. To the extent that the commissioner in charge of the police force there was thus being criticized, such allegations surely concerned his "official conduct." Beyond that, we learn nothing from the Supreme Court's 1964 decision to help future litigants determine the difference between criticisms of official conduct and more personal attacks that would presumably not trigger the actual malice rule.

In a pair of later decisions, however, the Court does provide some guidance. The first of these, decided just shortly after *New York Times Co. v. Sullivan*, involved New Orleans–area district attorney Jim Garrison, who was the defendant in a criminal libel prosecution stemming from a press conference during which he criticized several local criminal court judges.[11] Their huge backlog of cases, he alleged, could be attributed to their "inefficiency, laziness, and excessive vacations," and the difficulty of prosecuting local vice cases was a direct result of their failure to reimburse the expenses incurred by undercover police officers. The *Garrison* decision overturning the criminal libel conviction is remembered today for two reasons. First, the Court used the occasion to apply the actual malice rule to criminal libel cases. In so doing, the Court recognized, but did not answer, the larger question of whether criminal libel statutes could *ever* be constitutionally applied against those who criticize public officials. (You may recall from chapter 3 that, despite the seeming inconsistency with the notion that we don't believe in sedition laws in this country, seventeen states still have criminal libel statutes on the books.)[12]

The second historically important feature of the *Garrison* case is how the Court handled the state's argument that the actual malice rule should be inapplicable, in that Garrison's criticisms—especially the charge of "laziness"—dealt not only with the judges' official conduct but also with their overall personalities. "Any criticism of the manner in which a public official performs his duties will tend to affect his private, as well as his public, reputation," Justice Brennan wrote for the Court. "Few personal attributes are more germane to fitness for office than dishonesty, malfeasance, or improper motivation, even though these characteristics may also affect the official's private character."

Seven years later the Court gave a bit more guidance as to what constitutes "official conduct" for purposes of applying the actual malice doctrine. The *Monitor Patriot*, a Concord, New Hampshire, newspaper, referred to U.S. senatorial candidate Alphonse Roy as a "former small-time bootlegger"; that is, as someone who had profited from

---

11. *Garrison v. Louisiana*, 379 U.S. 64 (1964).

12. As recently as 2010 a federal court in New Mexico declined an invitation to strike down that state's criminal libel law. *Mata v. Anderson*, 685 F. Supp. 2d 1223 (D. New Mexico 2010). On the other hand, the State of Washington's criminal libel statute was struck down in 2008. *Parmelee v. O'Neel*, 186 P. 3d 1094 (Wash. Appel. 2008).

the illegal sale of hard liquor during the Prohibition era. In overturning the jury's $20,000 damages award to Roy, Justice Stewart concluded that "a charge of criminal conduct, no matter how remote in time or place, can never be irrelevant to an official's or a candidate's fitness for office."[13]

Who Else Should Be Required to Prove Actual Malice?

One of the Supreme Court's chief rationales for constitutionalizing the libel tort in *New York Times v. Sullivan* was our national commitment to the principle "that debate on public issues should be uninhibited, robust, and wide-open." Public issues, of course, do not always involve public officials. They might involve captains of industry and scientists, and both celebrities and obscure persons caught up in a controversial matter. The Supreme Court showed its recognition of this fact when, in ruling simultaneously on two cases in 1967, it extended the actual malice rule to allegedly libelous statements made about "public figures." The two cases—*Curtis Publishing Co. v. Butts* and *Associated Press v. Walker*—share the same citation,[14] but have very different facts and produced opposite outcomes. The first case came about because the *Saturday Evening Post* had accused Wally Butts, then–athletic director of the University of Georgia, of fixing a football game between that school and the University of Alabama. Butts could not be considered a public official, because the athletic program at Georgia was administered by a corporation funded wholly by the private sector.

The article, "The Story of a College Football Fix," quotes an Atlanta businessman who claims that his phone's wires got crossed with those of Butts, thus allowing him to listen in on the Georgia coach's conversation with his counterpart at Alabama, during which he revealed what sounded like the kinds of team secrets that can determine game outcomes. At trial, however, it came out that the overheard phone conver-

---

THINGS TO REMEMBER

What Is "Official Conduct"?

- In addition to commonsense notions of "official conduct," the Court has said that
  - some attributions of personal characteristics (such as laziness) have clear implications for the performance of one's official conduct and
  - any allegation of criminal behavior, no matter how long ago, is relevant to one's official conduct.

---

13. *Monitor Patriot Co. v. Roy*, 401 U.S. 265, 266, 277 (1971).
14. 388 U.S. 130 (1967).

The Supreme Court ruled that features of this article were actionable, in part because the news value was not so "hot" as to justify failing to check sources further.

sation had been greatly misunderstood by the eavesdropper, that the substance of the two coaches' banter did not involve any kind of inside facts or "trade secrets" about game plans. By a 5–4 vote, the Supreme Court upheld the lower court's award of almost a half million dollars to Butts, concluding that the magazine had engaged in reprehensibly shoddy journalism, failing to take even "elementary precautions." Their main source had a criminal background, yet his story was accepted without independent support. In addition, the magazine should have made at least some attempt "to find out whether Alabama had adjusted its plans after the alleged divulgence of information." The magazine's conduct represented "an extreme departure from the standards of investigation and reporting ordinarily adhered to by responsible publishers."

The companion case resulted from a reporter's eyewitness dispatch to the Associated Press (AP) wire service describing a riot at the University of Mississippi in response to the use of the National Guard to help calm the campus as it received its first African American student. The AP account said that former major general Edwin Walker (a private citizen at the time of the riot) had "taken command of the violent crowd and had personally led a charge against federal marshals." It also described Walker as encouraging rioters to use violence and giving them technical advice on combating the effects of tear gas. At his libel trial against the Associated Press, Walker testified that he was on the university campus and did talk to a group of students, but that his message to them was to exercise self-restraint and to remain peaceful. The jury awarded him $500,000 in compensatory damages.

The Supreme Court unanimously overturned the award to Walker. The Court emphasized that the story of the events on the University of Mississippi campus, unlike the one about coach Butts, was "news which required immediate dissemination." Also unlike the situation in the companion case, in this case the AP's news source was a correspondent who "gave every indication of being trustworthy and competent," especially to staffers "familiar with General Walker's prior publicized statements on the underlying controversy."

These companion cases are remembered today for two important issues related to the actual malice standard. First and most important, the Court used the cases as a vehicle to make clear that the *Sullivan* rule would apply not only to public officials but to public figures as well. Second, the Court also began to offer judges guidance in determining whether a journalist is guilty of actual malice. Specifically, the Court will be a bit more forgiving of journalistic errors if the news being disseminated to the public is "hard" news about important political events, if it is "hot" news that must be gotten out quickly, and perhaps too if the specific media outlet's tight deadline precludes careful verification of every single last fact.

What Are *Sullivan*'s Implications for the Truth Defense?

In the common-law tort of libel, it will be recalled from chapter 3, one of the most powerful defenses was to establish that the gist or "sting" of the defamatory remarks was substantially true.

How does the *New York Times Co. v. Sullivan* actual malice rule affect the place of truth and falsity in libel law? Plaintiffs who are able to prove actual malice by the first of the two options provided in the Supreme Court's definition—that the defendant published a "knowing falsehood"—will obviously have laid to rest any ambiguity about the truth or falsity of the defamation. It seems also that the second route, prov-

THINGS TO REMEMBER

Public Figures

Within three years of the *Sullivan* case, the Court decided to demand that not only public officials but also public figures prove actual malice to establish a libel claim.

ing actual malice as the dissemination of libel with "reckless disregard" as to truth or falsity, carries with it at least a strong implication that the publication's allegations must have been false. True, people do sometimes sue for recklessly publishing the *truth*, but that is not what libel is all about.[15]

To prove actual malice, then, is to prove falsity, but what of plaintiffs who do not have to prove actual malice? These plaintiffs are neither public figures, nor are they public officials whose official conduct has been called into question. Do these private libel plaintiffs have the burden of proving falsity? The Supreme Court gave at least a partial answer to this question in 1986, when it decided *Philadelphia Newspapers, Inc. v. Hepps.*[16] At issue were articles in the *Philadelphia Inquirer* linking local businessman Maurice Hepps to organized crime. The Court reversed the state high court, which had faulted the trial judge for failing to instruct jurors that Hepps did not have the burden of proving falsity. Justice O'Connor admitted that an ironclad rule requiring all libel plaintiffs to prove falsity would be imperfect in that there will be times when defamatory statements, while untrue, cannot be *proven* untrue. Yet always placing the burden of showing truth on the defendants, she argued, would stifle too much speech. She emerged with a compromise position, holding that "the common-law presumption that defamatory speech is false cannot stand *when a plaintiff seeks damages against a media defendant for speech of public concern*" (emphasis added).

The holding in *Hepps* provides a clue to a larger truth about the Supreme Court's post–*New York Times Co. v. Sullivan* defamation jurisprudence generally. That body of case law can be understood and organized far more easily if three important questions are kept in mind:

- Who is the plaintiff (a public official or public figure, or a private individual)?
- Who is the defendant (media or nonmedia)?
- What was the libel about (an issue of public importance or a private matter)?

The Court has in essence set up a two-by-two-by-two matrix, creating eight possible combinations of situations. More often than not, the answer to a question about the constitutional dimension of libel law is "it depends," and what it depends on is how these three questions are answered. If the question is "Who has the burden of proof regarding truth or falsity?" the answer seems to be that in at least five of the eight situations, the burden is shouldered by the plaintiff. Why five of eight? In all four situations in which the answer to the first question is that the plaintiff is a public person (assuming for public officials that their official conduct is at issue), that plaintiff has the burden of proving actual malice, and thus falsity. As a result of *Hepps*, in at least one set of circumstances, even purely private plaintiffs must prove falsity:

15. As we will see in the next chapter, there is a tort action for public disclosure (of true but embarrassing facts), but we shall also see that nowadays it is almost impossible to win such a suit.
16. 475 U.S. 767 (1986).

when the defendant is the media *and* the offending publication is about a matter of public interest. With respect to the remaining three boxes, the First Amendment as interpreted by the Supreme Court offers no guidance as to who shoulders the burden of proof regarding truth or falsity.

A Legal or a Factual Question?

In chapter 1, the distinction between questions of fact and questions of law was introduced. That distinction becomes crucial in the Supreme Court's libel jurisprudence; it becomes a big money issue in that the vast majority of libel suits are lost by the media at the trial level, but a majority of those are overturned in favor of the defendants at the appellate level. Libel defendants are therefore hungry to find plausible and fruitful grounds for appeal.

Given that so much of the constitutionalized tort of libel focuses on the level of fault manifested by defendants, whether a trial court finding of actual malice is a **question of fact** (generally not appealable) or a **question of law** (appealable) was a crucial question left unanswered in *New York Times Co. v. Sullivan*. Twenty years later, the Court provided an answer in *Bose Corp. v. Consumers Union*,[17] a case that resulted from "an unusual metaphor in a critical review of an unusual loudspeaker system." The speaker system was Bose's 901 model, and the review was published in the May 1970 issue of *Consumer Reports*. The reviewers, after offering some positive comments about the speaker system, cautioned that listeners "could pinpoint the location of various instruments much more easily with a standard speaker than with the Bose system." With this system, the reviewers added, "individual instruments . . . seemed to grow to gigantic proportions and tended to wander about the room." Prospective buyers, in the reviewers' opinion, might not be very happy with the system "after the novelty [wears] off."

The trial court ruled that Bose would be considered a public figure for the purposes of this product disparagement suit because of the unusual nature of the speaker system and the aggressive advertising by the company to promote it. Thus, actual malice

---

THINGS TO REMEMBER

The First Amendment and the Truth Defense

- Proving actual malice includes the proof of falsity.
- Those who do not have to prove actual malice will still have to prove falsity if they sue a media defendant about a story on a topic of public concern.

---

17. 466 U.S. 485 (1984).

The Bose case, which Justice Rehnquist disparaged as "The Case of the Wandering Instruments," found the Court ruling that the question of "actual malice" is an issue appellate courts can examine on their own.

was the required level of fault, and the trial court was satisfied that this level of fault had been demonstrated at trial. Where the magazine's panel of listeners reported that sound from the speakers seemed to "wander about the room," the court took it to mean "all over the room," not simply (as the evaluators *said* at trial that they meant) "along the wall," *between* the two speakers. The court concluded that the difference between what the evaluators meant and what they actually wrote was substantial enough to constitute actual malice. A federal appellate court overturned this decision, finding that the editors were guilty at most "of using imprecise language in the article—perhaps resulting from an attempt to produce a readable article for its mass audience." The question in front of the Supreme Court, then, was whether the appellate court had overstepped its bounds by assessing anew and independently the question of whether the magazine manifested actual malice. Is actual malice a question of law or of fact?

Intuitively, one might suppose that actual malice can be either a question of fact or a question of law. A jury that finds that the defendant published a "knowing falsehood"—in other words, that he lied—would seem to be making an inference of fact. Trying to guess what was going on in another person's mind at some relevant time in the past is difficult; it is more art than science, but it is an issue of fact. Either he knew or he did not know that he was publishing a falsehood.

Conversely, the intuitive approach would also suggest that if the jury depends instead upon the alternative definition of actual malice, that the defendant published with "reckless disregard as to truth or falsity," it will have settled a question of law rather than of fact. How far must a publisher deviate from accepted journalistic practices before we are ready to say that she has crossed over the line between mere negligence and actual malice? This kind of judgment is precisely what is normally thought of as a question of law.

Justice Stevens's majority opinion does not really answer the question, but it does provide a rule to guide lower courts in the future. Stevens emphasized that independent appellate review has been held by the Court to be required by the First Amendment in many contexts, from commercial speech to obscenity. Here similarly, the Court concluded that appellate courts may determine the actual malice question for themselves, that they can thus overrule a trial judge's decision on the matter without having to accuse that judge of having made a "clearly erroneous" decision. (Recall our discussion of the Clearly Erroneous Rule of federal civil procedure, discussed in chapter 1).

Does Editorial Pressure Lead to Actual Malice?

In the spring of 1985, media outlets nationwide were using their editorial pages to express dismay and even a bit of panic over a decision issued by the Court of Appeals for the D.C. Circuit. Mobil Oil president William Tavoulareas had sued the *Washington Post* for suggesting, in an article published in November 1979, that he had improperly used his influence to help set up his son Peter as a partner in a huge shipping business that had multimillion-dollar contracts with Mobil. The majority of the three-judge appellate panel hearing the case in 1985 made much of the fact that *Post* editor Bob Woodward put his staff under great pressure to produce, in his words, the kind of "holy shit story" for which he himself became famous during Watergate. Might not reporters who are under the gun to write such "high-impact investigative stories

THINGS TO REMEMBER

Appealing Actual Malice

- A trial court finding that a libel defendant has manifested actual malice with convincing clarity is an appealable finding.
- This rule has significant financial implications for media libel defendants, who tend to lose most libel cases at the trial level but often win on appeal.

of wrongdoing" be likely to see an international scandal where others would see only a father trying to help out his son? The appellate panel concluded that Woodward's colorful phrase "is relevant to the inquiry of whether a newspaper's employees acted in reckless disregard of whether a statement is false or not."[18]

The *Post*'s appeal to the full appellate court produced a very different result. The en banc court overturned the panel, holding that "managerial pressure to produce [hard-hitting investigative] stories cannot, as a matter of law, constitute evidence of actual malice" and adding that investigative reports serve "one of the highest functions of the press in our society."

The Supreme Court never heard the *Tavoulareas* case, and the media celebration of the en banc decision may have been both overly jubilant and premature. In the years since *Tavoulareas*, the notion that juries cannot use as evidence of actual malice the fact that reporters felt obliged to write hard-hitting investigative pieces has not spread beyond the D.C. Circuit.[19] Even before *Tavoulareas*, Chief Justice Warren's concurring opinion from the case discussed earlier involving University of Georgia football coach Wally Butts had suggested one reason the plaintiff there correctly prevailed: the *Saturday Evening Post* staff had been under enormous pressure to increase circulation and advertising revenues through stories that Warren described as "sophisticated muckraking," those that are designed to "provoke people," to "make them mad."[20]

Editors pressuring reporters to come up with "holy shit" stories is but one possible indication of actual malice. Courts, including the Supreme Court, have pointed to other factors that might legitimately lead to findings of actual malice, although judicial guidance has been limited, in that rulings tend to focus on highly specific facts of particular cases. In one case, the Supreme Court suggested that a newspaper's "deliberate decision not to acquire knowledge" of facts at odds with the allegedly libelous comments it eventually published could be used as evidence of actual malice. In that case reporters apparently relied on one highly questionable source and failed not only to interview easily identifiable persons likely to present contrary evidence, but also to even listen to a highly relevant tape recording they knew to exist.[21] In another case, the Supreme Court said that purposely changing a source's direct quotes in ways that produce "a material change in the meaning conveyed" could count as evidence of actual malice.[22] (Much more recently, a federal court in Georgia, in throwing out a

---

18. *Tavoulareas v. Piro*, 759 F.2d 90 (D.C. Cir. 1985), *rev'd en banc*, 817 F.2d 762 (D.C. Cir. 1987).

19. The Sixth Circuit has said, for example, that libel juries should not be required to "blind [themselves] to evidence of editorial pressure for sensationalistic stories." *Connaughton v. Harte-Hanks Communications, Inc.*, 842 F.2d 825, 834 (6th Cir. 1988), *aff'd*, 491 U.S. 657 (1989).

20. *Curtis Publishing Co. v. Butts*, 388 U.S. 130, 169 (1967) (Warren, C.J., concurring). A Supreme Court majority later cited this language with approval. See *St. Amant v. Thompson*, 390 U.S. 727, 732 n.3 (1968).

21. *Connaughton v. Harte-Hanks Communications, Inc.*, 491 U.S. 657 (1989).

22. *Masson v. New Yorker, Inc.*, 501 U.S. 496 (1991).

libel suit against comedians Penn and Teller's cable series *Bullshit,* held that using a plaintiff's own video speech clips to condemn him could be the basis of defamation, unless there was independent evidence the defendants had distorted the tapes.[23])

In yet another case, the Supreme Court offered a nonexhaustive list of transgressions that might constitute actual malice:

- A story is fabricated by the defendant, is the product of his imagination, or is based wholly on an unverified anonymous telephone call. . . .
- The publisher's allegations are so inherently improbable that only a reckless man would have put them in circulation. . . .
- There are obvious reasons to doubt the veracity of the informant or the accuracy of the informant's reports.[24]

Is There Such a Thing as a Defamatory *Opinion*?

In chapter 3, mention was made of the common-law libel defense known as fair comment, which reminds us that defamation plaintiffs must be able to prove that the damaging utterances made about them contained specific *factual* allegations. Pure opinions, at least theoretically, would not be actionable. The Supreme Court—and lower courts attempting to apply relevant Supreme Court doctrine—has applied a First Amendment analysis to the fact-versus-opinion distinction.

The somewhat confusing story of the Court's "protected opinion" doctrine began with an off-the-cuff bit of dicta in a 1974 decision. *Gertz v. Robert Welch, Inc.* involved

Plaintiff Russ Brock was unsuccessful in his libel suit against Penn and Teller, in part because the most damning factual "allegations" in the suit came from Brock's own speeches.

23. *Brock v. Viacom International,* 2005 U.S. Dist. LEXIS 12217 (N.D. Ga. 2005).
24. *St. Amant v. Thompson,* 390 U.S. 727, 732 (1968).

THINGS TO REMEMBER

Evidence of Actual Malice

- The Court of Appeals for the D.C. Circuit has held that juries may not consider as evidence of actual malice the fact that reporters may have been under pressure to produce hard-hitting investigative pieces.
- The Sixth Circuit seems to have rejected this approach, and it is not yet clear how the Supreme Court would rule on the issue.
- Juries might find actual malice if the media
  - depend on a single, anonymous phone call as their source;
  - publish without checking a charge that seems very likely, on its face, to be false; or
  - show no skepticism toward a source who is almost certainly lying.
- Juries may not find actual malice in the inaccuracy of exact quotes attributed to a source unless the meaning of the source's words has been materially changed.

a conservative magazine publisher who accused a civil rights attorney of being part of a Communist conspiracy to discredit law enforcement officials. The majority opinion included the following words: "We begin with the common ground. Under the First Amendment there is no such thing as a false idea. However pernicious an opinion may seem, we depend for its correction not on the conscience of judges and juries but on the competition of other ideas."[25]

At least two questions arise from this passage. The first, to which the Court would not provide any answer until sixteen years later, was whether it meant by its dramatic tone to create absolute immunity from liability for any utterance that could plausibly be called an opinion. Many lower courts took the Court to mean precisely that. The second question was whatever special measure of First Amendment protection against libel suits would be granted to opinions, how would one *distinguish* facts from opinions? In the years following *Gertz*, several lower courts offered their own thoughts regarding this second question.[26]

In 1990, the Supreme Court weighed in again on the fact-versus-opinion distinction in *Milkovich v. Lorain Journal Co.*[27] There is a great degree of ambiguity in the

---

25. 418 U.S. 323, 339–340 (1974).

26. One of the most influential suggestions was provided by the Court of Appeals for the D.C. Circuit, in *Ollman v. Evans*, 750 F.2d 970 (D.C. Cir. 1984) (en banc), in which newspaper columnists accused a political science professor of having "no status within the profession [except as] a pure and simple activist." The plurality opinion of the en banc panel in *Ollman* offered this test to distinguish facts from opinions: (1) What is the common usage or meaning of the words? (2) How verifiable is the statement at issue? (3) What is the immediate context in which the words appear? (4) What is the larger social context in which the words appear?

27. 497 U.S. 1 (1990).

case—courts have gone in about a dozen directions trying to apply it.[28] Still, it is fair to say that as a result of *Milkovich,* many libel suits that previously would have been dismissed in response to defendants' motions for summary judgment have instead gone to trial.

The *Milkovich* case stemmed from a high school wrestling coach's having testified in front of the Ohio High School Athletic Association, which was investigating a wrestling match altercation resulting in some injuries. A local newspaper article commenting on the proceedings seemed to accuse Milkovich of perjury.

Writing for a 7–2 majority, Chief Justice Rehnquist expressed concern that lower courts had made too much of the dicta from *Gertz* that "there is no such thing as a false idea." That passage was never intended "to create a wholesale defamation exemption for anything that might be labeled 'opinion,'" Rehnquist added. A contrary reading would "ignore the fact that expressions of 'opinion' may often imply an assertion of objective fact." Rehnquist went on to conclude that the newspaper article did raise very specific *factual* allegations about Milkovich that should be considered by a jury rather than subject to summary judgment for the defendant. "The dispositive question in the present case," he wrote, is "whether or not a reasonable factfinder could conclude that the statements . . . imply an assertion that petitioner Milkovich perjured himself in a judicial proceeding. We think this question must be answered in the affirmative."

Perhaps throwing a bone to the defendants, Rehnquist went out of his way to remind us that in many situations, existing Supreme Court precedents already serve to protect statements of opinion. Certainly in any case where actual malice is the required level of fault, a finding of false fact is necessarily a part of the plaintiff's burden. So too, after the *Hepps* case discussed earlier, plaintiffs suing media defendants over matters of public concern have the burden of proving that *false* allegations of fact have been made. *Milkovich*'s effects would thus chiefly be felt by defendants, especially nonmedia defendants whose utterances are not deemed to touch on matters of public concern.

A 2009 case from Massachusetts is a good example of *Milkovich* at work. The *Boston Herald* had published a series of articles about the dangers of answering online dating ads posted by inmates. One inmate featured in the articles sued unsuccessfully for libel. To be sure there were several factual misstatements in the articles, such as reporting that the plaintiff was convicted of manslaughter (in fact it was for aggravated rape). Unsurprisingly, the court found that such an error was not libelous—the gist or "sting," that here was a dangerous fellow whom one probably should not trust too easily, was still true. Among the protected opinions in the article were a quote from a corrections employee to the effect that the plaintiff was "a piece of work," and a headline alleging that his online self-descriptions were "greatly exaggerated." There

---

28. Nat Stern, "The Certainty Principle as Justification for the Group Defamation Rule," 40 *Arizona State Law Journal* 951, 977 (2008).

Maple Beat the Law with the "Big Lie" from the *News-Herald*, January 8, 1975

Yesterday in the Franklin County Common Pleas Court, Judge Paul Martin overturned an Ohio High School Athletic Association decision to suspend the Maple Heights wrestling team from this year's state tournament. . . .

But there is something much more important involved here than whether Maple was denied due process by the OHSAA, the basis of the temporary injunction.

When a person takes on a job in a school, whether it be as a teacher, coach, administrator or even maintenance worker, it is well to remember that his primary job is that of educator.

There is scarcely a person concerned with school who doesn't leave his mark in some way on the young people who pass his way—many are the lessons taken away from school by students which weren't learned from a lesson plan or out of a book. They come from personal experiences with and observations of their superiors and peers, from watching actions and reactions.

Such a lesson was learned (or relearned) yesterday by the student body of Maple Heights High School, and by anyone who attended the Maple-Mentor wrestling meet of last Feb. 8. . . . A lesson which, sadly, in view of the events of the past year, is well they learned early. It is simply this: If you get in a jam, lie your way out.

If you're successful enough, and powerful enough, and can sound sincere enough, you stand an excellent chance of making the lie stand up, regardless of what really happened.

The teachers responsible were mainly head Maple wrestling coach, Mike Milkovich, and former superintendent of schools H. Donald Scott.

Last winter they were faced with a difficult situation. Milkovich's ranting from the side of the mat and egging the crowd on against the meet official and the opposing team . . . resulted in . . . a brawl. . . .

Naturally, . . . the two men were called on the carpet to account for the incident. But they declined to walk into the hearing and face up to their responsibilities. . . . Instead they chose to come to the hearing and misrepresent the things that happened to the OHSAA Board of Control. . . .

I was among the 2,000-plus witnesses of the meet at which the trouble broke out, and I also attended the hearing before the OHSAA, so I was in a unique position of being the only non-involved party to observe both the meet itself and the Milkovich-Scott version presented to the

> board. Any resemblance between the two occurrences is purely coinci-
> dental.
> Anyone who attended the meet, whether he be from Maple Heights,
> Mentor, or impartial observer, knows in his heart that Milkovich and
> Scott lied at the hearing after each having given his solemn oath to tell
> the truth.
> But they got away with it. Is that the kind of lesson we want our young
> people learning from their high school administrators and coaches? I
> think not.

certainly were some exaggerations and inaccuracies in the plaintiff's personal ad, and who is to say when an exaggeration becomes a "great" one?[29]

Can Libel Plaintiffs Sue for Intentional Infliction of Emotional Distress?

In the early 1980s, the makers of Campari liqueur embarked on a clever ad campaign designed to capitalize on what might otherwise be considered a shortcoming of the product. The drink, which has been described as "distinct," "bittersweet," and "strictly an acquired taste," often does not appeal to persons tasting it for the first time. Madison Avenue's solution was to produce slick print ads featuring a celebrity talking about his or her "first time." On the surface, personalities such as actor Tony Roberts would be talking about their first time tasting Campari, but there would always be a naughty double entendre suggesting that the spokesperson's first sexual experience was the real subject under discussion.

Someone at *Hustler* magazine determined that a parody of the Campari campaign,

---

THINGS TO REMEMBER

Facts and Opinions

- In an offhand comment from *Gertz v. Robert Welch, Inc.* (1974), the Supreme Court implied that libel suits could never succeed against pure statements of opinion. Several lower courts then tried to find ways of distinguishing facts from opinions.
- In 1990 (*Milkovich v. Lorain Journal Company*), the Supreme Court tried to put the matter in perspective by emphasizing that libel defendants cannot escape liability simply by prefacing their defamatory utterances with "I think that . . ."

---

29. *LaChance v. Boston Herald*, 2009 Mass. Super LEXIS 340.

Jerry Falwell talks about his first time.*

FALWELL: My first time was in an outhouse outside Lynchburg, Virginia.

INTERVIEWER: *Wasn't it a little cramped?*

FALWELL: Not after I kicked the goat out.

INTERVIEWER: *I see. You must tell me all about it.*

FALWELL: I never *really* expected to make it with Mom, but then after she showed all the other guys in town such a good time, I figured, "What the hell!"

INTERVIEWER: *But your mom? Isn't that a bit odd?*

FALWELL: I don't think so. Looks don't mean that much to me in a woman.

INTERVIEWER: *Go on.*

FALWELL: Well, we were drunk off our God-fearing asses on Campari, ginger ale and soda—that's called a Fire and Brimstone—at the time. And Mom looked better than a Baptist whore with a $100 donation.

INTERVIEWER: *Campari in the crapper with Mom . . . how interesting. Well, how was it?*

FALWELL: The Campari was great, but Mom passed out before I could come.

INTERVIEWER: *Did you ever try it again?*

FALWELL: Sure . . .

lots of times. But not in the outhouse. Between Mom and the shit, the flies were too much to bear.

INTERVIEWER: *We meant the Campari.*

FALWELL: Oh, yeah. I always get sloshed before I go out to the pulpit. You don't think I could lay down all that bullshit *sober,* do you?

© 1983—Imported by Campari U.S.A., New York, NY 48°proof Spirit Aperitif (Liqueur)

Campari, like all liquor, was made to mix you up. It's a light, 48-proof, refreshing spirit, just mild enough to make you drink too much before you know you're schnockered. For your first time, mix it with orange juice. Or maybe some white wine. Then you won't remember anything the next morning. *Campari. The mixable that smarts.*

CAMPARI® **You'll never forget your first time.**

*AD PARODY—NOT TO BE TAKEN SERIOUSLY

The Supreme Court held that this ad parody was protected speech, even if it hurt Reverend Falwell's feelings.

using Reverend Jerry Falwell as the celebrity spokesperson, would be a handy vehicle for expressing the publication's distaste for the well-known leader of the Christian right. The parody, which appeared in the magazine's November 1983 issue, boasted Falwell's photo alongside the caption, "Jerry Falwell talks about his first time." The "ad" was presented as the transcript of a fictitious interview with its subject. Unlike the Campari ads, here the double entendre was more than a hint. Indeed, the text made clear that Falwell's first time sampling the liqueur was also his first time having sex—with his mother, as it turns out, in an outhouse.

Mr. Falwell was not amused, and he instructed his attorneys to sue the magazine and publisher Larry Flynt. They employed three legal theories in their quest for damages: libel, invasion of privacy, and a third tort called intentional infliction of emotional distress. Invasion of privacy is the subject of the next chapter and need not be of concern here, save to say that the State of Virginia, where Falwell brought his suit, did not recognize the category of privacy invasion for which he sought recovery. The jury ruled against Falwell on his libel claim, finding unsurprisingly that no one could possibly take the text of the ad parody seriously and that his reputation was therefore not damaged.

It is the playing out of the third claim that makes the case an important one beyond the mere fact of the litigants' celebrity. The jury provided Falwell with a fairly sizable damages award on his emotional distress claim, and this award was in front of the U.S. Supreme Court on appeal.[30] Would Falwell be permitted to keep the award even though the jury held that there was no libel here?

A little history of the emotional distress tort will help us answer that question. Emotional distress is a relative newcomer to the American scene, having been recognized only sporadically in the past hundred years or so. As its name implies, the tort is supposed to provide a remedy for persons whose feelings have been hurt by the malicious, intentional acts of others. That the tort sometimes goes by the name "outrage" serves to remind us that the conduct of the perpetrator—typically an overly zealous bill collector or a prankster with a perverse sense of humor—has to be truly outlandish. Sometimes the offensive behavior is much more *conduct* than *communication*. If you shoot my treasured family pet in my presence and in the presence of my young child, you will certainly have caused us both enormous emotional distress. Falsely telling someone that a loved one has died is also an example of this tort.

The *Falwell* case did not present the typical emotional distress set of facts, and indeed the plaintiff's attorneys added the claim almost as an afterthought. Yet it seemed a sensible legal strategy. In Virginia, and in many jurisdictions, the tort has four elements:

---

30. *Hustler Magazine v. Falwell*, 485 U.S. 46 (1988). See also *Peterson v. Grisham*, 594 F. 3d 723 (10th Cir. 2010) (law enforcement officials' libel suit against famed crime author Grisham failed; so too must his alternative claim of intentional infliction of emotional distress).

- The wrongdoer's conduct is intentional or reckless.
- The conduct is so "outrageous" as to offend generally accepted standards of decency.
- The conduct is in fact the cause of the plaintiff's emotional distress.
- The emotional distress thus caused is severe.

It is probably not surprising that Falwell's attorneys were able to persuade the jury that the four elements had been satisfied. In one deposition, Flynt candidly admitted that he had set out to "get" Falwell, to "assassinate" his reputation. Further, how many acts that could be attributed to a man would be more "outrageous," more beyond any reasonable standards of decency, than that he had sex with his mother in a stinking, fly-infested toilet? Would not seeing oneself, and one's mother, so depicted cause severe emotional distress, even if we know "intellectually" that no one would actually believe that the outlandish allegation is true? As Chief Justice Rehnquist allowed in his opinion for a unanimous Supreme Court, the *Hustler* ad parody was obviously offensive to Falwell, "and doubtless gross and repugnant in the eyes of most others."

Nonetheless, the Court ruled against Falwell, holding that public figures and public officials may not recover damages for intentional infliction of emotional distress resulting from publications concerning them unless they are first able to demonstrate actual malice. In other words, if your libel suit fails, so too must your cause of action for emotional distress. The damages award was reversed.

Is a Reporter's "State of Mind" Relevant?

One of the most famous catchphrases in Washington, D.C., born of Watergate is "What did the President know, and when did he know it?" The question reminds us that an agent's state of mind is often more important than his or her actual conduct. The *Sullivan* actual malice test is an example of just such an instance. That a media outlet published a false and defamatory remark does not alone make the publisher liable for damages; we need to know more. The actual malice inquiry seeks to answer the question, "What did the reporters and editors know (regarding the truth or falsity of that which they were about to publish), and when did they know it?"

Libel plaintiff Anthony Herbert thought it only fair that he be able to ask reporters these questions directly as he was preparing his case against the producers of CBS's *60 Minutes* program. A retired army officer, Herbert had served extended duty in Vietnam. He came to public attention when he accused superiors of covering up various wartime atrocities. *60 Minutes* did a piece about the accusations, suggesting that they were invented by Herbert as a way of rationalizing his having been disciplined by the army, including having been relieved of his command. The Supreme Court ruled that Herbert should have a chance to inquire as to the CBS staff's state of mind. To hold otherwise "would constitute a substantial interference with the ability of a

Herbert v. Lando tells us that libel plaintiffs who must prove actual malice may ask defendants what they were thinking when they went to press.

defamation plaintiff to establish the ingredients of malice as required by *New York Times*."[31]

How Has the Court Fine-Tuned the Actual Malice Rule?

Before we begin our extended discussion of *Gertz v. Welch, Inc.*, the Supreme Court's most important libel decision save for *New York Times v. Sullivan* itself, brief mention must be made of four additional ways in which the Court has applied the actual malice rule:

- *Seattle Times Co. v. Rhinehart*[32]—Media outlets do not necessarily have a right to publish things they learn about individuals or groups with whom they are in litigation (in this case, a newspaper being sued by a local religious leader for defamation)

31. *Herbert v. Lando*, 441 U.S. 153, 170 (1979).
32. 467 U.S. 20 (1984).

in the pretrial discovery process itself. Only if the press independently learns the information from other sources may they print it.

- *Anderson v. Liberty Lobby, Inc.*[33]—Just as actual malice must be proven *with convincing clarity* in an actual libel trial, so too must libel plaintiffs establish to a judge's satisfaction with the same level of certainty their ability to prove actual malice when combating a defendant's pretrial motion to dismiss a libel suit.
- *Keeton v. Hustler Magazine, Inc.*[34]—Libel plaintiffs may "forum shop"; they may bring suit in any state in which the defamatory statements were circulated. They need not restrict themselves to their or the defendants' state of residency.
- *Miami Herald, Inc. v. Tornillo*[35]—Print media may not be forced to publish aggrieved politicians' replies to what they see as personal attacks. The Court's invalidation of state **right-of-reply statutes** presumably applies to any target in the print media. The decision does not, however, invalidate **retraction statutes**, which do not *demand* that media print corrections, but rather give the media a measure of protection against any future libel suit if they *choose* to publish an admission of error.

Gertz v. Robert Welch, Inc.: The Other Landmark Libel Decision

Lower court judges were beseeching the Supreme Court for a bit of clarity regarding when the actual malice test applies. Why? Because in 1971, the Court produced anything *but* clarity when, in *Rosenbloom v. Metromedia, Inc.*, its members penned five separate opinions, not one of which commanded more than three votes.[36] Justice Brennan's *plurality* opinion offered much confusion in that it rejected the whole public official versus private plaintiff distinction, arguing instead that whether or not the alleged defamations were on a topic of public interest should determine in which cases the actual malice burden would apply. The confusion ended in 1974 in Gertz, in which a clear Court *majority* reaffirmed the actual malice rule originally articulated in *New York Times Co. v. Sullivan.*

---

33. 477 U.S. 242 (1986). Technically the *Anderson* rule applies only in federal courts, but almost all the states have embraced the rule. David A. Anderson, "Rethinking Defamation," 48 *Arizona Law Review* 1047, 1050, n.25 (2006).

34. 465 U.S. 770 (1984). In more recent years the issue of *international* forum shopping has become more prominent, as plaintiffs bring suit against American media companies in countries whose libel laws are more plaintiff-friendly. Some states in the U.S. have passed laws prohibiting the enforcement of a foreign-imposed libel judgment against American defendants. And in 2010, President Obama signed H.R. 2765, the Securing the Protection of our Enduring and Established Constitutional Heritage Act ("Speech Act" for short), preventing American courts from enforcing foreign libel judgments in cases that would not have been winnable in American courts. The law is now found at 28 USCS § 4101 (2010).

35. 418 U.S. 241 (1974).

36. 403 U.S. 29 (1971).

THINGS TO REMEMBER

Yet More on Actual Malice

- If an emotional distress suit is prompted by a publication about the plaintiff, he or she can prevail only by first proving actual malice.
- Because proving actual malice requires plaintiffs to probe the minds of reporters and editors, they will be permitted, in pretrial discovery, to examine and question defendants about their notes and their outtakes (footage they shot but chose not to air).
- There is no First Amendment violation in enjoining the media from publishing information learned only through the discovery process.
- The same "convincing clarity" burden of proof that applies to actual malice trials also dictates the level of proof that a libel plaintiff must demonstrate to defeat a defendant's motion to dismiss.
- Libel plaintiffs may bring their suits in any state where the allegedly defamatory statements were generally circulated.
- The print media cannot be forced by statute to publish a reply from an aggrieved party: Right-of-reply statutes should not be confused with retraction statutes, which provide media with a form of relief in libel suits if they first publish a requested retraction.

Here, briefly, are the facts of the case. Chicago-based civil rights attorney Elmer Gertz was hired by the family of a young man who had been killed by the police. The officer at fault had already been convicted of second-degree murder; Gertz was to handle the family's civil litigation against him. Robert Welch's magazine *American Opinion* published an article alleging that testimony against the cop was perjured and that Gertz was part of a Communist conspiracy to discredit law enforcement officials.

A $50,000 damages award for libel against Welch was rejected by a federal appellate court, in part because the confusing *Rosenbloom* decision had been handed down while the Gertz suit was pending. In a 5–4 ruling, the Supreme Court held that the civil rights attorney was a private figure who should not have to prove actual malice. Let us look at the several principles that *Gertz v. Robert Welch, Inc.* added to the law of libel.

A Reaffirmation of the "Who Is the Plaintiff?" Question

Earlier in this chapter it was suggested that much of the Supreme Court's libel doctrine can be organized around three questions: Who is the plaintiff? Who is the defendant? Does the alleged libel concern a matter of public interest? In *Rosenbloom*, the Court flirted with discarding the question of the plaintiff's identity. But the *Gertz* majority rejects the *Rosenbloom* plurality position and emphasizes the continued wisdom of looking toward the identity of the plaintiff as the proper gauge of the level of fault required to recover for libel.

It is appropriate to focus on whether the plaintiff is a public or a private individual, Powell explained, for two reasons. First, public plaintiffs do not need to sue to be vindicated in that they can engage in "self-help" remedies instead. If they call a press conference to combat charges made against them, people will come. Powell's second reason for treating public plaintiffs differently is that they usually have *chosen* to be media personalities. People who seek public office, or fame, "run the risk of closer public scrutiny."

Two Kinds of Public Figures

In the *Butts* and *Walker* cases discussed earlier, the Supreme Court extended the *Sullivan* actual malice rule to public figures. The *Gertz* decision clarifies and extends those holdings by pointing out that there are actually two kinds of public figures. "For the most part those who attain this status," Justice Powell wrote, "have assumed roles of especial prominence in the affairs of society." These people are household names, the truly famous. Criticize them, and they will have to prove actual malice to recover damages from you, regardless of the specific subject matter of the defamatory remarks. Since *Gertz*, these plaintiffs are often referred to as "general" or "all-purpose" public figures to distinguish them from the second category.

The second group, "limited" or "limited-purpose" public figures, might not be truly famous, but they have "thrust themselves to the forefront of particular public controversies in order to influence the resolution of the issues involved," thus inviting both "attention" and "comment." When these personalities become libel plaintiffs, the First Amendment demands that they prove actual malice only if the defamatory remarks concern the specific political issue in which they have become involved. An automobile company middle manager who gives speeches around the country on driving safety will have to prove actual malice if you accuse her of having a string of traffic violations on her record, but not if you point out she has had an abortion. (The reverse would be true of a pro-life activist.)

The Fault Element and Private Plaintiffs

Public officials always have to prove actual malice when they sue for libel, as do general public figures. Limited public figures will at least sometimes have to prove actual malice. What, though, does the First Amendment say about the degree of fault that a truly *private* plaintiff—or a limited public figure who is maligned in an area of life wholly unrelated to his or her political activism—must prove? Very little, Justice Powell told us. Consider Powell's assessment of the truly private libel plaintiff's plight: "He has not accepted public office or assumed an influential role in ordering society. . . . He has relinquished no part of his interest in the protection of his own good name, and consequently he has a more compelling call on the courts for redress of injury inflicted by defamatory falsehood." The Court majority therefore interpreted the First Amendment to give the individual states enormous latitude should they wish to tip the scales in favor of private parties' reputational interests. As long as states do not permit recovery under a strict liability standard (one requiring no finding of fault at all), they will be on sound constitutional footing. The majority of states require that private plaintiffs prove that defamatory remarks were made with negligence. About a dozen states demand a somewhat higher demonstration of fault, which they call "gross negligence." In some jurisdictions, which of these two standards applies to private plaintiffs is a function of whether the article triggering the libel suit is deemed to be on a matter of public or private interest. Finally, a small handful of states demand that all libel plaintiffs, public or private, prove actual malice.

Punitive or Presumed Damages and Actual Malice

"The common law of defamation," Justice Powell's majority opinion in *Gertz* reminds us, "is an oddity of tort law, for it allows recovery of purportedly compensatory damages without evidence of actual loss. Under the traditional rules pertaining to actions for libel, the existence of injury is presumed from the fact of publication. Juries may award substantial sums as compensation for supposed damage to reputation without any proof that such harm actually occurred."[37]

The awarding of presumed and punitive damages must be kept in check, Powell argued, because it can inhibit the vigorous exercise of First Amendment freedoms, and because it invites juries to punish those who hold unpopular political opinions. The *Gertz* majority opinion thus limits the damages available to libel plaintiffs who do not prove actual malice to an award designed to compensate for "actual injury." Powell did not try to provide a single definition for actual injury, but he made clear that it is not limited to "out-of-pocket loss" (the kinds of damages described in chapter 3 as "special damages"). States may feel free to include within actual injury such harms as "impairment of reputation and standing in the community, personal humiliation, and mental anguish and suffering"; moreover, there "need be no evidence which assigns an actual dollar value to the injury."

The "if you want punitive or presumed damages, you must prove actual malice" rule articulated in *Gertz* was limited in a later decision to those situations in which the allegedly libelous remark is on a matter of public interest. (Again we see the two-by-two-by-two matrix in play.) The case, *Dun & Bradstreet, Inc. v. Greenmoss Builders*,[38] involved an erroneous report to the effect that a local business was in bankruptcy, which appeared in a financial newsletter with limited circulation. Although the Court voted 5–4 and failed to produce a majority opinion, five of the justices determined that the false report concerned a matter of private rather than public interest and distinguished the *Gertz* rule concerning punitive or presumed damages.

---

37. *Gertz*, 418 U.S. at 349.
38. 472 U.S. 749 (1985).

The original judgment from the trial court, consisting of both compensatory and punitive damages, would be permitted to stand.

Proof of Damages

In the chapter 3 review of the elements of the common law of libel, the distinction between libel per se (utterances that are obviously defamatory) and libel per quod (statements whose defamatory nature is not apparent unless the audience has additional facts at its disposal) was introduced. Traditionally, in libel per se situations the plaintiff did not need to prove damages; it was assumed that a person falsely accused of being a criminal or an incompetent had been damaged.

The *Gertz* majority expresses concern that the ready availability of presumed damages (the kind of award that most logically fits libel per se situations) gives juries too much freedom to stifle debate on important issues of the day. The Supreme Court fashioned a two-part remedy. First it established the rule, from which it retreated a bit in the later *Dun & Bradstreet* decision, requiring plaintiffs seeking presumed damages to prove actual malice. Second, it required plaintiffs who were not otherwise required to prove actual malice to show some kind of actual harm. Only the second rule is relevant to the libel per se category, and it surely represents a partial repudiation of the category. Under the first rule, however, presumed damages are still permitted, and proving actual malice is really quite irrelevant to whether or not the plaintiff

---

THINGS TO REMEMBER

Gertz v. Robert Welch, Inc. (1974)

- The plaintiff's category (public figure or public official, or private citizen) is still the main determinant of whether actual malice must be proved.
- There are two public policy reasons for treating public plaintiffs differently:
  - They generally chose the limelight.
  - They often have access to the media to refute any damaging remarks.
- There are two kinds of public figures:
  - All-purpose or general public figures, who always must prove actual malice
  - Limited public figures, who must prove actual malice only if the libelous remarks concerned the controversy they sought out
- With respect to private plaintiffs, individual states are free to determine what level of fault such plaintiffs must show (mere negligence, actual malice, or something in between).
- All plaintiffs must prove harm to win damages (diluting the libel per se category from common law).
- Plaintiffs who wish to receive punitive damages must prove actual malice (in a later case, the Court limited this rule to situations involving libel on a matter of public interest).

has been harmed. Thus the majority opinion does not quite sound the death knell for the distinction between libel per se and libel per quod.

A fascinating feature of *Gertz*, however, is that Justice White's dissenting opinion makes clear that he assumed the Court *had* in fact gotten rid of presumed damages and thus the whole category of libel per se. "The impact of today's decision on the traditional law of libel is immediately obvious and indisputable," he wrote. "No longer will the plaintiff be able to rest his case with proof of a libel defamatory on its face or proof of a slander historically actionable per se." For whatever combination of reasons, Justice White's interpretation of what the *Gertz* majority had done has been accepted by many courts and commentators. Section 569 of the *Restatement of Torts*, for example, assumes that *Gertz v. Robert Welch, Inc.* discredited traditional notions of libel per se.

Chapter Summary

The landmark 1964 libel case, *New York Times Co. v. Sullivan*, establishes that public officials who sue for libel because of criticisms relevant to their official conduct must prove actual malice—that is, that the defendant either knew the accusations were false or at least published with "reckless disregard of truth or falsity"—with "convincing clarity." The Supreme Court emphasized that making it too easy for governmental officials to recover damages for libel is too hauntingly reminiscent of criminal prosecutions for sedition. Journalists must be given enough "breathing room" to make honest errors, the Court said, or they will experience the "chilling effect" of self-censorship.

Later cases have fine-tuned and extended the actual malice rule in many ways:

- "Public officials" include those who have policymaking authority and whose positions invite public scrutiny.
- Criticisms of "official conduct" include any accusations of criminal wrongdoing, as well as attributions of certain kinds of personal characteristics that have clear implications for public life.
- Not only public officials but also "public figures" must prove actual malice. So too must anybody who wants punitive damages (if the alleged libel touches on a matter of public importance).
- Even private plaintiffs, if suing the media over a matter of public importance, must prove falsity as an element of their cases.
- Appellate courts are free to assess anew the question of actual malice.
- Statements of pure opinions, ones that do not carry explicit or implicit factual allegations, cannot be the impetus for a libel suit.
- Plaintiffs who must prove actual malice may have access to reporters' notes and outtakes as part of the pretrial discovery process.

- "Convincing clarity" is the burden of proof on plaintiffs seeking to defeat a motion to dismiss.
- Libel plaintiffs may bring suit in any state where the allegedly libelous remarks were in general circulation.
- All libel plaintiffs must prove some degree of harm to win damages.
- Individual states are given a great degree of leeway to determine what level of proof of fault is required of private plaintiffs.

Chapter 5

INVASIONS OF PRIVACY

We need to begin with a short discussion about what this chapter is *not* about. It is not about the *constitutional* law of privacy, which focuses on the delicate relationship between individual autonomy and the need for governmental regulation. Whether Fourth Amendment "search and seizure" issues,[1] or Fourteenth Amendment "fundamental liberties" such as contraception, abortion, and homosexual conduct,[2] the constitutional right to privacy is fascinating and complicated, but generally beyond the scope of this book.

Beyond the Constitution itself, but still part of the delicate relationship between individual and state, sometimes the government passes laws that are designed to protect personal information about individuals. For example, the federal Fair Credit Reporting Act gives us the right to review our credit histories and to require that the credit rating bureaus include our side of the story concerning any items we contest. Another federal statute, the Family Educational Rights and Privacy Act, forbids schools to release students' educational records without parental consent. In 2002 the Supreme Court held the law did not forbid such practices as "peer grading," in which students are asked to review each others' papers.[3]

In the field of communication law, privacy refers to issues quite different from the kinds of controversies so far presented. Instead of concerning themselves with ways

---

1. See, for example, *City of Ontario v. Quon*, 130 S. Ct. 2619 (2010) (Fourth Amendment does not protect employees' personal text messaging on employer-provided hardware); *Safford United School Disctict #1 v. Redding*, 129 S. Ct. 2633 (2009) (Fourth Amendment protects public school student from underwear search); *Arizona v. Gant*, 129 S. Ct. 1710 (2009) (having already moved a suspect to their patrol car, police violated Fourth Amendment when searching his car without permission).

2. *Griswold v. Connecticut*, 381 U.S. 479 (1965) (contraception); *Roe v. Wade*, 410 U.S. 113 (1973) (abortion); *Lawrence v. Texas*, 539 U.S. 558 (2003) (homosexual relations); see generally Jamal Greene, "Liberty: The So-Called Right to Privacy," 43 *U.C. Davis Law Review* 715 (2010).

3. *Owasso Independent School District v. Falvo*, 534 U.S. 426 (2002).

in which government might infringe on our personal autonomy, students of the law of privacy in communication focus on the relationship between the media and the people from whom they seek information and about whom they write. We now begin our more formal exploration of this body of law with a discussion of two seminal publications, seventy years apart.

A Tale of Two Law Review Articles

There is a great degree of concern in this country about the use of technology—surveillance cameras, software that can monitor the strokes we make on a computer keyboard, sophisticated databases that create elaborate profiles of our purchasing habits, and so on—to invade our privacy. Such concerns are not new, of course. Indeed, it is not much of an exaggeration to say that when two prominent lawyers wrote about their similar concerns in the nineteenth century,[4] they laid the foundation for modern U.S. privacy law. Compared with the centuries-old body of libel law, then, privacy is a relative newcomer to the American legal scene, even if it does pre-date the microchip. Boston attorneys Samuel Warren and Louis Brandeis—the latter of whom would later achieve lasting fame as a U.S. Supreme Court justice—expressed their concern that such "recent inventions" as *instantaneous photographs . . . have invaded the sacred precincts of private and domestic life.*" The italicized phrase does not refer to global positioning systems or digital cameras but to photographic technology having advanced to the point where subjects did not have to remain motionless for twenty minutes to have their images captured on film. At the time, this advance seemed a huge encroachment on personal privacy. In the early days of photography, subjects may have always appeared stiff and ghostlike, but at least the potential for being photographed in a "candid" moment had not yet arrived.

Warren and Brandeis recognized that technological advances were not the only cause of privacy invasion. Indeed, citizens' privacy was most threatened by the combination of the "prurient taste" of the masses and the willingness on the part of the working press to satisfy that taste by filling "column after column . . . with idle gossip," by "overstepping in every direction the obvious bounds of propriety and of decency." (Contemporary social critics say much the same thing about cable networks' filling their twenty-four-hour "news hole" with salacious details of the latest homicide or child abduction). To combat these journalistic excesses, Warren and Brandeis concluded, nothing less than the creation of a new legal cause of action aimed at protecting the right to privacy, the "right to be let alone," would do.

Whereas Warren and Brandeis's essay was *pre*scriptive, telling readers what the law *should* do, a second law review article written seventy years later served as a *descriptive*

---

4. Samuel Warren and Louis Brandeis, "The Right to Privacy," 4 *Harvard Law Review* 193 (1890).

model of how the American law of privacy had developed in the first half of the twentieth century. William Prosser, then the dean of the University of California–Berkeley's law school, reviewed thousands of court cases and concluded that privacy law had really become four separate torts.[5] **Appropriation** occurs when our name or "likeness" (i.e., face, voice, or anything so closely associated with us so as to transmit our identity) is used without permission for commercial purposes. The aggrieved party's interest in such conflicts seems to be more a proprietary one—"How dare you make money by exploiting me?"—than the more psychological harm to one's feelings that we normally associate with privacy invasions. As such, this category of cases really is more closely aligned to the issue of copyright (the subject of chapter 6) than to any intuitive notion of privacy. **Intrusion** refers to an invasion of one's personal space. The use of telephoto lenses or hidden microphones, or the incessant shadowing and stalking of a subject, might be deemed actionable intrusions. Such ex-

We have likely all seen old photos such at this one from the Library of Congress's Brady Handy collection in which the subject was told to remain stoic rather than to try to hold a smile for the twenty minutes or so needed to capture the image.

cesses, whether committed by media employees or others, would seem to have much in common with ordinary trespass. **False light** invasions of privacy, as we see later, closely resemble libel actions, with the key distinction being that the statements made about the unwilling subject need not be technically defamatory. The final tort is the one that Warren and Brandeis themselves seem to have had in mind. It has come to be called the "public disclosure of true but embarrassing facts," or more succinctly, **public disclosure**. This category expresses the proposition that there are some kinds of highly personal but true information that no one has a right to publicize about us.

A caveat is in order before we examine these four torts in more depth. We must remember that privacy law varies tremendously from state to state. Only about half the states recognize all four torts identified by Prosser in 1960. Which states recognize which torts is not a static set of facts; state supreme courts continue to decide either

---

5. William Prosser, "Privacy," 48 *California Law Review* 383 (1960).

Warren and Brandeis's concerns about how "news" coverage often bordered on voyeurism is certainly echoed by today's media critics.

to embrace or to reject one or more of the Prosserian torts. For example, Florida explicitly rejected the false light tort in a 2008 decision.[6]

Appropriation

In 2010 wrestler Hulk Hogan filed suit against Post Foods, manufacturer of Cocoa Pebbles cereal, over a TV commercial featuring a character identified as "Hulk Boulder." Hogan claimed, not surprisingly, that the character was clearly based on his own persona and was used without his authorization.

Appropriation, sometimes called *misappropriation*, consists of the unauthorized use of a person's name or "likeness"—voice, picture, and the like—for commercial purposes. This tort was the first of the four to develop in U.S. law following the publication of the famous Warren and Brandeis law review article. The first state to officially recognize the tort was New York, which did so by statute in 1903 in response to a ruling from that state's highest court the year before permitting the unauthorized use of a child's photo to advertise a milling company's flour.[7] The first state court to

6. *Jews for Jesus v. Rapp*, 967 So. 2d 1098 (Fla. 2008); see also *Denver Publishing Co. v. Bueno*, 54 P.3d 893 (Colo. 2002) (also rejecting the false light tort).

7. *Roberson v. Rochester Folding Box Co.*, 64 N.E. 442 (N.Y. 1902).

THINGS TO REMEMBER

The Development of Tort Privacy Law

- Compared with libel, the law of privacy is a newcomer to American law.
- It can be traced back to the 1890 publication of a *Harvard Law Review* article by Samuel Warren and Louis Brandeis.
- Most states now recognize at least one of the four distinct privacy actions identified by William Prosser in 1960:
  - **Appropriation** of one's name or likeness for commercial gain
  - **Intrusion** into another person's personal space
  - **False light** invasions (similar to libel)
  - **Public disclosure** of true but embarrassing facts
- All four of these actions are part of the tort law of privacy, which should not be confused with the constitutional right to privacy.
- Apart from the Prosser torts, specific laws and regulations are often created that are designed to further our privacy rights.

recognize a common-law right (i.e., prior to passage of any explicit statutes) to sue for misappropriation was Georgia.[8] By 1939, so many states had embraced a right of privacy against unauthorized appropriations that the tort was included in the American Law Institute's treatise called *Restatement of Torts*.

Hulk Hogan's suit against Post Foods was settled out of court.

Two Actions or One?

Appropriation is actually a hybrid tort. There are two different kinds of grievances involved. The first is the feeling of shame, humiliation, or even damaged reputation associated with having our name or photo disseminated widely in ways over which we have no control. The harm is likely most severe when our name is associated with a cause or a product with which we wholly disapprove, as in a strict vegetarian seeming to endorse a fast-food hamburger chain. The second is simply lost income. If you steal my name or photo to sell your product, you will have enriched yourself unfairly at my expense. If anyone deserves to make money off my name, it is me. Sometimes this claim is referred to separately in the law as the **right to publicity**, and it applies primarily to celebrities. At least thirty-five states have explicitly embraced the right to publicity.

In some situations, plaintiffs are able to argue plausibly both that the commercial value of their name has been stolen and that the nature of the theft is one that personally embarrasses them. This was comedian Johnny Carson's dual claim when he sued

8. *Pavesich v. New England Life Insurance Co.*, 50 S.E. 68 (Ga. 1905).

Johnny Carson won his suit against a portable toilet manufacturer, in part because he had a history of exploiting his own "name and likeness" for commercial purposes.

the manufacturer of a line of portable toilets called—you probably guessed it—"Here's Johnny!"[9] The defendant-entrepreneur in this case continued the wordplay by labeling his product "the world's foremost commodian." Carson was not amused, arguing that it went beyond embarrassing to "odious" to be associated with such a product. Although the court determined that the applicable right to privacy did not protect celebrities' hurt feelings in such commercial situations, it ruled for Carson on the more tangible publicity claim. Carson had shown over the years his awareness that he could profit from the commercial exploitation of his own celebrity status, such as through his marketing of a sportswear line bearing his name.

What Is a Likeness?

In a sense, the *Carson* case staked out new ground, in that the product did not usurp the comedian's name, but rather a phrase that had come to be closely associated with that name (and with Ed McMahon's slow, rising-pitched delivery). Indeed, the appellate majority emphasized, there would have been no violation of Carson's right of publicity had the defendant called his product the "John William Carson Portable Toilet," which would have been a more literal taking of Carson's name but would not have amounted to a taking of his identity as a celebrity.

In 2010 Lindsay Lohan sued E-Trade over its Super Bowl commercial in which one baby asks another if "that milkaholic Lindsay" had been over to visit recently.[10] Had she not dropped the case a few months later, she would have had to demonstrate that her first name alone— perhaps juxtaposed with the playful reference to substance abuse?—is enough to have viewers think of her.

Another individual often accused of being "famous for being famous," Paris Hilton, sued Hallmark for producing a greeting card that attached Hilton's face to a drawing of a diner waitress. The Ninth Circuit Court of Appeals denial of defendant's

---

9. *Carson v. Here's Johnny Portable Toilets, Inc.*, 698 F. 2d 831 (6th Cir. 1983).

10. Kieran Krowley, "Tot Shots and Lindsay—E Trade Baby Poops All Over Her," *New York Post*, May 10, 2010, p. 3.

motion to dismiss the suit was based not only on the visual image, but also the card's use of the phrase, "that's hot," often associated with Hilton's appearances on the TV reality program *The Simple Life.*[11]

Lindsay Lohan filed a $100 million misappropriation suit against E-trade over this commercial.

Certainly an identifiable photo of an individual can be a likeness, as we saw in the early New York case against the flour milling company. A sketch or drawing can also be actionable, as the publishers of *Playgirl* mag- azine discovered when their February 1978 issue in- cluded a drawing of a nude black male seated in the corner of a boxing ring. "Even a cursory inspection of the picture," a federal district court in New York concluded, "strongly suggests that the facial characteristics of the black male portrayed are those of Muhammad Ali.[12]

Even a fictional character can constitute a likeness. Groucho Marx's estate, for ex- ample, sued the producers of the Broadway musical *A Day in Hollywood, A Night in the Ukraine*, the second act of which playfully inserted the Marx Brothers characters into a Chekhovian plot. The defendants eventually prevailed on the grounds that the right of publicity could not, in the state of California, be passed on to Marx's heirs. More impor- tant for our purposes is the fact that the federal district court made clear that the right of publicity is broad enough to pro- tect the fictional characters audiences worldwide know as "the Marx Brothers," characters which "hav[e] no relation to [the] real personalities" of Julius (Groucho), Leo (Chico), or Adolf (Harpo) Marx.[13]

Hilton's suit against Hallmark was based on the use not only of her photo, but also of the catchphrase, "That's hot."

An infringement can also be found when the actors are less than human. Samsung Corporation created a series of humor- ous TV ads that pictured the company's 1980s models of audio and video products in whimsical futuristic scenes, as if to sug- gest that such equipment would still be working many years hence. One ad featured a robot wearing a wig, gown, and jew- elry reminiscent of Vanna White, posed next to a game board like that featured in *Wheel of Fortune*. The caption read, "Lon- gest-running game show. 2012 AD." White sued. The federal appellate court recog- nized that this case could not be handled as a "name or likeness" dispute. A "likeness" must truly resemble the original, and no sane viewer would think that the robot in

11. *Hilton v. Hallmark Cards*, 599 F. 3d 894 (9th Cir. 2010).

12. *Ali v. Playgirl*, 447 F. Supp. 723 (S.D.N.Y. 1978). The court also took note of the ad's use of the phrase "The Greatest." While we have decided not to run the somewhat graphic drawing here, it is reprinted on the website www.paulsiegelcommlaw.com under "Additional Images" (chapter 5).

13. *Groucho Marx Productions v. Day and Night Co.*, 523 F. Supp. 485 (S.D.N.Y. 1981), *over- turned on other grounds*, 689 F.2d 317 (2d Cir. 1982).

The right of publicity can cover even fictional "likenesses" such as the Marx Brothers. Although the decision was overturned on other grounds, this finding remains intact.

the ad really *was* Vanna White. Accordingly, the court expanded the right of publicity (in California, at least) to cover celebrities' "identities."[14]

Look-Alikes and Sound-Alikes

The law of privacy has developed to cover situations in which defendants have not misappropriated an *actual* image of a celebrity, but rather have done their best to create an *ersatz* image of that celebrity, often using the services of persons who make their living as celebrity imposters. We usually refer to these as the "look-alike" and "sound-alike" cases. In one such case, Jackie Onassis won a judgment against Christian Dior for employing the services of Jackie O. look-alike Barbara Reynolds in a slick magazine ad campaign appearing in publications such as *Esquire, Harper's Bazaar*, the *New Yorker*, and the *New York Times Magazine*. The New York statute governing the case addressed only situations in which a plaintiff's "name, portrait or picture" is used without consent for a commercial purpose. The court, however, in ruling for Onassis, concluded that the use of look-alikes could not be permitted as a means of skirting the intent of the law, asserting that "the commercial hitchhiker seeking to travel on the fame of another will have to learn to pay the fare."[15]

Film director Woody Allen was a plaintiff in a similar case, which was prompted by print ads for National Video that used celebrity look-alike Phil Boroff. That readers would think of Allen was ensured not only by Boroff's physical resemblance to Allen but also by the *Annie Hall* and *Bananas* videotapes shown on the store counter. Although Boroff was not a dead ringer for Allen in the way Reynolds was for Onassis, Judge Constance Baker Motley granted summary judgment to Allen on the grounds that readers might be misled to believe that Allen consented to the campaign.[16]

14. *White v. Samsung Electronics America, Inc.*, 971 F.2d 1395 (9th Cir. 1992), *reh'g denied*, 989 F.2d 1512 (1993); see also *Wendt v. Host International, Inc.*, 125 F. 3d 806 (9th Cir. 1997) (stars of *Cheers* sue over "Bob and Hank," robots in airport bars allegedly designed to resemble "Norm" and "Cliff").

15. *Onassis v. Christian Dior*–New York, Inc., 472 N.Y.S.2d 254, 261 (N.Y. Sup. Ct. 1984).

16. *Allen v. National Video, Inc.*, 610 F. Supp. 612 (S.D.N.Y. 1985); see also *Allen v. Men's Wear Outlet*, 679 F. Supp. 360 (S.D.N.Y. 1988) (similar result).

The Ninth Circuit ruled that this Samsung ad was an actionable misappropriation of Vanna White's image.

Celebrities have also brought suit complaining about advertisements that mimic their distinctive speaking or singing voices. Early cases involving celebrities such as actor Bert Lahr, singer Nancy Sinatra, and the 1960s rock group The Fifth Dimension were unsuccessful.[17] In each of these cases, the courts ruled that the right of appropriation was not designed or intended to cover such sound-alike situations. The legal climate seems to be changing, however, largely as a result of Bette Midler's suit against Ford Motor Company and its advertising agency for hiring one of her former backup singers to imitate the *The Divine Miss M* rendition of the old Beach Boys tune "Do You Want To Dance?" in a Mercury Sable commercial.[18] The *Midler* court saw its ruling as a relatively narrow one, having demanded that the plaintiff establish both that the imitation was deliberate and that the plaintiff's vocal style was distinctive and well known.

---

17. *Sinatra v. Goodyear Tire and Rubber Company*, 435 F.2d 711 (9th Cir. 1970), *cert. denied*, 402 U.S. 906 (1971); *Davis v. TWA*, 297 F. Supp. 1145 (C.D. Cal. 1969); *Lahr v. Adell Chemical Company*, 195 F. Supp. 702 (D. Mass. 1961), *aff'd*, 300 F.2d 256 (1st Cir. 1962).

18. *Midler v. Ford Motor Co.*, 849 F.2d 460 (9th Cir. 1988).

Christian Dior: Clothing for Men and Sportswear for Women

Suits, Dress Shirts, Neckwear and Accessories for Men. Jewelry for Women.

The wedding of the Diors was everything a wedding should be: no tears, no rice, no in-laws, no smarmy toasts, for once no Mendelssohn. Just a legendary private affair.

The portion of the head behind Gene Shalit (the bespectacled, mustached fellow) is Jackie Onassis impersonator Barbara Reynolds. So striking is the resemblance that readers would incorrectly assume Ms. Onassis had participated in the ad campaign.

Even though the fellow depicted here was not deemed an exact Woody Allen look-alike, there were enough cues in the ad to suggest falsely that Allen had endorsed the National Video chain.

The Political Figures Exception

The movie *Contact*, the faith-versus-science parable in which Jodie Foster spends her professional life listening for extraterrestrials and then goes traipsing off to meet them, boasts guest appearances, "as themselves," by several CNN journalists and President Clinton. While the CNN reporters contracted to appear on film, Clinton appeared against his will. Footage of actual speeches was cleverly spliced into the film's narrative. White House counsel Charles Ruff fired off a letter to *Contact* director Robert Zemeckis, complaining of the "improper" use of Clinton's public statements. The White House made clear that it had no intention to sue the filmmaker; indeed, the pattern of relevant precedents suggests that Clinton could not have prevailed.[19]

---

19. *Paulsen v. Personality Posters, Inc.*, 299 N.Y.S. 2d 501, 503 (N.Y. Sup. Ct. 1968) (TV comedian who conducted a tongue-in-cheek run for the presidency could not sue the distributor of a "campaign poster"); *Pam Media, Inc. v. American Research Corp.*, 889 F. Supp. 1403 (D. Colo. 1995) (producers of Rush Limbaugh's radio program have no cause of action against a competing radio program called *After the Rush*).

President Clinton would almost certainly have failed had he tried to sue the producers of the feature film *Contact* for its unauthorized use of excerpts from his speeches.

That public officials will almost certainly lose their misappropriations suits does not always deter them from trying to silence those who use their name or likeness without permission. New York City mayor Rudy Giuliani once ordered the local transit authority to remove ads that had been placed on the sides of buses by the publishers of *New York* magazine. The ad campaign's theme took advantage of the mayor's reputation for self-aggrandizement, with a caption that read "*New York* magazine— possibly the only good thing in New York Rudy hasn't taken credit for." The magazine sued the Metropolitan Transit Authority and obtained an injunction precluding the agency from refusing the ads.[20] Three years later, the mayor's image was used without his permission in a much-criticized public-education campaign conducted by People for the Ethical Treatment of Animals (PETA). A takeoff on the dairy industry's famous "Got Milk?" campaign, PETA's ad used a milk-mustached Giuliani to make a serious point about a posited correlation between dairy-product intake and prostate cancer. News reports indicated that Giuliani considered suing, but a sheepish PETA promptly withdrew the campaign and apologized to the mayor for making light of his own cancer diagnosis. As tasteless as this particular use of the mayor's likeness may have been, it is highly unlikely that a lawsuit for misappropriation would have succeeded.

Newsworthiness

We have already seen that public officials pretty much give up their right to sue for misappropriation whenever political commentary is involved. Courts have sometimes gone a bit further, creating what has come to be known as the "newspaper exception"

---

20. *New York Magazine v. Metropolitan Transportation Authority*, 136 F.3d 123 (2d Cir. 1998).

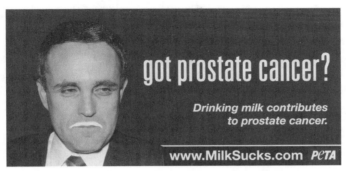

Even though neither New York magazine nor PETA had Mayor
Giuliani's permission to use his name or image in these ads, the
First Amendment protects them both.

to misappropriation torts. Newspapers and other news media are often permitted to
create printed works and other artifacts, the marketing of which would likely be actionable if engaged in by any other entity. San Francisco 49ers quarterback Joe Montana found out about this exception when he unsuccessfully attempted to enjoin the
San Jose Mercury News from selling posters bearing an artist's drawing of him that
had previously appeared in a special section of the newspaper celebrating the team's
record of four Super Bowl championships in ten years.[21] The court ruled that just as
the publisher surely had the right to print the drawing shortly after the 1990 Super
Bowl, so too must he still have the right to republish it a few weeks later.

The pattern of judicial results involving the highly litigious Elvis Presley estate is
also instructive. Elvis Presley Enterprises has aggressively litigated against those it perceives to be infringing on the King's name and likeness, the offenses having ranged
from the unauthorized marketing of posters to the naming of a bistro "The Velvet
Elvis." In general, whenever the presiding court has applied the laws of a state that
itself recognizes a right of publicity descendible to one's heirs or estate, those seeking
to present the unauthorized exploitation of Presley's work (usually the estate itself)
have prevailed.[22] A striking counterexample is found in a legal conflict surrounding
Elvis's famous Madison Square Garden concerts in 1972. RCA had an exclusive contract with him to market recordings of those events, but this contract was deemed

21. *Montana v. San Jose Mercury News*, 34 Cal. App. 4th 790 (1995).
22. *Elvis Presley Enterprises v. Elvisly Yours, Inc.*, 936 F.2d 889 (6th Cir. 1991); *Elvis Presley Enterprises v. Capece*, 950 F. Supp. 783 (S.D. Tex. 1996); *Estate of Presley v. Russen*, 513 F. Supp. 1339
(D.N.J. 1981); *Factors Etc., Inc. v. Creative Card Company*, 444 F. Supp. 279 (S.D.N.Y. 1977). Compare those cases with *Factors Etc., Inc. v. Pro Arts, Inc.*, 652 F.2d 278 (2d Cir. 1981) (applying Tennessee law and finding no inheritable right of publicity).

unenforceable against *Current Audio* magazine, which planned to use as its cover a playable LP recording of excerpts from the press conference given by Presley on the evening of one of the New York performances. Whatever might be the scope of Presley's right of publicity, the court concluded, it "has no application to the use of a *picture or name in connection with the dissemination of news or public interest presentations, notwithstanding that such activities are also carried on for a profit.*"[23]

Even though the model here had nothing to do with the awful narrative, New York's highest court held that the magazine could not be held liable for damages, because the general topic of rape is highly newsworthy.

New York allows a very broad newsworthiness defense, as is apparent from a case involving a professional model who had consented to having her photos used in *YM* magazine but was shocked at the specific nature of the use. Three photos of the plaintiff illustrated the magazine's Love Crisis column, which featured a letter ostensibly written by a fourteen-year-old reader who had "gotten trashed and had sex with three guys." New York's Court of Appeals (the state's highest court) held the state privacy law inapplicable to such a clearly newsworthy use, noting that the column confronted important issues such as underage drinking and date rape.[24] In many other jurisdictions the use of the photos might have been actionable as a false light invasion of privacy, but New York recognizes only misappropriation.

Another unsuccessful New York plaintiff was Jeffrey Lemerond, one of several individuals who sued the producers of the motion picture *Borat*. Lemerond is the fellow who hastens to get out of Sasha Baron Cohen's path on a busy Manhattan sidewalk, yelling "Get away! What are you doing?!" The encounter itself may not have been particularly newsworthy, but federal district judge Loretta Preska found that the overall theme of the movie—that modern society may be more "bizarre and offensive" than Borat—was newsworthy enough to preclude liability for misappropriation.[25] *Borat* was a lightning rod for other suits as well, including two of the three

---

23. *Current Audio, Inc. v. RCA*, 337 N.Y.S.2d 949, 954 (N.Y. Sup. Ct. 1972).
24. *Messenger v. Gruner + Jahr Printing and Publishing*, 727 N.E.2d 549 (N.Y. 2000).
25. *Lemerond v. Twentieth Century Fox Film Corp.*, 2008 U.S. Dist. LEXIS 26947 (S.D.N.Y. 2008).

fraternity members caught on film making racist and misogynist utterances and the driver education instructor.

A kind of newsworthiness defense also protected political activist Dan Frazier, whose Carryabigsticker.com website sells bumper stickers and similar merchandise boasting messages that are often whimsical but sometimes quite serious. At issue in *Read v. Lifeweaver, LLC*[26] was a T-shirt carrying the words, "Bush Lied, They Died." The "they" refers to the many American soldiers who had died to date in the Iraq War, and all their names are printed in very tiny type on the shirts. When the mother of one of the fallen soldiers sued Frazier's company, the court ruled that the defendant's action was not a misappropriation, in part because he was engaging in "core political speech."

The breadth of the newsworthiness exception in New York was enough to preclude Jeffrey Lemerond's misappropriation suit from going forward.

The newsworthiness defense is not so liberally interpreted in the Eleventh Circuit. In 2009 the court interpreted Georgia's misappropriation law so as to permit recovery for Nancy Benoit's surviving relatives. Nude photos of Benoit, a professional wrestler with a previous life as a model, who was murdered by her husband in 2007, found their way into *Hustler* magazine the year after. Benoit's murder was of legitimate public interest, the court allowed, but that did not make this nude layout newsworthy. Indeed, "the article was incidental to the photographs," Judge Wilson wrote.[27]

What might otherwise be an actionable misappropriation of a celebrity's name and likeness may escape liability if it entails a degree of parody. Thus, for example, when the Major League Baseball Players Association sued the distributor of a line

The suit against *Borat* by University of South Carolina students Justin Seay and Christopher Rotunda was dismissed. Also unsuccessful has been driver education instructor Michael Psenicska.

---

26. 2010 U.S. Dist. LEXIS 43879 (E.D. Tenn. 2010). See also *Frazier v. Boomsma*, 2007 U.S. Dist. LEXIS 72427 (D. Ariz. Sept. 27, 2007).

27. *Toffoloni v. LFP Publishing Group*, 572 F. 3d 1201 (11th Cir. 2009).

Dan Frazier, pictured here, was not liable for misappropriation, in that he was using the names of fallen soldiers (in very small print) to make a serious political point. Used by permission of carryabigsticker.com and Dan Frazier.

of baseball cards that made satiric comments about the players depicted rather than reporting the usual statistics, the Ninth Circuit Court of Appeals found that the cards "provide social commentary on public figures," and are no less protected by the First Amendment just because they do so with humor and caricature.[28]

The line between news and advertising is sometimes a fine one, a lesson learned by Dustin Hoffman when he sued the publishers of *Los Angeles* magazine for imposing his face from a poster publicizing his starring role in *Tootsie* on a professional model's body in a photo spread that included similarly superimposed contemporary designer garments on fifteen other movie stars as well. The photo spread was accompanied by a playful article called "The Ultimate Fashion Show: Grand Illusions," which made clear that Hoffman had been reoutfitted in a "butter-colored silk gown by Richard Tyler"—rather than the red sequined dress from the original movie poster—and shoes by Ralph Lauren. Although the designers with products featured in the article no doubt were happy with the free publicity, this was not the kind of *commercial* exploitation envisioned under California law, the court found. Rather, it was journalism, "a combination of fashion photography, humor, and visual and verbal editorial comment on classic films and famous actors."[29]

Similarly, an activist group supporting President George W. Bush's proposal to privatize Social Security (and thus critical of AARP's opposition to the proposal) was permitted to use a photo of a gay male couple kissing without the couple's authorization, because the point the group intended to make—that AARP could not be trusted, because it opposed the Iraq War and supported gay marriage—was clearly political.[30]

Cingular Wireless was not permitted to use without permission a reference to pioneering test pilot Chuck Yaeger in an online promotion for its advances in emergency notification procedures. Here is the part of the company's posting that caught the plaintiff's eye: "Nearly 60 years ago, the legendary test pilot Chuck Yeager broke the sound barrier and achieved Mach 1. Today, Cingular is breaking another kind of barrier with our MACH 1 and MACH 2 mobile command centers, which will enable us to respond rapidly to hurricanes and minimize their impact on our

---

28. *Cardtoons v. Major League Baseball Players Association*, 95 F.3d 959 (10th Cir. 1996).

29. *Hoffman v. Capital Cities/ABC, Inc.*, 255 F.3d 1180, 1185 (9th Cir. 2001).

30. *Raymen v. United States Seniors Association*, 409 F. Supp. 2d 15 (D.D.C. 2006). See the ad at www.paulsiegelcommlaw.com, "Additional Images," chapter 5.

customers." A federal district court ruled that Yaeger's misappropriation suit could go forward.[31]

In Florida the misappropriation doctrine is applied very narrowly, only to unauthorized uses of a plaintiff's name or likeness in *advertising*. Thus, for example, the movie *The Perfect Storm* could not be subject to a misappropriation suit brought by a surviving child of Captain Billy Tyne (played in the movie by George Clooney), because a movie was not deemed a commercial use.[32] A similar decision was reached in New York when a McDonald's employee sued unsuccessfully over her involuntary appearance in the documentary film *Supersize Me*. The court held that the use was not commercial in nature, that it was merely incidental (i.e., that the appearance was very brief, and the film's editing did not especially call attention to her), and that the subject matter of the film was highly newsworthy.[33]

That wrestler Benoit had been murdered did not make nude photos of her newsworthy, the Eleventh Circuit ruled. The court took note of the fact that neither the cover nor the table of contents even make mention of the *article* accompanying the photos.

As you have likely surmised already, whether and when the newsworthiness defense protects misappropriation defendants is hard to predict, in part because the law varies from state to state. The U.S. Supreme Court has not been much help, given the very strange set of facts that produced the Court's only decision to date in a misappro-

---

31. *Yaeger v. Cingular Wireless*, 673 F. Supp. 2d 1089 (E.D. Cal. 2009).

32. *Tyne v. Time Warner*, 901 So. 2d 802 (Fla. 2005). The ruling suggested that the plaintiff might have a valid false light claim, but the Florida Supreme Court has since rejected the false light cause of action altogether. See *Jews for Jesus v. Rapp*, 967 So. 2d 1098 (Fla. 2008).

33. *Candelaria v. Spurlock*, 2008 U.S. Dist. LEXIS 51595 (E.D.N.Y. 2008).

The distributor of Cardtoons demonstrates it was possible to make fun of Barry Bonds long before the steroid scandal.

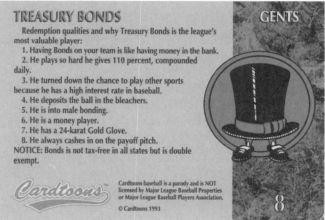

priation case. That *Zacchini v. Scripps-Howard Broadcasting Co.*[34] is typically referred to in the literature as "the human cannonball case" gives some indication of the unusual dispute involved. Circus performer Hugo Zacchini was in the habit of allowing himself to be shot out of a cannon into a net some two hundred feet away. In late summer of 1972, he was slated to perform his act, which takes approximately fifteen seconds from start to finish, at the Geauga County Fair in Burton, Ohio. A local TV reporter, without Zacchini's permission, filmed the act and broadcast it on the 11 p.m. news. By a 5–4 vote, the Supreme Court determined that the First Amendment would not protect the news media here from an otherwise legitimate suit for misappropriation, because the station had used Zacchini's entire act on the air. The *Zacchini*

34. 433 U.S. 562 (1977).

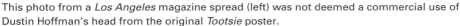

This photo from a *Los Angeles* magazine spread (left) was not deemed a commercial use of Dustin Hoffman's head from the original *Tootsie* poster.

case has been much criticized over the years. Zacchini's act lasted all of fifteen seconds, so how could the station have covered it *without* appropriating the whole thing?

The *Booth* Rule

Courts have also recognized a more specialized news media defense that protects promotional materials. Sometimes known as the *Booth* rule after a case involving the actress Shirley Booth, this doctrine tells media outlets that they are free to use materials they have already published in future advertisements for the same magazine or newspaper. Your local TV news no doubt does this all the time in slick spots containing short sound bites from previous stories, trumpeting its ability to get the news "first" and "best." In Booth's case, *Holiday* magazine, which had run an authorized

Candelaria's suit failed because the subject matter of the film, *Supersize Me*, was deemed newsworthy.

photo of the actress vacationing in Jamaica in one issue, the next year reprinted that photo in a full-page ad for the magazine. The court held that such media self-promotion is protected speech that cannot be the subject of misappropriation suits.[35]

In some jurisdictions the *Booth* rule has been broadened to permit a media outlet to use previously published materials not only for self-promotion within its own pages but also in advertisements placed in other media. Former New York Jets quarterback Joe Namath, for example, was unsuccessful in his suit against *Sports Illustrated* for using a photo of him that had previously appeared in that magazine in a later advertising campaign to drum up subscriptions that ran in *Cosmopolitan* using the heading "The Man You Love Loves Joe Namath."[36]

Consent

Permission is an additional, if obvious, defense worthy of at least passing mention. Misappropriation is, after all, the *unauthorized* use of another's name or likeness for commercial benefit. Authorized uses typically come in the form of licensing contracts, such as those entered into by just about all the celebrity endorsers we see in advertising campaigns. Even in the case of noncelebrity models, wise photographers will insist on a signature on a release form explicitly authorizing use of the individual's likeness. Whether such permission will be for a single specified use or will allow the photographer to reuse the image in unlimited future media and perhaps even alter the image can be subjects of negotiation. When dealing with models who are minors, a parent or legal guardian must sign such a release. Just how much power parents have to give such permission on behalf of their children was the source of litigation involving Brooke Shields, whose mother signed away their rights to photos taken of Brooke by noted artist Garry Gross and destined initially for a Playboy Press book called *Sugar and Spice*, but which were used in many magazines internationally. The courts eventually held that the permission was binding.[37]

How explicit permission must be is a question that has resulted in contradictory decisions. Consider first a rather bizarre case involving a former news anchor from

---

35. *Booth v. Curtis Publishing*, 182 N.E.2d 812 (N.Y. 1962). See also *Alfano v. NGHT, Inc.*, 623 F. Supp. 2d 355 (E.D.N.Y. 2009) (use of newsworthy photo of plaintiff helping John Gotti into his car in later advertisement for TV documentary *In The Mafia* not a misappropriation).

36. *Namath v. Sports Illustrated*, 363 N.Y.S.2d 276 (N.Y. Sup. Ct. 1975), *aff'd*, 371 N.Y.S. 2d 10 (N.Y. App. Div. 1975), *aff'd*, 352 N.E.2d 584 (1976).

37. *Shields v. Gross*, 58 N.Y.2d 338, 345–346 (1983).

the Youngstown, Ohio, market, Catherine Bosley. While vacationing with her husband in Florida, Bosley participated in a wet T-shirt contest. Imagine her embarrassment when video of her fully nude performance appeared in numerous online and other outlets, including a video in the "Dream Girls" series. The defendant had some strong arguments. Signs throughout the bar warned contestants that their participation constituted release to the rights of their images. Also, several of the shots of Bosley were hardly candid. That she was looking directly at the camera in a knowing pose might be seen as a nonverbal form of consent. Nonetheless the court held that more explicit consent was needed—if not in writing then at least orally—to negate Bosley's misappropriation claim.[38]

Compare the *Bosley* case with an Alabama Supreme Court decision involving Sam and Joseph Schifano, who often attended dog races at a local park and on one occasion were photographed while sitting in "the Winner's Circle," a special section of the park that could be reserved upon payment of additional fees. That photo later was used by the Greene County Greyhound Park in a brochure touting the advantages of the Winner's Circle. The plaintiff's suit alleging (among other things) misappropriation was unsuccessful. The unanimous court opinion emphasized that the plaintiffs had given implicit permission because a clear announcement had been made within the park about the photo to be taken

Pictured is "Hugo Zacchini, the younger son of Edmond," often billed as The Human Cannonball. His suit against an Ohio TV station resulted in what is still the Supreme Court's only "right of publicity" decision. Reprinted with permission.

---

38. *Bosley v. WildwetT.Com*, 310 F. Supp. 2d 914 (N.D. Ohio 2004). We chose not to reprint a nude photo of Ms. Bosley here, though it will come as no surprise to readers that such photos are all over the Internet.

Shirley Booth and chapeau, from a recent issue of Holiday

YOU'RE UP TO YOUR EARS IN OPULENCE

Holiday wades right in at Jamaica's Round Hill colony for a close-up look at how the other half of one per cent lives it up. The company is entertaining; the mood is delightfully intimate. Slim Aaron's perceptive camera captures these elusive spirits in mid-flight.

This is rich, it's Holiday, it's wonderful. With Holiday's highly personal point of view —expressed in a creative blend of words and pictures—the exotic scenes, places and pleas-

ures become familiar, and the familiar becomes freshly exciting.

It's exhilarating to Holiday readers—some 875,000 high-income families who are just naturally goers, doers, buyers, trend starters. Holiday whets their appetites for more of the good things in life, puts them in an expansive Holiday mood.

What a provocative selling opportunity for advertisers!

There's a rewarding new world for you in **HOLIDAY**

New York's highest court held that *Holiday* magazine needed no further permission from Shirley Booth to run this advertisement, a look back at an article from the previous year.

and the camera was mounted on a tripod in clear view and only a few feet away from the plaintiffs, neither of whom objected or moved.[39]

How can we reconcile the *Bosley* and *Schifano* cases, apart from the fact that they deal with laws in two different states (Florida and Alabama)? Perhaps one distinguishing feature is that once the Florida promoters learned that they had been blessed with a celebrity's image, they touted that fact aggressively in their marketing of the nude footage. By contrast, the Schifanos are not celebrities, and their names were never even mentioned in the brochure for the park.

Intrusion

Unique among the four privacy torts, intrusion concerns news *gathering* rather than news *reporting*. If, for example, shoving a microphone into a subject's face can ever

---

39. *Schifano v. Greene County Greyhound Park, Inc.*, 624 So. 2d 178 (Ala. 1993).

The man you love loves Joe Namath.

Of course he loves you best. But he also loves sports. So why fight it? This Christmas, give him what any sports lover is sure to want—a year of Sports Illustrated.

Does he like pro football, basketball, baseball, hockey? Tennis, golf, sailing, scuba-diving? Sports Illustrated covers them all, with yards of great color pictures and some of the most vivid writing anywhere.

So you can be sure—this is one gift that will fit him perfectly, no matter what size or age he is.

And it's one gift that won't be put away and forgotten soon after Christmas. Every week...season after season...52 times next year...he'll be opening up a new surprise package from you. You save $2 on every subscription after the first

one. So it pays to give Sports Illustrated to all the sports lovers in your life.

Just fill in and mail the attached order card—it's the easiest shopping trip you'll make this Christmas season.

As soon as we get your order, we'll send you handsome gift announcements to sign and put under the tree. And if you act soon, we'll be able to start your gift subscriptions right at the holidays with our spectacular year-end Double Issue.

Think about it—is there any other gift that gives a man so much good healthy pleasure...for so long...for so little money?

Mail the attached card right now. He'll love Sports Illustrated—and love you for it.

SPORTS ILLUSTRATED FOR CHRISTMAS

Jets quarterback Joe Namath had no legal recourse against *Sports Illustrated* for using this news photo to drum up subscriptions from readers of *Cosmopolitan*.

be an actionable intrusion, it will be so even if no news story ever results. The *Restatement (Second) of Torts* says that we can be held liable for intrusion if we "intentionally intrude, physically or otherwise, upon the solitude or seclusion of another or his private affairs or concerns," and if that intrusion "would be highly offensive to a reasonable person."[40] Depending on the jurisdiction—about four-fifths of the states recognize the tort—actionable intrusions may consist of the use of telephoto lenses or hidden recording equipment, incessant surveillance, or the failure to identify oneself as a reporter.

Precisely because the actionable harm in intrusion cases occurs via the news-*gathering* process, the First Amendment offers the press only very limited, if any, protection. As one writer put it, "To deny holding the tabloid media liable for an intrusive invasion of privacy is similar to holding a local television news crew immune from

---

40. *Restatement (Second) of Torts* § 652B (1977).

Brooke Shields was not happy having this photo continuing to be exploited after she reached majority, but the authorization granted by her mother was deemed binding.

tort liability for its van intentionally running over someone on its way to cover a big story."[41]

Reasonable Expectation of Privacy

Intrusion cases are very much bound by context, and courts often ask whether the plaintiff had a reasonable expectation of privacy in the situation that gave rise to the complaint. This is a concept borrowed from the Fourth Amendment constitutional right to privacy against unreasonable searches and seizures.[42] In constitutional cases, the person complaining of a privacy invasion is typically a criminal defendant. By contrast, in media privacy cases the person whose privacy was purportedly invaded tends to be the civil plaintiff. In one of the more frequently cited media intrusion cases, a federal appellate court upheld a judgment against a pair of *Life* magazine reporters who, acting pursuant to an agreement with the Los Angeles district attorney's office, pretended to be potential patients and entered the premises of a disabled veteran who apparently was practicing medicine without a license. The magazine's liability was based not so much on the reporters' lack of candor with the plaintiff as on their having used a hidden camera and audio-recording device. "One who invites another to his home or office takes a risk that the visitor may not be what he seems," the court allowed, "and that the visitor may repeat all he hears and observes when he leaves. But he does not and should not be required to take the risk that what is heard and seen will be transmitted by photograph or recording, or in our modern world, in full living color and hi-fi to the public at large or to any segment of it that the visitor may select."[43] In other words, it is not reasonable to expect that reporters will tell us the truth, even in gaining access to our place of business, but it is reasonable to expect they will not record us surreptitiously while deceiving us about their identity.

41. Eduardo W. Gonzalez, "'Get That Camera out of My Face!' An Examination of the Viability of Suing 'Tabloid Television' for Invasion of Privacy," 51 *University of Miami Law Review* 935, 952 (1997).

42. *Safford United School District #1 v. Redding*, 129 S. Ct. 2633 (2009); *Arizona v. Gant*, 129 S. Ct. 1710 (2009); *Virginia v. Moore*, 553 U.S. 164 (2008); *Weeks v. United States*, 232 U.S. 383 (1914); *Terry v. Ohio*, 392 U.S. 1 (1968); *Katz v. United States*, 389 U.S. 347 (1967); *Smith v. Maryland*, 442 U.S. 735 (1979).

43. *Dietemann v. Time, Inc.*, 449 F.2d 245, 249 (9th Cir. 1971).

THINGS TO REMEMBER

Appropriation

- There are two distinct grievances:
  - Purely financial ("How dare you profit from my good name?")
  - Personal dignity ("You could not pay me enough to be associated with that particular product!")
- A "likeness" for purposes of appropriation suits is anything that conjures up in readers' minds the image of the plaintiff.
- Even fictional characters can have recognizable "likenesses."
- "Look-alike" and "sound-alike" takings can be actionable.
- Politicians who sue over appropriations of their likenesses almost always lose, usually because courts conclude that the resulting "speech" is a form of political commentary.
- An otherwise actionable appropriation can be saved if it is part of a legitimate news story.
- Some courts have created a "newspaper exception" to the tort, permitting the media to sell posters or similar items that would almost certainly be considered commercial misappropriations if marketed by nonmedia companies.

Despite the quoted words from the *Dietemann* case offered above, more recent decisions citing it as a precedent case often emphasize the fact that the reporters lied about their identities as the more important violation of the plaintiff's reasonable privacy expectation. For example, an American Airlines flight attendant interviewed outside her doorway by an ABC news producer the day after her service as part of the crew on O. J. Simpson's flight from Los Angeles to Chicago (the night Nicole Brown Simpson and Ron Goldman were found murdered) was unsuccessful in her intrusion suit against the network, even though she was unaware she was being taped. The federal appellate court distinguished these facts from those of the *Dietemann* case described earlier, in that here no one "had gained entrance into another's home by subterfuge."[44]

While it is generally true that we must expect less privacy when we are out and about than when we are in the sanctity of our homes, even in public we might enjoy some privacy against photographers hounding us. The leading case here, though many years ago, concerned Jacqueline Onassis and children Caroline and John, Jr. Her nemesis for years had been freelance photographer Ronald Galella, who trailed Onassis everywhere, hiding in bushes and behind coatracks in restaurants and even intruding into her children's schools. The remedy applied by the court was an injunction against further harassment by Galella; it did not prohibit him from photograph-

---

44. *DeTeresa v. ABC*, 121 F.3d 460, 466 (9th Cir. 1997).

Dr. Dietemann (right) would have had a viable intrusion case against *Life* magazine even if the article about him had never appeared in print.

ing the family, although it required that he stand as far as one hundred yards away from his subjects.[45]

Recall that the *Restatement*'s definition of intrusion depends in part on "offensiveness." In particular contexts, especially offensive intrusions may violate our expectations of privacy. Consider a California Supreme Court decision involving automobile accident victim Ruth Shulman, whose conversations with an attending nurse while she was rescued from her car and while being transported to a local hospital in a rescue helicopter were filmed without her consent.[46] Writing for the majority, Judge Werdegar admitted that there normally would be no reasonable expectation of privacy against the media's coverage of an accident scene. But here the attending nurse herself was induced by the media representatives to wear a microphone, a practice the

---

45. *Galella v. Onassis*, 353 F. Supp. 196 (S.D.N.Y. 1972), *aff'd*, 487 F.2d 986 (2d Cir. 1973). The appellate decision generally reduced the restricted zone to twenty-five feet.

46. *Shulman v. Group W Productions, Inc.*, 955 P.2d 469 (Cal. 1998).

court found a "highly offensive" way "to intercept what would otherwise be private conversations with an injured patient."

In Fourth Amendment cases, there is no reasonable expectation of privacy in—and thus the police need not obtain a warrant to seize—materials that are not hidden, that are in plain sight. Analogously, in the tort law governing privacy and the media, courts have held that there is no intrusion when the media photograph or record, from a public place, what disinterested passersby could just as easily have seen or heard for themselves. In a frequently cited case, a Seattle TV station camera had been set up to peer inside a drugstore window, recording actions of a pharmacist who had recently been indicted for Medicaid fraud. There was no intrusion, the Washington Supreme Court held, in that the camera recorded "a public sight which anyone would be free to see."[47]

The plain-sight exception to intrusion is apparently not limited to mass media defendants. Consider an odd case involving feuding neighbors in Illinois, one of whom affixed a surveillance camera to his own home that recorded activities in his neighbor's driveway and garage twenty-four hours a day. The neighbor sued, but a state appellate court pointed out that any attentive passerby, and certainly a roofer or tree trimmer, would have had access to the same spaces monitored by the camera.[48]

"Ride-Along" Intrusions

In a fascinating example of art imitating life, the ABC TV network announced in 2010 that the cop drama *Detroit 1-8-7* was being reshot so as to eliminate any suggestion that the fictional police were being shadowed by a camera crew. The posited relationship between law enforcement and media was no longer tenable in a show set in Detroit, whose mayor had recently forbidden the police department to invite TV crews on "ride-alongs." Apparently the impetus for Mayor Bing's decision was the tragic death of a seven-year-old during a police raid which was itself being covered by a cable channel.[49]

The *Detroit 1-8-7* story is reminiscent in some ways of a tragic incident surrounding a much better-known media "franchise." Perhaps you are familiar with the NBC *Dateline* series called *To Catch a Predator*, in which the network's Chris Hansen lies in wait to confront individuals who show up ostensibly to have a sexual encounter

---

47. *Mark v. Seattle Times*, 635 P.2d 1081 (Wash. 1981); see also *Haynik v. Zimlich*, 508 N.E.2d 195 (Ohio Com. Pleas 1986) (no intrusion where cameras saw only what others could have seen in the public areas of a police station); but see *Sanders v. ABC, Inc.*, 978 P.2d 67 (Cal. 1999) (protecting at least a "limited expectation of privacy" in conversations among office coworkers in close quarters); see *generally* Lyrissa Barnett Lidsky, "Prying, Spying and Lying: Intrusive Newsgathering and What the Law Should Do about It," 73 *Tulane Law Review* 173 (1998).

48. *Schiller v. Mitchell*, 828 N.E.2d 323 (Ill. App. Ct. 2005).

49. "Coming ABC Cop Show Drops Its Documentary-Style Look," *New York Times*, July 9, 2010, C2.

with someone who had posed as a minor in an Internet chat room. Hansen chastises the alleged pedophiles, who typically make a hasty exit soon after they learn that their conversation has been videotaped for possible future airing on the network.

These "predators" may have broken state and federal laws simply by their online conduct—especially if they have sent sexually explicit photos to someone they had reason to believe was underage. In an incident that never aired on the NBC series, Hansen and crew staked out the home of an individual in Texas (a former prosecutor) as the local police were preparing to arrest the individual. But Louis W. Conradt, Jr., committed suicide rather than be arrested. Conradt's surviving family members' suit against NBC was settled out of court in 2008.[50]

The Conradt incident was a departure from the usual *Dateline* formula, in that the police apparently invited NBC along, rather than NBC inviting local police into the homes where the network had set up stings. Actually, most of the case law involving plaintiffs upset at interactions between media and law enforcement flow from situation in which media "ride along" with the police.

In a unanimous 1999 decision, the Supreme Court held that law enforcement agencies may be found in violation of the Fourth Amendment for inviting media to observe their activities conducted in a private residence.[51] Dominic Wilson was wanted by federal authorities for violating his probation on previous charges of robbery, theft, and assault with intent to rob. When U.S. Marshals stormed what they thought was Wilson's home—they in fact had the wrong address and mistakenly pointed guns at the suspect's father—they invited *Washington Post* reporters along. The Wilsons sued the government (not the *Post*), and the Supreme Court made clear that police may invite to events such as the execution of search and arrest warrants only nonparticipants who have a direct stake in the event, such as crime victims who can identify their stolen property. The Court did not provide guidance as to what the newspaper's own liability might have been.

Generally the pattern of lower court case law suggests that media are most vulnerable when they not only ride along but also act in tandem with law enforcement, For example, a panel of the Ninth Circuit Court of Appeals declared that CNN could be sued not only for trespass but also for violating a Montana plaintiff's civil rights. The network had accompanied U.S. Fish and Wildlife agents, who suspected Paul Berger of poisoning endangered species, on a search of Berger's ranch. The court was especially concerned by the fact that CNN entered into an elaborate agreement with the government agency, under which the network was granted permission to film as long as it promised not to air the footage until a jury was impaneled or a plea bargain

---

50. Matea Gold, "NBC Pulls Online Predator Suicide Footage," *Los Angeles Times*, June 26, 2008, E12.

51. *Wilson v. Layne*, 526 U.S. 603 (1999).

struck.[52] More recently, the Biography Channel's motion to dismiss was denied in a bizarre case involving *Female Force*, a *Cops*-like reality series focusing exclusively on the work of female police officers. Plaintiff Chelsea Frederick alleged that the TV producers worked so closely with the Naperville, Illinois, police department that when a male officer arrived to execute an arrest for her having failed to appear in court on an old traffic charge, her actual (on-camera) arrest was delayed until a female officer made the scene.[53]

By contrast, a police search of a St. Louis, Missouri, home, one of whose residents was suspected of keeping illegal weapons, produced a federal appellate ruling relieving the media of any constitutional liability. The court emphasized that the crew from local station, KSDK, although *invited* by the police to accompany them as they executed a search warrant, were not in any way *directed* by the officials to enter or not to enter, to film or not to film.[54]

In short, the more the media's presence and on-site conduct are controlled directly by the police, the more likely that presence can lead to media liability.[55] Some courts have emphasized also that media intrusions must be highly offensive to be actionable, that accepting law enforcement's invitation to enter a private dwelling even against the occupants' wishes is not itself sufficient evidence of offensiveness.[56] Finally, note that newsworthiness is generally not a defense in intrusion cases (since the tort does not require publication).[57]

Intrusions and Fraud

In the *Dietemann* case, it will be recalled, the *Life* magazine reporters were held liable not because they engaged in deception to obtain their story (by pretending to be in need of medical attention) but because of the surreptitious use of recording equipment. Does this mean that the media are always free to lie with impunity to obtain access to a residence or business? Does a newsworthy end justify a deceptive means?

As several courts have pointed out, deception is a necessary component of some kinds of reportage, from the restaurant critic who dons a disguise to avoid VIP treat-

---

52. *Berger v. Hanlon*, 129 F.3d 505, 515 (9th Cir. 1997). Technically, the Supreme Court, in *Wilson v. Layne*, affirmed this decision as well, although no separate discussion of the case's facts are presented. See also *Ayeni v. CBS, Inc.*, 848 F. Supp. 362 (E.D.N.Y. 1994), *aff'd sub nom. Ayeni v. Mottola*, 35 F.3d 680 (2d Cir. 1994), *cert. denied*, 514 U.S. 1062 (1995) (TV crew acting closely with Secret Service could be considered a "state's agent" capable of violating plaintiff's constitutional rights).

53. *Frederick v. The Biography Channel*, 683 F. Supp. 2d 798 (N.D. Ill. 2010).

54. *Parker v. Boyer*, 93 F.3d 445 (8th Cir. 1996).

55. But see *Prahl v. Brosamle*, 205 N.W.2d 768 (Wis. Ct. App. 1980) (no media intrusion when a search warrant explicitly authorizes videotaping of evidence).

56. *Magenis v. Fisher Broadcasting, Inc.*, 798 P.2d 1106 (Or. Ct. App. 1990).

57. *Miller v. National Broadcasting Co.*, 232 Cal. Rptr. 668 (Ct. App. 1986).

ment to the use of paired "testers" to uncover discriminatory housing and employ-ment practices.[58] In a 1995 decision, Judge Richard Posner of the Seventh Circuit Court of Appeals concluded that reporters cannot be held liable for trespass as long as their deceptions do not grant them access to truly private areas and they do not reveal "intimate details" of their subjects' lives.[59]

A few years later, a damage award of over $300,000 was assessed against producers of the ABC television newsmagazine *Primetime Live* after their reporters fraudulently obtained employment as Food Lion meat wrappers to research a story on unsafe meat preparation and marketing practices. On appeal, only a nominal award of two dollars for "breach of loyalty" (taking wages from an employer while engaged in practices designed to hurt the interests of that employer) was permitted to stand. The Fourth Circuit Court of Appeals threw out the huge punitive damages award, which had been based on the reporters' fraudulent misrepresentation of their employment and educa-tional backgrounds, finding that the real harm suffered by Food Lion was a function not of those false statements but of the broadcast story resulting from the undercover operation.[60]

Wiretapping

As we have already seen, one cannot discuss the privacy tort called intrusion with-out also talking about such related torts as trespass and fraud. It is also important to realize that certain kinds of news-gathering practices, whether or not they technically meet the definition of the intrusion tort in your state, might open you up to criminal prosecution. Chief among these are the use of mechanical devices to monitor or re-cord conversations (whether in person or telephonic) or to read another person's e-mail or similar computer communications. Both federal and state statutes can gov-ern these behaviors.

The law generally recognizes a difference between **third-party monitoring** (wherein person A records a conversation between persons B and C) and **participant monitoring** (person A records her own conversation with person B). The federal Elec-tronic Communication Privacy Act (ECPA) criminalizes third-party monitoring of oral messages as well as those sent by e-mail, satellite, and cell phones.

Other laws against participant and third-party monitoring are generally less strict than the ECPA. Most media representatives would agree that tape-recording other people's comments without their permission is ethically questionable at best. If you decide that you have a compelling need to engage in such behavior, you certainly will

---

58. Anthony L. Fargo and Laurence B. Alexander argue that courts need to more consistently recognize a "testers' privilege" for reporters. "Testing the Boundaries of the First Amendment Press Clause: A Proposal for Protecting the Media from Newsgathering Torts," 32 *Harvard Journal of Law and Public Policy* 1093 (2009).

59. *Desnick v. American Broadcasting Company*, 44 F.3d 1345 (7th Cir. 1995).

60. *Food Lion v. Capital Cities Cable/ABC*, 194 F.3d 505 (4th Cir. 1999).

THINGS TO REMEMBER

Intrusion

- Unique among the four privacy torts, intrusion does not require that anything be published. Therefore, the First Amendment is not a very helpful defense.
- There is generally no intrusion if the media capture images of scenes that any passerby could have seen (unless the media otherwise act egregiously).
- The Supreme Court has ruled that law enforcement officials might be in violation of suspects' constitutional privacy rights when they invite the media on "ride-along" observations; some courts have held that the media themselves may be sued for both tortious claims and for civil rights violations when they participate in the execution of a search warrant.
- That employees of news organizations sometimes lie to their subjects to gain access to property and obtain information is usually not sufficient to create an actionable intrusion claim.
- Reporters who surreptitiously record phone conversations with subjects not only run the risk of civil suit; they may be in violation of federal and state criminal statutes as well.

want to know if your jurisdiction criminalizes participant monitoring. Under federal law there is no criminal liability for surreptitious participant taping. Your local phone company, however, acting under directions from the FCC, likely has a policy prohibiting you from taping conversations unless all parties consent.

The majority of states use the same rules as the federal model, permitting recording of phone conversations as long as at least one party is aware of the taping. A dozen states, however, require that all parties consent to the taping of phone conversations.

Can wiretapping laws make reporters liable for broadcasting or publishing illegally taped conversations even if the media had no role in the taping? In a 2001 decision, the Supreme Court ruled that there was no liability against a radio station that had broadcast excerpts from cell phone conversations surreptitiously taped by someone else, at least when the issue involved is of public interest.[61]

False Light

The next of the four privacy torts identified by Prosser has much in common with libel. False light plaintiffs, like libel plaintiffs, sue because falsehoods have been spread about them. There is one very important difference between false light and libel, however. Plaintiffs in false light privacy suits need not prove that the falsities told about

---

61. *Bartnicki v. Vopper*, 532 U.S. 514 (2001). The newsworthy issue in the case was heated teacher union negotiations.

them are actually defamatory, only that they are offensive. Plaintiffs must show not just that they were offended by their portrayals, but that a reasonable reader or viewer would also find the depiction offensive. Thus Debbie Sue Croyle was unsuccessful in her suit against the producers of the independent film *Pittsburgh*. The film's plot finds Jeff Goldblum (playing himself) enticed by friends to come to the eponymous city to star in a local theater company production of *The Music Man*. Croyle, the theater company's makeup artist, is shown blowing gently while swabbing the star's neck with rubbing alcohol in preparation for taping down his wireless mike. Croyle's suit alleged that the scene, in which Goldblum coos at her to "blow some more," falsely depicts her as "a woman who would engage in fellatio."[62] Croyle may have been offended, but no reasonable viewer would have been.

Perhaps a few generations ago, when "a glimpse of stocking was looked on as something shocking," Croyle would have sued for defamation, too. In actuality, the vast majority of false light plaintiffs sue because of defamatory statements about them. In such cases, the false light claim seems to be a fallback option in controversies that should be litigated as libel actions. Indeed, when these plaintiffs prevail, it is usually on the defamation claim; moreover, false light's reputation as a "backdoor" libel vehicle has led many states to reject the tort altogether.[63]

The Hill Family

That the inaccuracies alleged in false-light claims need not be defamatory is apparent from the facts surrounding the leading Supreme Court false light decision; the falsity at issue might even be described as laudatory, as painting the plaintiffs in an inappropriately heroic light. *Time, Inc. v. Hill* began in 1952, when James Hill and his family were held hostage in their own Philadelphia-area home by three escaped convicts. A novel called *The Desperate Hours*, loosely based on the Hill family's ordeal, came out soon after. The novel was turned into a Broadway play starring Robert Montgomery. The February 1955 *Life* magazine article that became the subject of the lawsuit also reported on the then-upcoming movie version. The magazine article caused his family anguish, Hill alleged, not only because it exposed them anew to national attention for an episode of their lives that they would have preferred to put behind them but also because the article was fundamentally false. *Life* readers were led to the incorrect belief that the play was a completely factual retelling of the Hill family's experiences. As awful as the real ordeal was, Hill claimed, the *Life* account made it appear far worse.

In overturning a lower court's award of $30,000 in compensatory damages to Hill, the Supreme Court unanimously held that false light privacy actions involving news-

---

62. *Croyle v. Roar*, #07-1491 (W.D. Pa. 2007) (denying motion to stop distribution of the film). Croyle's companion claim for misappropriation also failed in that her name and likeness had no known marketability.

63. See for example, *Jews for Jesus v. Rapp*, 967 So. 2d 1098 (Fla. 2008).

worthy events cannot stand in the absence of a finding of actual malice—that is, that the defendant knew the story was false or published with reckless disregard as to its truth or falsity. By constitutionalizing the tort in this way, the Court demonstrated its concern that false light plaintiffs not be able to circumvent too easily the First Amendment protections granted the press three years earlier in the landmark *New York Times Co. v. Sullivan* libel decision.[64]

Debbie Sue Croyle failed to show that Jeff Goldblum's having said "blow some more" to her would suggest to viewers that she regularly performed fellatio.

Distortion

When text or photos appear out of context or in ways that omit key information, false light claims sometimes result. Let us look at two early cases from California that both stemmed from publication of the same photograph. The opposite rulings in the cases are a function of the photo's being used appropriately by one publication but in a distortive manner by the other.

John Gill and his wife were photographed without their knowledge while they were "seated in an affectionate pose" at a candy and ice-cream stand in the Los Angeles Farmers' Market. In one of the two cases, the Gills sued *Harper's Bazaar* magazine, which used their photo to illustrate a whimsical article titled "And So the World Goes Round," described by Justice Spence of the California Supreme Court as "a short commentary reaffirming the poet's conviction that the world could not revolve without love."[65] With respect to this use of the photo, the magazine publishers prevailed. The photo was not used in a context that would offend persons of reasonable sensibility.

The very same photo also showed up in the *Ladies' Home Journal*, but this time it was part of an article whose theme was that only some kinds of love—those based on an enduring affection, rather than simply physical attraction—are desirable and praiseworthy. Associated with the Gills' photo was a caption reading, "Publicized as glamorous, desirable, 'love at first sight' is a bad risk." The article refers to this kind of love as "wrong," as "founded upon 100 percent sex attraction," and as likely to lead to divorce. The Gills claimed that the article cast them, a "happily married" couple of "high moral reputation," in a hurtfully false light. The California Supreme Court agreed, finding that this use of the photo was "seriously humiliating and disturbing" in that it calls to mind "the intimate and private relationship between the opposite sexes and marriage."[66]

In another classic case, the publishers of the *Saturday Evening Post* erred when they

---

64. *Time, Inc. v. Hill*, 385 U.S. 374 (1967). See also *Cantrell v. Forest City Publishing Co.*, 419 U.S. 245 (1974) (false light claim is legitimate where reporter misled readers into believing that the subject of an article about a bridge collapse had been interviewed).

65. *Gill v. Hearst Publishing Co.*, 253 P.2d 441, 442 (Cal. 1953).

66. *Gill v. Curtis Publishing Co.*, 239 P.2d 630 (Cal. 1952).

ACTUAL EVENT, as reported in newspaper, took place in isolated house about 10 miles from Philadelphia. There three convicts from | Lewisburg penitentiary held family of James Hill as prisoners while they hid from manhunt. All three convicts were later captured.

TRUE CRIME INSPIRES TENSE PLAY

The ordeal of a family trapped by convicts gives Broadway a new thriller, 'The Desperate Hours'

Three years ago Americans all over the country read about the desperate ordeal of the James Hill family, who were held prisoners in their home outside Philadelphia by three escaped convicts. Later they read about it in Joseph Hayes's novel, *The Desperate Hours*, inspired by the family's experience. Now they can see the story re-enacted in Hayes's Broadway play based on the book, and next year will see it in his movie, which has been filmed but is being held up until the play has a chance to pay off.

The play, directed by Robert Montgomery and expertly acted, is a heart-stopping account of how a family rose to heroism in a crisis. LIFE photographed the play during its Philadelphia tryout, transported some of the actors to the actual house where the Hills were besieged. On the next page scenes from the play are re-enacted on the site of the crime.

As awful as the Hill family's experience was, the *Life* magazine article made it seem more so. (Additional photos from the article are available at www.paulsiegelcomm law.com.)

used a 1947 photo depicting a young girl who was lying in the street after having been almost run over by a car. The photo, which had previously run in a Birmingham, Alabama, newspaper, was used in an article about pedestrian carelessness, "They Ask to Be Killed," and was accompanied by the text "Safety education in schools has reduced child accidents measurably, but *unpredictable darting through traffic* still takes a sobering toll."[67] The magazine's use of the photo, even though some twenty months after the accident, was not the problem, the court explained. Instead, liability stemmed from the article's false implication that the young victim was responsible for her own duress.

Context is clearly important in false light cases. In a case involving *Baywatch* heart-throb José Solano, distortion was found not so much in a photo as in the way the photo was touted. The January 1999 issue of *Playgirl* magazine boasted a cover photo of a barechested Solano. In the upper left-hand corner of the cover were the words "TV Guys," accompanied by the headline "Primetime's Sexy Young Stars Exposed." The cover also promised "12 Sizzling Centerfolds Ready to Score with You." And in the cover's lower right-hand corner were the words "Baywatch's Best Body, José Solano."

Think about it: "Exposed." "Centerfold." "Best Body." Perhaps it was no surprise that Solano's false light suit alleged that a reasonable reader of the cover would infer

---

67. *Leverton v. Curtis Publishing*, 192 F.2d 974 (3d Cir. 1951).

This photo was the common feature of the two *Gill* cases.

that a nude layout of the star could be found in that issue's pages. In fact, Solano's only appearance within the magazine was a tame quarter-page head-and-shoulders photo "showing him fully dressed in a tee shirt and sweater, alongside a brief profile of the actor." The court determined that Solano should have his day in court (that the lower court erred in granting summary judgment to *Playgirl*) because "a jury reasonably could conclude that the *Playgirl* cover conveyed the message that Solano was not the wholesome person he claimed to be, that he was willing to—or was 'washed up' and had to—sell himself naked to a women's sex magazine."[68]

Whether a given context is distortive is an audience-focused inquiry, of course; put another way, distortion is in the eye of the beholder. Thus, for example, a plaintiff who is the aunt and godfather to a mobster's young son could not establish false light when the mobster's autobiography included a photo of her holding young Joey at his christening. Yes, the court allowed, many of the book's other photos were of mob-related incidents. But no reasonable reader would believe that the plaintiff's photo on this page reveals anything more than her family relationship to the book's author.[69]

---

68. *Solano v. Playgirl*, 292 F.3d 1078 (9th Cir. 2002).
69. *Raveling v. HarperCollins*, 33 Media L. Rep. (BNA) 1417 (7th Cir. 2005).

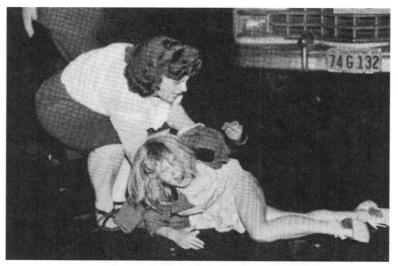

The *Saturday Evening Post* used this photo to imply that the young girl, rather than the driver, was responsible for her having almost been run over.

Fictionalization

Another group of false light cases result from the deliberate use of falsehood for the purpose of creating fictional accounts. TV docudramas, movies whose plots are based on real events but that take liberties with events, and historical novels have been the typical works to prompt such lawsuits.

Supermarket tabloids have a reputation for creating wholly fictional works more for the entertainment than for the edification of their readers. It is not surprising that they have frequently been defendants in libel and invasion of privacy suits. A particularly hilarious case involved the publishers of the *Sun*, which ran a completely fictitious story about one "Audrey Wiles," described as having quit her paper route—at the age of 101!—because an extramarital affair with a millionaire client on her route had left her pregnant. Since the story was a complete fabrication about a nonexistent subject—there was no Audrey Wiles—one would think that the article would have resulted in nothing more than a few chuckles. The newspaper, however, made the mistake of illustrating the story with photographs of the very real Nellie Mitchell, who was herself just a few years shy of the century mark and who was well known in Baxter County, Arkansas, as the operator of a local newsstand who did indeed deliver papers. Mitchell prevailed on her false light claim, with the court emphasizing that readers who looked only at the cover page of the newspaper would not necessarily realize that the story to be found inside was complete fiction.[70]

70. *People's Bank and Trust Company of Mountain Home v. Globe International*, 978 F.2d 1065 (8th. Cir. 1992).

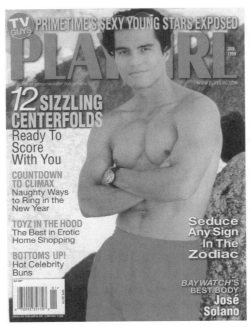

Mr. Solano alleged that this cover of *Playgirl* magazine strongly hinted readers would find a nude layout of him inside.

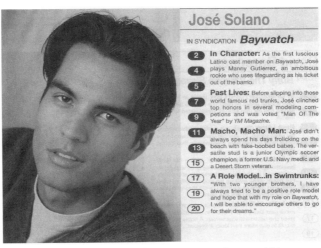

In the context of the *Solano* case, the magazine would have been on stronger legal footing if Mr. Solano's photo here *were* nude.

Public Disclosure

The first three torts discussed in this chapter add very little to American law. Intrusion is very similar to ordinary trespass. Misappropriation, as will be better understood after you have read chapter 6, has much in common with copyright law[71] (and to the extent that misappropriation suits are designed in part to protect consumers from confusion, also with trademark law). As for false light, plaintiff's claims are often merely fallback positions in a libel suit.

Public disclosure, then, is the only one of the four torts that truly adds anything new to the law. It should be admitted at the outset that plaintiffs rarely win these suits, and media defendants are especially likely to prevail.[72] Why bother learning about this feature of privacy law, then? Perhaps at least as much as a matter of ethics than as a matter of law. It is usually clear that we *may* publish truths that will embarrass the subject of our disclosures. The meatier question is often, *should* we publish?

Even textbook authors face such ethical considerations. There was a California court case in 2001 stemming from a *Sports Illustrated* exposé of high school sports coaches with police records as pedophiles.[73] This cover story included a photo of a Little League baseball team, and the article made it clear that the coach had molested five of the eight players pictured. From a purely pedagogic perspective, this would have been a wonderful photo to reprint in this chapter, indeed to begin the chapter.[74]

---

71. For now, suffice it to say that copyright is designed to protect an artist or writer's finished product (a book, a play, choreographic notations, etc.). At first blush, it would thus seem that the misappropriation tort is conceptually distinct from copyright, in that the former protects us from the unauthorized use of our "name or likeness," of our identity. We do not usually think of our name or our identity as finished products, as things we have created. Consider, though, that the most typical misappropriation cases involve celebrity plaintiffs who have worked hard to instill a commercial value to their name or likeness. What they seek to protect with this kind of misappropriation suit is thus every bit as much a "product" of the celebrity's sweat equity as is the artist's painting or the author's monograph.

72. Diane L. Zimmerman, "Requiem for a Heavyweight: A Farewell to Warren and Brandeis's Privacy Tort," 68 *Cornell Law Review* (1983) (only eighteen successful suits over the years); Randall Bezanson, Gilbert Cranberg, and John Soloski, *Libel Law and the Press: Myth and Reality* (New York: The Free Press, 1987), 116 (media defendants prevailed in 97 percent of cases).

73. *M. G. v. Time Warner*, 107 Cal. Rptr. 2d 504 (Ct. App. 2001).

74. After all, the case is a perfect springboard to talk about the difference between false light and public disclosure privacy claims, as well as the relationship between privacy and libel. The five students who had been molested would have a public disclosure claim against the magazine because their outrage was caused by the *true* revelation of their victimhood. For the remaining Little Leaguers in the photo, the cause of action would instead be false light, in that the photo *falsely* implied

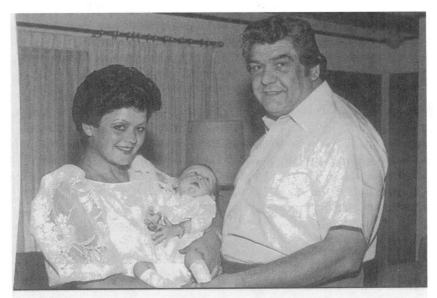

My son Joey's christening in 1983 was one of the proudest moments of my life. Here, my sister-in-law, Gail Barone, cradles him in her arms while Joey's godfather, Sal Bastone, beams into

The woman holding the child—correctly identified as the mobster-author's sister-in-law—could not maintain a false light invasion of privacy suit, because reasonable readers would understand that one can be related to the mob without being a mobster. Think Meadow Soprano?

Moreover, despite the fact that the California court told the plaintiffs their suit against Time Warner could go forward, my own educational use of the photo here would be protected both from invasion of privacy and copyright infringement claims (for the latter, see the discussion of fair use in chapter 6). But for obvious reasons, I could not bring myself to do it. The incidents of sexual abuse discussed in the magazine article were only a few years old, and the victims (and their teammates) are now young adults, no doubt trying to move on from this terrible memory. I suppose the argument could be made that the damage has already been done. Many more thousands of people have already seen the photo in *Sports Illustrated* than would ever see it in this textbook, and that same photo was used in a later HBO special, which was likely seen by over a million people. Yet there was that gnawing feeling that I should not be

that they too had been victims. For none of the pictured youngsters would there be a viable defamation claim, since to be thought of (even falsely) as a crime victim is not libel; it does not diminish one's reputation.

The subject matter may have been pure fabrication, but the fact that "Granny's" photo was of a very real Nellie Mitchell was enough to result in a successful lawsuit for false light invasion of privacy.

THINGS TO REMEMBER

False Light

- The false light tort is similar to libel, except that the remarks that cast the plaintiff in a false light need not be defamatory; they can simply be embarrassing (and false).
- In 1967, the Supreme Court ruled that false light plaintiffs who sue over stories on a matter of public interest must prove actual malice, just as if they had sued for libel.
- Falsity often results from the distortive use of photos or from purposive fictionalization (as in docudramas).

---

adding to the plaintiffs' grief or making the readers of this textbook even symbolic accomplices in the prolonging of that discomfort.

Although the public disclosure tort is not recognized in all American jurisdictions, those that do recognize it generally agree on its elements. A plaintiff must prove that

- the defendant publicly disclosed information about the plaintiff;
- the information was private (i.e., previously unknown to others);

- the disclosure would be highly offensive to a reasonable person; and
- the information is not newsworthy.

Let us examine each element in turn.

Publicly Disclosing Information

Unlike in defamation law, where all that is required is for one third party to hear the libelous statement, here the private facts must be made available to a wide audience to be actionable. "Wide" does not necessarily mean millions, however, and the mass media are not the only potential defendants in such cases. Employers who reveal intimate details of an employee's life to her coworkers, for example, have sometimes been found liable for damages under this tort. For example, a former town marshal in Winthrop, Washington, was permitted to sue the town for revealing that the reason for his termination was his epilepsy.[75] Also, a federal court applying Missouri law ruled that a Jane Doe's lawsuit could go forward against the doctors who disseminated "before" and "after" photos of her surgery for removal of excess skin to a wider audience than would be necessary for legitimate medical consultation.[76]

Previously *Private* Information

One cannot be held accountable for violating another's privacy if what is revealed was already widely known or readily available to all who wished to see. An often-cited case for this point is *Neff v. Time, Inc.*, in which a particularly enthusiastic Pittsburgh Steelers fan was upset enough about a *Sports Illustrated* photo narrative about him to bring suit against the magazine's publisher.[77] Neff and several other fans were, in the court's words, "jumping up and down in full view of the fans in the stadium" and "waving Steeler banners and drinking beer." That the magazine chose to run a picture showing Neff's fly open was deemed "utmost bad taste" by the court; nonetheless, he could not recover damages in that he "was photographed in a public place for a newsworthy article."

More recently, the Tenth Circuit Court of Appeals held that an invasion of privacy suit against *Harper's Magazine* resulting from the unauthorized taking and publishing of an open-casket photo at the funeral of a young man who was killed in Iraq could not go forward. The deceased was the first member of the Oklahoma National Guard to be killed in action since the Korean War; as such his funeral was deemed a highly newsworthy event, with over twelve hundred in attendance, including the state's governor.[78]

---

75. *White v. Town of Winthrop*, 116 P.3d 1034 (Wash. Ct. App. 2005).

76. *Doe v. Young*, 2009 U.S. Dist. LEXIS 101781 (E.D. Mo. 2009).

77. 406 F. Supp. 858 (W.D. Pa. 1976).

78. *Showler v. Harper's Magazine Foundation*, 222 Fed. Appx. 755 (10th Cir. 2007). The photo at issue is reprinted in chapter 7, where the case is again discussed.

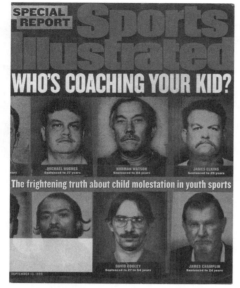

Do you agree with my compromise position, reprinting here the *Sports Illustrated* cover photo from *M.G. v. Time Warner*, but not the interior photo of the Little Leaguers themselves? Would your answer be affected at all by the fact that I typically do show the photo to my own students, and will even provide it to your instructor, upon request?

Another unsuccessful privacy plaintiff was Oliver Sipple, who achieved a degree of fame in the autumn of 1975, when President Ford was visiting San Francisco. Sipple foiled Sara Jane Moore's attempt to shoot Ford by grabbing her arm and deflecting the shot. As one can imagine, the national news media were abuzz with the story. When newspapers in San Francisco and elsewhere reported that Sipple happened to be gay—the first time most of his family learned of his sexual orientation—he took umbrage and sued. His invasion-of-privacy claims failed, at least in part because what was revealed about him was not deemed sufficiently *private* to meet the tort's demands. He was well known within the gay community, the court pointed out, having participated in numerous gay pride parades and even having developed a friendship with openly gay San Francisco Board of Supervisors member Harvey Milk.[79]

Some courts have had a slightly different take on the requirement that the facts revealed be *private*. Instead of focusing on how readily available the information was prior to the offensive disclosure, these courts concentrate on the nature of the information itself. For example, Minnesota gubernatorial candidate Jon Grunseth, whose high-level lobbying position frequently brought him to Washington, D.C., sued a Marriott hotel there for releasing to Minnesota newspapers a copy of a receipt that helped the media corroborate an allegation of a longtime affair he had apparently conducted with a Washington-area woman. The receipt at issue did not contain "private facts," the court pointed out. The receipt showed only that he had booked a room, not whether and with whom he might have been having an affair.[80]

Highly Offensive Revelations

The public disclosure tort also requires that the private information revealed be of a kind that would be found highly offensive by reasonable people. Consider the text

79. *Sipple v. Chronicle Publishing Co.*, 201 Cal. Rptr. 665 (Ct. App. 1984).

80. *Grunseth v. Marriott Corp.*, 872 F. Supp. 1069, 1075–1076 (D.D.C. 1995), *aff'd*, 79 F.3d 169 (D.C. Cir. 1996). Technically this was only dicta, in that the court's actual decision was based on the statute of limitations having run out.

of a *Time* magazine article from March 13, 1939, which resulted in one of the most often-cited invasion-of-privacy suits:

STARVING GLUTTON

One night last week pretty Mrs. Dorothy Barber of Kansas City grabbed a candy bar, packed up some clothes, and walked to General Hospital. "I want to stay here," she said between bites. "I want to eat all the time. I can finish a normal meal and be back in the kitchen in ten minutes, eating again."

Dr. R. K. Simpson immediately packed her off to a ward, ordered a big meal from the hospital kitchen while he questioned Mrs. Barber. He found that although she had eaten enough in the past year to feed a family of ten, she had lost 25 pounds. After a preliminary examination Dr. Simpson thought that Mrs. Barber's pancreas might be functioning abnormally, that it might be burning up too much sugar in her blood and somehow causing an excessive flow of digestive juices, which sharpened her appetite.

While he made painstaking laboratory tests and discussed the advisability of a rare operation, Mrs. Barber lay in bed and ate.[81]

Plantiff Neff could not recover for invasion of privacy, in that his conduct was recorded in a highly public place.

Accompanying the brief article was a photo of Mrs. Dorothy Barber in bed in a long-sleeved hospital gown, a close-up picture showing only her face, head, and arms, with the bedclothes over her chest. The caption read, "Insatiable Eater Barber—She Eats for Ten." The Missouri Supreme Court, emphasized that the right to privacy "should include the right to obtain medical treatment at home or in a hospital . . . without personal publicity."

---

81. *Barber v. Time, Inc.*, 159 S.W.2d 291, 292 (Mo. 1942).

Oliver Sipple shown foiling President Ford's would-be assassin (indicated by the black arrow). ©1975. AP Photo/*San Francisco Examiner*, Gordon Stone. Reprinted with permission.

International

INSATIABLE-EATER BARBER
She eats for ten.

Although Barber's suit against *Time* magazine was based on the public disclosure tort, it had strong "intrusion" elements, in that we usually think of our hospital room as a very private place.

Another case frequently cited in support of the principle that unconscionable intrusions into individuals' privacy should be restrained concerned Frederick Wiseman's documentary *Titicut Follies*.[82] The film depicted conditions in the Massachusetts Correctional Institution at Bridgewater, which housed "insane personscharged with crime, and defective delinquents." As a result of the suit, for many years showings of the film were restricted to audiences of mental health and similar professionals. Only in recent years, largely owing to most of the patients having passed away, has the film been made available for general release. Although the restrictions were apparently based on fear that the film would subject the inmates to intense humiliation, several commentators suggested that the real impetus behind the suit was government officials' fear that the unconscionable conditions at Bridgewater would be exposed to public view.

Although the cases involving Ms. Bar-

82. *Commonwealth of Massachusetts v. Wiseman*, 249 N.E.2d 610 (Mass. 1969), *cert. denied*, 398 U.S. 960 (1970).

ber and the patient-stars of *Titicut Follies* are important in the history of privacy law, it should be emphasized that courts today rarely rule for plaintiffs in public disclosure cases, even when the publication is deemed offensive. This pattern of results is largely owing to the importance of the tort's final element—a lack of newsworthiness.

A Defense Swallowing the Tort?

Newsworthiness is often referred to somewhat inaccurately as a defense to public disclosure suits. But this statement misplaces the burden of proof. In actuality, the burden is on the plaintiff to demonstrate that the offensive revelations of private information are *not* newsworthy, are *not* of public concern. In any event, it is clear that courts have made it very difficult indeed for plaintiffs to establish that revelations of embarrassing truths about them lack newsworthiness.

One of the leading cases on this point concerned mathematics prodigy William Sidis. Sidis was a Harvard graduate at age sixteen, but then dropped out of public sight for many years and became something of a recluse, at least until the *New Yorker* found him. The magazine often included within its pages a feature called "Where Are They Now?" which, as its name implies, sought to bring readers up-to-date on the once famous. The article's subtitle, "April Fool," neatly encapsulates what the Second Circuit Court of Appeals saw as the piece's condescending and abusive tone toward Mr. Sidis. The magazine focused on the "bizarre ways" in which Sidis's genius was manifested, such as his penchant for collecting streetcar transfers.

Although the court concluded that the essay was "merciless in its dissection of intimate details of its subject's personal life," Sidis's privacy claim was rejected. There are times, Judge Swan wrote, when "the public interest in obtaining information becomes dominant over the individual's desire for privacy."[83] After all, how better to determine if society's treatment of child prodigies is for the good than to examine the lives of such persons when they are no longer children?

The documentary *Titicut Follies* was subject to a restrictive order for many years, in deference to the privacy interests of the mental patients.

---

83. *Sidis v. F-R Publications*, 113 F.2d 806 (2d Cir. 1940).

"Newsworthiness" was defined quite broadly in the case of Carl DeGregorio's suit against CBS. The plaintiff was a construction worker upset at the station's having included in a story on "romance in New York" video footage of him walking hand in hand with an unmarried female coworker. DeGregorio unsuccessfully pleaded with the CBS crew to not run the footage. "It would not look good," he argued, because he was married and the young woman was herself engaged to be married. In dismissing the suit, the court interpreted "newsworthiness" as broad enough to include "an exploration of prevailing attitudes towards [romance]."[84]

Does newsworthiness wear off over time? Do persons whose fame has faded have a right to live in relative anonymity? Although the *Sidis* case seems to stand for the principle "once newsworthy, always newsworthy," courts have sometimes been deferential to plaintiffs trying to turn over a new leaf and start anew, to forget and have their neighbors not learn of embarrassing features of their past. But the pattern is shifting. Notably, in 2004 the California Supreme Court rejected the notion that a subject matter ever loses its newsworthiness for purposes of a public disclosure suit. At issue was an episode of the Discovery Channel's documentary series *The Prosecutors*, which aired in 2001 and recalled the facts of a hired-gun homicide from thirteen years earlier, for which plaintiff Steven Gates was charged as a coconspirator.[85]

The media have little to fear from public disclosure suits these days because courts asked to adjudicate the issue of newsworthiness most frequently let the press decide what is newsworthy.[86] The familiar and enduring masthead of the *New York Times* boasts that readers will find within "all the news that's fit to print." Courts seem to take these words to heart, ruling in perhaps circular fashion that if a subject matter has appeared in the news media, it must be news—that is, it must be news*worthy*.

The Supreme Court and Public Disclosure

The Supreme Court has weighed in on the public disclosure tort, and in two noteworthy decisions has come rather close to immunizing the press for reports of the truth. Both cases involved press reports of rape that included the victim's name. In *Cox Broadcasting Corp. v. Cohn*, WSB-TV in Georgia reported the name of the victim of a vicious gang rape and homicide, information its reporter had obtained from the official indictment provided to him by the clerk of the court.[87] The deceased's father then brought a privacy suit against the owner of the broadcast station.

The Court declined in *Cox Broadcasting* to rule on the central question—"whether

---

84. *DeGregorio v. CBS, Inc.*, 473 N.Y.S.2d 922 (Sup. Ct. 1984).

85. *Gates v. Discovery Communications*, 101 P.3d 552 (Cal. 2004). The ruling was based in part on the TV network's having gotten information from official government documents. See also *Uranga v. Federated Publications, Inc.*, 67 P.3d 29 (Idaho 2003) (unearthing a public record from forty years ago not a violation of privacy).

86. Zimmerman, "Requiem for a Heavyweight," supra note 72.

87. 420 U.S. 469 (1975).

truthful publications may *ever* be subjected to civil or criminal liability consistently with the First Amendment" (emphasis added)—instead emphasizing the specific facts of the case to produce a narrow holding. Cohn may not prevail, the Court held, but only because the broadcaster obtained the private information from a governmental source.

Florida Star v. B. J. F.[88] also involved the reporting of a rape victim's name, but there were two important differences between the facts here and in the earlier *Cox Broadcasting* case. First, the rape victim was still alive (and her rapist still at large). Indeed, as a result of the publication from which the suit flowed, the rapist phoned the victim's mother, threatening to attack her again. Second, although here too the media obtained the victim's name from a governmental source, the reporter clearly was on notice from the outset that the information was given to him by mistake. To be sure, BJF's name was included in the sheriff department's incident report, but prominently displayed in the same courtroom where that paper was distributed to reporters was a sign reminding the media that Florida law prohibited publication of the names of sex-crime victims.

Here, as in *Cox Broadcasting*, the Court makes clear that it does not intend to close the door on the possibility that a future public disclosure plaintiff might prevail against the press for its reporting of admittedly true information. "Our cases have carefully eschewed reaching [the] ultimate question" of whether "truthful publication may [ever] be punished consistent with the First Amendment," the majority further cautioned. The Court came rather close to reaching that ultimate question, however. Whereas it could simply have followed *Cox Broadcasting* to rest its holding on the basis that the *Florida Star* reporter had obtained the victim's name from a governmental source, it chose not to do so. The Court held instead that the *Florida Star*'s

---

THINGS TO REMEMBER

Public Disclosure

- Public disclosure is the only one of the four privacy torts that really added anything new to the law.
- The tort consists of four elements:
  - Information is published.
  - That information was previously private.
  - The revelation offends public sensibilities.
  - The revelation is not newsworthy.
- The "newsworthiness defense" seems to have swallowed the tort—it is virtually impossible for public disclosure plaintiffs to prevail against the media, except perhaps in cases involving especially distressing revelations about a child.

---

88. 491 U.S. 524 (1989).

story could not be sanctioned because the victim's name was "lawfully obtained." Although the Court later suggests that even truthful, lawfully obtained information might be the impetus for a successful public disclosure suit, it emphasizes even here that the state would need to be furthering a "narrowly tailored" interest of "the highest order." If helping to protect the life of a rape victim whose assailant has not yet been apprehended does not constitute such a compelling state's interest, one wonders if anything possibly could.

Chapter Summary

The law of privacy is a relative newcomer to the United States, owing much of its birth to an 1890 law review article in which Louis Brandeis and Samuel D. Warren argued that private citizens should have a cause of action against the nosy media and their intrusive technologies, such as "instantaneous photography" that no longer required the targets' cooperation in the capturing of their own images.

Writing seventy years after Warren and Brandeis, William Prosser catalogued the hundreds of tort cases nationwide that seemed to deal with privacy. He concluded that the states had come to recognize one or more of four distinct privacy torts: appropriation, intrusion, false light, and public disclosure.

Appropriation is the exploiting of another person's name or likeness for commercial gain. As we shall see in the next chapter, the tort shares many of the philosophical underpinnings of copyright law. Plaintiffs are more likely to succeed if they demonstrate an awareness of the marketability of their images (such as by having licensed that image to commercial products). Suits can be prompted by the use of models chosen to look like or sound like a celebrity. Uses that can plausibly be considered political speech rarely result in liability, even where the plaintiff is a comedian who was only pretending to engage in political discourse. Indeed, the fact that what would otherwise be an actionable appropriation resulted in an article on a newsworthy topic can help a defendant escape liability. Additionally, under the *Booth* rule the media have virtual carte blanche to commercially exploit images that they have previously used in a legitimate news context.

The intrusion tort is not too terribly different from ordinary trespass. It is the only one of the four privacy torts that does not necessarily involve publication at all. The offense occurs at the news-gathering stage, as in stalking a news subject or otherwise intruding relentlessly into his or her personal space. News media have been put on alert by a number of recent decisions that if they cooperate too closely with law enforcement officials in the live coverage of the execution of search warrants or police raids, they might be sued along with the government for violation of the subject's civil rights.

False light actions are similar to libel claims, so similar in fact that some courts and some states have rejected the tort as an attempted "back door" defamation suit. For those many states that do recognize false light, the key difference between it and libel is that the publication need only be embarrassing; it need not be defamatory. The Supreme Court has ruled that, when suing over revelations of matters of public concern, false light plaintiffs must prove actual malice.

The tort of public disclosure, which makes actionable the reporting of true but embarrassing, previously private, non-newsworthy facts, is the only one of the four privacy torts that adds much to the law. It is also the tort that is most like that which Warren and Brandeis proposed back in 1890. But at least in the past twenty years or so, in large part because the courts embrace the newsworthiness defense so wholeheartedly, public disclosure plaintiffs almost never prevail against the media.

Chapter 6

COPYRIGHT AND TRADEMARK

I n 2010 U.S. District Judge Alvin K. Hellerstein in New York pressed litigants to produce a settlement in a fascinating copyright lawsuit involving artist Shepard Fairey's ubiquitous "Hope" poster using President Obama's image in a Peter Max–like color scheme.[1] As you will recall from the previous chapter, the political speech exception to misappropriation law means that President Obama himself would have no recourse against Fairey. But Fairey admitted that he did not just conjure up Obama's image from memory. Rather he followed very closely (in terms of angle and facial expression) a photograph taken by Mannie Garcia for the Associated Press. Thus the AP likely would have a plausible claim against Fairey (Garcia dropped out as a plaintiff).

Article I, Section 8 of the Constitution tells Congress that it may create laws to protect "for limited times to authors and inventors the exclusive right to their respective writings and discoveries." The body of law designed to protect inventors is patent law. Most patents remain in force for seventeen years, although patents issued after 1995 last for twenty years. To be sure, there are occasional patent disputes surrounding communication technologies. For example, in 2005 we learned that our TiVo digital recording systems were not a violation of a similar unit patented by a company called Pause Technology.[2] But since patent law can cover just about any technology—including the proverbial "better mousetrap"—it is generally beyond the scope of this book.

The two more relevant areas of law flowing from Article I, Section 8 are copyright and **trademark**. Copyright protects a creative work itself, such as a book, movie, play,

---

1. Dave Itzkoff, "Judge Urges Resolution in Use of Obama Photo," *New York Times*, May 29, 2010, C2.
2. *Pause Technology v. TiVo*, 419 F.3d 1326 (Fed. Cir. 2005).

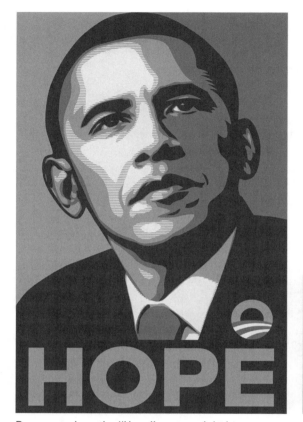

Do you see how the "Hope" poster might be seen as an unauthorized copying of the Mannie Garcia photo image of then-candidate Obama?

photograph, or song. (Again, note that the photograph of then-candidate Obama, not Obama's "name and likeness," is at issue in the lawsuit against the "Hope" poster). Trademark is designed to protect the slogans, logos, and trade names used by companies to identify their products and to avoid consumer confusion. If you think you are buying a pair of Nike sneakers, you would be very upset if your purchase was not in fact manufactured by that particular company. Although the two bodies of law protect different things, the philosophy behind them is remarkably similar. Both copyright and trademark are designed to protect the interests of the public itself, although the immediate beneficiary may be an individual artist or corporation. In the case of copyright, protection of the financial interests of authors and other creative artists exists to encourage them to produce so that we all can enjoy the fruits of their labors. Trademark also creates a financial incentive for businesses to create worthwhile goods and services. Such companies want the public to have pleasant mental associations with their brand names and logos. Again, a body of law designed in the end to benefit the public at large does its work by giving financial incentives to others who will then create things we will want to consume.

One key difference between the two bodies of law is that copyright protection lasts for a fixed period of time, whereas trademark protection can continue as long as a company is in the business of marketing the products identified by a particular trademark (and as long it renews the trademark every ten years). The distinction was crucial in a court decision involving the Three Stooges. The company that owns the rights to market the Three Stooges sued the producers of *The Long Kiss Goodnight*, a popular film that used, without permission, a thirty-second segment of the Three Stooges' film *Disorder in the Court* as the background for one scene. The court ruled for the defendant because the copyright on the Three Stooges' film had long since expired.

The court opinion indicates, however, that a different case would have been presented—one involving trademark rather than copyright—had the defendant instead been in the business of selling T-shirts with pictures of Moe, Larry, and Curly on them.[3] Indeed, the very next year the California Supreme Court upheld damages against an artist who had used the Three Stooges' likeness without authorization for his charcoal drawings, which were also sold as T-shirts.[4]

Under the terms of the Copyright Term Extension Act of 1998 (CTEA), new copyrights for works created by individuals last for the artist's life plus 70 years. This represents a 20-year extension in protection compared with the previous law. Works with

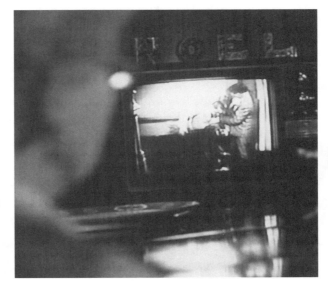

The copyright to *Disorder in the Court* had run out, thus precluding a copyright infringement suit against the distributors of *The Long Kiss Goodnight*.

---

3. *Comedy III Productions, Inc. v. New Line Cinema*, 200 F.3d 593, 596 (9th Cir. 2000).
4. *Comedy III Productions, Inc. v. Saderup*, 21 P.3d 797 (Cal. 2001).

The artist here was liable for damages because he had taken the Three Stooges' trademarked image.

corporate authorship will now be protected for 95 years after the date of first publication, or 120 years after the work's creation, whichever comes first.

The CTEA provided a measure of retroactivity in that works already created and otherwise due to enter the public domain will also enjoy a twenty-year extension in protection. This latter provision seemed to some constitutionally suspect. After all, Article I, Section 8 tells Congress that it may enact copyright laws "to promote" the creation of artistic and literary works. Retroactive extensions of a copyright's term promote nothing, the argument goes, because the affected works are already in existence. Also, it was argued that Congress's practice of extending the duration of copyright again and again, to the point of preventing any relatively recent works from entering the public domain, was at odds with Article I, Section 8's admonition that the monopolies granted by intellectual property law should be "for *limited* times." But the Supreme Court upheld the law. The twenty-year extension made sense for several reasons, Justice Ginsburg's majority opinion concluded. The CTEA brought American copyright law in closer harmony with European law, as articulated in the Berne Convention for the Protection of Literary and Artistic Works, which the United

THINGS TO REMEMBER

Basics of Intellectual Property Law

- Article I, Section 8 of the U.S. Constitution gives Congress the right to protect intellectual property.
- The three main branches of intellectual property law are patent, trademark, and copyright.
  - Patent protects functional devices and is beyond the scope of this book.
  - Copyright protects creative works such as writing, music, and art.
  - Trademark protects trade names, slogans, logos, and other images used to identify a company's goods.
- Copyrights for new works last for the life of the author, plus seventy years; trademarks can last as long as they are used in commerce.

States joined in 1989. Further, extending copyright's duration made sense because Americans live longer than we used to, and we have children later in life than we used to. "Life plus fifty years" provides less of a legacy for our children if we die when they are fifty rather than when they are twenty-five.[5]

The Law of Copyright

Let us suppose that twenty years from now, you have achieved a level of fame in your chosen field that makes yours a household name as much as the best-known and admired movie stars, sports figures, or political leaders. Imagine further that a former boyfriend or girlfriend, out of spite or greed, decides to write a "kiss and tell" book in which you will feature prominently and that this author intends to reprint several love letters from you still in his or her possession. You bring suit, seeking an injunction against the use of your letters in the book, as well as the return of the original letters to you. The chances are that your first wish will be honored but not your second, because the love letters, the actual papers with your handwriting on them, are the physical property of your ex-flame. You gave them freely, and a gift is a gift. The words you used to express your feelings at the time may still belong to you, however, and only you can decide if and when they will ever be published. That is the essence of the law of **intellectual property**, of which copyright is part. We use the word "property" to describe it, even though what is possessed is somewhat ethereal or intangible.

---

5. *Eldred v. Ashcroft*, 537 U.S. 186 (2003).

Scope

U.S. copyright law protects "original works of authorship, fixed in any tangible medium of expression." The statute enumerates many general categories of creative works, including literary works; musical works (both the musical notes and the lyrics, if any); dramatic works (i.e., plays, including musicals); pantomimes and choreographic works; pictorial, graphic, and sculptural works; motion pictures and other audiovisual works; sound recordings; and architectural works.[6]

A few clarifying points are in order. First, do not get carried away by the word *literary* in the first category. Yes, works of great literature are protected here, but so too can be the letter a college student writes to her parents asking for more money. This book you are reading is copyrighted, and so too are the sample examination questions in the instructor's manual. In other words, *words* is the key. The first category protects creative works that are made up of words.

As with literary works, we should not assume that "pictorial," "graphic," and "sculptural" works will always be the kinds of high-art creations collected by museums. Copyright also covers such useful art as clothing design. In a suit involving competing dress designers, for example, the Court of Appeals for the Second Circuit accepted as copyrightable a design consisting of "a geometric arrangement of color blocks banded in heavy lines" used on women's pullover tops.[7]

With respect to musical works, it is important to note that copyright protection can apply to the composition itself (as expressed typically in sheet music) and also to a particular performance of the composition (as set down in a "tangible" medium such as a CD). A particular arrangement of a well-known melody can itself be copyrightable and indeed quite valuable, as is the case, for example, with Nelson Riddle's arrangements of many of the tunes made popular by Frank Sinatra.

Characters in books generally cannot be copyrighted—thus when J. D. Salinger sought to prevent publication of the novel *60 Years Later: Coming Through the Rye*), his claim was that the work was an unauthorized adaptation of *Catcher in the Rye*, not that Salinger enjoyed a separate copyright in the Holden Caulfield character.[8] But sometimes the visual depictions of characters on TV and in movies can be copyrighted. This is the lesson of a fascinating case claiming that the 2000 remake of the 1974 cult film, *Gone in 60 Seconds* was a rip-off of the original. Allowing the suit to go forward, the Ninth Circuit Court of Appeals found that "Eleanor," a yellow 1971 Fastback Ford Mustang, functioned as a character in the earlier film.[9]

What does it mean to say that a work must be "fixed" in some kind of "tangible

---

6. See for example, *Peter F. Gaito Architecture, LLC. v. Simone Development Corporation*, 602 F.3d 57 (2nd Cir. 2010) (copyright dispute surrounding two companies' architectural plans for a development in New Rochelle, New York).

7. *North Coast Industries v. Jason Maxwell, Inc.*, 972 F.2d 1031 (2d Cir. 1992).

8. *Salinger v. Colting*, 607 F. 3d 68 (2nd Cir. 2010).

9. *Halicki Films v. Sanderson Sales and Marketing*, 547 F. 3d 1213 (9th Cir. 2008).

A federal appellate court held that the version of Eleanor the car from the 1974 film *Gone in 60 Seconds* (left) may have been protected by a copyright infringed upon in the 2000 Disney remake.

medium of expression" to be copyrightable? Consider the "pantomimes and choreographic works" category as an example. If you dance up a storm at a party, no matter how much you impress the other guests and how many of them try to mimic your steps, your creation is not yet copyrightable. The reason is not just because it was live and spontaneous. Your dazzling artistry will not be copyrightable even if you can repeat it step by step, move by move, on command. If, however, you commit to writing something resembling choreographic notation for your dance steps—and you need not be very professional about it—you will have a potentially copyrightable work. The requirement that a work be set down in some fixed medium applies to all the categories.

To be copyrightable, a work must also be "original." Being original does not mean that a work must be the expression of an earth-shattering, paradigm-shifting revelation. The law is not nearly so strict. In one case, a copyright was issued for a rectangular-shaped rock with the words of a poem—itself in the public domain—inscribed on it;[10] in another, a court found that an arrangement of percussive sounds lasting just one measure could be protected.[11]

The law is especially lenient with the copyrightability of photographs. Even when dozens of photojournalists cover the same event, each of the individual photos they produce is copyrightable, even though most of us would have a hard time telling one from the other. Photographs of things that are themselves copyrightable, such as a sculpture or a painting, can similarly be granted their own copyright protection. In 2009 a federal appellate court held that photographer Daniel Schrock held a legitimate copyright to photos he took of toys fashioned after the *Thomas and Friends* children's TV show.[12]

What is original in your work might be simply the way you have organized others' materials. Newspapers' sports pages frequently include very detailed information about the records of two baseball pitchers about to face each other in an important game. The statistics that are included in such a feature—overall win-loss record, more focused win-loss record against this particular opponent, and so on—are themselves

10. *Kay Berry, Inc. v. Taylor Gifts*, 421 F.3d 199 (3d Cir. 2005)
11. *Vargas v. Pfizer, Inc.*, 418 F. Supp. 2d 369 (S.D.N.Y. 2005).
12. *Schrock v. Learning Curve, International*, 586 F.3d 513 (7th Cir. 2009).

not copyrightable because they are readily available facts.[13] The writer's choice of which statistics to present and how to present them, however, may enjoy copyright protection.[14] This kind of work is referred to by the U.S. Copyright Office as a **compilation**, which the Copyright Act defines as "a work formed by the collection and assembly of preexisting materials or of data that are selected, coordinated, or arranged in such a way that the resulting work as a whole constitutes an original work of authorship."[15]

Collective works are special kinds of compilations in which the individual components are themselves original works of authorship eligible for copyright (and, indeed, that may have been granted copyright protection previously).[16] A collection of previously published short stories or poems is a good example. The collection itself becomes copyrightable, although the editor of the compilation will not then take over ownership of the copyrights already accruing to the individual contributors to the volume. Note, too, that the editor must obtain permission to reprint each of the works still covered by copyright.

What about movie adaptations of novels or stage plays? These works fit into the category of **derivative works**, which build on preexisting works by recasting, transforming, or adapting them. A colorized version of a previously black-and-white movie is such a derivative work, as can be a movie or TV program that has been made accessible to the deaf or the blind through the addition of closed captioning or descriptive video services. Creators of the derivative work are granted copyrights only for those creative elements that they added to the original, however. The people who add closed captioning to a TV program, for example, do not by this action earn a copyright to the program itself, only to the captioned version of it. It should be noted too that one must generally obtain permission from whoever holds the right to the original work if one wants to create a derivative work. Thus J. D. Salinger swiftly went to court to prevent publication of an unauthorized sequel to *Catcher in the Rye*.[17]

Things That Can't Be Copyrighted

Not everything that can be set down into some fixed medium of communication is copyrightable. The *Feist* case involving the competing telephone directories (see footnote 15)—serves as a reminder that mere facts cannot be copyrighted.

---

13. *National Basketball Association v. Motorola*, 105 F.3d 841 (2d Cir. 1997).

14. *Kregos v. Associated Press*, 3 F.3d 656 (2d Cir. 1993).

15. *Feist Publications, Inc. v. Rural Telephone Service Co.*, 499 U.S. 340, 362 (1991). The specific compilation at issue in *Feist*—a regional phone directory whose creators did not much more than cull together and realphabetize names and numbers from several smaller area directories—was not itself protected by copyright law.

16. See for example, *Bryant v. Media Rights Productions*, 603 F. 3d 135 (2nd Cir. 2010) (record album or CD is copyrightable as a collective work separate from the individual copyrights accruing to each of the songs on the album).

17. *Salinger v. Colting*, 607 F. 3d 68 (2nd Cir. 2010). The appellate court remanded the case to a lower court, finding it had used an incorrect standard of review.

Consistent with the Copyright Act's insistence that the law is designed to protect works that are already created (rather than in the nascent planning stages), mere ideas are not copyrightable, even if they seem to be fairly well-developed ideas. This was a lesson learned by Hwesu Murray, a former NBC employee who claimed that the idea for *The Cosby Show* was stolen from him.[18] Murray had written a memo to his superiors suggesting that Cosby be enticed to star in a family sitcom that would fuse comedy and serious subjects. Whatever NBC may have appropriated from Murray's memo, the court found, was not copyrightable. It would be different had Murray submitted a script for a pilot episode and had NBC "borrowed" too freely from it. But the mere idea for a new TV series was not protectable.

At issue in *Lapine v. Seinfeld*[19] was the "idea" of trying to fool fussy children into eating their vegetables by sneaking them into kid-friendly foods like puddings and brownies. That same idea formed the core of both Lapine's *The Sneaky Chef* and Jessica Seinfeld's *Deceptively Delicious*. Defendant Seinfeld (comedian Jerry's spouse) thus prevailed.

If only the expression of ideas is copyrightable, then even fairly complex combinations of ideas can be copied with impunity. The trust fund holding rights to the short

A federal appellate court determined that much of what *Deceptively Delicious* had taken from *The Sneaky Chef* was the uncopyrightable "idea" that kids can be fooled into eating more healthily.

---

18. *Murray v. National Broadcasting Co.*, 844 F.2d 988 (2d Cir. 1988).
19. 2009 U.S. Dist. LEXIS 82304 (S.D.N.Y. 2009), *aff'd*, 375 Fed. Appx. 81 (2nd Cir. 2010).

story that begat the Hitchcock film (and the later remake) *Rear Window* learned this when it sued Steven Spielberg in his capacity as producer of the 2007 film *Disturbia*. Even while dismissing the suit, federal judge Laura Swain admitted that both films inarguably "tell the tale of a male protagonist, confined to his home, who spies on neighbors to stave off boredom and, in so doing, discovers that one of his neighbors is a murderer." She refers to the shared "idea" of the two works in shorthand as "voyeur-suspicion-peril-vindication." But the expressions of that shared idea were very different in the two films, in terms of time frame (four days in *Rear Window*, over a year in *Disturbia*), development of characters and plotting, and even number of physical settings.[20]

Also not copyrightable are works that the case law often refers to as "trivial," which is simply another way of emphasizing that originality is one requirement for copyright. The Copyright Office has set forth four categories of such trivial materials.[21] The

One of the reasons that a copyright infringement suit against *Disturbia* failed was that the film's antagonist (played by David Morse) is a serial killer, whereas the villain in *Rear Window* killed only his wife.

first category consists of words and short phrases such as names, titles, and slogans. In a 2005 case, the First Circuit Court of Appeals rejected a songwriter's claim that the song title and lyric "You're the One for Me," merited protection. The phrase is "common" to the point of being "trite," the court said.[22] Had the court ruled otherwise, could not Neil Sedaka sue Led Zeppelin for use of the song title "Stairway to Heaven"?

The second category of trivial, uncopyrightable works consists of formulas or methods of instruction. Thus, for example, the folks who created Golden Tee, the popular golf video game, could not prevail against a competitor that used very similar language in its own in-game instructions for operating the trackball

mechanism common to both.[23] In another case, Richard Satava, a sculptor well known for his glass-in-glass "jellyfish" designs, was unsuccessful in his copyright infringement suit against a competing artist whose work was highly similar. To hold otherwise would make this method of sculpting—a "centuries-old art form"—subject to copyright protection, something the court was not ready to do.[24] In this case neither the glass-in-glass *method* nor the *idea* of depicting a jellyfish was deemed copyrightable.

The third category of trivial works, the "blank forms" category, includes time cards, graph paper, scorecards, and address books, which are all designed for record-

20. *Sheldon Abend Revocable Trust v. Spielberg*, 2010 U.S. Dist. LEXIS 99080 (S.D.N.Y. 2010).
21. 37 C.F.R. § 202.1 (2010).
22. *Johnson v. Gordon*, 409 F.3d 12 (1st Cir. 2005).
23. *Incredible Technologies, Inc. v. Virtual Technologies, Inc.*, 400 F.3d 1007 (7th Cir. 2005).
24. *Satava v. Lowry*, 323 F.3d 805 (9th Cir. 2003).

ing information but do not themselves convey any information.[25] The fourth and final category consists of works that are entirely dependent on information that is common property. Included here are standard calendars, height and weight charts, tape measures, and rulers. Obviously, if the author does add some originality to the commonplace, as we see in the decorative calendars sold by numerous companies, copyright can accrue to the unique design features involved.

Neither the method nor the idea of encasing a depiction of a jellyfish in glass was deemed protectable, thus halting the suit by Richard Satava (design on left) against fellow artist Christopher Lowry.

Protecting Your Copyright

At least since 1989, American law accepts that a copyright is born the moment a creative work is set down in writing or in some other appropriate finished form. Despite the ubiquity of copyright notices on everything from books to CD liner notes, the copyright holder is not legally required to take any affirmative steps to "earn" a copyright. It would be foolish, however, *not* to register a copyrightable work to which the writer attributes significant value. Should you ever need to bring suit against another person who has infringed on your copyright, registration of your work enables you to obtain money damages and sometimes attorneys' fees as well. Prominent notice of such registration also puts potential infringers on notice that this work is, in fact, protected.

Registration is very easy. One need only pay a modest fee to the federal Copyright Office, fill out the appropriate form depending on the specific medium involved, and place a copyright notice on existing copies of the work. You will also be asked to provide the office with two copies of the work to be copyrighted.[26]

Copyright notices generally consist of three elements:

- The internationally accepted symbol © (for sound recordings), or the word "copyright" or its abbreviation "copr."
- The date of the copyright (typically the date of publication).
- The name of the copyright holder.

---

25. See, e.g., *Tastefully Simple, Inc. v. Two Sisters Gourmet*, 134 Fed. Appx. 1 (6th Cir. 2005) (no protection in blank forms that impart no information but merely provide a space to enter information).

26. More information can be obtained from the Public Information Office, Library of Congress, Copyright Office, 101 Independence Avenue, S.E., Washington, DC 20559-6000, or at www.copyright.gov.

Who Owns a Copyright?

Usually the answer to the question of who owns a copyright is rather straightforward. The creator of a work—the author or artist—is the natural owner of a copyright to his or her work. Authors and artists do not always work alone, however. They may collaborate, as with a lyricist joining forces with a composer, or a small group of writers who coauthor a book. In such cases, in the absence of a contract to the contrary, the creators will jointly and equally own a copyright. In a 2009 decision, the Seventh Circuit Court of Appeals suggested that the line between merely asking a colleague for help in a creative project and having thus officially embarked on a joint project is often a state of mind. So be careful out there.[27]

Motion picture "ownership" presents special issues. In the United States, even though film critics are fond of using the French word *auteur* (as in "writer" or "creator") when speaking of a film's director, typically the film studio insists that it be granted the copyright to the finished work before it will risk millions of dollars and take on a project. Most other countries recognize what is called *le droit moral* (the "moral rights") of artists, which protects film directors' reputational interests in the integrity of their work even if they have signed away their financial rights to the studios. In those countries, directors have a great deal to say about whether or how their work can be altered, such as in the colorization of black-and-white films, the editing of films for television, and the creation of interactive CD-ROM versions of the movie narrative. The United States generally does not recognize such rights. Thus, for example, a former producer of some of Woody Allen's films was deemed to have the right to edit them for TV and airplane viewing, even over Allen's objections.[28]

The clash between the U.S. copyright system and *le droit moral* was at issue when media mogul Ted Turner purchased the MGM Studios film library and made clear his intention to colorize many of the collection's older black-and-white films. Directors and other artists cried foul and unsuccessfully lobbied Congress to bring U.S. law in line with the international standard. When Turner contracted with a French television station to air a colorized version of John Huston's *The Asphalt Jungle*, the director obtained an injunction—in France, based on French law—that prevented the distribution of the colorized film in that country.

Another complication affecting the ownership of copyrights is the **work-for-hire doctrine**. The general principle is quite straightforward. If your job description includes creating works that are copyrightable—such as drafting speeches for your company's president or writing and editing the company newsletter—your employer rather than you will be the owner of the copyright.

The issue becomes a bit more complex when the artist or author claims she is an

---

27. *Janky v. Lake County Convention and Visitors Bureau*, 576 F. 3d 356 (7th Cir. 2009) (courts should ask whether the contributors saw themselves as joint authors while they were working, not whether they agreed to claim joint authorship in their copyright application).

28. *Moses Productions v. Sweetland Films*, 819 N.Y.S. 2d 211 (Sup. Ct. 2006).

independent contractor rather than an employee. In this context, a contractor can be anyone from a freelance reporter to an advertising agency hired to create a marketing brochure to a photographer asked to take appetizing photos of a restaurant's main dishes for its website. The Supreme Court provided some guidance for situations such as these in a rather poignant 1989 decision, *Community for Creative Non-Violence v. Reid*.[29] The Community for Creative Non-Violence (CCNV), an organization dedicated to advocacy on behalf of the homeless, approached sculptor James Earl Reid to create a Nativity scene featuring, in lieu of the traditional Holy Family, an infant and two adult African American figures huddled for warmth on a steam grate. Reid and the CCNV each believed they owned the right to the sculpture and each filed competing certificates of registration with the Copyright Office.

In ruling for Reid the unanimous Court concluded that such factors as the hiring party's right to control the manner and means by which the project is accomplished, the nature of the skill required to complete the project, and the extent of the hired party's discretion over when and how long to work should determine whether a creator is a contractor or an employee.

The Supreme Court held that the creation of this work, *Third World America: A Contemporary Nativity*, was not covered by the work-for-hire doctrine, in part because the sculptor used his own artistic vision to settle upon key design elements. ©1985 James Earl Reid.

---

29. 490 U.S. 730 (1989).

THINGS TO REMEMBER

Recognition of Copyright

- Even the most mundane "literary works" are protected by copyright.
- Computer software is treated as a literary work.
- A work must be set down in some fixed medium before it becomes eligible for protection.
  - Copyright attaches to a work the moment it is set down.
  - Registering a work is necessary, however, to win damages against an infringer.
- At least a modicum of creativity in the work is also required.
- A collection of others' previously copyrighted works may itself be copyrightable.
- "Derivative" adaptations of earlier works can be copyrightable.
- Things that cannot be copyrighted include
  - mere facts (a creative compilation of facts, however, may sometimes be copyrightable)
  - mere ideas
  - methods of instruction, and
  - "trivial works" such as names, titles, slogans, and blank forms
- The artistic creator is the "natural" owner of the copyright, but often the "work for hire" doctrine dictates that the person or group footing the bill is the true owner.

Elements of a Copyright Infringement Suit

The word *copyright* seems to say it all. It grants the owner the right to "copy" the protected work. Copyright infringement is thus the unauthorized copying of that protected work. It can refer to obviously illegal actions such as marketing bootleg copies of movies or musical recordings. The creation of adaptations of protected works (e.g., making a movie of a popular novel) without permission is similarly forbidden. So too is the "public performance" of a work without permission. This part of the Copyright Act means that it is technically a violation of the law for a family restaurant, if it fails to pay licensing fees to the appropriate music clearinghouse, to have its staff sing "Happy Birthday" to its patrons on that special day.

In the real world, most copyright conflicts do not result in litigation. More typically, a letter is drafted by the potential plaintiff to the suspected infringer demanding that the infringement stop. If the case does go to court, typical remedies are an injunction, as well as damages that can include both the plaintiff's lost income and the income illegally obtained by the infringer. These are not necessarily the same thing. If, without your permission, I create a movie based on your book, I might create more income for you than you had been enjoying on your own, because the viewing of my film might create more demand for your book. You may nonetheless be entitled to receive my profits as part of your damages award. Alternatively, there are statutorily prescribed damage awards that plaintiffs may fall back on. As of 2011, these awards range from $750 to $30,000, with some exceptions. For example, judges have the discretion, in the case of defendants who can prove that they innocently infringed on a copyright—("I obtained permission from the person listed on the copyright notice. How was I to know that he did not really own the work?")—to reduce the minimum award to $200. At the other end, in the event of especially egregious violations, such as the kind of willful taking involved when the copyright holder explicitly rejects your request for rights to reprint a protected work, but you do it anyway, the maximum statutorily prescribed award can be as high as $150,000. The extreme case of systematic marketing of bootlegged works can be a criminal offense, punishable by a hefty fine and some jail time.

Copyright owners who choose to bring suit must prove three elements: originality, access, and substantial similarity.

Originality A copyright infringement plaintiff must first establish that the material alleged to have been stolen was original enough to have been legitimately copyrightable in the first place. We already know that works must be "creative" if they are to be copyrightable. The originality element of a copyright infringement suit might therefore be thought of as a reality check—was the plaintiff's work *really* creative or original enough? Or was the copyright given to the artist in error?

Access The element of access in copyright infringement suits is somewhat analogous to proving that a criminal defendant had the opportunity to commit the crime. One cannot steal what one never knew existed. It is not often possible to prove access in the sense of producing a witness to testify that the defendant became aware of the plaintiff's original work at a certain place and time. Often, access is demonstrated more inferentially. Thus, when former Beatle George Harrison was sued because his song "My Sweet Lord" seemed to be an unauthorized copying of the earlier hit song "He's So Fine," the plaintiff pointed to how popular the Chiffons hit had been in its day (it was at the top of the Billboard charts for five weeks).[30]

If the work you allege has been infringed upon is not in general circulation, you will have a harder time establishing access. Writer Craig Mowry claimed that the Jim Carrey film *The Truman Show* was a rip-off of his screenplay. But he had only distributed a few dozen copies of the work, and the closest he had gotten to studio decision-makers was a couple of real estate agents with Hollywood connections.[31]

Substantial Similarity Except in those instances in which a defendant has clearly marketed bootleg or otherwise unauthorized copies of an original work, it is necessary for a plaintiff to demonstrate that the fruit of the infringer's labors is so similar to his or her own copyrighted work as to constitute the theft of intellectual property. Courts typically employ a form of the familiar "reasonable person" test: are

---

30. *Bright Tunes Music v. Harrisongs Music*, 420 F. Supp. 177 (1976).
31. *Mowry v. Viacom International*, 75 U.S.P.Q.2d (BNA) (S.D.N.Y. 2005).

the two works being compared so similar as to suggest to a reasonable person that one was copied from the other? Sometimes the test is augmented by a more exacting comparison of specific features—for example, the plot, the melody, the setting—of the plaintiff's and defendant's works. In the case against George Harrison mentioned earlier, the court found it helpful to reprint short snippets from the sheet music to "He's So Fine" and "My Sweet Lord" in its decision.

In another case that turned on the issue of similarity, federal district court judge Gerhard Gesell had no difficulty determining that the publishers of the then-fledgling *Conservative Digest* had copied the cover design from the far more established *Reader's Digest*.[32] He thus issued an injunction against further infringement and awarded nominal damages. The cover design was protected both by copyright law (as an artistic work in its own right) and by trademark law (as a way of letting consumers know that this was indeed the popular magazine with which they were familiar). Judge Gesell analyzed design features such as composition (the placement of the table of contents, magazine name, date, and cover price), fonts, and the use of boldface type.

In an often-cited case from the Second Circuit, substantial similarity between photographer Art Rogers's photo of a couple cradling their eight German shepherd puppies and artist Jeff Koons's sculpture based on that photo was seen not only by using the "reasonable person" test but also because of the odd facts of the case.[33] The trial record makes clear that Koons purchased a note card depicting the Rogers photo and was sufficiently impressed that he instructed an Italian studio to fashion a wood sculpture faithful to the photo. There were several exchanges back and forth between Koons and the studio artisans in which he reminded them again and again that this or that feature (the size of the young woman's nose, the variety of hues in the dog's fur, etc.) needed to be "as per the photograph."

The same Jeff Koons escaped liability when he was sued by photographer Andrea Blanch over an *Allure* magazine spread, part of which Koons had used to create his painting *Niagara*. Certainly the feet in bejeweled sandals from Blanch's photo had found their way into the Koons painting, but they were but one of four pairs of feet. Koons had added enough of his own creativity that the two works were no longer substantially similar.[34]

There are at least two circumstances in which a court will permit a great deal of similarity between works without finding infringement. The first situation arises when a central idea common to both works (recall that ideas may not be copyrighted) can only be expressed in a very small number of ways. This is referred to in copyright law as the doctrine of **idea-expression merger**. In a fascinating case from Massachu-

---

32. *Reader's Digest Association v. Conservative Digest, Inc.*, 642 F. Supp. 144, 145 (D.D.C. 1986), *aff'd*, 821 F.2d 800 (D.C. Cir. 1987).

33. *Rogers v. Koons*, 960 F.2d 301 (2d Cir. 1992).

34. *Blanch v. Koons*, 467 F.3d 244 (2d Cir. 2007). In the vernacular of copyright law we would say that Koons's work was legitimate in that it was "transformative" (i.e., it had "transformed" Blanch's work into something more).

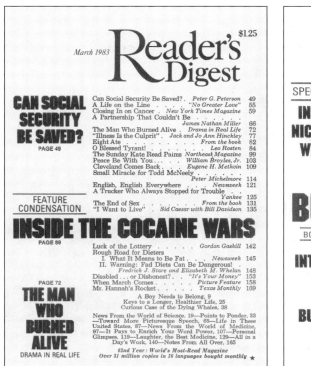

The substantial similarity element was the key for Judge Gesell in *Reader's Digest's* case against the now-defunct *Conservative Digest*.

The court in *Rogers v. Koons* determined that the similarity between the photo on the left and the sculpture depicted on the right would be apparent to any reasonable juror.

Koons's *Niagara* (at right) was seen to have built upon the one pair of legs in the Blanch photo so as to create a new, independently copyrightable work.

setts, the manufacturer of software designed to prompt trained emergency medical teams, step by step, through their performance of CPR, could not prevail over the manufacturer of a defibrillator device called the AED Plus. Not surprisingly, the case concerned both patent and copyright claims. The copyright claim centered around the exact words used by the two devices to teach or remind users how to perform CPR. One simply cannot own the right to such phrases as "stay calm," "give two breaths," and "if no pulse, continue" in this context, the court held. The "idea" of reminding people—in the moment when a life is at stake—how to perform CPR is inseparable from the expression of that idea.[35]

The second situation typically (though not always) arises in the context of litigation involving motion pictures and is governed by the **scènes-à-faire doctrine**. The doctrine posits that when directors choose a particular locale for their story, they commit themselves to including a number of highly predictable filmic moments. Thus, for example, the author of a series of children's books about a park filled with dinosaurs was unsuccessful in his suit alleging that *Jurassic Park* was an infringement

---

35. *Hutchins v. Zoll Medical Corporation*, 430 F. Supp. 2d 24 (D. Mass. 2006). See also *Yankee Candle Co. v. Bridgewater Candle Co.*, 259 F.3d 24 (1st Cir. 2001) (only a small number of words are likely to be used to describe familiar candle scents).

The producers of *John Q* defended themselves successfully against a copyright infringement suit in part because its differences with the plaintiff's work were many; for example, only *John Q* had the aggrieved father take his son's doctor hostage.

of his copyright. That both the plaintiff's and defendant's works took place in a "dinosaur park" meant that such features as electrified fences, automated tours, dinosaur nurseries, and uniformed workers were virtually unavoidable.[36] More recently a suit against the distributors of the film *John Q* failed because the Denzel Washington film and the plaintiff's screenplay for another apparently never-produced film both dealt with parents struggling with a health care system unresponsive to their child's needs. As such, certain scenes would almost inevitably be in common to the two works, such as "parents sitting in a hospital waiting room, nurses asking parents to fill out paperwork, [and] parents praying over the sick child's bedside."[37]

It should be noted that the scènes-à-faire doctrine is not limited to motion pictures. Although the book *Midnight in the Garden of Good and Evil* certainly became a highly successful film, the copyright infringement suit related to the work involved instead the eerie statue known as the *Bird Girl* featured on the cover of the book and later in posters promoting the film. A federal appellate court held that the overall notion of using eerie photography to evoke the mood of a cemetery is a classic example of unprotectable scènes à faire. The dispute arose because photographer Jack Leigh, who had been commissioned by Random House to create images appropriate for the original book cover, believed that the use by Warner Bros. of the same cemetery and the same *Bird Girl* image he had used for the book was a copyright violation. Likely not, the court held, in that the aspects of the Leigh photo that were legitimately copyrightable—the selection of lighting, shading, timing, angle, and film—were not taken, even if the book cover and the film posters are highly similar.[38]

Fair Use and the Supreme Court

As we have seen, plaintiffs in copyright infringement suits must prove three elements: originality, access, and substantial similarity. Thus, we already know some of

---

36. *Williams v. Crichton*, 84 F.2d 581 (2d Cir. 1996).

37. *Tillman v. New Line Cinema*, 295 Fed. Appx. 840 (7th Cir. 2008).

38. *Leigh v. Warner Brothers*, 210 F.3d 1210 (11th Cir. 2000); see also *Schrock v. Learning Curve, International*, 586 F. 3d 513 (7th Cir. 2009) (emphasizing that photographs of copyrighted artifacts—here, of a toy train—are usually themselves copyrightable).

The *idea* of using a cemetery to create an eerie mood is not copyrightable. Judge Phyllis Kravitch also found that the photo of *Bird Girl* at right was actually quite different from the one at left. What similarities and dissimilarities do you see?

the arguments that defendants in such suits are likely to make—that is, "the plaintiff has failed to establish one or more elements, and here is why." Technically, because the burden of proof in establishing these elements is on the plaintiff, defendants' counterarguments do not constitute legal defenses. A defense in this context is better thought of as an admission of copying, with an explanation. By far the most important defense in copyright infringement suits is the one that invokes the **fair use** doctrine, which is codified as section 107 of the Copyright Act.

The basic philosophy underlying fair use is that there are some instances of copying that must be protected, either because they provide some societal good or because they at least do not do a great deal of harm to the copyright holders. Many commen-

THINGS TO REMEMBER

Proving Copyright Infringement

- Copyright infringement plaintiffs may be awarded both their own lost profits and any profits illegally accrued by the defendant.
- The Copyright Act itself also provides specific dollar amounts of damages.
- Especially egregious infringements may also constitute a criminal offense.
- The main elements of an infringement suit are originality, access, and substantial similarity.
- The idea-expression merger and scènes-à-faire doctrines may excuse works that would otherwise be considered substantially similar to the plaintiff's work.

tators have suggested that if the Copyright Act did not provide this kind of defense, courts would have had to create it as a kind of First Amendment counterweight in favor of speech.

Section 107 is structured as a list of four questions that courts must ask as they try to determine if a particular taking that would otherwise be seen as an actionable copyright infringement should be excused as a fair use. The first question focuses on the actions of the alleged infringer: what is the nature of the use to which the defendant has put this copyrighted work? Some kinds of uses—such as for nonprofit educational purposes or to make critical commentary on or satirize the original work—are especially deserving of protection. The second question shifts the court's focus to the nature of the original copyrighted work. Here, too, the thrust of this question is that certain kinds of works are more protected than others. The third question asks how much of the work was taken, reflecting Congress's belief that writers should almost always be able to quote small sections of others' work without seeking permission. Finally, courts must ask what often turns out to be the most important inquiry of all: what is the likely financial effect of this unauthorized taking on the potential value of the original copyright?

The four questions are somewhat interdependent. Thus, for example, some kinds of uses (the first question) may permit a larger amount of taking from the original work (the third question) than would otherwise be the case.

Although we examine many examples of case law in the explication of the fair use questions to follow, three specific Supreme Court decisions are referred to over and over again. Therefore, a short description of the facts and rulings for each of the decisions is in order.

Home Videotapers Are Not Criminals
The "Betamax" case—a charmingly anachronistic nickname, not only because videotapes have given way to DVDs but also because Sony's Betamax format for VCRs had already lost much of the home

taping market to the competing VHS format—was filed because TV and movie production studios were afraid that large-scale home taping of their programs would greatly diminish the value of their copyrights. If you tape a daytime soap opera for viewing when you return home from work (a practice called **time shifting**), you may be tempted to fast-forward through the commercials. Copyright owners worry about this because the fewer the number of people known to view the commercials, the less advertisers will be willing to pay the TV networks for airtime, and thus the less TV networks will be willing to pay the program producers. Then too, you might like this specific episode of your favorite soap opera so much that you keep the tape to watch again and again. This practice, intuitively enough called **library building**, would have obvious implications for the market value of a TV series. Not only would reruns have an even smaller audience than they otherwise would have, but the customer base for commercially produced video of whole seasons of the series (nowadays done in the DVD format) would also be greatly diminished.

Naming millions of VCR purchasers as defendants would have been unwieldy, so the plaintiffs instead went after the Sony Corporation, as well as a small sample of retail outlets known to sell VCRs. Sony's advertising agency was also named as a defendant because it was alleged that the marketing campaign for Betamax machines encouraged purchasers to tape copyrighted programs from broadcast stations. Universal City Studios and Disney, the main plaintiffs, sought an injunction against the sale of video recorders or, barring that, some form of mandatory royalties on the sale

In the *Sony* case, the Court permitted home videotaping of copyrighted TV shows, partly because the practice of "time shifting" touted in ads such as this one was not itself seen as copyright infringement.

of each machine (and perhaps on the sale of blank videotapes as well). The Supreme Court denied the injunction. The majority's reasoning, which we examine in more detail when we return to an explication of section 107, was based largely on the first and fourth fair use inquiries—that is, the nature of the infringer's use of the copyrighted material and this use's effect on the value of the copyright.[39]

Newsworthiness and Copyright Infringement

The underlying facts in *Harper & Row, Publishers, Inc. v. Nation Enterprises* could have been part of a mystery novel.[40] Victor Navasky, editor of the *Nation* magazine, received a mysterious stranger one evening in March 1979 who had in his or her possession a copy of former president Gerald Ford's memoirs, scheduled to be published in the next few weeks by Harper & Row (jointly with the *Reader's Digest*) under the title *A Time to Heal*. Harper & Row had also contracted with *Time* magazine to publish excerpts from the book, timed to increase book sales. The mysterious stranger made clear that Navasky could look at the manuscript but could not keep it or make photocopies from it. Over the next twenty-four to seventy-two hours, Navasky took detailed notes from the Ford memoirs, including several hundred words of direct quotes. Believing that some of the revelations in the memoirs were so newsworthy that they should be brought to the public without delay, the *Nation* scooped the other publishers by including in its April 3, 1979, issue an article of about 2,250 words based on President Ford's manuscript.

Not surprisingly, the copyright owners of *A Time to Heal* sued the *Nation*, which defended itself in part by arguing that the specific words taken from Ford constituted a kind of contemporary history and were thus uncopyrightable facts. The Court rejected this argument as well as several arguments the defendant made based on the fair use doctrine. The majority ruling, as we shall see, says much about the Court's current interpretation of this most frequently raised defense to copyright infringement.

A Pretty (Hairy) Decision

The rap group 2 Live Crew took Roy Orbison's 1960s hit "Oh, Pretty Woman" and, depending on one's point of view, either created a work of biting social commentary on the song and on the hypocritical culture from which it sprang or simply ripped off the original for their own enrichment. The Orbison song tells the tale of a lonely man who, while walking the street late at night, encounters a woman who seems much too beautiful to consider spending time with him. "Don't walk on by," he pleads with her. "Don't make me cry." Just as he is about to leave for another lonely night at home, he finds he has guessed wrong and that the pretty woman is indeed walking his way.

---

39. *Sony Corporation of America v. Universal City Studios*, 464 U.S. 417 (1984). Note that the Court has never told us whether home recording to a DVD rather than a videotape is also protected. As we will see in chapter 13, the Digital Millennium Copyright Act complicates the issue.

40. 471 U.S. 539 (1985).

The Luther Campbell version recorded by 2 Live Crew has a quite different theme. Their "pretty woman" is likened to Cousin Itt of *Addams Family* fame, transmogrified into a "bald-headed," "hairy," and "two-timing" creature.

Fundamentally, *Campbell v. Acuff-Rose Music, Inc.* is about the relationship between the fair use doctrine and the long-accepted notion that comedians who use satire or parody should be allowed to point their audience's attention at various other cultural artifacts without having to obtain permission from those who own the copyright to such works.[41] Yet there has always been tremendous disagreement among courts as to the proper scope of the parodist's license. Should it cover any work that borrows from the original and that also happens to be funny, or must the comedy stem from a statement about the original work? Moreover, is the parodist's protection from copyright infringement suits something separate from and greater than the fair use doctrine, or should the defendant's satiric intent simply be one of the bits of data used in answering the four questions? The Supreme Court ruled unanimously in favor of 2 Live Crew, although it embraced the narrower definition of parody and made clear that defenses based on comedic intent will be handled as part of traditional fair use analysis.

Fair Use Inquiry #1: The Purpose and Character of the Use

Section 107 of the Copyright Act tells us that nonprofit educational uses of another's work are likely to be protected, as are unauthorized reproductions for the purposes of "criticism, comment, news reporting, teaching (including multiple copies for classroom use), scholarship, or research."

As the discussion of the 2 Live Crew case indicates, one kind of "criticism" or "comment" often at issue in copyright infringement litigation is parody. In that 1994 decision, Justice Souter's unanimous opinion makes clear that the Court's definition of parody is narrow.

Those comedic works most likely to be protected by fair use analysis are the ones that comment on the original work. Writers who borrow from earlier works only to make their own job easier will likely not enjoy any special degree of protection. As Souter put it, if the new work "has no critical bearing on the substance or style of the original composition," if the only reason the defendant borrowed from the original was "to get attention" or "to avoid the drudgery" of creating something truly new, the fairness of the use "diminishes accordingly, if it does not vanish."

Most parodists, and perhaps especially most parody songwriters, will not enjoy automatic protection under *Campbell*'s holding, because most comic songwriters borrow a melody for reasons other than making fun of the song itself. Let us take the example of the popular songwriting and performing troupe called the Capitol Steps, a Washington-based group whose founding members are all current or former con-

---

41. 510 U.S. 569 (1994).

gressional staffers. In "It Don't Mean a Thing if Your State's Not a Swing," their target is not Duke Ellington but our electoral system's encouraging presidential candidates to focus all their resources on the few states whose outcomes are up for grabs. "Strangers on Your Flight" is a send-up of the Transportation Security Administration's aggravating airport security rules, not of the song made famous by Frank Sinatra. And "You Can't Hide That Nobel Prize" is aimed at President Obama's peace prize, not at the Eagles hit "Lying Eyes."

Certainly some musical parodists do in fact make fun of the songs whose melodies (and sometimes lyrics) they borrow. Ray Stevens's tune, "I Need Your Help, Barry Manilow," is a respectful but also cutting critique of both Manilow and his fan base. "Into the Words," one of the cuts from the *Forbidden Broadway, Vol. 2* CD, is a highly sophisticated send-up of both the musical *Into the Woods* and Stephen Sondheim's work in general.

The producers of the long-running NBC program *Saturday Night Live* successfully defended against a copyright infringement suit stemming from a skit depicting the city fathers of the biblical town of Sodom devising a public relations campaign for their town reminiscent of the one that New York had recently embarked on. The skit's finale had the participants singing "I Love Sodom" to the tune of "I Love New York," the centerpiece of the New York campaign. The court got the joke and recognized that it was at the expense, at least in part, of the earlier tune's creators. Thus the *SNL* team had achieved a pure parody.[42]

Hollywood icon Carol Burnett lost a suit against the producers of the Fox animated series *Family Guy*, in which Ms. Burnett's famous cleaning lady character was shown mopping up in an X-rated bookstore while a slightly altered version of the *Carol Burnett Show* theme song played. The *Family Guy* scene was a classic example of protected parody, held federal judge Dean Pregerson.[43]

The Fox series also prompted a lawsuit from the owners of the copyright to "When You Wish Upon a Star," which cartoon character Jiminy Cricket famously croons in the Disney film *Pinocchio*. The suit sought damages because of an episode in which main character Peter Griffin sings "I Need a Jew," a melody at least highly similar to that of the Disney tune. (Griffin sought a Jewish accountant to solve his financial woes.) This was protected parody, held Judge Deborah Batts, in that it made fun of the naive notion that "wishing on a star" will solve one's problems.

A federal appellate court held that the music from this *Saturday Night Live* skit was a protected parody of the "I Love New York" campaign.

---

42. *Elsmere Music, Inc. v. National Broadcasting Co.*, 623 F.2d 252 (2d Cir. 1980). See also *Fisher v. Dees*, 794 F. 2d 432 (9th Cir. 1986) ("When Sonny Sniffs Glue" a protected parody of "When Sunny Gets Blue" and of singer Johnny Mathis).

43. *Burnett v. Twentieth Century Fox Film Corporation*, 491 F. Supp. 2d 962 (C.D. Cal. 2007).

More pointedly, that Peter is singing of Jewish stereotypes was clearly designed to conjure up in listeners' minds a long-standing belief in Walt Disney's own anti-Semitism.[44] Another notable parody decision involved the magazine *Vanity Fair*, which made quite a splash when it featured Annie Leibovitz's photo of a nude and very pregnant Demi Moore on its August 1991 cover. When Paramount Pictures, as part of its publicity campaign for the Leslie Nielsen film *Naked Gun 33 1/3: The Final Insult*, superimposed Nielsen's face on a torso chosen to closely resemble Moore's—the composite photo's caption was "Due This March"—Leibovitz sued. She did not prevail against Paramount Pictures, however, because the studio's promotional photo was at least partially a comment on her own work.[45]

In *Mattell, Inc. v. Walking Mountain Productions*,[46] photographer Tom Forsythe was defendant in a suit alleging that he infringed on one of the toy company's most famous icons in his *Food Chain Barbie* series of seventy-eight photographs depicting Barbie dolls in various comical settings all related to food preparation. Here, too, however, the use was deemed a legitimate parody.

The parody defense does not always work, of course. In one often-cited case, *The Cat Not in the Hat: A Parody by Dr. Juice* used the format of the famous children's book series, but did so to make fun of O. J. Simpson, not of Dr. Seuss.[47] The decision has been frequently criticized as a too-stingy interpretation of parody.[48]

Parody is really just a subset of a larger category of potential fair uses of copyrighted material: excerpting from another's work to comment on it or to criticize it.

Suits against *Family Guy* by Carol Burnett and by the company that holds rights to "When You Wish Upon a Star" failed, in that the uses were deemed protected parodies.

---

44. *Bourne Company v. Twentieth Century Fox Film Corporation*, 602 F. Supp.2d 499 (S.D.N.Y. 2009).

45. *Leibovitz v. Paramount Pictures Corp.*, 137 F.3d 109 (2d Cir. 1998).

46. 353 F.3d 792 (9th Cir. 2003).

47. *Dr. Seuss Enterprises v. Penguin Books*, 109 F. 3d 13943 (9th Cir. 1997).

48. See for example, Maureen McCrann, "Granting Presumptive Fair Use Protection for Musical Parodies," 14 *Roger Williams University Law Review* 96, 113–114 (2009).

The Leslie Nielsen photo at right was protected as clearly a satiric commentary on Annie Leibovitz's photo of Demi Moore.

Thus, a drama critic does not need to obtain permission to quote from a play's dialogue. A film critic can show excerpts from a copyrighted film in the course of doing a movie review for the TV news. In an especially ironic example of criticism as a protected use, Reverend Jerry Falwell and the Moral Majority were permitted to send copies of the famous Campari parody ad discussed in chapter 4 to his supporters as part of a direct-mail solicitation. Falwell escaped liability because he had used the ad "to rebut the personal attack upon Falwell and make a political comment about pornography."[49]

There was no parody defense in the *Sony* case, of course. The manufacture and distribution of VCRs was not halted because the machines could be used in many ways that do not violate the Copyright Act. Some broadcast programs, such as very old movies, are no longer protected by copyright. Other programs are "born in the public domain," such as C-SPAN's live coverage of congressional floor debates. Some copyright holders—PBS's *Mister Rogers* among them—would not be at all upset to

---

49. *Hustler Magazine, Inc. v. Moral Majority, Inc.*, 796 F.2d 1148, 1152 (9th Cir. 1986).

This is one of dozens of photos from Tom Forsythe's Food Chain Barbie series, which was protected as a parody of the doll. Additional photos can be found at www.paulsiegelcommlaw .com.

learn that consumers were time shifting their programs for later viewing. Such time shifting was seen also as a nonprofit use consistent with the Copyright Act.

Indeed, defendants who can demonstrate that their use of another's copyrighted materials was for a nonprofit educational purpose are given considerable deference in fair use analysis. The 1976 Copyright Act does not itself provide clear guidance as to how to balance the interests of copyright holders with those of educators, but the House of Representatives staff created a companion report popularly called the *Classroom Guidelines*. The guidelines are built around three main issues: **brevity**, **spontaneity**, and **cumulative effect**.

The brevity requirement permits teachers to make a single copy of a book chapter or an article for their own scholarly use or to prepare to teach a class about the work. Making multiple copies to distribute to students, however, triggers overall length limits (e.g., 250 words for a poem, 2,500 words for an article, no more than 10 percent of the total length of a book) that are quite rigid. Spontaneity means that a teacher is more likely to be permitted to make multiple copies if there is not enough time to contact the copyright holder for permission. The cumulative effect requirement limits teachers to copying no more than two works by the same author, no more than three from the same anthology, and no more than nine works total for classroom distribution during any single semester.

The guidelines also tell us that copying should not be used as a substitute for anthologies, compilations, or collective works, nor for works designed to be "consumable," such as workbooks, exercises, and standardized tests. All copying must be a result of the individual teacher's inspiration rather than directed by any higher administrative authority. Finally, students may not be charged any fees beyond the actual cost of the copying. Separate guidelines govern the use by teachers of homemade video from broadcast programs. The general rule here is that educators may retain and use any such videos only for forty-five days, after which the videos must be erased or destroyed.

It should be emphasized, however, that the *Classroom Guidelines* are for individual teachers. They do not protect for-profit commercial photocopiers, such as Kinko's, even when they produce customized textbooks culled from copyrighted works for use by teachers.[50] The guidelines also do not protect systematic, large-scale photocopying of copyrighted works by whole school systems or universities, or corporations preparing employee training materials.[51]

If educational uses can be exempt from copyright liability, what about uses for news reporting? In the Supreme Court case concerning President Ford's memoirs discussed earlier, the *Nation* magazine argued that its unauthorized use of purloined excerpts from the unpublished Harper & Row book should be protected as news reporting. The Court majority, however, emphasized that the magazine's motivation was commercial, that it intended to "scoop" the copyright holders. Moreover, the opinion rejects the newsworthiness defense outright, finding that "the public's interest in learning this news as fast as possible" does not necessarily outweigh the author's right to control the timing and circumstances of his work's publication. "The promise of copyright would be an empty one," Justice O'Connor wrote, "if it could be avoided merely by dubbing the infringement a fair use 'news report' of the book."[52]

Uses of copyrighted works that are "incidental" or "fortuitous" have often been protected as fair uses. The UCLA law professor Melville Nimmer uses the example of a motion picture in which an actor is seen reading a magazine, its cover clearly visible. The magazine would not be able to sue the film's producers for copyright infringement.[53] At one point in the motion picture *Seven (Se7en)*, about a deranged photographer who becomes a serial killer, detectives search the photographer's apartment and encounter on the wall a light box with a number of transparencies attached to it. Jorge Antonio Sandoval claimed that the transparencies were images of several of his own black-and-white photos, and New Line Cinema did not contest this allegation. The court ruled for the movie producers nonetheless, emphasizing that the images were seen on screen for such a short time and in such an obscured way as to make them almost unidentifiable as Sandoval's creations.[54]

In another dispute that never went to trial, sculptor Frederick E. Hart settled out of court with the producers of the Warner Bros. film *The Devil's Advocate*. In the film's climactic scene, a large sculpture that Hart thought a little too reminiscent of

50. *Basic Books, Inc. v. Kinko's Graphics Corp.*, 758 F. Supp. 1522 (S.D.N.Y. 1991); *Princeton University Press v. Michigan Document Services*, 99 F.3d 1381 (6th Cir. 1996).

51. David A. Simon, "Teaching Without Infringement: A New Model for Educational Fair Use," 20 *Fordham Intellectual Property, Media and Entertainment Law Journal* 453 (2010).

52. *Harper & Row, Publishers, Inc. v. Nation Enterprises*, 471 U.S. 539, 556–557 (1985).

53. Melville B. Nimmer and David Nimmer, *Nimmer on Copyright* (New York: Matthew Bender, 1997), § 13.05(D)3. See for example, *Italian Book Corp. v. ABC*, 458 F. Supp. 65, 68 (S.D.N.Y. 1978) (local news coverage of a festival not liable for airing moments of a band playing a copyrighted song).

54. *Sandoval v. New Line Cinema*, 147 F.3d 215 (2d. Cir. 1998). Technically this was not a fair-use finding at all. Rather, the court found that the images as used in the film were no longer "substantially similar" to the originals.

Although the images in the light box (upper left of this image) were under copyright, the use in *Seven (Se7en)* was permitted because it was brief and incidental.

his own famous *Ex Nihilo* (*Out of Nothing*) comes to life, its component characters engaging in a wide variety of sexual acts. Had the suit gone to trial, Warner Brothers likely would not have been protected by the "incidental use" defense, in that the scene emphasizes the sculpture, employing it as a kind of Greek chorus commenting on a Faustian offer extended by Al Pacino to Keanu Reeves.

Fair Use Inquiry #2: The Nature of the Work

We already know from the *Harper & Row* case that a not-yet-published work is especially protected, in that the Copyright Act gives authors the right to decide when, how, and if their work will be published. Thus, for example, J. D. Salinger biographer Ian Hamilton was not permitted to quote from any of the personal letters written by Salinger that had found their way into various university archives.[55]

Although a 1992 amendment to Copyright Act makes clear that a work's being not yet published will not automatically determine liability, the unpublished status of a protected work will still at least count against defendants. Note also that a not-yet-

---

55. *Salinger v. Random House*, 811 F.2d 90 (2d Cir. 1987). See also *New Era Publications International v. Henry Holt & Co.*, 873 F.2d 576 (2d Cir. 1989) (similar result regarding unauthorized use of L. Ron Hubbard's unpublished correspondence in a biography of the Church of Scientology founder). But see *Wright v. Warner Books*, 953 F.2d 731 (2d Cir. 1991) (biographer's unauthorized use of Richard Wright's unpublished letters permitted, because they were paraphrased rather than quoted directly, and because the letters provided mostly uncopyrightable facts).

Sculptor Frederick Hart's suit against Warner Brothers for the unauthorized use in *The Devil's Advocate* of his sculpture *Ex Nihlio* was settled out of court.

THINGS TO REMEMBER

The Nature of the Use

- Parody, a comedic work that makes fun of an earlier copyrighted work, may be protected as a fair use.
- Parody is a special case of the more general category of comment on the original work.
- Nonprofit and educational uses receive an extra weighting in fair use analysis.
- It is not always easy to determine if a use is commercial or educational (or both).
- The *Classroom Guidelines* accompanying the Copyright Act provide highly specific and rather strict rules for educators.
- Unauthorized uses that are so incidental or unintended as to be "fortuitous" will generally be excused.

---

published work is distinguished in copyright law from a work that is out of print. With respect to the latter, the *Classroom Guidelines* suggest an extra measure of leeway in copying. After all, consumers would likely not be able to buy even a single copy of the book, much less multiple copies for classroom distribution.

Another way that courts handle the "nature of the work" inquiry is to determine where the plaintiff's work fits along a continuum from what we might call "fact-heavy" to "truly artistic." At the extreme, the taking of purely factual material is necessarily a fair use, in that such material is not itself copyrightable in the first place.

THINGS TO REMEMBER

The Nature of the Work

- Not-yet-published works receive a special measure of protection, to preserve the author's right to determine how, when, and if such works will be published.
- Works that are out of print are given a bit less protection from unauthorized copying than are other works.
- The courts also give fact-laden works less protection than more artistic works.
- If the dissemination of a work is judged to be of strong public interest, or if it is the only way of bringing important information to the public (the Zapruder film of the JFK assassination being the best-known example), such a determination will also be factored into the fair use inquiry.

Even a legitimately copyrighted work, however, is less protected under this second fair use question if it is primarily an organization of facts.[56]

A special method of adjudicating the "nature of the work" issue arises when the work is truly unique and when its dissemination is of clear public interest. The long and complicated history of litigation and legislation surrounding the famous Zapruder film of President Kennedy's assassination is the most often cited example. Dallas dressmaker Abraham Zapruder just happened to be making a home movie of the JFK motorcade at the precise time the fatal shots were fired. His eight-millimeter film is surely one of the most important pieces of archival footage of the twentieth century. The publisher of *Life* magazine purchased the rights to the film from Zapruder for $150,000. A book critical of the government's investigation of the assassination called *Six Seconds in Dallas* appeared in 1967. The author of the book, who did not have access to the Zapruder film itself, instead used line sketches, each one copied from a different frame from the film, as reprinted earlier in *Life* magazine. The magazine publisher's resulting infringement suit was dismissed, because the public interest "in having the fullest information available on the murder of President Kennedy" necessitated that this particular film be made available to writers wishing to comment on this defining historical event.[57] In 1992, Congress passed the JFK Assassination Records Collection Act, and in 1997, a special review board created by that act declared the

---

56. *New York Times Co. v. Roxbury Data Interface, Inc.*, 434 F. Supp. 217 (D.N.J. 1977) (permitting defendant to create its own single-volume index of all persons ever named in *New York Times* articles, even though it used the newspaper's own annual indexes of persons named as its source material).

57. *Time, Inc. v. Bernard Geis Associates*, 293 F. Supp. 130 (S.D.N.Y. 1968). Elizabeth High has suggested that similar reasoning should be extended to other invaluable artifacts, most notably video of Martin Luther King, Jr.'s "I Have a Dream" speech, rights to which still reside with the King estate. "Holding History Hostage: Fair Use in the Context of Historical Documentary," 18 *Temple Political and Civil Rights Law Review* 753 (2009).

Zapruder film an official record that the government would thus be entitled to confiscate.[58]

Fair Use Inquiry #3: The Amount Taken

The precise wording of the third fair use criterion asks courts to consider "the amount and substantiality of the portion used in relation to the copyrighted work as a whole." This is Congress's way of saying that taking fifty words from a hundred-word poem is less likely to be considered a fair use than taking five hundred words from a full-length novel.

In the *Sony* case, the Court refused to enjoin the production or marketing of VCRs even though they are often are used to make copies of an entire work. That case was unusual, however, because, in a sense, the machines themselves were the defendants. The basis of the decision was that VCRs can be used in ways that are not violations of the Copyright Act. At most, the manufacturers of the units might have been guilty of **contributory infringement**, rather than **direct infringement**, on anyone's copyright.

The *Harper & Row* case posed an intriguing problem for the Court. If the question in section 107 was to be viewed as a purely quantitative issue, the *Nation* magazine surely should have won. After all, it quoted only a few hundred words from a full-length book manuscript. The Court's explanation for its ruling against the magazine is relevant to the "how much did you take?" inquiry in at least two ways. First, Justice O'Connor makes clear that this part of the fair use analysis has not only quantitative but also qualitative dimensions. Quoting from an earlier decision, she chided the defendant that "no plagiarist can excuse the wrong by showing how much . . . he did *not* pirate."[59] What the *Nation* took from President Ford's memoirs was the heart of the book, she emphasized. The magazine editor's testimony made clear that he purposely chose the book's most powerful passages, the ones that would convey the "absolute certainty with which [Ford] expressed himself."

A second important feature of the *Harper & Row* decision is that O'Connor's fair use analysis seems to deviate from the instructions, such as they are, in the Copyright Act itself. Whereas section 107 tells courts to adjudicate the third fair use inquiry by comparing what was stolen to the length of "the copyrighted work as a whole," O'Connor also considered the length of the resulting *Nation* magazine story. At one

---

58. 62 Fed. Reg. 27,008 (May 16, 1997). The board told the Zapruders to make whatever arrangements were necessary to transfer ownership to the government by August 1998. A year of negotiations resulted in payment of $16 million to the Zapruders. During those negotiations, the family arranged to have an Illinois company market a digitally enhanced copy of their original film. Thus *Image of an Assassination*, a forty-five-minute documentary incorporating a new version of the twenty-six-second film, became available in video stores.

59. 471 U.S. 539, 565 (1985) (quoting *Sheldon v. Metro-Goldwyn Pictures Corp.*, 81 F.2d 49, 56 (2d Cir. 1936), *cert. denied*, 298 U.S. 669 (1936)).

point she reports that 13 percent of the magazine article consisted of quotes from President Ford himself. Thus, the vast majority of the *Nation* essay was at least original enough not to have been lifted verbatim from someone else. Even here, though, her analysis becomes more qualitative than quantitative, as she concludes that the article "is structured around the quoted excerpts," that they "serve as its dramatic focal points," that they play a "key role in the infringing work."

The general topic of how parodies are treated within fair use analysis has already been introduced. With respect to the third inquiry, the general rule, not surprisingly, is that a parody is permitted to "take" more from the original than might other kinds of works. Parodists may, minimally, take whatever is necessary to "conjure up the original" in the minds of the listeners. Clearly this standard is not very precise. It is fair to say, however, based on the "Oh, Pretty Woman" case, that musical parodists may with impunity use the complete melody of the original if the new lyrics are indeed a critical commentary on the earlier work. Frequently parodists are a bit more cautious than this latitude would suggest. When *Family Guy* or *The Simpsons* employ musical parody, for example, they tend to alter slightly the melodies of original works even while faithfully following the rhythmic line.

Fair Use Inquiry #4: The Effect of the Taking on the Copyright's Value

Copyright law is at its core a property issue, thus making the fourth fair use inquiry, the one that considers whether and how the defendant has diminished the value of the plaintiff's copyrights, crucial. In the *Harper & Row* case, wherein *Time* magazine canceled its excerpting contract with the book publisher once the *Nation* had gone to press, Justice O'Connor wrote that the fourth inquiry "is undoubtedly the single most important element of fair use."

THINGS TO REMEMBER

The Amount Taken

- How much defendants are allowed to "take" is often a function both of the nature of their use and the nature of the original work.
- Although section 107 of the Copyright Act directs courts to consider "the amount and substantiality of the portion used in relation to the copyrighted work as a whole," courts often add to the equation the ratio of unoriginal to original words in the defendant's creation.
- There is also a qualitative dimension to the test, in that defendants are likely to be held liable for taking the "heart" of a work, no matter how few words are actually taken.
- Parodists are permitted to take, minimally, whatever is necessary to "conjure up the original" in the minds of readers.

In the *Sony* case, the Court had to deal with the VCR manufacturers' argument that their machines actually enhanced the value of the plaintiffs' copyrights. After all, the reasoning went, many people used video recorders primarily as video players for professionally prerecorded movies. Were there no VCRs, the whole home-video market, which produced a huge new stream of revenue for plaintiff Universal City and other studios, might never have developed. But Justice O'Connor rejected the argument. The fourth fair use inquiry, she reminds us, allows plaintiffs to say to defendants, "How dare you make money off of my copyright, without my permission, even if your doing so makes money for me as well!"

The fourth fair use inquiry concerns the copyright holders' financial interests not only in the work already created and marketed but also in any derivative works they may choose to market in the future. That is one of the key reasons the Court was not able to settle every issue in the case involving 2 Live Crew and had to remand the case to a lower court. What if Acuff-Rose, which owned the copyright to Roy Orbison's "Oh, Pretty Woman," had decided to license a rap music version of the song itself? Would the 2 Live Crew parody supplant the market for such a work, thus diminishing its value?

Parody might potentially dampen the market for the original. Ray Stevens's parody of Barry Manilow's music ("I Need Your Help, Barry Manilow"), for example, makes fun of the megastar and his fans ("No one knows how to suffer quite like you"). If listeners were to be swayed by Stevens's musical "argument" that Manilow is an overly sentimental songwriter whose devotees have a maudlin, masochistic streak, the value of the latter's copyrights would surely be diminished. This diminution, however, is not the kind the law is designed to protect.

Indeed, a "taking" of a copyrighted work, assuming it would not otherwise be actionable, cannot become so simply because the defendant's use of the work results in decreased sales of the original creator's works. Perhaps the leading example of this phenomenon is a 1977 decision involving the *Miami Herald* and *TV Guide*. The newspaper had decided to expand its coverage of television by offering a free weekly TV magazine. It launched the new supplement with an advertising campaign in the newspaper itself, the thrust of which was to suggest that here was quite a bargain compared with subscribing to *TV Guide* because consumers received a thick multifaceted newspaper plus a viewing guide. The ads included a pictorial comparison of the covers of the two magazines. In response to the resulting copyright infringement suit brought by *TV Guide*'s publishers, the court allowed that the ads "may have had the effect of drawing customers away," but concluded that any such result would stem from the logic of the *Herald*'s arguments to consumers, not from the use of the *TV Guide* covers.[60]

When diminution of the original copyright's value flows from the taking itself, the defendant is almost certain to lose both the fourth fair use inquiry and the litigation.

---

60. *Triangle Publications, Inc. v. Knight-Ridder Newspapers, Inc.*, 626 F.2d 1171 (5th Cir. 1980).

The Herald's new TV Book.
It's a little bit bigger
and a little bit better.

When you open the November 20, edition of the Sunday Herald, you're going to open your eyes to a very delightful little surprise: Our new, smaller, more convenient size TV Book.

Although we lopped off quite a few inches around the edges, we added quite a bit to the middle. We now have more listings. (More than TV Guide). Easier to read list-

ings. (Easier to read than TV Guide). More up-to-date listings. (More up-to-date than TV Guide). Plus a few more pluses TV Guide can't even come close to. Namely the umpteen different sections of the Sunday Herald.

Why did we make our new TV Book a little bit bigger than TV Guide?

Simple. We have a little bit more to say than TV Guide.

The TV Book. At no extra cost in Sunday's Miami Herald.

Even if the *Herald*'s unauthorized use of a *TV Guide* cover in this ad diminished sales, this is not the kind of financial harm copyright law prohibits.

This is apparent in a number of cases involving publishers of unauthorized "fan books" seeking to capitalize on the popularity of the *Twin Peaks*, *Seinfeld*, and *Star Trek* phenomena. In each case courts ruled for plaintiffs, who did not need to demonstrate either that the defendants' books would diminish their own profits, nor that they had plans to make money from licensing similar fan books themselves.

Finally, it is worth noting a 2006 decision involving a company called Clean Flicks, which was in the business of editing sex and gore from commercial movies. The company took so seriously this fourth fair use factor that it required all of its customers to buy an original unedited version of the requested movie title in addition to the edited version it provided. The major movie studios would not be losing money through this enterprise, Clean Flicks argued. After all, any customers seeking a sanitized version of a major movie clearly "would not have themselves purchased the [unedited] versions because of the objectionable content." Thus, if anything, Clean Flicks' and similar companies' business models resulted in more, not less, money flowing to the major studios. Perhaps true, but irrelevant, Judge Richard Matsch held. Copyright law dictates that the major studios have the right to decide for themselves whether or not to enter the "sanitized" movie market.[61]

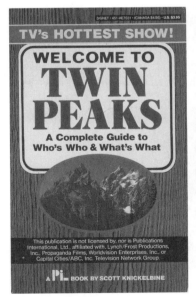  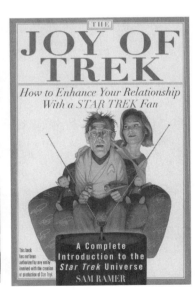

Publishers of each of these books infringed on the copyrights of the respective television programs.

---

61. *Clean Flicks of Colorado v. Soderbergh*, 433 F. Supp. 2d 1236 (D. Colo. 2006).

THINGS TO REMEMBER

Monetary Effect on the Plaintiff's Copyright

- Most courts treat this last fair use inquiry as the most important of the four.
- Infringers will be held liable even for profits they have earned from marketing works to new markets the original copyright owner may never have intended to reach or profit from.
- Even if an infringement can be shown to have increased the monies flowing to the copyright holder, defendants will still be held liable for the amount of their own profits.
- Diminution of the original copyright's value is actionable only if the taking itself (rather than, say, criticism hurled within the new work at the original work) is the cause of the diminished value.

The Law of Trademark

Imagine you are taking a long car trip, alone. You have been on the road for over ten hours, and your body is telling you to start seeking lodging for the night. You pass a number of motels with names that suggest a bit of local color but nothing about the cleanliness or overall quality of the property. Indeed, a few of them look a bit scuzzy. Then your eyes catch sight of a familiar name and logo—it really does not matter for present purposes whether it is Holiday Inn or Ramada or any of their well-known competitors—and you pull into the driveway, confident that you will enjoy a comfortable stay. If this narrative rings true for you, you already have a good intuitive feel for trademark law. Trademarks exist to give consumers a sense of predictability and thus to help businesses earn a deserved brand loyalty.

Kinds of Marks

In the United States, trademarks are protected by the Lanham Act of 1946. The act defines trademarks as any word, name, symbol, or device that a company may use to distinguish its products or services from its competition. Marks can be familiar brand names. They can also be slogans. In one case, the maker of a line of cosmetics sued the distributors of the Jerry Seinfeld film *Bee Movie*, claiming they had improperly used their "Give Bees a Chance" slogan.[62]

Distinctive shapes can also be marks, the best-known example probably being the

---

62. The case was settled out of court. "Bee Movie Suit Settled," *Los Angeles Times*, January 16, 2008, E3.

shape of Coca-Cola bottles. A color scheme, a series of sounds, and even smells can be protected by trademark law.[63]

The word *trademark* is used somewhat generically here. Technically, trademarks apply to a company's products, whereas a company that offers primarily a service (such as a hotel chain) seeks protection instead for its **service marks**. The law also recognizes an interest in protecting **collective marks**, which serve the needs of associations of businesses. The Chamber of Commerce, the National Restaurant Association, and the National Association of Broadcasters all represent many companies with overlapping interests and all are eligible to register their own marks. You have probably also seen **certification marks**, which do not refer to a product in its entirety but rather to a feature of that product (such as a promise that a given brand of pizza has "REAL" cheese). Finally, the Lanham Act provides for protection of the overall "look and feel" of product packaging or the building in which a service is provided.[64] This protection is called **trade dress**.

What Makes a Mark Protectable?

In copyright law, a creation is protected from the moment it is set down in some kind of finished form. Trademark law is quite different in this respect. You might create a terribly clever slogan or an eye-catching logo. Neither is protectable under trademark law until you actually establish a track record of using it in commerce, or at least what the U.S. Patent and Trademark Office calls a "bona fide intention" to use your mark within the next six months.

Just as not every conceivable "creation" is copyrightable, not every possible mark is protectable by trademark law. The law of copyright demands a measure of originality. Trademark law requires **distinctiveness**, which means that the mark does something more than simply describe the product or service. You cannot register the exclusive right to market "ink" pens because the use of ink is implicit in the definition of "pen." But even purely descriptive terms can sometimes become distinctive and thus protectable, over time. A **descriptive mark** is protected if a company can demonstrate that it has been marketing its wares under a specific name for so long and with such success that the public has developed a mental association between the name and the product. Consider "American Airlines," a name which seems to merely describe *any* U.S. (or Western Hemisphere)–based airline, but which most people clearly associate with a specific company. When a word or phrase that would otherwise be considered merely descriptive becomes distinctive in this way, it has acquired a **secondary meaning**, sometimes referred to instead as **acquired distinctiveness**. Com-

---

63. Melissa E. Roth, "Something Old, Something New, Something Borrowed, Something Blue: A New Tradition in Nontraditional Trademark Registrations," 27 *Cardozo Law Review* 457 (2005).

64. *Amazing Spaces, Inc. v. Metro Mini Storage*, 608 F. 3d 225 (5th Cir. 2010); *Wal-Mart v. Samara Brothers*, 529 U.S. 205 (2000); *Two Pesos, Inc. v. Taco Cabana, Inc.*, 505 U.S. 763 (1992).

pany owners' surnames generally must acquire distinctiveness before they can be protected. Frank Perdue's "Perdue" chicken is a good example.

It is generally preferable from the marketer's perspective if a mark can be distinctive from the time of its creation. Trademark law refers to such marks as "inherently distinctive," and they are sometimes called "strong" marks. Generally a mark can be inherently distinctive in three ways. The first way is if the mark is **fanciful**, if it has no life apart from its association with the product it seeks to market. Such marks are not found in any dictionary but are created out of thin air, often with the help of a high-powered advertising agency. The name "Prell" applied to a shampoo is a fanciful name. So too are marks such as "Xerox" copying machines and "Clorox" bleach. A mark can also be inherently distinctive if it is arbitrary. Arbitrary marks do have established dictionary meanings, but the specific product or service is not inherently related to that dictionary meaning. Apple computers and Camel cigarettes are examples. Finally, a mark can be inherently distinctive if it is **suggestive**, that is, if it suggests, without explicitly describing, a product or service's qualities or features. "Head and Shoulders" shampoo is such a mark, as is "Wet Kisses" pet store or the "Curl Up and Dye" salon.

Likelihood of Confusion

Generally plaintiffs can establish that their trademarks have been infringed in two ways. The first way is to show that the public is likely to be confused by the defendant's use of a highly similar mark, that it will presume incorrectly that the products or services are the plaintiff's or at least that the plaintiff authorized use of the mark. This is called the **likelihood of confusion** standard. Historically it has been limited both by geography and product line. A trademark infringement is less likely to be found if the alleged infringer is marketing goods or services in a geographic region

---

THINGS TO REMEMBER

The Basics of Trademark Law

- The Lanham Act protects trademarks, service marks, collective marks, certification marks, and trade dress. The word *trademark* is often used to refer to any of these categories of emblems.
- A trademark is any word, logo, slogan, or similar device used to call to mind a specific manufacturer's goods or services.
- The law protects only distinctive marks, those that do something more than simply describe the product or service.
- Marks can be distinctive from their birth (as in the case of fanciful, arbitrary, and suggestive marks), or they may be descriptive terms that have become distinctive over time through the acquisition of a secondary meaning.

far removed from where the plaintiff conducts business. Although this limitation is not as important with respect to large companies that market their goods nationally or internationally, it still comes into play when litigants are relatively local concerns. Thus, for example, the famous Sardi's restaurant in New York City was unable to enjoin the owner of a small neighborhood pub in California from using a highly similar name.[65]

Also, the law traditionally protected companies' trademarks only from those who sought to market product lines highly similar to their own. Often referred to as **product proximity**, this general rule says that trademark infringement is more likely to be found if the two products at issue are similar enough to compete plausibly with each other. To cite one early example, the manufacturer of "V-8" vitamin supplements was successfully sued by the manufacturer of the famous vegetable juice of the same name.[66]

Dilution

The second way a company might infringe on a competing company's trademark is through **dilution**. A claim for dilution does not require that the plaintiff's and defendant's product lines are similar. Rather a plaintiff must show that the defendant's use of its trademark has caused harm by either diminishing its effectiveness or disparaging the name in the public's mind. The first kind of dilution is sometimes called **blurring**. In the trademark-infringement literature, a hypothetical example of "Buick aspirin tablets" is often used. If the public began to believe mistakenly that General Motors had begun to sell analgesics, we might have a traditional likelihood-of-confusion suit. But what if the market were simultaneously flooded with a host of other "Buick" products, from toothbrushes to hammers? Infringement still might exist, but based on the alternative theory—blurring—that consumers would no longer think only of cars when they encounter the trademark Buick.[67]

The second category of dilution—**tarnishment**—is seen when a defendant's use of a company's mark creates unpleasant associations in consumer's minds. Thus, for example, the Coca-Cola Company sued distributors of a popular counterculture poster depicting an "exact blown-up reproduction of plaintiff's familiar 'Coca-Cola' trademark and distinctive format except for the substitution of the script letters 'ine' for '-Cola,' so that the poster reads 'Enjoy Cocaine.'" In the course of granting the plaintiff the requested injunction, the court emphasized that in the highly competitive soft drink industry, "even the slightest negative connotation concerning a particular beverage" may have a significant effect on market share.[68]

---

65. *Sardi's Restaurant Corp. v. Sardie*, 755 F.2d 719 (9th Cir. 1985); cf. *Good Earth Corp. v. M. D. Horton and Associates*, 1998 U.S. App. LEXIS 12572 (9th Cir. 1998).

66. *Standard Brands, Inc. v. Smidler*, 151 F. 2d 34 (2nd Cir. 1945).

67. Justin L. Gunnell, "Goldilocks and the Three Federal Dilution Standards: An Empirical Review," 17 *Texas Intellectual Property Law Journal* 101, 102 (2008).

68. *Coca-Cola Co. v. Gemini Rising*, 346 F. Supp. 1183 (E.D.N.Y. 1972)

Trademark Parody

A tarnishment claim will generally not succeed, however, if the defendant can demonstrate that the unauthorized use of the plaintiff's trademark was for the purpose of parody.[69] In 2010, for example, a federal judge threw out a trademark infringement suit by a group opposed to same-sex marriage in California whose logo was faithfully imitated while satirized by an opposing group.[70] See the logos on my website.

A trademark parody need not mimic closely a potential plaintiff's actual logo to be protected. Here, for example, is a poster for a popular restaurant in North Carolina. It is a fair bet that the McDonald's folks would have no recourse against this playful dig at fast food, even though it makes no attempt whatsoever to look like the golden arches.

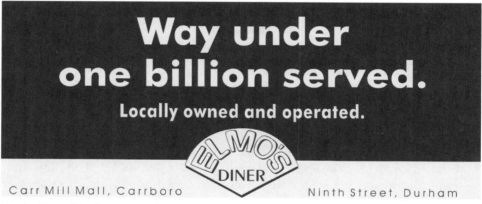

Used with permission.

Defendants who use another's trademark to make some kind of political commentary may generally do so even if that use is not primarily a comment on the trademark itself. The publisher of Al Franken's book certainly did intend by its cover design and use of the phrase "Fair and Balanced" to comment on Fox News and host Bill O'Reilly. Fox's trademark infringement suit was unsuccessful.[71] But so too was a suit by MasterCard International against presidential candidate Ralph Nader, who ran a TV spot using the company's "priceless" tag to argue for the pricelessness of "the truth," which the ad argued would emerge only if Nader were permitted to participate in the presidential debates. Look at the ad on my website, and I think you will agree that the

---

69. *L.L. Bean, Inc. v. Drake Publishers, Inc.*, 811 F.2d 26 (1st Cir. 1987) (protected parody of famous catalog store); *Lyons Partnership v. Giannoulas*, 179 F.3d 384 (5th Cir. 1999) ("San Diego Chicken" sports mascot a parody of the PBS "Barney" character).

70. *Protect Marriage.com—Yes on 8 v. Courage Campaign*, 680 F. Supp. 2d 1225 (E.D. Cal. 2010).

71. *Fox News Network v. Penguin Group*, 2003 U.S. Dist. LEXIS 18693 (S.D.N.Y. 2003).

target of Nader's criticism is the corrupt two-party system generally, that he has no beef with MasterCard.[72]

Use It or Lose It: The Fear of "Going Generic"

Have you ever "googled" something or someone? The Google corporation has mixed feelings about your nodding yes. On the one hand, the everyday use of the company's name is a reminder that theirs is one of the world's most ubiquitous brand names. But on the downside, the company's legal department surely fears overuse of the company's name, especially lowercased, as a verb, especially if the speaker really meant, "I used a search engine (perhaps Google, but maybe Yahoo! or Bing, etc.) to get some information." When a company's name comes to refer to a whole product line rather than to a specific company, it is said to have become **generic** and thus to have lost all protection of trademark law.

Companies will thus frequently write letters of admonishment to reporters who misuse their trademarks, such as by using "Xerox" as a noun or a verb instead of as

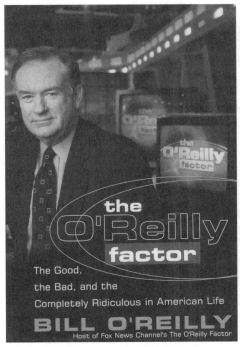
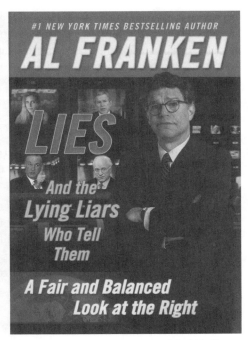

The Al Franken book cover was deemed a clear and protected parody of Fox and Bill O'Reilly.

---

72. *Mastercard International, Inc. v. Nader 2000 Primary Committee*, 70 U.S. P. Q. 2d 1046 (S.D.N.Y. 2004).

THINGS TO REMEMBER

Protecting Your Trademark

- Trademarks are infringed upon when the likelihood of confusion is introduced as to whose products or services a customer is actually buying.
- Even actions that do not necessarily create confusion may still result in liability if they diminish a trademark's distinctiveness by diluting it.
- Courts generally recognize two varieties of trademark dilution: blurring and tarnishment.
- Unauthorized uses that might otherwise be considered tarnishing dilutions may be protected nonetheless as trademark parodies.
- A trademark may lose its protectability if, over time, consumers come to perceive the mark as a generic word describing the entire product category. Words such as cellophane, aspirin, and escalator, all once trademarks of specific companies, have gone this route.

an adjective describing one particular company's photocopying machines. Although such letters sometimes read like threats of litigation, in fact corporations almost never sue reporters about these careless lapses. Indeed, the more important reason for sending the letter is that the company's file copy of it and other similar correspondence may become an important part of the company's proof, if it ever needs such proof, that it has not abandoned its trademarks.

Despite corporations' best efforts, over the years many brand names have in fact become generic. Among everyday words for whole product categories that once referred only to a specific company are aspirin, escalators, yo-yos, thermoses, and cellophane.

Chapter Summary

Copyright law is designed to protect the rights of authors and artists and to encourage them to create. It covers everything from music to literary works, from architectural drawings to computer software. A work must be set down in some fixed medium and must manifest some degree of creativity to be eligible for protection. Mere facts are not copyrightable, although a creative compilation of facts may sometimes be copyrightable. In some instances, the natural owner of a copyright will be an employer, rather than the actual creative artist.

Copyright infringement suits must establish originality (the plaintiff's work was legitimately copyrightable in the first place), access (the defendant was aware of the plaintiff's work), and substantial similarity (the defendant's work actually does constitute an infringement on the plaintiff's work).

The most important defense to a lawsuit is the fair use doctrine, which asks courts to make four inquiries, examining the nature of the use (whether for purely commercial or for educational or other productive purposes); the nature of the work (whether already published or not; whether factual or artistic); how much was taken; and the likely effect on the potential value of the original copyright.

Trademark law's province is commerce, and it is designed to avoid consumer confusion in the marketplace. The word *trademark* is often used as shorthand to refer to trademarks, service marks, collective marks, certification marks, and trade dress, all of which are protected by the Lanham Act.

The law protects only distinctive marks, those that do something more than simply describe the product or service. Marks can be distinctive from their birth (as in the case of fanciful, arbitrary, or suggestive marks), or they may be otherwise merely descriptive terms that have become distinctive over time through the acquisition of a secondary meaning.

Typically, trademark-infringement lawsuits seek to establish that consumers are likely to be confused by the defendant's conduct as to the true source of goods or services. Infringement suits based on dilution do not require such proof, especially in the case of tarnishment claims. But even a use that may tarnish the public image of a trademark may be protected speech if it serves as a parody of the original.

Trademark holders' biggest fear is that their marks will be so successful that they become generic; that is, the public starts associating them with the entire industry's offerings rather than just that of one company. For example, "aspirin," "escalator," and "yo-yo" are now generic terms, although at one time they were protected trademarks.

Chapter 7

ACCESS TO INFORMATION

O ur nation does not surrender to blackmail." In 2009 a federal appellate court quoted those words from a lower court decision holding that the government could not legitimately keep secret about twenty photos used by the Department of Defense during its investigation of America's alleged torture of detainees in Iraq and Afghanistan. The dramatic quote was the court's rejoinder to the government's argument that release of the photos and related documents could be a public relations bonanza for the Taliban. As this chapter was being prepared, the photos at issue had not yet been released, because the Supreme Court vacated the appellate court's ruling, asking it to reexamine the case in light of new federal legislation. The controversy is likely to come back to the high court again.[1]

The torture photos case began as a request under the federal Freedom of Information Act (FOIA). A more detailed description of that law is the subject of a later section of this chapter. For now suffice it to say that FOIA and its state-level companion legislation are the chief legal weapons the media have for compelling disclosure of government information. This is so because the First Amendment provides much more of a right to report what we already know than it does a right to learn information in the first place.

Before we examine FOIA, we will first look at what the First Amendment does tell us about a right to hear information from willing and sometimes unwilling speakers.

---

1. *ACLU v. DOD*, 543 F.3d 59 (2nd Cir. 2009), *vacated and remanded*, 130 S.Ct. 777 (2010). Later in 2010 the federal district court granted a motion to reconsider its earlier decision that had allowed the government to withhold documents describing the Department of Defense's interrogation policies. 2010 U.S. Dist. LEXIS 6524 (S.D.N.Y. 2010).

A First Amendment Right to Hear (From Willing Speakers)?

The First Amendment's guarantees of freedom of speech and freedom of the press, the U.S. Supreme Court has said on a number of occasions, at least imply a corollary right to hear, to listen, to read. A group of concerned students successfully challenged a Long Island, New York, school board's decision to remove books from high school and junior high school libraries. Announcing the decision of the Court in *Board of Education v. Pico* (there was no majority opinion), Justice Brennan remarked that the justices have frequently held, "in a variety of contexts," that the First Amendment protects not only the right to speak but also "the right to receive information and ideas."[2] Within the realm of sexually oriented speech (see chapter 11), although states are free to pass antiobscenity laws that comport with certain federal guidelines, no state may make criminal the mere act of *reading* obscene materials.[3] In the 1960s, when the postmaster general sought to prevent the use of the mails for sending "Communist propaganda" to any persons who did not explicitly request it, the Court ruled that he had overstepped his bounds by placing such a requirement on readers. "It would be a barren marketplace of ideas that had only sellers and no buyers," Justice Brennan wrote.[4] In another case, although choosing to defer to the attorney general's refusal of an entry visa to a well-known Marxist scholar who wished to offer a series of lectures at American universities, the Court went out of its way to say that whatever First Amendment interests were involved here were those of the potential audience members.[5]

These cases all have something in common: the pairing of a willing speaker and an equally willing listener. Whatever First Amendment right to hear might exist, it cannot compel others to speak. Reporters assigned to cover a local crime story understand that the victim's relatives and friends have no obligation to answer their questions. A press credential is not a **subpoena**. The First Amendment is also of limited use in compelling the release of official government information. As Justice Stewart put it in a famous lecture at Yale Law School, "the Constitution itself is neither a Freedom of Information Act nor an Official Secrets Act."[6]

To complete our setting the stage for a discussion of federal and state statutory provisions for disclosure of government information, we look at the somewhat limited First Amendment case law relevant to the general question of press access to government information and to government-controlled places.

---

2. 457 U.S. 853, 867 (1982).
3. *Stanley v. Georgia*, 394 U.S. 557 (1969).
4. *Lamont v. Postmaster General*, 381 U.S. 301, 308 (1965).
5. *Kleindienst v. Mandel*, 408 U.S. 753 (1972).
6. Potter Stewart, "Or of the Press," 26 *Hastings Law Journal* 631, 636 (1975).

News Gathering: The Constitutional Framework

It is a safe bet that the nation's founders did not presume that "freedom of the press" includes a constitutional right to *gather* news. That would not necessarily prevent a contemporary Supreme Court, of course, from interpreting the First Amendment more expansively. As we see in chapter 8, the Court has fashioned a fairly extensive First Amendment right to attend court proceedings and to write about what transpires in the courtroom. Yet the Court has refused to create a more expansive general First Amendment right to gather news from the government.

No Special Access Rights for the Press: A Tale of Three Prisons

In 1974 the Supreme Court handed down two cases on the same day that both rejected reporters' claims that their First Amendment right to gather news had been abridged. The first, *Pell v. Procunier*,[7] concerned a California Department of Corrections regulation providing that reporters would have access to prisons and might be able to interview inmates chosen by the prison staff but that reporters could not themselves select any particular inmates for interviews. Prison officials argued that the policy was necessary to prevent certain prisoners from becoming "celebrities."

Writing for the Court's majority, Justice Stewart upheld the prison regulation. The Constitution, he concluded, does not "require government to accord the press special access to information not shared by members of the public generally. . . . The right to speak and publish does not carry with it the unrestrained right to gather information." The second case, *Saxbe v. Washington Post Co.*,[8] involved a Federal Bureau of Prisons regulation virtually identical to the California rule against requesting a specific prisoner to interview. Writing for the same 5–4 majority, Justice Stewart emphasized that there were ample alternative means by which reporters could gather information about the correctional systems without enjoying carte blanche to interview anyone they chose. They could carry on correspondence with inmates. They could tour the prisons, even the most secure sections of the facilities, and interact with any inmates they happened to encounter. And, of course, they could always interview *former* prisoners.

Four years later, the Court dealt with yet another prison-access case. KQED sought radio and television access to a particular portion of the Alameda County Jail (in the San Francisco Bay area) that had been the site of an inmate suicide as well as a number of alleged beatings and rapes. Although the Court was highly fragmented, it is clear that the justices were again unwilling to put much stock in the notion of a First

---

7. 417 U.S. 817 (1974).
8. 417 U.S. 843 (1974).

Amendment right to gather news. The Court would grant reporters no more right of access than was enjoyed by the general public.[9]

Access to Other Places

The prison decisions just reviewed are very consistent with more general principles governing the relationship between the press and government authorities empowered to control the security of specific spaces. Thus, even though both the press and the public are generally free to traverse public streets and parks, anyone who disobeys a police officer's legitimate order to disperse in an emergency (such as the site of an automobile accident) may be prosecuted for crimes such as obstructing the law, resisting arrest, or trespassing.[10] More typically, media personnel with appropriate identification are permitted to cross police barricades, although in most jurisdictions this practice is entirely at the discretion of the officers on the scene.

In the case of spaces that might be *owned* by the public but generally not *open* to the public (such as military bases or power-generating plants), trespassers are even more likely to be arrested.[11] Also, elaborate procedures exist for determining how and when reporters will be permitted access by the military to international war zones. There have been ongoing tensions between the media and Pentagon officials about this issue for many years, resulting in cycles of openness and secrecy. It is commonly believed that reporting from Vietnam led to diminished public support for the war. A wary Pentagon thus succeeded for the most part in keeping the press away from the war zone in the early 1980s when the United States invaded Grenada. Media outrage spurred Congress to appoint an independent commission, which recommended that a small number of media organizations be allowed to serve as stand-ins for the press as a whole in a system of "pooled" reporting. This "pooled" reporting system was used in the 1991 Persian Gulf War, but the press complained about the "video game" aspect of the war, with Pentagon briefings consisting largely of replays of successful "smart bomb" target hits. How many of the bombs were *not* so smart, the press wondered. A 1991 lawsuit challenging the tight control maintained over the media during the Gulf War, however, was unsuccessful.[12]

In the military operations launched against Afghanistan following the September 11, 2001, attacks, the media were initially not permitted access to the actual ground operations, restricted instead to offshore stationing on U.S. military vessels in the

---

9. *Houchins v. KQED, Inc.*, 438 U.S. 1 (1978). See also *Hammer v. Ashcroft*, 570 F. 3d 798 (7th Cir. 2009), *cert. denied*, 130 S.Ct. 1735 (2010) (no right of access to prison's "special confinement unit"). Also in 2010 the Utah Department of Corrections denied the press access to Ronnie Lee Gardner, the first person to be executed by firing squad in America in fourteen years.

10. *Mitchell v. Baltimore Sun*, 883 A.2d 1008 (Md. App. 2005); *State v. Lashinsky*, 404 A.2d 1121 (N.J. 1979); *City of Oak Creek v. Ah King*, 436 N.W.2d 285 (Wis. 1989).

11. *Greer v. Spock*, 424 U.S. 828 (1976).

12. *Nation Magazine v. U.S. Department of Defense*, 762 F. Supp. 1558 (S.D.N.Y. 1991).

Arabian Sea. The Pentagon subsequently determined that both its interests and the interests of the press might best be served by "embedding" reporters with selected military units. In 2004, the RAND Corporation, a think tank, concluded that this embedding of reporters with the military in Iraq had worked well, that the media's objectivity had not been compromised by their close relationship with soldiers. Media companies themselves manifest ambivalence toward embedding. They relish the access but wonder if their credibility and objectivity are jeopardized by living with our soldiers.[13]

Equal Access to News as a First Amendment Right

Although courts have been very reluctant to find in the First Amendment an implicit right to gather news, several courts have held that once the government *chooses* to provide access to the news media, it may not discriminate among friendly and unfriendly media outlets. In one case, a federal judge held that a sheriff in the New Orleans area, who at the time was involved in libel litigation with the *Times-Picayune* newspaper, had trampled on the First Amendment when he announced that reporters for that particular media company would no longer receive advance word of upcoming press conferences and would be turned away at the door if they attempted to participate in any such press conferences.[14] A similar result was reached in Hawaii, where Honolulu mayor Frank Fasi sought to bar one particular *Honolulu Advertiser* reporter from official press conferences. Granting access to individual reporters on the basis of compatibility with the mayor is as much an act of censorship, Judge King concluded, as would be requiring a newspaper to submit its proposed news stories for prepublication clearance.[15]

Even the White House is not relieved of the obligation to treat media representatives evenhandedly. Reporter Robert Sherrill from the *Nation* magazine brought suit against the Secret Service for denying him access to the White House as a "security risk." Although the D.C. Circuit Court of Appeals did not require that the Secret Service's decision be reversed, it did insist that the Secret Service give any reporter denied a pass written notice and an opportunity to rebut whatever evidence was used to support the government's decision.[16]

Politicians might not be able to deny individual reporters access to press conferences or similar events open to large numbers of media representatives, but this does not mean that public officials must grant special access to any particular reporter.

---

13. David Ignatius, "Why the Inside Story Isn't Enough," *Washington Post*, May 2, 2010, B1.

14. *Times-Picayune Publishing v. Lee*, 15 Media L. Rep. (BNA) 1713 (E.D. La. 1988).

15. *Borreca v. Fasi*, 369 F. Supp. 906 (D. Haw. 1974). In an unpublished decision, the mayor of Toledo, Ohio, was similarly told that a "press conference is a public event," and that "to pick and choose who can attend" is a clear First Amendment violation. *Citicasters v. Finkbeiner*, #07-CV-00117 (N.D. Ohio 2007).

16. *Sherrill v. Knight*, 569 F.2d 124 (D.C. Cir. 1977).

Indeed, at least in some circumstances the reporter's calls need not even be returned. Thus, Governor Robert Ehrlich of Maryland was within his rights to instruct state agencies to refuse any contact beyond that required by law (such as to answer inquiries made under the state's Public Information Act) with two specific *Baltimore Sun* reporters whom he disliked.[17]

Hearing from Criminals and Bureaucrats

In two instances, the Supreme Court has struck down laws aimed squarely at reporters' potential sources rather than at media outlets themselves, at least in part because of the laws' effect on the "public's right to know." The term "news gathering" appears nowhere in either case, yet the philosophical bases for the decisions are very consistent with the media's often-repeated argument that the news-gathering process deserves special protection precisely because the public will otherwise be deprived of important information about weighty political matters.

The first of these cases involved New York State's "Son of Sam" law, named after the Son of Sam serial killer, David Berkowitz. The law required that any profits derived from writing about criminal wrongdoing be placed in a special escrow account for a period of five years, during which time the identifiable victims of any such crimes would be able to seek payment from that fund in partial compensation for

"Son of Sam" laws are designed to prevent this kind of profiteering from crime, but when such laws focus narrowly on profits made from *writing* about crime, they tend to have been struck down.

---

17. *Baltimore Sun Co. v. Ehrlich*, 437 F.3d 410 (4th Cir. 2006). See also *Youngstown Publishing Co. v. McKelvey*, 2005 U.S. Dist. LEXIS 9476 (N.D. Ohio 2005), *vacated on other grounds*, 189 Fed. Appx. 402 (6th Cir. 2006) (Youngstown, Ohio, mayor need not grant one-on-one interviews with disfavored reporters).

The *National Treasury Employees Union* case struck down portions of an ethics law prohibiting some employees from giving speeches or writing about topics related to their jobs.

their injuries. Justice O'Connor's majority opinion struck down the law as classic content-based censorship, finding that a financial disincentive to publish, when aimed only at some topics of discussion, is just as odious as an outright ban on the speech. Classic works like *The Autobiography of Malcolm X* and Henry David Thoreau's *Civil Disobedience* might never have been written if such a law had been in place.[18]

The second Supreme Court decision was handed down in 1995, invalidating por-

---

THINGS TO REMEMBER

A Constitutional Right to Gather News?

- The U.S. Supreme Court has at least hinted on several occasions that freedom of speech implies freedom to hear and to read.
- The Court has, however, refused to find an explicit First Amendment right to force the government to reveal information or to allow the press access to governmental venues.
- If, however, the government does grant press access to an event, it will not be allowed to discriminate among media outlets on the basis of a reporter's politics.

---

18. *Simon & Schuster, Inc. v. Members of the New York State Crime Victims Board*, 502 U.S. 105 (1991). See also *Keenan v. Superior Court*, 40 P.3d 718 (Cal. 2002), (striking down California's Son of Sam law); *Bretches v. Kirkland*, 335 Fed. Appx. 675 (9th Cir. 2009) (affirming prisoner's right to challenge order preventing him from publishing a book).

tions of the federal Ethics Reform Act that prohibited the vast majority of federal employees from receiving honoraria for writing or lecturing in their spare time, even if the topic of their communications was not at all related to their official duties. Here too, the Court emphasized the law's effect on the public's right to know, pointing out that literary giants Nathaniel Hawthorne, Herman Melville, Walt Whitman, and Bret Harte had all held "day jobs" as public servants.[19]

Access to Public Information: The Statutory Framework

Although the First Amendment does not provide the media an affirmative right to obtain government documents, the federal government and all state governments have passed laws that give varying degrees of such access. The federal and state laws often cover similar kinds of information and provide similar exemptions from disclosure. Even though forty states had freedom of information laws on the books before passage of the federal legislation in 1966, for convenience we begin here with a detailed examination of the federal Freedom of Information Act.

The Federal Freedom of Information Act

Congress passed the **Freedom of Information Act** (FOIA, pronounced "foy-uh") in 1966. It has been amended several times since. The philosophy undergirding the act, as interpreted by the federal courts, is that government works best when its work is open to public inspection. By exercising their rights accorded by the act, reporters and activists have helped us learn about issues such as the stalling in cleaning up after the *Exxon Valdez* oil spill, Poland's cooperation in the CIA's secret detainee program, the dangerous Ford Pinto gas tank, and the carcinogenic Red Dye #2. A FOIA request also resulted in release of some of the photos from Abu Ghraib prison in Iraq.

The act requires federal agencies, upon request, to make available any records that do not fit one of the law's nine exemptions. Most of the exemptions tell agencies only what they *may* withhold; government officials can usually choose to reveal more than the FOIA demands. Each year several million FOIA requests for government information are made. Because requesters who are denied the information they seek are explicitly given the right to bring suit in federal court, hundreds of federal FOIA cases are decided annually.

These cases typically involve the process of statutory construction introduced in chapter 1, as the courts' main role is to decide what the act means and whether a specific federal agency has conducted itself in ways consistent with the act. The courts

---

19. *United States v. National Treasury Employees Union*, 513 U.S. 454, 464–465 (1995).

generally do not look to the First Amendment to decide these cases, because there is no *constitutional* obligation for the government to open its records to the public.

It is also important to note that the act depends very much on the goodwill of the various federal agencies and the executive branch in fostering an atmosphere of openness. In response to the terrorist attacks of 2001, attorney general John Ashcroft circulated a memo in October 2001 to agency heads telling them to err on the side of nondisclosure of information requested under the FOIA and promising them the government's resources to defend them in any resulting litigation, just so long as there is "any sound legal basis" for a refusal to release information. Very soon upon taking office, President Obama circulated a new memo to department heads indicating that openness would be a hallmark of his administration (though a follow-up study released in 2010 expressed skepticism about Obama's track record).[20] It is likely that we may be in for a cycle of relatively secret government, and given that we have no way of knowing when a "war against terror" might be over, it is hard to predict how long that cycle might run.

We now continue our look at the federal FOIA by examining how courts have interpreted such basic issues as the definition of an "agency record" and the scope of the statutorily prescribed exemptions from disclosure.

What Is an "Agency"?   The FOIA defines a federal agency as "any executive department, military department, Government corporation, Government controlled corporation, or other establishment in the executive branch of the Government (including the Executive Office of the President), or any independent regulatory agency." Conspicuously missing from this list are Congress and the federal judiciary. The president is also not considered an "agency," nor is the presidential staff or any group whose sole function is to advise the president. Thus, for example, the National Security Council has been held to be beyond the reach of the FOIA. The council's function, as set forth in the National Security Act, is "to *advise* the President with respect to the integration of domestic, foreign, and military policies relating to the national security."[21]

The definition of "agency" in the act does cover many entities, however. It includes the departments of government headed by the various cabinet officers, such as the Department of the Treasury and the Department of Defense. The act also covers the various agencies that report to cabinet members; for example, the FBI, which reports

---

20. Eric Lichtblau, "Report Is Critical of Obama's Efforts at Transparency," *New York Times*, March 15, 2010, A12.

21. *Armstrong v. Executive Office of the President*, 90 F.3d 553 (D.C. Cir. 1996) (emphasis added); see also *Citizens for Responsibility and Ethics in Washington v. Office of Administration*, 566 F.3d 219 (D.C. Cir. 2009) (White House's Office of Administration, from which plaintiffs sought information about millions of lost presidential e-mails, not an "agency" for FOIA purposes—even though it has acted as if it were covered for over thirty years—because it provides only "operational and administrative support").

to the attorney general, is covered. The many agencies whose work is especially relevant to communication industries, such as the Federal Communications Commission, the Federal Trade Commission, and the Food and Drug Administration, are also covered by the act.

What Is a "Record"?

The FOIA does not define the word *record*, but the case law makes clear that it is to be interpreted broadly to include papers, reports, manuals, letters, and computer files, as well as audiotapes and other sound recordings, films, and photos. One thing that all these categories of materials have in common is their reproducibility. Physical objects that do not share this quality are generally beyond the scope of the FOIA. Thus, a reporter might obtain ballistic records from the FBI but will not be given access to actual guns and bullets. You may get reports on the efficacy of competing diet pills from the FDA, but you will not get samples of the pills studied by the agency.

What Is an "Agency Record"?

The phrase "agency record" has a more complicated meaning than the mere conjoining of the two words. In determining whether requested information is an agency record within the meaning of the act, courts often focus on whether the information was created by the agency, or at least obtained by the agency in the course of its normal duties.[22]

In one case, the Department of Justice was ordered to release numerous records of federal court decisions involving tax laws. Although the department does not create such records—they are created by the trial courts themselves—it keeps them on file because it provides the attorneys to represent the government in court on tax matters. This fact was enough to have the opinions considered Department of Justice agency records for the purposes of a FOIA request.[23]

More recently we learned that White House visitor logs are agency records under FOIA. True, they are eventually given to the White House, which is exempt from FOIA, but they are created by the Secret Service in the conduct of its duties.[24]

A quirky case involving the Department of Agriculture put government officials on notice that if they don't want their appointment calendars to be treated as agency records, they should not share them too widely within their agencies. A consumer group wanted to see the desk calendars of six department administrators to learn with which individuals and groups they had met before they loosened some meat-testing standards. A federal appellate court held that the appointment books for five of the six employees should be disclosed. They were agency records rather than merely personal

---

22. *Kissinger v. Reporters Committee for Freedom of the Press*, 445 U.S. 136 (1980) (transcripts of former secretary of state's conversations no longer State Department records after he donated them to the Library of Congress).

23. *U.S. Department of Justice v. Tax Analysts*, 492 U.S. 136 (1989).

24. 527 F. Supp. 2d 111 (D.D.C. 2009). The Secret Service is part of the Department of Homeland Security, which is covered by FOIA.

records, the court found, because they were created on company time and the employees had found it helpful to make their calendar entries available on a centralized computer system (apparently to keep coworkers and superiors appraised of their activities). The one employee whose calendar entries were shared only with his secretary was allowed to keep his data secret. But the five employees whose appointment books were subject to disclosure were told they could delete truly personal entries (dental appointments?) prior to complying.[25]

Making a FOIA Request   Perhaps the most difficult part of making a request under the FOIA is identifying the federal agency most likely to house the information sought. There is no single government-wide FOIA clearinghouse, so a fairly thorough understanding of the kinds of functions performed by the various agencies is needed. If you are interested in learning whether a particular toy is suspected by the government of being a safety hazard, for example, the Consumer Product Safety Commission is a logical place to start. A reporter desiring the latest report on the conditions at a specific nursing home that receives Medicare payments would likely contact the local Social Security office. If you are unsure which agency to contact, a good place to begin your research is the *Federal Register*, where each agency provides a description of its functions, as well as any FOIA contact information. Many federal agencies also have websites that provide varying degrees of helpfulness to potential FOIA requesters. The website of the Reporters Committee for Freedom of the Press (www.rcfp.org) also provides help in using the FOIA, including sample letters of request.

Once you identify the specific agency most likely to house the information you seek, a short letter to that agency's freedom of information (FOI) officer is the next step. Indicate early on (probably in the opening paragraph) that you are making a request "pursuant to the federal Freedom of Information Act" and, in as much detail as you possibly can, specify the precise information you seek. Mention if you are a representative of the news media, because the FOIA instructs agencies to give special consideration to reporters who intend to disseminate the information they gather. Perhaps most important is that agencies are supposed to charge such requestors only the cost of duplicating the records (waiving the often much larger cost involved in researching and organizing the records). Indeed, the act provides that *all* fees may be waived if the release of the information sought will be in the public interest. So add a sentence or two explaining why you believe the articles you intend to write will indeed benefit the public.

Because we are living in a digital age, indicate also in what form you would like the information (old-fashioned paper, CD-ROM, etc.). The FOIA was amended in 1996 by the Electronic Freedom of Information Act Amendments, which require that agencies comply with such instructions as long as the records sought are "readily re-

25. *Consumer Federation of America v. U.S. Department of Agriculture*, 455 F.3d 283 (D.C. Cir. 2006).

producible" in the format requested. In other words, an agency FOI officer will not be required to *create* a database according to the parameters you prefer, but if the database has already been created, it is considered an agency record every bit as much as is the hard paper version of the same data.

The FOIA requires that agencies respond to requests for information within twenty days of receipt. This requirement, however, does not necessarily mean you will have the information you seek in twenty days. Often the response is in the form of a request for additional specificity or an alert that the request is a huge one that will take a fair amount of time to fill. If the agency's FOI officer concludes that the information you seek falls within the scope of one of the nine exemptions enumerated in the act, your request may be denied. Or some material may be deemed releasable, and other portions subject to withholding. In that case, a redacted version of your request will be released, which often takes the decidedly low-tech form of sheets of paper with the exempted information blacked out. Agencies that deny requests either in whole or in part are generally required to provide descriptions of the kinds of documents being withheld, together with precise reasons for the withholding. This detailed listing of the kinds of documents in the agency's possession that are and are not being released is often referred to in the case law and commentary as a **Vaughn index**, named after an appellate decision from 1973.[26] If, however, an agency can demonstrate that the mere listing of the kinds of information available in the file will itself result in the same kind of serious harm that disclosure of the full documents would cause, the agency may be permitted to answer a request by refusing to indicate even whether the requested documents exist. Such answers are called *Glomar* responses, named after a commercial vessel, the records for which had been the subject of a FOIA request in a 1976 decision.[27] Agencies apparently can give such responses even when the existence of the records at issue is publicly known.[28]

If you are unhappy with an agency's response, you might go to court immediately, or you might instead seek out the Office of Government Information Services (OGIS), which was set up by the Open Government Act of 2007 to serve as a mediator of FOIA conflicts. The OGIS, part of the National Archives and Records Administration, first opened its doors in September 2009. It remains to be seen how successful it will be in resolving disputes between requesters and agencies.

The Supreme Court ruled in 2008 that even if an agency's rejection of a request for information has been upheld by the judiciary, a completely independent future litigant's request for very much the same information has to be processed anew by the agency. The agency cannot merely say, "but we already looked into that."[29]

---

26. *Vaughn v. Rosen*, 484 F.2d 820 (D.C. Cir. 1973).
27. *Phillippi v. CIA*, 546 F.2d 1009 (D.C. Cir. 1976).
28. *Wilner v. NSA*, 592 F.3d 60 (2nd Cir. 2009). The Supreme Court has never had occasion to rule on the legitimacy of *Glomar* responses; the *Wilner* case represents the first time the Second Circuit has embraced the concept.
29. *Taylor v. Sturgell*, 553 U.S. 880 (2008).

THINGS TO REMEMBER

Fundamentals of the Federal FOIA

- Passed in 1966 and amended several times since, the Freedom of Information Act tells government officials that they must make their agency records available to requestors, unless the requests fall within the scope of a handful of statutory exemptions.
- Under the act, "agencies" include departments headed by or reporting to cabinet officials, as well as many other kinds of executive offices; the president, Congress, and the judiciary are exempted, as are entities whose sole function is to advise the president.
- Virtually any reproducible data can be considered a "record" under the act, whether in the form of paper, film, photos, or computer records.
- Agency records must have been created by a covered agency or otherwise obtained in the course of carrying out its official functions.
- The act specifies the time frame in which FOI staff must respond to requests for information, as well as fees to be charged for searching and photocopying.

Exemptions from Disclosure

The Freedom of Information Act provides nine exemptions from the presumption that requests for information should be honored. Except for exemption 3, these exemptions are discretionary: FOI officers who conclude that a requested record falls within the scope of an exemption *may* withhold the information, but they are *not obligated* to withhold it.

Exemption 1: National Security. This first exemption permits agencies to withhold records that are "specifically authorized under criteria established by an Executive order to be kept secret in the interest of national defense or foreign policy" if the records are properly classified.[30] Not surprisingly, some agencies, such as the Central Intelligence Agency (CIA) and the National Security Agency (NSA), are in effect given virtual carte blanche to withhold information under this exemption. In 2004 a federal appellate court denied a law professor's request to see what documents the CIA had accumulated about him. The agency was willing to say only that they had a file. The court allowed this, reminding us the FOIA does not permit agencies to take into account the identity of a requestor. "Any information available to [Professor] Bassiouni is available to North Korea's secret police and Iran's counterintelligence service too," Judge Easterbrook explained.[31] More recently a FOIA request for information about past CIA clandestine activities in Guatemala was largely redacted for fear of revealing intelligence methods and identities of informants.[32]

---

30. *Baez v. U.S. Department of Justice*, 647 F.2d 1328 (D.C. Cir. 1980).

31. *Bassiouni v. CIA*, 392 F.3d 244 (7th Cir. 2004). In general, the court was right about the irrelevance of a FOIA requestor's identity, but there are exceptions, especially concerning prisoners' presentencing reports. See the discussion of exemption 5.

32. *Larson v. Department of State*, 565 F. 38 857 (D.C. Cir. 2009).

Federal judges who hear exemption 1 appeals are permitted to review the classified material to determine if the decision to classify was a proper one. In practice, judges very rarely exercise their right to perform such **in camera** reviews, relying instead on detailed affidavits from the government explaining why the material has been kept secret.[33]

Exemption 2: Internal Agency Personnel Rules.　　This exemption covers records of two very different kinds. FOIA attorneys often refer to them as the "low 2"and "high 2" categories.

The "low 2" exemption covers records "related solely to the internal personnel rules and practices of an agency." This part of exemption 2 is designed to protect some admittedly trivial materials from disclosure, such as the agency's rules for coffee or cigarette breaks and personal leave days. This exemption does not exist to protect delicate information, the kind that would violate employees' privacy. (Exemption 6 covers the more personal kinds of personnel files.) The Supreme Court has held that this part of exemption 2 seeks to "relieve agencies of the burden of assembling and maintaining for public inspection matter in which the public could not reasonably be expected to have an interest."[34] By contrast, the "high 2" portion of exemption 2 is designed to protect internal agency data that may very well have some public interest but that could make it difficult for the agency to function if it were publicly disseminated.

In *Sinsheimer v. U.S. Department of Homeland Security*, a "high 2" case, an accountant in the Department of Homeland Security who had a pending employment-discrimination suit and who had himself been a defendant in a couple of sexual-harassment complaints sought a memo that apparently gave supervisors instructions as to how to resolve sexual harassment complaints.[35] If this document were publicized, the department warned, future complainants and defendants might be able to foil an ongoing investigation. Our "low 2" example is a bit older. In *Schiller v. National Labor Relations Board*,[36] a private citizen had filed a FOIA request seeking documents related to the Equal Access to Justice Act, by which plaintiffs who successfully sue government agencies may sometimes receive court costs and attorney's fees. This may sound a bit too weighty to be a "low 2" case, but some of the documents withheld or at least blacked out in part by the National Labor Relations Board included references to information the court felt was fairly trivial and of primary interest only as internal personnel matters. Included were the agency's internal deadlines for com-

---

　33. An exception to the rule is seen in *American Civil Liberties Union v. FBI*, 429 F. Supp. 2d 179 (D.D.C. 2006), in which Judge Segal Huvelle's in camera review resulted in release of all but one of the documents sought.

　34. *Department of Air Force v. Rose*, 425 U.S. 352, 369–370 (1976).

　35. 437 F. Supp. 2d 50 (D.D.C. 2006).

　36. 964 F.2d 1205 (D.C. Cir. 1992).

pleting various tasks, names of persons individuals at the agency sometimes call for assistance, and even instructions to employees about how to keep records.

Exemption 3: Withholding Mandated by Other Federal Laws. Perhaps this part of the FOIA should be known as the "We bow down to other laws" exemption. It is sometimes referred to as the "catchall" exemption, and it is the only one of the nine wherein nondisclosure of requested files may be mandatory rather than discretionary. Agencies seeking to withhold data under this exemption must point to a specific federal law that either demands that this kind of information be kept secret or establishes clear criteria for determining whether the material must be withheld.[37] Dozens of federal laws sometimes are interpreted to require nondisclosure under FOIA's exemption 3. Among these are the Family Educational Rights and Privacy Act (FERPA, sometimes called the Buckley Act), the Health Insurance Portability and Accountability Act (HIPAA), and the more recently enacted Homeland Security Act of 2002, a section of which provides that information submitted to the government concerning "critical infrastructure" should be withheld from FOIA disclosure.

Perhaps the federal law FOIA requestors most frequently confront is the Privacy Act of 1974, which grants a qualified right to find out what information the government has about us, to correct such information where necessary, and to limit the ways in which the government may use that information (and to whom it may release it). In 1984 Congress amended the Privacy Act to clarify that the FOIA's presumption in favor of openness should prevail whenever the two laws might seem to conflict. Nonetheless, agencies will sometimes err on the side of nondisclosure, because persons may bring suit under the Privacy Act against any government agency that improperly reveals personal information about them to others. Such suits, if successful, can result in payment not only of court costs and attorney's fees but also of compensatory damages. By contrast, a FOIA requestor who sues an agency for improperly withholding data generally cannot receive actual damages (although the Open Government Act of 2007 provides for recovery of litigation costs and attorney's fees).

A good example of exemption 3 at work is found in *CIA v. Sims*, decided by the Supreme Court in 1985.[38] At issue was a FOIA request for information about MKULTRA, a multifaceted initiative in the 1950s and 1960s through which the CIA sought data on "the use of biological and chemical materials in altering human behavior," or "brainwashing." Part of the experiments had the government administering consciousness-altering drugs such as LSD to unwitting subjects, two of whom died during the course of the studies. The FOIA request sought copies of the grant proposals and contracts awarded under the MKULTRA program as well as the names of the individ-

---

37. See, for example, *Tax Analysts v. IRS*, 410 F.3d 715 (D.C. Cir. 2005) (IRS code legitimately used to deny FOIA request); *Public Citizen, Inc. v. Rubber Manufacturers Association*, 533 F.3d 810 (D.C. Cir. 2008) (wording of National Traffic and Motor Vehicle Safety Act does not prescribe withholding under FOIA exemption 3).

38. 471 U.S. 159 (1985).

uals, research universities, and other institutions that had performed the research. In denying that request, the CIA pointed to the National Security Act of 1947, which instructs the director of the agency to "protect intelligence sources and methods." The Supreme Court ruled unanimously in favor of the CIA.

Exemption 4: Confidential Commercial Information.   Often, in the course of conducting an investigation of a company or an industry (such as in deciding whether to approve a merger or to block it on antitrust grounds),[39] the government will learn things about one company that its competitors would love to learn but have no right to know. Exemption 4 reflects Congress's belief that neither competing companies nor the public in general necessarily have a right to learn such information, which after all had not started off as *government* information at all. For a FOIA request to be denied on the grounds that it includes such confidential commercial or financial information, the agency must conform to either of two rules set forth in a pair of decisions from the D.C. Circuit Court of Appeals. These rules are often referred to as the *National Parks* test,[40] as modified by the more recent *Critical Mass* decision.[41] The *National Parks* test governs information that a company has been *required* to provide to the government. When another entity makes a FOIA request for such data, an agency that seeks to deny the request under exemption 4 must be able to demonstrate that disclosure will either make it more difficult for the government to obtain such data in the future (because corporations will be less forthright) or do substantial harm to the competitive stance of the company that originally made the data available to the government. In *United Technologies Corporation v. U.S. Department of Defense*, for example, a federal appellate court told the government it could not reveal to the press some safety information it had required the corporation provide. The revelation may very well have had news value, but the plaintiff had made a strong showing to the effect that disclosure would give competing government contractors an unfair advantage.[42] Note that this decision is a "**reverse FOIA**" case, in that the plaintiff was not a media entity seeking disclosure, but rather the company that is the subject of the documents at issue, seeking *non*disclosure.

Data that a company has *voluntarily* submitted to the government are administered instead under the rule set forth in the *Critical Mass* decision. There, the D.C. Circuit Court of Appeals applied the first prong of the *National Parks* test but substituted for

---

39. *Inner City Press v. Board of Governors of the Federal Reserve System*, 380 F. Supp. 2d 211 (S.D.N.Y. 2005).

40. *National Parks and Conservation Association v. Morton*, 498 F.2d 765, 770 (D.C. Cir. 1974).

41. *Critical Mass Energy Project v. NRC*, 975 F.2d 871 (D.C. Cir. 1992).

42. 601 F.3d 557 (D.C. Cir. 2010). United Technologies argued that "a competitor with similar expertise could and would use th[e] information to gain insights into the strengths and weaknesses of [UTC]'s quality control system as well as manufacturing techniques and use those insights to revise and improve its own quality control and manufacturing systems."

the second prong a new test: that the information sought be of a kind that would not "customarily" be revealed by a corporation to the public in general.[43]

Exemption 5: Internal Agency Policy Discussions and Memoranda. The philosophy behind exemption 5 of the FOIA—often called the "working papers" or "executive privilege" exemption—is that the public has a right to know what policies a government agency has adopted but not all the details of the discussions that helped shape the completed policy. Such revelations would "chill" the speech of agency employees and advisors—who would fear that their words might come back to haunt them—and thus jeopardize the quality of decision making. The exemption is also consistent with a sense that public servants "should be judged by what they decided, not for matters they considered before making up their minds."[44]

Exemption 5 also permits withholding data related to a government agency's legal consultations with its own or outside attorneys (the "attorney-client privilege") as well as, more generally, any strategizing done by attorneys who are contemplating litigation on behalf of a government agency (the "attorney work-product privilege").[45] This latter privilege reflects the belief that the FOIA should not result in disclosure of information that would not normally be revealed to an adversary in litigation through the discovery process. In 1988, the Supreme Court issued a ruling on this facet of the exemption, in the context of a FOIA request by a group of federal prisoners for their "**presentencing reports**," which are made at the request of probation officers to the district court judge and which often include testimony from neighbors, therapists, and others who may have some knowledge about the circumstances surrounding a defendant's crimes. In a 5–3 vote, the Court determined that such reports might be withheld under exemption 5 from release to third parties but that the data should be given to the prisoners themselves.[46]

More recently the D.C. Circuit Court of Appeals found it helpful to distinguish the "working papers" and "attorney privilege" components of exemption 5.[47] At issue was a FOIA request made to the Department of Justice seeking a small number of e-mail messages sent within the department as it was considering whether to intervene in an unusual case in which Americans were suing a group of foreign associations they blamed for the death of their son in Israel. Intra-agency discussions that fall into the "working papers" category might be disclosed, at least in part, the court

---

43. See, for example, *ERG Transit Systems v. WMATA*, 593 F. Supp.2d 249 (D.D.C. 2009) (information submitted by company providing fare collection services to mass transit agency in support of a request for a contract modification had been provided voluntarily).

44. *Jordan v. U.S. Department of Justice*, 591 F.2d 753, 773 (D.C. Cir. 1978).

45. *Mead Data Central v. Department of the Air Force*, 566 F.2d 242 (D.C. Cir. 1977); *FTC v. Grolier*, 462 U.S. 19 (1983).

46. *U.S. Department of Justice v. Julian*, 486 U.S. 1 (1988).

47. *Judicial Watch v. U.S. Department of Justice*, 432 F.3d 366 (D.C. Cir. 2005). The underlying case involving Israel was *Boim v. Quranic Literacy Institute*, 291 F.3d 1000 (7th Cir. 2002).

found, because some utterances concerned relatively uncontroversial factual questions such as "Has this kind of litigation ever been attempted before?" or "How many attorneys do we have who know anything about the group Hamas?" Conversations between agencies and their attorneys, however, should be deemed completely and inarguably subject to withholding.

Exemption 6: Personnel, Medical, and Similar Files. As seen earlier, exemption 2 permits the nondisclosure of the kinds of trivial personnel matters (parking space allocations, coffee break policies) in which the public has no interest. Exemption 6 also provides for the nondisclosure of personnel matters, but those of a more personal nature. The latter exemption is not restricted to information about government personnel but extends to any individual about whom highly private information is included in a file.

The specific wording of the exemption tells FOI officers they may withhold information from "personnel and medical files and similar files the disclosure of which would constitute a clearly unwarranted invasion of privacy." There are thus two steps in adjudicating disputes arising under exemption 6: first, a court must determine whether the file is indeed a personnel or medical or "similar" file; second, a court must assess how "unwarranted" the privacy invasion, if any, would be if the file were disclosed.

Concerning the initial inquiry, it is not surprising that the word *similar* has been problematic. The key to determining relevant similarity is that the information sought is "of the same magnitude, as highly personal, or as intimate in nature, as that at stake in personnel and medical records."[48] In other words, the law does not care if the record physically resembles a medical chart; rather, it asks whether the record includes information as personal as might be seen in a medical chart.

Using this framework, the First Circuit Court of Appeals found that the names of scientists who had submitted unsuccessful proposals for National Cancer Institute grants would not be as "personal" a revelation as is envisioned by the exemption. The court pointed out that being rejected for such grants was "not so rare an occurrence as to stigmatize the unfunded applicant."[49]

Probably the most dramatic example of exemption 6 litigation involved the explosion of the *Challenger* space shuttle, which killed all the astronauts aboard, including high school teacher Christa McAuliffe. The *New York Times* sought from NASA the audiotape of the shuttle voice recorder. One of the threshold issues the courts had to confront was whether, given that NASA had already released what it claimed were the full transcripts of the tapes, the release of the tapes themselves would provide enough *additional* "personal" information to trigger exemption 6. The D.C. Circuit Court of

---

48. *Board of Trade of the City of Chicago v. Commodity Futures Trading Commission*, 627 F.2d 392, 398 (D.C. Cir. 1980).

49. *Kurzon v. Health and Human Services*, 649 F.2d 65 (1st Cir. 1981).

Appeals found that the tapes were in fact covered by the exemption. "While the taped words do not contain information about the personal lives of the astronauts," Judge Douglas Ginsburg wrote for the majority, "disclosure of the file would reveal the sound and inflection of the crew's voices during the last seconds of their lives."[50]

In more recent years exemption 6 was used to prevent disclosure of petitions filed by "American Taliban" John Walker Lindh as he sought to reduce his jail sentence, and the names and addresses of some Guantanamo detainees' family members.[51]

Records need not be very dramatic to be "personal" enough for exemption 6 purposes. In 1994 the Supreme Court adjudicated a FOIA request by union affiliates who wanted to organize federal workers in several agencies and thus sought workers' home mailing addresses. Disclosure of this information would constitute an unwarranted invasion of privacy, Justice Thomas concluded for the majority, because it would lead to an "influx of union-related mail, and, perhaps, union-related telephone calls or visits" that at least some employees would prefer to avoid.[52]

Exemption 7: Law Enforcement.   The purpose of exemption 7 is to prevent the premature disclosure of materials that would jeopardize criminal or civil investigations or cause some kind of demonstrable harm to informants who have assisted law enforcement personnel. This is the wordiest of the FOIA exemptions. Because it is set forth within the statute as subsections A through F, it is often thought of as six exemptions in one. Courts called on to adjudicate exemption 7 claims engage in a two-part analysis. First, they must determine whether the requested information was "compiled for law enforcement purposes." If the answer is yes, the courts must next ask if disclosing the information will interfere with law enforcement proceedings, jeopardize someone's right to a fair trial, constitute an invasion of privacy rights, reveal a confidential source's identity, reveal investigatory techniques, or endanger someone's life or physical safety.

Courts have generally been very deferential in their handling of the first inquiry, the question of whether the information sought was "compiled for law enforcement purposes." In 1982, for example, the Supreme Court held that the FBI files and other possibly derogatory materials that the Nixon administration had gathered to hurt persons on Nixon's famous "enemies list" should be considered exempt from FOIA disclosure. Even though the immediate reason for compiling the information may have been for rather shallow, and perhaps even illegal, political ends, the data had originally been gathered for legitimate law enforcement purposes.[53]

---

50. *NASA v. New York Times Co.*, 920 F.2d 1002 (D.C. Cir. 1990).

51. *Associated Press v. Department of Justice*, 549 F. 3d 62 (2nd Cir. 2008); *Associated Press v. Department of Defense*, 554 F. 3d 274 (2nd Cir. 2009).

52. *U.S. Department of Defense v. Federal Labor Relations Authority*, 510 U.S. 487, 501 (1994).

53. *FBI v. Abramson*, 456 U.S. 615, 631–632 (1982). See also *John Doe Agency v. John Doe Corp.*, 493 U.S. 146 (1989) (information not initially gathered for law enforcement purposes but later used for such can be withheld under exemption 7).

Recall that one of the negative results that exemption 7 tries to avoid is violation of the privacy interests of the person to whom the records refer. In its 2003–2004 term, the Court had to consider a novel issue—must the person objecting to disclosure be the subject of the files, or can that person's survivors also inject themselves into the litigation? You may recall Vincent Foster, who was deputy counsel to President Clinton and whose death shocked the Washington establishment and provided fodder for conspiracy theorists of many persuasions. At issue in the case before the Supreme Court were photographs of the death scene in a park outside Washington, D.C., including pictures of Foster's body. Allan Favish of the group Accuracy in Media was unconvinced that Foster's death was suicide and sought disclosure of the official police photos under the FOIA. When the case—actually a handful of consolidated related cases—reached the Supreme Court, Justice Kennedy concluded for a unanimous Court that the privacy interests of Foster's surviving family members were strong enough to outweigh Favish's interest in disclosure.[54]

The notion that such privacy interests can descend to surviving family members in a FOIA context is not applicable to the tort law of privacy (the subject of chapter 5). So ruled the Tenth Circuit Court of Appeals in *Showler v. Harper's Magazine Foundation*,[55] in which a fallen soldier's parents sued the magazine for having published a photo of their son's casket.

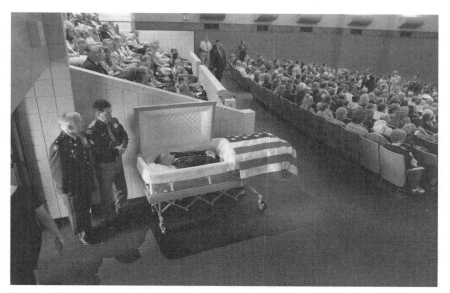

Sergeant Showler's father had no legally enforceable privacy interests against *Harper's Magazine* for the unauthorized publication of this photo.

54. *National Archives and Records Administration v. Favish*, 541 U.S. 1057 (2004).
55. 222 F. Appx. 755 (10th Cir. 2007).

It is also worth mentioning that the Third Circuit Court of Appeals has ruled that corporations can have "privacy" interests within the meaning of exemption 7. (It is not clear if their feelings can be hurt, too). The case dealt with a trade association that had requested documents related to AT&T's admitted overcharging of the government for services.[56]

Not surprisingly, the law enforcement exemption has been cited frequently in our post-9/11 world as a barrier to FOIA requests seeking information about our government's treatment of detainees and related responses to terrorist threats. In *Center for National Security Studies v. U.S. Department of Justice*, the plaintiff's request for information about the number of detainees held on immigration or criminal charges, or as material witnesses, was denied.[57] Thus remaining secret were detainees' names and citizenship, the charges filed against them, and the names of their attorneys (if any). And in 2009 an Associated Press request for documents related to mistreatment of Guantanamo detainees was denied, in part because of the presumed privacy interests—you read that right!—of the detainees themselves.[58]

Exemption 8: Financial Institutions. The purpose of this rather infrequently used exemption is to foster continued public confidence in banks, trust companies, securities exchanges, and similar entities. Surprisingly even the huge federal bailout of banks and auto companies has not resulted in case law invoking the exemption. A search conducted by this author in 2010 found only two cases citing the exemption in the past five years.[59]

Exemption 9: Geological and Geophysical Data. Exemption 9 is designed to protect the financial interests of companies that have filed with the government data concerning oil wells and natural gas deposits. It is the least used of all the nine FOIA exemptions; it has been cited in only a handful of court cases. Moreover, claims under this exemption often overlap with arguments made under other exemptions, such as exemption 8 (financial data) or exemption 4 (trade secrets).

The Government in the Sunshine Act

In 1976, Congress passed the Government in the Sunshine Act (also known as the federal open meetings law), which requires generally that certain federal agencies conduct their meetings in public. Most of the agencies covered by FOIA are covered by the Sunshine Act; to be subject to the open meetings requirement, an agency must be covered by FOIA, at least two of the agency's governing body members must be ap-

---

56. *AT&T v. FCC*, 582 F. 3d 490 (3rd Cir. 2009).

57. 331 F.3d 918 (D.C. Cir. 2003).

58. *AP v. U.S. Department of Defense*, 554 F. 3d 274 (2nd Cir. 2009).

59. *Abrams v. U. S. Department of the Treasury*, 243 Fed. Appx. 4 (5th Cir. 2007); *Gavin v. U.S. SEC*, 2007 U.S. Dist. LEXIS 62252 (D. Minn. 2007).

THINGS TO REMEMBER

The FOIA Exemptions

1. National Security
2. Routine Personnel Records
3. Deference to Other Federal Laws
4. Confidential Commercial Information
5. Internal Agency Discussions

6. Personnel, Medical, or "Similar" Files
7. Law Enforcement
8. Confidential Data from Financial Institutions
9. Geological and Geophysical Data

---

pointed by the president (with Senate approval), and it must have some policymaking powers. Thus, the Council of Economic Advisers is exempt from the act, precisely because its role is only to *advise* the president on economic matters.[60]

Agencies that are covered by the Sunshine Act must conduct their meetings in public. A "meeting" is defined in the act as any gathering of a quorum of the agency's members to talk together about their official business. A meeting can thus be in a government hearing room or in a coffee shop. It can be live or via telephone conference call, and likely in Internet chat rooms.

Under the act, agencies must announce upcoming meetings at least one week in advance. Should an agency determine that an upcoming meeting need not be open to the public because its subject matter is listed among the act's explicit exemptions, that determination must be included in the announcement. Persons who wish to appeal the agency's proposed closing can immediately bring suit in federal district court. Aggrieved parties can also sue after a closed hearing has been held, although such suits must be filed within sixty days. The burden of proof is always on the agency to justify closure, but even a successful suit will typically result only in release of a transcript or tape recording of the closed hearing. (Agencies are always required to produce such records and to retain them for at least two years.) There is no provision for damage awards, and the awarding of attorneys' fees and court costs is infrequent.

The statutory exemptions to open meetings for the most part mirror FOIA exemptions, including exemptions for meetings at which trade secrets will be discussed or where an open meeting would jeopardize a national security interest. A few of the Sunshine Act's exemptions are different from those of the FOIA, however. For example, the Sunshine Act includes an exemption for meetings that "involve accusing any person of a crime, or formally censuring any person." Meetings can also be closed if companies or individuals likely to be subject to a proposed regulation would want to attend only to learn ways of evading the law.[61]

---

60. *Rushforth v. Council of Economic Advisors*, 762 F.2d 1038 (D.C. Cir. 1985).
61. *Common Cause v. Nuclear Regulatory Commission*, 674 F.2d 921 (D.C. Cir. 1982).

The Federal Advisory Committee Act

We have seen that the Government in the Sunshine Act exempts agencies whose function is largely advisory. Many such advisory agencies' meetings must nonetheless be open to the press and public, because of separate legislation known as the Federal Advisory Committee Act (FACA) of 1972. Unsurprisingly, FACA has its own exceptions. The act specifically exempts committees "composed wholly of full-time, or permanent part-time, officers or employees of the Federal Government." The President's Task Force on National Health Care Reform, appointed by President Clinton and chaired by First Lady Hillary Clinton, was thus ruled beyond the reach of FACA.[62]

The Clinton administration produced another headline-making Federal Advisory Committee Act precedent when it set up the Presidential Legal Expense Trust to collect private donations toward the Clintons' private legal expenses from the Whitewater investigations and the Paula Jones sexual-harassment suit. When a private citizens' committee brought suit, alleging that the trust was not behaving in accordance with the FACA, a federal district court determined that the act was not implicated, that "a trust established by a government officer in his personal capacity without use of public funds, and which renders absolutely no advice on official government policy, simply is not within FACA's scope."[63]

Vice President Cheney was able to use the Federal Advisory Committee Act to avoid disclosing information about his leadership in the National Energy Policy Development Group, created by President George W. Bush shortly after his inauguration in 2001.[64] More recent litigation under FACA has suggested that an entity within the Department of Commerce devoted to working closely with Mexico and Canada on trade issues as well as an advisory group set up by the Forestry Service to study disease transmission between species of sheep were likely covered by FACA.[65]

State Freedom of Information Acts

All fifty states and the District of Columbia have some form of legislation providing for access to government records. Although there are many similarities between the state laws and the federal FOIA, in fact the states were the leaders here, with over forty states having some kind of freedom of information law on the books before the

---

62. *Association of American Physicians and Surgeons v. Clinton*, 997 F.2d 898 (D.C. Cir. 1993); *Association of American Physicians and Surgeons v. Clinton*, 989 F. Supp. 8 (D.D.C. 1997). The First Lady was treated as a federal employee, in part because separate federal law authorizes presidents to pay their spouses from public funds for any official assistance they provide.

63. *Judicial Watch v. Clinton*, 880 F. Supp. 1, 8 (D.D.C. 1995), *aff'd*, 76 F.3d 1232 (D.C. Cir. 1996).

64. *Cheney v. U.S. District Court*, 542 U.S. 367 (2004), *on remand, In re Cheney*, 406 F.3d 723 (D.C. Cir. 2005).

65. *Judicial Watch v. U.S. Department of Commerce*, 583 F. 3d 871 (D.C. Cir. 2009); *Idaho Wool Growers Association v. Schafer*, 637 F. Supp. 2d 868 (D. Idaho 2009).

THINGS TO REMEMBER

Federal Open Meeting Laws

- The Government in the Sunshine Act of 1976 generally requires meetings conducted by agencies covered by FOIA to be open to the public.
- Meetings need not be in person nor in formal meeting rooms.
- Exemptions generally mirror FOIA's own exemptions.
- Agencies wishing to meet in private must first alert the public of this intention, which is itself appealable.
- The Federal Advisory Committee Act also requires that certain meetings be open to the public.

federal law was adopted in 1966. In any event, it is not at all unusual for state supreme courts to cite federal case law interpreting the federal FOIA as precedent when they are called on to interpret their own state statutes.

State statutes typically define records rather broadly to include not only papers but also most other methods in which information might be retained, including computer databases. Several state laws make an explicit distinction between the information contained in a database (revealable) and the computer software that helps organize that information (not necessarily revealable). In Florida, the actual individual ballots cast in the contested 2000 election were given to a media consortium requesting them under the state's FOIA, but unused ballots from that same election were not deemed public records.[66]

A few states restrict informational access to citizens of that particular state. However, a federal court in Delaware invalidated such a restriction there, in part because of the disproportionate number of major national and multinational corporations that are incorporated in Delaware or set up their official headquarters in the tax-friendly state.[67] A nonprofit group called ProPublica has created a database of volunteers willing to make Freedom of Information Act requests in their home states on behalf of out-of-state reporters.[68]

Most states do not allow agencies to base access decisions on the requestors' motives (personal, educational, commercial), although several states do provide for a higher fee structure in the case of purely commercial uses. Within this framework, reporters seeking information for dissemination to the public are not considered commercial users, the profit motive of their employers notwithstanding. In 1999, the

---

66. *Rogers v. Hood*, 906 So. 2d 1220 (Fla. Dist. Ct. App. 2005). The state's supreme court refused to review the decision.

67. *Lee v. Minner*, 369 F. Supp. 2d 527 (D. Del. 2005), *aff'd*, 458 F. 3d 194 (3rd Cir. 2006).

68. Amanda Michel, "Reporting Network Doc Squad," *ProPublica Reporting Network*, April 5, 2010 (www.propublica.org/ion/reporting-network).

Supreme Court saw no constitutional impediment to a California statute permitting the release by law enforcement agencies of arrestees' home addresses only to persons willing to declare that the information would not be used for commercial purposes. (The company challenging the law routinely made the addresses available to attorneys, who would presumably contact the individuals named to solicit business.)[69] Although most states charge requestors only for photocopying costs, some also assess a fee for the agency's expenditure of human and other resources in researching a request. Overall fee waivers are common when requestors are able to demonstrate a public benefit from the release of the information sought. In practice, the result is that the media often do not have to pay fees.

Not surprisingly, all state access laws provide exceptions to the general presumption of openness. Often these exemptions are part of the statute itself, as is the case with the federal FOIA. Sometimes it has instead fallen to the state courts to create categories of exemptions. Whether an exemption requires or merely permits nondisclosure varies from state to state. Although many states have fashioned their own lists of exemptions after the federal statute, clearly some FOIA provisions make little sense in the context of a state law. The national security exemption, for example, is much more likely to be relevant to requests for federal rather than state information. Conversely, such information as tapes of 911 emergency calls are likely to be of more relevance at state and local levels than in federal FOIA requests.[70]

Requestors who are dissatisfied with a state agency's response may appeal, either initially via some administrative process or directly to state court. Many states provide for an expedited appeals process, so that these kinds of cases can be moved to the front of a court's calendar. Successful litigants will generally receive only the information they sought, not money damages, although attorneys' fees may be awarded under some circumstances.

Requests for certain categories of information have generated substantial public interest and litigation under state law. One such recurring issue has been the need to balance the public's right to know the details of searches to fill high-level job vacancies against the danger of discouraging the candidacies of applicants who fear publicity. Cases have involved applicants for such positions as state university president and municipal town manager.[71]

Individuals' medical records and birth certificates are generally not disclosable under state FOIA provisions.[72] Coroners' records, however, are generally revealable

---

69. *Los Angeles Police Department v. United Reporting Publishing Corp.*, 528 U.S. 32 (1999).

70. "States Push to Exempt 911 Calls," *News Media Update* (Reporters Committee for Freedom of the Press), March 15, 2010.

71. *City of Farmington v. The Daily Times*, 210 P. 3d 246 (Ct. App. New Mexico 2009); *Star Tribune Company v. University of Minnesota Board of Regents*, 667 N.W. 2d 447 (Minn. Ct. App. 2003).

72. Roxanne Moore Saucier, "Legislature Passes Limits on Vital Records Access," *Bangor Daily News*, April 12, 2010, D2. In another part of the country, investigative reporting revealed that Oklahoma had been selling vital records that it would not reveal under the state's freedom of informa-

(unless they are part of an ongoing police investigation), on the grounds that our privacy rights expire along with us. The Florida legislature, in response to the media's voyeuristic appetite for photos of deceased NASCAR racer Dale Earnhardt, passed a law declaring that autopsy photos should generally be withheld under the state's public records act.[73]

The increasingly common phenomenon of states contracting out traditional government functions—for example, the operation of schools, prisons, and other institutions and programs—to private companies has often meant that the records of those private companies are treated as public records covered by state freedom of information laws. This happened in Tennessee, when the records of a private company that provided day care programs for the state were treated as public records.[74] A similar concern has been expressed about federal government privatization.[75]

Until 1994 it had been left to each state's discretion whether to keep information found in driver's license records open to the public. The public policy implications of this question had become controversial for at least two reasons. First, there was growing resentment in some quarters at the states' profiting from selling their motor vehicle license databases to commercial users, as in letting Toyota have a list of the state's Honda owners. To many this policy was seen as an unwarranted invasion of privacy. Second, such personally identifying information could be used for criminal wrongdoing. An actress in California was murdered by a stalker who was able to obtain her address from the state because he knew the woman's license plate number. Antiabortion protesters can similarly obtain names and addresses not only of clinic physicians and staff but often of their clients as well, which has sometimes led to harassing mail and phone calls. Concerns such as these led to passage of the federal Drivers Privacy Protection Act in 1994, which requires that states give motorists the option of keeping their data confidential. The Supreme Court upheld the law in 2000.[76]

State Open Meetings Laws

All fifty states and the District of Columbia also have some kind of legislation providing for the opening up of governmental meetings to the press and public. The majority of these laws pre-date the federal government in the Sunshine Act of 1976,

tion act. John Estus, Paul Monies, and Gavin Off, "State Brings in Millions by Selling Personal Data," *The Oklahoman*, April 4, 2010, 1A.

73. *Campus Communications v. Earnhardt*, 821 So. 2d 388 (Fla. Dist. Ct. App. 2002). See generally Samuel A. Terilli and Sigman L. Splichal, "Public Access to Autopsy and Death-Scene Photographs: Relational Privacy, Public Records, and Avoidable Collisions," 10 *Communication Law and Policy* 313 (2005).

74. *Memphis Publishing Co. v. Cherokee Children and Family Services*, 87 S.W.3d 67 (Tenn. 2002).

75. Celeste Pagano, "Proceed with Caution: Avoiding Hazards in Toll Road Privatizations," 83 *St. John's Law Review* 351, 379 (2009).

76. *Condon v. Reno*, 528 U.S. 141 (2000).

which was itself modeled after the law in Florida. These statutes also require that some form of advance public notice be provided of an upcoming meeting, often in the form of a formal announcement in the local newspaper. In some states, openness means not only that the public and press may attend but also that citizens may address the meeting during a public comment period. Some statutes also explicitly provide for a right to broadcast meetings live. Typically, state-level laws govern meetings held by city, county, and town entities as well. Whether a group is covered by an open meetings law depends on a number of factors, including whether the group performs government-like functions or has policymaking authority, whether it was created by state law (or the state constitution), whether its membership consists mostly of public officials, and whether its expenses are paid out of public funds.

Reporters often complain that public officials will try to skirt their state's open-meetings law by having informal or "spontaneous" gatherings over lunch or in some other seemingly social milieu. State laws and judicial interpretations vary in the zeal with which they will try to prevent such abuses. Most open meetings laws provide that any gathering of a quorum (the smallest number needed to take official action) of a governmental body will be considered a "meeting," wherever such gatherings may take place, as long as some official business is discussed. The Texas Supreme Court held that when two of the state's three water commissioners discussed a case before them while in the men's room on recess, they held a "meeting" that should have been open to the public (although not necessarily in the men's room, one can assume).[77]

Another popular way of trying to evade the law's demand for openness is the use of "serial communication," a succession of private communications, each one of which involves a number of participants fewer than necessary to trigger the statute, but where the cumulative effect is to conduct via this "telephone game" the equivalent of a prohibited meeting of the whole. Some state statutes specifically prohibit this procedure, and in other states the judiciary has stepped in to accomplish the same thing.[78]

Not surprisingly, state statutes provide exceptions to the assumption of openness. Public bodies can meet in secret "executive session" when the matters they intend to discuss fall into certain specified categories, such as consultations with an attorney about ongoing litigation or internal personnel matters that would likely result in an unwarranted invasion of privacy. Typically, the decision to move into executive session must itself be in the form of a motion that is made and voted on in open session. Moreover, many states dictate that executive sessions are designed for discussions only, that any formal actions taken by the government body after participating in such private discussions must then again be voted on in public.

---

77. *Acker v. Texas Water Commission*, 790 S.W.2d 299 (Tex. 1990); see also *Newspaper Guild v. Sacramento County Board of Supervisors*, 69 Cal. Rptr. 480 (Ct. App. 1968) (a luncheon at the Elks Club deemed a "meeting" under the state law).

78. John F. O'Connor and Michael J. Baratz, "Some Assembly Required: The Application of State Open Meeting Laws to E-mail Correspondence," 12 *George Mason Law Review* 719 (2004).

THINGS TO REMEMBER

State Freedom of Information and Open Meeting Laws

- All fifty states and the District of Columbia have FOI and open meetings laws.
- State FOI laws, although generally modeled after the federal law, vary greatly in terms of who may obtain information and for what purposes and whether any statutory exemptions require, or merely permit, nondisclosure.
- Most state open meetings laws pre-date the federal law, and many give the public the right not only to attend but also to speak.
- States have often been called on to apply their laws to "spontaneous, off-the-record" meetings.

States vary in the kinds of sanctions to be applied against public officials who hold closed meetings that should have been open to the public. Some statutes provide for criminal fines and even imprisonment,[79] but these penalties are rarely invoked. It is also possible in several jurisdictions to have a state court nullify any government actions that were taken in an improperly convened executive session.

The (Mixed) Value of Being Nice: A Final Thought on Getting Information

One commonality between federal and state freedom of information and open meetings laws is that requestors have varying and limited legal options when government agencies deny their requests. A natural question arises, then—is it wiser to present a tough, no-nonsense front from the outset (so as to suggest you won't hesitate to sue, if need be), or should you appear cooperative and open to compromise? In an intriguing field study, Professor David Cullier from the University of Arizona sent threatening or cooperative cover letters seeking specific information covered by state law to police chiefs. A disturbing 42 percent of chiefs of police did not reply at all, in seeming violation of state law. Of those chiefs who did reply, far more provided the requested records when confronting a threatening as compared to a polite letter.[80]

---

79. *Rangra v. Brown*, 566 F. 3d 515 (5th Cir. 2009) (criminalizing with possible penalties of $500 and six months in jail the mere act of exchanging e-mail messages "discussing whether to call a council meeting" might be a violation of public officials' First Amendment rights).

80. David Cuillier, "Honey v. Vinegar: Testing Compliance-Gaining Theories in the Context of Freedom of Information Laws," 15 *Communication Law and Policy* 203 (2010). A second study seeking information from school districts about employee contracts yielded consistent but less dramatic results.

Chapter Summary

Although Supreme Court decisions have often included dicta to the effect that the First Amendment has some relevance to the news-gathering process, there is no constitutional right to obtain information from the government. Congress and the state legislatures, however, have created a limited statutory right through the passage of freedom of information and open meetings laws. These laws all provide categories of exemptions from disclosure, which have in turn resulted in a voluminous case law seeking to determine if a specific information request is exempted.

Chapter 8

REPORTING ON THE JUDICIARY

In June 2010 court junkies could watch the Senate Judiciary Committee's hearings on Elena Kagan's nomination to the Supreme Court gavel to gavel. How very different from actual day-to-day Supreme Court oral arguments, which are not televised. That same Senate committee, also in June 2010, passed a resolution expressing the "sense of the Senate" that the Court should make a "yes" to television the default option.[1] We will return later in this chapter to the question of whether courtroom proceedings should be televised. For now suffice it to say that the issue is one of many involving perceived clashes between freedom of the press and the need for an impartial and efficiently functioning judiciary.

You may wonder why there is a separate chapter on media coverage of the courts. Shouldn't the judiciary be treated as just one more topic of government information to which the press would want to gain access? In other words, couldn't the subject matter of this chapter have been handled in the previous chapter instead, the one dealing with access to information? The main reason is one of happenstance: the law in this area has developed separately from the "access to information" case law. Also, the kinds of issues encountered in this chapter concern not only access to judicial venues and information but also the core right to publish what the press already knows.

A Clash of Rights

In many legal disputes concerning information about the judiciary, both litigants favoring disclosure and those seeking secrecy have constitutional arguments on their

---

1. S. Res. 339, 111th Congress, 2nd Session (passed by Senate Judiciary Committee on June 8, 2010). At her hearings, Kagan expressed enthusiastic support for televising the Court's oral arguments.

side. Indeed, these disputes are often referred to as "First versus Sixth Amendment" clashes, reflecting the fact that the free press guarantee is pitted against the various "fair trial" rights—the right to a speedy trial, the right to an impartial jury of one's peers, and so forth—enumerated in the Sixth Amendment. The U.S. Supreme Court has handed down dozens of cases involving the clash between the First and Sixth Amendments.[2] Whereas the case law from the previous chapter dealt mostly with statutory construction (the process of figuring out what laws mean), litigation involving access to and freedom to report information about a court case is at its core a battle over competing constitutional rights. As we shall see, for example, there is a constitutional right to attend a criminal suspect's trial, even though there is not a right (as we saw in chapter 7) to interview that same suspect in jail. On the other hand, media are often prohibited from publishing what they already know about a judicial proceeding, whereas such a restriction on publishing information about other governmental proceedings is almost unthinkable.

The Contempt Power

It is especially important for professional communicators to understand their obligations under the Sixth Amendment because those who disobey orders from a trial judge risk being issued a contempt citation. To be held in **contempt of court** means to be fined or imprisoned for taking any action that a trial judge perceives as disobedient or disrespectful. The judiciary is not the only branch of government that can hold an offender in contempt. Congress held in contempt several uncooperative witnesses called before it during the McCarthy era and has often threatened to hold presidential appointees in contempt for failing to give complete and accurate testimony. The contempt power, however, is wielded most often by the judiciary. Most forcefully, too, in that the founders borrowed from the English common law the power of judges to issue **summary contempt** orders, through which persons disrupting the courtroom can be cited and punished on the spot, without a right to any further due process.

The law recognizes two broad categories of contempt citations: civil and criminal. **Civil contempt citations** are designed to persuade ("coerce" might be a better word) a reluctant party to do something she or he has thus far failed to do. In the case of reporters, this most typically means revealing the identity of one's sources. Many reporters have incurred daily fines and have even been imprisoned as part of a judge's efforts to compel disclosure. So important is the overall issue of reporters' relationships with their confidential sources that it is the subject of the next chapter. (Any trial participant—witnesses, jurors, attorneys[3]—might be found in contempt of court.

2. See, for example, *Presley v. Georgia*, 130 S. Ct. 721 (2010).
3. See, for example, Rochelle Olson, "Judge Clarifies Demand for Apology," *Star Tribune*, June 18, 2010, 4B (attorney threatened with contempt if he failed to write a letter of apology to his client's arresting police officer).

We focus on reporters because threatening them with contempt raises special First Amendment issues.) **Criminal contempt citations** are issued as punishment for actions already taken. Overzealous attorneys may incur the wrath of trial judges if they disobey orders. The order might be to "stop badgering a witness" or to accept an adverse ruling from the bench without any vocal complaints. Criminal contempt citations are of most relevance to communication law when they are aimed at trial participants who disobey a judge's order not to speak to the press. In Pennsylvania, for example, a judge conducting a trial of a man accused of shooting three police officers warned everyone in the courtroom that they should obey a gag order he had imposed, lest he have to "snatch [them] out of the clutches of a news camera and hold them in contempt."[4] When media professionals themselves are found in criminal contempt of court, it is most frequently for publishing information that had been subject to a judge's gag order prohibiting such publication.[5] Reporters have gotten into trouble in other ways as well, such as for filming in off-limits areas.[6]

Trial Judges' Burden of Proof

In the law the phrase "burden of proof" often comes up. Usually we think in terms of a prosecutor's burden of proof in a criminal case, to establish the defendant's guilt "beyond a reasonable doubt." In First versus Sixth Amendment conflicts, there is another kind of burden of proof involved, imposed by appellate courts (and especially by the U.S. Supreme Court) on trial judges who wish to rein in press coverage of trial proceedings. Sometimes judges try to do so by explicitly forbidding the dissemination of particular facts related to a trial. Such gag orders (judges usually prefer to call them restrictive orders) might be imposed directly on the media or on the trial participants—lawyers, witnesses, jurors—from whom the media might gather news. Judges often instead determine that the best way to retain some control over courtroom proceedings is to close the trial and deny the press and the public access to the courtroom altogether. **Closure orders** may apply to a trial itself or to any of several steps in the pretrial process. Trial judges may also deny press access to certain categories of court documents.

As it turns out, the Supreme Court has heard numerous cases involving closure orders, and a small number of cases involving gag orders. To varying degrees, the doctrines that emerge from those cases give trial judges a sense of the burden of proof they incur when they contemplate issuing such orders. Sometimes it is the press that brings suit against the trial judge, either because they have been "gagged" or closed

---

4. Gabrielle Banks, "Jury a Tough Find in Poplawski case," *Pittsburgh Post-Gazette*, December 17, 2009, A1.

5. See, e.g., *In re Court Order Dated October 22, 2003*, 886 A.2d 342 (R.I. 2005).

6. *State v. Angelico*, 328 So. 2d 378 (La. 1975) (hallways of criminal justice building); *Duffy v. State*, 567 S.W.2d 197 (Tex. Crim. App. 1978) (jurors leaving the courtroom).

THINGS TO REMEMBER

An Overview of First versus Sixth Amendment Controversies

- Conflicts in which the press is prevented from learning or reporting information about the judiciary usually pit the First Amendment against the Sixth Amendment.
- Judges may hold reporters in contempt of court for violating their orders:
    - Civil contempt citations are designed to produce compliance.
    - Criminal contempt citations are designed to punish noncompliance.
- Trial judges assume a "burden of proof" when they consider either closing their courtrooms or placing gag orders on those who are permitted in.

---

out of the courtroom or because gag orders placed on trial participants arguably infringe on the press's right to *gather* news. Sometimes the trial participants themselves, most frequently attorneys or witnesses, will seek to have a gag order lifted. Sometimes criminal defendants will argue that their convictions should be overturned because a judge's closure order (or refusal to issue a closure order) resulted in an unfair trial. Whatever the specific legal posture of a case, it makes sense to think in terms of the trial judge's burden of proof when answering to a higher judicial authority.

The Supreme Court and the Fugitive

Sometimes First and Sixth Amendment values work well together. The First Amendment, of course, includes among its provisions the constitutional guarantees of freedom of speech and freedom of the press. The Sixth Amendment promises criminal defendants the right to "a speedy and public trial, by an impartial jury." The Sixth Amendment's guarantee of a public trial seems wholly consistent with freedom of the press. To the extent that unfettered public and press access to the workings of the judiciary can uncover governmental abuses, such access would seem also to be at least one means of giving breath to the Sixth Amendment's promise of a trial by "impartial" jurors.

Yet the two amendments do sometimes conflict. Before enumerating the types of conflicts that arise, a bit of perspective is in order. The vast majority of criminal cases nationwide attract little or no media attention. In the absence of a pretrial media spectacle, there is no conflict between First Amendment values and the equally compelling interest in impaneling an impartial jury. Further, more than 90 percent of criminal prosecutions do not result in a trial at all. Rather, the typical defendant, after having been given a sense of the kinds of evidence the state would be able to present should a trial be held, will choose instead to plea bargain. In return for saving the state the time and expense of a full-blown trial, the district attorney's office, with the cooperation of the presiding judge, will accept a guilty plea to some lesser offense or promise to seek a lesser penalty than might otherwise be requested.[7]

We should realize, then, that the discussion of conflicts between the First and Sixth Amendments involves a tiny portion of criminal prosecutions. That being said, what are some of the ways that media coverage of the criminal justice system may make it difficult for a suspect to receive a fair trial? Consider the plight of Dr. Sam Sheppard, whose conviction for the murder of his wife provided the basic source material for the TV series and later movie *The Fugitive*. After several unsuccessful appeals in the Ohio state court system, and after he had spent a dozen years in jail, the U.S. Supreme Court overturned Sheppard's conviction on the grounds that the media circus surrounding his prosecution made a fair trial impossible.[8]

Within a few days of Marilyn Sheppard's death, newspaper stories made clear that the doctor was the prime suspect and that local police were frustrated by his refusal to take a lie detector test or to be injected with "truth serum." Such accounts were followed by what Justice Clark's majority opinion referred to as the "editorial artillery," the first of which asserted boldly that Sheppard was "getting away with murder." Prejudicial pretrial publicity continued. One story reported a detective's assertion that "scientific tests" had "definitely established" a particular trail of blood that would conflict with Sheppard's account of the murder. Yet no such evidence was produced at trial. Other articles reported on Sheppard's alleged extramarital affairs with numerous women, although only one such relationship was ever discussed at trial. Sheppard's difficulties with the media followed him into the courtroom as well; the press were seated so close to him that he and his attorney often needed to leave the room to confer in confidence.

It was not difficult for the Supreme Court to conclude that jurors had been tainted by both pretrial publicity and by events in the courtroom. Justice Clark thought it highly relevant that the jurors' photographs and life stories showed up frequently in the media and that they were not questioned about their own media consumption habits once they were chosen.

Justice Clark's majority opinion amounted to a public scolding of the trial judge. He had allowed the courtroom to become a circus, Clark charged, and failed to take any meaningful actions to minimize the effects of pretrial publicity on the jury pool or of media coverage of the trial itself on the jurors. The Court also made clear that the vast majority of avenues available to trial judges seeking to ensure that defendants receive a fair trial do not infringe on the First Amendment at all. Before examining the development of Supreme Court doctrine concerning closures and gag orders, we consider some of these other remedies.

---

7. Frequently such plea bargains include "flipping," providing evidence against one's criminal associates. An intriguing development in recent years has been the proliferation of "antisnitching" sites that publicize the names of such government informants. Dan Horn, "Anti-Snitching Sites Proliferate," *Cincinnati Enquirer*, May 17, 2009, 1A (mentions such sites as Whosarat.com).

8. *Sheppard v. Maxwell*, 384 U.S. 333 (1966).

Remedies That Do Not Infringe upon Freedom of the Press

As we shall see, the Supreme Court has imposed a rather strict burden of proof on trial judges who seek to further Sixth Amendment interests in a fair trial by using methods such as courtroom closures or gag orders. With respect to the latter kind of remedy, there exists a problem above and beyond any First Amendment counter-weights to be applied. Most of the truly damaging material, from the defendant's perspective, is likely to emerge long before a trial is held, long before a trial judge is even selected. Trial judges cannot prevent dissemination of such TV images as the defendant being handcuffed and arrested, often juxtaposed with sound bites of community members expressing outrage at the heinousness of the crime. Nassau County legislator Roger Corbin learned as much when he sought unsuccessfully to enjoin the media from using images of his arrest in handcuffs on federal tax evasion charges.[9] Judge Spatt agreed that Corbin's Sixth Amendment concerns were legitimate, but concluded that the kinds of traditional methods of ensuring a fair trial to be considered in the next section would suffice. Among these are the issuing of a continuance, a change of venue or of venire, and sequestration of the jury, as well as the everyday process of conducting careful voir dire of potential jurors.

Nassau County, New York, legislator Roger Corbin was unable to enjoin media from using images of his arrest for tax evasion.

Continuance

A fair amount of social science evidence suggests that news stories are rather ephemeral and soon forgotten.[10] Defendants who seek a **continuance** (i.e., a delay) of their trial are banking on the forgetfulness of community members from whom the jury pool will be drawn. Any harmful effects of prejudicial pretrial publicity should diminish, the reasoning goes, as citizens cease to focus on the sordid details of any particular crime and return to their normal day-to-day concerns.

Courts are reluctant to grant motions for a continuance. Delaying a trial places a burden on the judicial system. Witnesses may become unavailable and their memories may fade, records may be lost or otherwise become less usable. Another problem with trial delay is that the Sixth Amendment provides that defendants should be granted a "speedy" trial. The Speedy Trial Act of 1974 provides quantitative defini-

---

9. *U.S. v. Corbin*, 620 F. Supp. 2d 400 (E.D.N.Y. 2009).

10. See sources cited in Laura Donnelly, "Proximity, Not Story Format, Improves News Awareness among Readers," 26 *Newspaper Research Journal* 59, 64 n.1 (2005).

tions of "speedy" judicial proceedings, at least for defendants in the federal courts. The act requires, with some flexibility, that defendants generally be indicted within thirty days of arrest and brought to trial within seventy days of indictment. The Supreme Court has told us that the proper remedy for violations of the act is dismissal of charges against the defendant.[11]

Change of Venue or Venire

In extraordinary circumstances, where a community is so saturated with prejudicial publicity that a trial judge concludes it will be impossible to impanel an impartial jury,[12] the trial may be moved to another jurisdiction. While state trials may generally only be moved to another county within the state, federal trials can be moved just about anywhere. For example, the trial of Timothy McVeigh for the bombing of the Alfred P. Murrah Federal Building in Oklahoma City took place in Denver, Colorado. The McVeigh example notwithstanding, trial judges very rarely grant defendants' motions for a **change of venue**. Most Americans probably assume the practice is much more commonplace than it is, because the few successful motions for a change of venue tend to be, not surprisingly, in media-saturated cases.

It is a very difficult thing for judges to make a ruling admitting they are powerless to ensure a fair trial in their own jurisdiction. Even the judge presiding over the original trial of Jack Ruby for murdering accused JFK assassin Lee Harvey Oswald refused to grant the defendant a change of venue, despite the fact that so many millions had seen Ruby shoot Oswald on television. This decision weighed heavily in an appellate court's decision to overturn the conviction.[13] A change of venue is also an extremely expensive remedy. The transportation, housing, and boarding expenses for attorneys, court personnel, and an often large group of witnesses can be staggering.

There is an additional problem associated with changes of venue: defendants who accept a new venue as a means of maximizing their chances of obtaining a fair trial must waive their Sixth Amendment right to a trial of their peers, at least as the Constitution's drafters envisioned it. The Sixth Amendment promises the accused a jury of "impartial" citizens "of the State and district wherein the crime shall have been committed." Defendants are thus guaranteed both an impartial jury and a *local* one, and often they must choose between the two guarantees.

Finally, trial judges may be incorrect in their faith that the news media in the new

---

11. *Zedner v. United States*, 547 U.S. 489 (2006).

12. See for example, *Skilling v. U.S.*, 130 S. Ct. 2896 (2010), in which the Court ruled that an Enron defendant's rights had not been violated by the denial of a request for a change of venue, in part because the jury pool was based in the greater Houston area, drawing from a population of 4.5 million people. "Given this large, diverse pool of potential jurors, the suggestion that 12 impartial individuals could not be empaneled is hard to sustain," Justice Ginsburg wrote.

13. *Rubenstein v. State*, 407 S.W.2d 793 (Tex. Crim. App. 1966). Ruby died of cancer while awaiting retrial.

locale will avoid the kind of sensationalist coverage that prompted the defense to seek the change. Because there is typically a delay of several weeks or even months between the granting of a venue change request and the actual commencing of a trial, the problem of pretrial publicity may simply start all over again.

Some of these problems can be avoided through a **change of venire** instead of a change of venue: the trial is conducted in the locale where the crime was committed, but the jury is imported from another jurisdiction. A change of venire is generally less costly than a change of venue, although the living and traveling expenses of the jury have to be considered. It also is no less a violation of the Sixth Amendment guarantee of a local jury than is a change of venue. Whether the imported jurors will themselves be bombarded by prejudicial publicity back in their hometowns will be a function of both media interest and the delay between the trial judge's decision to change the venire and the actual seating of the jurors.

Sequestration of the Jury

Sequestration is a remedy that does not prevent bias caused by *pre*trial publicity but does effectively shield jurors already impaneled from any ongoing news coverage of the trial itself. To sequester jurors is to house them in seclusion, at the government's expense,[14] monitoring their media consumption to make sure that the trial itself is their only source of information.

The life of a sequestered juror resembles that of an inmate in a minimum-security prison. Long trials can take a hefty toll on jurors' morale, mental health, and family relationships. Juror pay is minimal, and although employers are generally required to make their workers available for jury duty, they are not typically required to pay them their full salaries during the trial. Because sequestration is a remedy disproportionately used in trials that are predicted to be quite lengthy, the financial burden on individual jurors can be immense.

In some states sequestration of the jury is mandatory in cases that might lead to capital punishment, although even here the procedure can be waived by the defendant (or, in a subset of states, if both the state and the defense agree to waive the right to a sequestered jury).[15]

Voir Dire

Mark Twain once quipped that the U.S. criminal jury system is the best in the world, its only blemish being "the difficulty of finding twelve everyday men who don't know anything and can't read." Twain was commenting on excesses in the **voir dire** process. The term *voir dire* refers to the process of questioning potential jurors in an effort to identify any sources of bias. It is by far the most frequently employed technique for ensuring that defendants—and the state—receive a fair trial. Voir dire is also used in civil trials.

The process may be as simple as a judge addressing the entire group of potential jurors, asking them if there is any reason they will not be able to render a verdict based solely on the evidence to be presented in the trial itself. Or potential jurors may be asked to fill out a lengthy questionnaire drafted jointly by counsel for both sides, under the judge's supervision.

Twain and other critics notwithstanding, voir dire, when conducted properly, does not need to result in the impaneling of ignoramuses as jurors. Indeed, the Supreme Court has made clear that because we live in an era of "swift, widespread and diverse methods of communication"—these words were written in the early 1960s, so the point is surely even more true today—it is unrealistic to expect to find many jurors who have heard nothing about a particularly notorious crime. All that is necessary to ensure a fair trial, Justice Clark wrote, is that a juror be able to "lay aside his impression or opinion and render a verdict based on the evidence presented in court."[16]

---

14. Daniel Malloy, "Sequestered Juries Prove the Price of Justice Is High," *Pittsburgh Post-Gazette*, May 11, 2009, A1 ($17,000 cost for a jury sequestered for only three days).

15. Marcy Strauss, "Sequestration," 24 *American Journal of Criminal Law* 63 (1996).

16. *Irvin v. Dowd*, 366 U.S. 717, 722, 723 (1961); see also *Mu'Min v. Virginia*, 500 U.S. 415 (1991) and *Skilling v. U.S.*, 130 S. Ct. 2896 (2010), both of which reinforce the importance of voir dire to ensure an unbiased jury.

What happens when a potential juror's bias is uncovered? An attorney for either side can have that juror removed **for cause** if the trial judge is persuaded of the likely bias. Attorneys are granted an unlimited number of such motions for removal. In addition, attorneys for both sides are permitted to seek the exclusion of other jurors whose bias is not alleged. These **peremptory challenges** form the art of jury selection. Those who can afford it often hire highly paid jury consultants to help identify the kinds of jurors, in terms of demographic variables or patterns of answers to specific questions, who are likely to be predisposed either for or against the defendant. In addition to the limit on the number of such challenges, which varies from venue to venue and among types of cases, the Supreme Court has said that attorneys may not systematically use their peremptory challenges to exclude jurors based on either race or gender.[17]

It would be constitutionally permissible for peremptory challenges to be forbidden altogether, and many critics have so suggested. As one proponent of such reform has put it, the whole process encourages "trivializing gamesmanship," whereas "trials are [supposed to be] about truth detection, not about whose lawyer is the cleverest."[18]

The voir dire process is designed to work hand in hand with the use of clearly worded instructions to the jurors by the trial judge. Except in the rare cases where juries are sequestered, judges must rely on juror compliance with admonitions such as "Do not discuss the case with friends or family members" and "Do not permit yourselves to view any news accounts of this trial." Judges may insist that jurors not read newspapers or magazines at all, for fear that a headline alone will prove prejudicial. Although jurors probably take such admonitions quite seriously, social science evidence suggests that the more forceful the instructions from the judge, the *less* likely

---

THINGS TO REMEMBER

Traditional Remedies

- In *Sheppard v. Maxwell*, the Supreme Court expressed displeasure with a trial judge's failure to keep control over the courtroom.
- Traditionally, trial judges have numerous strategies at their disposal to minimize the effects of prejudicial publicity:

  - Continuance
  - Sequestration of the Jury
  - Change of Venue
  - Careful Voir Dire
  - Change of Venire
  - Instructions to Jurors

---

17. *Batson v. Kentucky*, 476 U.S. 79 (1986) (race in jury selection); *J. E. B. v. Alabama*, 511 U.S. 127 (1994) (gender in jury selection); *Campbell v. Louisiana*, 523 U.S. 392 (1998) (systematic use of race in jury foreperson selection).

18. Morris Hoffman, "Unnatural Selection," *New York Times*, March 7, 2006, A1.

jurors will be able to ignore "evidence" from beyond the courtroom.[19] This reaction might be a function of what social psychologist Jack Brehm calls *reactance*: if we coerce people into doing things that they were planning to do anyway, resentment and noncompliance may result.[20] A perhaps more benign explanation is that focusing on the instruction itself necessitates focusing on what the instruction forbids: an adult version of the childhood admonition "Don't think of pink elephants."

Preventing Prejudicial Publicity: Gag Orders

There are at least some disadvantages to each of the traditional remedies trial judges may use to minimize the effects of prejudicial publicity. It is not surprising, then, that judges have sometimes tried to employ the seemingly more efficient strategy of simply forbidding the press to report potentially prejudicial information. Judges call these instructions restrictive orders, although the decrees are often referred to as gag orders. Judges also sometimes impose gag orders on trial participants. This section considers both kinds of restrictions.

Gag Orders Applied to the Press

One autumn evening in 1975, police in the town of Sutherland, Nebraska (population 850), found six members of the Henry Kellie family murdered in their home. Suspect Erwin Charles Simants was arraigned the next morning. Both the prosecutor's office and Simants's attorney asked the court to issue a gag order to minimize the extent of pretrial publicity. The county judge issued a rather broad one, forbidding the press from publishing "any testimony given or evidence adduced." A group of media entities appealed the order. The Nebraska Supreme Court modified and narrowed the order but continued to prohibit discussion of the suspect's confession to police, as well as of any other matter that would be "strongly implicative of the accused"—in other words, that would imply his guilt.

The U.S. Supreme Court held unanimously that the restrictive order, even as construed by the state's highest court, violated the First Amendment.[21] Chief Justice Burger's opinion emphasized that gag orders, although they sometimes seem the best way to ensure a fair trial, are still prior restraints on communication, which come to the Court with a presumption of their unconstitutionality. In this particular case, the trial judge failed to demonstrate that less restrictive remedies—such as careful voir dire coupled with clear and strict judicial instructions to the jurors—could not have

---

19. Geoffrey P. Kramer, Norbert L. Kerr, and John S. Carroll, "Pretrial Publicity, Judicial Remedies, and Jury Bias," 14 *Law and Human Behavior* 409 (1990); J. Alexander Tanford, "The Law and Psychology of Jury Instructions," 69 *Nebraska Law Review* 71 (1990).

20. Jack Brehm, *A Theory of Psychological Reactance* (New York: Academic Press, 1966).

21. *Nebraska Press Association v. Stuart*, 427 U.S. 539 (1976).

produced a fair trial. The gag order in the Simants case was especially troublesome in that it prohibited discussion of the suspect's confession, which had been presented in a preliminary hearing open to the press and public. It is a "settled principle," Burger wrote, that "once a public hearing [has] been held, what transpired there [cannot] be subject to prior restraint."

Several justices wrote separate concurring opinions that, taken together, depicted a majority of the Court at least flirting with an *absolute* ban on gag orders. Over time, the most influential of all the *Nebraska Press* opinions was Justice Powell's concurrence. Powell went out of his way to offer lower court judges what they hunger for from the high Court—a set of rules to apply in future cases. A gag order would only be permitted, Powell suggested, if there is a "clear threat" to a fair trial posed by precisely the narrowly crafted categories of publicity the order seeks to contain, and if no less restrictive alternatives are available.

The *Nebraska Press* decision has been interpreted by lower courts as a requirement that trial judges demonstrate a "clear and present danger" to the fairness of a trial before a gag order on the press can be entertained. It is now very rare for an appellate court to uphold restrictive orders applied against the media. For example, the Ohio Supreme Court struck down a gag order that had banned media reporting about the trial of Jayme Schwenkmeyer for involuntary manslaughter of her daughter until the jury had been seated in the separate prosecution of her boyfriend in the same incident.[22]

Knowing that they are likely to be overturned on appeal, wise trial judges will be very loath to accept even the most sympathetic arguments in favor of imposing a gag order against the press. Thus, in a bizarre federal trial involving charges of sadomasochistic sex trafficking, U.S. district judge Allyne Ross denied a defense motion for a gag order prohibiting the press from revealing some of the witnesses' identities. The judge, while admitting that witnesses would be testifying about some very sensitive and unpopular kinds of behaviors and could be jeopardizing (at least) their livelihoods, determined that a remedy less restrictive than a gag order should be employed. The solution ultimately embraced by the court was to allow the witnesses to testify using only their first names.[23]

In only a tiny handful of instances in recent years have appellate courts upheld gag orders applied to the press itself. Probably the best-known example involved Manuel Noriega, the former leader of Panama who was brought to the United States to face drug-trafficking charges. When Judge William Hoeveler learned that prison officials had surreptitiously taped conversations between Noriega and his attorneys and that

---

22. *State ex rel Toledo Blade Company v Henry County Court of Common Pleas*, 926 N.E. 2d 634 (Ohio 2010); see also *Shingara v. Skiles*, 420 F. 3d 301 (3rd Cir. 2005) (invalidating gag order about state police officer's suit alleging he had been fired for criticizing traffic radar systems).

23. *United States v. Marcus*, 2007 U.S. Dist. LEXIS 7226 (E.D.N.Y. 2007). The defendant's conviction was overturned by an appellate court, then reinstated by the Supreme Court, for reasons unrelated to the request for a gag order. 538 F. 3d 97 (2nd Cir. 2008), *rev'd*, 130 S. Ct. 2159 (2010).

CNN had copies of the tapes, he ordered the cable network not to broadcast any excerpts from them. An appellate court upheld Judge Hoeveler's order, and the U.S. Supreme Court, by refusing to hear the case, let the gag order stand.[24]

The CNN case is but one example of a body of case law that places the media on warning: disobey a judge's order at your own peril. Even if the original judicial decree is later found unconstitutional, the contempt of court citation issued to punish the press for disobeying the judge may be upheld. This is called the **Collateral Bar rule**, or the *Dickinson* rule, referring to a federal appellate decision from 1972 concerning two reporters for a Baton Rouge, Louisiana, newspaper who disobeyed a local judge's order by printing details of a federal hearing convened to examine an indictment for conspiracy to kill the city's mayor.[25] This rule, which is not restricted to gag orders but has general applicability to any rescinded court order that is disobeyed while in force, has been accepted in some jurisdictions and rejected in others.[26]

Gag Orders Applied to Trial Participants

As we have seen, the U.S. Supreme Court has placed a very high burden of proof on trial judges who seek to ensure a fair trial by imposing restrictive orders on the media. The Court's *Nebraska Press* decision, however, had very little to say concerning the appropriateness of imposing gag orders instead on the media's most likely news sources: lawyers, witnesses, litigants, and jurors. Indeed, the Supreme Court has never dealt with a case involving this precise issue, and lower courts are in disagreement as to the burden of proof to be imposed on trial judges who contemplate the use of gag orders aimed at trial participants rather than the media. At least in some jurisdictions, a trial judge's showing of a "reasonable likelihood" of an unfair trial is often sufficient to support the issuance of such a gag order.[27] Other courts invoke a stricter standard, permitting only those gag orders aimed at speech that is "substantially likely to materially prejudice ongoing criminal proceedings."[28] Still others, emphasizing the First

---

24. *United States v. Noriega*, 752 F. Supp. 1032 (S.D. Fla.), *aff'd sub nom. In re Cable News Network*, 917 F.2d 1543 (11th Cir. 1990), *cert. denied*, 498 U.S. 976 (1990). After listening to the tapes and satisfying himself that Noriega's rights to a fair trial would not be jeopardized by their dissemination, Judge Hoeveler rescinded his own order. *United States v. Noriega*, 752 F. Supp. 1045 (S.D. Fla. 1990). CNN had already aired English translations of some of the tapes while Hoeveler's gag order was still in place. As a result, the network was held in contempt of court, which was eventually settled in 1995 when it ran an on-air apology and reimbursed the government the approximately $85,000 incurred in prosecuting the case.

25. *United States v. Dickinson*, 465 F.2d 496 (5th Cir. 1972).

26. *Dever v. Kelly*, 348 Fed. Appx. 107 (6th Cir. 2009) (accepting the rule); *U.S. v. Straub*, 508 F. 3d 1003 (11th Cir. 2007) (accepting the rule); *In re Providence Journal Co.*, 820 F.2d 1342, 1347 (1st Cir. 1986) (rejecting the rule), *upheld en banc*, 820 F.2d 1354, 1355 (1st Cir. 1987) (but advising press to obey even blatantly unconstitutional court orders while appealing to a higher court).

27. *In re Dow Jones & Co.*, 842 F.2d 603, 610 (2d Cir. 1988).

28. *U.S. v. Wecht*, 484 F.3d 194 (3rd Cir. 2007).

Amendment right to hear, have concluded that gag orders imposed on those likely to speak to the press are indistinguishable from those imposed on the press directly.[29] In this section we look first at gag orders imposed on attorneys and then at orders targeted at other trial participants (such as jurors and witnesses).

Attorneys   Although the U.S. Supreme Court has never heard a case involving a gag order issued against an individual attorney, it did, in 1991, assess the constitutionality of a state supreme court rule governing the out-of-courtroom speech of Nevada lawyers. The **appellant** in that case was Las Vegas criminal defense attorney Dominic Gentile, who had been disciplined for holding a press conference in which he not only proclaimed his client's innocence but also suggested that the guilty party may have been a police detective who Gentile had concluded was a cocaine addict. Although the U.S. Supreme Court held that the state rule was improperly applied to Gentile's speech, it did not find the rule itself unconstitutional.[30]

Most states have such rules, modeled after the rules of professional conduct of the American Bar Association (ABA), which warn lawyers not to make any "extrajudicial statement that a reasonable person would expect to be disseminated by means of public communication if the lawyer knows or reasonably should know that it will have a substantial likelihood of materially prejudicing an adjudicative proceeding."[31] The ABA rules offer several categories of statements that might result in such prejudice, including references to a suspect's confession or refusal to take a polygraph test or the possibility of a plea bargain. It is not surprising, then, that trial judges' gag orders aimed at attorneys are a far more acceptable part of the legal landscape than similar orders targeting the press directly. Attorneys, after all, are often referred to as "officers of the court," a label that emphasizes their special responsibility to avoid behaving in ways that will likely result in an unfair trial.

None of this discussion is meant to suggest that trial judges issue gag orders against attorneys whenever one or both parties in litigation request it. Thus, for example, when entertainer Bill Cosby was accused by Andrea Constand of drugging and raping her, the trial court judge refused a request to impose a broad gag order on the parties' attorneys that would forbid them to speak to the press. Yes, there had been sensational coverage in the media, but that coverage was based on the actual pleadings filed by Cosby and Constand, not on anything an attorney had said to the press.[32]

Jurors and Witnesses   Often restrictive orders are targeted at jurors and witnesses instead of—or, more frequently, in addition to—attorneys. There is no U.S. Supreme Court majority opinion giving trial judges clear guidelines as to whether

---

29. *Journal Publishing Co. v. Mechem*, 801 F.2d 1233 (10th Cir. 1986); *CBS, Inc. v. Young*, 522 F.2d 234 (6th Cir. 1975); *Connecticut Magazine v. Moraghan*, 676 F. Supp. 38 (D. Conn. 1987).
30. *Gentile v. State Bar of Nevada*, 501 U.S. 1030 (1991).
31. *ABA Model Rules of Professional Conduct*, rule 3.6 (1994).
32. *Constand v. Cosby*, 232 F.R.D. 486 (E.D. Pa. 2006).

restrictions placed on witnesses and jurors should be granted more or less deference than those aimed at attorneys. In the *Gentile* case involving the Nevada attorney, Justice Kennedy argued that trial judges should be able to "require an attorney's cooperation to an extent not possible of nonparticipants," but that section of his opinion was joined by only three other justices. Jurors and witnesses are not "officers of the court" in the same way that attorneys are, and thus one might suppose that gag orders aimed at trial participants other than attorneys would be less likely to be upheld on appeal.

With respect to jurors, however, such a supposition would ignore the long tradition in this country of *secret* jury deliberations. Part of what it means to have a fair trial is that jurors feel comfortable expressing themselves openly and candidly during their deliberations. If jurors fear that their statements and their votes will be revealed publicly by other jurors, might their candor be thus diminished? Keep in mind, of course, that we are considering restrictions on the *post*trial statements of jurors. During trials, jurors are always required not to speak to anyone about the case before them. The other side of the equation is that jurors are uniquely qualified to set the record straight about controversial trials. Several jurors from the O. J. Simpson criminal trial felt the need to explain their not-guilty verdict. Indeed, three of them coauthored a book toward that end, called *Madam Foreman*.

Typically, gag orders aimed at jurors in completed cases are really directed at the press, telling reporters whether they may contact jurors and, if so, what they may or may not ask them. As a general rule, broadly worded gag orders prohibiting jurors in completed trials from ever being interviewed by the press or prohibiting such interviews from eliciting jurors' broad impressions about their experiences have been invalidated.[33] By contrast, orders prohibiting former jurors from talking about how they or others on the jury voted, or from characterizing the jury room discussions, or from sabotaging judges' efforts to keep jurors' names secret in those cases where the practice is allowed (e.g., when there has been evidence of attempted jury tampering) have been upheld.[34]

Trial witnesses are rarely singled out for gag orders; rather they tend to be covered by global orders affecting all trial participants. Witnesses will generally not be restricted in the same way that former jurors are; after all, they will not have had access to such traditionally confidential proceedings as jury deliberations. A state appellate court in Georgia threw out an unusually prescriptive gag order in a case involving allegations of child cruelty and assault made against a local church. The gag rule had instructed all trial participants, if contacted by the press, to say either "no comment,"

---

33. See, e.g., *Clyma v. Sunoco, Inc.*, 594 F. 3d 777 (10th Cir. 2010); *Journal Publishing Co. v. Mechem*, 801 F.2d 1233 (10th Cir. 1986); *United States v. Sherman*, 581 F.2d 1358 (9th Cir. 1978).

34. See, e.g., *United States v. Brown*, 250 F. 3d 907 (5th Cir. 2001); *United States v. Cleveland*, 128 F.3d 267 (5th Cir. 1997); *United States v. Antar*, 38 F.3d 1348 (3d Cir. 1994); *United States v. Harrelson*, 713 F.2d 1114 (5th Cir. 1983).

THINGS TO REMEMBER

Gag Orders

- In the *Nebraska Press* case, the Supreme Court ruled that trial judges may impose gag orders on the media only when
  - there is a clear threat to the fairness of trial;
  - the gag order is narrowly tailored, to remedy just that threat;
  - more traditional means of ensuring a fair trial would not work; and
  - it is not too late for the gag order to be effective.
- Gag orders placed on the press are likely to be invalidated or at least limited.
- In most jurisdictions, trial judges have a far lower burden of proof when they impose a gag order on trial participants rather than on the media.
  This lower burden of proof applies especially to attorneys, whose own ethical code demands that they refrain from out-of-court utterances likely to make a fair trial more difficult.
- Contempt citations issued against reporters who disobey even an obviously unconstitutional order from a trial judge may still be upheld by an appellate court.

or "whatever I have to say will be said in court."[35] Indeed, some state courts, Montana's among them, have found in their state constitutions a public "right to know" beyond that implicit in the First Amendment and have thus held that even gag orders aimed only at trial participants (rather than the press) can survive only if violation of such orders would produce a "substantial probability" of an unfair trial.[36]

Barring Reporters from the Courtroom

Restrictive orders seek to prevent the media from reporting what they already know. Sometimes judges have instead tried to ensure a fair trial by preventing the media from learning potentially prejudicial information in the first place. Language from two Supreme Court decisions handed down not long after the *Nebraska Press* case may have emboldened some trial judges to issue such closure orders. In the first case, decided in 1978, the Court ruled that a Virginia newspaper had a right to publish a story identifying a state judge whose conduct had been the subject of hearings conducted by the state's judicial review committee. A gag order was not at issue in *Landmark Communications, Inc. v. Virginia*, but rather a state statute specifically prohibiting dissemination of information concerning the committee's investigations.[37] Writing for the Supreme Court's majority, Chief Justice Burger allowed that the com-

---

35. *Atlanta Journal-Constitution v. State*, 596 S.E.2d 694 (Ga. Ct. App. 2004).
36. *The Missoulian v. Montana Twenty-First Judicial District Court*, 933 P.2d 829 (Mont. 1997).
37. 435 U.S. 829 (1978).

mittee certainly had the right to conduct its business secretly but concluded that the press could not be forbidden to publish whatever it learns about the committee's work (even if the source who "leaked" the material may have violated the statute). The majority decision seems to be telling the states, "If you want to keep certain judicial proceedings secret, make sure that they are indeed secret."

The second case, *Smith v. Daily Mail Publishing Co.*, also concerned a state statute rather than a gag order.[38] West Virginia law prohibited the publication of juvenile defendants' names without prior written approval of the juvenile court. When newspapers in Charleston published the name of a fourteen-year-old accused of killing a junior high school classmate—the information was obtained by interviewing witnesses at the scene—the state prosecuted them for violation of the statute. When the appeal reached the Supreme Court, Chief Justice Burger concluded that the statute violated the First Amendment. Yet he added that this ruling was a narrow one, in that the Court had not been asked to determine whether the state could legitimately close juvenile proceedings to the press and public, nor was this case one of a newspaper reporter somehow gaining "unlawful access" to such proceedings.

This section examines judicial closure orders as applied to trials and to various kinds of pretrial hearings. We also look at orders sealing court documents from press and public inspection. In addition, we consider the history and current status of televising trials.

Closing the Trial Itself

The U.S. Supreme Court has given trial court judges fairly clear guidance concerning when closing an actual criminal trial to the press and public can be permitted. The burden of proof demanded by the Supreme Court is a rather strict one, especially considering the circumstances surrounding the closure order at issue in the leading precedent, *Richmond Newspapers, Inc. v. Virginia*.[39] The unusual feature about the case was that this murder trial was defendant John Stevenson's *fourth*. His first trial had resulted in a conviction, but the judgment was reversed on the grounds that some inadmissible evidence had been presented to the jury. His second and third trials ended in mistrial. If ever a trial judge could be excused for a bit of zealotry in his attempt to ensure a fair trial, this was it, especially because the defense sought the closure order, and the prosecution had no objection to it. But when two newspaper reporters demanded a hearing on the closure order, the trial judge determined that the hearing should be considered a part of the trial itself, and thus subject to the closure order. As a result, and somewhat ironically, the reporters were closed out of their own hearing! Their interests were represented at the hearing by their attorneys.

Chief Justice Burger announced the judgment of the Court, a 7–1 decision that the

---

38. 443 U.S. 97 (1979).
39. 448 U.S. 555 (1980).

public and the press have a First Amendment right to attend criminal trials. Only two other justices joined Burger's opinion. Although it was not a majority opinion, it has been treated as such, because the pattern of concurring opinions suggests that a clear majority actually did support his reasoning, as far as it went. "The right to attend criminal trials," Burger wrote, "is implicit in the guarantees of the First Amendment; without the freedom to attend such trials, which people have exercised for centuries, important aspects of freedom of speech and the press could be eviscerated." Could criminal trials ever be closed? Burger maintained that trial judges must have an "over-riding interest" in doing so and that the interest must be "articulated in findings" that include an inquiry as to whether remedies less intrusive on First Amendment might have sufficed.[40] The various concurring opinions revealed the Court's lack of consensus as to whether the right to a *public* trial is a Sixth Amendment right, a First Amendment right, or both, and whether the right should extend to civil trials as well.

The only other case in which the Supreme Court has dealt with the closure of a criminal trial was in the context of a closure order issued by a Massachusetts judge presiding over a sex-crime trial. The trial judge was required by state law to issue such an order, in that the victims were juveniles. When the *Boston Globe* appealed the order, the state supreme court interpreted the statute to require clearing the court-room only during times when a juvenile victim was actually testifying. That interpretation would not help the *Globe* in this particular instance, because the rape trial had already been completed, with the press and the public completely closed out of the proceedings. The newspaper pursued the litigation to the U.S. Supreme Court, which held that statutes *requiring* closure violate the First Amendment. Writing for the majority, Justice Brennan admitted that although at least one of the state's interests involved—"the protection of minor victims of sex crimes from further trauma and embarrassment"—was a compelling one, it did not justify a broad statutory requirement of closure. Rather, he said, the trial judge must be permitted to determine these matters case by case, taking into account the victim's willingness to testify in open court, tempered by his or her age and psychological maturity.[41]

Overall the impact of the *Richmond Newspapers* and *Globe Newspaper* cases together is that actual trials are almost always kept open to the press and the public, except when the trial is part of the juvenile justice system. At least since the 1820s, juvenile law in the United States has been premised on the belief that youthful offenders can and should be rehabilitated. Several differences between the adult and juvenile justice systems have thus been part of the U.S. legal landscape throughout much of the country's history. Although juveniles are incarcerated, we send them to separate detention centers rather than prisons. The residents of such facilities are typically re-

---

40. See for example *State of Minnesota v. Bobo*, 770 N. W. 2d 129 (Minn. 2009) (trial judge legitimately closed the courtroom during testimony of a witness who apparently had been subject to intimidation).

41. *Globe Newspaper Co. v. Superior Court*, 457 U.S. 596 (1982).

ferred to as "delinquents" or "juvenile offenders" rather than "criminals." Punishment for crimes committed as a juvenile typically ends at the attainment of the age of majority, at which time the individual's record is expunged. Seen in this light, that trial proceedings involving juvenile defendants have traditionally been conducted in secret is just one more difference.[42]

In most states, anyone who does not have a "direct interest" in the outcome of a juvenile proceeding, or at least in the judicial operations of the court, is excluded from the courtroom. There is tremendous variation across jurisdictions, however, as to whether the media are considered to have such an interest. Many statutes explicitly invite trial judges to make this determination on a case-by-case basis. The wording of other statutes seems to suggest to judges that, when in doubt, they should exclude the media. Media representatives would thus be wise to become familiar with the applicable statutes and judicial interpretation of those statutes in their own jurisdictions.

Closing Pretrial Hearings

Most of what the Supreme Court has had to say about conflicts between First and Sixth Amendment rights emerges from a handful of its decisions governing public and press access to pretrial hearings. Because it is important to understand the evolution of that case law, in this section the cases are discussed in chronological order.

Suppression Hearings   The Court's doctrine concerning when pretrial hearings can be closed began with its 1979 decision in *Gannett Co. v. DePasquale*.[43] At issue was whether the press had a right to attend a pretrial suppression hearing, even when the defendant asked that it be closed and the prosecution and trial judge agreed. The case stemmed from a homicide trial in the Rochester, New York, area; the trial

---

THINGS TO REMEMBER

Closing Actual Trials

- In the *Richmond Newspapers* case, the Supreme Court told trial judges that they may close the courtroom to the press and public only for an "overriding interest."
- Later, in the *Globe Newspaper* case, the Court indicated that even in highly sensitive sex-crime trials, closures must be made on a case-by-case, perhaps even a moment-by-moment, basis; they cannot be mandated by statute.
- Actual trials, other than juvenile trials, are very rarely closed to the public these days.

---

42. Tamar R. Birckhead, "Toward a Theory of Procedural Justice for Juveniles," 57 *Buffalo Law Review* 1447 (2009).

43. 443 U.S. 368 (1979).

judge, Daniel DePasquale, excluded the public and the press from the suppression hearing and further denied the local newspapers' request to be provided immediately with a transcript of that hearing. The homicide case ended quickly with a plea bargain, at which point the transcript to the suppression hearing was released. The newspapers decided to press the constitutional issue further, however, which ultimately resulted in a 5–4 vote by the Supreme Court upholding Judge DePasquale's original closure order.

Writing for the majority, Justice Stewart concluded that the most important right at stake in the dispute was that to a public trial. Such a right is granted by the Sixth Amendment to the accused, not to the press and the public. In situations such as this one, where the defendant specifically requests closure, the Sixth Amendment inquiry would be concluded. None of this discussion is to deny that the public may have interests that generally coincide with the rights enumerated in the Sixth Amendment. A public trial benefits the public in many ways, Justice Stewart admitted, but that does not mean that the public has a Sixth Amendment *right* to a public trial.

Justice Stewart allowed that the press and the public *might* be able to argue under the First Amendment for an open suppression hearing, but he was not ready to commit himself to the proposition that such a right exists. Even if such a right does exist, Stewart continued, the defendant's Sixth Amendment rights would prevail, at least in this case. After all, the press was granted a hearing to present through counsel its interests in keeping the hearing opening. Also, the closure did not amount to a permanent denial to the press and public of information about the judiciary, in that the transcript of the suppression hearing was released immediately upon the entering of the defendant's plea bargain.

Justice Powell wrote a separate concurring opinion, destined to become majority doctrine a few years later.[44] Although agreeing with the majority that the defendant's wishes must prevail in this particular case, Powell went one step further than Stewart, committing himself to the view that there *is* a First Amendment right on the part of the press and the public to attend even pretrial hearings. Access to suppression hearings is especially deserving of protection, Powell asserted, precisely because such hearings are often the only trial; depending on their outcome, they most often lead either to a defendant very anxious to plea bargain or to a district attorney dropping the prosecution in frustration.

Powell's concurring opinion also provided lower courts with a set of guidelines to use in determining whether a suppression hearing should be closed to the press and public. Upon receiving a defendant's motion for closure, trial judges should consider whether any of the more traditional means of preserving a fair trial might work as well as closure. Should they be leaning toward closure, they must make sure that the closure order extends no further than necessary. They must also permit any press representatives present to express their views on the matter. Although these sugges-

---

44. *Press-Enterprise Co. v. Superior Court II*, 478 U.S. 1 (1986).

tions were not majority doctrine, many lower courts have since quoted the "Powell standard" with approval, and it has been adopted by both the Judicial Conference of the United States, which makes rules governing the federal judiciary, and the Department of Justice.

After the *Gannett* case, mass media companies soon got into the habit of providing their reporters on the "courtroom beat" a carefully worded statement that would enable them to object immediately and more effectively to any proposed courtroom closure. Printed on what are often called Gannett cards, these statements are designed to prevent a closure order from being instituted before the media's attorneys have had a chance to make legal arguments against it. Typically, the reporter will make clear in delivering the statement that he or she is not prepared to make the necessary arguments and will request a short break so that attorneys can be called in.[45]

In 1984, the Court handed down a decision in which the appeal for an open pretrial hearing came to the Court from the criminal defendant himself. Guy Waller appealed his conviction on commercial gambling charges on the grounds that the closing of the pretrial hearing convened to assess the admissibility of wiretap evidence was a violation of his constitutional right to a fair trial.[46]

The state had moved for closure, on two grounds. First, publicly playing some of the wiretap tapes would invade the privacy of innocent persons whose names or voices could be heard. And secondly, other persons identified on the tapes had been indicted but not yet tried, and the playing of the tapes in open court might, under Georgia law, make it difficult or impossible for the state to use such "tainted" evidence in later trials with other defendants. The suppression hearing was closed for its entire seven-day duration, even though only a few hours were taken up in actually playing tapes from the wiretaps.

Writing for a unanimous Court, Justice Powell concluded that Waller's constitutional rights had indeed been violated. Powell's opinion emphasizes the importance of suppression hearings in the overall judicial system. He repeated the point he had made in his concurring opinion from *Gannett Co. v. DePasquale*: such hearings are often the only "trial" a suspect will experience because suppression hearings usually end in either plea bargains or the dismissal of charges, with no trial to follow.

Perhaps the most interesting part of the *Waller* case was the Court's struggle to fashion an appropriate remedy. To set Waller free seemed a bit extreme, as did the suggestion that he be granted a new trial. Principles of equity demanded only that Waller be given what he had been denied: a new suppression hearing, this time open to the press and public. If and only if that new hearing were to result in the suppres-

---

45. In at least one case involving a motion to close a suppression hearing, the reading of the Gannett card backfired. The Kansas Supreme Court upheld a trial judge's decision to close a suppression hearing in a homicide case, partly on the basis that the judge had conducted a hearing on the matter. That "hearing" consisted of a *Kansas City Times* reporter standing up and reading her Gannett card to the judge! *Kansas City Star Company v. Fossey*, 630 P.2d 1176 (Kan. 1981).

46. *Waller v. Georgia*, 467 U.S. 39 (1984).

sion of significant evidence that had earlier been deemed admissible would Waller be granted a whole new trial.

In 2004, the Washington Supreme Court went a step further and actually overturned a murder conviction because a voir dire hearing was improperly closed to the public.[47] The decision, which resulted in a new trial rather than just a new voir dire hearing, was based on state constitutional guarantees of openness.

Voir Dire Hearings   Technically, the process of jury selection and questioning (voir dire) is the beginning of a trial. Still, the Supreme Court's case law concerning motions to close voir dire proceedings has developed separately from cases involving closure of trials themselves. The Court has provided us with two decisions on the issue of open voir dire hearings—one from the 1980s and one in 2010.

Two 1980s cases, while unrelated, bear the same name, *Press-Enterprise Co. v. Superior Court*.[48] The first of these stemmed from a racially tinged (white victim, black defendant) rape and homicide trial in Riverside, California. The prosecution sought to close the voir dire proceedings, fearing that media presence would make it difficult for potential jurors to answer candidly the highly personal questions likely to be posed to them. The trial judge decided to close virtually the entire voir dire hearing, which lasted six weeks, to the press and public.

Immediately after the selection of the jury, the *Press-Enterprise* sought a transcript of the hearing. The trial judge denied this request, on the grounds that the privacy of individual jurors would be compromised. A second request for the transcripts, made after the trial itself had concluded—the defendant had been convicted and sentenced—was similarly denied. The newspaper then commenced litigation to obtain the transcripts and have the original closure order ruled unconstitutional. By a unanimous vote, the Supreme Court sided with the press on both counts. Chief Justice Burger wrote the opinion for the Court. In it he reviewed the available historical evidence dating back to even before the Norman conquests to demonstrate that the jury-selection process had been a presumptively open one under English law for many centuries. "The process of juror selection is itself a matter of importance," he explained, "not simply to the adversaries but to the criminal justice system." Openness helps the community see "that offenders are being brought to account for their criminal conduct by jurors fairly and openly selected."

Because the defendant in this case had wanted the voir dire hearing open as much as the press did, Burger did not need to determine whether the right to this openness was enjoyed only by the accused (as a Sixth Amendment right) or by the press and the public as well (whether as a Sixth Amendment or a First Amendment right). He

---

47. *In re Personal Restraint Petition of Orange*, 100 P.3d 291 (Wash. 2004).

48. *Press Enterprise Co. v. Superior Court I*, 464 U.S. 501 (1984). The "I" is a handy way to distinguish it from a case with an otherwise identical name which is not about voir dire hearings but which merits discussion a bit later in this chapter.

did, however, feel the need to give trial judges some kind of guidance as to their burden of proof should they contemplate closing a voir dire hearing: "The presumption of openness may be overcome only by an overriding interest based on findings that closure is essential to preserve higher values and is narrowly tailored to serve that interest. The interest is to be articulated along with findings specific enough that a reviewing court can determine whether the closure order was properly entered."

Note Chief Justice Burger's reference to "higher values," rather than to "a fair trial." The protection of individual jurors' privacy rights may itself constitute such a "higher value." Although the trial judge's desire to produce an impartial jury and to protect participants' privacy was laudable, Burger concluded, the closure order was overkill. A more narrowly tailored closure might have been permissible, he added. For example, if a juror were to tell the judge and attorneys of her own or a loved one's experience as a rape survivor, that specific part of the voir dire might legitimately be held in the judge's chambers, away from the press and public. As part of the voir dire process, the trial judge could explicitly invite any jurors who have any reluctance about answering specific questions in the open courtroom to request the same level of privacy. The closure of virtually the entire hearing to the press and public, however, was a far greater encroachment on the presumption of openness than was warranted.

We skip ahead for a moment to 2010, and *Presley v. Georgia*,[49] in which the Court answered the question left hanging by Chief Justice Burger in *Press-Enterprise I*. The earlier Court was not ready to determine whether the right to keep voir dire hearings open belongs to the press, or the defendant, or would be honored only when both the defendant *and* the press want open hearings. In the more recent *Presley* decision, the Court tells us that the defendant's Sixth Amendment interests in a public voir dire hearing will be sufficient. During the voir dire for Eric Presley's cocaine trafficking trial, his uncle (a likely witness later on) was told to leave so he would not cross paths with the pool of potential jurors. While this state's interest was legitimate, the Supreme Court's per curiam opinion held that the trial judge had an obligation to fulfill that need while maintaining a completely open voir dire proceeding.

It is too early to tell whether *Presley* will result in more open voir dire hearings. Despite Chief Justice Burger's suggestions to trial courts from *Press Enterprise I*, there have been several instances since in which trial judges have succeeded in closing most or all of a voir dire hearing, without being overturned on appeal.[50]

Still, trial judges must demonstrate more than conjecture if they wish to have their voir dire closures upheld by an appellate court. The judge in Martha Stewart's securities law trial closed the voir dire hearing, an action later ruled unconstitutional by the Second Circuit Court of Appeals. True, the appellate panel agreed, many potential jurors will have prejudged the defendant, but that is true of any high-profile trial, and

49. 130 S. Ct. 721 (2010).
50. See, for example, *United States v. Koubriti*, 252 F. Supp. 2d 424 (E.D. Mich. 2003), and *United States v. Don King Productions*, 140 F.3d 76 (2d Cir. 1998).

there was no reason to assume that the members of the jury pool would be loath to admit their biases during an open voir dire hearing.[51]

Preliminary Hearings   Two years after the first case bearing the same name, the Court ruled in what has come to be known as *Press-Enterprise Co. v. Superior Court II*.[52] The case stemmed from a multiple homicide case involving a nurse named Robert Diaz, who was accused of killing a dozen patients in California by administering overdoses of a heart drug. The defendant's preliminary hearing was closed to the press and public at his own request. In California's penal system, these hearings function very much like full-blown trials; the prosecution produces evidence and witnesses, and the defense is invited to do so also. Witnesses can be cross-examined by either side. Indeed, almost the only differences between the preliminary hearing and the trial are the absence of a jury and the lower standard of proof of guilt ("probable cause" to proceed to trial compared to "beyond a reasonable doubt" to convict).

By a 7–2 vote, the U.S. Supreme Court ruled that the standard employed in deciding to close Diaz's preliminary hearing was not sensitive enough to the public's First Amendment interest and that, in any event, a transcript of the proceedings should have been made available to the press at the first possible moment.

Chief Justice Burger's majority opinion is notable for at least three reasons. First, he committed the Court for the first time to the principle that the interest in keeping judicial proceedings open to the press and public is primarily a *First* Amendment issue. (Remember, however, that in the much later *Presley* case, the Court says that the defendant's Sixth Amendment interests are also sufficient to keep a pretrial hearing open).

Second, the Court came about as close as it possibly could to overturning the *Gannett* case without explicitly doing so. *Gannett*, it will be recalled, also involved a motion from the defendant to close a pretrial hearing. No doubt Burger did not feel compelled to overturn *Gannett*, precisely because the majority decision in that 1979 case, by leaving open the possibility that there *might* be a First Amendment right to attend pretrial hearings that *might* in some circumstances outweigh a defendant's wish for closure, left future Court majorities enough "wiggle room." Still, if *Gannett* ever stood for the principle that a defendant's wish for closure necessarily trumps the media's desire for openness, that notion was rejected in *Press-Enterprise II*.

Finally, and perhaps most important, *Press-Enterprise II* represents the Court's first attempt to give trial judges a rule that should cover *all* kinds of judicial hearings. This attempt is all the more important when we consider that the Supreme Court to date has only reviewed cases involving three kinds of judicial hearings beyond trials themselves: voir dire proceedings, suppression hearings, and the kind of quasi trial that California's preliminary hearings resemble. Trial judges, however, have to deal with

---

51. *ABC, Inc. v. Stewart*, 360 F.3d 90 (2d Cir. 2004).
52. 478 U.S. 1 (1986).

all sorts of other hearings as well, such as bail hearings, competency hearings, plea bargain hearings, posttrial hearings alleging prosecutorial or jury misconduct, and, increasingly in the wake of the September 11, 2001, attacks, detention and deportation hearings.

The *Press-Enterprise II* test asks trial judges to consider first whether the category of hearing involved is one that should be considered "presumptively open." To be considered presumptively open, a category of hearings must meet at least one half of what the Court calls the **"experience and logic test"**: either the category of hearings has historically been conducted in public (i.e., openness has been our practice, our "experience"), or we reason (logically?) that openness will make for a better hearing (i.e., it will enhance the hearing's "function in the judicial process.").

Once it is determined that a category of judicial hearing is, in fact, presumptively open, then a burden of proof applies to any persons seeking to close the proceeding. Before approving a motion for closure, a trial judge must be able to demonstrate that there is a *substantial probability* of jeopardizing a "higher value" and that the closure is narrowly tailored to preserve that higher value.

In 1993, the Supreme Court had occasion to consider application of the *Press-Enterprise II* test to preliminary hearings conducted in the Commonwealth of Puerto Rico.[53] The hearings were structured very similarly to those in California, but local law explicitly stated that they were to be conducted in secret unless the defendant requested otherwise. Puerto Rico's highest court upheld this provision against a challenge by local newspaper reporters, having concluded that the hearings function differently in the commonwealth's "unique history and traditions, which display a special concern for the honor and reputation of the citizenry." The court also emphasized that the openly conducted preliminary hearings were far more likely to result in biased trial juries, given the commonwealth's small size and dense population.

In a relatively short, per curiam opinion, a unanimous U.S. Supreme Court rejected Puerto Rico's analysis, emphasizing that when the *Press-Enterprise II* test asks that trial courts look at whether certain categories of hearings have historically been "presumptively open," that inquiry is to be based on U.S. history as a whole, not the history of any smaller jurisdiction within.

Lower Courts Apply the *Press-Enterprise II* Test

As we have seen, the Supreme Court has heard closure cases involving only suppression hearings, voir dire hearings, and the kind of elaborate preliminary hearings conducted in California and some other jurisdictions. In this section we examine the pattern of lower court case law in which other kinds of hearings were at issue.

One-Sided Preliminary Hearings

One-Sided Preliminary Hearings   Recall that the preliminary hearing conducted in the *Press-Enterprise II* case from California was itself very similar to a trial,

---

53. *El Vocero de Puerto Rico v. Puerto Rico*, 508 U.S. 147 (1993).

especially in that both sides were permitted to present evidence and to question each other's witnesses, and that the defendant had an absolute right to such a hearing. In most states, however, preliminary hearings are far more one-sided. They provide an opportunity for the prosecution to present a truncated version of its case to a magistrate, who will then decide if probable cause exists to hold the defendant over for trial. Given the kinds of damaging evidence often heard in such hearings, it is no surprise that defendants often move for closure. The pattern of post–*Press-Enterprise II* lower court decisions suggests, however, that trial judges are very reluctant to approve these motions, in part because the preliminary hearing, like a suppression hearing, typically results in either a plea bargain or in the dismissal of charges and may thus be the only opportunity for the press and the public to monitor the criminal justice system.[54]

Hearing on a Motion to Disqualify

In the 1980s, officers of the Teamsters union being prosecuted on embezzlement charges moved to disqualify Judge Ann Aldrich from hearing the case, alleging that her past conflicts with one of their attorneys would bias her. Defendants requested further that the hearing on this motion be conducted in secret, and a district court judge chosen to hear the motion agreed. The Sixth Circuit Court of Appeals overturned this ruling, finding that disqualification hearings met both parts of the *Press-Enterprise II* test for presumed openness. First, the court reviewed many decades of history within the circuit and found that all such hearings had been open in the past. Writing for the appellate panel majority, Judge Lively concluded also that openness served a valuable societal function. "The background, experience, and associations of the judge are important factors in any trial," Lively wrote. "When a judge's impartiality is questioned, it strengthens the judicial process for the public to be informed of how the issue is approached and decided."[55] As of 2010, the Sixth Circuit was still the only court to have issued a ruling on the openness of disqualification hearings.[56]

Bail, Plea, and Sentencing Hearings

Probably some of the most dramatic recurring media narratives about the judiciary are tales of violent criminal acts

---

54. *New York Civil Liberties Union v. New York City Transit Authority*, 675 F. Supp. 2d 411 (S.D.N.Y. 2009) (transit authority hearings concerning passengers accused of violating its "Rules of Conduct" presumptively open); *Cowles Publishing Co. v. Magistrate Court*, 800 P.2d 640 (Idaho 1990) (closure denies the public "the opportunity to observe the criminal justice system at work"); *Des Moines Register & Tribune Co. v. District Court*, 426 N.W.2d 142 (Iowa 1988) (public access functions as "a curb on prosecutorial and judicial misconduct"); *Rivera-Puig v. Garcia-Rosario*, 983 F.2d 311, 323 (1st Cir. 1992) (*Press Enterprise II* rule applied to Puerto Rico, despite that jurisdiction's traditions to the contrary); *State v. Easterling*, 137 P.3d 825 (Wash. 2006) (convicted drug dealer given new trial because plea hearing at which his codefendant agreed to provide evidence against him should have been open to the public).

55. *In re National Broadcasting Co.*, 828 F.2d 340, 345 (6th Cir. 1987).

56. However, a federal district court in Massachusetts—which is in the First Circuit—ruled that hearings on motions to disqualify *attorneys* should similarly be open. *United States v. DiMasi*, 2009 U.S. Dist. LEXIS 68417 (D. Mass. 2009).

committed by persons out on bail while awaiting trial on wholly unrelated charges. Thus there is tremendous public interest in at least the end results, if not the mechanics, of hearings at which defendants plead to charges, and where judges set (or deny) bail and pass sentence. Courts have often held that such hearings are presumptively open.

The Court of Appeals for the First Circuit has emphasized that just as pretrial hearings are often a defendant's only trial, a bail hearing may represent the public's only chance to witness a suspect's interaction with the criminal justice system. This situation would occur, of course, if bail is granted and the suspect then flees. Conversely, the decision not to grant bail, or to set it so high as to effectively ensure that suspects will remain in jail pending trial, necessarily deprives defendants of their liberty before they have been convicted of any crime.[57]

Other jurisdictions have also come down on the side of open sentencing and plea hearings.[58] Courts have emphasized that taking a plea is by far the most common method of adjudicating criminal cases, and that sentencing is the natural culmination of cases. The First Amendment right to attend bail hearings, however, is not absolute. Limited closure has often been permitted when inadmissible evidence, such as tapes or transcripts from improperly conducted wiretaps, is to be presented as part of the prosecution's argument for denying bail.[59]

Competency Hearings   Although there have not been many cases involving the issue of closing competency hearings, courts that have addressed the matter have generally found a First Amendment interest in favor of openness. Some of these cases pre-date the *Press-Enterprise II* rule.[60] Not surprisingly, post–*Press-Enterprise II* cases have continued the trend toward openness of competency hearings. For example, a state appellate court in Virginia held that the press must be given access to a videotape of the competency hearing already held for a multiple homicide defendant. "Public access can play a significant positive role in criminal competency hearings," the court wrote, in that such hearings "can postpone, sometimes indefinitely, the trial of an accused."[61]

---

57. *In re Globe Newspaper Co.*, 729 F.2d 47 (1st Cir. 1984).

58. *United States v. Ketner*, 2008 U.S. Dist. LEXIS 108438 (W.D. Tex. 2008); *United States v. Alcantara*, 396 F. 3d 189 (2nd Cir. 2005); see also *United States v. Haller*, 837 F.2d 84 (2nd Cir. 1998); *In re Washington Post Company*, 807 F. 3d 383 (4th Cir. 1986); *Oregonian Publishing Company v. U.S. District Court*, 920 F. 2d 1462 (9th Cir. 1990).

59. See, for example, *United States v. Giordano*, 158 F. Supp. 2d 242 (D. Conn. 2001); *United States v. Leonardo*, 129 F. Supp. 2d 240 (W.D.N.Y. 2001); see also *United States v. Gotti*, 753 F. Supp. 443 (E.D.N.Y. 1990) (bail hearing closure appropriate to avoid "premature disclosure of inflammatory evidence").

60. *Westchester Rockland Newspapers Corp. v. Leggett*, 399 N.E.2d. 518, 523 (N.Y. 1979); *Miami Herald Publishing Co. v. Chappell*, 403 So. 2d 1342 (Fla. Dist. Ct. App. 1981).

61. *In re Times-World Corp.*, 488 S.E.2d 677, 682 (Va. Ct. App. 1997). See also, *Ashworth v. Bagley*, 351 F. Supp. 2d 786 (S.D. Ohio 2005); *Society of Professional Journalists v. Bullock*, 743 P.2d 1166, 1178 (Utah 1987).

Deportation Hearings   In response to the September 11, 2001, terrorist attacks, the federal government sought and obtained many new law enforcement investigatory powers; it also sought to increase the level of secrecy surrounding its use of
those powers. Some of these changes in law and in everyday practice by the executive
branch have been challenged in the courts.

One of the key unresolved issues is whether deportation hearings should be open
to the press and the public. Two federal appellate courts have reached opposite conclusions, and the Supreme Court has thus far failed to give us any guidance. The Sixth
Circuit ruled that deportation hearings should be open,[62] but the Third Circuit decided in favor of closure.[63] The latter decision minced no words when it came time
to articulate the higher values at stake: "This case arises in the wake of September 11,
2001, a day on which American life changed drastically and dramatically. The era that
dawned on September 11, and the war against terrorism that has pervaded the sinews
of our national life since that day, are reflected in thousands of ways in legislative and
national policy, the habits of daily living, and our collective psyches."[64]

Access to Judicial Documents

Some of the same Supreme Court precedents that have established a qualified First
Amendment right to attend judicial proceedings have also had something to say about
access to judicial documents. The transcript of a voir dire proceeding is, after all, a
judicial document. In *Press-Enterprise Co. v. Superior Court I*, one of the issues before
the Supreme Court was whether the press should have at least been given a transcript
of the voir dire proceeding in a timely fashion. The Court's majority came out
strongly in favor of such disclosure. Similarly, in *Press-Enterprise Co. v. Superior Court
II*, the Supreme Court concluded that by denying the press's repeated requests for a
transcript of the elaborate preliminary hearing, the trial judge had frustrated "the
community therapeutic value of openness."[65]

If voir dire hearings are presumptively open, should additional information about
jurors—such as their names, addresses, occupations, or even the questionnaires they
may have had to complete about their knowledge and attitudes—be revealed to the
media? Whether the media have a constitutional right to the data is a matter that has

---

62. *Detroit Free Press v. Ashcroft*, 303 F.3d 681 (6th Cir. 2002).

63. *North Jersey Media Group, Inc. v. Ashcroft*, 308 F.3d 198 (3d Cir. 2002).

64. For an intriguing argument to the effect that deportation hearings should be open at least
to the extent that are military court-martial hearings, see Dale L. Edwards, "If It Walks, Talks and
Squawks like a Trial, Should It Be Covered like One? The Right of the Press to Cover INS Deportation Hearings," 10 *Communication Law and Policy* 217 (2005).

65. 478 U.S. 1, 13 (1986).

never reached the U.S. Supreme Court, and the lower court case law is mixed.[66] Note, however, that the media likely have no right to private communications between jurors and trial judges, such as when jurors seek clarification of instructions,[67] though sometimes the gist of conversations between a judge and a juror can be revealed at the end of the trial.[68]

Trial judges have a burden of proof when they seek to close judicial records that closely mirrors the burden of proof for closing judicial hearings. Often this means demonstrating that there is not a history of openness with respect to a particular category of judicial documents (such as details of the negotiations that may lead to a plea agreement). Sometimes the judge meets the burden of proof by identifying reasons for closure compelling enough to override whatever common-law or constitutional interests may exist in openness.

Given the traditional secrecy surrounding grand jury proceedings, it is no surprise that judges overseeing such matters are given great deference should they wish to deny media access to related documents. Thus, for example, the press was not permitted access to many documents it requested related to the highly complex relationship among President Clinton, special prosecutor Kenneth Starr, and the grand jury convened to look into charges against the president.[69]

Often, the media are granted access to judicial documents under the *Press-Enterprise II* test. But what if those "documents" are in the form of audio or video recordings? Do the media then have a corollary right to copy and broadcast those recordings? The Supreme Court has given us one ruling on the issue, but because the facts of that case are intertwined with a unique federal statute, the value of the precedent is somewhat limited. The case was the trial of former attorney general John Mitchell for Watergate-related offenses.[70] The Supreme Court denied a request made by the media for the right to broadcast and sell copies of the several hours of Oval Office tape recordings that had been admitted in evidence. This case was unusual, Justice Powell admitted, in that Congress had already instituted a process for orderly release of the Nixon tapes to the public when it passed the Presidential Recordings Act.

Lower courts have thus been free to find a right—most frequently a common-law right based on tradition rather than a First Amendment right—for the media to copy

---

66. *United States v. Blagojevich*, 612 F. 3d 558 (7th Cir. 2010) (trial judge must at least hold hearing before allowing use of anonymous juries); *United States v. Wecht*, 537 F. 3d 222 (3rd Cir. 2008) (jurors' names to be public, even if not uttered during voir dire hearing); *United States v. Ochoa-Vasquez*, 428 F. 3d 1015 (11th Cir. 2005) (permitting anonymous jurors).

67. *United States v. Kemp*, 366 F. Supp. 2d 255 (E.D. Pa. 2005); *In re Application of Daily News*, 787 F. Supp. 319 (E.D.N.Y. 1992).

68. *United States v. Edwards*, 823 F.2d 111 (5th Cir. 1987).

69. *In re Motions of Dow Jones & Co.*, 142 F.3d 496 (D.C. Cir. 1998); *In re Sealed Case*, 199 F.3d 522 (D.C. Cir. 2000).

70. *Nixon v. Warner Communications, Inc.*, 435 U.S. 589 (1978).

and broadcast copies of audiotapes or videotapes played as evidence in court. And indeed the general rule seems to be that if tapes are played in open court and if the media are permitted into the court, the materials can be copied and broadcast.[71] There are exceptions, however. For example, just as portions of bail and detention hearings during which evidence likely to be inadmissible at trial is presented may be closed to the press and public, so too access to, and permission to broadcast, such inadmissible evidence (often tapes from "wired" informants) may be denied.[72] Also, if a witness makes a request to provide testimony via videotape, rather than live in the courtroom, the resulting video will not necessarily be considered a judicial record, even if it is played in open court. Thus when President Clinton provided a videotape deposition in the Arkansas trial of his Whitewater associate Jim McDougal, the media were not permitted to copy and broadcast the tape.[73] After all, the Eighth Circuit Court of Appeals reasoned, cameras are generally not permitted into federal courtrooms—more about that later—so why should the media be given a video record of this one witness's testimony? More generally, courts can apply the same "experience

---

THINGS TO REMEMBER

Closure of Other Court Proceedings

- In 1979, in *Gannett v. DePasquale*, the Court ruled that a defendant's wish to exclude the press from a pretrial hearing might outweigh whatever rights the press may have to attend.
- In *Press-Enterprise Co. v. Superior Court I* (1984), the majority ruled that voir dire hearings may be closed only when an "overriding interest" is established, and closure is determined to be "essential" by "findings" (i.e., the judge must prove it, not just say it). The "overriding interest" might be something other than a fair trial; it might be to protect jurors' privacy.
- In *Presley v. Georgia* (2010), the Court emphasized that the defendant's wishes alone are sufficient to demand opening of voir dire to the press and public.
- In *Press-Enterprise Co. v. Superior Court II* (1986), the Court instructed trial judges to consider whether the kind of hearing they are considering closing has historically been open and whether the function of the hearing will be enhanced by openness.
- Presumptively open categories of hearings may be closed only if the closure is narrowly tailored to ward off a "substantial probability" of jeopardizing a "higher value."
- This *Press-Enterprise II* test has since been applied by lower courts to several additional categories of pretrial hearings.
- Lower courts have fashioned similar rules to determine whether judicial documents may be sealed.

---

71. *In re National Broadcasting Co. (United States v. Criden)*, 648 F.2d 814 (3d Cir. 1981); *In re National Broadcasting Co. (United States v. Myers)*, 635 F.2d 945 (2d Cir. 1980).

72. *United States v. Andreas*, 1998 U.S. Dist. LEXIS 11347 (N.D. Ill. 1998).

73. *United States v. McDougal*, 103 F.3d 651 (8th Cir. 1996).

and logic" test from *Press-Enterprise II* and find that there is no history of openness in specific categories of judicial documents. Thus, for example, the *New York Times* was denied access to the police's application for a wiretap of the Emperors Club prostitution ring that led to the political downfall of New York governor Eliot Spitzer.[74]

TV Cameras in Court

The question of whether electronic media such as TV should be permitted in courtrooms is quite different from the issues of gag orders and closure discussed earlier. Unlike a judge's decision to issue a gag order or close a hearing, a trial judge's discretionary decision to prohibit cameras in the courtroom is generally not appealable. From the perspective of those who favor televised coverage of the judiciary, even this state of affairs represents a major step forward from the 1960s.

It was in 1965 that the Supreme Court overturned the fraud conviction of Billie Sol Estes, a friend of President Johnson's who had apparently "sold" farmers imaginary tanks of fertilizer and other agricultural equipment.[75] The majority accepted Estes's argument that his constitutional rights had been violated by the introduction of TV cameras into the courtroom. Writing for a 5–4 majority, Justice Clark expressed dismay over the cables and wires that "snaked across the courtroom floor," and the "considerable disruption" caused by the dozen cameramen and their equipment.

Because the *Estes* decision depended a great deal on the especially disruptive nature of cameras in this one particular courtroom, the individual states still felt free to experiment cautiously with television in the courtroom. By 1980, twenty-eight states had already permitted some trials to be televised, and another dozen states were studying the issue. In 1982, the American Bar Association abandoned its own decades-long opposition to TV cameras in courtrooms.

Sixteen years after *Estes*, the Supreme Court revisited the issue of TV in courtrooms. *Chandler v. Florida* involved two Miami Beach police officers appealing their burglary conviction on the grounds that the trial judge's decision to permit the televising of portions of their trial had violated their constitutional rights.[76] In a unanimous ruling, the Supreme Court upheld the conviction and determined that the televising of a trial, even over a defendant's objections, is not itself a violation of the

---

74. *In the Matter of the Application of the New York Times Company to Unseal Wiretap and Search Warrant Materials*, 577 F. 3d 401 (2nd Cir. 2009). In addition to the "experience and logic" test, the Second Circuit embraces an "attendance at proceedings" test in which it determines if the documents sought are related to judicial proceedings that are themselves typically open. Since wiretap applications are generally presented to a judge ex parte (with only the state, not any potential defendant or suspect, represented) and *in camera* (in judge's chambers, not in open court), this approach also did not bode well for the newspaper.

75. *Estes v. Texas*, 381 U.S. 532 (1965).

76. 449 U.S. 560 (1981).

right to a fair trial. *Chandler* was not an outright overturning of the earlier *Estes* doctrine, however. Using the vocabulary from chapter 1, we might say that the 1981 decision is best thought of as having *modified* the 1965 precedent. The introduction of TV cameras into the courtroom was no longer deemed inherently violative of a defendant's rights because something in the real world had changed—technology had improved to the point that TV cameras were no longer automatically intrusive. They had become smaller, as well as quieter, and they were now less dependent on the glare of high-intensity lighting.

Since *Chandler*, the pace of states' approval of televising court proceedings has increased dramatically. All fifty states now permit cameras in civil appellate courts, and most states permit television coverage in both trial and appellate courts in connection with both civil and criminal litigation. *Chandler*, however, stands only for the principle that trial judges *may* have cameras in court; it does not instruct them to do so. Trial judges typically are the final decision-makers on the matter, although in 2009 Arizona's Supreme Court placed on trial judges the burden of providing "clear, on the record findings" if they determine that honoring a media request to televise a trial would be a danger to some higher value. In other words, in Arizona a trial judge's decision to exclude cameras will generally be appealable.[77]

The various state supreme court rules that permit audio and video technologies in courtrooms typically provide rather strict guidelines. Jurors are not to be shown, nor may private consultations among attorneys and the judge be broadcast. There may also be strict limitations on the number and positioning of cameras, which may not bear the name or logo of any particular network or station.

Some states have permitted televised coverage of that traditionally secret venue, the jury room. Thus PBS was able to produce a documentary in the 1980s, *Inside the Jury Room*, focusing on jury deliberations in a Milwaukee case involving a mentally retarded ex-felon accused of violating parole when, following the instructions from a correspondence course for security guards, he purchased a firearm. But when PBS sought permission more recently to televise a jury at work in a capital murder trial in Texas, a state appellate court nixed the idea as a violation of state law prohibiting any person from "being with" the jury during their deliberations.[78]

Several news outlets over the years have sought judicial permission to film an execution, but none have prevailed.[79] Most recently, the Eighth Circuit Court of Appeals upheld the State of Missouri's policy against cameras in or around the execution

77. Electronic and Photographic Coverage of Public Judicial Proceedings, Ariz. Sup. Ct. Rule 122 (c).

78. *State ex el. Rosenthal v. Poe*, 98 S.W. 3d 194 (Tex. Ct of Criminal Appeals 2003).

79. *Garrett v. Estelle*, 556 F.2d 1274 (5th Cir. 1977), *cert. denied*, 438 U.S. 914 (1978); *Entertainment Network, Inc. v. Lappin*, 134 F. Supp. 2d 1002 (S.D. Ind. 2001); *Lawson v. Dixon*, 446 S.E.2d 799 (N.C. 1994); *Halquist v. Department of Corrections*, 783 P.2d 1065 (Wash. 1989). The Ninth Circuit has held that executions must be open to the public (though not necessarily televised). *California First Amendment Coalition v. Woodford*, 299 F.3d 868 (9th Cir. 2002).

THINGS TO REMEMBER

TV in Courts

- There is no First Amendment right to have a trial televised.
- Nonetheless, all states permit cameras in at least some courts, and most states permit cameras at both the trial and appellate levels in both civil and criminal cases.
- In most states, state trial judges retain complete discretion to refuse a request to televise a trial (but some states are beginning to ask judges who seek to prohibit cameras to explain their reasoning).
- TV is highly unusual in federal courtrooms, despite generally positive feedback from pilot programs.

chamber. The court agreed that there was a strong public interest in just about every aspect of the capital punishment debate but concluded that First Amendment rights were not implicated by the state's policy.[80]

While state courts are generally very open to the electronic media, in federal courts the story is quite different. In the early 1990s the Judicial Conference of the United States, which promulgates rules governing the federal judiciary, initiated a three-year experiment allowing cameras in two federal appellate courts as well as district courts in a handful of states. Although the Judicial Conference staff report was highly positive, the Judicial Conference decided to continue the long-standing tradition against permitting cameras in federal courtrooms. The ultimate decision was left up to each circuit court, and the lines of decision making between the circuit level and the individual (district) trial-level judge are complex. In two high-profile cases—one involving suits by Sony against online file sharing, the other a federal suit against California's anti–gay marriage Proposition 8—trial court judges' decisions to permit broadcasting or webcasting of judicial proceedings have been struck down by higher courts.[81] We may be reaching a point at which state judges need a good reason to keep cameras out, while federal judges need a good reason to let cameras in.

Most observers agree that the U.S. Supreme Court itself is unlikely to permit cameras to cover its oral arguments anytime soon, although it does sometimes permit immediate release of audiotapes after some high-profile cases. The majority of the justices seem to be against inviting cameras in, some for fear that the incessant replaying of emotionally charged sound bites will diminish the Court's stature, others likely because they relish wielding as much power as they do without having to suffer the

---

80. *Rice v. Kempker*, 374 F.3d 675 (8th Cir. 2004).

81. *Hollingsworth v. Perry*, 130 S. Ct. 705 (2010); *In re Sony BMG Music Entertainment*, 564 F. 3d 1 (1st Cir. 2009). Bucking the trend, in 2010 the Ninth Circuit permitted televising of a federal challenge to California's Proposition 8, which prohibits same-sex marriage.

inconvenience of celebrity. (How many of the current Court's members would you be able to recognize on sight, without using their group photo in chapter 1 as a guide?)

Chapter Summary

Reporters covering the judiciary often confront a clash between First Amendment and Sixth Amendment values. If a trial judge issues an order that unconstitutionally restricts the press, wise reporters obey the order even while taking an appeal to a higher court, lest a contempt citation be upheld.

Trial judges have many strategies at their disposal to minimize the damage caused by pretrial publicity. Among these options are issuing a continuance, granting a change of venue or of venire, or sequestering the jury. By far the most common techniques are a carefully conducted voir dire and clear instructions to the jurors.

Sometimes trial judges also embrace one of two other strategies: either preventing the press from publishing what it already knows (a "gag" order) or barring the press and the public from the judicial proceedings at which they might learn potentially prejudicial information. In a number of decisions handed down since the late 1970s, the Supreme Court has set forth rules governing the burden of proof trial judges assume if they choose to use either strategy.

Although the Court has said that there is a qualified First Amendment right to attend and report about judicial proceedings, there is no such constitutional right to bring TV cameras into courtrooms. Nonetheless, the states do permit cameras in their courtrooms (in most states the trial judge has the ultimate say). Cameras are virtually unheard of, however, in federal courts.

Chapter 9

PROTECTING NEWS SOURCES

I n a move that disappointed but did not necessarily surprise media rights advocates, the Obama Administration in 2010 renewed a subpoena that had been issued by the Bush Administration to *New York Times* reporter James Risen. Sought by the government were some of Risen's sources for his book *State of War: The Secret History of the CIA and the Bush Administration*.[1]

Another *New York Times* reporter—Judith Miller—was imprisoned for three months in 2005 for failing to reveal her confidential sources related to a story she never even wrote. But newspaper columnist and frequent TV pundit Robert Novak did write the story, two years earlier, in which he cited "two senior administration officials" in revealing that Valerie Plame, wife of former U.S. ambassador to Iraq Joseph Wilson, was a CIA operative.[2] In 2006 Novak revealed that presidential adviser Karl Rove was one of his sources for the Plame story. (It later emerged that his other source, former deputy secretary of state Richard Armitage, was the first leaker and that Rove was used to confirm the story.) Numerous Washington insiders have suggested that Rove may have intended to retaliate against Wilson for his public statements contradicting the Bush administration's insistence that Saddam Hussein had obtained materials from the African nation of Niger that could assist him in making nuclear weapons.

Whereas Novak apparently cooperated with the grand jury investigating the Plame leak, Judith Miller and *Time* magazine reporter Matthew Cooper were held in contempt for refusing to cooperate, and the D.C. Circuit Court of Appeals upheld the

---

1. Scott Shane, "Obama Steps Up Prosecution of Leaks to the News Media," *New York Times*, June 12, 2010, A1.

2. "The Mission to Niger," *Chicago Sun-Times*, July 14, 2003, 31.

contempt citation.[3] Unlike Miller, Cooper avoided jail time because his source (also Karl Rove) released him from his promise of confidentiality, allowing him and the magazine to obey Judge Thomas Hogan's orders to testify. Only after Judith Miller had served eighty-five days in jail did her source, former vice presidential chief of staff I. Lewis "Scooter" Libby, release her from her promise of confidentiality, paving the way for her release. Libby himself was convicted in 2007 on perjury and obstruction of justice charges related to the Plame leak.

While going to prison is not part of a reporter's usual job description, it should be pointed out that Judith Miller is hardly unique in this regard. Well over a dozen reporters have gone to jail for failure to testify (most often about confidential sources) in the past twenty years. The journalist with the unhappy distinction of having been jailed longest is freelance photojournalist and political activist Josh Wolf, who served 226 days in jail after refusing to turn over video footage he had taken of political demonstrations in San Francisco that resulted in a police officer being seriously injured. As part of the agreement leading to his release, he uploaded all the video outtakes sought by prosecutors to his website, and he stated under oath that he had no firsthand information about how or by whose hand the officer was injured.[4]

Wolf's time behind bars broke the record previously held by Vanessa Leggett, a part-time college teacher in Texas who had been conducting research for a book about the murder of a Houston-area socialite. A federal grand jury subpoenaed notes from Leggett, who argued that the First Amendment and the Texas Constitution together create a strong enough reporters' shield to protect her from being forced to produce her notes or testify. Federal judge Melinda Harmon held Leggett in contempt of court, and the Fifth Circuit Court of Appeals, in an unpublished opinion, upheld the citation. The Supreme Court later denied review.[5] Leggett spent 168 days in jail.

Reporters and Confidential Sources

In this chapter we look at what happens when the government seeks information from reporters. Whether reporters will have to turn over information to the government depends on a number of factors. One consideration is the kind of information sought. Is the reporter merely being asked to tell what he or she has seen firsthand as a witness to an event, or does the government instead want the reporter to repeat information that an informant has provided? Other factors include whether the gov-

---

3. *In re Grand Jury Subpoena (Judith Miller)*, 397 F.3d 964 (D.C. Cir. 2005), *reh'g denied*, 405 F.3d 17 (D.C. Cir. 2005).

4. Joe Mozingo, "Imprisoned Blogger Is Freed in Deal with Federal Prosecutor," *Los Angeles Times*, April 4, 2007, B3; *In re Grand Jury Subpoena* (Joshua Wolf), 201 Fed. Appx. 430 (9th Cir. 2006).

5. *Leggett v. United States*, 535 U.S. 1011 (2002).

ernment seeks disclosure of an informant's identity and whether the reporter explicitly promised anonymity to his or her source.

This area of law is complicated, since whatever rights reporters may have to avoid compelled disclosures come from a patchwork of federal and state case law interpreting First Amendment and state constitutional provisions, state "reporter shield laws," judicial rules, and even attorney general guidelines.

It is fair to say that the media have a love-hate relationship with confidential sources. The dangers of overreliance on such sources are obvious; it is equally obvious, however, that many important stories would never be reported without promises of anonymity. Perhaps the best example in modern American journalism is "Deep Throat," Bob Woodward's Watergate source, who remained anonymous for thirty-plus years until he finally "outed" himself as W. Mark Felt, once the second in command at the FBI. Consider for a moment if you would prefer that the Watergate break-in and cover-up, or the more recent stories about CIA secret prisons and warrantless government wiretaps of Americans' phone conversations, had never been reported. Without reporters' freedom to promise their sources confidentiality, many stories such as these likely would never be revealed.

A whole lexicon has developed governing the degree of anonymity a source may expect when conversing with a reporter. There is no ambiguity about the meaning of talking "on the record"—the reporter is free to use everything the source says and to quote the source directly. "Off the record" means, minimally, that the source is not to be quoted. Some assume that it also means that paraphrases are equally forbidden, and still others think that the reporter should pretend that off-the-record conversations never took place. If a source insists on speaking "on background," the reporter can repeat everything that is said and attribute it, although somewhat vaguely. Certainly the source's name should not be associated with any quotes. Sources sometimes will speak only "on deep background," which most reporters take to mean that para-

---

THINGS TO REMEMBER

Reporters and Confidential Sources

- Reporters, especially in Washington, D.C., have a love-hate, interdependent relationship with confidential sources.
- Journalists and writers have occasionally gone to jail to protect the confidentiality of their sources.
- A special lexicon exists describing the degree of anonymity demanded by a source, including such phrases as speaking "off the record," "on background," and "on deep background."

phrasing is permitted, but not attributions, even to such vague entities as "informed sources."[6]

Most of the remainder of this chapter concerns the legal conflicts that arise when government officials ask reporters to break their bonds of confidentiality with their sources. We begin that exploration by looking closely at the one time the U.S. Supreme Court has issued an opinion addressing whether the U.S. Constitution protects reporters who wish to shield the identities of their confidential sources.

The First Amendment and Confidential Sources: *Branzburg v. Hayes*

It all began with a story written by reporter Paul Branzburg of the Louisville *Courier-Journal* in November 1969 about a pair of local residents—given the pseudonyms Larry and Jack—and their partnership in the synthesis of hashish from marijuana plants. Not surprisingly, local law enforcement officials ordered Branzburg to appear in front of a grand jury to question him about his subjects' true identities. Although the reporter did appear as ordered, he refused to answer any questions he felt would tend to reveal the identities of his sources. Moreover, he refused to honor later requests to appear at all before other grand juries investigating the local drug trade. Because grand jury proceedings are traditionally sealed, Branzburg argued, the moment it became known that he had appeared before the grand jury, he would have no way of persuading his informants that he did *not* betray them.

Counting the Votes

Branzburg v. Hayes resulted in a 5–4 split among the justices.[7] Much of Justice White's opinion for the Court was majority doctrine, joined by Chief Justice Burger as well as justices Blackmun, Powell, and Rehnquist. Yet the odd nature of Justice Powell's separate concurring opinion leads to the conclusion that, although Powell officially voted with the majority, some sections of Justice White's opinion really commanded only a plurality of four votes. Moreover, because Justice Powell's concurring opinion shared some common ground with those of the four dissenters, *Branzburg* represents one of those quirky situations in which lower courts have followed the dissenting opinion more than the majority opinion.

Looking first at the majority opinion, we note that Justice White rejected the reporter's claim that core First Amendment values will be jeopardized if confidential sources become afraid to talk to the media. Only when reporters' sources are sus-

6. Norman Pearlstine, *Off the Record: The Press, the Government, and the War over Anonymous Sources* (New York: Macmillan, 2008).
7. 408 U.S. 665 (1972).

Could Be a Pot of Gold
THE HASH THEY MAKE ISN'T TO EAT
By Paul M. Branzburg
(excerpts from the Louisville *Courier-Journal* article,
November 15, 1969)

Larry, a young Louisville hippie, wiped the sweat off his brow, looked about the stuffy little room and put another pot on the stove over which he had been laboring for hours. For over a week, he has been proudly tending his pots and pans. . . . Larry and his partner, Jack, are engaged in a weird business that is a combination of capitalism, chemistry, and criminality.

They are operating a makeshift laboratory in south-central Louisville that may produce them enough hashish, or "hash," a concentrate of marijuana, to net them up to $5,000 for three weeks of work. . . .

"I don't know why I'm letting you do this story. . . . To make the narcs (narcotics detectives) mad, I guess. That's the main reason. . . ."

"The trouble we're having is finding the right base," Larry said, as he continued to chop stems. "The hash we've produced gets you stoned, but it doesn't smoke the same as foreign hash. I tried to use incense as a base, but it gives too much of a sweet taste. In the Middle East they use camel manure, so I'm thinking of going out to the zoo. . . ."

---

pected of criminal wrongdoing would the question of compelled testimony surface. To rule for the reporters here would send the message that "it is better to write about crime than to do something about it."

Branzburg was not prohibited from publishing, Justice White emphasized, nor was he told he had to eschew the use of confidential sources. "The sole issue before us is the obligation of reporters to respond to grand jury subpoenas as other citizens do and to answer questions relevant to an investigation into the commission of crime." For the Court to create a First Amendment right on the part of reporters to refuse to testify in front of grand juries would create a logistic nightmare, White added: "Sooner or later it would be necessary to define those categories of newsmen who qualified for the privilege, a questionable procedure in light of the traditional doctrine that liberty of the press is the right of the lonely pamphleteer who uses carbon paper or a mimeograph just as much as of the large metropolitan publisher who utilizes the latest photo composition methods."

As we see later in this chapter, state legislatures have had to deal with this precise issue—defining who is a "reporter"—in connection with the enactment of reporter shield laws. Congressional committees pondering a federal law—none has yet been enacted—have had to deal with the same issue.

Let us examine Justice Stewart's dissent, which was joined by justices Brennan and Marshall. (Justice Douglas wrote a separate dissent, which need not concern us here). The Stewart opinion offered lower courts a set of principles by which to balance a reporter's interest in keeping information confidential with the grand jury's interest in compelling disclosure. The reporter's interest should prevail, he suggested, unless the government can prove three elements:

- There is probable cause to believe that the reporter possesses information relevant to a criminal investigation.
- The government has a compelling need for this information (i.e., its disclosure or nondisclosure will likely affect the outcome of the case).
- The reporter is the only identifiable source of the needed information.

Why, though, should the government have to meet such a high burden of proof? For Justice Stewart, the special interdependent relationship between informants and reporters provides the answer. "The promise of confidentiality," he proposed, is "a necessary prerequisite" to the nurturance of that relationship. The institutionalized press needs such informants "if it is to perform its constitutional mission." Without them the media would be reduced to "print[ing] public statements" and "publish[-ing] prepared handouts."

Justice Powell's brief concurring opinion in *Branzburg* is the key to understanding how and why the three-part test from Justice Stewart's dissenting opinion has been so very influential. Powell cautions that the majority "does not hold that newsmen, subpoenaed to testify before a grand jury, are without constitutional rights." Should a reporter called before a grand jury conclude that "the investigation is not being conducted in good faith," that the information sought has "only a remote and tenuous relationship to the subject of the investigation," a motion to quash (i.e., to invalidate) the subpoena would appropriately be sought. A court asked to intervene in this way would make its decision by "striking a proper balance" between the reporter's First Amendment claims and competing state's interests.

At its core, Justice Powell's opinion was far more consistent with the philosophy espoused by the dissenters than that of the majority. He, unlike the majority, accepted that the First Amendment is implicated when reporters are called on by the government to reveal confidential information. Like Justice Stewart, he argued for a balancing test. Perhaps it should not be surprising, then, that many lower court judges counted up the *Branzburg* votes and concluded that a majority of the Court—the four dissenters plus Justice Powell—insisted that reporters' First Amendment claims of confidentiality be taken seriously.

THINGS TO REMEMBER

Branzburg v. Hayes

- In *Branzburg v. Hayes* (1972) the Supreme Court held that even if reporters do enjoy First Amendment protection, their claims must yield to the need of grand juries investigating criminal wrongdoing.
- Justice Stewart's dissenting opinion—which has proved more influential than the majority opinion—argued that states wishing to compel reporter testimony must prove that:

  (1) there is probable cause to believe that the reporter possesses information relevant to a criminal investigation; (2) the government has a compelling need for this information (i.e., its disclosure or nondisclosure will likely affect the outcome of the case); and (3) the reporter is the only identifiable source of the needed information.

The Lower Courts Apply *Branzburg*

In the decades since *Branzburg* was decided, most courts that have confronted the issue have recognized at least a limited First Amendment privilege for reporters who wish to avoid compelled disclosure of information in their possession. The two exceptions are the Sixth and Seventh Circuits, but even these exceptions do not represent a complete repudiation of a reporters' privilege.

The Seventh Circuit, covering Illinois, Indiana, and Wisconsin, rejected a First Amendment privilege for reporters, but Judge Richard Posner suggested that his ruling might have been different had the identity of a confidential source been at issue.[8] In the Sixth Circuit, which includes Kentucky, Michigan, Ohio, and Tennessee, the privilege was seemingly rejected in 1987,[9] but later cases from the same circuit have interpreted the decision very narrowly and have allowed that reporters do have some constitutional confidentiality rights,[10] or at least that a "balancing of interests" must be conducted.[11]

Because the Supreme Court has never clarified the confusing array of opinions from the *Branzburg* case and has never heard a similar dispute, lower courts have

---

8. *McKevitt v. Pallasch*, 339 F.3d 530 (7th Cir. 2003). There has since been some conflicting case law from the circuit. See *Thayer v. Chiczewskii*, 257 F.R.D. 466 (N.D. Ill. 2009) (no First Amendment reporters' privilege); *Solaia Technology v. Rockwell Automation*, 2003 U.S. Dist. LEXIS 20196 (N.D. Ill. 2003) (extending First Amendment protection for reporter's confidential sources).

9. *Storer Communications v. Giovan*, 810 F.2d 580 (6th Cir. 1987).

10. *Southwell v. The Southern Poverty Law Center*, 949 F. Supp. 1303 (W.D. Mich. 1996); *Marketos v. American Employers Insurance Co.*, 460 N.W.2d 272 (Mich. Ct. App. 1990); *King v. Photo Marketing Association International*, 327 N.W.2d 515 (Mich. Ct. App. 1982).

11. *In re Daimler Chrysler AG Securities Litigation*, 216 F.R.D. 395 (E.D. Mich. 2003).

fashioned their own assessments as to the scope of any First Amendment protection for journalists' sources. How much protection courts grant is a function of three variables: (1) Is the judicial proceeding at issue a grand jury or some other kind of civil or criminal hearing? (2) Is the information sought truly "confidential"? and (3) Is the person being asked to testify really a "reporter"?

Before reaching the constitutional issue, courts often find it helpful to determine whether a subpoena issued to a reporter comports with Rule 17(c) of Federal Rules of Civil Procedure, which tells us that subpoenas must have three characteristics to be proper: relevancy, specificity, and admissibility. *Relevancy* is clear enough: the information sought must be relevant to the legal proceeding in which the litigant claims to need the reporter's help. *Specificity* is another way of saying that the motion cannot be part of the kind of "fishing expedition" Justice Powell warned against in *Branzburg* itself. *Admissibility* means that the subpoena must seek information that would itself be admissible in the court where the litigant's ongoing case is being adjudicated. If any of these criteria are not met, the subpoena will be quashed without any need to address whether the reporters' privilege exists in the jurisdiction where the dispute arises.

If, however, the subpoena is well constructed and properly executed as per Rule 17(c), courts will generally next consider whether and to what extent *Branzburg v. Hayes* provides reporters with a privilege not to produce documents or not to testify in court. The first factor that may inform such an inquiry is the kind of legal proceeding in which information is being sought.

What Type of Judicial Proceeding?

Lower courts have applied the *Branzburg* precedent in three different circumstances: when a reporter is compelled to testify in a criminal trial; when civil litigants seek information from a reporter; and when a reporter is compelled to testify before a grand jury, the same situation that was at issue in *Branzburg*.

Criminal Trials.

In chapter 8 we considered conflicts between the media's First Amendment interest in reporting on judicial proceedings and the accused's Sixth Amendment right to a fair trial. Those two constitutional provisions are again in conflict here. Reporters claim a First Amendment privilege in keeping information from the judiciary, but criminal suspects also have a Sixth Amendment interest in compelling disclosure of such information. The relevant portion of the Sixth Amendment says that the accused has a right "to have compulsory process for obtaining witnesses in his favor."

Because criminal defendants enjoy an explicit constitutional right, some courts—they are in the minority, however—have been especially skittish about recognizing a confidentiality privilege for reporters seeking to quash a subpoena to testify at criminal trials. When John Phillip Walker Lindh, dubbed the "American Taliban" because he was captured by U.S. forces during their post-9/11 invasion of Afghanistan, was facing trial, his attorneys subpoenaed freelance journalist Robert Young Pelton. Pelton's interviews with Lindh during his hospital stay in Afghanistan had appeared on CNN, and Lindh contended that Pelton's testimony at his suppression hearing would be invaluable. Even assuming that a First Amendment privilege might apply to Pelton in this circumstance, "Lindh's Sixth Amendment right to prepare and present a full defense" would have to prevail, Judge T. S. Ellis III held.[12]

Another celebrated defendant, former vice presidential chief of staff Lewis "Scooter" Libby, was similarly permitted to compel disclosure of some key documents from numerous media sources when he was charged with perjury and obstruction of justice charges in connection with the media "outing" of CIA operative Valerie Plame. Libby sought notes from NBC and correspondent Andrea Mitchell, *Time* magazine and reporter Matthew Cooper, and the *New York Times* and reporter Judith Miller. Since charges of perjury against Libby stemmed from possible falsehoods told by him to law enforcement officials about his conversations with these and other journalists, the journalists' own notes about the conversations were highly relevant. Judge Reggie Walton compared Libby's situation to the factual situation in *Branzburg v. Hayes* itself. Unlike Paul Branzburg, who merely "report[ed] on alleged criminal activity," here the reporters being subpoenaed "were personally involved in the conversations with the defendant that form the predicate for several charges in the indictment." Although the *Branzburg* case concerned a grand jury and this case involved an actual criminal proceeding, the same logic that compelled Branzburg to testify would apply here. If reporters must testify in front of grand juries, Judge Walton reasoned, they surely may not "invoke the First Amendment to stonewall a criminal defendant who has been indicted by that grand jury and seeks evidence to establish his innocence."[13]

Two cases decided in 2005 also refused to find a reporters' privilege. In one, the Vermont Supreme Court held that a local TV station must turn over outtakes from its coverage of a riot at the University of Vermont in the aftermath of—I am not making this up, honestly—a game between the Boston Red Sox and the New York Yankees.[14] In the other case, New York's highest court overturned a criminal manslaughter conviction and granted a new trial because the defendant's pretrial motion to compel disclosure of some documentary TV footage of his interrogation had been denied.[15]

The first time a military court was asked to decide whether the media enjoy a privilege when confronted with a subpoena was in 2009. *United States v. Wuterich*[16] found

---

12. *United States v. Lindh*, 210 F. Supp. 2d 780 (E.D. Va. 2002).

13. *United States v. Libby*, 432 F. Supp. 2d 26 (D.D.C. 2006). Libby, it will be recalled, was convicted in 2007.

14. *In re Inquest Subpoena* (WCAX), 890 A. 2d 1240 (Vt. 2005).

15. *People v. Combest*, 828 N.E.2d 583 (N.Y. 2005).

16. 68 M.J. 511 (U.S. Navy–Marine Court of Criminal Appeals 2009). The underlying case was a court-martial, of course, rather than a civilian criminal proceeding.

the government seeking to compel CBS to turn over unaired footage from interviews conducted by *60 Minutes* with an American soldier accused of atrocities in Iraq. The court decided that there is no reporters' privilege in the military.

In most American jurisdictions, however, at least a qualified reporters' privilege has been recognized even in the context of criminal trials, though not always based on the First Amendment. The Supreme Court of Washington, for example, has held that the tradition of that state's common law provides for a qualified reporters' confidentiality privilege, even with respect to criminal trials.[17]

Some of the federal circuits apply a balancing test not too different from that proposed by Justice Stewart's *Branzburg* dissent. In a case from the Second Circuit involving charges of conspiring to "fix" college basketball games, the Second Circuit held

that media representatives may be compelled to reveal confidential information in criminal proceedings only when the information cannot be obtained from any other source. The material sought must also be "highly material and relevant," and "necessary or critical" to the trial outcome.[18]

In the Third Circuit, the press has been told that its qualified confidentiality privilege applies with equal force in civil and in criminal proceedings. The relevant ruling emerged from a case involving a subpoena of statements made to CBS's *60 Minutes* program by likely government witnesses in a fraud prosecution against the owners of a chain of fast-food restaurants in the Newark, New Jersey, area. As the appellate court put it, "the interests of the press that form the

CBS was told to turn over footage from its interview with Staff Sergeant Frank Wuterich, in preparation for a court-martial.

foundation for the privilege are not diminished because the nature of the underlying proceeding out of which the request for the information arises is a criminal trial"[19] Criminal defendants' Fifth Amendment due process rights and Sixth Amendment right to compel the testimony of witnesses could be weighed against the press's First Amendment rights, case by case, but they did not count as reasons for denying the existence of the journalistic privilege.

Civil Proceedings.   When the person seeking to compel a reporter to testify is a civil litigant rather than a criminal defendant, courts are even more likely to recognize a reporters' privilege, since there is no Sixth Amendment right to balance against the journalist's asserted First Amendment interests.

---

17. *State v. Rinaldo*, 689 P.2d 392 (Sup. Ct. Wash. 1984).
18. *United States v. Burke*, 700 F.2d 70 (2d Cir. 1983).
19. *United States v. Cuthbertson*, 630 F.2d 139, 147 (3d Cir. 1980).

The privilege against disclosure in civil litigation was recognized very soon after the *Branzburg* decision was handed down. The precipitating incidents were the Watergate break-in and the Democratic National Committee's (DNC's) subpoena issued against several media outlets seeking information that would help the DNC in its civil suit against the burglars. A federal district court in the District of Columbia quashed the subpoena.[20]

Several years later the U.S. Court of Appeals for the District of Columbia produced a decision very strongly supportive of the reporters' privilege. In the early 1970s *Detroit News* reporter Seth Kantor published a series of articles about organized crime's influence on that city. Local residents Anthony T. Zerilli and Michael Polizzi, whose phones had been illegally tapped by the Justice Department, concluded that some of the factual assertions in those articles could only have been obtained from transcripts of their recorded conversations. To aid them in their civil lawsuit against the Justice Department, the plaintiffs sought the identity of Kantor's sources. The D.C. Circuit Court of Appeals denied the request. Although the information sought was unquestionably crucial to their case, the court reasoned, the plaintiffs had not exhausted all other possible ways of obtaining it, especially since the Justice Department had already provided them with a list of other persons who had had access to the transcripts. The court also concluded that when balanced against civil litigants' interests, the reporters' privilege should prevail in "all but the most exceptional cases."[21]

As a general rule, reporters will not be compelled to disclose confidential information to civil litigants unless it can be shown that the material sought is of clear relevance to the litigation, that the case's outcome will likely be determined by the disclosure, and that the information is not available from any other source. Again, these criteria parallel closely the guidelines offered by Justice Stewart in his *Branzburg* dissent.

The reporters' interests do not always prevail, of course. Documentary filmmaker Joe Berlinger was told to turn over at least some of the outtakes from his *Crude: The Real Price of Oil*, requested by Chevron, which was defending itself against civil litigation claiming it had behaved recklessly in contaminating the Amazon.[22]

And in an almost comic case from Vermont, an unsuccessful applicant for a road foreman position with the town of Topsham, who had been told publicly (at the local equivalent of a town council meeting) that he was too old, was permitted to subpoena

20. *Democratic National Committee v. McCord*, 356 F. Supp. 1394 (D.D.C. 1973).

21. *Zerilli v. Smith*, 656 F.2d 705 (D.C. Cir. 1981). One such "exceptional" case to the contrary was *Lee v. U.S. Department of Justice*, 413 F.3d 53 (D.C. Cir. 2005) (former government scientist's need for confidential sources whose information led to the apparently inaccurate reportage to the effect that he was a spy for the People's Republic of China is essential enough to prevail against any reporter's privilege).

22. *In re Application of Chevron Corporation*, 709 F. Supp. 2d 283 (S.D.N.Y. 2010). The Second Circuit Court of Appeals agreed that at least limited disclosure was warranted. 2011 U.S. App. LEXIS 629 (2nd Cir. 2011).

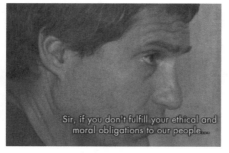

Sir, if you don't fulfill your ethical and moral obligations to our people...

In 2010 the Second Circuit Court of Appeals ordered Joe Berlinger to turn over to Chevron a few categories of outtakes, including any additional footage of attorney-consultants like Mr. Steven Donziger.

the testimony of a newspaper reporter who had covered the meeting, in preparation for his age discrimination suit against the town.[23] These two decisions can be explained by the fact that plaintiffs did not seek *confidential* information from the reporters, a point to which we will return in a later section.

A bit more complicated are those civil cases in which reporters are themselves litigants. Most typically this situation occurs in a libel suit stemming from an article that relied on one or more anonymous sources. We already know from *Herbert v. Lando* (discussed in chapter 4) that libel plaintiffs who need to prove actual malice will be granted access to reporters' notes and outtakes as part of the pretrial discovery process.[24] The same logic often requires that the media reveal the identity of their confidential sources to libel plaintiffs. Thus, comedian Rodney Dangerfield finally got some respect when he sued the publishers of the *Star* tabloid, which quoted several unnamed employees of Caesars Palace in Las Vegas in an article that depicted the comic as a rude and destructive hotel guest. The court granted Dangerfield's request to compel disclosure of these confidential sources because challenging the very existence of the sources, or demonstrating their lack of credibility, would have to form the heart of his proof of actual malice.[25]

Media outlets that find themselves as libel defendants and that refuse to reveal the name of a confidential source may in some jurisdictions be subject to a specially fashioned sanction. The court adjudicating the libel claim may rule, as a matter of law, that no such source exists. The logical conclusion of such an assumption is that the media simply made up whatever libelous statements had been attributed to the unnamed source. In short, the plaintiff will have proven actual malice by default.[26]

Grand Jury Proceedings. Courts are least likely to recognize a confidentiality privilege when the forum seeking information from a reporter is a grand jury. This generalization may seem counterintuitive. After all, the Sixth Amendment's explicit right of the accused to compel witness testimony applies to trials, not to grand juries. The seeming logical inconsistency can be explained by the principle of *stare decisis*

---

23. *Spooner v. Town of Topsham*, 937 A. 2d 641 (Vt. 2007).

24. 441 U.S. 153 (1979).

25. *Dangerfield v. Star Editorial*, 817 F. Supp. 833 (C.D. Calif.), *aff'd*, 7 F.3d 856 (9th Cir. 1993).

26. See, e.g., *Downing v. Monitor Publishing Co.*, 415 A.2d 683 (N.H. 1980); but see *Maressa v. New Jersey Monthly*, 445 A.2d 376 (N.J. 1982).

introduced in chapter 1. Supreme Court precedents, to the extent they offer clear guidance, should be followed. The *Branzburg* case itself dealt with reporters whose grand jury testimony was sought. Because the majority ruled against the journalists, the decision provides little "wiggle room" to lower court judges who might otherwise be inclined to recognize a journalistic privilege against compelled grand jury testimony. Indeed, a general rule has developed, consistent with the majority and concurring opinions in *Branzburg*, that reporters must testify unless the grand jury is engaged in a bad faith "fishing expedition" or is otherwise intent merely on harassing the media.

Perhaps the strongest reaffirmation in recent years of the principle that reporters must share what they know with grand juries comes from the D.C. Circuit Court of Appeals 2005 decision ordering journalists Judith Miller (eventually jailed for several months for disobeying) and Matthew Cooper to reveal the identities of whoever told them that Valerie Plame was a CIA operative.[27] Judge Sentelle's decision makes clear his view, shared by the lower court judge whose ruling he affirmed, that there is no First Amendment privilege to refuse to testify before a grand jury. The thrust of the holding is worth repeating. He did not say that there might be such a privilege, but that it is outweighed in this particular instance. He said that there is *no* such privilege, period.

What Kind of Information?   Whether courts will recognize a qualified reporter's privilege is also in large part a function of whether the information sought is truly *confidential* information. Generally, confidential information is what a source tells a reporter under an agreement of anonymity. Certainly this also includes the confidential source's identity. Nonconfidential information refers to things that re-

---

THINGS TO REMEMBER

Applying *Branzburg* to Various Judicial Proceedings

- As a general rule, reporters are most likely to succeed in their efforts to keep information confidential when confronting a subpoena to testify in an ordinary civil proceeding, a bit less likely to succeed if the proceeding is a criminal trial, and least likely to succeed when they wish to keep information from a grand jury.
- In some jurisdictions, reporters who refuse to reveal a confidential source when they are sued for libel risk a judicial determination that no such source exists; such a declaration virtually ensures that the plaintiff will prevail.

---

27. *In re Grand Jury Subpoena (Judith Miller),* 397 F.3d 964 (D.C. Cir. 2005). See also *New York Times Co. v. Gonzales,* 459 F.3d 160 (2d Cir. 2006) (government may compel release of phone numbers called by reporters to ascertain the sources who had apparently alerted them that two Islamic organizations were under investigation).

porters witness for themselves firsthand, as well as any other materials gathered without a promise of confidentiality. Thus, for example, if an interview with a nonconfidential source is aired on a TV news program, the footage that was shot but not aired is no more confidential than what was broadcast. Similarly, information found in a print reporter's notes that did not survive the editor's red pen is usually no more confidential than the words that were actually printed.

Perhaps, then, the best way to explain the case involving the documentary film *Crude*, discussed earlier in this chapter, is that the people who were interviewed in the film had not sought confidentiality. Indeed, they sought quite the opposite—to tell their story to as wide an audience as they could reach. And the job applicant in Vermont who wished to sue the town of Topsham for age discrimination was not seeking *confidential* information from the newspaper reporter. He sought only an official recounting of what the reporter and every other attendee at the public meeting had heard with their own ears (when the town officials admitted candidly that the other candidate would be hired because he was younger).[28]

In some jurisdictions, federal appellate courts stop short of concluding categorically that reporters enjoy no First Amendment rights in challenging a subpoena for nonconfidential information, asserting that there is a First Amendment interest to be placed in the balance. One court has enumerated four plausible interests raised by reporters seeking to protect even nonconfidential information: (1) the threat of intrusion into the news-gathering and editorial processes; (2) fear that the media will seem to become an investigative arm of the government; (3) concern that media will have a disincentive to compile and preserve outtakes; and (4) the burden on journalists' time and resources in responding to subpoenas.[29] Even in those jurisdictions favoring a balancing test, however, the scales are weighted a bit more against the press when the information sought is nonconfidential.[30]

From Whom Is the Information Sought?

It would be unthinkable to have a rule that an investigative journalist, such as Bob Woodward, would be protected by the privilege in his capacity as a newspaper reporter writing about Watergate, but not as the author of a book on the same topic.[31]

---

28. *In re application of Chevron Corporation*, 709 F. Supp. 2d 283 (S.D.N.Y. 2010); *Spooner v. Town of Topsham*, 937 A. 2d 641 (Vt. 2007); see also *Wilson v. O'Brien*, 2009 U.S. Dist LEXIS 22967 (N.D. Ill. 2009) (no reporters' privilege in unused portions of interviews with crime victim who later admitted she may have identified the wrong man as her assailant, in that she was a very public, on-record source, not a confidential one).

29. *United States v. La Rouche Campaign*, 841 F. 2d 1176, 1182 (1st Cir. 1988).

30. *Shoen v. Shoen*, 5 F.3d 1289 (9th Cir. 1993); *von Bulow v. von Bulow*, 811 F.2d 136 (2d Cir. 1987).

31. *Shoen v. Shoen*, 5 F.3d 1289, 1293 (9th Cir. 1993).

THINGS TO REMEMBER

Applying *Branzburg* to Various Kinds of Information

- Whereas the *Branzburg* case involved reporters' *confidential* information, courts are very loath to recognize a media right not to testify about *non*confidential information.
- The usual press arguments in favor of nondisclosure do not apply to such situations, courts reason; there is, for example, no danger of "the well of confidential sources running dry" when there is no *confidential* source at all.

If the lesson of *Branzburg* and subsequent cases is that there exists at least a limited First Amendment reporters' privilege, we should ask the question that the Supreme Court avoided in that case: what does it mean to be a reporter?

The question has been addressed by several courts, dating back to the 1970s. *Apicella v. McNeil Laboratories, Inc.* stemmed from a damages suit against the manufacturer of Innovar, an anesthetic used during operations.[32] The defendant sought to compel testimony from the editor of a bimonthly professional medical journal called the *Medical Letter on Drugs and Therapeutics*, which had run an article critical of Innovar. That article included anonymous testimony from a physician claiming to have seen three patients die from heart problems as a result of using the drug. The federal district court denied the defendant's request, finding that the journal performed as valuable a public service as any general-circulation newspaper and that the reporters' confidentiality privilege would thus apply to the publication's contributors.

The reporters' privilege was also extended to documentary filmmaker Buzz Hirsch, who was researching the suspicious death of Karen Silkwood, the whistle-blower who had alleged various public-safety violations at a nuclear generating plant. That the Kerr-McGee Corporation (the target of Silkwood's complaints) was making such a "major legal effort" to obtain Hirsch's testimony was seen by a panel of the Tenth Circuit Court of Appeals as evidence that he must have been doing serious reporting.[33]

A 1987 case involving another notoriously suspicious turn of events led the Second Circuit Court of Appeals to devise a set of guidelines to determine what categories of persons may claim the reporters' confidentiality privilege. The case was an offshoot of the criminal prosecution and later civil litigation against Claus von Bulow alleging that he assaulted his wife, Sunny, with intent to kill by injecting her with insulin and other drugs. (He was acquitted of the criminal charges.) In the civil litigation, Sunny von Bulow's family members sought testimony and document disclosures from Andrea Reynolds, a longtime friend of Claus von Bulow's, who was at the time writing

---

32. 66 F.R.D. 78 (E.D.N.Y. 1975).

33. *Silkwood v. Kerr-McGee Corp.*, 563 F.2d 433 (10th Cir. 1977).

THINGS TO REMEMBER

Applying *Branzburg* to Various Kinds of Writers

- The First Amendment "reporters' privilege" has been applied not only to employees of well-known media outlets but also to writers for professional journals with far more limited circulation, to book authors, and to documentary filmmakers.
- Many courts will apply the privilege to any persons who, at the time of gathering information or "news," intended to disseminate their findings to the public eventually. Such individuals need not be employees of media organizations.

a book based on the criminal case. The court determined that a "reporter" need not be an employee of a newspaper or other traditional media outlet; all that was required was that she intended, at the time she was gathering information, to disseminate it to the public. Reynolds herself, however, failed even this test. Her primary motivation at the outset of her fact gathering, the court determined, was to clear Claus von Bulow's name, not to write a book.[34]

The *von Bulow* test has been accepted in the Third and Ninth Circuits.[35] The Fifth Circuit skirted the issue of whether Vanessa Leggett, the Texas writer jailed for almost half a year for refusing to reveal her confidential sources, should be considered a journalist for purposes of applying whatever reporters' privilege is found in the *Branzburg* precedent. The appellate panel deemed it unnecessary to decide this question, because the fact that a grand jury was the entity seeking disclosure would outweigh whatever privilege might exist. Still, the judges went out of their way to describe Leggett as a "virtually unpublished freelance writer, operating without an employer or a contract for publication,"[36] thus hinting that the determination of whether the reporters' privilege applied to her likely would have focused on whether her ultimate goal while she was collecting information about the underlying homicide case was to publicly disseminate such information.

State Reporter Shield Laws

Reporters who wish to avoid testifying before judicial proceedings are not limited to making First Amendment arguments. In 1972, when *Branzburg v. Hayes* told the press that any First Amendment claims would necessarily be limited by the judiciary's

---

34. *von Bulow v. von Bulow*, 811 F.2d 136 (2d Cir. 1987).

35. *Shoen v. Shoen*, 5 F.3d 1289 (9th Cir. 1993); *In re Madden (Titan Sports v. Turner Broadcasting)*, 151 F.3d 125 (3d Cir. 1998).

36. Petition for Writ of Certiorari, *Leggett v. United States*, 535 U.S. 1011 (2002) (No. 01-983).

needs, seventeen states already had statutes on the books providing reporters with a limited right to keep their confidential sources confidential. The first such law was enacted by Maryland in 1896.

Thirty-nine states plus the District of Columbia have some form of reporter shield law on the books, the most recent one having been enacted in Wisconsin in 2010. The majority of the remaining states that do not have an actual statute still provide some protection for confidential sources through judicial interpretation of either the state constitution[37] or the common law.[38] In only a handful of remaining states—Hawaii, Mississippi, Utah, and Wyoming—has the state supreme court not produced a ruling committing itself to at least some kind of reporters' privilege.[39]

Specific provisions of state shield laws vary in ways that generally parallel the three criteria already seen with respect to the federal constitutional privilege: whether the reporter is asked to testify before a civil proceeding, a criminal trial, or a grand jury; the nature of the information being sought; and who should be considered a reporter.

What Type of Proceeding?

For the press, one advantage of living in a state with a strong shield law is that such statutes need not be constrained by the specific holding from *Branzburg v. Hayes* that there is no First Amendment right to refuse to testify in front of a grand jury. Still, several states do provide more protection to reporters seeking to quash a subpoena emerging from civil litigation rather than from a criminal prosecution. The logic here is much the same as that offered by the various federal courts that have adjudicated the issue from a constitutional perspective. A criminal defendant's right to a fair trial figures prominently in the balance. The shield law in Michigan, for example, requires reporters to produce subpoenaed materials when sought by a criminal defendant facing a possible life sentence.[40] The New Jersey statute offers absolute protection from compelled testimony in civil cases, but only qualified immunity in criminal cases.[41]

What Kind of Information?

Shield statutes vary as to the kinds of information that are protected. Some jurisdictions—Arizona is an example—provide absolute immunity from compelled disclosure of a source's identity.[42] The Illinois statute provides a qualified privilege to

---

37. See, e.g., *O'Grady v. Superior Court*, 139 Cal. App. 4th 1423 (Cal. Ct. App. 2006); *In re Contempt of Wright*, 700 P.2d 40 (Idaho 1985); *Winegard v. Oxberger*, 258 N.W.2d 847 (Iowa 1977); *In re Letellier*, 578 A.2d 722 (Me. 1990); *Opinion of the Justices*, 373 A.2d 644 (N.H.1977).

38. See, e.g., *Sinnott v. Boston Retirement Board*, 524 N.E.2d 100 (Mass. 1988).

39. Anthony L. Fargo and Paul Mcadoo, "Common Law or Shield Law? How Rule 501 Could Solve the Journalist's Privilege Problem," 33 *William Mitchell Law Review* 1347 (2007).

40. Mich. Compiled Laws Service § 767.5a (2010).

41. N.J. Statutes § 2A:84A-21.1 (2010).

42. Arizona Revised Statutes 12-2214 (2010).

shield a source's identity, but no other protections.[43] New York's statute provides absolute immunity for both a source's identity and for any information obtained from that source in confidence.[44] The privilege in New Jersey extends also to reporters' notes and outtakes in general—the statute has been interpreted to protect the news-gathering process itself.[45]

Although one might assume that New York and California, the two states in which media industries are especially concentrated, would boast the most far-reaching shield statutes, laws in some of the other states actually offer more protection. New Jersey, for example, provides reporters absolute immunity from having to testify in civil cases. Reporters in that state are sometimes required to testify when called before criminal proceedings, but only if they have witnessed a crime taking place or an accident happening. The privilege will remain intact, in other words, if the reporter arrived on the scene so late as to only see the *aftermath* of the crime or the accident.[46] The Pennsylvania statute is unusually protective; it cannot be circumvented even where there is an allegation that an individual may have leaked confidential grand jury information, in violation of state law.[47]

Who Is Protected?

Most state shield laws define *reporter* fairly narrowly, limiting protection to those who are "employed by" such traditional media outlets as newspapers, magazines, and broadcast stations. Such wording seems to exclude freelance writers. The Florida statute explicitly excludes from its scope "book authors and others who are not professional journalists."[48] Other statutes more broadly protect not only persons employed by the media industry but also those "connected with" the media.[49] The Delaware statute lists "scholars," "educators," and even "polemicists" among those who enjoy the reporters' privilege,[50] whereas the law in Nebraska provides immunity to anyone "engaged in procuring, gathering, writing, editing, or disseminating news *or other information* to the public.[51]

Oddly, the Alabama shield law protects reporters for newspapers (and radio and TV outlets) but not magazines. That quirky feature of the statute was most unfortunate from the perspective of *Sports Illustrated* reporter Don Yaeger, who tried to withhold information about a confidential source from University of Alabama football

43. Illinois Compiled Statutes § 735 5/8-901 (2010).
44. New York Consolidated Law Services, Civil Rights § 79-h (2010).
45. N.J. Statutes § 2A:84A-21.1 (2010).
46. *In re Woodhaven Lumber and Mill Work*, 589 A.2d 135, 143 (N.J. 1991).
47. *Castellani v. The Scranton Times*, 956 A. 2d 937 (Pa. 2008).
48. Florida Statutes § 90.5015 (2010).
49. See, for example, Code of Alabama § 12-21-142 (2010).
50. 10 Delaware Code Annotated § 4320 (2010).
51. Nebraska Revised Statutes Annotated § 20-146 (2010).

coach (and libel plaintiff) Mike Price, who Yaeger's article claimed had manifested "boorish" behaviors since assuming his duties, including hanging out in strip clubs and hiring the "dancers" there for sex.[52] Judge Edward Carnes looked to several dictionaries to justify his conclusion that a defining distinction between newspapers and magazines is that the former tend to be printed on folded, unstapled sheets of paper, while magazines such as *Sports Illustrated* tend to be stapled or bound. He also noted that the Pulitzer Prize for newspaper journalism, the guidelines for which never actually *define* "newspaper," nonetheless has never been awarded to any publication we would normally think of as a magazine.

Often the question of whether freelance writers are protected is not spelled out clearly in the statute itself, requiring state courts to weigh in with their interpretations of the law's wording. An appellate court in Arizona, for example, refused to apply its shield law to author Dary Matera, who at the time was writing a book about undercover "sting" operations that had resulted in the prosecution of several state officials. One of those state officials subpoenaed Matera for materials he thought would help him in preparing his defense. Although the statute was worded broadly, the court

COLLEGE SPORTS

BAD BEHAVIOR

Associating with strippers and carousing with coeds proved costly for Alabama's Mike Price and Iowa State's Larry Eustachy, respectively, as they lost their jobs, embarrassed their schools and stoked the debate over the duty of college coaches to set a good example on and off the field

How He Met His Destiny at a Strip Club
BY DON YAEGER

MIKE PRICE: FIRED

The Party Ends for an Admitted Alcoholic
BY GRANT WAHL WITH REPORTING BY GEORGE DOHRMANN

LARRY EUSTACHY: FORCED OUT

The *Sports Illustrated* reporter responsible for this cover story was not offered any protection by the Alabama reporter shield law, which covers newspapers but not magazines.

---

52. *Price v. Time*, 416 F.3d 1327 (11th Cir. 2005).

THINGS TO REMEMBER

State Reporter Shield Laws

- Thirty-nine states, plus the District of Columbia, have reporter shield statutes, and the majority of the remaining states recognize a reporter's privilege either in their state constitutions or in the common law.
- Many reporter shield statutes give the media a stronger presumption in favor of nondisclosure of information in civil, as opposed to criminal, proceedings.
- The statutes vary widely with respect to what kinds of information are protected and who is considered a reporter.

noted that *Webster's Ninth New Collegiate Dictionary* defined "news" as "material reported in a newspaper or news periodical or on a newscast." Matera's motion to quash the subpoena was thus denied.[53]

It is likely but not certain that freelance reporters are protected by California's shield law. A 1982 lower court case held that authors who have not yet entered into a contract with a news organization or book publisher cannot claim the reporters' privilege.[54] A decade later, however, the state supreme court declined to review a lower court ruling that had extended the privilege to a freelance writer. The lower court had made much of the fact that the freelancer in question had many years of experience as a regular media employee, however, so it is not entirely clear what the state supreme court would do with a less seasoned freelancer who had never been a salaried media professional.[55] Although we again have no definitive word from the California state supreme court on the matter, an appellate court applied the shield law to an online news magazine,[56] which would seem logically consistent with a trend toward a liberal interpretation of the law.

U.S. Department of Justice Guidelines

In the wake of *Branzburg*, several bills were introduced in Congress that sought to provide some measure of protection for reporters' confidential sources, but none passed. The attorney general's office has, however, promulgated guidelines imposing certain restrictions on the federal government's ability to obtain information from

---

53. *Matera v. Superior Court*, 825 P.2d 971 (Ariz. Ct. App. 1992).

54. *In re Van Ness*, 8 *Media Law Reporter* 2563 (Cal. Super. Ct. 1982).

55. *People v. Von Villas*, 13 Cal. Rptr. 2d 62 (Cal. Ct. App. 1992).

56. *O'Grady v. Superior Court*, 139 Cal. App. 4th 1423 (Ct. App. 2006). See also *Krinsky v. Doe 6*, 159 Cal. App. 4th 1154 (Ct. App. 2008) (shielding, on First Amendment rather than statutory grounds, the identity of an online speaker accused of defamation).

reporters. The guidelines,[57] which have been in the *Federal Register* in their current form since 1973, are in some ways modeled after Justice Stewart's dissenting opinion from *Branzburg v. Hayes*. Department of Justice officials are instructed in the guidelines to make "all reasonable attempts" to obtain needed information elsewhere before seeking a subpoena against the news media. Moreover, the information must be deemed "essential" to building the government's case. There has not been a lot of litigation stemming from the guidelines, however, in large part because they provide no judicial remedy against a Justice Department official who violates them. It should also be emphasized that the guidelines govern only the Department of Justice, which is not the only federal entity empowered to issue subpoenas. In one case from Charleston, West Virginia, a federal appellate court vacated a lower court injunction against the National Labor Relations Board subpoena, thus permitting the NLRB to compel disclosure from a local newspaper reporter.[58]

Newsroom Searches

From a law enforcement perspective, issuing a subpoena to a reluctant informant—whether a reporter or anyone else—can be a rather inefficient means of obtaining data. If the subpoena's recipient is well heeled or well insured or both, the motions to modify or quash a subpoena can be time consuming and expensive for both sides. No wonder, then, that police sometimes find it more expedient to knock on the media's door with search warrant in hand.

No Constitutional Immunity: *Zurcher v. Stanford Daily*

Stanford University enjoys an international reputation as a top-ranked institution with a beautiful campus of bicyclists, inline skaters, and mission revival–style sandstone buildings with red tile roofs, the essence of "West Coast laid-back." On one particular Friday afternoon in April 1971, however, the Stanford campus was the site of a violent political demonstration pressing several employee demands and protesting the firing of a janitor by the university hospital. When local police were brought in to remove the protesters, there were twenty-two arrests, several injuries, and over $100,000 in damages. The incident also resulted in a major Supreme Court decision and an important piece of federal legislation aimed at undoing that decision.

The campus newspaper published a special Sunday edition focusing on the demonstration. The very next day, the local district attorney obtained and executed a warrant to search the offices of the *Stanford Daily* in hopes of recovering photo negatives that

---

57. 28 C.F.R. § 50.10 (2010).

58. *Maurice v. National Labor Relations Board*, 691 F.2d 182 (4th Cir. 1982). The trial court had found the subpoena inconsistent with the attorney general's guidelines.

might serve to identify those demonstrators who had engaged in violence or vandalism. The police affidavits accompanying the application for the warrant made clear that the newspaper staff itself was not suspected of any wrongdoing.

The search was unsuccessful; only photographs already published in the newspaper were on hand. The newspaper staff, upset that the search could have laid bare reporters' notes that had been gathered from confidential sources, brought suit against the Palo Alto police chief, James Zurcher, alleging that the search violated the First and Fourth Amendments.

When the case reached the Supreme Court, it resulted in a 5–3 vote (Justice Brennan did not participate) rejecting the newspaper's claims. Justice White disposed of the Fourth Amendment argument first. That this was a "third-party search"—the newspaper staff was not itself under investigation—was of no constitutional consequence, he concluded. "Under existing law," he wrote, "valid warrants may be issued to search any property, whether or not occupied by a third party, at which there is probable cause to believe that fruits, instrumentalities, or evidence of a crime will be found."[59]

The plaintiffs had also argued that whatever Fourth Amendment protections might apply to third-party searches in general, the First Amendment interests that come into play when the site to be searched is a newspaper office necessitated judicial recognition of an added measure of privacy. Justice White expressed sympathy for the media's First Amendment claims. Newsroom searches are often physically disruptive, he admitted, thus jeopardizing "timely publication" of the news. In addition, confidential sources might dry up if things they tell a reporter in confidence may be revealed to the police by coercion. The proliferation of such searches might give reporters an incentive toward sloppy journalism, because they would be reluctant to maintain detailed notes or recordings. Important though these interests might be, White concluded, there was no need to create any special measure of Fourth Amendment protection for the press against third-party searches. "Properly administered," he wrote, "the preconditions for a warrant—probable cause, specificity with respect to the place to be searched and the things to be seized, and overall reasonableness—should afford sufficient protection against the harms that are assertedly threatened by warrants for searching newspaper offices."

The Privacy Protection Act

The *Zurcher* case prompted media industries to lobby Congress for some legislative remedy. In response, Congress passed the Privacy Protection Act of 1980,[60] which provides that law enforcement officials at any level of government who seek testimony from reporters or from anyone "reasonably believed to have a purpose to dissemi-

---

59. *Zurcher v. Stanford Daily*, 436 U.S. 547, 554 (1978).
60. 42 USCS § 2000aa (2010).

nate" information to the public, should generally use subpoenas rather than search warrants. Subpoenas are far preferable from the media's perspective. They invite a chance to argue, through counsel, why some or all of the sought materials should not be turned over. More important, they do not result in the ransacking of a newsroom, which disrupts the reporting operation and often turns up confidential materials not at all related to the specific law investigation at hand.

The use of the word *newsroom* in the previous sentence carries perhaps more meaning than you might think at first blush. Although litigation under the Privacy Protection Act is scant, it is clear that not every law enforcement seizing of media materials such as film, videotape, reporters' notes, and the like is considered a search at all. In one case, an animal rights group sought to document what they feared would be cruel practices in an Ohio park's use of expert marksmen to cull a local deer over-population. The group hid video cameras in the park during evening hours when the area was closed to the public. But the cameras must not have been hidden very well, because the park's rangers stumbled upon them in the course of their workday. When the rangers confiscated the cameras, the animal rights group sued, alleging a Privacy Protection Act violation, but the courts found that there was no "search" here, within the meaning of the act.[61]

The Privacy Protection Act provides that there will be occasions when law enforcement *will* need to conduct a search of the newsroom. These exceptions to the general rule that a subpoena should be issued instead vary according to what kinds of materials are sought. The act recognizes two broad categories: **work product** and **documentary materials**.

To help distinguish between these two categories, let us imagine that you are a reporter assigned to cover a recurring story in the United States: the competing political protests that take place each year in late January, the anniversary of the Supreme Court's famous abortion decision, *Roe v. Wade*. As you prepare to do the story, you will likely gather together many materials that have been written by others. These might include position statements from both pro-life and pro-choice organizations, excerpts from any of the scores of books and thousands of articles that have been written about abortion, and the Supreme Court opinion itself (and later abortion opinions that have cited *Roe* as a precedent). These are all examples of documentary materials, as defined in the Privacy Protection Act.

Your story will likely also flow from materials you produce yourself. These might include transcripts of interviews you conduct with leaders on both sides of the abortion debate, notes you make to yourself as you observe the street demonstrations, and any early drafts of your article. These materials all fit into the work product category.

Work product is the more protected of the two categories; after all, your work product is unique to you and is not as easily reproducible as the documentary materials you gather. Hence there will be fewer exceptions to the "get a subpoena, not a

---

61. *S.H.A.R.K. v. Metro Parks Serving Summit County*, 499 F. 3d 553 (6th Cir. 2009).

search warrant" rule if law enforcement officials seek your work product. Indeed, under the act, when seeking a reporter's work product, law enforcement may obtain a search warrant only in two situations. The first situation is if the police can demonstrate that someone is likely to die or suffer serious bodily harm should the sought material not be immediately uncovered. The second situation is where the reporter is suspected of criminal wrongdoing, rather than just possessing information about other people's wrongdoing.

When law enforcement officials seek a reporter's documentary materials (rather than his or her work product), the same two exceptions already articulated still apply, plus two more. First, the police will be permitted to search a newsroom if using a subpoena would likely result in the "destruction, alteration, or concealment" of the materials. Alternatively, if the reporter has disobeyed a subpoena seeking the production of the material in question, a search of the premises may be justified. Prior to the authorization of such a search, however, the reporter must be given a chance to submit an affidavit arguing why the materials in question should not be subject to seizure.

There is yet one additional complication we need to consider, and it can be applicable to work product and documentary materials alike. Section 215 of the Patriot Act, passed by Congress in the aftermath of the 2001 terrorist attacks, lowered the federal government's burden of proof when seeking a warrant (from the FISA court, a special entity created decades earlier in the Foreign Intelligence Surveillance Act) to search the records of a business. Department of Justice officials have testified before Congress that media outlets are not exempted from this change in law. As a result, there may be a new, unwritten exception to the Privacy Protection Act's general rule to use a subpoena rather than a search warrant—that is, if the government asserts to the FISA court that it needs to obtain media records in order to further an investigation relevant to terrorist activity.

Ignoring the FISA complication for the moment, what remedies are available to news media representatives whose premises have been searched in violation of the Privacy Protection Act? The act gives aggrieved parties the right to sue the government for the improper conduct of any law enforcement official. This could mean suing the federal government, or state or local governments, with one caveat: the Eleventh Amendment to the U.S. Constitution tells individual states that they need not permit citizens to sue them. Because the Constitution supersedes any individual piece of federal legislation, the individual states may be sued for Privacy Protection Act violations only with their consent.

Plaintiffs may obtain damage awards either large enough to reimburse them for actual losses or up to $1,000, whichever is larger. Attorneys' fees and other related litigation costs are also recoverable. No damages will be paid, and the plaintiff's suit will fail, if the state is able to show that its agents acted in the "good faith" belief that they were not, in fact, violating the law.

If the specific facts of a case might permit a search under the act, a failure on the part of police to state clearly in their application for a search warrant which of the act's provisions support issuance of the warrant will not itself constitute a violation of law. This lesson was learned in a case involving WDAF-TV in Kansas City, which purchased from a tourist one evening in August 1994 a videotape depicting a brutal murder that had been committed earlier in the day. (The tourist was not himself suspected of any criminal activity; apparently he and his wife had been videotaping a local park from the Liberty Memorial Tower and "stumbled" upon the crime in progress from that vantage point.) The local police were able to make an arrest in the homicide, but they would not be able to hold the suspect very long without the additional evidence they presumed the videotape could provide. It is at least arguable that the act's exception aimed at preventing death or serious injury would apply to this situation; after all, here is a person suspected of homicide, who may very well commit additional crimes if released. The majority of a federal appellate court panel ruled that the district attorney should be permitted to defend herself against the station's Privacy Protection Act suit by citing this exemption, despite the defectiveness of the affidavit in support of the search warrant application.[62]

One might suppose that a search conducted in violation of the Privacy Protection Act is, by definition, an *unconstitutional* search. The act itself, however, makes clear that the question of whether a search is constitutional or not—that is, whether it is in keeping with the Fourth Amendment's prohibition against unreasonable searches and seizures—is a completely separate issue. This point is important because it means that the fruits of a search conducted in violation of the Privacy Protection Act are not by that fact alone subject to the exclusionary rule of Fourth Amendment jurisprudence. Such evidence is not automatically suppressed; it can still be used in a criminal prosecution.

Betraying a Pledge of Confidentiality

Thus far this chapter has focused on reporters' efforts to protect the identity of their confidential sources and the information obtained from them. In 1991 the Supreme Court ruled in a dispute that turned the usual relationship between the media and their sources on its head.[63] The case emerged out of a hotly contested gubernatorial election in Minnesota.

Dan Cohen, who had been working in 1982 as a public relations consultant for the gubernatorial campaign of Independent-Republican Wheelock Whitney, brought to the attention of several Twin Cities–area reporters the fact that the Democratic-Farmer-Labor candidate for lieutenant governor, Marlene Johnson, had been convicted many years earlier of petty larceny. With each reporter he approached, Cohen

---

62. *Citicasters DBA WDAF-TV v. McCaskill*, 89 F.3d 1350 (8th Cir. 1996).
63. *Cohen v. Cowles Media Co.*, 501 U.S. 663 (1991).

THINGS TO REMEMBER

Newsroom Searches

- Although there is no federal reporter shield law, the Department of Justice has issued guidelines to its own agents that greatly limit the circumstances in which media representatives should be compelled to reveal their sources or other confidential information.
- In *Zurcher v. Stanford Daily* (1978), the Supreme Court ruled that the First Amendment does not protect the media from a newsroom search that is conducted in the furtherance of a properly issued warrant.
- In response to the *Zurcher* case, Congress passed the Privacy Protection Act of 1980, which creates a general presumption that law enforcement officials at all levels of government should use subpoenas instead of searches to compel testimony from reporters.
- The act is especially protective of a reporter's work product (things the reporter created, such as notes or interview tapes) and a bit less protective of documentary materials gathered by the reporter from other sources.
- Searches conducted in violation of the act are not necessarily unconstitutional under the Fourth Amendment.

performed a ritual of sorts. Prior to opening the envelope containing Johnson's court records, Cohen would indicate that he had "some documents which may or may not relate to a candidate in the upcoming election" and offer to hand them over only if the reporter promised "that I will be treated as an anonymous source, that my name will not appear in any material in connection with this," and that "you're not going to pursue me with a question of who my source is."

Some of the reporters shooed Cohen away, concluding that Johnson's criminal act was too minor and too long ago to be newsworthy. Reporters for the *St. Paul Pioneer Press Dispatch* and the *Minneapolis Star and Tribune*, however, felt otherwise and decided to write articles incorporating Cohen's information. They both readily agreed to their source's request for confidentiality.

The two papers, in independent editorial meetings, determined that the news about Johnson's petty larceny conviction was sufficiently newsworthy to be placed before their readers on the eve of this hotly contested election. The editors also decided that Cohen's identity was too integral to the story to be omitted. The *Minneapolis Star and Tribune* unmasked Cohen in its very first paragraph. The article carried Wheelock Whitney and his campaign manager's denial of having prior knowledge of Cohen's intentions; both nonetheless told the reporter that "such information about a candidate's past ought to be available to the public before an election."

On several occasions in the next few years—in depositions, at trial, and in other court documents—the *Minneapolis Star and Tribune* staff was called on to describe the editorial process that day. In their brief before the U.S. Supreme Court, the newspaper's publishers noted that several options had been open to them. They could publish no article at all, but that would be unacceptable. Not only were the allegations themselves newsworthy, but, because other local media had gone forward with the story, for the *Minneapolis Star and Tribune* not to publish would open it to charges of being biased in favor of the Democratic candidate (whom the paper had endorsed editorially a few days earlier). Attributing the charge in a deliberately vague way, such as to a "Whitney supporter," was also deemed unacceptable because the Whitney campaign denied (falsely, as it later turned out) any involvement in the dissemination of the information.

So it was that two newspapers in the Twin Cities decided to override their own reporters' promises of confidentiality to Cohen, who lost his job with a public relations firm almost immediately upon publication, and who promptly brought suit in a Minnesota state court for fraudulent misrepresentation and for breach of contract. A jury awarded damages totaling $700,000 on both claims. The trial judge determined that the First Amendment had nothing to say about this dispute, that it was governed instead by the purely commercial relationship between reporter and source.

The Minnesota Supreme Court overturned both judgments against the newspapers. The U.S. Supreme Court reviewed the case, allowing at the outset that there was indeed no formal contract between Cohen and either of the reporters. The legal doctrine known as **promissory estoppel**, however, dictates that if failure to enforce an agreement would be inequitable or would otherwise be against the public interest, the state may enforce the agreement, even in the absence of a contract.[64] From the justices' point of view, the *Cohen* case asked whether the First Amendment should preclude the state from applying promissory estoppel against the press. Justice White, writing for the majority, concluded that the First Amendment does not bar application of the doctrine in situations such as these. Newspaper publishers have "no special immunity from the application of general laws," he wrote. They must obey the National Labor Relations Act and the Fair Labor Standards Act, as well as laws against breaking and entering. Application of such general laws to the media, White wrote, "is not subject to stricter scrutiny than would be applied to enforcement against other persons or organizations."

Nothing in the *Cohen* decision limits the application of promissory estoppel to guarantees of confidentiality. Reporters who mislead their sources in other ways can also incur liability. In 2000, the First Circuit Court of Appeals permitted a truck driver to sue NBC because the network's *Dateline* producers falsely promised the source that the story they were preparing would not include testimony from a group called Par-

---

64. But see *Pierce v. The Clarion Ledger*, 236 Fed. Appx. 887 (5th Cir. 2007) (if a reporter violates a pledge of confidentiality to person A, and writes a story that embarrasses person B, the latter has no breach of contract claim against the paper).

ents Against Tired Truckers.[65] A reporter can also be sued simply for asking specific questions during an interview if an earlier agreement had included a guarantee that certain subject matters would be off-limits.[66]

The *Cohen* case represents a cry for improved communication between reporters and editors. If reporters are not truly empowered to make promises of confidentiality to their sources, such promises should not be made, or at least they should be made conditionally. This solution is not wholly satisfying, of course. There is no way of knowing how many important stories will be lost because sources are not sufficiently comforted by a promise of confidentiality that is "contingent on my editor's signing off on it later."

At least one court has concluded that a *Cohen*-like promise is not binding on a reporter when the source is a liar. The CBS television newsmagazine *60 Minutes* conducted an interview with former White House employee Kathleen Willey, who claimed that President Clinton had "groped" her in the Oval Office when she came to speak with him about a personal problem. Seeking to bolster her credibility, Willey apparently asked longtime friend Julie Steele to tell a *Newsweek* reporter, falsely, that Willey had confided in her immediately after the incident with Clinton. Steele agreed to do so only on the condition that her name never appear in print. When Steele later confessed to the *Newsweek* reporter that she had lied, the magazine felt relieved of any moral responsibility to keep its promise of confidentiality. A federal district court in Washington, D.C., concluded that the publication was also relieved of any legal contractual obligation to keep its promise under these circumstances.[67]

THINGS TO REMEMBER

Betraying a Source

- In *Cohen v. Cowles Media Co.* (1991), the Supreme Court relied on the principle that the media are not exempt from obeying laws applied to all, and thus upheld a damage award against newspapers that published a source's name after having promised confidentiality.
- The *Cohen* doctrine might not apply when a source has obviously lied to the media defendants.

---

65. *Veilleux v. National Broadcasting Co.*, 206 F.3d 92 (1st Cir. 2000). The producers' more general promise to the effect that the broadcast would depict the driver in a positive light was deemed too vague to be actionable.

66. Kyu Ho Youm and Harry W. Stonecipher, "The Legal Bounds of Confidentiality Promises: Promissory Estoppel and the First Amendment," 45 *Federal Communication Law Journal* 63, 77–78 (1992).

67. *Steele v. Isikoff*, 130 F. Supp. 2d 23 (D.D.C. 2000).

Chapter Summary

In *Branzburg v. Hayes* (1972), the Supreme Court ruled that whatever First Amendment rights reporters might enjoy regarding the confidentiality of their sources, such rights do not extend so far as to outweigh a grand jury's demand for testimony. Because five members of the Court agreed that the First Amendment is at least implicated, however, lower courts in many jurisdictions have concluded that there is a qualified reporters' privilege to confidentiality. How much protection that privilege provides is a function of what type of judicial proceeding is involved (grand jury, or criminal or civil proceeding), what kind of information is being sought (sources' identities, other confidential information, or nonconfidential information witnessed firsthand by the reporter), and whether the person from whom the material is being sought is considered a "reporter."

Several jurisdictions have openly embraced a test endorsed by Justice Stewart in his dissenting opinion from *Branzburg*. Reporters should be compelled to testify, Stewart argued, only if they are the only identifiable source of information relevant to a criminal investigation and for which the government has a compelling need.

The vast majority of the states either have a reporter shield law in their statute books or recognize a confidentiality privilege as a matter of state constitutional or common law. Here, too, the same three factors tend to determine how much protection is provided.

Although there is no federal reporter shield law, the Department of Justice has created guidelines for its own agents that emphasize a preference for negotiating with media representatives rather than creating an adversary relationship by using a subpoena or a search warrant.

In *Zurcher v. Stanford Daily* (1978), the Supreme Court held that the First Amendment does not provide reporters with any special measure of protection against newsroom searches, that the Constitution requires only that such searches be conducted in accordance with standard Fourth Amendment limitations.

The Privacy Protection Act of 1980, designed to undo the effects of the *Zurcher* decision, proceeds on the general assumption that law enforcement officials seeking information from reporters should use subpoenas instead of search warrants. Exceptions may be made under certain specified circumstances, depending on whether the material sought was created by the reporters themselves (their work product) or was created by others and gathered by the reporters (documentary materials).

A promise of confidentiality made and then broken to a news source was the impetus for the 1991 case *Cohen v. Cowles Media Co.* There the Court held that media employees, like other citizens, may be sued for violating their promises, in accordance with the principle of promissory estoppel. That doctrine holds that the state may find it in the public interest to enforce promises even if they were not part of a formal contract.

Chapter 10

REGULATION OF ADVERTISING

Are you familiar with the Pizza Man He Delivers chain? Even if not, you likely can understand that when I first encountered the name—this was back when people used actual phone books instead of online search engines—I marveled at the strategy behind it. The name itself, after all, clearly tells consumers a "selling feature" of the business that could normally only be communicated in an expensive Yellow Pages display ad, but the clever folks behind the franchise need not pay for such an ad. Their name alone, in the far less expensive alphabetical listings of the phone book, would say what needed to be said.

A recent federal appellate decision also involved the relationship between a name and an advertisement. The zoning commission in Pittsburgh allowed "advertising signs" only in certain neighborhoods, though it would permit in all parts of the city onsite signs that do no more than indicate a company's or location's name. What to do then with a company that *named* its buildings "wehirenurses.com" and "PALegal-Help.com"? Could the company erect signs touting those buildings' names on the buildings themselves? The zoning board denied the request, concluding that such signs were prohibited advertisements and that the clever proposal amounted to a "strategy of evasion." A panel of the U.S. Court of Appeal for the Third Circuit upheld the zoning board.[1]

We Americans have a love-hate relationship with advertising. We express dismay at the ubiquity of commercial messages on shopping carts, on movie screens, and even in public toilet stalls. Yet we also cannot help but admire the art of the sell. Super Bowl viewers are often more likely to talk the next day about the commercials premiered during that annual event than about the game itself, which should not

---

1. *Melrose, Inc. v. City of Pittsburgh*, 613 F. 3d 380 (3rd Cir. 2010).

be surprising given the production and airtime costs associated with a thirty-second commercial seen by so many hundreds of millions of eyeballs.

It is no surprise, however, that a company such as the one at issue in the Pittsburgh signage case would want to have its messages categorized by the state as something other than advertising. As we shall see, commercial speech is less protected by the First Amendment than political speech is, and litigants therefore often claim that their messages are not purely commercial, that they have political elements.

The Supreme Court and Commercial Speech

The first part of this chapter examines the Supreme Court's commercial speech doctrine. Supreme Court pronouncements, however, are intended only to tell the other branches of government how much regulation is consistent with the First Amendment. It is also important to understand the government's day-to-day regulation of advertising. The second part of the chapter therefore considers statutory and regulatory approaches. That section begins by considering state and local regulation of advertising and then moves to an extensive discussion of the most important regulatory body in this area, the Federal Trade Commission (FTC). Next is a discussion of the federal Lanham Act—which allows a company to sue a competitor it feels has hurt its market share through deceptive advertising—and a short discourse on industry self-regulation. The chapter concludes with a discussion of political campaign advertising.

Saying Yes to Advertising

The Supreme Court first brought purely commercial speech within the First Amendment's protection in 1976, in a challenge to Virginia's law prohibiting pharmacists from advertising prescription drug prices.[2] The *Virginia Pharmacy* decision, as it is called, overturned a somewhat distant precedent which had held that advertising is beyond the reach of the First Amendment.[3]

Justice Blackmun's majority opinion in *Virginia Pharmacy* cited surveys of local prescription drug prices, which revealed tremendous disparity among drug dispensers, as much as 650 percent for some drugs. Keeping consumers ignorant as to who in town offered the best prices served only to bilk the poor. Surely that would have been enough to justify the Court's decision, but Blackmun went further and, in so doing, demonstrated the Court's continuing ambivalence about *pure* advertising by purposely blurring the line between commercial and political speech. "So long as we

---

2. *Virginia State Board of Pharmacy v. Virginia Citizens Consumer Council*, 425 U.S. 748 (1976).

3. *Valentine v. Chrestensen*, 316 U.S. 52 (1942). Valentine involved an entrepreneur arrested for distributing commercial leaflets on the streets of New York City.

preserve a predominantly free enterprise economy," he wrote, "the allocation of our resources in large measure will be made through numerous private economic decisions. It is a matter of public interest that those decisions, in the aggregate, be intelligent and well informed." What better way to ensure that this public benefit is achieved than through "the free flow of commercial information"? Justice Blackmun seemed to be equating smart shopping with patriotism.

In its next term, the Court continued its tendency to emphasize the political elements of commercial messages, even though it had already extended First Amendment protection to purely commercial speech. At issue was a Willingboro, New Jersey, town ordinance—designed to curb "white flight" and retain its integrated community—which forbade the use of For Sale and Sold signs on residential lawns. The Court unanimously struck down the ordinance, in part because it stifled the flow of information "of vital interest to Willingboro residents, since it may bear on one of the most important decisions they have a right to make: where to live and raise their families."[4] Here too we see the elevation of the commercial ("I have a house for sale here") to the political (a statement about racial harmony?).

The *Linmark* decision notwithstanding, local governments are free to prohibit not only For Sale signs but just about any commercial signs, if they do so through zoning ordinances that leave ample alternative venues for signs or billboards. Twin decisions in 2010 upheld such laws in Los Angeles and New York City.[5]

How Much Protection? The *Central Hudson* Test

The *Virginia Pharmacy* case says that commercial speech enjoys at least some First Amendment protection, but not how much. The answer to that question emerged a few years later in a case involving a New York law, borne of the 1970s energy crisis, prohibiting advertising by any electric company that would tend to promote the in-

THINGS TO REMEMBER

Saying Yes to Advertising

- In the *Virginia Pharmacy* case (1976), the Supreme Court held for the first time that even purely commercial speech is protected by the First Amendment.

---

4. *Linmark Associates v. Township of Willingboro*, 431 U.S. 85, 96 (1977).

5. *World Wide Rush v. City of Los Angeles*, 606 F. 3d 676 (9th Cir. 2010); *Clear Channel Outdoor v. City of New York*, 594 F. 3d 94 (2nd Cir. 2010). See also *Pagan v. Fruchey*, 453 F.3d 784 (6th Cir. 2006) (upholding a Glendale, Ohio, law forbidding For Sale signs in the windows of cars left on public streets).

creased use of electricity.[6] Writing for an 8–1 majority, Justice Powell struck down the law as unconstitutional. In so doing, he established the four-part *Central Hudson* test, intended to give lower courts guidance as to how to adjudicate disputes involving the regulation of commercial speech. In step one, courts ask if the advertisement is misleading, or if it is promoting an illegal product or service. If so, then a law regulating or prohibiting it is constitutional.

Call to mind for a moment the "Your Money or Your Life!" cartoon from chapter 2, the lesson of which was that illegal acts do not become innocent if speech is part of the conduct. This commonsense notion is part of the Supreme Court's commercial speech doctrine, and was so even before the *Central Hudson* test. In the leading decision, from 1973, the Court said that newspapers could be forbidden to accept gender-specific employment ads ("HELP WANTED—MALE"), in that the ads themselves were best seen as part of the act of job discrimination.[7]

A fascinating offshoot of the first *Central Hudson* question about deceptive speech is whether commercial fortune tellers are entertainers or liars (claiming falsely to be able to tell the future). The individual states have ruled differently on the issue.[8]

If the answer to the first *Central Hudson* question is no—if the ad is not deceptive, and not for an illegal product or service—we move on to ask three more questions about the state's interest behind the regulation under review: (1) Is that interest a substantial one? (2) Does the regulation really further that interest? and (3) Does the regulation abridge no more speech than necessary?

Applying the test to the law before it, Justice Powell found initially that electricity is a legal product and that Central Hudson's ads were not misleading. Moving to the second inquiry, he allowed that the state did in fact have a substantial interest at stake—energy conservation. Did the law under review further that substantial interest, as the third inquiry demands? Powell felt so. Common sense suggests that advertising for a product will result in more demand for that product. Why would Central Hudson contest the advertising ban unless it believed it could increase its own sales via advertising?

The fourth inquiry, regarding the extensiveness of the regulation, whether it

---

6. *Central Hudson Gas & Electric v. Public Service Commission of New York*, 447 U.S. 557 (1980).

7. *Pittsburgh Press Co. v. Pittsburgh Commission on Human Relations*, 413 U.S. 376 (1973). But see *Housing Opportunities Made Equal v. Cincinnati Enquirer*, 943 F.2d 644 (6th Cir. 1991) (allowing job seekers to place ads bringing to the attention of potential employers facts—e.g., an applicant's race, religion, age, or gender—that likely would be illegal for the employer to actually use in the hiring decision). More recently, an online roommate referral service was told that the Federal Housing Act might prohibit it from requiring its clients to reveal similarly personal data. *Fair Housing Council of San Fernando Valley v. Roommates.com*, 521 F. 3d 1157 (9th Cir. 2008). The case was remanded for additional fact-finding.

8. *Nefedro v. Montgomery County*, MD, 996 A.2d 850 (MD 2010) provides a handy summary of what other states have done; the Maryland Supreme Court itself held that fortune-telling could not be forbidden across the board; that it is entertainment, not inherently deceptive.

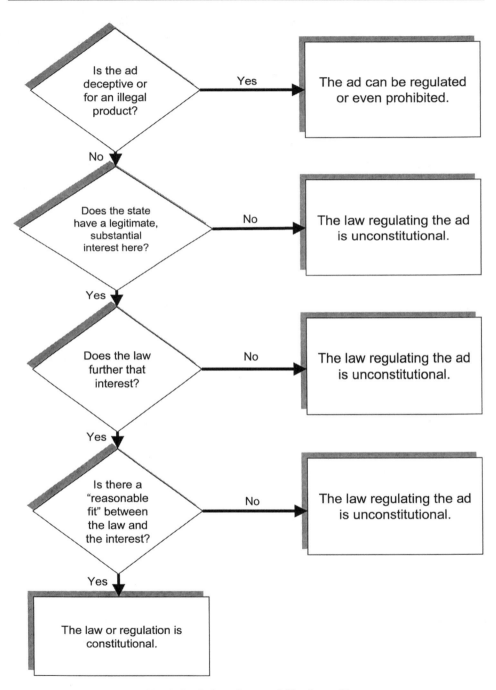

A Model of the *Central Hudson* Test

abridged more speech than necessary[9] to achieve the state's legitimate goals, proved to be the state's downfall. The prohibition on advertising was more extensive than necessary for two reasons, Powell concluded. First, the ban covered *all* promotional advertising, thus even prohibiting utility companies from marketing energy-*saving* devices. Second, the state's interest was in saving *energy*, not electricity, yet some people (depending on what systems they already were using) might waste less energy overall by switching to electricity.

Smoking, Drinking, Gambling, and Making Whoopee

The late 1990s saw a tremendous flurry of legal activity involving tobacco companies. Dozens of states' attorneys general prepared lawsuits against the big tobacco conglomerates, seeking reimbursement for billions of dollars in health care costs. In early 2000, the major tobacco companies entered into a "Master Settlement Agreement" that put to rest dozens of those suits in return for billions of dollars, plus several concessions concerning the future marketing of tobacco products. Among the concessions were the companies' promises to stop targeting the underage youth market, to cease using cartoon figures such as Joe Camel, and to refrain from any further outdoor advertising (such as highway billboards or ads placed on the exterior of buses). By signing the agreement, the tobacco companies hoped to avoid judicial resolution of a question that has stymied jurists and scholars for decades: would the First Amendment permit the government to forbid tobacco advertising altogether? The agreement, however, could not resolve all outstanding issues concerning advertising of tobacco products. For example, although it covers outdoor advertising placed by the tobacco companies themselves, it is mute with respect to such advertising placed by retail establishments that sell tobacco products.

Into this void stepped the State of Massachusetts, which established regulations affecting both the advertising and point-of-sale conduct of retailers. Among the regulations' provisions was a prohibition against any outdoor advertising for tobacco products within one thousand feet of schools and parks. The regulations also insisted that retailers eschew self-service displays of tobacco products, which must instead be placed out of reach of customers, available to them only upon asking a sales clerk for help.

Toward the end of its 2000–2001 term, the Supreme Court handed down a complex decision from a combination of cases challenging the various regulations. The state's regulations on cigarette advertising were struck down on **Supremacy Clause** grounds because Congress had already made clear its own intention to regulate cigarette advertising (by, for example, demanding health warning labels on packages and

---

9. In 1989, the Court substituted a less stringent final query, asking only that there be a "reasonable fit" between the regulation and the state's interest. *Board of Trustees of the State University of New York v. Fox*, 492 U.S. 469 (1989).

removing cigarette ads from TV and radio).[10] Since Congress had been silent about its intentions concerning advertising for cigars and smokeless tobacco, the Court turned to the *Central Hudson* test. The advertising regulations were struck down on the grounds that they failed the fourth prong of the test—there was not a "reasonable fit" between the rules and the state's interest, in that the rules prohibited much more speech than was warranted.

Rules demanding that in-store "point of sale" advertisements for tobacco products be placed at least five feet above the ground also failed the *Central Hudson* test. These rules, Justice O'Connor wrote for the majority, could not even be said to further the state's interest in keeping minors from smoking. "Not all children are less than 5 feet tall," she reminded us, "and those who are certainly have the ability to look up and take in their surroundings." The regulations providing that tobacco products must be placed out of reach behind the counter so that customers must first ask a clerk for help were the only ones at issue here to survive the Court's scrutiny. These regulations were plainly beyond the scope of the First Amendment, O'Connor held.

In a more recent decision, the Court held that the Supremacy Clause did not bar a group of activists in Maine from bringing a suit alleging that tobacco companies were in violation of a state Unfair Trade Practices law in deceptively advertising "light" brands. The suit intended to bring to bear scientific evidence to the effect that smokers tended to smoke more "light" and "low tar" cigarettes and inhale more deeply from them, thus eliminating any possible positive health effects of switching to such brands. Yes, relevant federal law promises that companies that are in compliance with it shall not be subject to a "requirement or prohibition based on smoking and health" stemming from state law claims. But the plaintiffs' allegation here was one of fraudulent advertising, which the Court held is not "based on smoking and health."[11] Gotcha!

In 2010, the Food and Drug Administration sent a well-publicized letter to the Atria Company, expressing displeasure with the company's seemingly having found a way to avoid at least the spirit of federal law prohibiting further labeling of cigarettes as "light." Not only was the new labeling of "Marlboro Gold" designed to match the color scheme of the old Marlboro Lights; the company also added labeling during the transition period, explicitly alerting customers that "Your Marlboro Lights pack is changing. But your cigarette stays the same," and advising them, "in the future," to "ask for 'Marlboro in the gold pack.'"[12]

---

10. *Lorillard Tobacco Company v. Reilly*, 533 U.S. 525 (2001). Under the same citation, the decision includes the Court's handling of *Consolidated Cigar Corporation v. Reilly*. The Supremacy Clause of the U.S. Constitution prohibits state and local governments from enacting laws that conflict with federal law. See for example, *United States v. Arizona*, 703 F. Supp. 2d 980 (D. Ariz. 2010).

11. *Altria Group v. Good*, 555 U.S. 70 (2008).

12. Letter from Lawrence R. Deyton of the FDA's Center for Tobacco Products to the Altria Group's General Counsel, June 17, 2010.

Federal rules prohibiting the use of the word "light" in cigarette labels took effect in mid-2010, resulting in these kinds of labeling changes.

Unless you are more than a bit older than the typical undergraduate student, your only familiarity with TV commercials for tobacco products will be through archival footage. Yet tobacco companies were among the biggest spenders on TV and radio airtime until the early 1970s. Indeed, in decades past, broadcast personalities often stepped out of role for a few moments to hawk cigarettes on their own programs. Lucille Ball and Desi Arnaz did it, as did the voices behind the Flintstones. That all stopped with the passage of the Public Health Cigarette Smoking Act, which as of 1971 forbade the advertising of cigarettes on TV and radio. A special three-judge panel of the federal district court for Washington, D.C., upheld the constitutionality of that act, and the Supreme Court, without writing an opinion, upheld the lower court's ruling.[13] Although the decision was based on the government's unique relationship to the electronic media, the district court majority added in dicta that "Congress has the power to prohibit the advertising of cigarettes *in any media.*"

How much weight this statement should be given is unclear. That broader question was not presented to the lower court. Moreover, the decision was written prior to the *Virginia Pharmacy* ruling, at a time when lower courts had no reason to expect that advertising enjoyed *any* First Amendment protection. Those who support a complete ban on tobacco advertising across all media took solace from a 1986 Supreme Court decision. Recall that the first part of the *Central Hudson* test from 1980 asks whether an advertisement is misleading or is for an illegal product or service. The 1986 ruling in *Posadas de Puerto Rico Associates v. Tourism Co.* prompted many to wonder whether the justices had secretly added a third prong to that inquiry.[14] The decision seemed to say that a very diluted version of the commercial speech doctrine would apply when the product or service being advertised was a *dangerous* (although legal) one. At issue was a Puerto Rico law that forbade some forms of advertising for casinos. More specifically, ads aimed at Puerto Ricans were banned, but ads aimed at tourists from elsewhere were permitted.

Perhaps the most puzzling part of Justice Rehnquist's opinion for the 5–4 Court was his reference to gambling as part of a category of products and services—he included cigarettes, alcoholic beverages, and prostitution—that governments may legitimately "deem harmful." Puerto Rico could surely have prohibited its residents from engaging altogether in such a harmful activity as casino gambling, Rehnquist suggested, and this broad power must surely include "the lesser power" to ban advertising designed to stimulate demand for the casinos.

---

13. *Capital Broadcasting Co. v. Mitchell*, 333 F. Supp. 582 (D.D.C. 1971), *aff'd mem.*, 405 U.S. 1000 (1972).
    14. 478 U.S. 328 (1986).

Did Rehnquist thus mean to suggest that governments would be given carte blanche to regulate (or indeed, to prohibit) advertising for any "products or activities deemed harmful"?

Surely not with respect to alcohol, right? After all, the Twenty-First Amendment had repealed prohibition quite some time ago. Indeed, more recent decisions involving alcohol advertising strongly suggest that the *Posadas* decision is perhaps best seen as an aberration, even though it has not yet been explicitly overturned.[15] A plurality of four justices in the latter *44 Liquourmart* decision concluded that the *Posadas* Court had performed an "erroneous . . . First Amendment analysis," and not a single justice expressed disagreement with this sentiment.

A death knell for *Posadas*? Perhaps, but a couple of recent federal appellate decisions suggest that advertising regulation of "dangerous" products or services can still be constitutional. In one, student editors at Virginia Tech were disappointed when a Fourth Circuit panel upheld a state regulation that prohibits most advertising for liquor in college newspapers, even where evidence made clear that most readers were over twenty-one.[16] The second case upheld a Nevada law prohibiting ads for prostitution in any county where the practice is illegal. Even while admitting that the *Posadas* case seems to have been discredited over the years, judges on the Ninth Circuit suggested that prostitution is unique among the usual vices (alcohol, tobacco, and gambling), in that society has numerous laws aimed at discouraging the "commodification" of human beings.[17]

What does all this bode for restrictions on tobacco advertising beyond those that might survive *Central Hudson* scrutiny anyway, or even for an outright ban on advertising for this still-legal product? The question cannot be answered with total certainty, but the Court has certainly signaled its reluctance to permit the censoring of true commercial information based on the fear that readers will act on the information.[18] The argument could be made, of course, that most tobacco advertising either does not impart any information or imparts mostly a kind of nonverbal misinformation. Do not most print ads for tobacco products, after all, seek to create a mental association of the product with athletic endeavors engaged in by healthy, young models with impeccably white teeth? Surely this is quite different from such mundane and verifiable kinds of information as the price of a bottle of beer or its alcohol content

---

15. *Rubin v. Coors Brewing Company*, 514 U.S. 476 (1995) (government may not prohibit beer distributors from listing their alcohol content on their product labels); *44 Liquourmart v. Rhode Island*, 517 U.S. 484 (1986) (government may not prohibit liquor distributors from advertising their prices).

16. *Educational Media Company at Virginia Tech v. Swecker*, 602 F. 3d 583 (4th Cir. 2010).

17. *Coyote Publishing, Inc. v. Miller*, 598 F. 3d 592 (9th Cir. 2010). The judges alluded to laws against slavery and the selling of our organs, and the practice in many states of refusing to enforce surrogate parent contracts.

18. Such an inference finds further support in *Greater New Orleans Broadcasting Association v. United States*, 527 U.S. 173 (1999).

(or the location of a brothel). Whether that difference is one that makes a difference in First Amendment analysis is a question for possible future litigation.

Can't Stop with Drugs: Advertising by Lawyers and Other Professionals

Back in the landmark *Virginia Pharmacy* decision, which first held that purely commercial speech is protected by the First Amendment, some of the justices tried carefully to limit the ruling to pharmacists only. In his majority opinion, Justice Blackmun went out of his way to say that he would "express no opinion as to other professions." He hinted, however, that lawyers and doctors would likely be treated differently because they "do not dispense standardized products" but rather "render professional services of almost infinite variety and nature." Chief Justice Burger's concurring opinion emphasized that he was voting with the majority only because he predicted it would be possible to restrict this ruling to pharmacists. He pointed to data showing that 95 percent of prescriptions are already in dosage units when they arrive at the pharmacy, thus implying that pharmacists spend most of their time simply pouring pills from big bottles into little bottles.

Only Justice Rehnquist's crystal ball seems to have been working. He alone, in his *Virginia Pharmacy* dissenting opinion, argued that there would be no way to avoid opening the door to advertising by all categories of professionals, including lawyers. "I cannot distinguish," he taunted his colleagues, "between the public's right to know the price of drugs and its right to know the price of title searches or physical examinations." Why "title searches" and "physical examinations?" Clearly this was his way of throwing the majority's words back at Justice Blackmun. Pharmacists are not the only professionals who render "standardized products."

It did not take very long for Justice Rehnquist to be proven right. In its very next term after deciding *Virginia Pharmacy*, the Court ruled 5–4 to strike down Arizona's

---

THINGS TO REMEMBER

Dangerous Advertising

- In the *Posadas* case, Justice Rehnquist seemed to add two very new rationales, above and beyond the *Central Hudson* test, for upholding the Commonwealth's ban on casino advertising:
  - The state's inarguable freedom to ban the activity altogether surely includes the "lesser" right to ban advertising for the activity.
  - Governments should have a large amount of leeway in regulating advertising for products or services deemed harmful, such as gambling, smoking, drinking, and the like.
- *Posadas* has since been discredited, though not explicitly overruled.

law banning lawyer advertising. A Phoenix law firm called Bates and O'Steen placed an ad in a local newspaper describing itself as a "legal clinic" offering "very reasonable rates." The ad went on to indicate the actual rates charged for services such as uncontested divorce or separation, adoption, change of name, and bankruptcy.

Among the state's arguments in defense of the law were that lawyer advertising would have an adverse effect on attorney professionalism and that lawyer ads are inherently misleading. With respect to the first concern, Justice Blackmun countered that clients are not foolish enough to think that all attorneys are giving away their time pro bono. The state's second concern he dismissed swiftly, finding an assumption of deceptive intent bizarre. The bar association could certainly find certain categories of attorney advertising deceptive, or rule on a case-by-case basis, but it could not assume all such ads were bound to be deceptive.

The Bates ad itself was not deceptive, the Court majority held. Even boasting "reasonable" prices was, for want of a better word, reasonable. Survey data showed that Bates's fees were toward the low end of the Phoenix market at the time. The majority cautioned, however, that lawyers should be very careful about making global pronouncements in their ads about the "quality" of their services, because such claims would not be "susceptible to measurement by verification."[19]

In 1990, the Court elaborated on, and perhaps stepped back a bit from, its concern about advertisements touting a professional's "quality" of service. By a 5–4 vote, the Court overturned the censuring of Illinois attorney Gary Peel for having advertised,

When Justice Blackmun, in his *Bates* opinion, suggested that lawyers and clients should come to a mutual understanding at the outset about legal fees, this is likely not what he had in mind.

---

19. *Bates v. State Bar of Arizona*, 433 U.S. 350 (1977).

on his personal letterhead, that he held a "Certificate in Civil Trial Advocacy from the National Board of Trial Advocacy." Although Peel did hold such certification, the state was concerned that readers would assume (incorrectly) that the National Board of Trial Advocacy (NBTA) is a government agency. The state also argued that Peel's boasting of his certificate was an impermissible statement, at least implicitly, about the quality of his services. Four of the five justices ruling in favor of Peel emphasized the difference between unsubstantiated promises of quality based on nothing more than a lawyer's own assessment of how wonderful he or she is and statements of objective facts that may support an inference of quality. Although Justice Marshall did not join in the plurality opinion, his separate opinion did not contradict the plurality on this point.[20]

Whether touting that one has been judged one of New Jersey's "super lawyers" by one's peers counts as such an unsubstantiated promise was at least implicitly at issue in a decision from the state's state supreme court. Rejecting an administrative ruling to the effect that such advertising was always beyond the pale, the court said such bragging is OK as long as the publication in which the ads appear clearly sets forth the methodology used and includes a disclaimer to the effect that the court itself has nothing to do with the accolades.[21]

The Supreme Court had more to say about lawyer advertising in a case involving a St. Louis attorney—identified in the court proceedings only as RMJ—who had been disciplined by the Missouri Supreme Court's Advisory Committee for placing advertisements containing text that deviated from the committee's strict guidelines. Chief among RMJ's sins were his having deviated from the precise wording demanded by the state to describe his practice—"personal injury" instead of "tort law" and "real estate" instead of "property law"—and his having indicated that he was a member of the U.S. Supreme Court Bar. Writing for a unanimous Court, Justice Powell overturned the reprimand issued against RMJ, telling the states that they may not "place an absolute prohibition" on whole categories of "*potentially* misleading information," but must instead target advertising practices that are, in fact, deceptive.[22]

That RMJ's ad also touted his membership in the Bar of the Supreme Court of the United States Justice Powell admitted was "somewhat more troubling." Consider for

20. *Peel v. Attorney Registration and Disciplinary Commission of Illinois*, 496 U.S. 91 (1990). See also *Ibanez v. Florida Department of Business and Professional Regulation, Board of Accountancy*, 512 U.S. 136 (1994) (attorney who also happens to be an accountant and a certified financial planner may tout those facts in Yellow Pages ads).

21. New Jersey Court Rules Annotated RPC 7. 1 (2010); *In re Opinion 39 of the Committee on Attorney Advertising*, 961 A. 2d 722 (N.J. 2008).

22. *In re R. M. J.*, 455 U.S. 191 (1982). See also *Harrell v. The Florida Bar*, 608 F. 3d 1241 (11th Cir. 2010) (critiquing the vagueness of several state proscriptions governing attorney advertising); *In the matter of Anonymous Member of the South Carolina Bar*, 684 S.E. 2d 560 (S. C. 2009) (advertising claim that an attorney will "work to protect your job" does not necessarily convey a promise to succeed).

The New Jersey Supreme Court held that attorneys whose ads tout their having been listed among the "best" or "super" lawyers must direct readers to the methodology resulting in their selection, and include the sentence, "No aspect of this advertisement has been approved by the Supreme Court of New Jersey." The text in the bottom right of the ad here satisfies those requirements.

Notice, in RMJ's ad here, his mention of his membership in the United States Supreme Court Bar.

a moment what it would mean to *you* to learn that an attorney had such membership. Would you be impressed? You probably should not be, at least not very much. Membership in the Supreme Court Bar means that you are permitted to make oral arguments in front of the nation's highest court, but there is no test to take or interview to pass. One must simply have been a practicing attorney for three years, pay a fee, and obtain a statement of "good character" from a current member of the bar. That RMJ chose to include this relatively uninformative fact about his qualifications was "at least bad taste," Powell concluded, but the Missouri rules did not specifically prohibit the disclosure, and in any event the state did not present clear evidence to support its contention that this particular boast was deceptive.

The Supreme Court had further occasion to advise the states on permissible regulations when it accepted a case involving attorney Philip Zauderer's ads for plaintiffs who might have been injured by the Dalkon Shield intrauterine device (IUD).[23] The ad featured a drawing of the device and the caption, "Did you use this IUD?" The text went on to enumerate the many health problems that had been associated with this particular IUD, admonish possible victims that it is "not too late to take legal

---

23. *Zauderer v. Office of Disciplinary Counsel*, 471 U.S. 626 (1985). Ohio also sought to discipline Zauderer over an advertisement for DUI defendants promising that "your full legal fee will be refunded if you are convicted of drunk driving." The deceptiveness in this ad, Ohio claimed, was its failure to inform readers that most criminal cases ripe for trial end in plea bargains. Any of Zauderer's clients who chose to plead guilty to a lesser offense would have to pay his full fee. As soon as the state expressed its displeasure to Zauderer, he withdrew the ad and pledged not to take on as clients any persons who might respond to it.

action," and inform them that "our law firm is presently representing women on such cases." The ad also promised that "no legal fees" will be owed unless a suit is successful.

The Dalkon Shield ad attracted the attention of the Supreme Court of Ohio's Office of Disciplinary Counsel for several reasons. First, the state had a clear rule against drawings or any other illustrations in lawyer advertisements. Second, Ohio had an anti–"ambulance chasing" rule that it interpreted as forbidding attorneys to recommend themselves to any potential client who has not specifically sought out their advice. In other words, attorneys were forbidden to give unsolicited legal advice, including the messages "You need an attorney" and "You ought to consider hiring *me*." Third, Zauderer's promise that "if there is no recovery, no legal fees are owed" seemed vague. Apparently the client would not have to pay the attorney his fee. But what about fees due to the court itself, such as filing fees, or fees for photocopying official documents? Moreover, if the client wins—and thus has to pay the attorney's fee—will that fee be calculated as a percentage of the gross amount awarded to the client, or the net (after the client pays all court costs out of pocket)?

Writing for the Court, Justice White had no trouble overturning the state's blanket prohibition against drawings or illustrations. "The use of illustrations or pictures in advertisements," he wrote, "serves important communicative functions: it attracts the attention of the audience to the advertiser's message, and it may serve also to impart information directly." But White upheld the judgment of the state on the contingency fees issue; after all, the state was not prohibiting attorneys from advertising this fee option, but merely requiring that any such claims be clear.

One key issue remained in the *Zauderer* case: the state's application of its antisolicitation rules to Zauderer for having suggested to readers both that they might need an attorney *and* that he might be a good one to hire. "All advertising is at least implicitly a plea for its audience's custom," Justice White reminded the Ohio Supreme Court. More to the point, there was nothing deceptive either in the ad's suggesting that women who have been hurt by the Dalkon Shield might need an attorney to help them recover damages or in its reporting that Zauderer's firm was experienced in this particular kind of litigation. Justice White made clear that it is quite legitimate for state regulations to protect the public from *in-person* attorney solicitations (from true "ambulance chasers"). Print advertising is different, however, in that it lacks "the coercive force of the personal presence of a trained advocate," and thus is "more conducive to reflection."

A few years later, the Court revisited the distinction between in-person solicitation of business by attorneys and attorney advertising. The case concerned a Louisville, Kentucky, attorney named Richard Shapero who was in the habit of culling through public records for lists of persons whose homes were being foreclosed. He would then write to these individuals and offer his services. The Kentucky Bar Association had strict rules forbidding most kinds of direct-mail advertising, and its logic was interesting. States can surely prohibit attorneys from mailing an individually targeted letter of solicitation to a specific individual, Kentucky reasoned, in that such a communication is very similar to in-person solicitation. As the science of information retrieval and direct-mail list development grows more precise, lawyers may know so much about the persons on a carefully created mailing list that writing a letter to the entire list might also come to approximate in-person self-promotion. The Kentucky Bar Association therefore prohibited attorneys from sending direct mailings to any group of people who are somehow systematically different from the general public because of some "specific event or occurrence" (such as an auto accident or, indeed, a home foreclosure).

The wording of the rule was not terribly clear, which is part of the reason the Supreme Court struck it down. The rule prohibited mailings to persons "known to need legal services of the kind provided by the lawyer in a particular manner," but permitted mailing to persons "who are so situated that they *might* in general find such services useful." Perhaps, then, Shapero could have mailed to whole zip codes in the poorer parts of town? Justice Brennan's opinion for the Court, like Justice White's in the earlier *Zauderer* case, emphasizes the key difference between in-person solicitation and direct-mail appeals. "A letter, like a printed advertisement (but unlike a lawyer)," Brennan wrote, "can readily be put in a drawer to be considered later, ignored, or discarded."

Brennan admitted that a targeted mail campaign does carry with it the danger that recipients will overestimate the lawyer's qualifications—"He knows so much about me, he must be a good attorney!"—but this danger counts as a reason for carefully monitoring direct mail, not for banning it altogether. The Court suggests here that states may require all attorneys who wish to send direct mailings to have them prescreened by an appropriate regulatory body.[24]

If the *Shapero* decision tells attorneys that it is all right to target for direct mail someone who may need their services because of a specific catastrophic life event, a 1995 decision cautions that they may have to wait a suitable period of time before sending any letters. In a 5–4 ruling, the Court upheld a Florida statute prohibiting attorneys from sending targeted direct-mail solicitations to accident or natural catastrophe victims or their relatives for thirty days following the event. Justice O'Connor applied the *Central Hudson* test on behalf of the Court. The state's purported interest in "protecting the privacy and tranquility of personal injury victims and their loved ones against intrusive, unsolicited contact by lawyers" was clearly substantial.[25] Moreover, the state's regulation served to further that interest in a narrowly tailored way.

---

24. *Shapero v. Kentucky Bar Association*, 486 U.S. 466, 475–476 (1988). See also *Harrell v. The Florida Bar*, 608 F. 3d 1241 (11th Cir. 2010) (upholding state requirement that attorneys' TV and radio ads be prescreened by the bar association, which pledged a twenty-day turnaround); *Florida Bar v. Went For It, Inc.*, 515 U.S. 618 (1995) (upholding state rule requiring attorneys to wait thirty days after an auto accident or natural catastrophe before soliciting victims' business by direct mail).

25. *Florida Bar v. Went For It, Inc.*, 515 U.S. 618 (1995).

After all, attorneys do not have to wait thirty days to do other kinds of outreach, such as newspaper ads, billboard placements, or broadcast spots.

The Supreme Court has heard a disproportionate number of *attorney* advertising cases, but other professions have also been represented in its decisions. For example, the whole issue of in-person solicitation was treated somewhat differently by the Supreme Court when the professional involved was an accountant rather than an attorney. Florida was one of a tiny handful of states that forbade accountants to engage in "direct, in-person, uninvited solicitation" to obtain new clients. Accountant Scott Fane wanted to do just that and so sought a declaratory judgment on the rule's constitutionality. Writing for an 8–1 majority, Justice Kennedy rejected the state's argument that any accountant who solicits clients in that manner "is obviously in need of business" and might be a bit too willing to bend the rules when it comes time each year to certify that the client's accounting practices are appropriate. Indeed, the opposite—that accountants with *long-standing* clients would be most likely to bend reality a bit at certification time—is equally plausible. Why, then, permit accountants but not attorneys to solicit business in person? Because unlike accountants, whose clients tend to be "experienced business executives," initial contacts between attorneys and potential clients often occur "at a moment of high stress and vulnerability."[26]

The last case we consider in this section involved advertising and marketing by optometrists. Consider the plight of Dr. N. Jay Rogers, a Texas optometrist who unsuccessfully challenged a state rule prohibiting members of his profession from doing business under a trade name. A trade name in this context would mean virtually any wording on the shingle other than "N. Jay Rogers, OD." You are probably familiar with numerous trade names used by optometrists; sometimes they are clever puns such as "For Eyes" or "Make a Spectacle." Rogers's chosen trade name was the more mundane "Texas State Optical." Writing for a 7–2 majority, Justice Powell upheld the constitutionality of the state's prohibition, contrasting the Texas rule here with the Virginia rule that had prohibited pharmacists from advertising their prescription drug prices. It is difficult to imagine any commercial information more crucial to consumers than the prices of goods and services, Powell suggested. The speech Texas prohibits here, by contrast, is not valuable information, and indeed "has no intrinsic

---

26. *Edenfield v. Fane*, 507 U.S. 761, 766, 774–776 (1993); cf. *Ohralik v. Ohio State Bar Association*, 436 U.S. 447 (1978) (explaining the Court's embracing of antisolicitation rules applied to attorneys). Attorneys are almost unique among professionals in that they are "trained in the art of persuasion."

A pair of conflicting federal appellate decisions tried to apply the Supreme Court's lawyer-solicitation cases to chiropractors. In the Fifth Circuit, a Louisiana statute forbidding chiropractors to solicit individuals on targeted lists, such as victims of recent auto accidents, was struck down—*Speaks v. Kruse*, 445 F.3d 396 (5th Cir. 2006). But in the Seventh Circuit, the State of Illinois was allowed to prevent a chiropractor from similar solicitations. *Goodman v. Illinois Department of Financial and Professional Regulation*, 430 F.3d 432 (7th Cir. 2005). The difference? In the Illinois case the chiropractor intended to use paid telemarketers (as opposed to his own office staff, or making calls himself).

THINGS TO REMEMBER

Advertising by Lawyers and Other Professionals

- The 1977 *Bates* case first opened the door to lawyer advertising.
- The Court has since *said* it would be very leery of attorneys whose ads were designed to tout the high quality of their services, yet the justices have never upheld any state sanction against an attorney for doing just that.
- The only sanctions the Court has upheld were for advertising in potentially deceptive ways with respect to fees.
- There is a long history of forbidding in-person solicitation by attorneys; neither traditional mass media advertising nor direct-mail appeals are considered solicitation.
- States may, however, insist that attorneys wait a suitable time after an accident or other catastrophic event before sending a mailing to the victims.
- States may not constitutionally prohibit accountants (nor, presumably, other professionals who are not "trained in the art of persuasion") from engaging in in-person solicitation.
- States may prohibit professionals from doing business under a trade name.

meaning" at all. Moreover, Powell pointed out, trade names are at least as likely to deceive consumers as to inform them. A company can continue to use a trade name even after one or more optometrists whose reputation first attracted the public to the practice have departed. Conversely, an optometrist with a terrible reputation, perhaps owing to his or her own "negligence or misconduct," can simply change the name of the practice. A single optometrist could even, "by using different trade names at shops under his common ownership, give the public the false impression of competition among the shops."[27]

Statutory and Regulatory Approaches

The First Amendment, as interpreted by the Supreme Court in such landmark decisions as *Virginia Pharmacy* and *Central Hudson*, puts the government on notice as to how much regulation of advertising will be permissible. One thing that has remained constant throughout and even before the development of the Supreme Court's commercial speech doctrine is the commonsense notion that the government should protect us from deceptive advertising. Not surprisingly, most of the ongoing regulatory interactions between the government and advertisers are aimed at identifying and eliminating deceptive statements from commercial messages. This section looks first at state and local regulation of advertising, then at the most important source of federal regulation—the Federal Trade Commission (FTC). We then examine the federal

---

27. *Friedman v. Rogers*, 440 U.S. 1, 13 (1979).

Lanham Act, which permits one competitor to sue another for damages without having to persuade the FTC to intervene. After considering nongovernmental efforts at self-regulation by media and by the advertising industry, we conclude with a brief look at Supreme Court decisions concerning corporate advertising that seeks to "sell" political candidates rather than products and services.

State and Local Regulation

State regulation of advertising pre-dates any meaningful intervention by the federal government. A magazine based in New York, reacting to an array of newspaper and magazine exposés of medical quackery, proposed in 1911 that individual states draft laws criminalizing the use of deceptive advertising. Such *Printers' Ink* statutes, named after that magazine, were eventually passed by the majority of states.

Many state laws governing advertising practices are fashioned after federal laws and regulations, and some explicitly instruct state courts to consider FTC and federal court rulings. Some go further. Massachusetts, for example, makes it easier than most states for plaintiffs alleging deceptive advertising to bring a class-action suit. A mere threat of a class-action suit by the nonprofit Center for Science in the Public Interest resulted in the Kellogg company agreeing to no longer use cartoon characters such as SpongeBob SquarePants to market unhealthy foods to children. The more global issue of marketing sugary foods to children, with or without the aid of cartoon characters, remains very much in the news, especially with First Lady Michelle Obama's having chosen childhood obesity as one of her causes.[28]

At times state laws have been found to violate the federal Constitution's Supremacy Clause, which prohibits state and local governments from enacting laws that conflict with federal law. Courts speak of the state laws having been "preempted" in such situations. State laws governing the marketing of airfares and prohibiting wine advertising on cable television have been struck down on Supremacy Clause grounds.[29] Note, however, that state and federal laws can peacefully coexist, as long as the structure of the relevant federal law is not designed to preempt state law. Thus, for example, a federal appellate court ruled in 2009 that the federal law did not automatically prevent a New Jersey fraud statute from being used against the Snapple Beverage Corporation's labeling its drinks "all natural."[30]

Actually, the federal government frequently takes its lead from the states. In 1998, for example, American Family Publishers had to pay damages totaling over $1 million to several states that had sued the magazine subscription service best known for its annual sweepstakes using Ed McMahon and Dick Clark as pitchmen. The large print

28. William Newman, "Ad Rules Stall, Keeping Cereal a Cartoon Staple," *New York Times*, July 24, 2010, A1.

29. *Morales v. Trans World Airlines*, 504 U.S. 374 (1992); *Capital Cities Cable v. Crisp*, 467 U.S. 691 (1984).

30. *Holk v. Snapple Beverage Corporation*, 575 F. 3d 329 (3rd Cir. 2009).

A threatened class-action lawsuit using Massachusetts law was enough to pressure Kellogg's to halt the use of popular cartoon characters on packaging for sugary foods aimed at children.

in mailings from the company trumpeted that the recipient "has won" millions of dollars; only by reading the very fine print would one learn that this joyful event will only have come to pass if "you have and mail in the winning number." Some recipients of the mail piece, convinced that they were millionaires, had flown cross-country at their own expense to pick up their prizes! Publicity generated from state prosecutions spurred the federal government into action. In December 1999, President Clinton signed into law the Deceptive Mail Prevention and Enforcement Act; among its provisions is a requirement that qualifying language contradicting the bold assertion that the recipient "has won" must be "clearly and conspicuously displayed." The law also requires sweepstakes mailings to make clear that participants' odds of winning are not affected by whether they purchase the promoter's products, such as magazine subscriptions.[31]

The Federal Trade Commission

The main vehicle for the day-to-day federal regulation of advertising is the FTC, created appropriately enough by the Federal Trade Commission Act of 1914. The FTC has five commissioners, who are appointed by the president with the consent of the Senate, and who serve for seven-year staggered terms. The FTC was originally em-

---

THINGS TO REMEMBER

State and Local Regulation

- State Printers' Ink statutes were adopted early in the twentieth century to protect consumers from deceptive advertising.
- The Supremacy Clause of the U.S. Constitution prevents states or localities from passing regulations that conflict with federal law.

---

31. 39 USCA §3001, 3017 (2010).

powered only to police business practices that could unfairly hurt a competing company's bottom line. Congress's passage of the Wheeler-Lea amendments to the Federal Trade Commission Act, in 1938, gave the commission the broader power to protect consumers from unfair and deceptive business practices as well.

A word is in order about that phrase from the preceding sentence—"unfair and deceptive." Much of what the FTC does is not actually concerned with deceptive advertising. The commission's definition of *unfairness*, as laid down by Congress, points to any business practice that "causes or is likely to cause substantial injury to consumers which is not reasonably avoidable by consumers themselves and not outweighed by countervailing benefits to consumers or to competition." There is nothing in the act that restricts the commission to considering only issues related to advertising messages. Thus, for example, in 2010 a federal court upheld the FTC's complaint against an online checking service whose security procedures were inadequate, resulting in numerous examples of con artists accessing customers' records and misappropriating funds.[32]

Deceptive Advertising

The FTC uses a three-step process to determine whether it should take action against an allegedly deceptive advertisement. The first step involves a textual analysis of the ad and its context to determine just what it is saying and whether it appears on the surface to be deceptive. The second step, almost inseparable from the first in practice, requires the commission to consider whether a *reasonable* consumer would be deceived by the ad. Assuming that there is some deception at work, the last inquiry is whether that inaccuracy is *material*—that is, whether it is likely to affect the purchasing decision. Let us examine these three inquiries in turn.

Finding the Meaning of the Ad. Some advertisements, such as one that falsely claims the surgeon general has endorsed a product, are obviously deceptive. More typically, deceptive messages are implied rather than expressly stated. I offer here a list of four categories of deceptive advertising: "And I can prove it!" "More than I can say," "Did I hear that right?" and "Who said that?"[33]

"And I can prove it!" At one level, almost all advertising copy includes the implication "And I can prove it!" Make virtually any factual claim about your product, and consumers will assume that you have some reasonable basis for making the claim, that you can prove it. Sometimes ads teasingly go a step further, hinting at a particular kind of proof for their claims. Suppose an advertiser said that "90 percent of all teach-

---

32. *FTC v. Neovi, Inc.*, 604 F. 3d 1150 (9th Cir. 2010); see also *Philip Morris, Inc.*, 82 F.T.C. 16 (1973) (complaint against giving away free razor blades in newspaper inserts, an obvious danger to consumers).

33. My categories owe much to Ivan Preston's fifteen-category system. Ivan Preston, "The Federal Trade Commission's Identification of Implications as Constituting Deceptive Advertising," 57 *University of Cincinnati Law Review* 1243 (1989).

ers surveyed recommended the Grok Reading Program." That seems like pretty compelling testimony, doesn't it? But what if the 90 percent figure refers, literally, to nine out of ten teachers, and all ten were employees of the company? The deceptiveness then becomes apparent. The moment survey data or other statistical evidence are offered as proof for a claim, consumers have a right to expect that the figures were gathered in a scientifically valid way. Thus, for example, the makers of Fleishmann's margarine were told by the FTC to stop advertising that twice as many doctors recommended their margarine as any other brand. The manufacturer failed to include the sobering caveat that almost 70 percent of the physicians surveyed did not express a preference for any particular brand.[34]

Frequently the FTC is just not satisfied that a company's purportedly scientific evidence is sufficient to back up its claims. Thus, Tropicana was told to stop making dramatic claims about how its Healthy Heart orange juice formula could raise good cholesterol and lower bad in a few short weeks. The studies cited by the company had been based on too few subjects for too short a time.[35]

When a company offers "proof" of its product effectiveness in the form of an actual demonstration, the FTC requires that the demonstration not be rigged in any material way. Campbell Soup Company, for example, concerned that the solid chunks of meat and vegetables in their product would tend to sink to the bottom of the bowl over time, dropped a number of marbles into soup bowls so that the TV camera would not make it seem as if the soup was merely broth. The FTC charged Campbell's with making a visually deceptive claim.[36]

Probably the most famously deceptive advertising demonstration to attract the FTC's attention was that engaged in by the makers of Rapid Shave, who wanted to show viewers that their lather made shaving so effortless that it could strip sandpaper of its grain. Apparently, it would have been possible for the product to shave very fine sandpaper if the paper had been soaking long enough in advance of the demonstration. Fine sandpaper, however, did not "read" like sandpaper at all on analog TV back then—you couldn't see the grain. Very coarse sandpaper would produce the right picture for the cameras, except that it would be impossible to actually shave. So the manufacturer instead affixed grains of sand onto a piece of Plexiglas. The announcer then informed the audience that the purpose of the demonstration was "to prove Rapid Shave's super-moisturizing power," and that the process was as simple as "apply, soak, and off in a stroke." The FTC ordered the company to take the ads off the air, and the manufacturer appealed all the way to the Supreme Court, which upheld the commission's decision. The commercial included three misrepresentations, the Court held: that sandpaper could be shaved by Rapid Shave, that an experi-

34. *Standard Brands, Inc.*, 97 F.T.C. 233 (1981).
35. *In re Tropicana Products*, 140 F.T.C.176 (2005).
36. *Campbell Soup Co.*, 77 F.T.C. 150 (1970).

ment had been conducted verifying this claim, and that viewers were seeing this experiment for themselves.[37]

"More than I can say!"   Advertisements fit into the "More than I can say" category when their text is cleverly crafted to imply erroneous conclusions. That a line of clothing may have begun as bamboo fibers, with all the positive environmental statements one might legitimately make about how bamboo forests do not require pesticides, seems not terribly relevant when the fibers are ultimately transformed by a chemically harsh process into the artificial product known as rayon.[38]

Actually, since there likely is not a reasonable way for humans to determine if the new dog food really has an "improved" flavor, the only claim the FTC would likely require this company to *prove* is that it had changed the formula.

37. *FTC v. Colgate-Palmolive Co.*, 380 U.S. 374 (1965).

38. *In the matter of Pure Bamboo, LLC*, 2009 FTC LEXIS 235 (2009); see also *Firestone Tire & Rubber Co. v. FTC*, 481 F.2d 246 (6th Cir. 1973) (truthful claim that tires have passed all of its own manufacturer's inspections may imply falsely that the tires were therefore without any defects); *J. B. Williams & Co. v. FTC*, 381 F.2d 884 (6th Cir. 1967) (claim that dietary supplement can treat leth-

Sometimes, by touting a specific property inherent to its product, an advertiser may suggest that this brand is the only one on the market with that quality. For example, Whirlpool got the commission's attention when it boasted that its air conditioners had a "special Panic Button to cool you off extra fast." The FTC found that such a button was hardly unique to Whirlpool's products, but was "merely a control which activates the highest of the three fan speeds, substantially similar to controls on comparable air conditioners made by other companies."[39]

Distortion can also occur when advertisers offer, often in a dramatic way, true but not terribly important information about their product. One of the best-known examples was when the makers of Carnation Instant Breakfast emphasized in their ads that their product has "as much mineral nourishment as two strips of crisp bacon." But bacon actually has very few mineral nutrients, so the comparison was not terribly meaningful.[40]

Or consider ads that never quite make any direct claims about what a product does, yet invite erroneous conclusions. The FTC found that the manufacturer of Ab Force belts had engaged in deceptive advertising, even though the ads merely reminded consumers of competing companies' ads that touted wearing similar belts, which administer small electric shocks to the abdominal muscles, as "the latest fitness craze." Those other companies promise that their units will "get our abs into great shape—without exercise." Although the Ab Force ads never said what its own machines were supposed to do, the commission determined that touting the units as "just as powerful and effective" (but less expensive) was to promise, without substantiation, that they would help consumers shed inches and pounds. Since the commission had never been persuaded that any of these kinds of machines work, the Ab Force manufacturers could not be let off the hook by seeming not to promise anything.[41]

"Did I hear that right?"   Advertisers will often choose their words carefully, perhaps even injecting new words into the lexicon, to lead consumers to make conclusions based on a kind of auditory confusion. If you heard that a sweater was made of "cashmora," for example, isn't it likely that you will think of "cashmere?"[42] Or consider "plyhide" as a descriptive name for an upholstery material. Does it not suggest

---

argy associated with "iron-poor blood" ignores fact that very few cases of fatigue are caused by anemic blood).

39. *Whirlpool Co.*, 83 F.T.C. 1830 (1974). See also *American Home Products Corp.*, 98 F.T.C. 136 (1981) (Anacin's touting its having more aspirin than competing brands may lead to erroneous conclusion that it is therefore better an pain relief than competing over-the-counter drugs based on other formulas); *Sun Oil Co.*, 84 F.T.C. 247 (1974) (claim that lower-octane gasoline blends had the "action" of company's highest, 260-octane fuel, promised a bit more than was likely being delivered).

40. *Carnation Co.*, 77 F.T.C. 1547 (1970).

41. *Telebrands Corporation v. Federal Trade Commission*, 457 F. 3d 354 (4th Cir. 2006).

42. *Elliot Knitwear*, 59 F.T.C. 893 (1961).

some kind of leather, or at least the hide of some unnamed animal, rather than the vinyl it really was?[43]

Advertisers do not have to invent new words to create linguistic ambiguity. Given how the recent recession has been blamed at least in part on "subprime" mortgage lending, in which folks who really could not afford to buy real estate were enticed to do so, it is no surprise that the FTC has been cracking down on lenders whose advertising touts an absurdly low and misleading interest rate.[44] The commission's suspicions were similarly aroused by America Online's ubiquitous offers of "ten free hours" of online time. Consumers would easily miss the barely visible warnings that the hours must all be used in one month, that any use exceeding the ten hours or going beyond the one-month trial would result in automatic charges to their credit card, and that users needed to take the affirmative step of contacting the company to cancel their membership prior to the month's passage or they would begin to incur hourly fees.[45]

If advertisers can get into trouble for offering their wares "free," they certainly can attract the FTC's attention when they offer merchandise at sale prices. Look at the typical full-page department store ad in your local newspaper, telling readers that this or that product is now "on sale" for a hefty "percent off." What does this wording mean? The commission demands that the percentage shown be a comparison with a bona fide "regular" price and that the regular price shall have been in place for a reasonable period of time prior to the beginning of the special sale days. Ideally, too, a substantial number of sales will have occurred at the regular price. If not, this very fact must be affirmatively disclosed in the ad. Thus, if you look at the fine print of such ads, you will often see words to the effect that "our regular and original prices are offering prices only and may or may not have resulted in sales."[46]

"Who said that?" Advertisements often rely just as heavily on the attributed source for their messages as on the text itself. Madison Avenue is constantly on the lookout for appropriate spokespersons, celebrity or otherwise, to endorse their clients' goods and services. FTC regulation in this area is rather complex.

The commission does not consider all instances of people saying nice things about products in commercials "endorsements." Advertising narratives in which one character teaches another about a product, whether food storage bags or laxatives, would not usually be of commission concern. Viewers understand that these are fictional relationships depicted by paid actors. Nor does a spokesperson who does not enjoy any special brand of notoriety beyond appearing in a commercial typically count as

---

43. *Robbin Products*, 62 F.T.C. 1461 (1963).

44. *In the Matter of American Nationwide Mortgage Company*, 2009 FTC LEXIS 24 (2009). Some of the company's ads had touted a 1.95 percent mortgage rate, where only very fine print admitted that the rate could really adjust as high as 7.5 percent.

45. *America Online*, 1998 F.T.C. LEXIS 25 (1998).

46. *Home Centers, Inc.*, 94 F.T.C. 1362 (1979).

an endorser. Actress Stephanie Courtney, for example, is (at least as of this writing) hardly a household name, but you likely know her face and voice as "Flo," the perky young sales clerk in the mythical Progressive Insurance store. Ms. Courtney's appearance in the insurance company's campaign would not be considered an "endorsement."

A true celebrity endorsement must represent the genuine beliefs and experiences of the person or group to whom it is attributed. In a classic case, a cigarette company's advertisements implied that a *Reader's Digest* article had endorsed its product line. The appellate court that upheld the FTC's order to cease the advertisement campaign referred to the ads as "a perversion of the meaning of the *Reader's Digest* article." Whereas the article itself emphasized that the differences in tar and nicotine levels of competing cigarette brands were so negligible that a smoker could be confident that any of them could "effectively nail down his coffin," the manufacturer made it seem as if the magazine had endorsed Old Gold cigarettes as an especially healthful brand.[47]

Endorsers who claim to be users of products they advertise must in fact be users. Actor Wilford Brimley would have to have been a genuine user of Quaker oatmeal. Former surgeon general C. Everett Koop had to be truly a client of those Life Alert medical bracelets.[48] Advertisers have the responsibility to keep in touch with endorsers periodically to make sure that they still are users of products they endorse for as long as the campaign runs.

If an endorser's experience with a product is more dramatically positive than most consumers should expect, that fact must be disclosed. In 2009 the FTC went further, demanding that companies using such "true success stories" also provide realistic normative data. You can claim truthfully that client A lost forty-five pounds in eight weeks, but if the average weight loss in that time was closer to ten pounds, the ads must say so.[49]

When an advertisement purports to be using ordinary consumers rather than paid actors, that representation must itself be truthful. In its guide to advertisers, the FTC uses the example of a company seeming to have a hidden camera catch real consumers in a candid scene at a cafeteria giving spontaneous testimonials about a new brand of breakfast cereal. Such a production technique would be deceptive if the on-screen spokespersons are instead paid actors.

The commission employs a special measure of scrutiny concerning the use of "experts" giving testimonials. When an advertisement either expressly or implicitly states that an endorser has some special expertise vis-à-vis a product, FTC policy is that "the endorser's qualifications must in fact give him the expertise that he is represented as

---

47. *P. Lorillard Co. v. FTC*, 186 F.2d 52 (4th Cir. 1950).

48. Singer Pat Boone's hawking of Acne-Statin skin medication was seen as deceptive because, among other reasons, he claimed falsely that all his daughters used it. *Cooga Mooga*, 92 F.T.C. 310 (1978).

49. Guides Concerning the Use of Endorsements and Testimonials in Advertising, 74 FR 53124 (2009).

possessing." Beatrice Foods, makers of Milk Duds candies, got into a bit of trouble with the commission for its TV ads depicting baseball player Lou Brock getting a base hit, catching an opponent's fly ball, and stealing second base. The voice-over interviewer asks Brock his "secret for stealing second," and Brock's reply suggests that Milk Duds might have had something to do with his success. The FTC allowed that Brock is an expert with respect to athletic pursuits, but surely not with respect to nutrition.[50]

Interestingly, the FTC has not gotten involved in advertising campaigns exploiting the "expertise" attached to actors because of particular roles with which they are best associated. The commission never asked the Sanka people to refrain from using actor Robert Young to tout the benefits of drinking decaffeinated coffee, yet it is clear that the manufacturer was primarily interested in exploiting the public's identification of Young as the title character on *Marcus Welby, M.D.* More generically, advertisers are perfectly free to seek out celebrity spokespersons whose best-known roles make them seem trustworthy. Actor Dennis Haysbert, for example, was likely seen by Allstate as a desirable spokesperson in large part due to audiences' memory of him as President David Palmer from *24*, the popular FOX TV series.

Deceptive to a "Reasonable" Consumer?   In fulfilling its mission to protect the consumer against deceptive advertising, the FTC has at times presumed complete gullibility on the part of the citizenry. In one often-criticized case, the commission refused to permit a cosmetics company to advertise that its product could "color hair permanently." The commission felt this was misleading because hair that had not yet grown in would emerge in one's natural color.[51] The commission abandoned that entirely paternalistic approach some years later. In 1963, for example, it determined that a company marketing a device called Swim-Ezy to help novice swimmers stay afloat had not advertised deceptively by describing the small device as "invisible"; obviously, the product was not "invisible or impalpable or dimensionless," the FTC allowed, and consumers would be no more likely to think so than they would be to assume that "Danish pastry" must, as a matter of law, come from Denmark.[52]

Whether a reasonable consumer is likely to be misled can sometimes become a numbers game. What percentage of consumers need to be led astray before an ad will be found deceptive? The commission recognizes also that some ad campaigns are targeted to very specific markets. If the persons targeted are likely to be particularly vulnerable, the FTC may employ a more fluid definition of what it means to be "reasonable" or to be "likely to deceive." Thus, for example, the commission indicated its concern about companies that aggressively market loans to persons who may have very poor credit histories but lots of equity built up in their homes. Such persons may

---

50. *Beatrice Foods*, 81 F.T.C. 830 (1972).

51. *Gelb v. FTC*, 144 F.2d 580 (2d Cir. 1944).

52. *Heinz W. Kirchner*, 63 F.T.C. 1282 (1963).

be in need not only of money but also the chance to improve their credit ratings. Often these "predatory" mortgage companies, as the FTC calls them, make loans that they surmise will lead to default, thus allowing them to foreclose on their clients' homes.[53]

Not surprisingly, the commission has often expressed concern about children as an especially vulnerable target audience. Youngsters are, in the commission's words, "unqualified by age or experience to anticipate or appreciate the possibility that representations may be exaggerated or untrue."[54] Back in the 1970s the commission tried to ban just about all advertising aimed at young children, but the proposal was seen as politically unpalatable, and was swiftly rescinded.[55]

In 1998 Congress passed the Children's Online Privacy Protection Act, designed to protect children from the gathering of personal information about them without their parents' explicit consent. The law instructed the FTC to create and enforce specific rules in furtherance of the act's goals. The commission's rules prohibit websites from requiring children under thirteen to post information about themselves in order to participate on the site. Site operators must also delete promptly any personal information such youngsters might voluntarily post about themselves (such as in chat rooms).[56]

"Material" Information.   Not all potentially deceptive marketing messages are actionable. Only those that are material, that will likely affect the consumer's purchasing decision, will catch the FTC's attention. In practice, the FTC considers any factual claim about a product expressed in words to be material. The logic seems to be that if the advertiser chooses to make a claim, it is likely doing so to influence the consumer's purchasing decision. That is the whole point of running the ad in the first place.

Nontextual, visual elements become a bit trickier. If your product line is children's sportswear and your TV ads depict kids running around having fun while wearing your product, the FTC will not be terribly concerned that the ice cream cones the child actors seem to be consuming with such glee are actually filled with colored mashed potatoes. Ice cream just does not hold up very well to the hot lights in the TV studio. Indeed, even if you are selling ice cream itself, you will be able to use mashed potatoes in your ads, as long as you do nothing special to make the switch material. Thus, for example, if your ad touts the large number of flavor choices your company offers, there is no problem. If, however, your ad instead emphasizes the rich color and texture of the ice cream and the "fact" that it will help keep your kids neat

---

53. Complaint, *F.T.C. v. Capital City Mortgage Corp.*, No. 1:98-CV-00237 (D.D.C. filed Jan. 29, 1998).

54. *Ideal Toy Corp.*, 64 F.T.C. 297 (1964).

55. M. Neil Browne, Lauren Frances Biksacky, and Alex Frondorf, "Advertising to Children and the Commercial Speech Doctrine: Political and Constitutional Limitations," 58 *Drake Law Review* 67, 79–80 (2009).

56. Children's Online Privacy Protection Rule, 16 CFR 312.1–312.12 (2010).

Since the label "action figure" has become so common (perhaps as a way of allowing boys to play with dolls without being teased), the FTC would likely not see the label as a "material" reason for purchasing the product.

and clean because it does not melt as quickly as other brands, you will have serious problems with the commission.

The finding of materiality must come from the ads themselves. Thus, for example, Pizza Hut was able to demonstrate that many consumers believed Papa John's advertising claim that its pies have "better ingredients than other national pizza chains." Pizza Hut claimed this was a deceptive claim, in that its competitor's ads suggested that a small handful of differences in the two companies' production techniques made Papa John's "better," even though consumers apparently had no taste preferences for pies made with one or the other set of techniques. Even if the claims were deceptive, however, Pizza Hut failed to prove materiality, a federal appellate court held, because consumers' beliefs might have been based on their firsthand experiences with the two companies' products, rather than on the ad campaign.[57]

There is a special category of assertions about products that the commission has determined would not be used by reasonable consumers in making purchasing deci-

---

57. *Pizza Hut, Inc. v. Papa John's International, Inc.*, 227 F.3d 489 (5th Cir. 2000).

sions. This is called **puffery**, those unsubstantiated statements of opinion about a product's overall quality that consumers theoretically listen to with only one ear and do not take very seriously. We buy Hallmark greeting cards when we "care enough to send the very best." We are told that Carnival cruises are "the most popular in the world." If we "bring out the Hellmann's" mayonnaise, we "bring out the best." The FTC presumes that such claims about products serve no higher purpose than to keep the brand names alive in the collective consciousness, that they do not affect purchasing decisions in a material way.

Procedures and Powers of the FTC   The totality of the FTC's powers and responsibilities goes far beyond the subject matter of this book. Over the years, Congress has asked the agency to enforce no fewer than three dozen federal statutes, many of which have nothing to do with communication. We limit the consideration here to the commission's actions against deceptive advertising.

How does the FTC decide which cases to pursue? It often makes these determinations independently, after its own staff has monitored a specific ad campaign or concluded that a whole industry could benefit from the commission's guidance concerning consumers' likely inferences from the claims made in a category of advertising. Or the commission may first learn about a potentially deceptive practice from a company's competitors, or even from a member of the public.

The FTC would not get involved in this kind of advertising claim but would treat the labeling of an "all-day" lollipop as an example of puffery, protected speech precisely because no reasonable consumer would take the claim literally.

However an advertising campaign comes to the commission's attention, the FTC staff may, if it believes a violation of the law has occurred, attempt to obtain voluntary compliance. The staff will thus seek to enter into what is called a **consent order** with the company. This is similar to a **consent decree**, except that there is no judge and no court of law in charge of enforcing the order. A company that signs a consent order need not admit that it violated the law, but it must agree to stop the disputed practices, which the commission will have outlined in an accompanying complaint.[58] Most FTC actions against particular advertisers are such consent orders. Skeptics often point out that the FTC succeeds in getting this level of agreement from the targets of its investigations because the commission takes so long to act that the offending ad campaign is likely already over, or at least scheduled to soon be retired.

Sometimes a company is unwilling to sign a consent order. It may dispute the FTC's findings, believing that its advertising is not deceptive and should not be subject to any governmental sanctions. In this event, the commission staff will often issue an **administrative complaint**, which leads to a formal proceeding that is much like a court trial, except that the judge hearing the dispute is not an ordinary federal district judge but rather an **administrative law judge** (ALJ). Should the ALJ determine that the advertisement in dispute is indeed deceptive, a **cease and desist order**—the term is self-explanatory—will typically be issued.

If the defendant advertiser is dissatisfied with the ALJ's initial ruling, it may appeal to the five FTC commissioners themselves. These commission rulings are also appealable, first to a federal appellate court (usually the one for the District of Columbia) and ultimately to the Supreme Court (if it chooses to hear the case).

The FTC may in some circumstances opt to circumvent the often laborious administrative process of seeking a consent order and going to an ALJ. It can instead apply directly to a federal district judge for an injunction ordering the advertising to cease. The direct adjudicative route has the advantage of surprise, in that offending advertisers will not learn of the FTC's interest in them until the suit is actually filed. The commission typically reserves this action for egregious and continuing ad campaigns, as well as for those that may have direct and immediate implications for consumers' health.

The FTC is empowered not only to stop the use of an advertisement's deceptive wording but also to require advertisers to insert specific language, called **affirmative disclosures**, into future advertisements. Consent orders (agreements between the FTC and an advertiser) and consent decrees (issued by a federal court at the commission's request) frequently include such a requirement. In one case, the FTC reached an agreement with a maker of sunscreen that the commission's staff felt had made unrealistic claims about its product's ability to protect users from dangerous rays. The

---

58. The Kellogg Company, for example, entered into such an agreement with the FTC when the commission found the company exaggerated the results of a study on how Frosted Mini-Wheats cereal made youngsters more attentive. *In the Matter of Kellogg Company*, 2010 FTC LEXIS 45 (2010).

final order required, among other things, that the company's future advertising include such caveats as "tanning in sunlight or under tanning lamps can cause skin cancer and premature skin aging—even if you don't burn," and (with respect to lotions not having at least an SPF value of two) that "this product does not contain a sunscreen and does not protect against sunburn."[59]

Many disclaimers found in commercial messages, however, are offered voluntarily by the individual advertiser, with no direct input from the FTC or any other regulatory body. As a practical matter, marketers know that consumers are often unable to make sense of such disclaimers, especially in TV ads, since they flash on the screen too quickly and in print far too small to read.[60] (This is really no surprise to you, is it?)

In rare circumstances, an advertiser will be required to insert specific language into future advertising to undo a long history of past deceptions. Such **corrective advertising** has been required by the FTC only twice since its creation. The first case involved Warner-Lambert Company, makers of Listerine mouthwash, which had for many years suggested in its advertisements that the product could prevent the common cold. In 1975 the FTC ordered the company to insert into its next $10 million worth of advertising the admission that the mouthwash "will not help prevent colds or sore throats," a requirement upheld by a federal appellate court.[61]

The second instance of corrective advertising was in a 1999 FTC action requiring the manufacturer of Doan's pills, which the commissioners felt had implied falsely for many years that its product was superior to other analgesics for the relief of back pain, insert in its next $8 million of advertising a candid admission that there was no such evidence. The ruling was a vehicle for the commission to assert that corrective advertising is an appropriate remedy whenever prior advertising has "substantially created or reinforced a misbelief, and the misbelief is likely to linger into the future."[62]

The commission need not wait until a specific company's advertising campaign comes to its attention. Often the agency acts proactively, offering general guidelines concerning advertising of particular products or within a particular industry. Such **industry guides,** as they are called, offer highly specific instructions concerning the

59. *California Suncare*, 1997 F.T.C. LEXIS 24 (1997).

60. Jim Shea, "Small Print, Big Problems: You've Been Warned," *Hartford Courant*, June 16, 2007, B1; Daniel D. Lovil and Allan B. Padderud, "Video Disclaimers in Television Advertising: Are They Effective?" 31 *Journal of Communication* 72 (1981).

61. *Warner-Lambert Co. v. FTC*, 562 F.2d 749 (D.C. Cir. 1977). The commission also wanted the new ads to make explicit reference to the falsity of earlier messages—"contrary to prior advertising"—but the court deemed this unnecessarily punitive. When the court-imposed ads eventually ran on TV, Warner-Lambert cleverly deemphasized the forced disclaimer by making it the dependent clause in a compound sentence, thus turning a negative into a positive: "Although Listerine will not help prevent colds or sore throats or lessen their severity, it kills germs on contact, the germs that can cause bad breath." "Turning Warner-Lambert into a Marketing Conglomerate," *Business Week*, March 5, 1979, 60.

62. *In re Novartis Corporation and Novartis Consumer Health, Inc.*, 1999 F.T.C. LEXIS 63 (1999).

proper use of product claims and may have relevance for manufacturers of many kinds of products rather than just one. In one such guide, the commission provides a lengthy policy statement explaining when products may legitimately be marketed as "recyclable" or "made from recycled materials."[63] A related kind of action is the **trade regulation rule**, which looks very much like an industry guide but carries the force of law. The commission is therefore required to follow elaborate public notice procedures in advance of issuing such rules. In 2010, after reviewing hundreds of public comments on a proposal made the year before, the commission created a trade regulation rule governing telemarketers who offer "debt relief" services. The rule demands that companies offering such services not require payment up front, and that they make clear disclosures about costs, how the complicated process works, and whether it is likely to affect the client's credit rating.[64]

The Lanham Act: Suits by Competitors and Consumers

The FTC investigates what it wishes and passes on any issue for which it does not have sufficient resources or the enthusiasm to pursue. Bringing a claim of deceptive advertising to the attention of the commission, however, is not the only remedy avail-

THINGS TO REMEMBER

The Federal Trade Commission

- When created in 1914, the commission was only able to protect competing companies from each other's excesses; today the FTC is also empowered to protect consumers from unfair and deceptive practices.
- To determine if an advertisement is deceptive, the commission first performs a textual analysis of the ad, then determines whether a reasonable consumer is likely to be misled, and finally decides whether any such deception would be material to the purchasing decision.
- Deceptiveness can be explicit or implicit; it can appear in text or in visual demonstrations.
- Remedies available to the FTC include the consent order (whereby the FTC staff itself typically requires, at a bare minimum, that the offending company cease making a particular claim that the commission has decided is deceptive), the cease and desist order (issued by an administrative law judge after a full hearing), and a demand that the advertiser engage in affirmative disclosures or corrective advertising in future commercial messages.
- The commission can also issue industry guides and trade regulation rules, both of which put companies on notice about the kinds of claims the FTC staff is likely to find deceptive.

---

63. Guides for the Use of Environmental Marketing Claims, 16 C.F.R. §§ 260.1–260.8 (2010).
64. Telemarketing Sales Rule, 75 FR 48458 (2010).

able to aggrieved parties. The federal Lanham Act, adopted in 1946 and initially designed to protect against trademark infringements, also includes prohibitions against deceptive advertising. Section 43(a) of the act forbids advertisers to "misrepresent the nature, characteristics, qualities, or geographic origin of [their] or another person's goods, services, or commercial activities."[65] Perhaps the section's most important feature is that it allows "any person who believes that he or she is or is likely to be damaged" by the misrepresentation to sue. Certainly this means that competing companies may bring suit. In some jurisdictions the courts have interpreted the act to give individual consumers a right to sue as well. Consumers rarely litigate under the Lanham Act, however. Indeed, they rarely take advantage of state or common-law remedies against deceptive advertising, because the harm they might be able to prove generally is not large enough to justify the expense of hiring an attorney.[66]

Perhaps the most frequent category of Lanham Act advertising claims concerns comparative advertising, in which one company's commercials mention and criticize the competition by name. Time Warner Cable (TWC), for example, sued DirecTV because the latter's highly comical ads with such spokespersons as Jessica Simpson and William Shatner at least implicitly claimed that the satellite provider's digital picture quality was superior to TWC's cable picture, whereas the court ruled that the quality of the pictures was identical.[67]

A federal appellate court allowed Time Warner's suit against DirecTV to go forward, finding the latter's ads conveyed at least implicitly a deceptive claim that its digital picture quality was superior to cable.

A company need not be named by a competitor's ad to bring a Lanham Act complaint. In 2007, the manufacturers of the sweetener Equal sued their counterparts who produce Splenda, alleging that the latter's labeling and advertising claim that the product is "made from sugar" and therefore "tastes like sugar" was misleading, in that Splenda's cane sugar is burnt off early in the manufacturing process. The suit was settled out of court just as the case was to be handed to the jury.[68]

Sometimes the named competitor is an entire product line. Pfizer, the current maker of Listerine, was sued under the Lanham Act in 2005 by a company that makes dental floss, because the ads in question claimed swirling and gargling the product "is as effective as floss in fighting plaque

65. *Groden v. Random House*, 61 F.3d 1045, 1051 (2d Cir. 1995). Section 43(a) of the Lanham Act is codified at 15 U.S.C. § 1125(a) (2010).

66. Lee Goldman, "The World's Best Article on Competitor Suits for False Advertising," 45 *Florida Law Review* 487, 505 (1993).

67. *Time Warner Cable v. DirecTV*, 497 F. 3d 144 (2nd Cir. 2007); but see *Schering-Plough Healthcare Products v. Schwarz Pharma*, 586 F. 3d 500 (7th Cir. 2009) (there is no literal falsity when one laxative manufacturer indicates that its product is available "by prescription only" even though a generic form is available over the counter).

68. James P. Miller, "Bitter Sweets Fight Ended," *Chicago Tribune*, May 12, 2007, C1.

and gingivitis." After determining that the claim was false, federal district judge Denny Chin enjoined Pfizer from continuing to make such a claim. One result of the suit was that Pfizer spent a few million dollars sending folks to drugstores and other outlets nationwide to remove the "as effective as floss" labels from bottles.[69]

Lanham Act suits can result in an injunction against the defendant company's ads. Damage awards can also be made and can include the defendant's full profits attributable to the deception, the plaintiff's damages (such as lost market share), and court costs. In especially egregious cases the award can be triple the actual amount of damages and can include attorneys' fees. Corrective advertising can be ordered as well.

Industry Self-Regulation

Companies that think their competitors are engaged in deceptive advertising

The makes of Equal sued Splenda under the Lanham Act, alleging that the "made from sugar, tastes like sugar" claim was deceptive.

campaigns but that wish to avoid the costs and long delays inherent in litigation and governmental intervention may instead choose to bring a complaint to the National Advertising Division (NAD). The NAD is a self-regulatory system created by major advertising associations and the Council of Better Business Bureaus in 1971 to hear such complaints. Comparative advertising cases have always been a large part of the NAD's docket.

The procedure for bringing an NAD complaint is in some ways very similar to that for going to court. After the complaint is filed, an investigation ensues, and a process like pretrial discovery takes place. The NAD's inquiry will generally be limited to determining whether the company whose advertising is the target of the complaint can offer sufficient substantiation of the claims made in the advertisement. If the NAD determines that the ad lacks substantiation, it will request that the campaign be stopped or changed. For example, in 2010 the NAD requested that the folks who make Charmin toilet paper, in future ads, no longer visually "claim" that their prod-

69. *McNeil v. Pfizer*, 351 F. Supp. 2d 226 (S.D.N.Y. 2005).

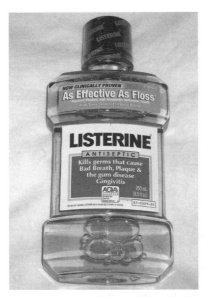

As a result of a suit brought under the Lanham Act, you will no longer find Listerine bottles claiming that the product is "as effective as floss."

uct leaves no pieces behind (versus the more modest textual claim of "fewer" pieces left behind in comparison to its competitors' products).[70]

This quasi–"cease and desist order" is the only remedy available to those filing a complaint with the NAD. There are no money damages to be awarded, no attorneys' fees, no court costs. Of course, because the NAD regularly publishes the results of its hearings in periodicals such as the *Wall Street Journal* and *Advertising Age*, adverse publicity must also be considered a remedy inherent in this self-regulatory process. If either party is dissatisfied with the ruling, it can appeal to the next and final level of decision making, the five-member National Advertising Review Board (NARB). This is a relatively infrequent occurrence. If a company refuses to adhere to an NAD or NARB ruling, these industry self-regulation groups may choose to turn the matter over to the FTC for possible investigation.

Compared with litigation or waiting for ultimate FTC action, the NAD/NARB process is timely, informal, and relatively inexpensive. Advertisers also often prefer to use this procedure because the decision makers are all experts in the fields of advertising and marketing. The industry self-regulatory procedure is not a panacea, however. The NAD restricts its inquiries to national advertising campaigns and reserves the right to refuse to hear any complaint that does not raise issues of public interest. That one company is losing market share to another is usually insufficient to trigger an investigation.

Regulation of Political Campaign Advertising

Not all advertising by corporate America is designed to sell a particular product or service. Exxon Mobil's frequent *New York Times* "advertorials," through which the company expresses its opinion on various political issues—not all directly related to the oil industry—are studied in university business schools and public relations programs nationwide. It is perfectly legal for corporations to use the advertising space or time they pay for to participate in the nation's political dialogue.

And although there have been some legal restrictions applied to corporate speech

---

70. "NAD Recommends P&G Modify Claims for Charmin Ultra Strong Toilet Tissue. Press Release, August 10, 2010, www.nadreview.org/DocView.aspx?DocumentID=8135&DocType=1.

THINGS TO REMEMBER

The Lanham Act

- Created in 1946, the act permits a company to sue a competitor for deceptive advertising.
- A successful suit can result in forfeiture of profits attributable to the deception, damages, court costs, attorneys' fees, and compelled corrective advertising.

dealing with a particular election, whether on behalf of a candidate or a public referendum issue, a 2010 Supreme Court decision greatly liberalized the law in this area. Before discussing that decision and the case from only a few years earlier that it partially overturned, two preliminary points need to be made.

First, we need to understand that there is a body of case law governing political campaign advertising that applies only to television and radio, largely as a result of specific provisions of the legislation that set up the Federal Communications Commission. We postpone a discussion of that case law until chapter 12, which deals with content regulation of the broadcast media. Second, although there is also a body of case law based on the Federal Election Campaign Act (and parallel state laws) that addresses the issue of limitations on financial

The NAD accepted that Charmin might leave "fewer" pieces of paper behind than its competitor, but chastised Proctor and Gamble's commercial for visually implying that Charmin left *no* pieces behind.

THINGS TO REMEMBER

Industry Self-Regulation

- The National Advertising Division (NAD) was created in 1971 to provide a forum to address complaints about competitors' allegedly deceptive national advertising campaigns.
- The NAD can request that an offending advertiser cease and desist and publishes its findings in media outlets that reach the advertising community as well as the general public.

Whether *Hillary: The Movie* really was a movie, or simply a very long political ad, did not turn out to be crucial to the Citizens United decision; the Court held that even if it was merely an ad, the First Amendment protects the plaintiff's right to air it in advance of a presidential election, as long as their expenditures were not being orchestrated by an opposing candidate.

contributions to political campaigns[71]—as well as cases dealing with contributions to committees set up to work for or against referendum proposals[72]—that area of law is beyond the scope of this book. After all, even though candidates do spend a high proportion of contributions on political advertising, they might also spend donations on travel expenses or on any number of other things not directly related to communication. Suffice it to say that in general there are far more restrictions on contributions to political campaigns than on independent expenditures in support of those campaigns.

In 2003 the Supreme Court decided *McConnell v. Federal Election Commission*, which upheld much of the Bipartisan Campaign Reform Act of 2002 (BCRA), popularly known as the McCain-Feingold campaign finance law.[73] For our purposes, the most relevant section of BCRA upheld by the *McConnell* Court requires that candidates who wish to qualify for the lowest ad rates from broadcasters include in their ads a clear message indicating that the candidate approves of the communication—for example, "I'm Hillary Clinton, and I approved this ad."

The BCRA also forbade TV and radio stations from airing ads from special interest groups (i.e., from anyone other than candidates or parties themselves) within sixty days of an election (thirty days of a primary) if those ads mention the name of any candidate for federal office. Although the *McConnell* Court upheld this provision, in 2010 the Court changed its mind, holding that such outside voices (corporations, unions, etc.) should have an unfettered right to spend their money in support of or in opposition to a candidate, as long as such expenditures are truly independent of the candidate's own organizations.[74] "Unfettered" may be overstating things a bit—to avoid some donor disclosure provisions imposed by the FEC and more general Internal Revenue Service provisions concerning what it means to be a bona fide charitable organization, some nonprofits avoid advertising that explicitly admonishes citizens to vote for or against a given candidate. Instead such groups run ads—we all have seen

71. *Nixon v. Shrink Missouri Government PAC*, 528 U.S. 377 (2000).

72. *Citizens Against Rent Control v. Berkeley*, 454 U.S. 290 (1981).

73. 540 U.S. 93 (2003).

74. *Citizens United v. FEC*, 130 S. Ct. 876 (2010). The *Citizens United* decision resulted from a nonprofit group's desire to air on cable TV a documentary (or a very long political commercial, depending on one's perspective) highly critical of Hillary Clinton, at the time the Democratic Party's presumptive presidential nominee. Nonprofit corporations were already free to spend from their own coffers on elections—see *FEC v. Massachusetts Citizens for Life*, 479 U.S. 238 (1986).

THINGS TO REMEMBER

Regulation of Spending for Political Advertising

- There are more restrictions on contributions to candidates' campaigns than on independent expenditures in support of candidates or issues.
- The *Citizens United* decision in 2010 greatly liberalized regulations governing corporate, union, and nonprofit independent expenditures (not coordinated by candidates or parties) on behalf of candidates.
- To obtain the lowest per-minute charges from stations, broadcast ads placed by candidates themselves must include the candidate's name and an indication that the candidate approved of the ad.

them, no doubt—expressing disfavor with a candidate's voting pattern, ostensibly requesting that viewers "call Senator Jones and tell her to rethink her position."[75]

Chapter Summary

The Supreme Court currently uses the *Central Hudson* test to determine whether a regulation on commercial speech is consistent with the First Amendment. The test requires that we ask whether the product or service being offered is itself legal or the advertisement deceptive, whether the state has a legitimate interest in this regulation, and whether there is a reasonable fit between the regulation and the interest.

The Court has on a number of occasions dealt with the issue of advertising by attorneys and other professionals. In general, the rule seems to be that we should focus on the first *Central Hudson* question: is the advertisement inherently deceptive? If not, the Court has been very reluctant to allow much state intrusion on the content of communications between professionals and potential clients.

Although individual states and even municipalities are in the business of regulating advertising, by far the most active agent in this area is the Federal Trade Commission. To determine if a given ad is deceptive, the commission first examines the text of the ad and then considers whether a reasonable consumer would likely be deceived and whether any such deception would be material to the purchasing decision. The majority of commission investigations go no further than the consent order stage, at which time the offending company agrees to meet certain requests by the commission staff, such as to stop making a deceptive claim. The FTC also is empowered to require

---

75. Michael Luo, "Groups Push Legal Limits in Advertising," *New York Times*, October 18, 2010, A10.

advertisers to insert specific wording into future ads. Companies can also sue competitors for deceptive advertising under the federal Lanham Act.

A 2010 Supreme Court decision greatly liberalized restrictions on "special interest groups" wishing to spend their money in support of or opposition to a specific candidate for office. Generally such expenditures are now permissible, as long as they are genuinely independent of the candidate's own organization.

SEXUALLY ORIENTED SPEECH

I t was a classic scene from HBO's *The Sopranos*—New Jersey Mafia chieftain Tony and wife Carmela pulled over for speeding and wondering aloud, with no sense of irony, why the cops can't instead be going after "real" crime. Court watchers often make similar comments about obscenity prosecutions—should not prosecutors be devoting resources instead to violent crimes, especially in a post-9/11 world?[1]

Americans are a horny people. By most accounts, the "adult" film industry is far bigger than Hollywood, with some estimates as high as $13 billion annually.[2] And this figure does not begin to tap the dollars we spend on media designed to help us "hook up." Somewhat paradoxically, we Americans are also seen as highly puritanical in our approach to sexual matters. Award-winning European film directors often produce a toned-down print for distribution in the U.S. market to obtain an "R" rather than the dreaded "NC-17" rating. Although we don't usually see obscenity prosecutions for dirty books anymore, the Fourth Circuit Court of Appeals recently ruled that obscenity can be still be found in words alone.[3] Emotional debates over what to tell youngsters about sex and morality regularly consume the time and energy of school boards nationwide.

In the 1940s the U.S. Supreme Court, in one of the most often-quoted passages in the history of First Amendment jurisprudence, placed "the lewd and obscene" at the

---

1. Alan Lengel, "Will Failed DC Porn Case Dampen Prosecutors' Zeal?" AolNews.com, July 29, 2010, www.aolnews.com/nation/article/will-failed-dc-porn-case-dampen-prosecutors-zeal/19574219.

2. Aoife White, "Internet Porn Sites Closer to .xxx Address," *San Jose Mercury News*, June 25, 2010.

3. *United States v. Whorley*, 550 F. 3d 326 (4th Cir. 2008), *petition for rehearing en banc denied*, 569 F. 3d 211 (4th Cir. 2009). Whorley was not exactly a poster child defendant, having previously been convicted on child pornography charges.

head of its list of categories of speech deemed "of such slight social value" as to be outside the Constitution's protection.[4] Sexual speech that meets the current legal definition of **obscenity** can be criminalized. Even nonobscene sexual expression can be regulated in several ways. It can be banned from TV and radio broadcast hours or zoned into certain restricted parts of town. Communicators of sexual messages might not be permitted to use their chosen mode of presentation; the state can insist, for example, that they keep their clothes on.[5]

Thinking about the Obscene

Although this chapter is primarily about *obscenity* and the law, a few related constructs that often produce confusion need to be defined first. The word **pornography** refers to any printed text, drawing, picture, film, or other communication in which the explicit depiction or description of sexual conduct occurs. Although journalists, scholars, and even lawyers and judges often use the word to refer to sexual materials, it has no *legal* definition, nor does its publication carry any legal penalty.

When the word *child* is added however, the phrase **child pornography** results, and it does have legal definitions under both federal and state law.[6] A later section of this chapter is devoted to the law regarding child pornography. For now suffice it to say that depictions of real children in sexually provocative poses, even if partially clothed, are generally what the courts have in mind when they adjudicate child pornography cases.

Indecency is a word used to describe a wider set of sexual materials that meet some but not all of the components of the Supreme Court's current definition of obscenity.[7] Although it would be unconstitutional for the government to ban writings that are merely indecent, such materials may not generally be broadcast during daytime hours on radio and TV stations that use the public airwaves. **Profanity** has been defined by courts as "vulgar, irreverent, or coarse language, . . . personally reviling epithets . . . so grossly offensive as to amount to a nuisance."[8] Because the law regarding indecent and profane speech is restricted to the broadcast media, we postpone a more extensive discussion of these matters until chapter 12, which deals with regulation of the elec-

---

4. *Chaplinsky v. New Hampshire*, 315 U.S. 568, 571 (1942).

5. *FCC v. Pacifica Foundation*, 438 U.S. 726 (1978) (broadcasting); *Young v. American Mini Theatres*, 427 U.S. 50 (1976) (zoning); *City of Erie v. Pap's A.M.*, 529 U.S. 277 (2000); *Barnes v. Glen Theatre*, 501 U.S. 560 (1991) (nude shows, nude dancing).

6. *United States v. Faulds*, 612 F. 3d 566 (7th Cir. 2010); *Osborne v. Ohio*, 495 U.S. 103 (1990).

7. *Fox Broadcasting Stations, Inc. v. FCC*, 613 F. 3d 317 (2nd Cir. 2010).

8. *In re Complaints against Various Broadcast Licensees Regarding Their Airing of the "Golden Globe Awards" Program*, 199 F.C.C. Rcd. 4975 (2004).

THINGS TO REMEMBER

Thinking about Obscenity

- Under the law, obscenity is viewed as something other than speech, thus wholly outside the First Amendment's protection.
- Related concepts to be examined in this chapter include indecency, child pornography, and profanity.
- In everyday conversation, obscenity seems to refer to anything outrageously offensive, not narrowly to sexual matters.

tronic media. As we see in chapter 13, the government has also attempted, mostly unsuccessfully, to outlaw indecent speech on the Internet.

What does it mean to be obscene? In everyday parlance, the word can attach to anything deemed outrageous or offensive, from the high price of funerals to the exorbitant salaries paid to professional sports figures. For most of us, the label is not limited to matters of sex. The philosopher Harry Clor has suggested that the term *obscenity* refers to making offensively public that which should be private, which is consistent with some etymologists' belief that the word *obscene* is derived from Greek words referring to that which happens "off the stage." Certainly the notion of obscenity as graphic depictions of others' sexual behavior would fit within this definition, but there can also be obscene depictions of such physical acts as eating, scratching, grooming, or picking one's nose while driving. For Clor, the key is that the persons depicted are degraded by having their humanity reduced to animalistic behaviors. If *dining* is too genteel a word to describe the way you might attack that lamb chop when no one is watching, you can surely understand Clor's point.[9]

The Supreme Court Defines Obscenity: *Miller v. California*

The Court accepted many obscenity cases for consideration in its 1972–1973 term and handed down eight of them in June 1973. By far the most important one was *Miller v. California*,[10] which represented the first time since 1957 that a majority of the Court would grapple with the actual definition of obscenity.

The factual situation was an unusual one. Most obscenity convictions involved the selling or mailing of materials to willing recipients, or at least to undercover police

---

9. Harry M. Clor, *Obscenity and Public Morality: Censorship in a Liberal* Society (Chicago: University of Chicago Press, 1966), 225.

10. 413 U.S. 15 (1973).

officers masquerading as such willing recipients. Here the defendant instead had mailed unsolicited brochures advertising books bearing titles such as *Intercourse* and *Sex Orgies Illustrated*. The brochure itself was not for the squeamish, consisting primarily of "pictures and drawings very explicitly depicting men and women in groups of two or more engaging in a variety of sexual activities, with genitals often prominently displayed." The prosecution commenced after a restaurant owner in Newport Beach opened the brochure (in the company of his mother) and complained to the police. The Supreme Court, by a 5–4 vote, upheld Miller's conviction.

Although the *Miller* decision does not provide a single comprehensive definition of obscenity, it does give the individual states several important guidelines. Most fundamentally, the chief justice told the states that "the permissible scope" of their regulations must be limited to "works which depict or describe sexual conduct," and that the regulations themselves, whether in statutes or in judge-made common law, must "specifically define" what is prohibited. The First Amendment requires also that government regulations prohibit only "works which the average person, applying contemporary community standards, would find, taken as a whole, appeal to the prurient interest,"[11] which "portray sexual conduct in a patently offensive way" and "do not have serious literary, artistic, political, or scientific value." (This latter provision is often referred to in shorthand as the "SLAPS test.") That obscene works must both turn us on (appeal to our prurient interest) and gross us out (be "patently offensive") is a contradiction that has not escaped the wrath of the Court's critics.[12]

Chief Justice Burger's opinion sought to clarify the meaning of "community" in the phrase "contemporary community standards." Whereas lower courts had flirted

---

11. Many sexually oriented works apply to subgroups who embrace particular fetishes. Since "average" persons might not find these fetishes arousing, the Court, in an earlier decision, told us that jurors should ask if the target audiences for these works would have *their* prurient interests aroused. *Mishkin v. New York*, 383 U.S. 502 (1966).

12. Jeffrey Rosen, "*Miller* Time," *New Republic*, October 1, 1990, 17 (quoting Stanford University law professor Kathleen M. Sullivan).

with the notion of a single nationwide standard, the *Miller* jury had been asked to apply *statewide* standards, and Chief Justice Burger agreed with this instruction, suggesting that a smaller "community" might also be invoked.

Asking jurors to apply a *local* community standard has important implications, depending in part on the technology involved. If a book or a magazine is found obscene in only a few venues in relatively conservative areas of the country, distribution can still proceed in the rest of the country. Suppose, though, that the work at issue is a film, distributed using direct broadcast satellite. The cost of maximizing the number of viewers who can see the film (and maximizing profits) while ensuring that potential viewers who live in parts of the country where the film has been judged obscene will not be able to access it can be large. In chapter 13, we will address the special complication of defining an Internet "community."

Local communities' judgments must sometimes be kept in check by appellate review, however, as the Supreme Court made clear in its very next term after handing down *Miller*. The State of Georgia had ruled that the film *Carnal Knowledge*, starring Jack Nicholson, Art Garfunkel, Candice Bergen, and Ann-Margret, was obscene. This story of two male college roommates' difficulties in relating to women (after years of marriage, Garfunkel's character wonders aloud if sex is "just not supposed to be fun anymore when you love her") made many critics' "best ten films of the year" lists, and resulted in an Academy Award nomination for Ann-Margret. The film did include brief bits of nudity. There were also several instances where the characters seemed to be engaging in sexual activity—notably in the final scene, where Nicholson's character can achieve orgasm only through a highly ritualized act of fellatio performed by a high-class call girl played by Rita Moreno—but all of these acts were only hinted at, with the camera focused elsewhere. The Supreme Court held that this film was plainly not obscene, that no reasonable jury could have found it patently offensive.[13]

Go to www.paul siegelcommlaw .com and click on "Video Clips" to see the ritualized fellatio scene with Jack Nicholson and Rita Moreno.

In a decision handed down in 1987, the Supreme Court clarified that jurors' adjudication of the "serious value" question—unlike the questions concerning whether a work is "patently offensive" and whether it appeals to the "prurient interest"— should be based on a national standard. Moreover, when determining whether a work boasts enough serious value to be protected from an obscenity charge, jurors should conjure up as best they can their image of what a "reasonable" person would say, rather than an "average" person.[14] This latter point may on its surface seem a bit insulting, as if the Court is suggesting that the "average" American is not very reasonable. It also makes an already confusing set of legal instructions even more so. In any event, the clear intent of the decision is in the direction of making obscenity convictions a bit more difficult to obtain against works of value.

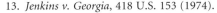

13. *Jenkins v. Georgia*, 418 U.S. 153 (1974).
14. *Pope v. Illinois*, 481 U.S. 497 (1987).

THINGS TO REMEMBER

The *Miller* Test

- In *Miller v. California* (1973), the Supreme Court created the test for obscenity still used today.
- Under the *Miller* test, a work is obscene if
  - the average person, applying contemporary community standards, would find that the work, taken as a whole, appeals to the prurient interest;
  - the work depicts or describes specified sexual conduct in a patently offensive manner; and
  - the work lacks serious literary, artistic, political, or scientific value.
- Although "community" generally means local, the Supreme Court told the state of Georgia it could not find the popular film *Carnal Knowledge* obscene.

Fine-Tuning the Legal Definition of Obscenity

The Supreme Court has offered additional guidelines for states trying to fashion constitutional obscenity statutes. Some of these guidelines can be culled from *Miller* itself, others from new interpretations of previous cases, and others still from cases decided in more recent years.

What Kind of Sexual Conduct?

Under *Miller*, obscenity prosecutions can succeed only against "patently offensive" works aimed at our "prurient" interests. Neither phrase is self-defining. Even as it cautioned that "it is not our function to propose regulatory schemes for the states," that is in fact what the *Miller* majority did. A constitutionally acceptable statute might be one, Burger wrote, that prohibits either "representations or descriptions of ultimate sexual acts, normal or perverted, actual or simulated," or "representations or descriptions of masturbation, excretory functions, and lewd exhibition of the genitals."[15] Not surprisingly, many states simply quote this language in their statutes.

The *Miller* Court also required that obscenity laws "specifically define" what was to be prohibited. A few years later, however, the Court made clear that whatever due process guarantees seemed to flow from such a requirement would not be strictly enforced. Defendants in *Ward v. Illinois* had been convicted for selling magazines that depicted sadomasochistic sexual practices.[16] By a vote of 5–4, the Court upheld Ward's conviction, even though the state law nowhere mentioned sadomasochistic practices.

---

15. *Miller v. California*, 413 U.S. 15, 25 (1973).
16. 431 U.S. 767 (1977).

Thematic Obscenity

States may not use obscenity law to stifle debate *about* sexual matters. The leading case on this issue is from 1959, when the Supreme Court told the State of New York that it could not deny a distribution license for the showing of a film version of D. H. Lawrence's *Lady Chatterley's Lover*. One of the state's arguments had been that the film glorifies the commission of adultery, which is "contrary to the moral standards, the religious precepts, and the legal code of its citizenry." Writing for the Court, Justice Stewart chided the state for "misconceiving what the Constitution protects." The First Amendment "protects advocacy of the opinion that adultery may sometimes be proper," as well as all sorts of other views not necessarily shared by the majority of citizens.[17]

The doctrine of **thematic obscenity** established in the 1959 decision means that artistic works with a sexual theme or thesis cannot be the targets of government sanctions in this country unless actual sexual depictions in the films meet the *Miller* definition of obscenity. Martin Scorcese's 1988 film *The Last Temptation of Christ* posited a sexual relationship between Jesus and Mary Magdalene. Kevin Bacon's performance in the 2004 independent film *The Woodsman* offers a humanizing, almost heroic depiction of a pedophile. Both films were highly controversial. But neither could be held obscene by dint of their provocative themes.

Smut at Home

Georgia state police suspected Robert E. Stanley of being a small-time bookmaker and obtained a search warrant for his home. They did not find any helpful evidence on the gambling charge, but while looking through a desk drawer in an upstairs bedroom, they found three reels of film. Using Stanley's own film projector, they examined the films, which they concluded were obscene.

Stanley was placed under arrest for possession of obscene materials, in violation of state law. The state obtained a conviction, which was upheld by the Georgia Supreme Court. The U.S. Supreme Court, however, unanimously overturned Stanley's conviction. Justice Marshall's opinion for the Court articulated a fusion of First and Fourth Amendment values, emphasizing that the government "has no business telling a man, sitting alone in his own house, what books he may read or what films he may watch."[18]

Some lower courts, citing *Stanley*'s emphasis on a right to receive information, reasoned that the right should have a life beyond one's own four walls, and these

---

17. *Kingsley International Pictures Corp. v. Regents*, 360 U.S. 684 (1959).
18. *Stanley v. Georgia*, 394 U.S. 557, 565 (1969).

expansive rulings were often struck down by the Supreme Court.[19] In an often-quoted dissent, Justice Douglas expressed dismay with the Court's having decided to interpret *Stanley* narrowly. He "fail[ed] to comprehend how the right to possession enunciated in *Stanley* has any meaning when States are allowed to outlaw the commercial transactions which give rise to such possession."[20] Perhaps the death knell for broad interpretations of *Stanley* occurred in 1973, when, on the same day the Supreme Court produced the *Miller* test, it also handed down *Paris Adult Theatre I v. Slaton*, upholding the constitutionality of an obscenity prosecution against a pair of adult-movie-theater owners in Atlanta. The theater owners argued that their patrons were consenting adults, each of whom would, under *Stanley*, have a right to view the same films at home that they saw at the theater. A 5–4 Court rejected the "consenting adults" defense and made clear that *Stanley* "was hardly more than a reaffirmation that 'a man's home is his castle,'" not the creation of a "zone of privacy that follows a distributor or a consumer of obscene materials wherever he goes."[21]

The "consenting adults" defense had a short-lived resurrection in 2005, when a federal district judge refused to enforce federal obscenity statutes, having found that the Supreme Court's ruling in *Lawrence v. Texas*[22] (which struck down the state's sodomy law) could be interpreted so as to prevent the government from basing sex laws solely on a claimed state's interest in promoting traditional moral codes. But the Third Circuit Court of Appeals reversed the district court.[23]

It should also be noted that a parolee's freedom can be rescinded for having otherwise legal pornography in the privacy of his home. This was a lesson learned by convicted sex offender Christopher Farrell, who argued that conditioning his parole on his not possessing any "pornographic" material was both vague (what is pornography?) and overbroad (in that the construct clearly includes materials he would have a perfect right to own were he not on parole). The Third Circuit Court of Appeals disagreed in a 2006 decision that does not even mention the *Stanley* case.[24]

---

19. *Karalexis v. Byrne*, 306 F. Supp. 1363, 1366 (D. Mass. 1969) (arguing one must also have a right to view obscene films at a movie theater); *United States v. Thirty-Seven Photographs*, 309 F. Supp. 36 (C.D. Cal. 1970) (a right to have obscene works must include a right to receive them, thus calling into question federal law against importing them), *rev'd*, 402 U.S. 363 (1971); *United States v. Orito*, 338 F. Supp. 308 (E.D. Wisc. 1970) (right to own must include right to transport across state lines), *rev'd*, 413 U.S. 139 (1973).

20. *Carlson v. Minnesota*, 414 U.S. 953, 954 (1973) (Douglas, J., dissenting).

21. 413 U.S. 49 (1973). The "I" in the name of the case is not an indication that there is a later court decision by the same name, but rather that there were two theaters, side by side, the Paris Adult I and the Paris Adult II.

22. 539 U.S. 558 (2003).

23. *United States v. Extreme Associates*, 352 F. Supp. 2d 578 (E.D. Pa. 2005), *rev'd and remanded*, 431 F. 3d 150 (3rd Cir. 2005).

24. *Farrell v. Burke*, 449 F.3d 470 (2d Cir. 2006).

Variable Obscenity

On occasion the Supreme Court has recognized that its definition of obscenity has to be adjusted or modified—sometimes making it stricter, sometimes making it more relaxed—depending on a pornographer's intended audience or the manner in which he advertises his wares. Collectively, such instances have come to be called the doctrine of **variable obscenity.**

The government claims a special interest in seeing to it that obscene materials do not fall into the hands of children. Thus one important instance of variable obscenity concerns materials that are marketed to children or at least where the purveyors do not take sufficient steps to block access by children. The leading case on this point is *Ginsberg v. New York.* The defendant's and his wife's troubles began when they sold two otherwise nonobscene "girlie magazines," as the Court put it, to a sixteen-year-old, in violation of a state law prohibiting the distribution to minors of photos showing "female buttocks . . . or female breasts with less than a fully opaque covering." The Supreme Court upheld Ginsberg's conviction, with Justice Brennan finding that it is "altogether fitting and proper for a state to include in a statute designed to regulate the sale of pornography to children special standards, broader than those embodied in legislation aimed at controlling dissemination of such material to adults."[25]

Variable obscenity permits convictions for actually showing even nonobscene sexual materials to minors, not for publishing or selling materials that would be deemed harmful to a hypothetical minor who *might* come across them. Indeed, the Supreme Court has made clear that states may not, in pursuit of the laudable goal of protecting children, create obscenity laws so restrictive that adults are limited to what would be suitable for children.[26] Still, managers of bookstores and magazine stands would be wise to take reasonable precautions to prevent minors from accessing sexually explicit materials. In recent years statutes have sprung up in numerous locales requiring such businesses to cover up titillating magazine covers or to keep such materials where minors can't see them (such as behind the counter). When these statutes have narrowly and carefully specified the kinds of materials within their scope, they have generally been upheld.[27] The U.S. Supreme Court has yet to rule on such a statute, however.

---

25. 390 U.S. 629, 640 (1968); see also *People v. Jackson,* 832 N.E.2d 418 (Ill. App. Ct. 2005) (upholding conviction of employee of residential home for boys for showing to them a likely nonobscene home video of him having sex).

26. *Butler v. Michigan,* 352 U.S. 380 (1957).

27. *Davis-Kidd Booksellers v. McWherter,* 866 S.W. 2d 520 (Tenn. 1993); *American Booksellers v. Webb,* 919 F.2d 1493 (11th Cir. 1990); *M.S. News Co. v. Casado,* 721 F.2d 1281 (10th Cir. 1983); *Upper Midwest Booksellers Association v. City of Minneapolis,* 602 F. Supp. 1361 (D. Minn. 1985); *American Booksellers Association v. Rendell,* 481 A.2d 919 (Pa. Super. Ct. 1984). But see *American Booksellers Association v. Virginia,* 792 F.2d 1261 (4th Cir. 1986); *Rushia v. Town of Ashburnham,* 582 F. Supp. 900 (D. Mass. 1983); *American Booksellers Association v. McAuliffe,* 533 F. Supp. 50 (N.D. Ga. 1981); *Tattered Cover, Inc. v. Tooley,* 696 P.2d 780 (Colo. 1985).

The doctrine of variable obscenity also permits states to take into account the manner in which sexual materials are marketed, specifically whether the defendant has engaged in what is called "pandering." The leading case is *Ginzburg v. United States*[28] (do not confuse this with the *Ginsberg* case discussed earlier). Ralph Ginzburg appealed his convictions for having used the U.S. mails to distribute three issues of his magazine, *Eros*, which consisted of articles, essays, and photos. Some of the material in one of the issues had appeared previously in professional journals. That same issue also included "an interview with a psychotherapist who favors the broadest license in sexual relationships." In other words, this was not the sort of material one usually considers hard-core pornography. One reason the Supreme Court upheld Ginzburg's conviction was that he had engaged in pandering, "the business of purveying textual or graphic matter openly advertised to appeal to the erotic interest of [one's] customers." The mailed advertisements, Justice Brennan wrote, "stressed the sexual candor of the respective publications, and openly boasted that the publishers would take full advantage of what they regarded as an unrestricted license allowed by law in the expression of sex and sexual matters." That Ginzburg had tried unsuccessfully to obtain mailing privileges for his wares from the postmasters of Blue Ball and Intercourse, Pennsylvania—in the end, he had to settle for the post office in Middlesex, New Jersey—also merited the Court's mention.

The *Ginzburg* case did not create a separate cause of action or enhanced punishment for pandering (as the dissenting justices claimed). One cannot be prosecuted for advertising *non*obscene materials in a sexy manner, unless the advertisements

---

THINGS TO REMEMBER

Fine-Tuning Obscenity

- In *Ward v. Illinois* (1977), the Court told states that their obscenity statutes need not spell out every possible component of what might make a sexual depiction obscene.
- The doctrine of "thematic obscenity" says that works cannot be found obscene because they seem to glorify or condone immoral sexual practices or values.
- We have a right to *own* obscene material (but not to buy it, or import it, or transport it across state lines).
- The mere fact that the only attendees at a viewing of obscene materials are consenting adults does not protect the proprietor of that establishment from prosecution.
- The "variable obscenity" doctrine says that the definition of obscenity can be modified to reflect the specific audience targeted (e.g., persons with unusual sexual interests or children) or to reflect the manner in which materials are marketed (e.g., that a pornographer has marketed his or her wares in a "pandering," leering way).
- Parolees' conditions of release can sometimes include prohibitions on consuming sexually oriented works that would otherwise be protected by the First Amendment.

---

28. 383 U.S. 463 (1966).

themselves are obscene. Pandering is an indicator of crime; it is not itself a crime. In essence, the decision means that a purveyor's having marketed sexy wares in a pandering manner may be used only as one piece of evidence "in determining the ultimate question of obscenity."

Child Pornography and "Sexting"

The variable obscenity doctrine, as we have seen, is in part a manifestation of society's desire to protect children from sexually explicit messages. That protectiveness is apparent even more clearly in the existence of child pornography laws. These statutes, which began to spring up in the late 1970s and 1980s, generally prohibit the use of minors as actors or models in the production and later distribution of sexual images. Clearly, then, one of the government's interests in criminalizing the production of "kiddie porn," as it is often called, is preventing the sexual abuse of children. Whereas the traditional impetus behind obscenity laws is to safeguard the morals of pornography's consumers, child pornography laws are designed to protect the actors.

It matters not, then, if child pornography meets all the components of the *Miller* test. Child abuse is child abuse, whether the photographic record of the event appeals to consumers' prurient interests, regardless of a lack of patent offensiveness, and despite whatever serious literary or other value the work as a whole may possess. Therefore, child pornography statutes do not require that these issues be addressed to justify a conviction. Similarly, the finished product need not be judged as a whole, for what difference would it make whether a scene involving child abuse takes up 5 percent or 75 percent of a film's total running time?

If the only state interest in prosecuting child pornography cases were the prevention of the child abuse inherent in the production of the materials themselves, it would at least be open to debate whether such statutes should reach beyond the producers to the distributors and to individual consumers. Governments argue, however, that they have other related interests as well. The Supreme Court, in a 1982 decision upholding New York's child pornography law, pointed to several harms flowing from the production and distribution of these materials.[29] Sexually exploited children, Justice White pointed out, are often unable to develop healthy, affectionate relationships in later life and are likely to become sexual abusers themselves. The existence of a photographic or film record of an episode of sexual abuse continues to victimize the child participants by invading their privacy as adults.

The *Ferber* decision makes clear that the state may legitimately criminalize not only the production but also the distribution of child pornography. One of the most efficient ways of providing a disincentive for the production of such pornographic images designed for commercial distribution is choking off the distribution network

---

29. *Ferber v. New York*, 458 U.S. 747 (1982).

itself. It is much easier for the state to go after marketers because the production of this kind of material tends to be a "low-profile" and "clandestine" enterprise.

Virtually the only portion of the *Miller* obscenity test that the Court did apply to child pornography statutes is the due process requirement that such laws clearly specify precisely what kinds of representations or depictions are covered. The only guidance the majority opinion provides to the states is that the laws criminalize only "works that visually depict sexual conduct by children below a specified age" and that the phrase "sexual conduct" itself needs to be "suitably limited and described."

That the courts take very seriously the state's interest in protecting children from the production and dissemination of child pornography is apparent from a number of later decisions, which together establish the following principles:

- Despite the lofty language in *Stanley v. Georgia* about the right to enjoy even obscene works in the privacy of our own homes, we have no such right to own child pornography.[30]
- Journalists will not be immune from prosecution by claiming that they were viewing child pornography only in order to write about its evils.[31]
- Pictures of fully clothed children may still be deemed child pornography.[32]
- Although federal laws are supposed to be triggered only by interstate commerce, the mere fact that pornographic photos depicting children in the possession of a Florida man were printed on Kodak paper (produced in New York) was sufficient to permit application of federal law.[33]

There have been government excesses in this area of law. In one notorious instance, child pornography was found in words alone, without pictures. Brian Dalton, on probation for possession of photographs of children in compromising positions, was found to keep a diary that included fantasies of sexually abusing children. Dalton was pressured to plead guilty to new charges that could have resulted in a seven-year prison term. He was eventually permitted to rescind his guilty plea, and the new charges were dropped.[34] Also, in 2002 the Supreme Court struck down the "virtual porn" portions of the Child Pornography Prevention Act of 1996, which would have criminalized the production, distribution, and possession of images that even *appear* to depict children engaged in sexual acts. The law was so broad, Justice Kennedy wrote for the majority, that it would seem to outlaw such popular films as *American*

---

30. *Osborne v. Ohio*, 495 U.S. 103 (1990).
31. *United States v. Matthews*, 209 F.3d 338 (4th Cir. 2000).
32. *United States v. Knox*, 32 F.3d 733 (3d Cir. 1994).
33. *United States v. Smith*, 459 F.3d 1276 (11th Cir. 2006).
34. *State v. Dalton*, 793 N.E.2d 509 (Ohio Ct. App. 2003).

Beauty and *Traffic*, both of which included scenes with minors appearing to have sex. Even some film versions of *Romeo and Juliet* could have been banned, he added.[35]

In response to the 2002 decision, Congress passed the PROTECT Act (the acronym stands for Prosecutorial Remedies and Other Tools to End the Exploitation of Children Today) as an amendment to the Child Pornography Prevention Act. And in 2008, the Supreme Court upheld the act, in a truly bizarre case. Defendant Michael Williams had offered in an online chat room to provide to an undercover federal agent photos of various men molesting his four-year-old daughter. Williams attempted to have the act declared unconstitutional, in that its wording would seem to make even the false offer of child pornography a crime. Justice Scalia's majority opinion makes clear that since it is illegal to sell forbidden products, and illegal to advertise fraudulently, it surely can be illegal to fraudulently market banned products.[36]

"Sexting" is an offshoot of child pornography that has entered the public's consciousness in recent years. The phenomenon, while lacking a standard legal definition,

Go to www.paul siegelcommlaw .com and click on "Video Clips" to see the most relevant scene from *American Beauty*.

THINGS TO REMEMBER

Child Pornography and Sexting

- Child pornography laws are aimed at sexually oriented materials that use children as actors or models.
- Such laws differ from obscenity statutes in that
  - works need not be judged as a whole;
  - there is no exemption for works with serious value;
  - the works need not appeal to the prurient interest, nor be obscene; and
  - the state may criminalize the mere possession of child pornography.
- Even photos of fully clothed youngsters may be child pornography if the children are engaged in lewd poses or conduct, or if the focus is on the genital area.
- It is a violation of the First Amendment to criminalize images that merely *appear to be* of children in sexual poses.
- Parolees might be reincarcerated for producing or reading stories involving minors' sexual activity, even where such works would not meet a legal definition of child pornography.
- The government may criminalize even an insincere or fraudulent offer of providing child pornography to others.
- States have struggled with "sexting," and some have exempted from prosecution teens who send provocative images of themselves (but not of others) to recipients who are themselves at least fifteen years old.

---

35. *Ashcroft v. Free Speech Coalition*, 535 U.S. 234 (2002). Justice O'Connor, in a separate concurring opinion, suggested that the government's interest will become stronger as technology improves to the point where computer-generated images of children become "virtually indistinguishable" from real children, at which point pedophiles might use the images to lure very real children into engaging in sexual practices.

36. *United States v. Williams*, 553 U.S. 285 (2008).

usually involves teens using social networking sites to send erotic photos to friends, sometimes of themselves, sometimes of classmates and others. Traditional child pornography laws don't seem well suited to address sexting, and some states have amended their laws to exempt teens who send naked photos of themselves to willing recipients who are themselves at least fifteen years old.[37]

Pornography as a Civil Rights Issue: The Feminist Response

In the early 1980s, the feminists Andrea Dworkin and Catherine MacKinnon drafted a model ordinance that would take a novel approach to sexually explicit communications. The ordinance sought to define *pornography* rather than *obscenity* as a legal construct. It provided for civil actions rather than criminal prosecutions. Most crucially, the purported state interest in providing for such civil actions was the promotion of equal rights rather than a desire to foster a traditional view of morality.

Pornography, the law's feminist sponsors argued, harms women in several ways. The women who appear in pornography are often physically and sexually abused in the course of producing films. As MacKinnon has written, pornography "forces, threatens, blackmails, pressures, tricks and cajoles women into sex for pictures."[38] Proponents of the civil rights approach also point to the plethora of social science research showing that people who are exposed to many pornographic images develop misogynist attitudes and beliefs (for example, that women enjoy pain or that they want to be raped). There is also considerable evidence that those who commit sex crimes are disproportionately likely to have been voracious consumers of pornography.[39]

The city council in Minneapolis passed the model ordinance, but the law was promptly vetoed by the city's mayor. Then conservative organizations in Indianapolis cleverly co-opted the feminist model and succeeded in passing a similar ordinance. The law was challenged in court by a coalition of groups and individuals headed by the American Booksellers Association. A federal district court, affirmed by the Seventh Circuit Court of Appeals, held the statute unconstitutional.[40]

The statute defined pornography as "the graphic sexually explicit subordination of women, whether in pictures or in words" when such depictions also include any of several specified exacerbating features. Depictions of women enjoying pain or humili-

---

37. See, for example, Nebraska Revised Statutes Annotated §28-1463.03 (2010).

38. Catherine A. MacKinnon, *Only Words* (Cambridge, Mass.: Harvard University Press, 1993), 15.

39. Gail Dines, Robert Jensen, and Ann Russo, *Pornography: The Production and Consumption of Inequality* (New York: Routledge, 1998).

40. *American Booksellers Association v. Hudnut*, 598 F. Supp. 1316 (S.D. Ind. 1984), *aff'd*, 771 F.2d 323 (7th Cir. 1985).

THINGS TO REMEMBER

Pornography and Feminism

- Some feminists joined forces with conservative groups in the 1980s to lobby for laws giving women the right to sue pornographers for depicting women in sexually degrading ways.
- An Indianapolis ordinance that took this approach was held unconstitutional.

ation would trigger the law, as would depictions of them tied up, mutilated, or penetrated by objects or animals. More broadly, the law also would reach depictions of "degradation"—of women as "inferior" or in "postures or positions of servility or submission."

Writing for the appellate panel, Judge Easterbrook emphasized that the statute lacked many of the constitutional protections provided under the *Miller* test. First, there was no requirement that a work be judged as a whole. Also conspicuously absent from the ordinance was an exception for works of serious value, akin to *Miller*'s SLAPS test. In addition, the statutory definition required neither a finding of patent offensiveness nor a finding of the work's appeal to the prurient interest. The statute's more fundamental constitutional flaw, however, was that it prohibited the expression of specific *ideas* about women. Speech that portrays women in positions of equality or superiority, Easterbrook pointed out, would be beyond the law's reach, no matter how graphic the content, whereas speech that presents women in submissive roles would be subject to civil actions, no matter how tame. Such legislation seeks to establish "an approved view of women," and thus amounts to "thought control."

Although the Indianapolis statute is often characterized as *the* feminist answer to sexually explicit images, in fact many women who describe themselves as feminists are strong opponents of any government censorship in this arena. Nadine Strossen's book *Defending Pornography* is probably the best-known articulation of the feminist civil libertarian view. Members of a group called the Feminist Anti-Censorship Task Force (FACT) also oppose obscenity laws.

Other Means of Regulating Sexual Materials

As we have seen, the Supreme Court defines obscenity as categorically beyond the protection of the First Amendment, as if it were not speech at all. There is also a wide variety of sexual texts and images that do not necessarily fit the definition of obscenity but that the government has been permitted to regulate in numerous ways. In this section, we examine several kinds of such regulations, including the zoning of adult businesses (sometimes called "sexually oriented businesses," and yes, cities often refer to them as SOBs for short), declaring such businesses to be "public nuisances," and treating pornographers as practitioners of organized crime. We conclude by taking a brief look at government funding of the arts and humanities, and U.S. Postal Service regulations governing the mailing of adult-oriented materials.

Zoning Laws

Government zoning commissions wield tremendous power in the United States. They can decide where you may live, tell you that you may not convert your attic into a separate apartment, and even dictate what colors you may or may not paint your home's exterior. Many communities have used zoning ordinances either to cluster all "adult businesses" into a single red-light district or to disperse them widely so that they do not become too big an eyesore for any one neighborhood. Generally the courts have upheld such zoning plans if they further a clearly articulated and substantial state interest, are aimed at the "secondary effects" of adult businesses (not at the adult content itself), provide for expedited judicial review,[41] restrict no more speech than necessary, and do not have the real-world effect of forcing the targeted businesses to go *out of* business[42] (though it might be permissible to force one of two adult-oriented businesses operating under the same roof to move to another part of town).[43]

The Supreme Court first ruled on this kind of zoning law in 1976. At issue were Detroit statutes requiring that adult movie theaters—defined in the statute as those that present material "characterized by an emphasis" on any of a list of "sexual activities" or "anatomical areas" enumerated in the law itself—obtain a city license to operate and prohibiting them from locating within a thousand feet of any two other adult theaters (or adult bookstores, cabarets, bars, or hotels). Clearly, then, Detroit's aim was to prevent the creation of a red-light district. Equally clear is that the definition of affected businesses was not at all related to obscenity itself; a theater could be subject to the licensing and zoning scheme without ever having been accused of showing obscene movies. Justice Stevens's majority opinion upholding the ordinances rested in part on his assertion that nonobscene sexual speech, although it may enjoy some First Amendment protection, is not nearly as central to our system of freedom of expression as is political speech. "Few of us would march our sons and daughters off to war," Stevens wrote, "to preserve the citizen's right to see 'Specified Sexual Activities' exhibited in the theaters of our choice."[44]

Five years later, the Court struck down a zoning ordinance in Mount Ephraim, New Jersey. Although the defendant was in the business of providing coin-operated

---

41. *City of Littleton, Colorado v. Z. J. Gifts D-4*, 541 U.S. 774 (2004).
42. *Executive Arts Studio v. City of Grand Rapids*, 391 F.3d 783 (6th Cir. 2004).
43. *City of Los Angeles v. Alameda Books*, 535 U.S. 425 (2002).
44. *Young v. American Mini Theatres*, 427 U.S. 50, 70 (1976).

booths through which patrons could watch live nude dancers perform, the applicable ordinance was worded so broadly as to preclude *any* live entertainment from the entire downtown area. The Court's decision was based in large part on the borough's failure to clearly articulate a substantive state interest in preventing its citizens from partaking of such a wide variety of protected expression.[45]

Then in 1986, the Court upheld a zoning law from Renton, Washington, that forbade adult movie houses from locating within a thousand feet of any residential area, church, park, or school. It is in this decision that the Court most clearly articulated the criteria to be used in assessing the constitutionality of such zoning schemes. Justice Rehnquist admitted at the outset that these kinds of laws constitute a unique category. In a way, they are based on the content of the theater owners' message, in that only movie houses that predominantly show "adult" films are affected. Traditional First Amendment jurisprudence dictates that content-based regulations come to the Court with a presumption of unconstitutionality, unless the state can show a *compelling* interest furthered by the regulation. However, since these zoning ordinances are aimed at the adverse "secondary effects" of adult businesses on neighborhood children and on attempts at urban development, rather than at the content of any specific film, the laws will be judged by a far less exacting standard.[46] Using that standard, the Court has also allowed communities to ban (not merely zone) nude-dancing clubs as long as the statute aims at secondary effects.[47]

Concerning this whole notion of secondary effects, social science research makes clear that municipalities' assumptions about how adult-oriented businesses will increase crime rates are not supported. Indeed, quite the opposite happens, perhaps in part because proprietors of such businesses have so much at stake that they willingly incur additional costs to maintain well-lit parking areas and to hire security guards.[48]

An interesting twist on zoning ordinances emerged in New York in 1999, when a number of businesses featuring strippers decided to avoid the impact of local laws simply by admitting minors. They could thus no longer be considered adult-oriented businesses, or so they argued. A state judge in New York City agreed with one club's owners, whose attorney argued that if "you could take your 15-year-old to see the

---

45. *Schad v. Mount Ephraim*, 452 U.S. 61 (1981).
46. *Renton v. Playtime Theatres, Inc.*, 475 U.S. 41 (1986).
47. *City of Erie v. Pap's A.M.*, 529 U.S. 277 (2000).
48. Daniel Linz, Mike Yao, and Sahara Byrne, "Testing Supreme Court Assumptions in *California v. LaRue*: Is There Justification for Prohibiting Sexually Explicit Messages in Establishments That Sell Liquor?" 7 *Communication Law Review* 23 (2007); Daniel Linz, Bryant Paul, and Mike Yao, " Peep Show Establishments, Public Place and Time: A Study of Secondary Effects in San Diego, California," 43 *Journal of Sex Research* 182 (2006); Bryant Paul, Daniel Linz, and Bradley J. Shaffer, "Government Regulation of 'Adult' Businesses through Zoning and Antinudity Ordinances: Debunking the Legal Myth of Negative Secondary Effects," 6 *Communication Law and Policy* 355 (2001); Daniel Linz, Kenneth Land, Jay Williams, and Bryant Paul, "An Examination of the Assumption that Adult Businesses Are Associated with Crime in Surrounding Areas," 38 *Law and Society Review* 69 (2004).

movie 'Striptease,'" you should also be able to take him to see a live striptease. The state's highest court disagreed, however, finding that the state may legitimately base its definition of "adult" establishments on the nature of the entertainment provided within, regardless of whether admission is limited to those who have achieved the age of majority.[49]

It should also be noted that the Twenty-First Amendment, which ended Prohibition, gave the states wide leeway in how they wanted to regulate the sale of liquor. Relevant for our purposes, laws against expressive activity (such as topless dancing, for example) which would otherwise almost certainly be unconstitutionally overbroad may be legitimately enforced in establishments that serve alcohol.[50]

Public-Nuisance Laws

For many years communities have attempted, through the use of public-nuisance laws, to protect citizens from having unwanted sexual images thrust at them. These laws have not always demanded that the images be obscene ones. A Dallas ordinance, for example, prohibited the public display of photos depicting human genitals or buttocks. Newsstand workers thus had to paste over a famous *Newsweek* magazine cover in 1975 that showed a Vietnamese mother carrying her young, wounded, *nude*, daughter. In 1975, the Supreme Court struck down the Jacksonville, Florida, public-nuisance law, which had been applied to a drive-in movie theater showing nonobscene films that included nudity and could be seen from a nearby church parking lot.

THINGS TO REMEMBER

Zoning

- Some local governments have decided to control the proliferation of adult-oriented businesses through the use of zoning ordinances, intended either to cluster all such businesses together into a red-light district or to disperse them to avoid the creation of such a zone.
- Such laws have generally been upheld if they further a clearly articulated and substantial state interest, are aimed at regulating the "secondary effects" of adult businesses, restrict no more speech than necessary, and do not make it impossible for such businesses to exist.

---

49. *City of New York v. Stringfellows*, 749 N.E.2d 192 (N.Y. 2001); see also *East Brooks Books Inc. v. Shelby County*, 588 F. 3d 360 (2009) (bookstore's policy of allowing only adults to enter can be basis for assumption that the store is likely to produce adverse secondary effects on the town)

50. The leading case is *California v. Larue*, 410 U.S. 948 (1973); see also *Imaginary Images, Inc. v. Evans*, 612 F. 3d 736 (4th Cir. 2010) (upholding state law permitting clubs with erotic dancers to serve beer and wine but not mixed drinks).

Those who might be offended by these images could always avert their eyes, the Court held.[51]

At the other extreme, businesses that happen to sell books or rent or sell videotapes cannot find First Amendment protection when the government seeks to enjoin activity that is inarguably prohibitable as a public nuisance. Thus, the operators of the Village Books and News Store in Kenmore, New York, were put out of business for violating the state's public-nuisance statute by permitting their premises to be used by patrons for masturbation, oral sex, and solicitation of prostitution. Writing for the Supreme Court majority, Chief Justice Burger chided the defendants for making the "ludicrous" argument that closing the bookstore was an unconstitutional sanction. Such an assertion, he wrote, is akin to "a thief who is sent to prison . . . complain[ing] that his First Amendment right to speak in public places has been infringed because of the confinement."[52]

While generally beyond the scope of a book on *communication* law, it should be noted that the Supreme Court has never held that the constitution provides a right to enjoy what might be called "sex toys" (and in more delicate times were termed "marital aids"). The Supreme Court of Alabama upheld that state's law restraining the sale of "sexual devices" as recently as 2010.[53]

Some courts have concluded that the First Amendment requires that a company's "expressive activity" be permitted to continue even while activity that truly is a public nuisance is enjoined or punished. Thus, an adult establishment in Allen County, Ohio, that included a bookstore and an arcade of private booths in which patrons would masturbate while viewing films was allowed to retain its inventory and stay in business (although the arcade area was shut down).[54] Similarly, rules in Chattanooga, Tennessee, requiring that viewing booths not provide enough privacy to engage in sex and that establishments with such booths not be permitted to remain open twenty-four hours a day were upheld, although other rules affecting the owners and investors in the bookstore in which such booths were located were struck down.[55]

Racketeering Statutes

Both the federal government and many states have embraced a controversial weapon against pornographers, similar to public-nuisance laws but with a few twists. The federal Racketeer Influenced and Corrupt Organizations Act, popularly known as RICO, was enacted in 1970 as a way of curtailing the influence of organized crime on otherwise legitimate businesses. Today, RICO is used against many different kinds

---

51. *Erznoznik v. Jacksonville*, 422 U.S. 205 (1975).
52. *Arcara v. Cloud Books*, 478 U.S. 697, 706 (1986).
53. *1560 Montgomery Highway, Inc. v. City of Hoover*, 45 So. 3d 319 (Ala. 2010).
54. *Ohio v. Elida Road Video & Books*, 696 N.E.2d 668 (Ohio Ct. App. 1997).
55. *Broadway Books v. Roberts*, 642 F. Supp. 486 (E.D. Tenn. 1986); see also *Ellwest Stereo Theater v. Boner*, 718 F. Supp. 1553 (M.D. Tenn. 1989) (concerning similar rules in Nashville).

THINGS TO REMEMBER

Public Nuisances

- Some communities have used public nuisance statutes, traditionally aimed at public sexual conduct, to close down adult businesses.
- Not all such laws require a finding that a business has sold obscene literature.
- Nuisance laws vary with respect to whether they result in businesses losing their licenses or being shut down for a specified period of time.
- These laws are most likely to be found constitutional if they are perceived as punishments for past offenses, rather than as prophylactic measures designed to prevent future wrongdoing (thus falling into the category of "prior restraints" on speech).
- States are apparently still free to prohibit the sale of sex toys as public nuisances.

of activities that at first blush might not seem the stuff of the Mafia. For example, the Supreme Court has held that RICO can be used against pro-life protestors at abortion clinics to the extent that they are involved in organized conspiracies to shut down the clinics through illegal means.[56] In addition, state and federal prosecutors nationwide have used RICO and similar state laws against persons who peddle pornography. It has been assumed for some time that organized crime has a hand in pornography industries. Still, RICO and similar state statutes are worded and interpreted broadly enough to reach even relatively mainstream publishers and bookstores. All that is usually required to obtain a conviction is to show that the accused has sold obscene materials at least two times over a ten-year period.

As in the case of public-nuisance statutes, the fact that a defendant has engaged in the peddling of obscenity is used as a means of triggering a legal action other than enforcement of an ordinary obscenity statute. Under racketeering laws, defendants face punishments not contemplated in the typical obscenity law or public-nuisance statute. A racketeering conviction can result in a twenty-year jail sentence and hundreds of thousands of dollars in fines. Moreover, any property used by the defendant in racketeering activities or purchased with the profits from such activities is often forfeitable. Not only can the defendant's place of business and entire inventory (obscene and nonobscene) be seized, but the seizure might extend to personal property such as a place of residence. After all, placing a phone call to order a supply of magazines or videotapes for the store or giving instructions to employees—activities often conducted from a store owner's private residence—are both "associated with" committing the crime of selling obscene materials.

The Supreme Court has twice had occasion to rule on the application of racketeering laws to pornography. In 1989, it held that the State of Indiana violated the First

---

56. *National Organization for Women v. Scheidler*, 510 U.S. 249 (1994).

Amendment when, under its state racketeering law, it seized an adult bookstore's inventory before any convictions had been obtained. The Court gave its approval, however, to the use of racketeering statutes and their forfeiture provisions, as long as no confiscation occurs prior to a conviction.[57] Four years later, in *Alexander v. United States*, the Court made a similar ruling concerning RICO, emphasizing that the forfeiture here of the defendant's entire business and approximately $9 million in profits was not a prior restraint on feared future pornography peddling, but rather permissible punishment for past violations of the law.[58]

Government Sponsorship of the Arts

There is a long and complicated body of case law on the question of what First Amendment limitations apply when the government itself is the speaker. It is clear that the government as speaker may engage in viewpoint-based discrimination that would be impermissible in other contexts. The state may not censor private speech arguing for or against drug legalization, but when was the last time you saw a government-sponsored public service announcement on the issue calling for anything other than complete abstinence? In another context, the Supreme Court has said that when the federal government pays for health care, the professionals delivering that care can be prohibited not only from performing abortions but also from even mentioning the topic.[59]

THINGS TO REMEMBER

Sex and Racketeering

- The federal Racketeer Influenced and Corrupt Organizations Act (RICO), originally enacted in 1970, has been amended to provide for the prosecution of pornographers as one would prosecute organized crime figures.
- Many states have passed their own racketeering laws as well.
- These laws provide for hefty fines and lengthy prison terms, as well as forfeiture of any and all possessions purchased with proceeds from the commission of such racketeering crimes or that have been used in the furtherance of the criminal activity.
- The Supreme Court has upheld the constitutionality of such forfeitures as long as they do not happen before any convictions are obtained.

---

57. *Fort Wayne Books v. Indiana*, 489 U.S. 46 (1989).

58. 509 U.S. 544 (1993). The majority sent the case back to the lower courts, however, to determine if this huge forfeiture violated the Eighth Amendment's prohibition against cruel and unusual punishment. On remand, the lower courts upheld the forfeiture amount, and the Supreme Court declined to review the case, under the name *Schledit v. Souval*, again. 522 U.S. 869 (1997).

59. *Rust v. Sullivan*, 500 U.S. 173 (1991).

The National Endowment for the Arts (NEA) was created in 1965. Since then it has made over $4 billion in grants to artists and arts organizations. A tiny handful of controversial grants prompted Congress to instruct the NEA that it should make grants not only on the basis of artistic excellence but also "taking into consideration general standards of decency and respect for the diverse beliefs and values of the American public." Four performance artists with reputations for creating feminist, gay, and other provocative works—Karen Finley, John Fleck, Holly Hughes, and Tim Miller—challenged the new provision. Each had previously received an NEA grant, and each had a pending proposal accepted by an endowment advisory panel but ultimately disapproved by the director. Two lower federal courts held the "decency" amendment unconstitutional, but the Supreme Court, in an 8–1 ruling, overturned these judgments in 1998. Justice O'Connor's majority opinion was based on the rather narrow grounds that the amendment was merely "hortatory," that it told the NEA director what the grants application *should* look like, rather than explicitly prohibiting the funding of indecent art. Had the NEA in fact developed an unwritten policy against funding art espousing specific political messages, the decision might have been different.[60]

Washington is not the only source of government funding for the arts, of course. From time to time state and local governments create their own First Amendment nightmares. In 1999 the Brooklyn Museum included as part of an exhibit entitled *Sensation* a painting by Chris Ofili—an impressionistic rendering of the Virgin Mary created from, among other materials, elephant dung. Outraged by what he perceived as the artist's desecration of the Catholic faith, New York City mayor Rudolph Giuliani promptly withheld funds already appropriated to the museum for operating expenses and maintenance. He also commenced litigation seeking to eject the museum from the city-owned land and building in which its collections had been housed for over a hundred years. Federal district judge Nina Gershon enjoined the city from imposing any such tangible sanctions against the museum.[61]

Postal Regulations and Sexually Oriented Junk Mail

Earlier in the chapter we examined the federal laws making it illegal to send obscene materials through the mails and giving post office investigators the right to open and seize obscene materials. In this section we see two additional pieces of federal legislation that, taken together, can save individuals the embarrassment or inconvenience of receiving any "adult" mailings. Under what is popularly known as the Goldwater amendment to the Postal Reorganization Act,[62] individuals who do not wish to

---

60. *National Endowment for the Arts v. Finley*, 524 U.S. 569 (1998).

61. *Brooklyn Institute of Arts and Sciences v. City of New York*, 64 F. Supp. 2d 184 (E.D.N.Y. 1999); see also *Cuban Museum of Arts and Culture, Inc. v. City of Miami*, 766 F. Supp. 1121 (S.D. Fla. 1991).

62. 39 USCS §3010 (2010).

THINGS TO REMEMBER

Government Sponsorship

- A small handful of the thousands of grants made by the National Endowment of the Arts have been very controversial and have led Congress to demand that the funding agency include general notions of "decency" into its decision making.
- The Supreme Court has upheld this provision but has warned the NEA that it must not engage in flagrant viewpoint-based discrimination.

---

receive sexually oriented mail of any kind may fill out a form at their local post office informing the postmaster of this wish. The U.S. Postal Service in turn alerts all companies that it has previously determined to be in the business of sending such mail to purchase the list—updated monthly—of all such mail patrons who have filled out the requisite paperwork. These companies are then required by law to remove the names and addresses of all those on the list from any mailing lists and to never mail *anything* to those individuals (whether the companies think a particular mailing is "adult" or not). The constitutionality of this provision has been upheld.[63] More wide-reaching is the Pandering Advertisements Statute,[64] under which mail patrons who fill out a different form at the post office indicating their belief that a specific company's mailing was "erotically arousing" will thus put that company on notice that it may no longer send mail to those patrons. Yes, this means that you may use this law to avoid

---

THINGS TO REMEMBER

Sex and the Mails

- In addition to laws criminalizing the mailing of obscene materials, the U.S. Postal Service is empowered by two other congressional provisions to control the mailing of nonobscene, but sexually oriented, messages.
- Title 39, section 3010 of the U.S. Code requires companies that mail "adult" materials to purchase, and respect, a periodically updated list from the U.S. Postal Service of all mail patrons who do not want to receive any such mailings.
- Section 3008 gives mail patrons themselves the absolute right to determine that a given mailing is "sexually arousing" and to notify the post office of this determination. The U.S. Postal Service will then notify the offending company that it may not send any mail to that patron again.

---

63. *Pent-R-Books v. U.S. Postal Service*, 328 F. Supp. 297 (E.D.N.Y. 1971).

64. 39 USCS §3008 (2010). The provision was upheld in *Rowan v. U.S. Post Office Department*, 397 U.S. 728 (1970).

getting those bulky mail-order catalogs that take up so much room in your mailbox. The catalog need not be from Victoria's Secret; it can be from L.L.Bean.

Chapter Summary

The Supreme Court has said that obscenity is not speech and is thus wholly outside the First Amendment's protection. The current rules for defining obscenity are found generally in the 1973 decision *Miller v. California*. The *Miller* test provides that allegedly obscene works should be judged as a whole, not by isolated passages, and by their likely effects on average, or reasonable, community members. To be judged obscene, a work must describe or depict sexual matters in a patently offensive way and in a way that appeals to the prurient interest. Whether a work meets that definition is a determination to be made using contemporary community standards (not a single national standard). Moreover, works that have serious literary, artistic, political, or scientific value—as judged by a national standard—cannot be found obscene. Materials cannot be found obscene merely because they seem to condone or glorify immoral sexual values.

There exists a right to privacy in the home that extends far enough to protect an individual's right to possess obscene materials but not so far as to permit an individual to import such materials, carry them across state lines, or use the mails to ship them.

Child pornography laws are aimed at sexually oriented materials that use children as actors or models. Such laws differ from obscenity statutes in many ways: works need not be judged as a whole; they are not exempted from the law by dint of having serious value; and they need not appeal to the prurient interest, nor be obscene. Moreover, the state may criminalize the mere possession of child pornography. States have struggled in recent years to construct appropriate remedies for "sexting," in which teens send sexually charged images of themselves or often classmates to each other.

In the 1980s a feminist response to pornography developed, emphasizing the material's degrading depiction of women rather than its overall effect on a society's moral tone. An Indianapolis ordinance based on this new theory was struck down as unconstitutional.

In recent years, communities have embraced legal strategies beyond a reliance on obscenity laws per se to stem the proliferation of adult-oriented businesses. These include zoning ordinances, public-nuisance statutes, and the use of federal and state racketeering laws. In addition, individuals have rights under laws governing the U.S. Postal Service to avoid receiving unwanted sexual mailings, whether obscene or not.

Chapter 12

BROADCAST, CABLE, AND SATELLITE TV REGULATION

Politician or newscaster? Once and future candidate or media personality? Sometimes it is hard to tell the players without a scorecard. George Stephanopoulos, former White House Communications director for President Clinton, cohosts ABC's *Good Morning America* (after a gig as moderator of the Sunday talk show *This Week*). Former Alaska governor and likely future presidential candidate Sarah Palin is a paid commentator for Fox News. Actor and former U.S. senator Fred Thompson stepped through the revolving door several times.

At the point when today's electronic media personality seeks to become tomorrow's candidate, the **Equal Time rule** kicks in, requiring (with some exceptions) that every opposing candidate for the same office be given equal time on any broadcast station in which the personality-candidate appears. We will be examining that rule in much more detail later in this chapter. For now, suffice it to say that, should Palin decide to seek the presidency, she will likely be fired by Fox, because the rule's provisions would make it prohibitively expensive to keep her.

In this chapter we review the complicated regulatory framework governing the electronic media—chiefly, broadcast radio and TV, but also cable, satellite, and microwave means of delivery. Then chapter 13 explores the new and challenging field of Internet law. A sense of humility should accompany us as we try to make sense of the rapid changes that have characterized the regulation of electronic media. New court cases and new Federal Communications Commission rules (or more often, the discarding of old rules) emerge on the scene every week. Also of relevance are the frequent announcements of mergers among major players in the telecommunications industry and the new ways of playing out old turf wars among broadcast, cable, satellite, local and long-distance telephone, and Internet companies.

We are often reminded that we live in an era not only of rapid deregulation of the electronic media industry but also of **convergence**. Industry analysts use the word to describe the fact that from the end user's perspective, how one gets access to media content—whether on TV sets, radios, computers, or smart phones—matters much less than that one indeed has access. But for a combination of reasons, traditional American communication law has assumed a small handful of neatly defined and separate categories of communications media. The print media are governed by one body of law, and the broadcast media have had additional laws and regulations imposed on them. Cable TV systems have been subject to a body of regulations somewhat more restrictive than those applied to the print media but less restrictive than those applied to over-the-air TV and radio. Rather separate has been the body of law governing telephone companies, often called "common carriers" because their traditional function has been to serve as a mere conduit for others' transmissions—anyone able and willing to pay the price (the connection costs, the monthly phone bill) gets to send messages. Which model shall we use, then, to regulate a single home appliance that can perform all our communications functions? The short answer is that no one knows.[1]

In the next section we explore the general structure of electronic media regulation. The most prominent feature of that structure is the Federal Communications Commission (FCC), which governs through its rule-making authority and through its interactions with Congress, the courts (especially the D.C. Circuit Court of Appeals), and industry trade groups.

This chapter next considers the traditional rationales used by the FCC, Congress, and the courts for treating print and electronic media differently. The government has regulated electronic media more strictly because of the scarceness of available frequencies (not everyone who wants to obtain a broadcast license may get one), the pervasiveness of TV and radio in our daily lives, and the electronic media's unique power to influence the young.

We next focus on three broad categories of regulations governing TV and radio: those affecting the licensing of individual stations, those aimed at improving the technical and engineering aspects of broadcasting (including the goal of making signals accessible to the hearing impaired and the visually impaired), and those more directly aimed at specific kinds of content. As we shall see, electronic media are subject to regulations concerning political content (especially speech by and about political candidates), sexually oriented messages, and programming aimed at children. Content regulations that apply uniquely to public broadcasters, such as National Public Radio (NPR) and Public Broadcasting Service (PBS) stations, are also discussed.

---

1. See, for example, *Comcast v. Federal Communications Commission*, 600 F. 3d 642 (D.C. Cir. 2010) (FCC does not have the authority to treat the Internet as a "common carrier," akin to traditional telephone companies); *Fox Television Stations, Inc. v Federal Communications Commission*, 613 F. 3d 317 (2nd Cir. 2010) (recognizing that what was once thought of only as "broadcast" TV is now accessible as easily over cable systems and via the Internet).

THINGS TO REMEMBER

A Changing Media Landscape?

- Traditionally, media in the United States have been regulated by one of three models: print, broadcasting, and "common carrier" (e.g., telephone and telegraph), with cable TV treated as something in between print and broadcasting.
- But now that much of our mobile hardware (e.g., the iPad) can perform as a telephone, radio, newspaper, and TV, there is great pressure on government to permit media law to "converge" to a single system.

Then we examine the complicated development of laws and regulations affecting the cable industry. Even to this day, the Supreme Court has refused to commit itself to a determination of how much free speech cable TV operators should enjoy, save to say that it will be an "intermediate" amount, somewhere between the free speech accorded to the print media and that accorded to the electronic media. We will also see how the law has affected the direct broadcast satellite (DBS) industry, which thus far has been the cable industry's chief competition.

The Birth of Broadcast Regulation

Part of my morning ritual involves my straining to listen to *Morning Edition* on my local NPR station while fixing breakfast. "Straining" because my station's signal often experiences interference from a jazz station .2 megahertz higher up on the dial. This minor annoyance points to one of the primary reasons that electronic media have from the outset been regulated more vigorously than print. Newspapers and magazines cannot block each other out in the way that TV and radio stations can. It became apparent not long after amateur and commercial radio stations came on the scene in the early part of the twentieth century that federal intervention was necessary if the broadcast industry was to thrive. As then–Secretary of Commerce Herbert Hoover exclaimed, "this is probably the only industry in the United States that is unanimously in favor of having itself regulated."[2]

Congress's first comprehensive response was the Radio Act of 1927, which provided an elaborate licensing scheme and established a "public trustee" model to govern radio in America. Because the electromagnetic spectrum, which includes not only radio waves but also X-rays, gamma rays, and both infrared and ultraviolet light, is inherently limited, not every applicant who would like to obtain a broadcasting li-

---

2. Quoted by Sidney Head, *Broadcasting in America: A Survey of Television and Radio*, 3d ed. (New York: Houghton Mifflin, 1976), 126.

THINGS TO REMEMBER

Early Broadcast Regulation

- The Radio Act of 1927 created the Federal Radio Commission and first authorized the federal government to rescind licenses from those who were not operating "in the public interest."
- In 1934, Congress passed the Federal Communications Act, which, as modified over the years, is the basis for government regulation of electronic media as well as telecommunications.

cense can do so. Congress therefore asserted that the airwaves belong to the public and that individual licensees, in their roles as trustees of that valuable public resource, must use their broadcasting licenses in a manner consistent with the "public interest, convenience, and necessity." The act also created the Federal Radio Commission (FRC), a five-member board granted broad powers not only to issue licenses but also to deny applications and to revoke licenses already granted. As interpreted by the Supreme Court in a 1933 decision, the 1927 act also clarified that regulation of the radio spectrum must take place at the national rather than at the state level, because "no state lines divide the radio waves."[3]

In 1934 Congress entered further into the regulation of electronic media with the passage of the Federal Communications Act which, as amended over the years, still governs American broadcasting. The 1934 act disbanded the FRC and created in its stead the Federal Communications Commission, aptly named in that its seven commissioners (since reduced to five) were to be charged with regulating not only radio but also the common-carrier technologies of the day (telephone and telegraph).

Structure and Powers of the FCC

The Federal Communication Commission's five commissioners are appointed by the president with the consent of the Senate. They serve five-year staggered terms. No more than three of the five commissioners may be registered in the same political party. The president designates one of the five to serve as the commission's chairman. As of this writing, Julius Genachowski is the chairman of the FCC, appointed by President Obama. A graduate of Harvard Law School, Genachowski has a background in public service and as an executive in telecommunication industries.

---

3. *Federal Radio Commission v. Nelson Brothers*, 289 U.S. 266, 279 (1933).

The FCC's Bureaus

As with any large bureaucracy, most of the nuts-and-bolts work in the FCC is done by its professional staff, who are primarily attorneys, engineers, and economists. The staff is organized into seven divisions or bureaus. The Media Bureau regulates AM and FM radio, and both broadcast and cable television. The Wireless Telecommunications Bureau deals with, among other systems, cell phone and personal communication and paging services. The Wireline Competition Bureau deals with corded and cordless phones, as well as broadband Internet service. The Public Safety and Homeland Security Bureau, as its name implies, addresses national security and emergency-preparedness issues related to communication. The International Bureau represents the commission at international conferences involving telecommunications matters and administers any relevant provisions of treaties and other international agreements. The Consumer and Governmental Affairs Bureau deals with public inquiries and informal consumer complaints, maintains relationships with all levels of government, and makes policy recommendations concerning disability access. Finally, the Enforcement Bureau's responsibilities cut across the other bureaus' domains for the purpose of investigating alleged violations of law or FCC policies by licensees. In this bureau agents quite literally bring out the hatchets when they hear of unauthorized, "rogue" radio transmitters.

Rulemaking and Enforcement

The process of creating new FCC regulations typically begins when the commission's professional staff—sometimes on their own initiative, sometimes after complaints by external constituencies—brings to the commissioners an outline of a problem and its proposed solution. That solution is usually in the form of a "notice of proposed rule making." If accepted by the commissioners, the notice is then widely disseminated to the affected industries and, through publication in the *Federal Register*, to the public at large. Public comments are sought over a period of months, and the text of those comments is also made available for review by any interested parties, which typically results in a second round of comments. At that point, the commissioners review staff reports and the public's feedback and articulate their final decision, called a "report and order."

The FCC not only creates new policies, of course, it must also enforce existing policies and relevant statutes. One might suppose that the most frequent impetus for the commission to commence an investigation against a broadcast licensee would be a complaint from an offended viewer or listener. The FCC, however, requires that a *pattern* of abuse be demonstrated before it will take on a case for review, and the average consumer simply does not have the time and resources to monitor a station for a long enough period to meet this standard. More typical, therefore, are complaints from organized interest groups or from licensees whose own economic interests are tangibly affected by another station's alleged wrongdoing.

If a matter brought to the FCC's attention is seen as warranting investigation, a typical next step is to draft a letter of inquiry (LOI) to the licensee against whom a complaint has been brought, seeking additional information. This initial inquiry is popularly known as "regulation by raised eyebrow" and is often sufficient to bring licensees' behaviors into compliance with FCC policies. The licensee's written response to the LOI might elicit a slight escalation from the FCC staff in the form of a notice of apparent liability. Sometimes too, the "raised eyebrow" does not consist of singling out individual stations at all but instead takes the form of a speech or other formal statement by the chairman or other commissioners criticizing an overall industry practice. Current chairman Julius Genachowski made frequent speeches in 2010 arguing for "**net neutrality**," which would prevent Internet service providers such as Comcast or Verizon from giving some content access to faster "pipelines" than others.

The commission is also empowered to issue cease and desist orders and to levy fines against offending licensees. A yet more extreme measure available to the commission include granting a license renewal on a probationary basis—for a shorter time than the usual eight years—and refusing to renew a license altogether. This latter action is very rarely taken and in recent decades is almost never taken on the basis of broadcast content itself. Licensees found to have engaged in fraud, however, may very well lose their licenses. The FCC has revoked licenses when licensees have purposely overbilled advertisers or have been untruthful in dealings with the commission itself.[4]

Ancillary Powers

Technically, the FCC is empowered only to regulate government licensees; with respect to broadcast regulation, that means the FCC may regulate only the individuals and companies who have been granted a license to run specific local TV or radio stations. Even more narrowly, because Congress's right to establish the FCC in the first place flows from the Constitution's Commerce Clause (which gives Congress the power to regulate *interstate* commerce), one might expect that a station with a small broadcast radius capable of only *intra*state transmissions would be beyond the commission's purview. Enter the **ancillary powers** doctrine, through which the courts have granted the FCC authority to regulate matters not specifically enumerated in the Federal Communications Act but which the commission must oversee if it is to effectively regulate interstate transmissions by individual licensees.

The doctrine has been invoked to permit regulation of purely intrastate signals, on the theory that such transmissions could interfere with neighboring broadcast stations whose *interstate* transmissions inarguably bring them into the commission's domain.[5]

---

4. See, for example, *In re Application of Trinity Broadcasting of Florida*, 144 FCC Rcd 13570 (1999) (revoking license for having set up a "puppet," ostensibly minority-owned, company, seeking to qualify for more licenses than those to which it would normally be entitled).

5. *Nelson Brothers*, 289 U.S. 266.

THINGS TO REMEMBER

FCC Structure and Powers

- The FCC has five commissioners, each appointed by the president with the consent of the Senate, and no more than three of whom may be of the same political party; they serve for staggered five-year terms.
- The FCC is empowered to enforce existing regulations as well as to promulgate new regulations consistent with federal law.
- To punish stations found in violation of relevant regulations, the FCC is empowered to use any of several sanctions, including the rarely invoked revocation of a license.
- The ancillary powers doctrine has been used to extend the commission's authority to TV and radio networks, cable systems, and small stations with wholly *intra*state signals. But the doctrine does not permit the commission to directly regulate the Internet.

The FCC has also been permitted to maintain some oversight of radio and TV *networks*, which are not themselves licensed entities. In this instance, two theories are involved. First, although networks are mostly composed of far-flung individual stations (affiliates) that they do not own, each network also does have a number of "O& O" (owned and operated) stations within its portfolio. Second, the contractual relationships between networks and their affiliate stations necessarily have an impact on local broadcasting.[6]

The FCC unsuccessfully invoked the ancillary powers doctrine in a quest to exercise oversight related to Internet service providers. As we will see in the next chapter, the D.C. Circuit Court of Appeals rejected the commission's move.[7]

Why Treat Broadcast and Print Media Differently?

Think back to the example of Sarah Palin from the chapter introduction. If she were working as a newspaper reporter prior to a possible run for the presidency, the Equal Time Rule would have no impact on the paper's publisher. The rule would only be triggered in response to certain kinds of TV and radio appearances. Indeed, a whole host of laws and regulations that govern the broadcast media would be clearly unconstitutional if applied to newspapers, books, magazines, or other print media. Some of these rules determine who may own a station license; others impose highly specific

---

6. *National Broadcasting Co. v. FCC*, 319 U.S. 190 (1943). The ancillary power doctrine has also provided some FCC power to regulate cable TV, even before Congress had passed laws governing cable. *United States v. Southwestern Cable Co.*, 392 U.S. 157 (1968).

7. *Comcast v. FCC*, 600 F. 3d 642 (D.C. Cir. 2010).

restrictions on message content. Over the years, several rationales have been offered in support of the differential treatment of print and broadcast media. The chief rationale has always been, as was seen in the earlier discussion of the Radio Act of 1927, Congress's assertion that the airwaves belong to the public. There have been other reasons offered as well. We look here at three of them: spectrum scarcity, pervasiveness, and accessibility to children.

Spectrum Scarcity

Spectrum scarcity forced the government to regulate radio broadcasting from the very beginning of the industry. It makes no sense to speak of a "right" to a broadcast license when there are not enough licenses to go around.[8]

The spectrum scarcity rationale is not without its critics. Many argue that the government creates, or at least exacerbates, the scarcity by *giving away* licenses worth tens or even hundreds of millions of dollars. If scarcity is determined by the ratio of the supply of and demand for a product, then giving away licenses, which increases demand, does much to exacerbate the scarcity of licenses. Congress has thus instructed the FCC to experiment with the use of auctions, rather than government giveaways, to distribute new kinds of licenses. The commission has since raised tens of billions of dollars auctioning off licenses to use portions of the spectrum for personal communication systems and other wireless telephone and radio services.

From an engineering perspective, the spectrum scarcity argument made much more sense when considering analog TV stations than it does in an era of digital broadcasting. It is fair to say that the main limitation on the number of commercially viable broadcast stations in any given market is actually the finite number of advertising dollars attracted to that market, not the potential for signal interference.[9]

Pervasiveness

Long before there was "web surfing," we spoke of "channel surfing." The phrase is a handy way of emphasizing that TV viewers often do not have a specific program in mind when they turn on the set. They are settling in to simply "watch some TV." Clearly in a cable or satellite world of DVR, TiVo, and "on demand" programming, things are quite different. But when our system of electronic broadcast regulation was created, we viewers had little control over what kinds of messages might be transmitted to us. Broadcast media were thus often described by regulators as "pervasive."[10] (Some critics have suggested that "intrusive" would have been a more appropriate word to express the government's real concerns.)

---

8. *Red Lion Broadcasting v. FCC*, 395 U.S. 367, 388–389 (1969).

9. FCC Quadrennial Regulatory Review, 47 CFR 33227 (2010) (citing dramatic decrease in advertising revenues for TV and radio station just in two years).

10. See for example *In re WUHY-FM*, 24 F.C.C. 2d 408, 411 (1970).

THINGS TO REMEMBER

Rationales for Broadcast Regulation

The three most frequently invoked reasons for regulating broadcast media more strictly than print are the scarcity of the electromagnetic spectrum, the pervasiveness or intrusiveness of TV and radio, and the stronger potential for these media to reach children.

Protecting the Children

Closely related to the pervasiveness rationale is the concern that the broadcast media are especially accessible (and therefore dangerous) to children. This concern is most frequently focused on the level of violence or sexual banter on TV. As we shall see, the FCC's definition of "broadcast indecency" includes a reference to the likelihood that there are large numbers of children in the audience. Moreover, the hard-fought compromise over how to regulate broadcast indecency, the creation of a "safe harbor" for such programming late at night and early in the morning, was settled on with children in mind.

Broadcast Regulation: Licensure and Ownership

Certainly the most fundamental difference between communication law as applied to the print media and as applied to the broadcast media is that one needs a federal *license* to engage in broadcasting. The requirements for licensure discussed below may seem commonsense and thus unremarkable; consider, however, how odd it would be if the same criteria were applied to the print media.

Requirements for Licensure

Licensees must be "of good character," which in recent years has generally meant only that they not be convicted felons or have a history of lying in previous dealings with the FCC. Applicants for a broadcast license must also be citizens of the United States. A corporate applicant may qualify if at least 75 percent of its assets are American owned. This latter rule was waived by the FCC to permit Rupert Murdoch's News Corporation (an Australian company) to retain licenses for several TV stations that formed the core of the Fox network.

Broadcast license applicants must have, or be able to hire people who have, the requisite engineering skills to run such a complicated operation. The applicant must also demonstrate sufficient financial resources to remain in business for three months even without one penny of advertising revenue coming in.

How Much Can You Own?

The age of deregulation that began in the early 1980s has all but eliminated limits on the total number of stations that any one individual or company may own. There are currently no limits on the number of radio stations a single entity can own nationwide. San Antonio–based Clear Channel Communications alone owns over eight hundred stations reaching over 110 million listeners.[11] As for television stations, the rules governing nationwide ownership are not based on the number of stations owned but on how many people those stations can reach. Currently a single company can own as many stations as it would like, as long as those stations, taken together, do not reach more than 39 percent of America's TV households.

The commission still has on the books an array of rules governing how many media companies one can own in the same local market, which is a function of how competitive that market is (i.e., how many other stations operate there). In its 2010 "regulatory review" document, the FCC has indicated it will be considering whether to keep in place the following rules:

- The Local TV Ownership Rule, which generally says that no single company may own more than two TV stations in the same market, and does not allow even that second station if both will be in the top four in the market;
- The Local Radio Ownership Rule, which limits any single company to no more than eight radio stations even in the very top markets (those with over forty-five stations), and which requires that no more than five of those eight can be the same service (i.e., AM or FM);
- The Newspaper/Broadcast Cross-Ownership Rule, which had held generally that no single company can own a major daily newspaper and a TV or radio station in the same market. In 2006 the Commission voted to liberalize this rule so as to allow newspapers to also own a single TV or radio station in the very largest markets. A challenge to that liberalization was in front of the Third Circuit of Appeals as we were going to press.
- The Radio-Television Cross-Ownership Rule, which allows companies in the biggest markets to own up to two TV stations and up to six radio stations (as long as those totals for a given market do not exceed the numbers prescribed by the other rules); and
- The Dual Network Rule, which would prohibit any of the four TV networks (ABC, CBS, Fox, and NBC) from buying or merging with any of the others.

---

11. http://clearchannel.com/Radio/PressRelease.aspx?PressReleaseID = 1563&p = hidden (visited September 4, 2010).

THINGS TO REMEMBER

Licensure and Ownership Issues

- Basic requirements for obtaining a broadcast license include U.S. citizenship, "good character," technical expertise, and financial solvency.
- Many long-standing limits on the number of TV and radio stations any one person or company can own have been eliminated.
- Every few years the FCC must report to Congress on additional regulations that might be eliminated; in 2010 the commission pointed to a number of regulations it might like to rescind.
- The FCC and the courts have been receptive to low-power FM radio stations as a truly local alternative to the major chains.
- The courts have been less receptive to the commission's various strategies for enhancing minority ownership of stations.

In recent years the FCC has begun issuing licenses for noncommercial low-power FM (LPFM) stations, which operate at up to one hundred watts of power with a broadcast antenna no higher than thirty meters, and which generally are designed to have a broadcast radius of only about three and a half miles. There are now over eight hundred such stations on the air. In 2009 a federal appellate court accepted the FCC's argument that the goal of providing true "localism" justifies such stations being regulated a bit less strictly than larger, more traditional stations.[12]

Preferences for Minority Ownership

One additional issue related to ownership and licensure is whether the federal government could require or encourage broadcast licensees to embrace affirmative action or minority-hiring preferences. For decades the FCC has assumed this would be the most feasible way to foster a diversity of viewpoints on the air. However, the courts have usually restrained the commission.[13]

The commission's logic has been assailed by the D.C. Circuit Court of Appeals, which in one case said that to expect that a black owner would play hip-hop music and would somehow embrace a "black editorial viewpoint" would be akin to assuming that "an Italian station owner would primarily program Italian operas, or would eschew Wagner in favor of Verdi."[14]

---

12. *National Association of Broadcasters v. Federal Communications Commission*, 569 F. 3d 416 (D.D.C. 2009).

13. *MD/DC/DE Broadcasters Association v. FCC*, 236 F.3d 13 (D.C. Cir. 2001); *Lutheran Church, Missouri Synod v. FCC*, 141 F.3d 344, 350 (D.C. Cir. 1998), *reh'g en banc denied*, 154 F.3d 494 (D.C. Cir. 1998). See also *Gratz v. Bollinger*, 539 U.S. 244 (2003) (indicating the Court's skepticism about affirmative action in higher education admissions).

14. *Steele v. FCC*, 770 F.2d 1192, 1198 (D.C. Cir. 1985).

In recent years courts have expressed skepticism about predicting the diversity of radio station formats from the diversity (in terms of gender, race, or ethnic background) of licensees.

Broadcast Regulation: Consumers and Technology

The FCC, sometimes in direct response to a specific congressional mandate, at other times on its own initiative, has frequently taken steps to improve the technological aspects of broadcasting. Clearly technological considerations are always part of the licensing process. The management of a radio station with a history of engineering glitches that result in extended periods of "dead air" will find it harder to renew its broadcast license. We can also identify times in the history of broadcasting when the FCC has stepped in to bring the entire industry up to a higher standard. For example, over a period of more than twenty years—pursuant to the 1962 All Channel Receiver Act—the commission promulgated rules requiring that TV sets be able to receive UHF stations as conveniently as they did VHF stations. Two noteworthy other examples of FCC regulations governing technical broadcast standards are digital high-definition television and signal accessibility for persons with hearing or visual impairments.

The Switch to HDTV

After many years of internal debates about competing formats, the federal government in 1997 embarked on a long-term commitment to bring the U.S. system of TV transmission into the digital age. Existing TV license holders were granted a second frequency, gratis, to start making the transition to high-definition television (HDTV). After some false starts, the switch to digital broadcasting was accomplished in 2009, with the federal government subsidizing the purchase of converter boxes for poorer households not ready to make the switch to digital TV receivers.

Accessibility to Audio and Video Signals

Millions of Americans have limited visual or auditory acuity. They may have been born deaf or hard of hearing, or blind, or they may have lost some of their sense modalities with age. In recent years Congress has intervened to ensure that television programming is as accessible as practicable to all.

Closed Captioning   The Television Decoder Circuitry Act of 1990 (TDCA) mandated that as of July 1, 1993, all TV sets with thirteen-inch or larger screens would have to be capable of receiving closed-captioning signals. Thus most American TV households have access to captioning. Although the most obvious market for the service is persons who are deaf and hard of hearing, the technology can also benefit other identifiable groups, such as children learning to read and adults learning English as a second language. You have probably also seen TVs with captions on and volume off in commercial establishments such as bars and health clubs.

Section 713 of the Telecommunications Act of 1996 instructed the FCC to conduct a study of the current level of closed captioning and to "prescribe such regulations as are necessary" to significantly increase that level. The Commission's rules resulted in virtually 100 percent[15] of new programming, whether delivered on broadcast TV, cable systems, or direct broadcast satellite systems, being captioned as of January 1, 2006.

Video Descriptions   It is one of the most famous scenes from contemporary American cinema: young Elliott (played by Henry Thomas) befriends the creature we will all soon know as E.T. The scene lasts for almost five minutes. The audio is limited

---

15. Some categories of programming will be permanently exempted from the captioning requirement. Included among the exemptions are such commonsense categories as primarily textual programs (e.g., community bulletin boards) and programs consisting mostly of instrumental music. Advertisements are also exempted, as are "interstitial announcements" (e.g., "How did the city council vote go? News at 11."). Programs airing only between 2 a.m. and 6 a.m. need not be captioned, nor locally produced and distributed nonnews programs with limited repeat value (such as local parades, local high school or nonprofessional sports, and community theater productions).

to some pleasant but mysterious background music, a bit of breathing and chewing, the sound of something crashing to the floor and of a door slamming, and only one word spoken: Elliott's barely whispered "Wow!" In other words, if you were a blind child encountering the Spielberg film for the first time, you would have no idea what was going on.

Enter now the power of video description, the artistically complex method of adding a second audio track, a voice describing the action, to TV programs as well as to films, whether on the big screen or in home video format. WGBH-TV in Boston has been a pioneer in this area, with its trademarked Descriptive Video Service (DVS).

Perhaps you can appreciate that the elaborate nature of the *E.T.* video-description text prompted one critic to suggest that legislation placing on broadcasters the same kinds of demands for the service that the commission has imposed for closed captioning would have to be subtitled "The English Majors' Full Employment Act." The Telecommunications Act of 1996 required only that the FCC "commence an inquiry" as to the extent of available programming with video descriptions. But the Commission went further, promulgating rules requiring that network affiliate stations in the twenty-five largest markets provide fifty hours of video-described programming quar-

Video Description from *E.T.*

Elliott stands at the top of the staircase on the second floor. Holding a bag of candy in one hand, he drops a pile of Reese's Pieces onto the carpeted landing. He backs away to the door of his room, crouches on the floor, and keeps his eyes locked on the candy. The alien's long, pencil-thin fingers reach over the top of the stairs to pick up one of the pieces. . . . A faint smile spreads across Elliott's mouth.

The alien grabs the rest of the candy, leaving one piece behind. He steps onto the landing to get it. Elliott dumps more Reese's Pieces in the doorway of his room. The alien eagerly reaches for them and scoops them into his hands. . . .

As the creature stands in the light, we see him clearly for the first time. He has wrinkly, light-brown skin, his stubby torso rests on squat, inch-high legs connected to his webbed feet. Completely bald, he has a broad face, shaped like a squashed heart, with a button nose and great big blue eyes. . . .

THINGS TO REMEMBER

Technology and Access Issues

- After initial glitches and delays, the federally mandated switch to digital TV went smoothly in 2009.
- The Television Decoder Circuitry Act of 1990 mandated that TVs larger than thirteen inches be capable of reading closed captioning, and the Telecommunications Act of 1996 resulted in virtually all broadcast and cable programming being captioned beginning in 2006.
- The commission has thus far not been permitted, however, to require that TV stations provide video descriptions for the blind.

---

terly (about four hours weekly). A coalition of broadcasters and cablecasters successfully challenged those rules.[16]

Broadcast Regulation: Content

Section 326 of the Federal Communications Act reads: "Nothing in this Act shall be understood or construed to give the [FCC] the power of censorship over the radio communications or signals transmitted by any radio station, and no regulation or condition shall be promulgated or fixed by the Commission which shall interfere with the right of free speech by means of radio communication."

"*No* regulation or condition"? This is very reminiscent of the First Amendment's admonition that Congress shall pass "*no* law abridging . . . freedom of speech." Yet if that latter admonition were interpreted literally, this book would have been much shorter. Similarly, both Congress and the FCC frequently legislate and regulate the actual content of media messages. In this section we look at several categories of restrictions on broadcast media content. Included are the regulation of political speech and sexually oriented speech, children's programming, the V-chip as an answer to TV violence, special regulations applied to PBS and NPR stations, and some other miscellaneous content regulations.

---

16. *Motion Picture Association of America v. FCC*, 309 F. 3d 796 (D.C. Cir. 2002). Consumers wishing to purchase DVDs with video descriptions included generally must order them from services such as WGBH itself, rather than on the open market. But this began to change in 2009, when the very first commercially produced DVD for general retail with video descriptions (the Disney Studio's animated film *Up*) went on the market. "Disney-Pixar's 'Up' Released with Descriptive Video Service on Blu-Ray, DVD and iTunes," National Center for Accessible Media, November 13, 2009 (press release).

Regulation of Political Speech

As a result of the deregulation fervor of the 1980s and beyond, just about the only broadcast regulations governing political speech apply exclusively to times when political campaigns are underway. Chief among these are the **Candidate Access rule** and the **Equal Time rule.**

Candidate Access Rule   Section 312(a) of the Federal Communications Act authorizes the FCC to revoke the license of any TV or radio station that fails to "allow reasonable access to or to permit purchase of reasonable amounts of time . . . by a legally qualified candidate for Federal elective office on behalf of his candidacy." Section 312 further dictates that as an election grows near, stations must charge candidates the lowest rates they make available to their best commercial customers.[17] Although the act refers only to candidates for *federal* office, station managers understand that an absolute refusal to sell ads to candidates for state and local offices would be seen by the FCC as an abrogation of their overall obligation to broadcast "in the public interest."

The Candidate Access rule does not indicate its own triggering mechanism; when, exactly, has a campaign begun? The Supreme Court has offered some guidance (though not much). Such factors as candidates having formally announced their candidacy, as well as the imminence of the primary season by which the parties choose their nominees, will suggest that the time has come to trigger the rule.[18]

Equal Time Rule   Often referred to as the Equal Time rule (even though the statutory language is "equal *opportunities*"), section 315 has been part of the Federal Communications Act since its passage in 1934. Indeed, it was born as section 18 of the 1927 Radio Act. The essence of the rule is found in 315(a): anytime a "legally qualified candidate for any public office" is permitted to "use" a broadcasting station, the station's owner must "afford equal opportunities to all other such candidates for that office." The rule also prohibits stations from exercising the "power of censorship over the material broadcast under the provisions of this section." An important corollary: broadcast licensees are immune from liability, such as for defamation, stemming from the content of candidate-placed political ads over which the licensees, after all, have no control.[19]

---

17. Under the McCain-Feingold campaign finance law, upheld in relevant part by the Supreme Court, candidates must now include their faces in their TV ads, saying something to the effect that they "approved this message," in order to qualify for the lowest ad rates. *McConnell v. Federal Election Commission*, 540 U.S. 93 (2003).

18. *CBS, Inc. v. FCC*, 453 U.S. 367 (1981). The Candidate Access rule does not require that stations give their time away, only that they be willing to sell airtime. *Kennedy for President Committee v. FCC*, 636 F.2d 432 (D.C. Cir. 1980); *Kennedy for President Committee v. FCC*, 636 F.2d 417 (D.C. Cir. 1980).

19. *Farmers Educational & Cooperative Union of America v. WDAY*, 360 U.S. 525, 530 (1959).

Note two differences between the Equal Time rule and the Candidate Access rule discussed earlier. Unlike section 312, section 315 applies to candidates for office at all levels of government, from local dogcatcher to president of the United States. Also, candidates earn a right to access under section 315 only if another candidate for the same office has already been permitted to "use" the station's airwaves. That a political campaign has begun is not sufficient to trigger the rule.

What Is a "Legally Qualified" Candidate?   The FCC employs four guidelines to determine if an individual is a "legally qualified" candidate for purposes of applying Section 315. First, the candidate must have publicly announced his or her intention to run for office. This rule seems straightforward enough, although candidates are often quite coy about whether they are in fact running for office or reelection. The longer they can avoid making the official announcement, the longer they can continue to appear on camera in various capacities without triggering the Equal Time rule.

Second, the candidate must be legally qualified to hold the particular office. Winning enough votes is a necessary but not a sufficient condition to be elected to public office. For example, the president must be a natural-born citizen and must be at least thirty-five when assuming office. Anyone who has already served two terms as president can no longer be a legally qualified candidate for that office. Senators must be at least thirty years old, representatives at least twenty-five; members of both houses must be residents of the districts or states they represent. Similar age and residency requirements, and in some cases, term limits, apply to many state and local offices as well.

Third, the candidate must be qualified for a place on the ballot (or as a write-in candidate). In most circumstances, simply announcing that you are a candidate does not earn you a place on the ballot come Election Day. You must file a petition containing a sufficient number of qualified voters' signatures with the Board of Elections or similar governmental entity to meet local rules for ballot placement. If the office for which you are running is permitted to have write-in candidacies, you can be a legally qualified candidate for the purposes of section 315 by meeting whatever qualifications are prerequisite to that status.

Finally, candidates must have been nominated for the office by a recognized political party, or at least must have made a "substantial showing" of their candidacy. Making a "substantial showing" in this context does not necessarily mean that your polling numbers suggest that you have a good chance of winning the race. Rather, this part of the test for determining a candidate's status should be thought of as more of a "looks like a duck, quacks like a duck" yardstick. What kinds of behaviors do candidates generally engage in? the FCC asks itself. They make speeches about political topics, they establish a campaign headquarters (for low-budget candidates vying for minor offices, this might be their own home or the home of a supporter), they distribute campaign literature, they assemble a committee to help them with their campaigns. These are the kinds of behaviors that count as making a "substantial showing."

"Using" the Airwaves   The Equal Time rule is triggered when a broadcast station permits a candidate for elected office to use its airwaves. But what does it mean to *use* a station's airwaves? First, the appearance must be a "positive" one, which does not mean that the candidate has to come off well on camera, or say clever things. Rather, the rule is intended to exempt such scenarios as when candidate A, in the course of a media appearance, uses the voice or picture of opposing candidate B while criticizing the opponent. Such a scenario would not constitute a "use" by candidate B.

Use of the airwaves does not have to be for the purpose of delivering political messages at all. Indeed, TV stations had to be careful about showing old Arnold Schwarzenegger or Ronald Reagan movies at election time. When in 1994 NBC broadcast the movie *Necessary Roughness*, which included an appearance by lawyer-turned-actor-turned-politician Fred Thompson, it had to give free airtime to Democrat Jim Cooper, Thompson's opponent in the Senate race in Tennessee. As the FCC has ruled in numerous cases, Cooper was not entitled to an amount of time equivalent to the entire running time of the film, but only to the amount of time that Thompson appeared on screen—four minutes and thirteen seconds. Only if a candidate is in charge of the TV broadcast does "equal time" mean "equivalent to the entire broadcast's length."

Even tongue-in-cheek candidate appearances constitute a use for purposes of the Equal Time rule. Comedian Pat Paulsen, who made his own mock candidacy for president a running gag on the *Smothers Brothers Comedy Hour*, continued the joke in the 1972 campaign and actually filed as a candidate for the Republican nomination. A problem emerged, however. He was also to appear as a guest on a decidedly nonpolitical program called *The Mouse Factory*, owned by Disney. The FCC ruled that stations airing that episode would indeed incur the usual section 315 obligations, and a federal appellate court upheld the commission. The court rejected Paulsen's argument that the commission's ruling applied to entertainers as a class denied them the Constitution's promise of equal protection under law, because only they would have to choose between running for office and their usual way of making a living.[20]

Courts have generally interpreted the language in section 315 warning broadcast licensees not to censor "material broadcast under the provisions of this section" as applicable to more than just one candidate's free use of airtime to respond to another candidate's triggering "use." Rather, courts assume that the provision applies to all

---

20. *Paulsen v. FCC*, 491 F.2d 887 (9th Cir. 1974). TV personality Stephen Colbert likely would have been treated similarly had his own tongue-in-cheek run for the presidency in 2008 been carried further. Instead, he took no further action when South Carolina ruled he had not satisfied the state's requirements to be placed on the primary ballot. See also *In re William H. Branch*, 101 F.C.C. 2d 901 (1985), *aff'd*, *Branch v. FCC*, 824 F.2d 37 (D.C. Cir. 1987) (local newscaster's run for town council triggers section 315).

candidate speech during an election campaign, including political ads candidates place on TV and radio stations.[21]

The "no censorship" rule has frequently caused grief for station managers. In 1972, one of the candidates for the Democratic Party's nomination for U.S. senator from Georgia, J. B. Stoner, used a campaign ad that was as overtly racist as one can imagine: "The main reason why niggers want integration" is that they "want our white women," he charged. Stoner further disparaged all of his opponents for office as "race mixers," warning that "you cannot have law and order and niggers too." The NAACP and the mayor of Atlanta sought a declaration from the commission that stations could not be forced to run such an ad, in part because reactions to it could jeopardize public safety. But the commission rejected their challenge.[22] In 1980, the Citizens Party ran a radio ad on behalf of its presidential candidate, Barry Commoner, that began with an exasperated male voice shouting "Bullshit! . . . Carter, Reagan, and Anderson. It's all bullshit!" Commoner's voice then took over, with the candidate lamenting that he had to use "such strong language" to get anyone's attention. When NBC initially refused to run the ad, Commoner appealed to the FCC, which ruled in his favor.[23] And in the 1990s, several pro-life candidates sought to run ads that included highly graphic images of aborted fetuses. The management of WAGA-TV in Atlanta agreed to run such ads from congressional candidate Daniel Becker, but only at times of day when the number of children in the audience would be small. The FCC sided with the station, but the D.C. Circuit Court of Appeals reversed the commission's decision and held that even such "channeling" of offensive messages to late-night hours was a violation of both section 312(a) and section 315.[24]

Statutory Exemptions to the Equal Time Rule In 1959 Congress amended section 315 to exempt certain categories of candidate appearances from triggering stations' obligations to opposing candidates. The amendments cover candidate appearances on newscasts, news interview programs, and documentaries, as well as appearances in on-the-spot coverage of news events. Let us look at each of these in a bit more detail.

The newscast exemption covers not only such obvious kinds of programs as *NBC Nightly News* or *ABC World News Tonight* but also newsmagazines such as *20/20*, *Primetime Live*, and *Dateline NBC*, as well as the networks' morning news/variety programs, such as *Today* and *Good Morning America*. As part of its responsibility for the day-to-day administration of section 315, the FCC has also granted exemptions, on a case-by-case basis, to various syndicated talk shows.[25]

21. *Hammond for Governor Committee*, 69 F.C.C. 2d 946, 947 (1978).

22. *Letter to Lonnie King*, 36 F.C.C. 2d 635 (1972).

23. *In re Complaint of Barry Commoner and LaDonna Harris against NBC Radio*, 87 F.C.C. 2d 1 (1980).

24. *Becker v. FCC*, 95 F.3d 75 (D.C. Cir. 1996).

25. See for example, *Multimedia Entertainment, Inc.*, 56 Rad. Reg. 2d (P & F) 143 (1984) (covering the Phil Donahue program).

In 1989, the commission ruled that some but not all of the weekly *McLaughlin Group* was beyond section 315's reach. At the time of the FCC ruling, the typical *McLaughlin* program consisted of a short news clip, often borrowed from another network, followed by a few minutes of discussion about that event by the show's four panelists. This "news clip, then discussion" format was repeated two or more times during the course of the program. The FCC ruled that a candidate appearance on one of the prerecorded news clips was exempt from the Equal Time rule but that the same candidate's appearance in the studio, participating in a panel discussion with the small group of journalists, might not be exempt. The D.C. Circuit Court of Appeals upheld the FCC's decision.[26]

News interview programs are exempt if they are regularly scheduled programs, rather than ad hoc "meet the candidates" events. If a network or a local station pre-empted regular programming to interview one candidate for an hour, all other bona fide candidates for the same office would be able to make an Equal Time claim. Thus, any of the well-known Sunday morning programs on the various networks, such as *Meet the Press*, *This Week*, and *Face the Nation*, can invite one candidate for office onto the show without having to invite all other announced candidates onto that or later editions of the program. Regularly scheduled programs, only part of which involve the host interviewing political figures, have also been exempted from section 315. Included in this mix have been programs conducted by Jerry Springer, Sally Jessy Raphael, Bill Maher, and even Howard Stern.[27]

Documentary programs are exempt from section 315's provisions only if the candidate's appearance is "incidental" to the subject matter of the program. The candidate cannot *be* the subject matter. The commission has offered several criteria to help determine whether a candidate appearance is truly "incidental": the program should not have been designed to aid or advance the candidate's campaign, the decision to have the candidate appear in the documentary should have been made on the basis of "bona fide news judgment," and the candidate should not have had any control over the format or the production of the broadcast.

The on-the-spot news exemption covers a wide range of situations, most of which tend to favor the interests of incumbents seeking reelection. A public official might show up at the scene of a natural disaster or at a ribbon-cutting ceremony for a new shopping center. Both would be news events. So too would press briefings and press conferences. Indeed, in the context of twenty-four-hour news coverage, the real difference between the newscast and on-the-spot coverage exemptions seems to be whether the candidate participates in an event deemed sufficiently newsworthy for

---

26. *In re Oliver Productions, Inc.*, 4 F.C.C. Rcd. 5953 (1989), upheld in *Telecommunications Research and Action Center v. FCC*, 26 F.3d 185 (D.C. Cir. 1994).

27. See, respectively, *Request of Multimedia Entertainment*, 9 F.C.C. Rcd. 2811 (1994); *Request of Multimedia Entertainment*, 6 F.C.C. Rcd. 1798 (1991); *Request of ABC*, 15 F.C.C. Rcd. 1355 (1999); and *Request of Infinity Broadcasting*, 18 F.C.C. Rcd. 18603 (2003).

the TV news not just to cover but to cover *live* instead of waiting for the evening news.

Under what circumstances a staged debate between political candidates is exempted as an on-the-spot news event has been a long-running and complicated question for the FCC, Congress, and the courts. Strictly enforced, Section 315 would seem to suggest that every single bona fide candidate for a given office would have to be invited. Indeed, Congress felt the need to create special legislation suspending the rule so that the networks could have Kennedy and Nixon debate alone. The current rules are much more relaxed. Broadcast stations can "cover" a debate sponsored by a non-profit group such as the League of Women Voters, or by the candidates themselves (as long as the broadcasters retained editorial control). Indeed, broadcasters can themselves sponsor debates, without incurring an obligation to invite every single candidate.[28]

Regulation of Sexually Oriented Speech

It was the wardrobe malfunction seen around the world. And in this country, the effects on the broadcast industry of Justin Timberlake's baring of Janet Jackson's breast during their halftime performance at the 2004 Super Bowl have been profound. The FCC received over 500,000 complaints about the event—mind you, the vast majority of these were organized mailings by a single public interest group, but still, no government agency can afford to ignore that kind of outpouring. CBS itself was fined $550,000 for that Super Bowl moment. More significantly, after several false starts, in 2006 Congress increased the statutory fine for broadcast indecency tenfold, from $32,500 to $325,000 per incident.

THINGS TO REMEMBER

Broadcast Regulation and Political Campaigns

- The Candidate Access rule tells stations that they must make their airwaves available to persons running for federal office and that any advertising time they sell to candidates must be at the lowest rates available.
- The Equal Time rule provides that stations who permit one candidate (for *any* elected office) to "use" their airwaves must provide a comparable time slot to all other candidates for the same office. Not all appearances are "uses," however; among the exemptions are appearances on news and news interview programs, and on documentaries whose subject matter is something other than the candidate.
- Stations are not permitted to censor candidates' speech, whether on unpaid news programs or on paid advertisements.

---

28. *Amsterdam v. KITV 4 Television Station*, 2010 U.S. Dist. LEXIS 91021 (D. Haw. 2010).

The FCC fined CBS $550,000 for the Super Bowl "wardrobe malfunction." But a 2011 federal appellate decision involving an episode of NYPD Blue held that the FCC's indecency policies are unconstitutionally vague as applied to brief depictions of nudity, thus suggesting that the fine against CBS for the Janet Jackson incident also cannot stand. *ABC, Inc. v. FCC*, 2011 U.S. App. LEXIS 72 (2nd Cir. 2011).

Notice that reference was made to *indecency* in the preceding paragraph, not *obscenity*. To be sure, the U.S. Code also has a provision (section 1464) forbidding the use of the airwaves to broadcast obscenity. Such a prohibition has been part of our broadcasting system since the adoption of the Radio Act of 1927. But section 1464 also warns radio and TV station licensees that they may not broadcast either "indecent" or "profane" speech. There is virtually no case law concerning the latter,[29] but the courts have had much to say about indecency. The leading Supreme Court case, *FCC v. Pacifica Foundation*, resulted from an FM radio station in New York broadcasting on a Tuesday afternoon in October 1973 a George Carlin routine called "Filthy Words." The Commission, acting on a single complaint, determined that the station had violated section 1464's prohibition against indecent broadcasting. The broadcast was not obscene in that it was not designed to appeal to "the prurient interest," and it may very well have had "serious literary, artistic, political, or scientific value." The commission's definition of broadcast indecency, however, did not include these two features of the *Miller* obscenity test (see chapter 11 for a review of the test). It was enough that the monologue described sexual or excretory functions in a patently offensive way and that children were likely to be listening. But when are enough children likely to be listening to make an otherwise acceptable program indecent? After several years of sometimes comic wrangling among Congress, the FCC, and the federal judiciary, in 1995 it became clear that broadcast licensees must refrain from airing indecent programming during the hours from 6 a.m. to 10 p.m.[30] The remaining hours are referred to in the industry as broadcasting's "safe harbor."

When the "filthy words" case came to the Supreme Court, Justice Stevens's majority opinion (portions of it only commanded a plurality) emphasized radio's "pervasiveness" (especially its ability to intrude on one's privacy at home) and its accessibility to children, "even those too young to read."[31]

The *Pacifica* decision tells the FCC that it *may* impose sanctions against licensees who broadcast indecent, nonobscene speech; it does not tell the commission that it must or should do so.

After the *Pacifica* decision, the commission's enforcement of indecency restrictions on licensees was virtually nonexistent for a decade or so. Then, in 1987, the FCC imposed sanctions against a handful of licensees, including *The Howard Stern Show*.[32]

---

29. Even in *Fox TV, Inc. v. FCC*, 613 F. 3d 317 (2nd Cir. 2010), discussed a bit later, the FCC abandoned at the appellate level its finding that various programs were "profanity," focusing solely on its allegation that the programming had been indecent.

30. *Action for Children's Television v. FCC*, 58 F.3d 654 (D.C. Cir. 1995).

31. *FCC v. Pacifica Foundation*, 438 U.S. 726, 749 (1978).

32. *In re Infinity Broadcasting Corp. of Pennsylvania*, 2 F.C.C. Rcd. 2705 (1987). A few years later Stern cited the decision as a reason for his move to the Sirius satellite radio network, which is free to broadcast indecent speech at any time of day or night. See also *In re Pacifica Foundation*, 2 F.C.C. Rcd. 2698 (1987) (radio play *Jerker*, about a phone sex relationship between two gay men, offered serious social commentary on the AIDS crisis, but was still indecent).

The Super Bowl wardrobe malfunction incident was followed by a dramatic increase in FCC activity aimed at broadcast indecency. Key to its stepped-up enforcement was its insistence that even the fleeting and isolated occurrence of words like *fuck* and *shit* and compounds based on them could result in liability. Thus the FCC fined Fox TV when at its 2002 and 2003 Billboard Music Awards, Cher and Nicole Richie, respectively, used indecent language.[33] On appeal, the Supreme Court held that the FCC was not overstepping its regulatory authority by tightening the reins in this area, but the Court did not address the litigants' First Amendment claims. On remand, however, the Second Circuit Court of Appeals held that the Commission's indecency standards were unconstitutionally vague, and likely to result in arbitrary and discriminatory enforcement. The court expressed puzzlement, for example, at the Commission's having determined that the musicians' utterances in the PBS documentary *The Blues* were indecent, but that the many expletives used in the opening scenes of *Saving Private Ryan* were not.[34]

Regulation of Children's Television

For the first several decades of commercial radio and TV, there were virtually no legal requirements concerning children's programming, save for general statements from the FCC to the effect that meeting the needs of children was one of the many items included in broadcasters' overall obligation to function "in the public interest." The FCC also imposed limits on the numbers of commercials that could be aired during, as well as immediately before and after, a children's program, but these were rescinded in the 1980s, in keeping with the commission's fervor for deregulation. In the Children's Television Act in 1990, Congress reimposed limits on the number of commercial minutes that could be aired during children's programming (defined as programs aimed at viewers age twelve and younger). Current maximums are ten and a half minutes per hour on weekends and twelve minutes per hour on weekdays. The act's requirement that broadcasters provide programming designed to further the "development" of children was, however, often criticized for its vagueness. It was not at all unusual for TV stations to petition the FCC to accept as evidence of their having met the law's requirements their airing of cartoon programs such as *The Flintstones*, *The Jetsons*, and *Yogi Bear*.[35] The FCC insisted that licensees take the act more seri-

---

33. Specifically, Cher said "People have been telling me I'm on the way out every year, right? So fuck 'em," and Nicole Richie, making reference to her work on the reality series *The Simple Life*, said, "Have you ever tried to get cow shit out of a Prada purse? It's not so fucking simple."

34. *Fox TV, Inc. v. FCC*, 613 F. 3d 317, 333 (2nd Cir. 2010). "It is hard not to speculate," suggested Judge Pooler, "that the FCC was simply more comfortable with the themes in *Saving Private Ryan*, a mainstream movie with a familiar cultural milieu, than it was with *The Blues*, which largely profiled an outsider genre of musical experience."

35. Adam Candeub, "Creating a More Child-Friendly Broadcast Media," 2005 *Michigan State Law Review* 911, 916.

ously; in 1996 the commission adopted rules, still in place, specifying that all commercial stations must air an average of at least three hours per week of programming designed to foster the development of children's cognitive and social growth. The Spanish-language network Univision ran afoul of the requirements in a big way, and in 2007 had to pay $24 million in fines for repeated attempts to have various *telenovelas* (soap operas) count as children's programming.[36]

The Second Circuit Court of Appeals held in 2010 that the FCC's indecency standard was too vague to allow the commission to fine TV stations for having broadcast Cher and Nicole Richie's use of indecent language. Presumably, the ruling will also result in reversing of fines stemming from Bono's use of the phrase "fucking brilliant" to express pleasure at having won a Golden Globe award.

Federal law, then, imposes limits on the number of minutes per hour broadcasters may insert commercials into children's programming and sets extremely modest requirements on the number of hours of programming that must be dedicated to "core" educational TV. A third noteworthy limitation imposed by the FCC under pressure from the courts and the lobbying group Action for Children's Television hold that there can be no paid advertisements for merchandise associated with the characters on a specific program aired during the program.[37] Using as examples two animated programs from current Saturday animated fare, *Strawberry Shortcake* merchandise can still be advertised on *Sabrina* and vice versa.

One of the most dramatic changes in broadcast regulation in the 1990s was introduced in a section of the Telecommunications Act of 1996 requiring that all TV sets with thirteen-inch or larger screens have a microchip, often called the V-chip, preinstalled. The chip is designed to read electronic signals embedded in specified TV programs, thus enabling parents to screen out material they think inappropriate for their children. The chips work on entertainment programming, but not on bona fide news programs. To facilitate use of the chips, the major networks created a rating system that indicates each covered program's age appropriateness and offers warnings about specific features of a particular episode—V for violence (with FV for fantasy violence in children's shows), S for sexual situations, L for coarse language, and D for suggestive dialogue. That V-chips are now on the vast majority of TV sets led a federal appel-

---

36. 22 FCC Rcd 5842 (2007); See generally Lili Levi, "A 'Pay or Play' Experiment to Improve Children's Educational Television," 62 *Federal Communications Law Journal* 275 (2010) (arguing that stations not wishing to do their own children's programming should be given the choice instead of paying into a fund to subsidize stations that will do so).

37. *Children's Television Programming*, 56 Fed. Reg. 19,611 (1991).

THINGS TO REMEMBER

Sexually Oriented Broadcasts

- Section 1464 of the U.S. Code prohibits broadcasting of obscene, indecent, and profane programming.
- Nonobscene sexual programming (even if it includes indecency and, presumably, profanity) may be broadcast between 10 p.m. and 6 a.m.
- There has been a huge increase in FCC actions against indecent and profane broadcasts since the infamous 2004 Super Bowl ''wardrobe malfunction.''
- In response to that same incident, Congress increased tenfold the statutory fine for a single instance of broadcast indecency, to $325,000.
- A federal appellate decision in 2010 held that the FCC's stricter policy of punishing stations for even isolated, fleeting expletives was unconstitutionally vague and thus unenforceable.

late court recently to reject altogether the notion that broadcast content must be regulated to protect children.[38]

Special Regulations Imposed on PBS and NPR

Questions about how to fund public television and radio in the United States and what their programming should consist of have been matters of ongoing debate ever since the passage of the Educational Television Facilities Act of 1962, which first pro-

THINGS TO REMEMBER

Children's Television

- TV stations must air, on average, at least three hours of pro-social programs for children per week.
- Advertising on children's programs (those aimed at viewers aged twelve and younger) is limited to ten and a half minutes per hour on weekends and twelve minutes per hour on weekdays.
- Ever since 1998, most TV sets in the United States have been equipped with a V-chip to help parents filter out undesired categories of programs, but it appears that very few parents use the technology.

---

38. *Fox Television Stations, Inc. v. Federal Communications Commission*, 613 F. 3d 317 (2nd Cir. 2010). Interestingly, most surveys have found that very few parents use the V-chips. Jonathan Takiff, ''Radio Chips in Cell Phones Debated,'' *Philadelphia Daily News*, September 1, 2010, 33.

vided federal funding for noncommercial stations, and the Public Broadcasting Act of 1967, which created the Corporation for Public Broadcasting (CPB) as the system's funding mechanism. In the 1960s, the Carnegie Commission on Educational Television suggested that the United States should adopt the United Kingdom's practice of funding public broadcasting through a predictable, renewable source, such as a tax on the sale of each TV and radio set. This idea was rejected, however, thus setting up a system of oversight in which public broadcast representatives must appear before Congress regularly to justify their budget requests. In recent years, Congress has pressed public broadcasters to reduce their dependence on government monies by obtaining more favorable merchandising contracts with producers of its most popular programs.

Conservatives charge that too much of the programming on National Public Radio (NPR) and the Public Broadcasting Service (PBS) is left-leaning. Liberals also have their gripes with the programming, such as the network's high reliance on government spokespersons. Viewers of all political persuasions complain that during PBS's periodic fund-raising drives, programs with a proven track record of bringing in the pledge calls are repeated ad nauseam.

The Public Broadcasting Act of 1967 gives the CPB responsibility for maintaining "strict adherence to objectivity and balance in all programs or series of programs of a controversial nature." No such restrictions are imposed on commercial broadcasters. The law also dictates the manner in which the corporation's board of directors will be appointed.

Some of the legal differences between public and commercial broadcasting in the United States are directly related to program content. Perhaps most obviously, we do not talk about "advertisers" on PBS and NPR but instead of "underwriters." Messages alerting us as to which individuals, foundations, or corporations have underwritten a program may resemble commercials in some ways, but the legally prescribed purpose

of these messages is to inform viewers, not to persuade them.[39] A corporate sponsor can say who it is and display its logo. It can say what products it makes, which is especially important if its product line and its corporate name are not one and the same. A sponsor's message, however, may not tout the quality of the company's products or services the way most commercials do. Nor may a PBS or NPR station accept paid ads from corporations who wish to use the time to speak out on political issues.[40]

There are additional differences between the regulation of commercial and noncommercial broadcasters. Recall the earlier discussion of statutory exemptions to the Equal Time rule. One exemption, for "on-the-spot" coverage of news events, has been applied to candidate debates. In recent years, the FCC has held that this exemption applies even when the TV networks, or the candidates themselves, are the sponsors. This rule has not applied automatically to debates sponsored by PBS stations, however. Especially in the case of PBS stations owned by the state, which is not an unusual circumstance, candidates who are excluded from a debate can make a First Amendment attack on such editorial decisions. When an Arkansas congressional candidate protested his exclusion from a debate on the local PBS station, the Supreme

39. *Commission Policy Concerning the Noncommercial Nature of Educational Broadcasting Stations*, 97 F.C.C. 2d 95 (1984).

40. *Minority Television Project, Inc. v. Federal Communications Commission*, 649 F. Supp. 2d 1025 (N.D. Cal. 2009).

THINGS TO REMEMBER

Public Broadcasting

- Public broadcasting stations are governed by rules not applicable to commercial stations:
  - Each program or series is supposed to be objective and balanced.
  - Public stations may not have on-air "advertising" per se, although sponsors' names and products or service lines are mentioned in "enhanced underwriting" messages at the beginning or end of each program.
  - Station management may not endorse candidates for office.

Court ruled for the station, but made clear that public broadcasters have an obligation to demonstrate that such decisions are not based on favoritism for some speakers' messages over other speakers' messages.[41] Regular commercial networks would not have to make even this kind of a showing.

Another difference between public and commercial broadcasting stations is the management's freedom to editorialize on the air. Unlike their commercial counterparts, PBS and NPR stations are not permitted to endorse political candidates. As a result of a Supreme Court decision from 1984, however, additional regulations forbidding public broadcasting stations from editorializing about political issues and ballot initiatives were struck down.[42]

Regulation of Cable TV

The cable industry is behemoth. Far more Americans get their TV from cable than from a rooftop antenna. As this chapter was being prepared, the Comcast cable company was poised to purchase the NBC network. But when cable first came on the scene in the 1940s, things were quite different. Originally called community antenna television systems (CATV), cable stations' main function was to pick up and retransmit local TV signals to homes in rural communities otherwise too remote to receive high-quality signals with their own roof antennas. Broadcasters became a bit wary of the new industry in the 1950s, however, when cable systems began using microwave technology to import more distant TV stations. Local stations could thus lose market share.

---

41. *Arkansas Educational Television Commission v. Forbes*, 523 U.S. 666 (1998). The station's journalistic criteria were the candidate's unlikelihood of winning and the shortage of airtime.

42. *FCC v. League of Women Voters of California*, 468 U.S. 364 (1984).

The FCC Begins to Regulate Cable

The danger posed by cable systems to local broadcast stations' bottom lines was the rationale embraced by the Supreme Court in 1968 in support of the FCC's authority—asserted haltingly and tentatively—to regulate cable. Any industry that could interfere, technically or economically, with local broadcast stations was logically of interest to the commission.[43] At issue in this particular case were FCC restrictions on the ability of CATV systems to import distant signals into another market. The commission was afraid that distant stations would fragment local UHF stations' natural audience base.

In the 1960s, when cable companies began to create their own programming, a phenomenon emerged that is now taken for granted: use of the home television set to receive programs that had never been "broadcast." Suddenly the traditional rationale for regulating electronic media differently from print—the use of the public's airwaves—had to be rethought. This situation is even more true today, when the vast majority of U.S. homes are hooked up to cable or satellite systems and no longer have TV roof antennas.

In 1972 a 5–4 Supreme Court majority upheld FCC regulations, soon thereafter abandoned voluntarily by the commission, requiring that cable systems produce a certain percentage of their own programming rather than serve only as retransmitters of others' signals.[44] But the FCC went too far, a 6–3 majority held in 1979, when it required cable systems to open some of their channel capacity to public, educational, and local government uses, as well as for leased access by independent programmers.[45] The FCC was trying to regulate cable systems as if they were common carriers (like telephone and telegraph companies) that must send messages provided by anyone willing to pay the cost. Congress had decided long ago that over-the-air broadcasters could not themselves be regulated in this manner. Since whatever authority the FCC has to regulate cable stems from the industry's relationship to broadcasting, such authority could not allow common-carrier status to be imposed on cable.

Although cable systems do not necessarily use the public's airwaves, they inevitably use the public's telephone poles and streets to lay the miles of coaxial cable needed to connect each subscriber's home to the system's "head end" (its main switching area). Typically, a cable system will sign a long-term contract with a city or similar local government for the right to lay the cable, and the cities have predictably expected much in return, such as annual franchise fees, promises about the quality of customer service, and the inclusion of certain kinds of programming or leased network access (e.g., a station for airing city council hearings and other government events). In 1984,

43. *United States v. Southwestern Cable Co.*, 392 U.S. 157 (1968).
44. *United States v. Midwest Video*, 406 U.S. 649 (1972).
45. *FCC v. Midwest Video*, 440 U.S. 689 (1979).

the Supreme Court placed significant restraints on state and local governments' claimed right to regulate cable programming.[46]

The Cable Communications Policy Act of 1984 was seen by the cable industry as its own Bill of Rights. Largely in response to a public perception that the cable industry abused those rights, however, Congress created the Cable Television Consumer Protection and Competition Act of 1992 to rein the industry in a bit. Under these two laws, as well as FCC and judicial interpretations of them, the federal government is given considerable power to regulate the cable industry, but local governments are given the authority to regulate individual cable system operators. A complication has arisen in recent years, as telephone companies—which have begun to offer video services—persuaded about a dozen states to allow the companies to negotiate at the state rather than local level.

Thus, for example, cable system operators are assured by federal statute that their contracts with local governments for the ongoing right to use local streets, utility poles, and the like will carry at least a presumption of being renewed. At the same time, however, cities cannot artificially create a cable monopoly. Other companies that wish to compete may do so if they can afford to. The economic reality is such that a municipality with more than one cable system is highly unlikely (although in most areas of the country consumers now have a choice between a cable system and a DBS system). Cable systems are themselves not permitted to sign exclusive contracts with individual cable networks that would prevent such networks from appearing on other cable systems.[47]

Cities cannot dictate that the local cable system carry any specific network, although they can require that cable systems carry certain broad categories of programming, including public-access, educational, and government channels, sometimes "PEG" for short. Thus we find, for example, that most cable systems carry C-SPAN and likely too the channel that carries the state legislature and the local city and county governmental bodies. True public-access channels are made available to any interested community members on a first-come, first-served basis. Often the local cable system will train interested community groups on how to run cameras and in whatever other skills are necessary to get a program on air. Federal law dictates that neither the government nor the cable system may censor such public-access programming.

During cable's early decades, there was no question that your cable system would

---

46. *Capital Cities Cable, Inc. v. Crisp*, 467 U.S. 691 (1984). The case was not so much a victory for the cable industry as for the doctrine of federal preemption, pursuant to which valid federal laws trump state or local laws. At issue was an Oklahoma law forbidding advertising for alcoholic beverages. The state's attorney general had determined that this statute was applicable to out-of-state TV signals imported by Oklahoma-based cable systems. Writing for a unanimous Court, Justice Brennan found that the state's law was in conflict with legitimate FCC policies governing the relationship between broadcast stations and cable franchisees and thus struck down the Oklahoma law.

47. *Cablevision Systems Corporation v. FCC*, 597 F. 3d 1306 (D.C. Cir. 2010).

carry the local broadcast signals as part of their offerings. Indeed, retransmission of the broadcast signal was cable's main function. But as time went on and as the cable industry began creating its own programming, some cable systems balked at carrying less lucrative broadcast signals. Thus the FCC, Congress, and the courts struggled for many years with various versions of **"must carry" rules**, requiring that cable systems carry local stations. As a general rule, cable systems now indeed must carry any local stations that request such carriage and must carry them as part of the "basic tier" rather than as part of a premium level of service. Moreover, the local stations that request carriage must appear on the cable system as if they had been received over the air. That is, "channel 7" must appear as channel 7 on the cable system. When a cable system carries a local station that requests to be on the system, no payment is made by the cable company to the local station.

Local stations may, however, opt not to be carried for free by a cable system and may instead negotiate a fee for the cable system to have the privilege of carrying them. This is known as exercising the right to **retransmission consent**. Sometimes such negotiations involve a demand for higher payments;[48] other times they include a demand that the cable system also carry other cable networks in which the local station's parent company owns an interest. The overall system of "must carry," or retransmission consent, has been upheld by the Supreme Court.[49]

To a large extent the Cable Television Consumer Protection and Competition Act of 1992, as its name implies, was designed to curb cable industry excesses that led to numerous consumer complaints. The law requires, for example, that cable systems answer their phones within thirty seconds of the first ring and that they maintain some kind of telephone response system 24/7. Installation requests must be honored within one week, and there must be a system of rebating appropriate portions of monthly fees in response to system outages or similar malfunctions.

Not all of the 1992 act dealt with such minutiae, however. The law also explicitly empowered the commission to impose two kinds of ownership limits on cable companies. First, the FCC could impose vertical limits capping the percentage of channels on a cable system that could be owned by the system operator. Second, the commission could set a horizontal cap on the total percentage of U.S. households receiving some kind of multichannel programming (whether cable or satellite) that any one cable company could service. With respect to the latter, the commission's having settled on 30 percent as its cap was struck down as arbitrary by the D.C. Circuit Court of Appeals.[50]

The Telecommunications Act of 1996, generally intended to foster competition

---

48. Cablevision customers missed the first two games of the 2010 World Series, as Fox held out for higher payments from the cable provider. Joe Flint, "Fox, Cablevision Strikes a Deal that Ends TV Blackout," *Los Angeles Times*, October 31, 2010, A36.

49. *Turner Broadcasting System, Inc. v. FCC (II)*, 520 U.S. 180 (1997).

50. *Comcast Corporation v. NCTA*, 579 F.3d 1 (D.D.C. 2009).

among communications industries, also had some direct impact on cable. It eliminated some regulation of consumer cable fees immediately and provided for a phase-out of the remaining regulations. Also, the law eliminated most barriers that had prevented cable companies, long-distance phone companies, and local phone companies from competing in each other's domains. Many critics have concluded that the main effect of the Telecommunications Act of 1996 has been not the fostering of genuine competition in most markets but "merger (and acquisition) mania." To be fair, the move toward greater and greater consolidation in the media industry had begun long before the 1996 act went into effect; still, by most accounts the legislation has accelerated the rate of mergers and acquisitions.

Cable TV and the First Amendment

As we have seen, the reasons traditionally offered for regulating broadcast media more strictly than print media are spectrum scarcity (not everyone who would like a broadcast license could be given a frequency on "the people's airwaves") and the power of TV and radio to intrude on the privacy of the home and to influence young children. Does cable television manifest these same features of electronic media, and what are the First Amendment implications of the answer to that question? The Supreme Court has had a number of occasions to address this issue and has always approached it with caution. The Court's opinions have not always offered clear guidance, nor have they been completely consistent.

In 1986, in the course of ruling that the City of Los Angeles could not sign an exclusive cable contract with one company, the Court majority granted that cable operators perform an "editorial" role like "the traditional enterprises of newspapers and book publishers" when they decide which cable networks to include on their systems.[51] In the very next sentence, however, Chief Justice Rehnquist equated cable's First Amendment rights with those of "wireless broadcasters." The Court thus did not say which model of regulation it would use in cable cases: print, broadcast, or some kind of hybrid created especially for the new industry.

A few years later the Court was asked to rule on the constitutionality of a broad-based sales tax in Arkansas, from which the state decided to exempt the sales of subscriptions to magazines and newspapers. A local cable system and a cable subscriber sued on free speech and equal protection grounds since monthly cable bills were not also exempt from the tax. The Court held that there was no constitutional defect in the tax system, because it did not discriminate on the basis of taxpayers' speech.[52]

In 1994, the Supreme Court took its first look at the "must carry" rules imposed by the 1992 cable act and instructed a lower court on remand to subject the rules to a level of scrutiny somewhere between the strict scrutiny used for print media and

51. *City of Los Angeles v. Preferred Communications*, 476 U.S. 488, 194 (1986).
52. *Leathers v. Medlock*, 499 U.S. 439 (1991).

the far more lax standards applied to broadcast regulations.[53] The lower court then found the rules constitutional, and the Supreme Court, hearing the case a second time, agreed.[54]

In 1996 the Court had occasion to decide what level of scrutiny should apply to regulations that directly affect cable content. At issue were three related sections of the Cable Television Consumer Protection and Competition Act of 1992 that all governed how cable systems might deal with sexually indecent material on leased-access and public-access stations. Justice Breyer, in an opinion that only at some points commanded enough votes to constitute a majority, refused to commit the Court to any of the competing models—print, broadcast, or common carrier—for analyzing laws regulating cable content.[55]

In 2000, a Supreme Court majority applied the same kind of strict scrutiny to a cable regulation that it would normally apply to the print media. At issue were sections of the Telecommunications Act of 1996 requiring "sexually oriented" cable channels (a cable channel is considered "sexually oriented" if the majority of its programming is sexually oriented), and the local cable systems that retransmit their programming to subscribers, to "fully scramble" their signals or to limit their transmissions to between 10 p.m. and 6 a.m. The impetus for the regulation was that existing scrambling technologies were generally imperfect, resulting in "bleeding" of the video or audio messages to other channels; households not subscribing to and not interested in "adult" programming might receive it anyway.

In striking down the regulation, the majority found that the degree of self-censorship imposed on the cable industry was plainly unacceptable. Writing for the majority, Justice Kennedy suggested that the Court's decision to employ the strictest level of review in such a case was more a reflection of the regulation's structure than a judicial statement about the overall level of First Amendment protection due the cable industry. The regulation, after all, not only was triggered by the content of messages (sexually oriented ones) but also was limited only to certain speakers (sexually oriented cable channels). That is, HBO or Showtime, even if they aired an occasional program that might otherwise be covered by the rule, would escape liability, precisely because such programs are not their usual content. Far better, Kennedy said, for cable operators to fully block unwanted channels from a given household upon written request from the subscriber.[56]

When, then, are cable systems exempt from the kinds of regulations that are regularly imposed on the broadcast media but that would be clearly unconstitutional if applied to print media? Although the Court has not yet articulated a clear answer to this question, we can intuit a pattern emerging from relevant cases and statutes. In

---

53. *Turner Broadcasting System, Inc. v. FCC (I)*, 512 U.S. 622 (1994).
54. *Turner Broadcasting System, Inc. v. FCC (II)*, 520 U.S. 180 (1997).
55. *Denver Area Educational Telecommunications Consortium v. FCC*, 518 U.S. 727 (1996).
56. *United States v. Playboy Entertainment Group*, 529 U.S. 803 (2000).

THINGS TO REMEMBER

Cable Regulation

- Cable regulation was at first accomplished through a combination of sometimes conflicting FCC policies and rules set forth by local franchising authorities. Congress did not pass the first law governing cable until 1984. The 1984 act was very industry friendly.
- Charges of poor service and inordinately high monthly fees led Congress to create new legislation in 1992, which reimposed some controls and established minimal levels of acceptable service.
- The Telecommunications Act of 1996, however, eliminated most cable rate regulations; it also permitted cable companies, and local and long-distance phone companies, to compete in each other's industries.
- Currently, many of the best-known regulations regarding broadcast speech apply with equal force to cable programming.

---

general, in the case of regulations aimed at indecent speech—sexual programming that the print media may disseminate freely but that can be highly regulated if appearing on broadcast stations—cable is treated more like print. When regulations force broadcast licensees to speak or to otherwise take action—think in terms of speech about political campaigns or rules demanding accessibility for the disabled—cable is subject to the same controls, even though these regulations could not be applied to the print media.

As a general rule, Congress has in recent years included the cable industry within the purview of any new statutes governing broadcast content. Thus, for example, those sections of the Telecommunications Act of 1996 mandating closed captioning apply with equal force to broadcast and cable signals. Some of the older broadcast rules have been amended to apply to cable as well, such as the Equal Time rule and the Candidate Access rule.

Direct Broadcast Satellite Services

While most Americans get their TV signals these days from their local cable companies, about 27 million or so instead subscribe to one of the major direct broadcast satellite (DBS) services, the Dish network and DirecTV. The history of DBS regulation is a bit different from that of cable, in that the satellite industry never had to deal with the problem of getting public rights of way to run cables underground or on utility poles. They beam their signals to orbiting satellites, which then bounce the signals back directly to home subscribers' satellite dishes.

Although the FCC at first tried to exempt the satellite industry from those federal

THINGS TO REMEMBER

Satellite TV

- DBS systems transmit signals directly from satellites to subscribers' home satellite dishes.
- Although the FCC was at first reluctant to regulate DBS, the courts and Congress insisted that the industry be subject to the same kinds of political content regulations and children's TV regulations as are broadcasters.
- A special kind of must carry ("carry one, carry all") rule applies to satellite systems.

regulations governing the broadcast industry that have been applied to the cable industry, the courts[57] and Congress insisted otherwise. As it stands, the Candidate Access rule and the Equal Time rule, the various nonduplication rules[58] designed to protect local over-the-air broadcasters, and the limits on the total number of commercial minutes per hour on children's television all apply not only to cable but to satellite as well. Additionally, a special kind of "must carry" rule applies to DBS systems. Aptly named "carry one, carry all," the rule dictates that if a DBS system chooses to carry at least one of the local stations in a given community, it must carry all of them. This provision was upheld against a trade association challenge.[59] More recently, the D.C. Circuit Court has upheld the FCC's rule that satellite systems may not sign exclusive contracts with apartment buildings that would prevent individual tenants from signing with a competing company.[60]

Chapter Summary

The traditional reliance on distinctions between print, broadcast, cable, and other "new media" is very much in flux as we enter an era of media convergence, wherein communication services are increasingly being provided to end users in a single device.

The Federal Communications Act of 1934 created the FCC; it still provides the

---

57. *National Association of Broadcasters v. FCC*, 740 F.2d 1190 (D.C. Cir. 1984); *Daniels Cablevision v. United States*, 835 F. Supp. 1 (D.D.C. 1993); *rev'd sub nom. Time Warner Entertainment Co. v. FCC*, 93 F.3d 957 (D.C. Cir. 1996).

58. Nonduplication rules permit local broadcasters to demand that cable or satellite operators that import distant stations carrying a specific program a local station is carrying at the same time (say, a specific episode of a series now in syndication) block out the duplicated program.

59. *Satellite Broadcasting and Communications Association v. FCC*, 275 F.3d 337 (4th Cir. 2001).

60. *NCTA v. FCC*, 567 F. 3d 659 (D.C. Cir. 2009). The FCC rule, which uses the phrase "multiple dwelling unit" (or MDU), also applies to cable systems.

basic framework for regulation of electronic media. A major overhaul of the law was accomplished in the Telecommunications Act of 1996, through which Congress sought to encourage competition among and across segments of the communications industry.

The general trend since the early 1980s has been toward deregulating electronic media. Virtually all limits on the number of stations any single person or company may own have been eliminated; so too have several regulations governing media content. The FCC is mandated to conduct an inquiry every four years as to the wisdom of even further deregulation.

Some rules do still apply only to electronic media, however; among them are the Candidate Access rule, the Equal Time rule, prohibitions against indecent programming, and a requirement to provide at least three hours of weekly programming designed to aid youngsters' cognitive and social development. Special rules apply to NPR and PBS stations, which may not use their airwaves to endorse candidates for public office.

Cable television, once only a means of retransmitting broadcast signals to rural areas otherwise cut off from television service, has emerged as the primary delivery system for video in the United States. Regulations governing cable have historically been a confusing and sometimes contradictory array of actions by the FCC, Congress, the courts, and local governments. The Supreme Court in 1996 explicitly refused to indicate what standard of review should be used to evaluate regulations aimed at cable content.

Other means of delivering video programming have emerged in recent years, chief among these being DBS service. The FCC, Congress, and the courts have struggled to decide which, if any, regulations normally applied to broadcast stations should apply to DBS as well.

Chapter 13

COMMUNICATION LAW AND THE INTERNET

I n 2010 the media were abuzz with how seventeen states' attorneys general had pressured the Internet site craigslist into shutting down its "adult services" section, which they saw as the venue for prostitution ads. Richard Blumenthal, attorney general of Connecticut, who spearheaded the effort, expressed concern that current federal law governing the Internet might make it impossible to legally compel the website to permanently close the section. Internet service providers are generally not held liable under current law for violations of law perpetrated by their clients.[1]

Many people use the word **Internet** to describe the totality of the millions of websites and other content to which anyone with a computer and a modem has access. To "go online" is to "use the Internet." But actually the word *Internet* was coined to refer to the technical ways in which the innumerable computer networks worldwide connect to each other. The history of the Internet is intertwined with the Cold War (itself a quaint, anachronistic notion since the collapse of the Soviet Union and the new focus on the so-called war on terrorism).

In 1969 the Department of Defense created the Advanced Research Projects Agency Network (ARPANET) to ensure that the military could continue to carry on sensitive communications even in the event of nuclear war. Not long after, other similar computer networks were developed to link universities, research facilities, businesses, and individuals. The multiple layers of linkages of these and numerous other computer networks to each other formed the basis for the Internet.

The Internet is often thought of as a place, though of course this is a metaphor. It is rather the result of our all having agreed to hook our computers together. Indeed, it is not as much a bunch of computers as it is the way the computers talk to each

---

1. Ezra Silk, "Blumenthal Presses Craigslist Campaign," *Hartford Courant*, September 8, 2010, A1.

THINGS TO REMEMBER

Some Internet Basics

- Begun by the Department of Defense in the 1960s, the Internet was designed as a means of ensuring that government communications could continue even after a nuclear attack.
- The Internet is often thought of as an imaginary place called "cyberspace," leading some theorists to suggest it should be considered the purest of "pure public forums," subject to less government regulation than any other communications medium.

other. Still, the word *cyberspace* is often used as a synonym for the Internet, and we will sometimes be guilty of that practice here as well. The whole notion of the Internet as an imaginary place cannot help but call to mind the discussion of the U.S. Supreme Court's public forum analysis (see chapter 2). There we learned that the Court singled out public streets and parks as the quintessential public forums. But parks, though they may be fine for speech making, are also used for flying kites, jogging, and picnicking. By contrast, the Internet may be the first "place" whose *only* function is to facilitate communication. Some commentators have therefore argued that this new medium is the ultimate public forum, purer than pure, and that government would properly permit more freedom of speech in this place than in any other.

Whole books are written about Internet law, and whole law school seminars are devoted to it. This next section therefore discusses some of the characteristics of the Internet that, if not unique, at least set it apart for many purposes from other media of communication. Then, we examine the relevant Internet case law to date, including libel, trademark and copyright, invasion of privacy, and the sending of sexual messages. Our final section is a short discourse on the issue of what has come to be called "net neutrality."

What Makes the Internet Different?

Many theorists and jurists who have examined the issue agree that the Internet boasts several unique communication features, each of which has significant implications for the application of communication law to this new technology.

An Infinite Number of Information Sources

This feature of the Internet is important because it helps us distinguish cyberspace from the electromagnetic spectrum that governs more traditional electronic media, such as radio and television. As seen in chapter 12, one of the chief arguments used to justify regulations of broadcast media that would be unconstitutional if applied to the print media is "spectrum scarcity." Only so many TV or radio stations can fit onto the spectrum, so not everyone who wishes to obtain a broadcast license can get one. In 1997, the Supreme Court was asked to uphold the Communications Decency Act, which would have made it a criminal offense to transmit indecent sexual messages on the Internet. (A more detailed discussion of the act appears later in this chapter.) One of the government's arguments in favor of the law was that the Federal Communications Commission prohibits the broadcasting of such messages on TV and radio. The Supreme Court, however, found that the Internet is the antithesis of scarcity, in that it provides "unlimited . . . capacity for communication of all kinds."[2]

A Lack of Gatekeepers

Communication with at least the potential of reaching large audiences has traditionally entailed much editorial control. Potential book authors, for example, must find someone willing to incur the cost of publishing and distributing their words, and the publisher will often insist on changes in the original manuscript. Also, only the most established Hollywood movie directors obtain the rights to make the "final cut" on their films. Whatever the traditional mass medium, rarely do a writer's unfiltered ideas make their way to the audience.

By contrast, you get to say pretty much what you want on your own website or blog, in large part because it costs so little to publish in cyberspace. You need only find a unique website **URL** (or blog host or "self-hosting" service) and possess the skills and the software to get started. There is no guarantee you will get many hits, of course,[3] but at least you decide what you want to say, usually with no editorial interference.

Parity among Senders and Receivers

Because traditional mass media speakers often have the backing of huge corporate structures, we all know instinctively the difference in "production values" between a network broadcast or a big-city newspaper compared with home videos or a neighborhood association newsletter. The Internet seems to have changed much of this. Put plainly, there are only so many things one can do to a website to make it slick and professional, and most of these tricks of the trade are equally available to a huge media corporation or to talented, motivated individuals with limited funds. One of

---

2. *Reno v. American Civil Liberties Union*, 521 U.S. 844, 870 (1997).

3. How many people view your site will often be a function of how easily search engines such as Google can find it, a truth that has created a whole industry called "search engine optimization." Tim Barker, "New Lab Teaches How to Get Websites Noticed," *St. Louis Post-Dispatch*, January 15, 2010, B5.

Florida congressman Alan Grayson's critics created quite a buzz, for example, with a low-cost but well-designed site called MyCongressmanIsNuts.com.[4]

It has often been suggested that the growth of the Internet means that we are *all* publishers now. This admittedly glib assertion may come to have important long-term effects on the structure of U.S. communication law. Consider the many times throughout this book's earlier chapters that we saw the courts treat members of the institutional press differently from the rest of us. In chapter 9, for example, we saw the difficulty in deciding who is a "reporter" covered by state reporter shield laws. Should such laws, or a possible new federal law, protect Internet bloggers along with employees of the traditional media? States have been reluctant to apply their shield laws to bloggers who don't at least act like reporters (e.g., by doing their own research rather than just uploading others' work, or by having actual sources to whom they have promised confidentiality).[5]

There are also times when media industries are more protected from libel suits than other defendants.[6] Again, when will or should an Internet "publisher" be considered a mass media outlet? Consider also that the Privacy Protection Act (see chapter 9), the federal law that was enacted in response to the Supreme Court decision in *Zurcher v. Stanford Daily* and which requires in most circumstances that law enforcement officials issue a subpoena rather than searching newsrooms, offers its protection to all persons "reasonably believed to have a purpose to disseminate to the public a newspaper, book, broadcast, or other similar form of public communication." Does not the advent of the Internet mean that virtually *everyone* communicating online can fit this definition?

Extraordinarily Low Cost

Chapter 10 included discussion of a Supreme Court decision involving a ban on residential For Sale signs in Willingboro, New Jersey. One of the reasons Justice Marshall gave for overturning the statute was that it precluded homeowners from using the least expensive traditional means of letting people know they are looking for a buyer. To be sure, Marshall allowed, Willingboro residents were still free to advertise in the newspaper's real estate section or to hire a professional real estate agent, but both those options are more expensive than placing a sign on one's lawn.[7]

Although it would be overstating Marshall's point to suggest that the "free" in "free speech" means free from financial cost, his opinion reminds us that the vigor of our First Amendment rights should not depend on the size of our wallets. This

---

4. "Central Florida Blogwatch," *Orlando Sentinel*, May 11, 2010, B2. The online critic is admittedly sometimes an opposing candidate with traditional financial backing. Mark Lacey, "Clicking on candidate.com, but landing at opponent.com," *New York Times*, September 16, 2010, A1.

5. *Too Much Media, LLC v. Hale*, 993 A. 2d 845 (N.J. Super. 2010).

6. *Philadelphia Newspapers, Inc. v. Hepps*, 475 U.S. 767 (1986).

7. *Linmark Associates v. Township of Willingboro*, 431 U.S. 85, 93 (1977).

logic suggests that speech on the Internet should enjoy a special measure of protection. After all, the For Sale signs in Willingboro would reach the eyes only of those walking or driving by a specific home in the course of their daily activities; depending on the home's location, that could mean only a few dozen audience members. By contrast, the Internet permits speakers to reach an audience of thousands, even millions, at little or no cost.

That it is so inexpensive to reach huge audiences online can be a rationale for either furthering Internet speech or for inhibiting it. On the one hand, Internet speakers seem to be the modern-day equivalent of the "lone pamphleteers" whose outrage at the Crown's imposition of the stamp tax created at least part of the impetus for the American Revolution. The great ease with which Internet publishers can disseminate their messages, however, often irks their audiences in ways not often seen with other media. Perhaps the best example is the phenomenon called "spam," or junk e-mail. This issue is discussed at more length later in this chapter; for now suffice it to say that Internet service providers have often sought legal assistance in their efforts to eliminate such unwanted commercial messages from their systems.

Jurisdictional Ambiguity

Passing reference was made in chapter 4 to a case called *Keeton v. Hustler Magazine, Inc.*,[8] in which the Supreme Court told us that the plaintiff, a New York resident, could sue the Ohio-based magazine empire in a New Hampshire court because *Hustler* distributed some copies of its magazines to New Hampshire residents.

The *Keeton* case was actually a special case of the more general issue of **personal jurisdiction**, which helps courts decide when one state may adjudicate claims involving nonresidents of that state. In 1945, the Supreme Court articulated a general rule to the effect that there must be some kind of "minimum contacts" between a defendant and the "forum state" (the state in which personal jurisdiction is sought). The issue is really one of due process, because it would be fundamentally unfair for citizens of one state to be dragged into the courts of another state in which they had not and never intended to do business.[9] A more recent decision tell us that defendants need not have actually set foot in the potential forum state, as long as some of their activities were "purposefully directed toward" residents of the forum state.[10]

How should these principles apply on the Internet? The matter is complicated by the fact that websites, once they have been uploaded to the Internet, are accessible in every state (and indeed, around the world). Some courts have in fact held that the

---

8. 465 U.S. 770 (1984).
9. *International Shoe v. Washington*, 326 U.S. 310 (1945).
10. *Burger King Corp. v. Rudzewicz*, 471 U.S. 462, 476 (1985).

mere fact of a single resident of the forum state having visited a website is enough to provide jurisdiction against that out-of-state speaker.[11]

Other courts have fashioned a rule to the effect that, at least for some purposes, the creation of a website is not itself sufficient to create personal jurisdiction, especially if it is a "passive" site that does not function interactively—for example, it does not have "leave feedback" or "contact us" options, and it does not offer any products for sale online.[12]

Another kind of Internet jurisdiction issue has popped up in recent years, involving not when a particular court should be able to hear a case but rather when a public school system may have "jurisdiction" to punish students for off-campus website creation. The Supreme Court has not heard a case on this precise issue, and lower courts are in disagreement.[13]

It is an easy thing to engage in anonymous speech on the Internet. (Perhaps you have several different highly idiosyncratic screen names yourself.) What happens if a defendant in a communication lawsuit (or indeed any lawsuit) has to be named "John Doe" because of the anonymity of cyberspace? Some federal courts are very reluctant to accept jurisdiction in these cases, unless there is an allegation of a violation of federal law. Why? Because federal courts are only supposed to adjudicate state law claims when the plaintiff and defendant are from different states—when the court has diversity of citizenship jurisdiction. When the defendant is a "John Doe" hiding behind an Internet screen name, there is no way of knowing whether the litigants are from different states.[14]

The Internet is not merely a nationwide but rather a worldwide communication medium, which leads to some unusual jurisdictional and enforcement issues. Later in this chapter we discuss *Reno v. American Civil Liberties Union*, the 1997 case that produced the Supreme Court's very first Internet decision. The issue involved was the constitutionality of the Communications Decency Act, which sought to protect children from unsolicited transmission of sexual materials online. For now, it is worth noting that one of the problems involved in such legislation is that sexually oriented websites can originate halfway around the world just as easily as they can from the next state or the next block. How can we possibly enforce American obscenity law against a website operator doing business halfway around the globe?

---

11. See, for example, *Internet Solutions Corporation v. Marshall*, 39 So. 3d 1201 (Fla. 2010); *Kauffman Racing Equipment, LLC v. Roberts*, 930 N.E. 2d 784 (Ohio 2010). But see *Cornelius v. Deluca*, 2010 U.S. Dist. LEXIS 40640 (D. Idaho 2010) (online customers in forum state actually having purchased products from defendant necessary to establish jurisdiction).

12. Scott Brinkerhoff, "Traveling Through the Jungle of Personal Jurisdiction in the Internet Age," 12 *SMU Science and Technology Law Review* 83, 88 (2008).

13. See, for example, *Layshock v. Hermitage School District*, 593 F. 3d 249 (3rd Cir. 2010) (no "jurisdiction" where student used private, off-campus computer to create website mocking principal); but see *J.S. v. Blue Mountain School District*, 593 F. 3d 286 (3rd Cir. 2010) (jurisdiction does exist when such mocking runs risk of disrupting school).

14. *McMann v. Doe*, 460 F. Supp. 2d 259 (D. Mass. 2006).

THINGS TO REMEMBER

Unique Features of the Internet

- It is theoretically possible to carry an infinite amount of information on the Internet.
- Its basic structure does not require the use of "gatekeepers." Anyone who wants to post messages can do so.
- On the Internet, consumers and "publishers" are usually the same people.
- Even on a humble budget, individuals can make their online presence appear as slick and professional as that of a multibillion-dollar corporation.
- Because information posted on the Internet is available to anyone nationwide (and worldwide), courts have had to rethink the matter of personal jurisdiction (i.e., when it is appropriate for one state's courts to accept jurisdiction over a nonresident of that state).
- In recent years courts have struggled with how much authority school administrators should have in regulating students' off-campus use of the Internet.

Developments in Communication Law Online

Although the Internet is still young, a fair amount of relevant communications case law and legislative activity has already accumulated. In the next sections we examine six separate areas of communication law as applied to cyberspace: libel, trademark and copyright, privacy, regulation of advertising, sexually oriented messages, and net neutrality.

Libel Online

If one subscriber to an online service uses the Internet to engage in defamatory speech, should the plaintiff be able to recoup damages from the service provider, or only from the individual speaker? The case law was at first disturbingly mixed, creating a pattern in which service providers invited liability if they ever edited their users' postings.[15] Congress found this state of affairs unacceptable, not wanting to discourage Internet service providers (ISPs) from taming their clients' excesses, and so inserted into the Telecommunication Act of 1996 assurance that "no provider or user of an interactive computer service shall be treated as the publisher or speaker of any information provided by another information content provider." As a result of the provision, now found in section 230 of the Communications Decency Act, AOL es-

---

15. *Cubby, Inc. v. CompuServe, Inc.*, 776 F. Supp. 135 (S.D.N.Y. 1991) (no liability where the service provider makes clear in its marketing that it does not intend to edit users' postings); *Stratton Oakmont, Inc. v. Prodigy Services Co.*, 23 Media L. Rep. (BNA) 1794 (N.Y. Sup. Ct. 1995) (liability can obtain where the service indicates it does).

caped liability in a defamation brought against online columnist Matt Drudge, even though AOL actually contracted with Drudge to run his column on its system.[16]

By immunizing ISPs from most liability, Congress has thus answered at least one of the Internet's challenges for traditional libel law. Other issues must await future resolution. Consider, for example, the distinctions among categories of libel plaintiffs. In *Gertz v. Robert Welch, Inc.*, covered at length in chapter 4, the Supreme Court offered two reasons why the First Amendment demands that public officials and public figures have a difficult time obtaining a libel judgment. One of those rationales was that such persons "usually enjoy significantly greater access to the channels of effective communication and hence have a more realistic opportunity to counteract false statements than private individuals normally enjoy."[17]

Does this reasoning apply with full force on the Internet, one of whose defining

The truly global nature of Internet communication makes it somewhere between difficult and impossible to enforce one nation's laws against "renegade" websites based in other countries.

---

16. *Blumenthal v. Drudge*, 992 F. Supp. 44 (D.D.C. 1998). See also *Zeran v. America Online*, 129 F. 3d 327 (4th Cir. 1997) (no liability for AOL when one user created malicious postings falsely attributed to another user, who received death threats as a result).

17. *Gertz v. Robert Welch, Inc.*, 418 U.S. 323, 344 (1974).

characteristics is a relative equality of access for all, as both consumers and "publishers"? Persons who are maligned online can and do respond in kind. Flaming begets flaming. Moreover, the aggrieved individuals can reach an audience as large as the one exposed to the original defamation. Some commentators have suggested that the new communication dynamics of the Internet will soon require a rethinking of the *Gertz* doctrine. Might it not make more sense, some argue, for all Internet participants to be considered public figures?[18]

Not surprisingly given the use of screen names, Internet libel suits often involve anonymous defendants. Courts have struggled to fashion rules governing when it is appropriate to unmask the potential defendants.[19] Several courts have endorsed the "Dendrite test" from a 2001 New Jersey decision, which basically holds that plaintiffs must be able to attribute specific, likely defamatory statements to specific screen names, and that the users of those names must first be alerted by their ISP (or by the court itself) that a subpoena to unmask them may be issued.[20]

In a very different context but still relevant to online anonymity, a federal district court in Georgia held that the state may not require sex offenders to provide, in addition to all the other identifying information inherent in "registering," all of their Internet screen names and passwords. The rule was overly broad, the court ruled, in that the public need only be protected from such offenders' possible use of private e-mail, not their highly public and therefore easily monitored blogs designed for discussion of political issues.[21]

Trademark and Copyright Online

Cyberspace forces us to rethink some of the most basic tenets of intellectual property law. In the online world, we are not certain what it means to make a "copy" of a work, nor is the relationship clear between traditional trademarks and the Internet "addresses" called universal resource locators, or URLs. That the Internet is a computer-mediated form of communication where messages are sent digitally has enormous implications for intellectual property law for three related reasons. First, the Internet makes the mass production of protected works effortless. Second, unauthorized copies can be distributed worldwide in a matter of seconds. Finally, the enor-

---

18. Kaitlin M. Gurney, "MySpace, Your Reputation: A Call to Change Libel Laws for Juveniles Using Social Networking Sites," 82 *Temple Law Review* 241 (2009); Aaron Perzanowski, "Relative Access to Corrective Speech: A New Test for Requiring Actual Malice," 94 *California Law Review* 833 (2006).

19. *in re Anonymous Online Speakers v. U.S. District Court*, 611 F. 3d 653 (9th Cir. 2010); *Maxon v. Ottawa Publishing Company*, 929 N.E. 2d 666 (Ill. App. 2010).

20. *The Mortgage Specialists, Inc. v. Implode-Explode Heavy Industries*, 999 A. 2d 184 (N.H. 2010) (endorsing the *Dendrite* test); *Dendrite International, Inc. v. Doe Number 3*, 342 N.J. Super. 134 (App. Div. 2001); see also *John Doe #1 v. Cahill*, 884 A. 2d 451 (Del. 2005) (public officials should have an especially strict burden of proof in order to unmask an anonymous online critic).

21. *White v. Baker*, 696 F. Supp. 2d 1289 (N.D. Ga. 2010).

THINGS TO REMEMBER

Libel Online

- The Telecommunications Act of 1996 gives ISPs virtually complete immunity from liability for their clients' libelous postings.
- Some commentators have suggested that the traditional distinctions between public figures and private plaintiffs be discarded for Internet libel suits, that all persons who engage in "cyber chatter" should be considered public figures.
- Public officials and public figures may have a high burden of proof if they seek to unmask "John Doe" online libel defendants.

mous volume of copying makes it virtually impossible to track down the original infringer in a chain of Internet piracy.[22]

"Copying" in a Digital World   Traditional copyright law does not seem to fit well with the Internet. In the physical world, we recognize the difference between reading something and copying it. You might have seen a funny cartoon or a provocative article in your local newspaper, and perhaps you chose to show it to a friend or clip it and paste it on your door for any passersby to enjoy. You have not *copied* it. On the Internet, however, to read *is* to copy, because we access digital expression by *reproducing* it in our computer's random access memory (RAM) or on a hard drive, CD, or similar medium. Thus, the simple act of reading an online file would, in a predigital world, seem a clear violation of the copyright holder's right to decide if and when a work will be reproduced.

Many commentators have pointed to a fundamental irony here. The Internet is often touted as a revolutionary vehicle for the unlimited exchange of information, yet its infrastructure would seem to give copyright holders a veto over what will be seen and where, power far in excess of what Congress had ever intended. If you cannot even read a protected work on your computer screen without permission, what will happen to the fair use doctrine? After all, in virtually all protected works, some subset of the text consists of the recounting of historical facts, which are themselves not copyrightable.

We might be in violation of copyright law when we incorporate text or graphics created by others on our own websites, and perhaps even when we point visitors to others' protected works online with hyperlinks. Will copyright holders sue you for these kinds of transgressions? Usually not, because you are either "under the radar" or the cost of going after you is prohibitive. But the balance between the rights of

---

22. Jack E. Brown, "New Law for the Internet," 28 *Arizona State Law Journal* 1243 (1996).

copyright holders and the rights of users who may wish to read and to comment on others' works seems to have shifted.

Surely, if the technology itself seems to be tilted a bit too much toward rights holders, laws would be passed to reset the balance. Ah, but no. In fact, there has been a strong legislative trend toward strengthening the copyright holders' control over Internet content even more. The Digital Millennium Copyright Act (DMCA), enacted in late 1998, has been especially vexing. That statute contains a provision making it a criminal offense to circumvent any technological locking device that might be used by copyright holders to prevent unauthorized copying.

Luckily from the perspective of individuals wanting to make fair use of others' works, the law requires the librarian of Congress to report every three years on uses that should be deemed beyond the scope of the anti–encryption breaking provisions. The 2010 statement from the Library of Congress's James Billington tells documentary filmmakers that they may break the encryption of others' DVDs in order to include snippets in their own films for the purpose of comment or criticism. Billington also determined that e-book makers and users are permitted to break encryptions that would otherwise prevent "audio books" from working.[23]

Peer-to-Peer Websites In the Broadway musical *Avenue Q*, one of the characters ponders whether a friend's having made a "mix tape" for her is an expression of friendship, or something more. The reference is to a predigital age. If you owned some long-playing phonograph records (LPs), and some of the songs on them were coveted by a friend, you might make her a copy of her preferred tracks by playing the LP with the phonograph linked to a cassette tape deck. If your friend wanted to make a copy of that cassette for another person, the resulting second-generation copy would be of audibly inferior quality. Third- and fourth-generation copies would manifest yet further deteriorated sound. In short, there would not be much of an incentive or opportunity for the casual copyright infringer to do much damage.

Enter the digital age, and things change markedly. Websites that permit Internet users to upload and share music abound. Multiple copies and multiple generations of copies lose little if any of the fidelity of the original. Millions of Americans use peer-to-peer (P2P for short) sites, resulting in as much as a 25 percent reduction in legitimate sales of music.[24] Not surprisingly, the recording industry finds this unacceptable, and has repeatedly litigated to shut down such sites.[25] Record companies have sued not only the websites themselves, but individual users, and have used the courts to

---

23. "Statement of the Librarian of Congress Relating to Section 1201 Rulemaking," http://www.copyright.gov/1201/2010/Librarian-of-Congress-1201-Statement.html (accessed on September 22, 2010).

24. Dan DeLuca, "Rock's a Hard Place," *Philadelphia Inquirer*, September 19, 2010, H1.

25. *A&M Records v. Napster*, 284 F. 3d 1091 (9th Cir. 2002); *MGM Studios v. Grokster, Ltd.*, 545 U.S. 913 (2005).

unmask users based on their computers' Internet protocol (IP) addresses.[26] In the *Grokster* case, the Supreme Court admitted that the site's clients might use it to share perfectly legal material not protected by copyright, but found the defendant companies guilty of "actively inducing" users to share protected movies and music. The unanimous Court thus distinguished its earlier *Sony* decision (see chapter 6), even while admitting that Sony's ads for its VCRs decades ago also encouraged purchasers to "record favorite shows" and to "build a library" of recorded programs. Within a few months of the adverse ruling, Grokster went out business, with a terse message on its site: "There are legal services for downloading music and movies. This service is not one of them."

Today there are a number of websites that work on a newer business model, trying to establish a symbiotic relationship among artists, distributors, and fans alike. The Second Circuit Court of Appeals ruled in 2009 that such a structure was sufficient to save the LAUNCHcast site from otherwise rather odious copyright regulation.[27] Was LAUNCHcast the kind of interactive music service that must, under federal law, pay a fee to each and every copyright owner for every song in its system? (More traditional radio stations need only pay a single, blanket fee.) The court was persuaded that the site's clients did not have enough control over what songs they will be exposed to when they visit for it to be considered interactive.

A portion of the Digital Millennium Copyright Act, adopted in 1998, addresses the issue of liability for systems operators stemming from their subscribers' content. The DMCA exempts service providers and systems operators from liability if they do not know of their subscribers' infringing conduct. The exemption will hold also if the provider, once made aware of the existence on their systems of unauthorized copyrighted material, "acts expeditiously to remove or disable access to the material." The law further protects the service provider from lawsuits that might be brought by subscribers distraught over their noninfringing content having been removed from the system without their consent, as long as the provider believed in good faith that the materials had been posted in violation of copyright law. It is also important that the service provider not gain financially as a direct result of the users' infringing activities.

Trademark, URL Addresses, and Website Interactions   One of the most fascinating—and for those directly involved, perplexing—ways in which cyberspace has affected communication law concerns Internet domain names, which are the heart of a website's URL. In the real world many companies can use the same trademark for very different products or services. Thus we have Life cereal and also

---

26. *Arista Records, LLC v. Does 3*, 604 F. 3d 110 (2nd Cir. 2010). Completely legal for-pay downloading sites have carved out a sizable market, too, with iTunes leading the pack at over 160 million users.

27. *Arista Records v. Launch Media*, 578 F. 3d 148 (2nd Cir. 2009).

Life the board game, Thrifty Car Rental and Thrifty Drug Stores, Universal Van Lines and Universal Pictures. In trademark law, this is called **concurrent registration** of marks. Concurrent registration is the norm as long as two businesses are not in direct competition or marketing complementary products that consumers would presume must come from the same source.[28] In cyberspace, however, there can be only one www.life.com, one www.thrifty.com, and so on.

This restriction on the naming of Internet URLs is actually more a convention than an insurmountable technological barrier. It has been suggested, for example, that "master domain name masks" be created so that there would not be just one McDonalds.com, but rather McDonalds1.com, McDonalds2.com, McDonalds3.com, and so forth; such a system would be akin to finding *the* "John Smith" of interest from among a long list of John Smiths in the phone book.[29] At least for now, though, one and only one entity can be assigned the "space" of a particular URL address.

Since there is no universal Yellow Pages to help consumers associate domain names with company names—and Internet search engines such as Yahoo! and Google can produce overwhelmingly large numbers of "hits" in response to a request for one specific site—consumers are often left guessing. The wise company seeking an Internet presence needs to predict as best it can whatever addresses consumers will *guess* might be theirs. Such domain names are thus very valuable commodities and have been the impetus for a flurry of litigation.

There have been at least four identifiable categories of disputes between trademark holders and URL address holders. First are those situations in which the URL registrant legitimately is doing business under a name that just happens to be the cherished trademark of another company. In one often-cited case, a nightclub in Columbia, Missouri, used a URL that included the phrase "BlueNote," which is also the name of a well-known nightclub in New York City.[30] In that case, the court in New York refused to accept jurisdiction, because the smaller club's website was a "passive" one not set up for such interactions as actually buying tickets online. Had the site been more interactive, and especially if it could have been shown that some customers from the New York area had purchased tickets in preparation for a trip to the Midwest college town, the court would have been forced to address the conflict between one company's legitimately obtained URL address and the other's federally protected trademark.

A second kind of legal dispute, especially vexing from a trademark holder's perspective, involves "**cybersquatters.**" These are folks who never actually intend to do

---

28. Xuan-Thao Nguyen, "Selling it Fast, Stealing it Later: The Trouble with Trademarks in Corporate Transactions in Bankruptcy," 44 *Gonzaga Law Review* 1, 34 (2009).

29. Rosanne T. Mitchell, "Resolving Domain Name–Trademark Disputes: A New System of Alternative Dispute Resolution Is Needed in Cyberspace," 14 *Ohio State Journal on Dispute Resolution* 157 (1998).

30. *Bensusan Restaurant Corp. v. King*, 937 F. Supp. 295, 299 (S.D.N.Y. 1996), *aff'd*, 126 F.3d 25 (2d Cir. 1997).

An early Internet trademark dispute involved nightclubs sharing the same name in Columbia, Missouri (left) and New York City. © 2006 Benjamin Reed (Missouri photo). Used by permission.

business using the URL addresses for which they apply; rather, they make money by thinking a few steps ahead of large businesses that, for whatever reasons, did not establish an early Internet presence. One particularly well-known squatter is Dennis Toeppen, who received authorization for hundreds of domain names with familiar rings, from "aircanada.com" and "neiman-marcus.com" to "camdenyards.com."[31] Even though the legal climate is shifting against the squatter—Congress enacted the Anticybersquatting Consumer Protection Act in 1999, which explicitly prohibits buying up URLs one never intends to use in commerce but only to sell back to the more "logical" owner—corporations often find it cheaper to settle with squatters out of court.[32]

A third category of conflict involves URL addresses maintained by companies or individuals who intend to prevent consumers from reaching the "natural" owners of the addresses. As a general rule, such uses will be prohibited if the defendant is a business competitor fraudulently steering customers away, or a shady entrepreneur making advertising dollars on a website the URL of which is a predictable "typo" of the real site.[33] But even the potentially confusing use of a domain name may be permitted if the defendant seeks to make legitimate criticisms of a company.[34] Even more

---

31. *Panavision International v. Toeppen*, 945 F. Supp. 1296 (C.D. Cal. 1996)

32. Zorik Pesochinsky, "Almost Famous: Preventing Username Squatting on Social Networking Websites," 28 *Cardozo Arts and Entertainment Law Journal* 223, 264–265 (2010).

33. See, for example, *Southern Company v. Dauben, Inc.*, 324 Fed. Appx. 309 (5th Cir. 2009); *Wintice Group, Inc. v. Destiny Longleg*, 2010 U.S. Dist. LEXIS 92661 (D. Nev. 2010).

34. See, for example, *Career Agents Network, Inc. v. White*, 2010 U.S. Dist. LEXIS 17263 (E.D. Mich. 2010). There have been cases to the contrary, but these tend to have involved defendants who make otherwise protected political commentaries while steering visitors to other commercial sites.

so in electoral politics, where candidates often use website names that include their opponent's name to steer voters to their own sites, it is pretty clear that the victimized candidate has no legal recourse.[35]

Finally, there can be trademark concerns when one website provides hyperlinks that send visitors to another website, or uses misleading **meta tags** to exploit potential customers' interest in a competitor's products to steer them to a defendant's site. Site A's link to site B might include an unauthorized use of B's logo. Without an appropriate disclaimer, visitors may be misled to believe that B not only has permitted this use but also has in some way endorsed A's products or services.[36] Courts have been especially perplexed by disputes in which defendants "**deep link**" users to inside pages (a click or more away from the home page) of plaintiffs' websites. Such situations further mask the fact that a website detour has occurred.[37] The practice of **framing** (when site B pops up as a window within site A, also potentially hiding from users the fact that they have been detoured) has also raised trademark infringement issues, at least where plaintiffs can demonstrate likelihood of confusion.[38]

Meta tags are the keywords, invisible to the user, that website developers embed in their sites to help search engines such as Google find them. For example, suppose that two commercial websites are maintained by competing discount travel agencies, the aggressively marketed "cheapestfare.com" and the far more obscure "cheapflights .com." If Cheapflights includes "cheapestfare" among its meta tags, consumers who

During the 2010 electoral season, anyone inputting "bobmenendez.com" (Senator Bob Menendez of New Jersey was chair of the Democratic Senatorial Campaign Committee) would be surprised to be redirected to a site touting Republican candidates, such as Sharron Angle of Nevada or Christine O'Donnell of Delaware.

---

35. Mark Lacey, "When Candidate.com is Opponent.com," *New York Times*, September 15, 2010, A18.

36. *Playboy Enterprises, Inc. v. Universal Tel-A-Talk*, 1998 U.S. Dist. LEXIS 17282 (E.D. Pa. 1998); Robert Tucker, "Information Superhighway Robbery: The Tortious Misuse of Links, Meta-tags, and Domain Names," 4 *Virginia Journal of Law and Technology* 8 (1999).

37. Tan Pham, "Been Deep Linked? Apparent Authority Might Link You to Liability," 2004 *Boston College Intellectual Property & Technology Forum* 60802.

38. *Hard Rock Cafe International v. Morton*, 1999 U.S. Dist. LEXIS 8340 (S.D.N.Y. 1999).

use "cheapestfare" as a search engine keyword will also "hit" the Cheapflights web-site. The smaller company will be unfairly riding the coattails of the larger company in this scenario. As one court put it, "using another's trademark in one's meta tags is much like posting a sign with another's trademark in front of one's store."[39]

Databases and Authors' Rights   Another novel issue posed by the Internet is whether publishers, having contracted to purchase the rights to distribute an au-thor's work in traditional print media, may, without further payment or permission, redistribute the work in computer databases. The lesson of two leading cases—one from the Supreme Court, one from the Eleventh Circuit—is "it depends." If the data-base drastically enhances the search and formatting possibilities for users, then the medium is considered a large enough change to require a new contract.[40] But if the "new" medium looks very much like the traditional one, no new contract with the affected freelancers is required. Purchasers of National Geographic's CD-ROM ver-sion, for example, see on their computer screens mock-ups of the exact pages they could have seen in the print version of the magazine.[41]

Privacy Online

The Internet's impact on users' privacy dramatically demonstrates the complex and contradictory nature of this new medium. Certainly the Internet can be, for bet-ter or worse, a privacy-enhancing means of communication. Many pundits have sug-gested that 1993 will be looked back upon as the year the Internet finally "arrived" as a cultural phenomenon. That is when it first became the subject of a *New Yorker* car-toon, which showed two dogs sitting together, interacting intently with a computer screen; one, winking, advised the other that "on the Internet, no one *knows* you're a dog."

Shielding one's personal identity while online, such as by using a screen name un-related to one's real name, has become a cyberspace norm. Sophisticated software also exists for shielding the identity of the computer and the network from which e-mail is sent. The programs do this by stripping off the identifying information on an e-mail and substituting an anonymous code number or term. As any fan of the TV series *24* knows, some kinds of software also route messages through many different relay computers around the world, leaving no record of the path a message traveled.

Even to the extent that cyberspace increases our level of privacy, it is both a bless-

---

39. *Brookfield Communications Inc. v. West Coast Entertainment Corp.*, 174 F.3d 1036, 1064 (9th Cir. 1999); see generally Daniel Devoe, "Applying Liability Rules to Metatag Cases and Other In-stances of Trademark Infringement on the Internet: How to get to 'No Harm, No Foul,'" 90 *Boston University Law Review* 1221 (2010).

40. LEXIS/NEXIS fits into this category. *New York Times Co. v. Tasini*, 533 U.S. 483 (2001).

41. *Greenberg v. National Geographic Society*, 533 F. 3d 1244 (11th Cir. 2008).

THINGS TO REMEMBER

Trademark and Copyright Online

- The simple act of reading a file on a computer screen cannot help but also involve making a "copy" of the file; this fact alone poses a serious complication for traditional copyright law.
- The Digital Millennium Copyright Act makes it a criminal offense to circumvent any software attached to a work by the copyright holder.
- The DMCA also immunizes Internet service providers from liability for infringements made by their subscribers if they were unaware of such infringements.
- Many suits have been brought in recent years alleging that an Internet domain name is too similar to the plaintiff's trademark. Sometimes the defendant is a cybersquatter, someone who obtained the rights to the domain name only to sell it back to the more legitimate owner at a higher price.
- The ease of sharing music over peer-to-peer networks has resulted in as much as a 25 percent reduction in legitimate sales.
- Trademark law is also implicated by the unauthorized linking of one's own website to another, especially if the latter company's logo is used as the link.
- Links that do not fully move a visitor from site A to site B, but rather "frame" B within A, cause special problems; the use of inappropriate meta tags can also be an infringement.
- The Supreme Court has ruled that in the absence of a specific contract clause one way or the other, media outlets may not upload their freelancers' work into a database such as NEXIS without the freelance authors' permission.

ing and a curse. Privacy—perhaps "anonymity" is a better word in this context—is usually seen as a societal good; it permits us to try out new ideas without having to commit prematurely to those ideas. Personal and group privacy have been essential components of the American brand of liberty from the very beginning. Surely Thomas Paine would have been hanged if he had published *Common Sense* under his own name. Yet privacy can be a dangerous thing too, perhaps more so on the Internet than ever before. Cyberspace anonymity enables organized crime and terrorist networks to conspire and can make it far easier for petty crooks to defraud the unwary and abscond with their profits long before their nefarious deeds have been detected.[42]

The digitized world also diminishes our personal privacy in dramatic ways. By its very infrastructure, as a worldwide interconnected network of countless smaller computer networks, the Internet both makes the gathering of personal information much less expensive than ever and facilitates sophisticated cross-referencing of data to create highly detailed dossiers on us all. As one writer has suggested, updating the story of

---

42. Jonathan A. Orphardt, "Cyber Warfare and the Crime of Aggression: The Need for Individual Accountability on Tomorrow's Battlefield," 2010 *Duke Law and Technology Review* 3.

the canine *New Yorker* cartoon, "they not only know you are a dog, but they know your favorite leash color and whether or not you have been neutered."[43]

Online Privacy at Work   In the workplace, your employer may have installed software that allows him or her to monitor every single keystroke you make at your own office computer terminal. Inexpensive software abounds for companies wishing to keep track of every e-mail message employees send and every website they visit. According to one survey, over three-quarters of employers in the United States electronically monitor their workers.[44]

The law is clearly on the side of employers; after all, they own the office and the hardware. The Electronic Communications Privacy Act (ECPA), which under many circumstances prohibits anyone from eavesdropping on both voice telephone conversations and digitized transmissions such as e-mail, does not apply to your employer. The pattern of case law makes clear that as long as employers put their workforce on notice that they intend to monitor e-mail transmissions, employees will generally not have legal recourse.[45]

Online Privacy and the Government   Although the Electronic Communications Privacy Act now prohibits unauthorized interceptions of voice and digital messages by both governmental and private agents (including private-sector employers), the law was originally conceived of as an antiwiretapping statute aimed only at law enforcement officials.[46]

The ECPA protects newer e-mail messages more fully than it does older ones. If a message has been stored on an online system for fewer than 180 days, law enforcement officials must obtain a search warrant to read it. To read messages that have been on a server longer than that, only an "administrative subpoena" is required. Such subpoenas can be issued within a law enforcement agency without having to obtain an independent judge's approval.

Critics have pointed out that the length of time a message has been on a server is not a perfect measure of how old the message really is. When Google's Gmail system's users "read" their incoming e-mail, the message stays on Google's server. By contrast, in Microsoft's Outlook, to read a message is to transfer it to one's own hard drive.[47]

---

43. Paul Rosenzweig, "Privacy and Counter-Terrorism: The Pervasiveness of Data," 42 *Case Western Reserve Journal of International Law* 625, 632 (2010).

44. Ariana R. Levinson, "Carpe Diem: Privacy Protection in Employment Act," 43 *Akron Law Review* 331, 340 (2010).

45. *TBG Insurance Service Corp. v. Superior Court*, 96 Cal. App. 4th 443, 451–453 (2002).

46. Of course, often government *is* the employer. In such situations, while the case law is still evolving, it is clear that similar Fourth Amendment doctrines—for example, "did the employee manifest a reasonable expectation of privacy?"—will apply with equal force to interceptions of e-mails and text messages as they did to lower-tech invasions of privacy. See *City of Ontario v. Quon*, 130 S. Ct. 2619 (2010).

47. Achal Oza, "Amend the ECPA: Fourth Amendment Protection Erodes as E-mails Get Dusty," 88 *Boston University Law Review* 1043 (2010).

Federal law differs too depending on whether an e-mail message is intercepted by the government while still in transit to its intended recipient, or has already arrived at the recipient's server.[48] (In the latter case it matters not whether the recipient has actually read the message yet.) The logic for the disparity is that interception of live, in-transit messages involves greater invasion of privacy, in that law enforcement will not know in advance when a "real-time" message being sent is relevant to their investigations. Irrelevant discussions among innocent participants cannot help but be intercepted. With respect to stored e-mail, however, "technology exists [such as keyword searches] by which relevant communications can be located without the necessity of reviewing the entire contents of all of the stored communications."[49]

The Patriot Act, passed swiftly by Congress in response to the 9/11 terrorist attacks, amended the ECPA to give the government more power to monitor e-mail. Specifically, section 216 of the Patriot Act lets the government monitor the addresses to which a computer sends e-mail, the digital-age equivalent of a "pen register" search pursuant to which the government could obtain a list of phone numbers dialed from a specific phone but could not actually listen to the telephone conversations.

Online Privacy and the Private Sector   Going online is an enormously trusting endeavor. We typically must reveal much personally identifying information to ISPs and online vendors, and we trust that they will keep our information secure. Sometimes that trust is betrayed by inadequate software or by misbehaving employees.[50]

Especially complicated are situations in which an Internet service provider reveals clients' personal information to the government. When a properly executed subpoena is administered to the ISP, we expect that the information will be released, and that the affected parties will have no legal recourse. A section of the Homeland Security Act known as the Cyber Security Enhancement Act goes further, relieving ISPs from civil liability for releasing clients' personal data to the government even in the absence of a subpoena, as long as the ISP had a good-faith belief that some serious harm would otherwise result.[51]

ISPs' divulgence of clients' personal data to third parties is not the only controversial privacy issue in our online, private-sector dealings. Also of much concern is cor-

---

48. In-transit interceptions are governed by the ECPA, while the Stored Communication Act (SCA) governs interceptions of messages that have already arrived. Nicholas Matlach, "Who Let the *Katz* Out? How the ECPA and SCA Fail to Apply to Modern Digital Communications and How Returning to the Principles in *Katz v. United States* Will Fix it," 18 *Commlaw Conspectus* 421 (2010).

49. *Steve Jackson Games, Inc. v. U.S. Secret Service*, 36 F.3d 457, 463 (5th Cir. 1994).

50. Jessica Guynn, "Google Worker Fired for Alleged Snooping," *Los Angeles Times*, September 16, 2010, B10; Tim Feran, "Coding Weakness Allows Twitter to be Hacked," *Columbus Dispatch*, September 22, 2010, A9; Jennifer Martinez, "Internet Firms Grilled on Privacy," *Los Angeles Times*, July 28, 2010, B6.

51. 18 U.S.C. § 2702 (c) (4) (2010).

THINGS TO REMEMBER

Privacy Online

- The Internet both enhances and diminishes privacy.
- State wiretapping statutes have generally been interpreted to protect the privacy of e-mail only at the exact moment of transmission.
- The federal Electronic Communications Privacy Act covers both e-mail in transmission and in storage, but damages for unauthorized access are potentially much higher when the intrusion occurs at the time of transmission.
- As long as employers put their workforce on notice, they are generally free to "eavesdrop" on workers' online activities, even keystroke by keystroke.
- The Patriot Act gives the government explicit permission to keep track of the "e-mailing lists" used by any individual computer.
- The Homeland Security Act immunizes ISPs from civil lawsuits for turning over their clients' personal information to the government (even in the absence of a subpoena).
- There has been an increase in the incidence of "John Doe" suits filed by potential libel plaintiffs in an effort to unmask persons who had been maligning them in online discourse.
- The Children's Online Privacy Protection Act prevents websites from gathering information from youngsters under thirteen without parental permission.

porations' ability, exponentially enhanced by the Internet, to gather huge amounts of information about us. Such "data mining" can be spooky, even if it results in tangible benefits. How would you feel if, while you were visiting a website, a pop-up ad said: "We notice you have been here for 15 minutes but have not bought anything. Suppose we offered you free shipping today. Would that help?"[52]

Much outrage has been expressed in recent years by citizens' groups about commercial websites that have been used to gather information from children. In response, Congress passed the Children's Online Privacy Protection Act, which requires that websites targeted at children gain parental permission before collecting personally identifiable information from anyone under thirteen years old. The Federal Trade Commission has been empowered to enforce the law.

Advertising Online: Spam and Deceptive Meta Tags

Internet users express concerns not only about how information is gathered about them but also about the intrusion on their privacy by large numbers of unwanted commercial messages, or "**spam.**" Online mailboxes can quickly fill up with such junk

---

52. Stephen T. Watson, "Growth of Data Mining is Latest Threat to Privacy," *Buffalo News*, July 6, 2010, A1; Elizabeth Weise, "Online 'Cyberbazaars' Practice Fluid Pricing: Web Prices May Depend on Factors That Raise Serious Privacy Issues," *Detroit News*, May 17, 1999, S3.

mail, which is often disguised as personal messages rather than advertisements, a practice called "**spoofing**."

Federal legislation aimed at protecting computer users from unwanted commercial e-mail was signed into law by President Bush in 2003. The law prohibits the use of misleading subject lines and false identities on the part of commercial e-mailers. Sexually oriented e-mail must be clearly labeled as such. Violators may be fined up to $250 per violation, subject to a cap of $2 million. Especially egregious violators may have their fines tripled and may be subject to up to five years' imprisonment.

Critics point out that the so-called CAN-SPAM Act ("CAN-SPAM" is actually an acronym for Controlling the Assault of Non-Solicited Pornography and Marketing) is not as strict as some of the thirty or so state laws it may preempt, notably a California statute that prohibits almost all commercial e-mail to e-mail account holders who did not give explicit permission to send them spam (i.e., an "opt in," rather than an "opt out," system). The Supreme Court has not yet told us whether it sees CAN-SPAM preempting state and local law, and the lower court case law is not definitive.[53]

Spam is annoying to most of us, even when not it is not deceptive. As we learned in chapter 10, materially deceptive advertising is illegal in any communication medium. Thus it is no surprise that the FTC has been vigilant in bringing complaints against deceptive online advertisers. There is also, however, an issue related to deceptive advertising that is unique to the Internet. We have already seen how Internet search engines produce "hits" at least in part on the basis of hidden meta tags created by website managers to describe their own sites. Can there be deception in meta tags alone, even if the readily visible portions of the website itself are wholly truthful?

Suppose a desperate patient inputs "breast cancer alternative treatments." Suppose further that a website pops up touting the many health benefits of garlic (never suggesting that it has any efficacy as a cancer cure) among the first few "hits." If the search engine located that website because the site's meta tags touted garlic as a cancer cure, has the Internet user been deceived? While the vast majority of case law and scholarly commentary about the legal problems associated with meta tags has focused on the role they play in trademark-infringement cases, this generally invisible Internet indexing system can also be the stuff of deceptive advertising. The Federal Trade Commission has ruled in a few cases, but these cases are inconclusive as to this narrower issue because the visible portions of defendants' websites in these cases also included deceptive claims. Still, in recent years the commission has included language

---

53. *White Buffalo Ventures v. University of Texas at Austin*, 420 F.3d 366 (5th Cir. 2005) (University of Texas's anti-spam regulations not preempted by federal law); *Omega World Travel, Inc. v. Mummagraphics, Inc.*, 469 F. 3d 348 (4th Cir. 2006) (Oklahoma law preempted); *Gordon v. Virtumundo, Inc.*, 575 F. 3d 1040 (9th Cir. 2009) (Washington statute preempted). See also *Jaynes v. Commonwealth*, 666 S.E. 2d 303 (Va. 2008) (striking down Virginia's anti-spam law for failing to exempt political and religious mailings).

admonishing errant advertisers to avoid in future ads not only deceptive wording, but deceptive meta tags as well.[54]

Sexual Messages Online

"The Internet is for porn!" So exclaims Trekkie Monster, a lovable but worldly puppet character in the Tony Award–winning musical *Avenue Q*. Regardless of whether you agree with Trekkie Monster, the fact is that "adult-oriented" websites were among the first to turn a profit, and current estimates suggest that the industry is worth over $3 billion.[55] When sexual messages are too easily accessed by minors, or indeed when minors are the target of online predators, however, the state has a compelling interest to intervene. Frequently minors' online chat room acquaintances are middle-aged adults—mostly men but sometimes women—posing as teens themselves.[56] The Communication Decency Act makes clear, by the way, that ISPs are not themselves liable for the stalking and even sexual abuse of minor clients who falsely portray *themselves* as over eighteen.[57]

The desire to protect children from inappropriate sexual messages and content online led Congress to enact the Communications Decency Act (CDA), which was actually Title V of the Telecommunications Act of 1996. The CDA criminalized the use of

---

THINGS TO REMEMBER

Advertising Online

- Precisely because the cost of disseminating e-mail widely is so low, spam has become a major problem on the Internet.
- The federal CAN-SPAM Act is designed to enable computer users to opt out of getting a particular company's messages and offers some protection from unwanted sexually oriented messages, but it may preempt a number of stricter state laws already on the books.
- A unique and unsettled issue posed by the Internet is whether deceptive messages in websites' meta tags are actionable when the text of the visible portions of a site are not deceptive.

---

54. See, for example, *Federal Trade Commission v. Clark*, 2008 FTC LEXIS 97; *Federal Trade Commission v. Westberry Enterprises, Inc.*, 2008 FTC LEXIS 99; *Federal Trade Commission v. Nu-Gen Nutrition, Inc.*, 2008 FTC LEXIS 101.

55. John Horn, "'Middle Men' Advertising Takes Adult Approach," *Los Angeles Times*, August 5, 2010, D1.

56. Janice Morse, "Warren County Woman Allegedly Posed as Teenage Boy to Have Sex with Girl," *Cincinnati Enquirer*, July 8, 2010; Patrick M. O'Connell, "Bond Sought for Woman Accused of Enticing Boy," *St. Louis Post-Dispatch*, October 2, 2009, A2.

57. *Doe v. MySpace, Inc.*, 528 F. 3d 413 (5th Cir. 2008).

a computer network to knowingly transmit any obscene or indecent message to a child under eighteen years of age. Also prohibited was the posting of any such message in a manner that would be "available" to minors, as well as permitting a minor in one's charge (presumably including one's own child) to have access to such online messages. In 1997, however, in its very first foray into Internet law, the Supreme Court overturned key sections of the CDA.

The CDA had criminalized knowingly sending to minors not only obscene, but also indecent, messages. (Chapter 12 explains how indecent speech is by far the broader category.) Violators—who could even include parents sending birth control information to their seventeen-year-old college freshman child—could face up to two years in jail. The core of the Court's opinion is Justice Stevens's finding that there is no reason to subject the Internet to the kinds of special regulations reserved for broadcast TV and radio. Rightly or wrongly, Stevens concludes that sexually oriented material is "seldom encountered" online by accident. He thus applied the Court's least intrusive First Amendment model, the one applicable to the print media.[58]

The CDA soon begat the "son of CDA," as Congress passed the Children's Online Protection Act, which would have taken effect in November 1998 had it not been challenged successfully in federal district court,[59] a ruling followed by two trips up to

---

58. *Reno v. American Civil Liberties Union*, 521 U.S. 844 (1997).

59. *American Civil Liberties Union v. Reno*, 31 F. Supp. 2d 473 (E.D. Pa. 1999), *aff'd*, 217 F.3d 162 (3d Cir. 2000), *vacated and remanded sub nom. Ashcroft v. American Civil Liberties Union*, 535 U.S. 564 (2002), *aff'd*, 322 F.3d 240 (3d Cir. 2003), *aff'd and remanded*, 542 U.S. 656 (2004).

Whether children are likely to inadvertently encounter "adult-oriented" websites was a factual question with which the Supreme Court had to wrestle in *Reno v. American Civil Liberties Union*, its first Internet case.

the Supreme Court. COPA, as it was popularly called, was designed to eliminate some of the flaws the Supreme Court identified in the earlier Communications Decency Act. The law covered only certain kinds of online sexual materials defined within the statute as "harmful to minors." Companies whose websites include such materials could escape liability if they sought to screen out minors by requiring all visitors either to pay by credit card or to cooperate with the company in the creation of some form of adult access code.

In its second and final ruling on the matter, the Court's 5–4 majority was represented by Justice Kennedy, who, while stopping short of actually invalidating the statute outright, suggested that parental use of any of the filtering software on the market might be a more suitable means of protecting children from sexual messages. Not only would filtering software be less intrusive of the First Amendment, he concluded, but it also might be more effective than federal legislation, which cannot reach the huge number of sexually oriented websites that originate in other countries. As a result of the ruling, the case was sent back to the district court for the purpose of, among other things, updating the factual record concerning the performance of filtering software. In 2007, Judge Lowell Reed, of the same federal district court in Pennsylvania that had issued the 1999 ruling preventing COPA from taking effect, issued a permanent injunction against the law's enforcement.[60]

Many commentators have pointed out the irony of expecting the baby boomer generation to depend on computer software to prevent their far more computer-literate offspring from having free rein on the Internet.[61] Still, blocking software has become very popular in recent years. Such software will likely never be perfect, but, as both the Supreme Court majority and Judge Lowell Reed agreed, the First Amendment demands that parents, not the government, decide how much access to the Internet their children should enjoy.

Congress's next foray into the oversexed Internet was the Children's Internet Protection Act (CIPA), which requires all schools and libraries receiving special earmarked federal monies—a $2.25 billion expenditure aimed at "wiring" them to the Internet—to install filtering software to block sexually oriented websites whenever their juvenile patrons go online. In 2003 the Supreme Court concluded that the act did not violate the constitution, marking the first time the justices have upheld a congressional action aimed at protecting children from sexually charged Internet content.[62]

60. *American Civil Liberties Union v. Gonzales*, 478 F. Supp. 2d 775 (E.D. Pa. 2007), *aff'd sub nom. ACLU v. Mukasey*, 534 F. 3d 181 (3rd Cir. 2008).

61. "Technologically savvy teenagers always seem to be a step ahead of adults." Margaret Farley Steele, "For Parents, a New Concern: Teenagers and Laptops," *New York Times*, April 20, 2008, CT1.

62. *United States v. American Library Association*, 539 U.S. 194 (2003).

Writing for a four-justice plurality, Chief Justice Rehnquist rejected the plaintiffs' argument that the Court should, minimally, demand the library play by the rules of a "public forum" (as described in Chapter 2). The Internet, he replied, is merely one way of many that a library can organize its offerings, not too different from a bookshelf. The government should be free from First Amendment constraints when it decides how it wants to spend its money. Moreover, any inconvenience to library patrons wishing full access to the web was minimal, since the law required library staff to disable the filtering software for any adult patron.

There has also been some interesting lower court case law involving public library systems deciding on their own, without any pressure from Congress, to limit Internet access. In 1997, the Loudoun County, Virginia, public library system adopted a "Policy on Internet Sexual Harassment," aimed at least as much at protecting one computer station patron from being offended at what pops up on a neighbor's screen as at limiting any individual's Internet access. The board implemented the policy by installing X-Stop software on all its patron computers. Adult patrons were free to "appeal" the software's "decisions" by providing their name and address and their reason for wanting access to a specific site blocked by the software to the librarian on duty, who would then make a case-by-case determination.

When the policy was challenged, Judge Leonie Brinkema determined that the county's conduct was unconstitutional in that it was not the least restrictive means of achieving its laudable goals. Brinkema's characterization of the Internet stands in stark contrast to that offered by Justice Rehnquist. "Unlike a library's collection of individual books," the Internet is a "single, integrated system," she concluded. For a public library to use Internet blocking software is like its buying a set of encyclopedias and then "laboriously redact[ing] portions deemed unfit for library patrons."[63]

More recently and on the other coast, the Washington Supreme Court opined (at the request of a federal district court) that the state constitution was not offended by a public library's use of computer filters on all its patron terminals, even if the staff refused to unlock the filters on request. (Staff would on a case-by-case basis determine if a specific site sought by a patron had been "improperly" blocked by the filtering software.) The library's policy not only sought to block sexually oriented websites, but also prohibited access to any interactive sites, such as chat rooms.[64]

Regulation of sexual messages on the Internet raises at least one more novel issue beyond that of how best to protect children from harmful websites and chat rooms. Recall the mechanics of the Supreme Court's *Miller* test for defining obscenity, described in more detail in chapter 11. The test depends upon reference to "contemporary *community* standards," and the Court has made clear that this refers to a

---

63. *Mainstream Loudoun v. Board of Trustees of the Loudoun County Library*, 2 F. Supp. 2d 783, 793–794 (E.D. Va. 1998) (rejecting motion to dismiss), 24 F. Supp. 2d 552 (E.D. Va. 1998) (granting summary judgment to plaintiffs).

64. *Bradburn v. North Central Regional Library*, 231 P.3d 166 (Wash. 2010).

statewide or local standard, not a nationwide one. If sexual images are made available on a computer bulletin board, can its operators therefore be prosecuted anywhere, using the standards of a much more conservative community rather than their home state? The Sixth Circuit Court of Appeals concluded that the answer is "yes" in a case involving a sexually oriented site managed by a California couple who allowed an undercover cop from Tennessee to subscribe to their service and to purchase videos.[65]

Net Neutrality

Congress set up the Federal Commissions Commission (née the Federal Radio Commission in 1927) to regulate individual broadcast TV and radio stations. Nowhere in the Federal Communications Act is the commission given permission to regulate content on the Internet. But in 2008 the commission determined the "ancillary powers" doctrine (described in more detail in chapter 12) gave it authority to insist that Comcast stop disfavoring video-sharing sites like BitTorrent by making their streaming move more slowly on the network.[66] In 2010 the D.C. Circuit Court of Appeals agreed with Comcast that the commission had overstepped its authority.[67] In response, the Commission issued a Report and Order in December, 2010, asserting that several provisions of the Federal Communications Act other than the ancillary powers doctrine give it broad authority to regulate the Internet. The new rules, which cover only wired and not wireless broadband Internet service providers, demand that

---

THINGS TO REMEMBER

Sexual Messages Online

- The Communications Decency Act, Congress's first attempt to protect children from inappropriate sexual messages and content in cyberspace, was struck down by the Supreme Court in 1997.
- The Children's Online Protection Act also has never been permitted to take effect; the federal judge whose injunction was eventually upheld by the Supreme Court suggested parents use some form of Internet blocking device instead.
- To date, the only federal law designed to protect children from sexual messages online to be upheld by the Supreme Court is the Children's Internet Protection Act, which requires libraries receiving certain kinds of federal grants to use filtering software on any computers used by minors.
- We have no definitive word from the Supreme Court yet on if and how the First Amendment limits public libraries from, on their own initiative, blocking sexually oriented websites. The lower court case law is mixed.

---

65. *United States v. Thomas*, 74 F.3d 701 (6th Cir. 1996).
66. 23 F.C.C.R. 13028 (2008).
67. *Comcast v. FCC*, 600 F. 3d 642 (D.C. Cir. 2010).

THINGS TO REMEMBER

Net Neutrality

- Net Neutrality is the principle that Internet service providers cannot favor some clients over others in terms of the amount of bandwidth or speed.
- The FCC's attempt to use the auxiliary powers doctrine to foster net neutrality was struck down by an federal appellate court.
- It is possible that the commission will instead argue that the Internet is or should be regulated by a "common-carrier" model, akin to the old-fashioned phone company.

such companies not discriminate "unreasonably" in granting access and setting prices to clients wishing to user their network. The Commission warns such companies too that charging some clients more for higher-speed access (referred to as "pay for priority" in the document) would likely be deemed discriminatory.[68]

Chapter Summary

The Internet, developed as part of a Department of Defense program aimed at ensuring the survival of intragovernmental communications in case of nuclear war, has revolutionized the exchange of information. It boasts a number of unique features—a lack of gatekeepers (a not entirely uncontroversial assertion, given our new dependency on search engines), the potential for carrying infinite amounts of data, a kind of parity between content provider and consumers, and an extraordinarily low cost of data transmission—and each poses challenges to traditional legal doctrines.

Cyberspace law is still a new phenomenon. There have been only a handful of Supreme Court cases, but there has been a fair amount of congressional activity in this area, and a body of case law has begun to develop at the lower courts. Among some of the communication law issues posed by the Internet are the following evolving questions:

- Are bloggers "reporters" within the meaning of reporter shield laws?
- Who has a right to send us e-mail? To monitor our e-mail?
- What does it mean to be a public figure in cyberspace for the purpose of libel law?
- How much of a right to anonymous speech should be respected online?
- How should courts determine if they even have jurisdiction to hear an Internet dispute?

---

68. *In the Matter of Preserving Open Internet Broadband Industry Practices.* Report and Order. FCC 10-201 (Dec. 23, 2010).

- How should we balance the interests of copyright holders against those who envision a more free-form kind of communication online, in which we all build on each other's work?
- How much authority should the federal government have to regulate the flow of data online?

Perhaps most fundamentally, because the United States still has different models of regulation applied to different types of media (print, broadcast, cable), we need to know which model will apply to the Internet. Although the print model has thus far been embraced for the most part, it is not clear that this will always be the case.

Glossary

absolute privilege. Complete immunity from libel suits provided to elected officials while carrying out their official duties.

absolutist theory. Theory of First Amendment jurisprudence emphasizing the absolute prohibition ("Congress shall make *no* law") upon antispeech regulations provided in the First Amendment.

acquired distinctiveness. A characteristic attributed to a trademark that was once merely descriptive (e.g., "American" Airlines) but that has become associated in the public's mind with a specific company.

actual damages. Monies awarded to plaintiffs who prove that they have been damaged.

actual malice. The level of fault required in libel cases governed by *New York Times Co. v. Sullivan*: the defendant published defamatory material either knowing it was false or "with reckless disregard as to truth or falsity."

ad hoc balancing. Method of First Amendment adjudication that balances, on a case-by-case basis, free speech interests against whatever competing interests are involved.

administrative agency. Any of the many agencies, such as the Federal Communications Commission (FCC) and the Federal Trade Commission (FTC), created to engage in rule making consistent with established law.

administrative complaint. Document filed by a federal agency alleging specific wrongdoing to be adjudicated by an administrative law judge.

administrative law judge. A judge who hears disputes between individuals and regulatory agencies; a hearing before an administrative judge is usually required before proceeding to federal court.

affirmative disclosure. Specific facts that the Federal Trade Commission may require advertisers to disclose in future advertising.

Alien and Sedition Acts. Very early laws (1798) criminalizing statements critical of the government.

amicus brief. An argument filed in an appellate court by parties not directly involved in the litigation.

amicus curiae. Person or organization (literally, "friend of the court") filing an amicus brief.

ancillary powers. Powers granted to the Federal Communication Commission to regulate entities that do not themselves possess broadcast licenses but whose practices may affect such licensees.

answer. In a civil suit, the initial document filed by the defendant, which may deny the plaintiff's claims or may offer specific defenses under law.

appellant. The party who lost in a lower court and is bringing an appeal to a higher court.

appellate court. A court that hears an appeal from adjudication of a case from a lower court.

appropriation. The branch of privacy law involving the unauthorized use of someone's name or likeness for commercial purposes.

arraignment. A criminal defendant's initial appearance before a judge, at which time formal charges will be made, and a plea may be offered.

block-booking. A scheme, ended by the Supreme Court's 1938 *United States v. Paramount* decision, by which movie studios would force movie theaters to accept dozens of lesser films in a block in order to obtain the rights to exhibit a few "name" pictures.

blurring. Diminishing the value of a company's trademark by offering for sale many different kinds of wholly unrelated products or services using the same mark.

brevity. A provision of the Copyright Act's *Classroom Guidelines* that limits the length of material (e.g., a book chapter, no more than 10 percent of the book) teachers may copy for distribution to their students.

brief. An argument filed in an appellate court, arguing either for the affirmance or reversal of the decision from the lower court.

Candidate Access rule. Section 312(a) of the Federal Communications Act, which tells TV and radio stations that they must make available advertising time for purchase to legally qualified candidates for federal office.

cease and desist order. As its name implies, an order (issued by an agency such as the Federal Trade Commission) demanding that a company stop engaging in an allegedly illegal practice.

certification mark. A promise through which a company attests as to a particular quality of its product (e.g., that this frozen pizza uses "REAL" cheese).

change of venire. The importation of a jury from a location ostensibly far enough away from the crime site to be untainted by any pretrial publicity.

change of venue. Moving a trial to a new location to avoid the negative effects of pretrial publicity.

child pornography. Images of underage individuals in sexually provocative poses, as defined by statutes that need not satisfy *Miller v. California* obscenity-test requirements such as judging the work as a whole or exempting works that manifest serious value.

civil (case). Court action prompted by one private party suing another.

civil contempt citation. Finding by a judge against a party who fails to perform a particular action (e.g., a reporter who refuses to reveal the identity of a source).

Clearly Erroneous rule. A rule of federal civil procedure that states that appellate courts may review not only legal questions but also factual ones if the appellate judges determine that the trial court made a clearly erroneous finding of fact.

closure order. A judge's ruling that all or part of a judicial proceeding shall be conducted in private, with no members of the press or public present.

Collateral Bar rule ("Dickinson rule"). Accepted in only some jurisdictions, this rule holds that contempt citations may stand even if the defendant is found by an appellate court to have had a right to engage in the behavior that resulted in the citation.

collective mark. A phrase or logo, protected under trademark law, designed to call to mind an association or organization (e.g., the NAB, National Association of Broadcasters).

collective work. A creative work eligible for copyright, consisting of many elements, each of which is also eligible for copyright (e.g., a newspaper edition and its many individual articles).

common law. Law as created by judge-made precedent, rather than enacted by a legislature.

compensatory damages. Damages designed to make a victim "whole"; that is, to undo harm that has been done.

compilation. A work formed by the collection and assembly of preexisting materials or of data; it is eligible for copyright protection to the extent that the selection and arrangement of those materials are themselves creative.

complaint. Document filed by the plaintiff in a civil case alleging the wrongs done by the defendant.

concurrent registration. More than one company using the same brand name for very different products or services (e.g., Life cereal and Life, the board game).

concurring opinion. An opinion written by an appellate judge who agrees with the outcome of the case but not all of the majority's reasoning.

consent. A defense in a tort action (including libel and invasion of privacy) claiming that the plaintiff knew of and explicitly indicated approval of, or at least acquiescence to, the defendant's conduct.

consent decree. Agreement entered into by two or more parties (e.g., a regulatory agency and a regulated company) and approved by a court.

consent order. Ruling by an agency's staff directing a company to behave in prescribed ways.

conspiracy. A combination of two or more persons planning to commit a criminal act.

constitution. A government's most basic controlling document, setting forth the structure and powers of the government.

contempt of court. An act or failure to act that either obstructs a court's functioning or otherwise adversely affects the dignity of the court.

continuance. Delaying a trial's beginning.

contributory infringement. Actions that do not directly infringe on the plaintiff's rights but that enable others to do so (e.g., creating a website that enables users to make illegal copies of copyrighted works).

convergence. In media law, the state of affairs when the differences among traditionally separate communications media become less and less identifiable.

convincing clarity. A measure, somewhere between "beyond a reasonable doubt" and "by a preponderance of the evidence," of how satisfactorily plaintiffs have established their burden of proof.

copyright. The exclusive right to profit from one's own creative works.

corrective advertising. Advertising including text designed to undo in consumers' minds false impressions created by prior advertising.

courts of equity. Courts empowered to make litigants whole, as best as possible, even in the absence of a clear body of legal precedent (common law).

criminal (case). Legal action taken by a government accusing a defendant of violating a law.

criminal contempt citation. Order issued by a judge designed to punish agents who act in ways that may interfere with government function (e.g., disrupting the courtroom or violating a judge's gag order).

criminal libel. Defamatory remarks, whether aimed at an individual or a group, prosecuted by the state on the theory that such utterances will tend to lead to violence.

cumulative effect. One of the guidelines found in the *Classroom Guidelines* under the Copyright Act, which limits teachers to copying no more than two works by the same author, no more than three from the same anthology, and no more than nine works total for classroom distribution during any single semester.

cybersquatting. Obtaining the rights to an Internet address bearing the name of a famous person or company, with the purpose of later selling it to the "logical" owner for a higher price.

decision. Court decisions tell us who wins and who loses, not necessarily why.

deep link. To insert a hyperlink in one's own website that sends visitors to an internal page of another individual's website.

defamation. An utterance or printed material asserting the kinds of derogatory facts about another person that may lead to that person's reputation being damaged.

defamation by implication. *See* "implied libel."

defendant. A person accused by the state of a crime or by a civil plaintiff of a wrongful act.

deposition. A part of the discovery process in which potential witnesses for the opposing side are interviewed with attorneys present and with a transcript created.

derivative works. A creative work eligible for copyright protection that is based in some way on a separate work (e.g., a movie version of a book).

descriptive mark. A trademark that merely describes the product or service (e.g., *lead* pencils or *Korean* restaurant) and is thus not ordinarily eligible for legal protection.

dicta. Portions of a court's opinion that are not essential to the disposition of the case (*see* "holding").

dilution. In trademark law, a claim that defendant's use of plaintiff's mark has diminished its effectiveness by making consumers less likely to think immediately of plaintiff's products, or by disparaging the name of the mark.

direct infringement. Infringement on a copyright resulting from the defendant's own actions.

discovery. The pretrial process of fact-finding performed by both sides in a civil suit, which may include deposing (formally questioning) prospective witnesses for the opposing side.

dissenting opinion. An opinion written by an appellate judge who disagrees with the outcome of the case (with the majority's decision).

distinctiveness. The main quality that makes a trademark protectable; it sets one product or service apart from competing brands.

distinguish (a precedent). Deciding that an earlier case's facts were sufficiently different from the case at hand so as not to be a useful precedent.

doctrine of incorporation. Constitutional doctrine holding that the Fourteenth Amendment's Due Process Clause implies that some of the Bill of Rights' limitations on the federal government also apply to the states.

documentary materials. Information and other items gathered by, but not created by, a reporter working on a story.

due process. Fundamental fairness; the Fifth Amendment says that life, liberty, and property may not be taken by the state without "due process."

en banc. A ruling by an entire federal appellate court (instead of just a three-judge panel).

Equal Protection Clause. Provisions in the Fifth and Fourteenth Amendments admonishing the federal government and the individual states, respectively, to treat citizens equitably.

Equal Time rule. Section 315 of the Federal Communications Act, which provides that broadcast stations must provide all candidates for a particular elected office approximately equal airtime if the stations allow any such candidate to "use" their airwaves in an election cycle.

Espionage Act. A federal law from the World War I era that criminalized criticizing the government or the war effort.

Establishment Clause. Part of the First Amendment; used by the Supreme Court to establish the "separation of church and state."

executive order. A change in policy promulgated by the executive branch (e.g., the president or a governor), carrying the effect of law.

experience and logic test. In cases involving First versus Sixth amendment conflicts, a doctrine that asks whether a whole category of judicial hearings has traditionally been open ("experience") and/or whether openness can "logically" be expected to enhance the judicial process.

fact, question of. The kinds of "did it happen or didn't it?" questions decided by trial courts, rather than appellate courts.

fair comment. A common-law defense against libel suits in which the defendant claims that the alleged libel was an honestly held opinion based on facts reasonably believed to be true.

fair report. A common-law libel defense in which the defendant claims to have offered an accurate report of an utterance made by a public official conducting official duties.

fair use. A defense against a copyright infringement suit, based on section 107 of the Copyright Act, that tells courts to consider the nature of the original work, the nature of the alleged infringement, the amount taken, and the use's effect on the value of the original copyright.

false light. One of the privacy torts, similar to libel, but under which the falsity need not be defamatory.

fanciful. In trademark law, a name created as a neologism—a word that is not in the dictionary before—such as Clorox or Viagra.

fault. In libel law, the element of a defamation suit constitutionalized by the Supreme Court in *New York Times Co. v. Sullivan*.

federal circuit. The jurisdiction—generally several states—covered by any of thirteen federal appellate courts.

Federal Communications Commission (FCC). Federal agency established in 1934; it oversees broadcast, cable, satellite, and telephonic communications systems.

federal district court. Federal trial court whose jurisdiction is generally one state or a portion of a state.

Federal Election Commission (FEC). Federal agency charged with enforcement of the Federal Election Campaigns Act, which includes regulations applied to political contributions and expenditures as well as some content restrictions on political advertising.

Federal Trade Commission (FTC). Federal agency regulating, among other things, deceptive advertising practices.

first impression, case of. A case presenting a novel issue, a controversy never before adjudicated in a specific jurisdiction.

Food and Drug Administration (FDA). Federal agency that regulates the marketing of and the advertising for food and drug products.

for cause (challenge of juror). Each side in a lawsuit or criminal prosecution may request that a potential juror not be impaneled, providing the trial judge with a specific reason why the potential juror would not be able to make an unbiased decision in a given case. Generally, the number of "for cause" challenges to which a party is entitled is unlimited.

framing. Surreptitiously sending an online "visitor" from one website to another (i.e., site B pops up on-screen as if a part of site A).

freedom of association. A doctrine emerging from First Amendment adjudication—if we have a right to speak out about public issues, we also have a right to create associations that better enable us to speak out.

Freedom of Information Act (FOIA). Passed by Congress in 1967, the act provides the mechanism by which citizens can obtain information held in federal government agency files; states also have analogous laws.

Free Exercise Clause. The First Amendment's prohibition against congressional interference with citizens' right to practice (or "exercise") their religion.

Free Press Clause. The First Amendment's prohibition against congressional interference with freedom of the press.

Free Speech Clause. The First Amendment's prohibition against congressional interference with freedom of speech.

gag order (restrictive order). Judicial order requiring that the target (e.g., attorneys, witnesses, jurors, or the press) refrain from speaking about or publishing specific information associated with a trial.

generic. In trademark law, a mark that once referred to a specific company's product but that over time comes to refer to the whole product line. For example, "aspirin" once referred to a specific company's pills.

***Glomar* response.** Federal agency response to a Freedom of Information Act request, refusing to provide the information sought and refusing to confirm or deny the existence of the requested file.

grand jury. A jury impaneled for the purpose of determining whether sufficient cause exists to charge one or more possible defendants with a crime.

holding. The essence of a court's ruling, often in the form of a rule established by the court.

idea-expression merger doctrine. Consistent with the truism that one cannot copyright mere "ideas," when only a small number of possible expressions of an idea are imaginable, those expressions will themselves not be entitled to copyright protection, because they are too closely tied to a mere "idea." *See also* "scènes-à-faire doctrine."

identification. The element of a libel suit in which plaintiffs establish that the offensive utterance or publication was "of or about" them.

implied libel. Situations in which utterances or writings are not themselves alleged by a libel plaintiff to be untrue, but where the inferences to be naturally drawn from the admittedly true statements are untrue.

indecency. Sexually oriented speech that, unlike obscenity, may be regulated even if it has serious value.

indictment. The document by which the government articulates a list of charges against a criminal defendant.

industry guide. Document promulgated by the Federal Trade Commission that gives general guidelines concerning acceptable ways to advertise products or services (e.g., when a product can be called "natural," "low fat," or "recyclable").

injunction. Judicial action demanding that the target either perform, or cease engaging in, specific conduct.

intellectual property. The conjunction of protections provided by patent, copyright, and trademark law.

intensity of suspicion test. In libel law, the notion that individual plaintiffs may bring suit to the extent that a group to which plaintiffs belong and to which a defamatory quality is attributed is small or the percentage of the group said to have the quality is large.

Internet. A worldwide systems of communication networks; or, the manner in which those networks communicate with each other.

intrusion. One of the four privacy torts; the transgression occurs when another's solitude or seclusion is intruded upon, regardless of whether any information gathered as a result of the intrusion is ever published.

joint operating agreement (JOA). Federally approved arrangement in which otherwise competing local newspapers can share the cost of core functions such as printing and distribution.

judicial review. Courts deciding on the constitutionality of legislative or executive-branch actions.

jurisdiction. Geographic area governed by a specific court; or, subject matters which a court is empowered to adjudicate.

law, question of. Questions, generally adjudicated by appellate courts, that concern whether a given factual situation fits the parameters of a legal doctrine or definition.

libel. Factual allegations about another that, if believed, would tend to lower that person's reputation in the eyes of others.

libel per quod. Statements that would damage another's reputation only if other unreported facts are known by readers.

libel per se. Statements that, if believed, would themselves damage the target's reputation.

libel-proof plaintiff. Libel plaintiff whose reputation is presumed already so low that no additional criticisms could lower it.

library building. The use of VCRs to make copies of broadcast programs, which the user keeps over time rather than erases with subsequent use.

likelihood of confusion. The mainstay of a traditional trademark-infringement suit, alleging that consumers will be confused as to the source of goods or services.

majority opinion. A judicial opinion joined by the majority of the judges on an appellate court.

memorandum order. An appellate court ruling unaccompanied by a formal opinion.

meta tags. Language, akin to "keywords" in traditional indexing, that lead a computer search engine to include a specific website among the "hits" resulting from a search.

modify (a precedent). A court modifies a precedent when it determines that the general principle espoused in that precedent is relevant to the current case but that some extrajudicial societal changes dictate that the precedent not be followed closely (e.g., to accuse someone of having a "loathsome" disease might still be libelous, but attitudes toward cancer have changed sufficiently so that this particular disease is no longer thought of as loathsome).

"must carry" rules. Federal Communications Commission rules requiring that cable systems include local broadcast signals in their most basic tier of service.

net neutrality. Doctrine arguing that Internet service providers must permit all users equal access, with equal transmission speeds, to their networks.

neutral reportage. Libel defense, accepted in only a few jurisdictions, positing that an otherwise punishable republication of libelous remarks can be excused if done in a fair and neutral way.

Newspaper Preservation Act. Federal law adopted in 1970 that provided for the creation of joint operating agreements as a way of preserving some degree of competition among daily newspapers.

obscenity. Sexually oriented messages wholly unprotected by the First Amendment.

official conduct. Part of the *New York Times Co. v. Sullivan* libel rule; public officials can recover only for defamatory statements that criticize the way they perform their duties or that make allegations about personal characteristics likely to affect the performance of those duties.

opinion. A court's written discussion of its reasons for making a decision. (But note that the word often carries its everyday meaning in libel law, as when we ponder whether an alleged libel makes a factual claim or is merely a matter of opinion.)

oral arguments. Arguments made by opposing attorneys, each typically arguing for about half an hour, in front of the judges of an appellate court.

overbreadth. First Amendment doctrine suggesting that a defendant whose conduct was legitimately covered by a law's prohibitions may nonetheless be able to challenge the law for being worded so broadly as to also arguably cover conduct that should not be prohibited.

overturn. Ruling by which an appellate court in effect changes its mind, holding that one of its earlier precedents will no longer be honored. Appellate courts can also overturn lower court decisions, and "overturn" is often used interchangeably with "invalidate" to describe what happens when any court rules that a legislative action is improper or unconstitutional.

participant monitoring. One party to a telephone conversation taping the conversation without the other's knowledge.

per curiam opinion. An unsigned opinion (literally, "by the Court").

peremptory challenge. Motion made by a party to a lawsuit or criminal prosecution, without any reason offered, seeking to remove a potential juror from being impaneled. Unlike in the case of challenges for cause, each side typically is entitled to only a limited number of peremptory challenges.

personal jurisdiction. A doctrine whereby one state's courts may claim jurisdiction over a citizen from another state.

Petition Clause. Section of the First Amendment giving Americans the right to assemble peaceably and to petition their government for redress of grievances.

petit jury. In criminal law, the jury that actually decides the defendant's guilt or innocence.

plaintiff. The party bringing a civil suit against a civil defendant.

plea. A criminal defendant's answer to a charge or indictment, such as a plea of guilty or not guilty.

plea bargain. A criminal defendant's decision to plead guilty to a lesser offense than that for which the government was prepared to try him or her.

plurality opinion. Opinion signed by one or more appellate judges agreeing with the majority's ultimate decision, but not with all of its reasoning.

pornography. Communications that include somewhat graphic depictions of sexual conduct; might or might not meet legal definitions of indecency and/or obscenity.

precedent. A court decision made prior to the one being argued at present, which at least one litigant suggests counts as a reason for ruling in a specific way in the current case.

preferred-position balancing. Presumption in First Amendment cases that speech is more important than whatever competing interest is involved in a given case.

preliminary hearing. Any judicial hearing that occurs before the criminal trial itself.

presentencing report. Report given to the judge in a criminal trial, after a defendant has been found guilty, offering arguments for severity or lenience of sentence.

presumed damages. In libel cases, damages due the successful plaintiff even without proof of specific quantifiable harm.

Printers' Ink **statutes.** State laws aimed at deceptive advertising.

prior restraint. A law, executive order, or judicial decree prohibiting communicative conduct before it occurs (rather than punishing it after it occurs).

probable cause. The standard of proof required to hold a criminal defendant over for trial; also the standard used to determine if a search warrant should be granted.

product disparagement. Comments similar to libel, but directed at a company's product line, rather than at its management.

product proximity. Thematic or logical relationship between one product line and another; in trademark law, infringement is more likely to be found as proximity increases.

profanity. Language the Federal Communications Commission deems "vulgar and coarse" and so "grossly offensive" that it constitutes a "nuisance"; unlike indecency, the language need not be sexually oriented.

promissory estoppel. A common-law legal doctrine providing that even in the absence of a contract, an agreement may be enforced if failure to do so would result in gross inequity.

prosecute. For the government to bring legal action against a defendant, alleging a violation of criminal law.

publication. In libel law, dissemination of the allegedly libelous remarks to at least one third party. In most other areas of communication law, the word carries its everyday meaning.

public disclosure. A privacy tort in which highly private and embarrassing, but true, information about the plaintiff is disseminated.

public figure. In libel law, a plaintiff who is famous or associated with a specific political cause.

public forum. A place where, either by tradition (as in the sidewalks or public parks) or by government designation (as in a public auditorium), speech on a variety of topics and from a variety of viewpoints is generally welcomed.

publicity, right to. A hybrid privacy and property right to profit from the commercial exploitation of one's own name or likeness.

public official. In libel law, a government employee perceived to have decision-making authority and who occupies a position that is a frequent topic of public discussion.

puffery. Obviously exaggerated advertising claims (e.g., "we serve the best food in town") that are protected precisely because consumers do not take them literally.

punitive damages. Damage awards, above and beyond those granted to compensate the plaintiff for harm, which are designed to punish the defendant for outrageous conduct.

recuse. To remove oneself from participation (as judges will do if they believe their hearing a case would create a conflict of interest).

reporter shield laws. State laws providing media representatives some degree of immunity from having to testify in front of judicial bodies.

republication. In libel law, publishing a "defamation once removed" (e.g., "Ms. Jones asserted that her ex-husband sexually abused their daughter.").

retraction statutes. State laws that provide some measure of protection from damages in a libel suit for media outlets that have already published an admission of error.

retransmission consent. Permission granted by a broadcaster to a cable or satellite TV company to include the broadcaster's signal among the cable (or satellite TV) company's offerings to subscribers.

right-of-reply statutes. State laws providing persons who feel they have been unfairly criticized by a media outlet a right to air their side of the issue; in 1974, the Supreme Court struck down such laws as they apply to the print media.

right to publicity. *See* "publicity, right to."

scènes-à-faire doctrine. In copyright law, the notion that some film genres by their very nature virtually demand that certain stock scenes be included (e.g., a car chase in a crime drama) so that other directors' use of such scenes is not an infringement. *See also* "idea-expression merger doctrine."

search warrant. As provided for by the Fourth Amendment, a document given by a judge to a law enforcement officer permitting the search of a property where there is reason to believe helpful evidence will be found.

secondary meaning. *See* "acquired distinctiveness."

Securities and Exchange Commission (SEC). Federal agency of relevance to media law in that it can determine eligibility to write financial newsletters.

self-publication. In libel law, the unusual situation in which the publication element is established because the defamed person himself will, predictably, have to share the libelous statements with others (e.g., if he is blind and needs someone to read the publication to him).

service mark. A word, phrase, or logo designed to conjure up in consumers' minds a specific company's services.

slander. A spoken defamation (traditionally, *libel* referred only to printed defamations).

SLAPP suit. Strategic lawsuit against public participation; a libel suit designed to silence public criticism of a powerful individual or group.

Smith Act. Federal law from the 1940s making it a criminal offense to participate in an organization whose mission includes the violent overthrow of the government.

spam. Unwanted commercial e-mail messages.

special damages. Damages awarded for very tangible, demonstrable, out-of-pocket losses.

Speech or Debate Clause. Provision of the Constitution immunizing members of Congress from libel suits flowing from their conduct of their official duties.

spontaneity. A provision in the *Classroom Guidelines* accompanying the federal Copyright Act that immunizes teachers from infringement suits for unauthorized copying for classroom use if there was no time to seek official permission (i.e., the idea to use this material was too spontaneous).

spoofing. Designing a commercial e-mail message to appear noncommercial.

stare decisis. Literally "let the decision stand"; an admonition to follow precedent when possible.

statute. A law passed by a legislative body, usually at the state or local level.

statute of limitations. Time period, usually stemming from the date of an alleged transgression, during which legal action must be commenced for the plaintiff (or, in a criminal prosecution, the state) to prevail.

statutory construction. The process by which a court determines the meaning and effect of ambiguous language in a statute.

strict liability. Doctrine providing that the person whose action causes a certain result is civilly or criminally liable for such result, even if no degree of negligence can be shown.

subpoena. Judicial document demanding that the recipient appear before the court or produce requested documents.

suggestive. In trademark law, a mark that uses real words to hint at a product's qualities. For example, "Head and Shoulders" shampoo suggests it is for dandruff, but "Dandruff" shampoo would be too obviously descriptive to be protected.

summary contempt. A judge's power to charge, "convict," and punish a wrongdoer on the spot.

summary judgment. Judicial ruling to the effect that even if any facts in dispute are presumed in favor of the opposing party, the party seeking the order must prevail as a matter of law; such judgments avoid having to present facts to a jury, or even to have a full trial.

superior court. The name usually given to state trial courts.

Supremacy Clause. Federal constitutional provision telling the individual states that their laws may not conflict with established federal law.

tarnishment. Using another company's trademark in a way that will tend to bring that company's goods or services into disrepute.

thematic obscenity. Doctrine, long ago rejected by U.S. courts, that permitted works to be found obscene if their theme, or story line, was offensive (e.g., because an adulterer did not get punished).

third-party monitoring. Taping a conversation without the permission of any of the participants.

time shifting. Using a video recorder to tape programs only to view them at a more convenient later time (not to build a permanent library).

trade dress. Use of the overall look or feel of a product or place of business to conjure up in consumers' minds a specific company.

trade libel. *See* "product disparagement."

trademark. A word, phrase, or logo designed to conjure up in consumers' minds associations with a specific company's product line.

trade regulation rule. Federal Trade Commission guidelines governing general advertising practices (e.g., when a product can be called "natural" or "recyclable") rather than a specific company's conduct. A trade regulation rule is very similar to an industry guide (*see* "industry guide") but carries the force of law.

trial court. The court in which the first level of a judicial proceeding (the trial) takes place and from which the losing party may seek review by an appellate court.

underinclusive. A kind of challenge sometimes raised in First Amendment cases, suggesting that if a state's purported reasons for creating the law were legitimate, the law would prohibit far more conduct than it does.

URL. Universal Resource Locator, generally a website "address" such as www.paulsiegel commlaw.com.

variable obscenity. Legal doctrine holding that the definition of obscenity can be somewhat fluid depending on the target audience (especially if children are exposed to the materials).

Vaughn index. A federal agency's response to a Freedom of Information Act request in which the agency provides a list of relevant documents in the agency's possession but claims that some or all of the documents may not be released.

voir dire. The process of selecting a jury (from the Old French, "to say that which one has seen," or to bear truthful witness).

work-for-hire doctrine. In copyright law, an exception to the general rule that the artist or creator owns a copyright; if a work was created as part of an employee's job description, the rights may be enjoyed instead by the employer.

work product. Materials actually created by a reporter working on a story.

Case Index

Subject Index

Note: Page numbers in *italics* refer to illustrations.

AARP, 160–161
ABA (American Bar Association), 284, 301
ABC, 169, 172, 174, 399, 408, 417
ABC World News Tonight, 417
Abrams, Jacob, 34–34
absolute privilege, 98
access theory, 49–50
Action for Children's Television, 423
actual malice, 114–142; applied to public figures, 120–122, 139; and confidential sources, 316; convincing clarity standard, 114–115; and damages, 140–141; defined, 114; and emotional distress, 132–135; factual and legal question, 124–126; indications of, 122–124, 126–128, 136–137; and invasion of privacy, 176–177; and opinion, 128–132; and private plaintiffs, 139–140; and public officials, 117–120; state of mind, 135–136, 316; and truth defense, 122–124
Adams, John, 22, 43
administrative agencies as sources of law, 11–12. *See also names of specific agencies*

"adult" businesses, 7n17, 66, 382, 390–394, 432, 437, 458–463
Advanced Research Projects Agency Network (ARPANET), 437
advertising, 335–372; billboards, 9; *Central Hudson* test, 49, 337–340, 342; dangerous products, 340–344; direct mail, 221, 349–350; and the Federal Trade Commission, 12, 354–367; and the Food and Drug Administration, 12; and in-person solicitation, 349–351; by lawyers and other professionals, 344–352; and misappropriation, 160; less protection than "core" political speech, 46, 55; and the NAD, 369–370; and news, 160–161; political, 9, 370–373; *Printers' Ink* statutes, 353; and the Supreme Court's commercial speech doctrine, 60, 63–64, 336–352; sweepstakes, 353–354; testimonials, 359–361; trade names, 351–352
Advertising Age, 370
AED Plus, 211–212
Agriculture, Department of, 63–64, 250

Albright, James, 88
Alexander, Laurence B., 174n58
Ali, Muhammad, 151
Alien and Sedition Acts, 32, 116
Alito, Samuel, 18, *19*
All Channel Receiver Act, 410
Allen, Woody, 152, *155*, 206
American Bar Association (ABA), 284, 301
American Gangster, xviii, 103, *104*
amicus briefs, 22
Anderson, David A., 137n33
animal cruelty, 47n34, 69, 327
Anticybersquatting Consumer Protection Act, 450
antitrust laws, 71–73, 256
AP (Associated Press), 121–122, 195, 261
appellate courts, *23*, *125*; and actual malice, 124–125; and cameras, 302–303; place in judicial structure, 17–18, 21–23; publication of, 27–28; ruling on trial judges' orders, 273, 282–283, 293, 318, 379
Arnaz, Desi, 342
ARPANET (Advanced Research Projects Agency Network), 437
arraignment, 20

About the Author

Paul Siegel is professor of communication at the University of Hartford. For sixteen years Siegel taught at Gallaudet University, the world's only comprehensive university designed especially for deaf and hard of hearing students. He has also taught communication law courses at American University, the Catholic University of America, George Mason University, Illinois State University, Keene State College (New Hampshire), Quinnipiac University, Tulane University, the University of Connecticut, the University of Missouri–Kansas City, and the University of North Carolina.

Siegel has published dozens of essays in journals of communication, sociology, and anthropology, as well as in law reviews and as book chapters. Topics have ranged from product placement in movies and the development of the Supreme Court's commercial speech doctrine to the gays-in-the-military debate and the interaction of privacy and communication law. Siegel also edited a collection of readings on the Clarence Thomas hearings.

A graduate of Northwestern University's doctoral program in communication studies, Siegel also earned degrees from the University of Wisconsin and the University of New Mexico. Beyond work in the academy, Siegel was the founding executive director of the Kansas and Western Missouri office of the American Civil Liberties Union and has been on the ACLU's affiliate boards in Illinois, Washington, D.C., and Connecticut. He is also the immediate past president of the Text and Academic Authors Association.